Dodge Omni & Plymouth Horizon
Automotive Repair Manual

by Larry Warren, Mike Stubblefield and and John H Haynes
Member of the Guild of Motoring Writers

Models covered:
All Dodge Omni and Plymouth Horizon models
1978 through 1990
Does not include 1.6L engine information

(7W3 – 545)

ABCDE

Haynes Publishing Group
Sparkford Nr Yeovil
Somerset BA22 7JJ England

Haynes North America, Inc
861 Lawrence Drive
Newbury Park
California 91320 USA

Acknowledgements

We are grateful for the help and cooperation of Chrysler Corporation for assistance with technical information, certain illustrations and vehicle photos. The Champion Spark Plug Company supplied the illustrations of various spark plug conditions.

A book in the **Haynes Automotive Repair Manual Series**

Printed in the USA

ISBN 1 85010 745 9

Library of Congress Catalog Card Number 90-85098

Contents

1987 Dodge Omni America

1987 Dodge Shelby Charger

About this manual

Its purpose

The purpose of this manual is to help you get the best value from your vehicle. It can do so in several ways. It can help you decide what work must be done, even if you choose to have it done by a dealer service department or a repair shop; it provides information and procedures for routine maintenance and servicing; and it offers diagnostic and repair procedures to follow when trouble occurs.

We hope you use the manual to tackle the work yourself. For many simpler jobs, doing it yourself may be quicker than arranging an appointment to get the vehicle into a shop and making the trips to leave it and pick it up. More importantly, a lot of money can be saved by avoiding the expense the shop must pass on to you to cover its labor and overhead costs. An added benefit is the sense of satisfaction and accomplishment that you feel after doing the job yourself.

Using the manual

The manual is divided into Chapters. Each Chapter is divided into numbered Sections, which are headed in bold type between horizontal lines. Each Section consists of consecutively numbered paragraphs.

At the beginning of each numbered section you will be referred to any illustrations which apply to the procedures in that section. The reference numbers used in illustration captions pinpoint the pertinent Section and the Step within that section. That is, illustration 3.2 means the illustration refers to Section 3 and Step (or paragraph) 2 within that Section.

Procedures, once described in the text, are not normally repeated. When it's necessary to refer to another Chapter, the reference will be given as Chapter and Section number. Cross references given without use of the word "Chapter" apply to Sections and/or paragraphs in the same Chapter. For example, "see Section 8" means in the same Chapter.

References to the left or right side of the vehicle assume you are sitting in the driver's seat, facing forward.

Even though we have prepared this manual with extreme care, neither the publisher nor the author can accept responsibility for any errors in, or omissions from, the information given.

NOTE

A **Note** provides information necessary to properly complete a procedure or information which will make the procedure easier to understand.

CAUTION

A **Caution** provides a special procedure or special steps which must be taken while completing the procedure where the **Caution** is found. Not heeding a **Caution** can result in damage to the assembly being worked on.

WARNING

A **Warning** provides a special procedure or special steps which must be taken while completing the procedure where the **Warning** is found. Not heeding a **Warning** can result in personal injury.

Introduction to the Dodge Omni/Plymouth Horizon

Dodge Omni and Plymouth Horizon models are available in both two and four-door hatchback body styles. Many model variations, including the O24, TC-3, Charger and Turismo, were manufactured.

The transverse-mounted, inline four-cylinder engine used in these models is equipped with a carburetor or single-point fuel injection system. Turbocharged models are equipped with multi-point fuel injection. The engine drives the front wheels through either a four or five-speed manual or three-speed automatic transaxle via independent driveaxles.

Independent suspension, featuring coil springs and struts, is used at the front wheels. A beam-type axle, with struts and coil springs, is used at the rear wheels. The rack and pinion steering unit is mounted behind the engine.

The brakes are disc at the front and drums at the rear, with power assist as standard equipment.

1987 Plymouth Horizon America

1987 Plymouth Turismo

Vehicle identification numbers

Modifications are a continuing and unpublicized process in vehicle manufacturing. Since spare parts lists are compiled on a numerical basis, the individual vehicle numbers are essential to correctly identify the component required.

Vehicle Identification Number (VIN)

This very important identification number is stamped on a plate attached to the left side of the dashboard, just inside the windshield on the driver's side of the vehicle **(see illustration)**. The VIN also appears on the Vehicle Certificate of Title and Registration. It contains information such as where and when the vehicle was manufactured, the model year and the body style.

Body code plate

This plate is located in the engine compartment, either on the inner side of the left fender or on top of the radiator support **(see illustration)**. It contains information on the vehicle model, engine and transaxle as well as the paint code.

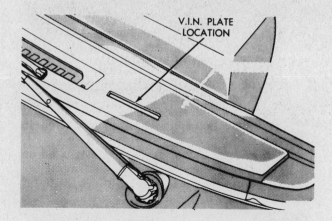

The Vehicle Identification Number is visible from outside the vehicle through the driver's side of the windshield

```
LINE
NO.
 6  1 2 3 4 5 6 7 8 9 10 11 12 13 14 15 16 17 18 19 20 21 22 23
 5  ○ 3 4 5 6 7 8 9 10 11 12 13 14 15 16 17 18 19 20 21      ○
 4  1 2 3 4 5 6 7 8 9 10 11 12 13 14 15 16 17 18 19 20 21 22 23
 3  1 2 3  5 6 7  9 10 11       14         17 18 19 20 21 22 23
 2  1 2 3  5 6 7 8  10 11 12   14 15 16      18 19 20 21 22 23
 1  1 2 3 4  6 7 8 9 10 11 12 13 14 15 16    18 19 20 21 22 23
```

FOR FACTORY USE ONLY

The body code plate is located in the engine compartment

Vehicle safety certification label

This label is affixed to the left front door pillar **(see illustration)**. The plate contains the name of the manufacturer, the month and year of production, the Gross Vehicle Weight Rating (GVWR) and the certification statement.

Engine Identification Number (EIN)

This number is stamped into the engine block on the transaxle end **(see illustration)**.

Engine serial number

In addition to the EIN, each engine has a serial number which must be referenced when obtaining replacement parts. On the 1.7L engine, the serial number is located behind the fuel pump, on the engine block **(see illustration)**. On the 2.2L engine, it's located on the transaxle end of the block, directly below the EIN.

Transaxle identification and serial numbers

The transaxle identification number is stamped into a boss on the upper surface of the housing **(see illustration)**. When obtaining parts for the transaxle, you may also be asked for the transaxle serial number. The serial number is located on a metal tag attached to the front side of the transaxle housing (manual transaxles) or stamped into the transaxle housing at the left front corner (automatic transaxles).

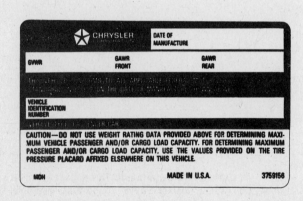

The vehicle safety certification label is located on the driver's door pillar

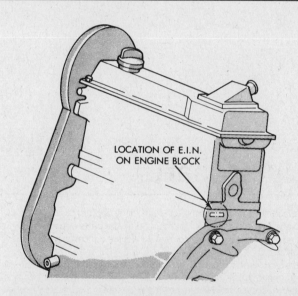

The engine identification number is located on the transaxle end of the engine block

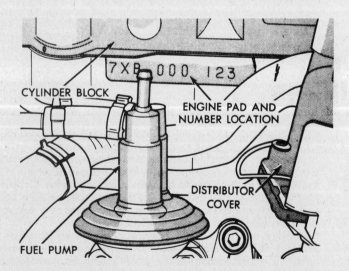

The engine serial number on the 1.7L engine (shown here) is on the side of the block, directly behind the fuel pump – on the 2.2L engine, the serial number is on the end of the block, directly below the identification number

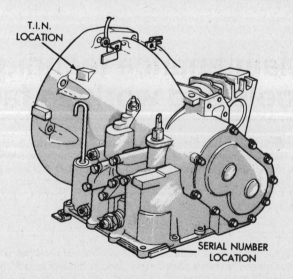

Locations of the transaxle identification number and serial number (automatic transaxle models)

Buying parts

Replacement parts are available from many sources, which generally fall into one of two categories – authorized dealer parts departments and independent retail auto parts stores. Our advice concerning these parts is as follows:

Retail auto parts stores: Good auto parts stores will stock frequently needed components which wear out relatively fast, such as clutch components, exhaust systems, brake parts, tune-up parts, etc. These stores often supply new or reconditioned parts on an exchange basis, which can save a considerable amount of money. Discount auto parts stores are often very good places to buy materials and parts needed for general vehicle maintenance such as oil, grease, filters, spark plugs, belts, touch-up paint, bulbs, etc. They also usually sell tools and general accessories, have con-

venient hours, charge lower prices and can often be found not far from home.

Authorized dealer parts department: This is the best source for parts which are unique to the vehicle and not generally available elsewhere (such as major engine parts, transmission parts, trim pieces, etc.).

Warranty information: If the vehicle is still covered under warranty, be sure that any replacement parts purchased – regardless of the source – do not invalidate the warranty!

To be sure of obtaining the correct parts, have engine and chassis numbers available and, if possible, take the old parts along for positive identification.

Maintenance techniques, tools and working facilities

Maintenance techniques

There are a number of techniques involved in maintenance and repair that will be referred to throughout this manual. Application of these techniques will enable the home mechanic to be more efficient, better organized and capable of performing the various tasks properly, which will ensure that the repair job is thorough and complete.

Fasteners

Fasteners are nuts, bolts, studs and screws used to hold two or more parts together. There are a few things to keep in mind when working with fasteners. Almost all of them use a locking device of some type, either a lockwasher, locknut, locking tab or thread adhesive. All threaded fasteners should be clean and straight, with undamaged threads and undamaged corners on the hex head where the wrench fits. Develop the habit of replacing all damaged nuts and bolts with new ones. Special locknuts

with nylon or fiber inserts can only be used once. If they are removed, they lose their locking ability and must be replaced with new ones.

Rusted nuts and bolts should be treated with a penetrating fluid to ease removal and prevent breakage. Some mechanics use turpentine in a spout-type oil can, which works quite well. After applying the rust penetrant, let it work for a few minutes before trying to loosen the nut or bolt. Badly rusted fasteners may have to be chiseled or sawed off or removed with a special nut breaker, available at tool stores.

If a bolt or stud breaks off in an assembly, it can be drilled and removed with a special tool commonly available for this purpose. Most automotive machine shops can perform this task, as well as other repair procedures, such as the repair of threaded holes that have been stripped out.

Flat washers and lockwashers, when removed from an assembly, should always be replaced exactly as removed. Replace any damaged washers with new ones. Never use a lockwasher on any soft metal surface (such as aluminum), thin sheet metal or plastic.

Fastener sizes

For a number of reasons, automobile manufacturers are making wider and wider use of metric fasteners. Therefore, it is important to be able to tell the difference between standard (sometimes called U.S. or SAE) and metric hardware, since they cannot be interchanged.

All bolts, whether standard or metric, are sized according to diameter, thread pitch and length. For example, a standard 1/2 – 13 x 1 bolt is 1/2 inch in diameter, has 13 threads per inch and is 1 inch long. An M12 – 1.75 x 25 metric bolt is 12 mm in diameter, has a thread pitch of 1.75 mm (the distance between threads) and is 25 mm long. The two bolts are nearly identical, and easily confused, but they are not interchangeable.

In addition to the differences in diameter, thread pitch and length, metric and standard bolts can also be distinguished by examining the bolt heads. To begin with, the distance across the flats on a standard bolt head is measured in inches, while the same dimension on a metric bolt is sized in millimeters (the same is true for nuts). As a result, a standard wrench should not be used on a metric bolt and a metric wrench should not be used on a standard bolt. Also, most standard bolts have slashes radiating out from the center of the head to denote the grade or strength of the bolt, which is an indication of the amount of torque that can be applied to it. The greater the number of slashes, the greater the strength of the bolt. Grades 0 through 5 are commonly used on automobiles. Metric bolts have a property class (grade) number, rather than a slash, molded into their heads to indicate bolt strength. In this case, the higher the number, the stronger the bolt. Property class numbers 8.8, 9.8 and 10.9 are commonly used on automobiles.

Strength markings can also be used to distinguish standard hex nuts from metric hex nuts. Many standard nuts have dots stamped into one side, while metric nuts are marked with a number. The greater the number of dots, or the higher the number, the greater the strength of the nut.

Metric studs are also marked on their ends according to property class (grade). Larger studs are numbered (the same as metric bolts), while smaller studs carry a geometric code to denote grade.

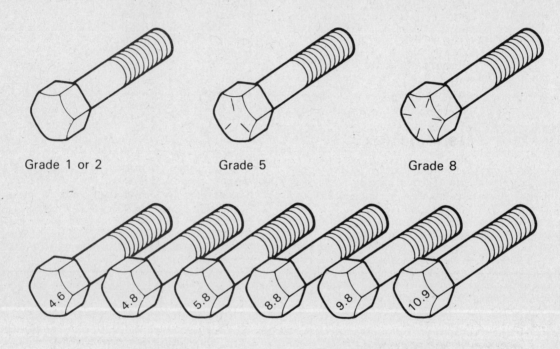

Grade 1 or 2   Grade 5   Grade 8

Bolt strength markings (top – standard/SAE/USS; bottom – metric)

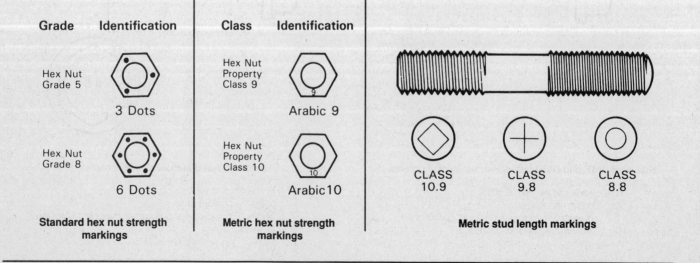

Grade	Identification	Class	Identification
Hex Nut Grade 5	3 Dots	Hex Nut Property Class 9	Arabic 9
Hex Nut Grade 8	6 Dots	Hex Nut Property Class 10	Arabic 10

CLASS 10.9   CLASS 9.8   CLASS 8.8

Standard hex nut strength markings   **Metric hex nut strength markings**   **Metric stud length markings**

It should be noted that many fasteners, especially Grades 0 through 2, have no distinguishing marks on them. When such is the case, the only way to determine whether it is standard or metric is to measure the thread pitch or compare it to a known fastener of the same size.

Standard fasteners are often referred to as SAE, as opposed to metric. However, it should be noted that SAE technically refers to a non-metric *fine thread* fastener only. Coarse thread non-metric fasteners are referred to as USS sizes.

Since fasteners of the same size (both standard and metric) may have different strength ratings, be sure to reinstall any bolts, studs or nuts removed from your vehicle in their original locations. Also, when replacing a fastener with a new one, make sure that the new one has a strength rating equal to or greater than the original.

Tightening sequences and procedures

Most threaded fasteners should be tightened to a specific torque value (torque is the twisting force applied to a threaded component such as a nut or bolt). Overtightening the fastener can weaken it and cause it to break, while undertightening can cause it to eventually come loose. Bolts, screws and studs, depending on the material they are made of and their thread diameters, have specific torque values, many of which are noted in the Specifications at the beginning of each Chapter. Be sure to follow the torque recommendations closely. For fasteners not assigned a specific torque, a general torque value chart is presented here as a guide. These torque values are for dry (unlubricated) fasteners threaded into steel or cast iron (not aluminum). As was previously mentioned, the size and grade of a fastener determine the amount of torque that can safely

Metric thread sizes

	Ft-lbs	Nm
M-6	6 to 9	9 to 12
M-8	14 to 21	19 to 28
M-10	28 to 40	38 to 54
M-12	50 to 71	68 to 96
M-14	80 to 140	109 to 154

Pipe thread sizes

1/8	5 to 8	7 to 10
1/4	12 to 18	17 to 24
3/8	22 to 33	30 to 44
1/2	25 to 35	34 to 47

U.S. thread sizes

1/4 – 20	6 to 9	9 to 12
5/16 – 18	12 to 18	17 to 24
5/16 – 24	14 to 20	19 to 27
3/8 – 16	22 to 32	30 to 43
3/8 – 24	27 to 38	37 to 51
7/16 – 14	40 to 55	55 to 74
7/16 – 20	40 to 60	55 to 81
1/2 – 13	55 to 80	75 to 108

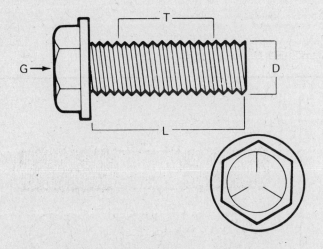

Standard (SAE and USS) bolt dimensions/grade marks

G   Grade marks (bolt length)
L   Length (in inches)
T   Thread pitch (number of threads per inch)
D   Nominal diameter (in inches)

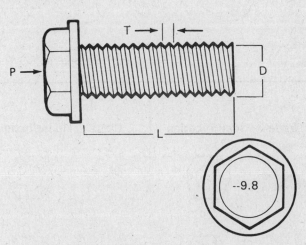

Metric bolt dimensions/grade marks

P   Property class (bolt strength)
L   Length (in millimeters)
T   Thread pitch (distance between threads in millimeters)
D   Diameter

be applied to it. The figures listed here are approximate for Grade 2 and Grade 3 fasteners. Higher grades can tolerate higher torque values.

Fasteners laid out in a pattern, such as cylinder head bolts, oil pan bolts, differential cover bolts, etc., must be loosened or tightened in sequence to avoid warping the component. This sequence will normally be shown in the appropriate Chapter. If a specific pattern is not given, the following procedures can be used to prevent warping.

Initially, the bolts or nuts should be assembled finger-tight only. Next, they should be tightened one full turn each, in a criss-cross or diagonal pattern. After each one has been tightened one full turn, return to the first one and tighten them all one-half turn, following the same pattern. Finally, tighten each of them one-quarter turn at a time until each fastener has been tightened to the proper torque. To loosen and remove the fasteners, the procedure would be reversed.

Component disassembly

Component disassembly should be done with care and purpose to help ensure that the parts go back together properly. Always keep track of the sequence in which parts are removed. Make note of special characteristics or marks on parts that can be installed more than one way, such as a grooved thrust washer on a shaft. It is a good idea to lay the disassembled parts out on a clean surface in the order that they were removed. It may also be helpful to make sketches or take instant photos of components before removal.

When removing fasteners from a component, keep track of their locations. Sometimes threading a bolt back in a part, or putting the washers and nut back on a stud, can prevent mix-ups later. If nuts and bolts cannot be returned to their original locations, they should be kept in a compartmented box or a series of small boxes. A cupcake or muffin tin is ideal for this purpose, since each cavity can hold the bolts and nuts from a particular area (i.e. oil pan bolts, valve cover bolts, engine mount bolts, etc.). A pan of this type is especially helpful when working on assemblies with very small parts, such as the carburetor, alternator, valve train or interior dash and trim pieces. The cavities can be marked with paint or tape to identify the contents.

Whenever wiring looms, harnesses or connectors are separated, it is a good idea to identify the two halves with numbered pieces of masking tape so they can be easily reconnected.

Gasket sealing surfaces

Throughout any vehicle, gaskets are used to seal the mating surfaces between two parts and keep lubricants, fluids, vacuum or pressure contained in an assembly.

Many times these gaskets are coated with a liquid or paste-type gasket sealing compound before assembly. Age, heat and pressure can sometimes cause the two parts to stick together so tightly that they are very difficult to separate. Often, the assembly can be loosened by striking it with a soft-face hammer near the mating surfaces. A regular hammer can be used if a block of wood is placed between the hammer and the part. Do not hammer on cast parts or parts that could be easily damaged. With any particularly stubborn part, always recheck to make sure that every fastener has been removed.

Avoid using a screwdriver or bar to pry apart an assembly, as they can easily mar the gasket sealing surfaces of the parts, which must remain smooth. If prying is absolutely necessary, use an old broom handle, but keep in mind that extra clean up will be necessary if the wood splinters.

After the parts are separated, the old gasket must be carefully scraped off and the gasket surfaces cleaned. Stubborn gasket material can be soaked with rust penetrant or treated with a special chemical to soften it so it can be easily scraped off. A scraper can be fashioned from a piece of copper tubing by flattening and sharpening one end. Copper is recommended because it is usually softer than the surfaces to be scraped, which reduces the chance of gouging the part. Some gaskets can be removed with a wire brush, but regardless of the method used, the mating surfaces must be left clean and smooth. If for some reason the gasket surface is gouged, then a gasket sealer thick enough to fill scratches will have to be used during reassembly of the components. For most applications, a non-drying (or semi-drying) gasket sealer should be used.

Hose removal tips

Warning: *If the vehicle is equipped with air conditioning, do not disconnect any of the A/C hoses without first having the system depressurized by a dealer service department or a service station.*

Hose removal precautions closely parallel gasket removal precautions. Avoid scratching or gouging the surface that the hose mates against or the connection may leak. This is especially true for radiator hoses. Because of various chemical reactions, the rubber in hoses can bond itself to the metal spigot that the hose fits over. To remove a hose, first loosen the hose clamps that secure it to the spigot. Then, with slip-joint pliers, grab the hose at the clamp and rotate it around the spigot. Work it back and forth until it is completely free, then pull it off. Silicone or other lubricants will ease removal if they can be applied between the hose and the outside of the spigot. Apply the same lubricant to the inside of the hose and the outside of the spigot to simplify installation.

As a last resort (and if the hose is to be replaced with a new one anyway), the rubber can be slit with a knife and the hose peeled from the spigot. If this must be done, be careful that the metal connection is not damaged.

If a hose clamp is broken or damaged, do not reuse it. Wire-type clamps usually weaken with age, so it is a good idea to replace them with screw-type clamps whenever a hose is removed.

Tools

A selection of good tools is a basic requirement for anyone who plans to maintain and repair his or her own vehicle. For the owner who has few tools, the initial investment might seem high, but when compared to the spiraling costs of professional auto maintenance and repair, it is a wise one.

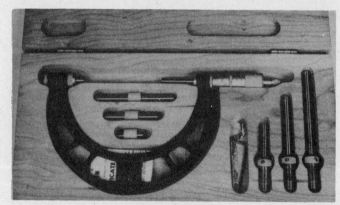

Micrometer set

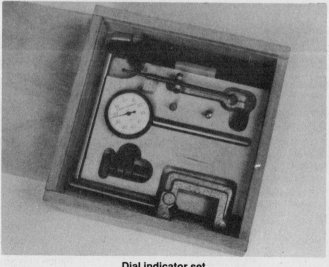

Dial indicator set

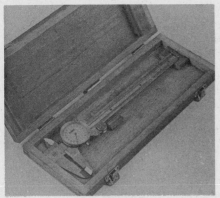

Dial caliper

Hand-operated vacuum pump

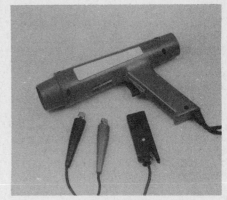

Timing light

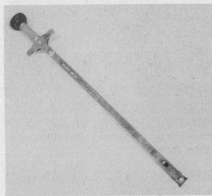

Compression gauge with spark plug
hole adapter

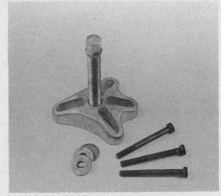

Damper/steering wheel puller

General purpose puller

Hydraulic lifter removal tool

Valve spring compressor

Valve spring compressor

Ridge reamer

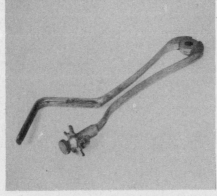

Piston ring groove cleaning tool

Ring removal/installation tool

Ring compressor

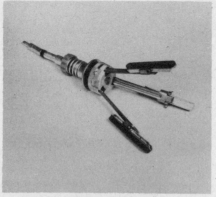
Cylinder hone

Brake hold-down spring tool

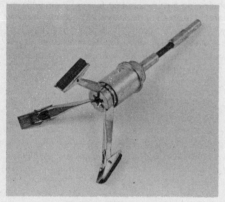
Brake cylinder hone

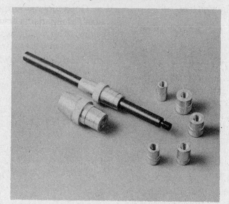
Clutch plate alignment tool

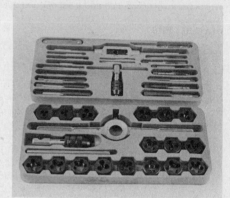
Tap and die set

To help the owner decide which tools are needed to perform the tasks detailed in this manual, the following tool lists are offered: *Maintenance and minor repair, Repair/overhaul and Special.*

The newcomer to practical mechanics should start off with the maintenance and minor repair tool kit, which is adequate for the simpler jobs performed on a vehicle. Then, as confidence and experience grow, the owner can tackle more difficult tasks, buying additional tools as they are needed. Eventually the basic kit will be expanded into the repair and overhaul tool set. Over a period of time, the experienced do-it-yourselfer will assemble a tool set complete enough for most repair and overhaul procedures and will add tools from the special category when it is felt that the expense is justified by the frequency of use.

Maintenance and minor repair tool kit

The tools in this list should be considered the minimum required for performance of routine maintenance, servicing and minor repair work. We recommend the purchase of combination wrenches (box-end and open-end combined in one wrench). While more expensive than open end wrenches, they offer the advantages of both types of wrench.

Combination wrench set (1/4-inch to 1 inch or 6 mm to 19 mm)
Adjustable wrench, 8 inch
Spark plug wrench with rubber insert
Spark plug gap adjusting tool
Feeler gauge set
Brake bleeder wrench
Standard screwdriver (5/16-inch x 6 inch)
Phillips screwdriver (No. 2 x 6 inch)
Combination pliers – 6 inch
Hacksaw and assortment of blades
Tire pressure gauge
Grease gun
Oil can
Fine emery cloth
Wire brush

Battery post and cable cleaning tool
Oil filter wrench
Funnel (medium size)
Safety goggles
Jackstands(2)
Drain pan

Note: *If basic tune-ups are going to be part of routine maintenance, it will be necessary to purchase a good quality stroboscopic timing light and combination tachometer/dwell meter. Although they are included in the list of special tools, it is mentioned here because they are absolutely necessary for tuning most vehicles properly.*

Repair and overhaul tool set

These tools are essential for anyone who plans to perform major repairs and are in addition to those in the maintenance and minor repair tool kit. Included is a comprehensive set of sockets which, though expensive, are invaluable because of their versatility, especially when various extensions and drives are available. We recommend the 1/2-inch drive over the 3/8-inch drive. Although the larger drive is bulky and more expensive, it has the capacity of accepting a very wide range of large sockets. Ideally, however, the mechanic should have a 3/8-inch drive set and a 1/2-inch drive set.

Socket set(s)
Reversible ratchet
Extension – 10 inch
Universal joint
Torque wrench (same size drive as sockets)
Ball peen hammer – 8 ounce
Soft-face hammer (plastic/rubber)
Standard screwdriver (1/4-inch x 6 inch)
Standard screwdriver (stubby – 5/16-inch)
Phillips screwdriver (No. 3 x 8 inch)
Phillips screwdriver (stubby – No. 2)

Pliers – vise grip
Pliers – lineman's
Pliers – needle nose
Pliers – snap-ring (internal and external)
Cold chisel – 1/2-inch
Scribe
Scraper (made from flattened copper tubing)
Centerpunch
Pin punches (1/16, 1/8, 3/16-inch)
Steel rule/straightedge – 12 inch
Allen wrench set (1/8 to 3/8-inch or 4 mm to 10 mm)
A selection of files
Wire brush (large)
Jackstands (second set)
Jack (scissor or hydraulic type)

Note: *Another tool which is often useful is an electric drill motor with a chuck capacity of 3/8-inch and a set of good quality drill bits.*

Special tools

The tools in this list include those which are not used regularly, are expensive to buy, or which need to be used in accordance with their manufacturer's instructions. Unless these tools will be used frequently, it is not very economical to purchase many of them. A consideration would be to split the cost and use between yourself and a friend or friends. In addition, most of these tools can be obtained from a tool rental shop on a temporary basis.

This list primarily contains only those tools and instruments widely available to the public, and not those special tools produced by the vehicle manufacturer for distribution to dealer service departments. Occasionally, references to the manufacturer's special tools are included in the text of this manual. Generally, an alternative method of doing the job without the special tool is offered. However, sometimes there is no alternative to their use. Where this is the case, and the tool cannot be purchased or borrowed, the work should be turned over to the dealer service department or an automotive repair shop.

Valve spring compressor
Piston ring groove cleaning tool
Piston ring compressor
Piston ring installation tool
Cylinder compression gauge
Cylinder ridge reamer
Cylinder surfacing hone
Cylinder bore gauge
Micrometers and/or dial calipers
Hydraulic lifter removal tool
Balljoint separator
Universal-type puller
Impact screwdriver
Dial indicator set
Stroboscopic timing light (inductive pick-up)
Hand operated vacuum/pressure pump
Tachometer/dwell meter
Universal electrical multimeter
Cable hoist
Brake spring removal and installation tools
Floor jack

Buying tools

For the do-it-yourselfer who is just starting to get involved in vehicle maintenance and repair, there are a number of options available when purchasing tools. If maintenance and minor repair is the extent of the work to be done, the purchase of individual tools is satisfactory. If, on the other hand, extensive work is planned, it would be a good idea to purchase a modest tool set from one of the large retail chain stores. A set can usually be bought at a substantial savings over the individual tool prices, and they often come with a tool box. As additional tools are needed, add–on sets, individual tools and a larger tool box can be purchased to expand the tool selection. Building a tool set gradually allows the cost of the tools to be spread over a longer period of time and gives the mechanic the freedom to choose only those tools that will actually be used.

Tool stores will often be the only source of some of the special tools that are needed, but regardless of where tools are bought, try to avoid cheap ones, especially when buying screwdrivers and sockets, because they won't last very long. The expense involved in replacing cheap tools will eventually be greater than the initial cost of quality tools.

Care and maintenance of tools

Good tools are expensive, so it makes sense to treat them with respect. Keep them clean and in usable condition and store them properly when not in use. Always wipe off any dirt, grease or metal chips before putting them away. Never leave tools lying around in the work area. Upon completion of a job, always check closely under the hood for tools that may have been left there so they won't get lost during a test drive.

Some tools, such as screwdrivers, pliers, wrenches and sockets, can be hung on a panel mounted on the garage or workshop wall, while others should be kept in a tool box or tray. Measuring instruments, gauges, meters, etc. must be carefully stored where they cannot be damaged by weather or impact from other tools.

When tools are used with care and stored properly, they will last a very long time. Even with the best of care, though, tools will wear out if used frequently. When a tool is damaged or worn out, replace it. Subsequent jobs will be safer and more enjoyable if you do.

Working facilities

Not to be overlooked when discussing tools is the workshop. If anything more than routine maintenance is to be carried out, some sort of suitable work area is essential.

It is understood, and appreciated, that many home mechanics do not have a good workshop or garage available, and end up removing an engine or doing major repairs outside. It is recommended, however, that the overhaul or repair be completed under the cover of a roof.

A clean, flat workbench or table of comfortable working height is an absolute necessity. The workbench should be equipped with a vise that has a jaw opening of at least four inches.

As mentioned previously, some clean, dry storage space is also required for tools, as well as the lubricants, fluids, cleaning solvents, etc. which soon become necessary.

Sometimes waste oil and fluids, drained from the engine or cooling system during normal maintenance or repairs, present a disposal problem. To avoid pouring them on the ground or into a sewage system, pour the used fluids into large containers, seal them with caps and take them to an authorized disposal site or recycling center. Plastic jugs, such as old antifreeze containers, are ideal for this purpose.

Always keep a supply of old newspapers and clean rags available. Old towels are excellent for mopping up spills. Many mechanics use rolls of paper towels for most work because they are readily available and disposable. To help keep the area under the vehicle clean, a large cardboard box can be cut open and flattened to protect the garage or shop floor.

Whenever working over a painted surface, such as when leaning over a fender to service something under the hood, always cover it with an old blanket or bedspread to protect the finish. Vinyl covered pads, made especially for this purpose, are available at auto parts stores.

Booster battery (jump) starting

Observe these precautions when using a booster battery to start a vehicle:

a) Before connecting the booster battery, make sure the ignition switch is in the Off position.
b) Turn off the lights, heater and other electrical loads.
c) Your eyes should be shielded. Safety goggles are a good idea.
d) Make sure the booster battery is the same voltage as the dead one in the vehicle.
e) The two vehicles MUST NOT TOUCH each other!
f) Make sure the transmission is in Neutral (manual) or Park (automatic).
g) If the booster battery is not a maintenance-free type, remove the vent caps and lay a cloth over the vent holes.

Connect the red jumper cable to the positive (+) terminals of each battery.

Connect one end of the black jumper cable to the negative (–) terminal of the booster battery. The other end of this cable should be connected to a good ground on the vehicle to be started, such as a bolt or bracket on the engine block **(see illustration)**. Make sure the cable will not come into contact with the fan, drivebelts or other moving parts of the engine.

Start the engine using the booster battery, then, with the engine running at idle speed, disconnect the jumper cables in the reverse order of connection.

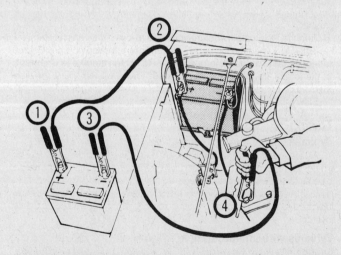

Make the booster battery cable connections in the numerical order shown (note that the negative cable of the booster battery is NOT attached to the negative terminal of the dead battery)

Jacking and towing

Jacking

Warning: *The jack supplied with the vehicle should only be used for raising the vehicle when changing a tire or placing jackstands under the frame. Never work under the vehicle or start the engine while the jack is being used as the only means of support.*

The vehicle must be on a level surface with the wheels blocked, the hazard flashers on and the transaxle in Park (automatic) or Reverse (manual). Apply the parking brake if the front of the vehicle must be raised. Make sure no one is in the vehicle when using the jack to lift it.

Remove the jack, lug nut wrench and spare tire (if needed) from the vehicle. If a tire is being changed, use the lug wrench to remove the wheel cover. **Warning:** *Wheel covers may have sharp edges – be very careful not to cut yourself.* Loosen the lug nuts one-half turn, but leave them in place until the tire is off the ground.

Position the jack under the vehicle at the indicated jacking point. There's a front and rear jacking point on each side of the vehicle **(see illustration)**. Turn the jack handle clockwise until the tire clears the ground. Remove the lug nuts, pull the tire off and install the spare. Thread the lug nuts back on with the beveled edges facing in and tighten them snugly. Don't attempt to tighten them completely until the vehicle is lowered to the ground.

Turn the jack handle counterclockwise to lower the vehicle. Remove the jack and tighten the lug nuts (if loosened or removed) in a criss-cross pattern. If possible, use a torque wrench to tighten them (see Chapter 1 for the torque figures). If you don't have a torque wrench, have the nuts checked by a service station or repair shop as soon as possible.

Stow the tire, jack and wrench and unblock the wheels.

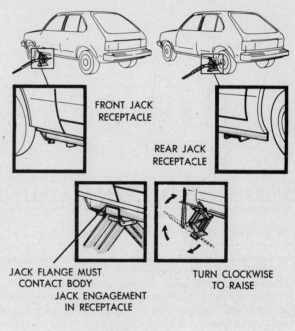

FRONT JACK RECEPTACLE

REAR JACK RECEPTACLE

JACK FLANGE MUST CONTACT BODY
JACK ENGAGEMENT IN RECEPTACLE

TURN CLOCKWISE TO RAISE

Jacking points

Towing

Vehicles with a manual transaxle

As a general rule, the vehicle should be towed with the front (drive) wheels off the ground. Be sure to release the parking brake. If the vehicle is being towed with the front wheels on the ground, place the transaxle in Neutral. Also, the ignition key must be in the Off position, since the steering lock mechanism isn't strong enough to hold the front wheels straight while towing.

Vehicles with an automatic transaxle

Caution: *Never tow a vehicle with an automatic transaxle from the rear with the front wheels on the ground. If the vehicle must be towed from the rear, place the front wheels on a towing dolly.*

Vehicles equipped with an automatic transaxle can be towed from the front only with all four wheels on the ground, provided that speeds don't exceed 40 mph and the distance isn't over 15 miles. Before towing, check the transmission fluid level (see Chapter 1). If the level is below the Hot mark on the dipstick, add fluid or use a towing dolly. Release the parking brake, put the transaxle in Neutral and place the ignition key in the Off position. A driver must be in the towed vehicle to steer and operate the brakes.

All vehicles

Equipment specifically designed for towing should be used. It should be attached to the main structural members of the vehicle, not the bumpers or brackets. Safety is a major consideration when towing and all applicable state and local laws must be obeyed. A safety chain must be used. Remember that power steering and brakes won't work with the engine off.

Automotive chemicals and lubricants

A number of automotive chemicals and lubricants are available for use during vehicle maintenance and repair. They include a wide variety of products ranging from cleaning solvents and degreasers to lubricants and protective sprays for rubber, plastic and vinyl.

Cleaners

Carburetor cleaner and choke cleaner is a strong solvent for gum, varnish and carbon. Most carburetor cleaners leave a dry-type lubricant film which will not harden or gum up. Because of this film it is not recommended for use on electrical components.

Brake system cleaner is used to remove grease and brake fluid from the brake system, where clean surfaces are absolutely necessary. It leaves no residue and often eliminates brake squeal caused by contaminants.

Electrical cleaner removes oxidation, corrosion and carbon deposits from electrical contacts, restoring full current flow. It can also be used to clean spark plugs, carburetor jets, voltage regulators and other parts where an oil-free surface is desired.

Demoisturants remove water and moisture from electrical components such as alternators, voltage regulators, electrical connectors and fuse blocks. They are non-conductive, non-corrosive and non-flammable.

Degreasers are heavy-duty solvents used to remove grease from the outside of the engine and from chassis components. They can be sprayed or brushed on and, depending on the type, are rinsed off either with water or solvent.

Lubricants

Motor oil is the lubricant formulated for use in engines. It normally contains a wide variety of additives to prevent corrosion and reduce foaming and wear. Motor oil comes in various weights (viscosity ratings) from 5 to 80. The recommended weight of the oil depends on the season, temperature and the demands on the engine. Light oil is used in cold climates and under light load conditions. Heavy oil is used in hot climates and where high loads are encountered. Multi-viscosity oils are designed to have characteristics of both light and heavy oils and are available in a number of weights from 5W-20 to 20W-50.

Gear oil is designed to be used in differentials, manual transmissions and other areas where high-temperature lubrication is required.

Chassis and wheel bearing grease is a heavy grease used where increased loads and friction are encountered, such as for wheel bearings, balljoints, tie-rod ends and universal joints.

High-temperature wheel bearing grease is designed to withstand the extreme temperatures encountered by wheel bearings in disc brake equipped vehicles. It usually contains molybdenum disulfide (moly), which is a dry-type lubricant.

White grease is a heavy grease for metal-to-metal applications where water is a problem. White grease stays soft under both low and high temperatures (usually from –100 to +190-degrees F), and will not wash off or dilute in the presence of water.

Assembly lube is a special extreme pressure lubricant, usually containing moly, used to lubricate high-load parts (such as main and rod bearings and cam lobes) for initial start-up of a new engine. The assembly lube lubricates the parts without being squeezed out or washed away until the engine oiling system begins to function.

Silicone lubricants are used to protect rubber, plastic, vinyl and nylon parts.

Graphite lubricants are used where oils cannot be used due to contamination problems, such as in locks. The dry graphite will lubricate metal parts while remaining uncontaminated by dirt, water, oil or acids. It is electrically conductive and will not foul electrical contacts in locks such as the ignition switch.

Moly penetrants loosen and lubricate frozen, rusted and corroded fasteners and prevent future rusting or freezing.

Heat-sink grease is a special electrically non-conductive grease that is used for mounting electronic ignition modules where it is essential that heat is transferred away from the module.

Sealants

RTV sealant is one of the most widely used gasket compounds. Made from silicone, RTV is air curing, it seals, bonds, waterproofs, fills surface irregularities, remains flexible, doesn't shrink, is relatively easy to remove, and is used as a supplementary sealer with almost all low and medium temperature gaskets.

Anaerobic sealant is much like RTV in that it can be used either to seal gaskets or to form gaskets by itself. It remains flexible, is solvent resistant and fills surface imperfections. The difference between an anaerobic sealant and an RTV-type sealant is in the curing. RTV cures when exposed to air, while an anaerobic sealant cures only in the absence of air. This means that an anaerobic sealant cures only after the assembly of parts, sealing them together.

Thread and pipe sealant is used for sealing hydraulic and pneumatic fittings and vacuum lines. It is usually made from a teflon compound, and comes in a spray, a paint-on liquid and as a wrap-around tape.

Chemicals

Anti–seize compound prevents seizing, galling, cold welding, rust and corrosion in fasteners. High-temperature anti-seize, usually made with copper and graphite lubricants, is used for exhaust system and exhaust manifold bolts.

Anaerobic locking compounds are used to keep fasteners from vibrating or working loose and cure only after installation, in the absence of air. Medium strength locking compound is used for small nuts, bolts and screws that may be removed later. High-strength locking compound is for large nuts, bolts and studs which aren't removed on a regular basis.

Oil additives range from viscosity index improvers to chemical treatments that claim to reduce internal engine friction. It should be noted that most oil manufacturers caution against using additives with their oils.

Gas additives perform several functions, depending on their chemical makeup. They usually contain solvents that help dissolve gum and varnish that build up on carburetor, fuel injection and intake parts. They also serve to break down carbon deposits that form on the inside surfaces of the combustion chambers. Some additives contain upper cylinder lubricants for valves and piston rings, and others contain chemicals to remove condensation from the gas tank.

Miscellaneous

Brake fluid is specially formulated hydraulic fluid that can withstand the heat and pressure encountered in brake systems. Care must be taken so this fluid does not come in contact with painted surfaces or plastics. An opened container should always be resealed to prevent contamination by water or dirt.

Weatherstrip adhesive is used to bond weatherstripping around doors, windows and trunk lids. It is sometimes used to attach trim pieces.

Undercoating is a petroleum-based, tar-like substance that is designed to protect metal surfaces on the underside of the vehicle from corrosion. It also acts as a sound-deadening agent by insulating the bottom of the vehicle.

Waxes and polishes are used to help protect painted and plated surfaces from the weather. Different types of paint may require the use of different types of wax and polish. Some polishes utilize a chemical or abrasive cleaner to help remove the top layer of oxidized (dull) paint on older vehicles. In recent years many non-wax polishes that contain a wide variety of chemicals such as polymers and silicones have been introduced. These non-wax polishes are usually easier to apply and last longer than conventional waxes and polishes.

Safety first!

Regardless of how enthusiastic you may be about getting on with the job at hand, take the time to ensure that your safety is not jeopardized. A moment's lack of attention can result in an accident, as can failure to observe certain simple safety precautions. The possibility of an accident will always exist, and the following points should not be considered a comprehensive list of all dangers. Rather, they are intended to make you aware of the risks and to encourage a safety conscious approach to all work you carry out on your vehicle.

Essential DOs and DON'Ts

DON'T rely on a jack when working under the vehicle. Always use approved jackstands to support the weight of the vehicle and place them under the recommended lift or support points.

DON'T attempt to loosen extremely tight fasteners (i.e. wheel lug nuts) while the vehicle is on a jack – it may fall.

DON'T start the engine without first making sure that the transmission is in Neutral (or Park where applicable) and the parking brake is set.

DON'T remove the radiator cap from a hot cooling system – let it cool or cover it with a cloth and release the pressure gradually.

DON'T attempt to drain the engine oil until you are sure it has cooled to the point that it will not burn you.

DON'T touch any part of the engine or exhaust system until it has cooled sufficiently to avoid burns.

DON'T siphon toxic liquids such as gasoline, antifreeze and brake fluid by mouth, or allow them to remain on your skin.

DON'T inhale brake lining dust – it is potentially hazardous (see Asbestos below)

DON'T allow spilled oil or grease to remain on the floor – wipe it up before someone slips on it.

DON'T use loose fitting wrenches or other tools which may slip and cause injury.

DON'T push on wrenches when loosening or tightening nuts or bolts. Always try to pull the wrench toward you. If the situation calls for pushing the wrench away, push with an open hand to avoid scraped knuckles if the wrench should slip.

DON'T attempt to lift a heavy component alone – get someone to help you.

DON'T rush or take unsafe shortcuts to finish a job.

DON'T allow children or animals in or around the vehicle while you are working on it.

DO wear eye protection when using power tools such as a drill, sander, bench grinder, etc. and when working under a vehicle.

DO keep loose clothing and long hair well out of the way of moving parts.

DO make sure that any hoist used has a safe working load rating adequate for the job.

DO get someone to check on you periodically when working alone on a vehicle.

DO carry out work in a logical sequence and make sure that everything is correctly assembled and tightened.

DO keep chemicals and fluids tightly capped and out of the reach of children and pets.

DO remember that your vehicle's safety affects that of yourself and others. If in doubt on any point, get professional advice.

Asbestos

Certain friction, insulating, sealing, and other products – such as brake linings, brake bands, clutch linings, torque converters, gaskets, etc. – contain asbestos. *Extreme care must be taken to avoid inhalation of dust from such products since it is hazardous to health.* If in doubt, assume that they *do* contain asbestos.

Fire

Remember at all times that gasoline is highly flammable. Never smoke or have any kind of open flame around when working on a vehicle. But the risk does not end there. A spark caused by an electrical short circuit, by two metal surfaces contacting each other, or even by static electricity built up in your body under certain conditions, can ignite gasoline vapors, which in a confined space are highly explosive. Do not, under any circumstances, use gasoline for cleaning parts. Use an approved safety solvent.

Always disconnect the battery ground (–) cable *at the battery* before working on any part of the fuel system or electrical system. Never risk spilling fuel on a hot engine or exhaust component.

It is strongly recommended that a fire extinguisher suitable for use on fuel and electrical fires be kept handy in the garage or workshop at all times. Never try to extinguish a fuel or electrical fire with water.

Fumes

Certain fumes are highly toxic and can quickly cause unconsciousness and even death if inhaled to any extent. Gasoline vapor falls into this category, as do the vapors from some cleaning solvents. Any draining or pouring of such volatile fluids should be done in a well ventilated area.

When using cleaning fluids and solvents, read the instructions on the container carefully. Never use materials from unmarked containers.

Never run the engine in an enclosed space, such as a garage. Exhaust fumes contain carbon monoxide, which is extremely poisonous. If you need to run the engine, always do so in the open air, or at least have the rear of the vehicle outside the work area.

If you are fortunate enough to have the use of an inspection pit, never drain or pour gasoline and never run the engine while the vehicle is over the pit. The fumes, being heavier than air, will concentrate in the pit with possibly lethal results.

The battery

Never create a spark or allow a bare light bulb near a battery. They normally give off a certain amount of hydrogen gas, which is highly explosive.

Always disconnect the battery ground (–) cable *at the battery* before working on the fuel or electrical systems.

If possible, loosen the filler caps or cover when charging the battery from an external source (this does not apply to sealed or maintenance-free batteries). Do not charge at an excessive rate or the battery may burst.

Take care when adding water to a non maintenance–free battery and when carrying a battery. The electrolyte, even when diluted, is very corrosive and should not be allowed to contact clothing or skin.

Always wear eye protection when cleaning the battery to prevent the caustic deposits from entering your eyes.

Household current

When using an electric power tool, inspection light, etc., which operates on household current, always make sure that the tool is correctly connected to its plug and that, where necessary, it is properly grounded. Do not use such items in damp conditions and, again, do not create a spark or apply excessive heat in the vicinity of fuel or fuel vapor.

Secondary ignition system voltage

A severe electric shock can result from touching certain parts of the ignition system (such as the spark plug wires) when the engine is running or being cranked, particularly if components are damp or the insulation is defective. In the case of an electronic ignition system, the secondary system voltage is much higher and could prove fatal.

Conversion factors

Length (distance)
Inches (in)	X	25.4	= Millimetres (mm)	X 0.0394	= Inches (in)
Feet (ft)	X	0.305	= Metres (m)	X 3.281	= Feet (ft)
Miles	X	1.609	= Kilometres (km)	X 0.621	= Miles

Volume (capacity)
Cubic inches (cu in; in³)	X	16.387	= Cubic centimetres (cc; cm³)	X 0.061	= Cubic inches (cu in; in³)
Imperial pints (Imp pt)	X	0.568	= Litres (l)	X 1.76	= Imperial pints (Imp pt)
Imperial quarts (Imp qt)	X	1.137	= Litres (l)	X 0.88	= Imperial quarts (Imp qt)
Imperial quarts (Imp qt)	X	1.201	= US quarts (US qt)	X 0.833	= Imperial quarts (Imp qt)
US quarts (US qt)	X	0.946	= Litres (l)	X 1.057	= US quarts (US qt)
Imperial gallons (Imp gal)	X	4.546	= Litres (l)	X 0.22	= Imperial gallons (Imp gal)
Imperial gallons (Imp gal)	X	1.201	= US gallons (US gal)	X 0.833	= Imperial gallons (Imp gal)
US gallons (US gal)	X	3.785	= Litres (l)	X 0.264	= US gallons (US gal)

Mass (weight)
Ounces (oz)	X	28.35	= Grams (g)	X 0.035	= Ounces (oz)
Pounds (lb)	X	0.454	= Kilograms (kg)	X 2.205	= Pounds (lb)

Force
Ounces-force (ozf; oz)	X	0.278	= Newtons (N)	X 3.6	= Ounces-force (ozf; oz)
Pounds-force (lbf; lb)	X	4.448	= Newtons (N)	X 0.225	= Pounds-force (lbf; lb)
Newtons (N)	X	0.1	= Kilograms-force (kgf; kg)	X 9.81	= Newtons (N)

Pressure
Pounds-force per square inch (psi; lbf/in²; lb/in²)	X	0.070	= Kilograms-force per square centimetre (kgf/cm²; kg/cm²)	X 14.223	= Pounds-force per square inch (psi; lbf/in²; lb/in²)
Pounds-force per square inch (psi; lbf/in²; lb/in²)	X	0.068	= Atmospheres (atm)	X 14.696	= Pounds-force per square inch (psi; lbf/in²; lb/in²)
Pounds-force per square inch (psi; lbf/in²; lb/in²)	X	0.069	= Bars	X 14.5	= Pounds-force per square inch (psi; lbf/in²; lb/in²)
Pounds-force per square inch (psi; lbf/in²; lb/in²)	X	6.895	= Kilopascals (kPa)	X 0.145	= Pounds-force per square inch (psi; lbf/in²; lb/in²)
Kilopascals (kPa)	X	0.01	= Kilograms-force per square centimetre (kgf/cm²; kg/cm²)	X 98.1	= Kilopascals (kPa)

Torque (moment of force)
Pounds-force inches (lbf in; lb in)	X	1.152	= Kilograms-force centimetre (kgf cm; kg cm)	X 0.868	= Pounds-force inches (lbf in; lb in)
Pounds-force inches (lbf in; lb in)	X	0.113	= Newton metres (Nm)	X 8.85	= Pounds-force inches (lbf in; lb in)
Pounds-force inches (lbf in; lb in)	X	0.083	= Pounds-force feet (lbf ft; lb ft)	X 12	= Pounds-force inches (lbf in; lb in)
Pounds-force feet (lbf ft; lb ft)	X	0.138	= Kilograms-force metres (kgf m; kg m)	X 7.233	= Pounds-force feet (lbf ft; lb ft)
Pounds-force feet (lbf ft; lb ft)	X	1.356	= Newton metres (Nm)	X 0.738	= Pounds-force feet (lbf ft; lb ft)
Newton metres (Nm)	X	0.102	= Kilograms-force metres (kgf m; kg m)	X 9.804	= Newton metres (Nm)

Power
Horsepower (hp)	X	745.7	= Watts (W)	X 0.0013	= Horsepower (hp)

Velocity (speed)
Miles per hour (miles/hr; mph)	X	1.609	= Kilometres per hour (km/hr; kph)	X 0.621	= Miles per hour (miles/hr; mph)

Fuel consumption*
Miles per gallon, Imperial (mpg)	X	0.354	= Kilometres per litre (km/l)	X 2.825	= Miles per gallon, Imperial (mpg)
Miles per gallon, US (mpg)	X	0.425	= Kilometres per litre (km/l)	X 2.352	= Miles per gallon, US (mpg)

Temperature
Degrees Fahrenheit = (°C x 1.8) + 32

Degrees Celsius (Degrees Centigrade; °C) = (°F - 32) x 0.56

*It is common practice to convert from miles per gallon (mpg) to litres/100 kilometres (l/100km), where mpg (Imperial) x l/100 km = 282 and mpg (US) x l/100 km = 235

Troubleshooting

Contents

Remember, successful troubleshooting isn't a mysterious black art practiced only by professional mechanics. It's simply the result of the right knowledge combined with an intelligent, systematic approach to a problem. Always use the process of elimination, starting with the simplest solution and working through to the most complex – and never overlook the obvious. Anyone can run the gas tank dry or leave the lights on overnight, so don't assume that it can't happen to you.

Finally, always try to establish a clear idea why a problem has occurred and take steps to ensure that it doesn't happen again. If the electrical system fails because of a poor connection, check all other connections in the system to make sure they don't fail as well. If a particular fuse continues to blow, find out why – don't just replace one fuse after another. Remember, failure of a small component can often be indicative of potential failure or incorrect functioning of a more important component or system.

Engine

1　Engine will not rotate when attempting to start

1　Battery terminal connections loose or corroded. Check the cable terminals at the battery. Tighten the cable or remove corrosion as necessary.
2　Battery discharged or faulty. If the cable connections are clean and tight on the battery posts, turn the key to the On position and switch on the headlights and/or windshield wipers. If they fail to function, the battery is discharged.
3　Automatic transaxle not completely engaged in Park or Neutral or clutch pedal not completely depressed.
4　Broken, loose or disconnected wiring in the starting circuit. Inspect all wiring and connectors at the battery, starter solenoid and ignition switch.
5　Starter motor pinion jammed in flywheel ring gear. If manual transaxle, place transaxle in gear and rock the vehicle to manually turn the engine. Remove starter and inspect pinion and flywheel at earliest convenience (Chapter 5).
6　Starter solenoid faulty (Chapter 5).
7　Starter motor faulty (Chapter 5).
8　Ignition switch faulty (Chapter 12).

2　Engine rotates but will not start

1　Fuel tank empty.
2　Faulty carburetor or fuel injection system (Chapter 4).
3　Battery discharged (engine rotates slowly). Check the operation of electrical components as described in the previous Section.
4　Battery terminal connections loose or corroded (see previous Section).
5　Fuel pump faulty (Chapter 4).
6　Excessive moisture on, or damage to, ignition components (Chapter 5).
7　Worn, faulty or incorrectly gapped spark plugs (Chapter 1).
8　Broken, loose or disconnected wiring in the starting circuit (see previous Section).
9　Distributor loose, causing ignition timing to change. Turn the distributor as necessary to start the engine, then set the ignition timing as soon as possible (Chapter 1).
10　Broken, loose or disconnected wires at the ignition coil or faulty coil (Chapter 5).

3　Starter motor operates without rotating engine

1　Starter pinion sticking. Remove the starter (Chapter 5) and inspect.
2　Starter pinion or flywheel teeth worn or broken. Remove the flywheel/driveplate access cover and inspect.

4　Engine hard to start when cold

1　Battery discharged or low. Check as described in Section 1.
2　Fault in the fuel or electrical systems (Chapters 4 and 5).
3　Carburetor needs overhaul (Chapter 4).
4　Distributor rotor carbon tracked and/or damaged (Chapters 1 and 5).
5　Choke control stuck or inoperative (Chapters 1 and 4).

5　Engine hard to start when hot

1　Air filter clogged (Chapter 1).
2　Fault in the fuel or electrical systems (Chapters 4 and 5).
3　Fuel not reaching the carburetor or fuel injection system (see Section 2).

6　Starter motor noisy or excessively rough in engagement

1　Pinion or flywheel gear teeth worn or broken. Remove the cover at the rear of the engine (if so equipped) and inspect.
2　Starter motor mounting bolts loose or missing.

7　Engine starts but stops immediately

1　Loose or faulty electrical connections at distributor, coil or alternator.
2　Fault in the fuel or electrical systems (Chapters 4 and 5).
3　Insufficient fuel reaching the carburetor or fuel injection system. Check the fuel pump (Chapter 4).
4　Vacuum leak at the gasket surfaces of the intake manifold, or carburetor/throttle body. Make sure all mounting bolts/nuts are tightened securely and all vacuum hoses connected to the carburetor/throttle body and manifold are positioned properly and in good condition.

8　Engine lopes while idling or idles erratically

1　Vacuum leaks. Check the mounting bolts/nuts at the carburetor/throttle body and intake manifold for tightness. Make sure all vacuum hoses are connected and in good condition. Use a stethoscope or a length of fuel hose held against your ear to listen for vacuum leaks while the engine is running. A hissing sound will be heard. A soapy water solution will also detect leaks.
2　Faulty fuel or electrical systems (Chapters 4 and 5).
3　Leaking EGR valve or plugged PCV valve (see Chapters 1 and 6).
4　Air filter clogged (Chapter 1).
5　Fuel pump not delivering sufficient fuel to the carburetor or fuel injection system (see Chapter 4).
6　Carburetor/throttle body out of adjustment (Chapter 4).
7　Leaking head gasket. Perform a compression check (Chapter 2).
8　Camshaft lobes worn (Chapter 2).

9　Engine misses at idle speed

1　Spark plugs worn or gap too wide (Chapter 1).
2　Faulty fuel or electrical systems (Chapters 4 and 5).
3　Faulty spark plug wires (Chapter 1).

10　Engine misses throughout driving speed range

1　Fuel filter clogged and/or impurities in the fuel system (Chapter 1).
2　Faulty or incorrectly gapped spark plugs (Chapter 1).
3　Faulty fuel or electrical systems (Chapters 4 and 5).
4　Incorrect ignition timing (Chapter 1).
5　Check for cracked distributor cap, disconnected distributor wires and damaged distributor components (Chapter 1).
6　Defective spark plug wires (Chapter 1).
7　Faulty emissions system components (Chapter 6).
8　Low or uneven cylinder compression pressures. Remove the spark plugs and test the compression with a gauge (Chapter 2).
9　Weak or faulty ignition system (Chapter 5).
10　Vacuum leaks at the carburetor/throttle body, intake manifold or vacuum hoses (see Section 8).

11　Engine stalls

1　Idle speed incorrect. Refer to the VECI label and Chapter 1.
2　Fuel filter clogged and/or water and impurities in the fuel system (Chapter 1).
3　Distributor components damp or damaged (Chapter 5).

4 Faulty fuel system or emission control system information sensors (Chapters 4 and 6).
5 Faulty emissions system components (Chapter 6).
6 Faulty or incorrectly gapped spark plugs (Chapter 1). Also check the spark plug wires (Chapter 1).
7 Vacuum leak at the carburetor/throttle body, intake manifold or vacuum hoses. Check as described in Section 8.

12 Engine lacks power

1 Incorrect ignition timing (Chapter 1).
2 Faulty fuel or electrical systems (Chapters 4 and 5).
3 Excessive play in the distributor shaft. At the same time, check for a damaged rotor, faulty distributor cap, wires, etc. (Chapters 1 and 5).
4 Faulty or incorrectly gapped spark plugs (Chapter 1).
5 Carburetor/throttle body not adjusted properly or excessively worn (Chapter 4).
6 Defective coil (Chapter 5).
7 Brakes binding (Chapter 1).
8 Automatic transaxle fluid level incorrect (Chapter 1).
9 Clutch slipping (Chapter 8).
10 Fuel filter clogged and/or impurities in the fuel system (Chapter 1).
11 Emissions control system not functioning properly (Chapter 6).
12 Use of substandard fuel. Fill the tank with the proper octane fuel.
13 Low or uneven cylinder compression pressures. Test with a compression tester, which will detect leaking valves and/or a blown head gasket (Chapter 2).

13 Engine backfires

1 Emissions system not functioning properly (Chapter 6).
2 Faulty fuel or electrical systems (Chapters 4 and 5).
3 Ignition timing incorrect (Chapter 1).
4 Faulty secondary ignition system (cracked spark plug insulator, faulty plug wires, distributor cap and/or rotor) (Chapters 1 and 5).
5 Carburetor in need of adjustment or worn excessively (Chapter 4).
6 Vacuum leak at the carburetor/throttle body, intake manifold or vacuum hoses. Check as described in Section 8.
7 Valves sticking (Chapter 2).

14 Pinging or knocking engine sounds during acceleration or uphill

1 Incorrect grade of fuel. Fill the tank with fuel of the proper octane rating.
2 Faulty fuel or electrical systems (Chapters 4 and 5).
3 Ignition timing incorrect (Chapter 1).
4 Carburetor out of adjustment (Chapter 4).
5 Incorrect spark plugs. Check the plug type against the VECI label located in the engine compartment. Also check the plugs and wires for damage (Chapter 1).
6 Worn or damaged distributor components (Chapter 5).
7 Faulty emissions system (Chapter 6).
8 Vacuum leak (Chapters 2 and 4).

15 Engine diesels (continues to run) after switching off

1 Idle speed too high. Refer to Chapter 1.
2 Faulty fuel or electrical systems (Chapters 4 and 5).
3 Ignition timing incorrect (Chapter 1).
4 Thermo-controlled air cleaner heat valve not operating properly (Chapters 1 and 6).

5 Excessive engine operating temperature. Probable causes of this are a malfunctioning thermostat, clogged radiator, faulty water pump (Chapter 3).

Engine electrical system

16 Battery will not hold a charge

1 Alternator drivebelt defective or loose (Chapter 1).
2 Electrolyte level low or battery discharged (Chapter 1).
3 Battery terminals loose or corroded (Chapter 1).
4 Alternator not charging properly (Chapter 5).
5 Loose, broken or faulty wiring in the charging circuit (Chapter 5).
6 Short in the vehicle wiring causing a continual drain on battery (refer to Chapter 12 and the Wiring Diagrams).
7 Battery defective internally.

17 Ignition light fails to go out

1 Defective alternator or charging circuit (Chapter 5).
2 Alternator drivebelt defective or loose (Chapter 1).

18 Ignition light fails to come on when key is turned on

1 Instrument cluster warning light bulb defective (Chapter 12).
2 Alternator faulty (Chapter 5).
3 Fault in the instrument cluster printed circuit, dashboard wiring or bulb holder (Chapter 12).

Fuel system

19 Excessive fuel consumption

1 Dirty or clogged air filter element (Chapter 1).
2 Incorrect ignition timing (Chapter 1).
3 Choke sticking or incorrectly adjusted (Chapter 1).
4 Emissions system not functioning properly (Chapter 6).
5 Faulty fuel or electrical systems (Chapters 4 and 5).
6 Carburetor internal parts excessively worn or damaged (Chapter 4).
7 Low tire pressure or incorrect tire size (Chapter 1).

20 Fuel leakage and/or fuel odor

1 Leak in a fuel feed or vent line (Chapter 4).
2 Tank overfilled. Fill only to automatic shut-off.
3 Evaporative emissions system canister clogged (Chapter 6).
4 Vapor leaks from system lines (Chapter 4).
5 Carburetor internal parts excessively worn or out of adjustment (Chapter 4).
6 Leaking fuel injector(s) (Chapter 4).
7 Leaking fuel pressure regulator (Chapter 4).

Cooling system

21 Overheating

1 Low coolant level (Chapter 1).
2 Water pump drivebelt defective or loose (Chapter 1).
3 Radiator core blocked or radiator grille restricted (Chapter 3).
4 Thermostat faulty (Chapter 3).

5   Fan blades broken or cracked (Chapter 3).
6   Radiator cap not maintaining proper pressure. Have the cap pressure tested by gas station or repair shop.
7   Ignition timing incorrect (Chapter 1).

22   Overcooling

Thermostat faulty (Chapter 3).

23   External coolant leakage

1   Deteriorated or damaged hoses or loose clamps. Replace hoses and/or tighten the clamps at the hose connections (Chapter 1).
2   Water pump seals defective. If this is the case, coolant will drip from the weep hole in the water pump body (Chapter 3).
3   Leakage from radiator core or header tank. This will require the radiator to be professionally repaired (see Chapter 3 for removal procedures).
4   Engine drain plug leaking (Chapter 1) or water jacket core plugs leaking (see Chapter 2).

24   Internal coolant leakage

Note: *Internal coolant leaks can usually be detected by examining the oil. Check the dipstick and inside of the cylinder head cover for water deposits and an oil consistency resembling a milkshake.*
1   Leaking cylinder head gasket. Have the cooling system pressure tested.
2   Cracked cylinder bore or cylinder head. Dismantle the engine and inspect (Chapter 2).

25   Coolant loss

1   Too much coolant in the system (Chapter 1).
2   Coolant loss caused by overheating (see Section 15).
3   External or internal leakage (see Sections 23 and 24).
4   Faulty radiator cap. Have the cap pressure tested.

26   Poor coolant circulation

1   Inoperative water pump. A quick test is to pinch the top radiator hose closed with your hand while the engine is idling, then let it loose. You should feel a surge of coolant if the pump is working properly (Chapter 1).
2   Restriction in the cooling system. Drain, flush and refill the system (Chapter 1). If necessary, remove the radiator (Chapter 3) and have it reverse flushed.
3   Water pump drivebelt defective or loose (Chapter 1).
4   Thermostat sticking (Chapter 3).

Clutch

27   Fails to release (pedal pressed to the floor – shift lever does not move freely in and out of Reverse)

1   Worn cable (Chapter 8).
2   Clutch plate warped or damaged (Chapter 8).
3   Worn or dry clutch release shaft bushing (Chapter 8).

28   Clutch slips (engine speed increases with no increase in vehicle speed)

1   Cable out of adjustment (Chapter 1).
2   Clutch plate oil soaked or lining worn. Remove clutch (Chapter 8) and inspect.
3   Clutch plate not seated. It may take 30 or 40 normal starts for a new one to seat.

29   Grabbing (chattering) as clutch is engaged

1   Oil on clutch plate lining. Remove (Chapter 8) and inspect. Correct any leakage source.
2   Worn or loose engine or transaxle mounts. The mounts move slightly when the clutch is released. Inspect the mounts and bolts (Chapter 2).
3   Worn splines on clutch plate hub. Remove the clutch components (Chapter 8) and inspect.
4   Warped pressure plate or flywheel. Remove the clutch components and inspect.

30   Squeal or rumble with clutch fully disengaged (pedal depressed)

1   Worn or damaged release bearing (Chapter 8).
2   Worn or broken pressure plate diaphragm fingers (Chapter 8).

31   Clutch pedal stays on floor when disengaged

Linkage or release bearing binding. Inspect the linkage or remove the clutch components as necessary.

Manual transaxle

32   Noisy in Neutral with engine running

1   Worn or damaged mainshaft bearing.
2   Worn countershaft bearings.
3   Countershaft endplay incorrect.

33   Noisy in all gears

1   Any of the above causes, and/or:
2   Insufficient lubricant (see the checking procedures in Chapter 1).

34   Noisy in one particular gear

1   Worn, damaged or chipped gear teeth for that particular gear.
2   Worn or damaged synchronizer for that particular gear.

35   Slips out of high gear

1   Transaxle loose on clutch housing (Chapter 7).
2   Shift rods interfering with the engine mounts or clutch lever (Chapter 7).
3   Shift rods not working freely (Chapter 7).
4   Dirt between the transaxle case and engine or misalignment of the transaxle (Chapter 7).
5   Worn or improperly adjusted linkage (Chapter 7).

36   Difficulty in engaging gears

1   Clutch not releasing completely (see clutch adjustment in Chapter 1).
2   Loose, damaged or out-of-adjustment shift linkage. Make a thorough inspection, replacing parts as necessary (Chapter 7).

37   Oil leakage

1   Excessive amount of lubricant in the transaxle (see Chapter 1 for correct checking procedure). Drain lubricant as required.
2   Defective driveaxle oil seal or speedometer oil seal (Chapter 7).

Automatic transaxle

Note: *Due to the complexity of the automatic transaxle, it's difficult for the home mechanic to properly diagnose and service. For problems other than the following, the vehicle should be taken to a dealer service department or a transmission shop.*

38   General shift mechanism problems

1   Chapter 7 deals with checking and adjusting the shift linkage on automatic transaxles. Common problems which may be attributed to poorly adjusted linkage are:
Engine starting in gears other than Park or Neutral.
Indicator on shifter pointing to a gear other than the one actually being selected.
Vehicle moves when in Park.
2   Refer to Chapter 7 to adjust the linkage.

39   Transaxle will not downshift with accelerator pedal pressed to the floor

Chapter 7 deals with adjusting the throttle cable to enable the transaxle to downshift properly.

40   Transaxle slips, shifts rough, is noisy or has no drive in forward or reverse gears

1   There are many probable causes for the above problems, but the home mechanic should be concerned with only one possibility – fluid level.
2   Before taking the vehicle to a repair shop, check the level and condition of the fluid as described in Chapter 1. Correct fluid level as necessary or change the fluid and filter if needed. If the problem persists, have a professional diagnose the probable cause.

41   Fluid leakage

1   Automatic transaxle fluid is a deep red color. Fluid leaks shouldn't be confused with engine oil, which can easily be blown by air flow to the transaxle.
2   To pinpoint a leak, first remove all built-up dirt and grime from around the transaxle. Degreasing agents and/or steam cleaning will achieve this. With the underside clean, drive the vehicle at low speeds so air flow will not blow the leak far from its source. Raise the vehicle and determine where the leak is coming from. Common areas of leakage are:
   a) *Pan:* Tighten the mounting bolts and/or replace the pan gasket as necessary (see Chapter 7).
   b) *Filler pipe:* Replace the rubber seal where the pipe enters the transaxle case.
   c) *Transaxle oil lines:* Tighten the connectors where the lines enter the transaxle case and/or replace the lines.
   d) *Speedometer connector:* Replace the O-ring where the speedometer cable enters the transaxle case (Chapter 7).

Driveaxles

42   Clicking noise in turns

Worn or damaged outer joint. Check for cut or damaged boots. Repair as necessary (Chapter 8).

43   Knock or clunk when accelerating after coasting

Worn or damaged inner joint. Check for cut or damaged boots. Repair as necessary (Chapter 8)

44   Shudder or vibration during acceleration

1   Excessive joint angle. Check and correct as necessary (Chapter 8).
2   Worn or damaged CV joints. Repair or replace as necessary (Chapter 8).
3   Sticking CV joint assembly. Service or replace as necessary (Chapter 8).

Rear axle

45   Noise

1   Road noise. No corrective action available.
2   Tire noise. Inspect tires and check tire pressures (Chapter 1).
3   Rear wheel bearings loose, worn or damaged (Chapter 1).

Brakes

Note: *Before assuming a brake problem exists, make sure the tires are in good condition and inflated properly (see Chapter 1), the front end alignment is correct and the vehicle isn't loaded with weight in an unequal manner.*

46   Vehicle pulls to one side during braking

1   Defective, damaged or oil contaminated disc brake pads on one side. Inspect as described in Chapter 1.
2   Excessive pad or disc wear on one side. Inspect and correct as necessary.
3   Loose or disconnected front suspension components. Inspect and tighten all bolts to the specified torque (Chapter 10).
4   Defective caliper assembly. Remove the caliper and inspect for a stuck piston or other damage (Chapter 9).

47   Noise (high-pitched squeal with the brakes applied)

Disc brake pads worn out. The noise comes from the wear sensor rubbing against the disc (does not apply to all vehicles) or the actual pad backing plate itself if the lining material is completely worn away. Replace the pads with new ones immediately (Chapter 9). If the pad material has worn completely away, the brake discs should be inspected for damage as well.

48   Excessive brake pedal travel

1   Partial brake system failure. Inspect the entire system (Chapter 9) and correct as required.
2   Insufficient fluid in the master cylinder. Check (Chapter 1), add fluid and bleed the system if necessary (Chapter 9).
3   Rear brakes not adjusting properly. Make a series of starts and stops while the transaxle is in Reverse. If this doesn't correct the situation, remove the drums and inspect the self-adjusters (Chapter 9).

49   Brake pedal feels spongy when depressed

1   Air in the hydraulic lines. Bleed the brake system (Chapter 9).
2   Defective brake hoses. Inspect all system hoses and lines. Replace parts as necessary.
3   Master cylinder mounting bolts/nuts loose.
4   Master cylinder defective (Chapter 9).

50   Excessive effort required to stop vehicle

1   Power brake booster not operating properly (Chapter 9).
2   Excessively worn linings or pads. Inspect and replace if necessary (Chapter 9).
3   One or more caliper pistons or wheel cylinder cups seized or sticking. Inspect and rebuild as required (Chapter 9).
4   Brake linings or pads contaminated with oil or grease. Inspect and replace as required (Chapter 9).
5   New pads or shoes installed and not yet seated. It will take a while for the new material to seat against the drum (or rotor).

51   Pedal travels to the floor with little resistance

Little or no fluid in the master cylinder reservoir caused by leaking wheel cylinder(s), leaking caliper piston(s), loose, damaged or disconnected brake lines. Inspect the entire system and correct as necessary.

52   Brake pedal pulsates during brake application

1   Caliper improperly installed. Remove and inspect (Chapter 9).
2   Disc or drum defective. Remove (Chapter 9) and check for excessive lateral runout and parallelism. Have the disc or drum resurfaced or replace it with a new one.

Suspension and steering systems

53   Vehicle pulls to one side

1   Tire pressures uneven (Chapter 1).
2   Defective tire (Chapter 1).
3   Excessive wear in suspension or steering components (Chapter 10).
4   Front end alignment incorrect.
5   Front brakes dragging. Inspect the brakes as described in Chapter 9.

54   Shimmy, shake or vibration

1   Tire or wheel out-of-balance or out-of-round.

2   Loose, worn or out-of-adjustment rear wheel bearings (Chapter 1).
3   Shock absorbers and/or suspension components worn or damaged (Chapter 10).

55   Excessive pitching and/or rolling around corners or during braking

1   Defective shock absorbers. Replace as a set (Chapter 10).
2   Broken or weak springs and/or suspension components. Inspect as described in Chapters 1 and 10.

56   Excessively stiff steering

1   Lack of fluid in power steering fluid reservoir (Chapter 1).
2   Incorrect tire pressures (Chapter 1).
3   Front end out of alignment.

57   Excessive play in steering

1   Excessively worn suspension or steering components (Chapter 10).
2   Steering gear damaged (Chapter 10).

58   Lack of power assistance

1   Steering pump drivebelt loose or defective (Chapter 1).
2   Fluid level low (Chapter 1).
3   Hoses or lines restricted. Inspect and replace parts as necessary.
4   Air in power steering system. Bleed the system (Chapter 10).

59   Excessive tire wear (not specific to one area)

1   Incorrect tire pressures (Chapter 1).
2   Tires out-of-balance.
3   Wheels damaged. Inspect and replace as necessary.
4   Suspension or steering components excessively worn (Chapter 10).

60   Excessive tire wear on outside edge

1   Incorrect tire pressures (Chapter 1).
2   Excessive speed in turns.
3   Front end alignment incorrect (excessive toe-in).
4   Suspension arm bent or twisted (Chapter 10).

61   Excessive tire wear on inside edge

1   Incorrect tire pressures (Chapter 1).
2   Front end alignment incorrect.
3   Loose or damaged steering components (Chapter 10).

62   Tire tread worn in one place

1   Tires out-of-balance.
2   Damaged or buckled wheel. Inspect and replace if necessary.
3   Defective tire (Chapter 1).

Chapter 1   Tune-up and routine maintenance

Contents

1

Specifications

Recommended lubricants and fluids

Engine oil
- Type . . . . SF, SF/CC or SF/CD
- Viscosity . . . . See accompanying chart

Manual transaxle lubricant
- A-412 4-speed . . . . API GL-4 SAE 90W gear oil
- All others
  - 1982 through 1986 . . . . DEXRON II ATF (DO NOT use gear oil!)
  - 1987 on . . . . SAE 5W30 engine oil

Automatic transaxle fluid
- 1978 through 1986 . . . . DEXRON II ATF
- 1987 on . . . . MOPAR ATF Plus Type 7176

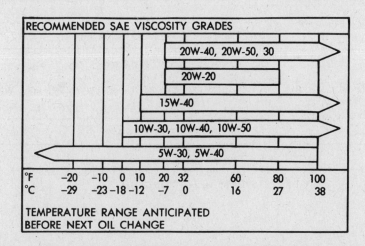

ENGINE OIL VISCOSITY CHART

Note: SAE 5W-30 and 5W-40 are not recommended for use in turbocharged engines when the temperature is above 60-degrees F

Recommended lubricants and fluids (continued)

Differential lubricant (1978 through 1982 automatic transaxle equipped models only)	DEXRON II ATF (DO NOT use gear oil!)
Power steering fluid	Mopar 4-253 power steering fluid or equivalent
Brake fluid	DOT 3 brake fluid
Engine coolant	50/50 mixture of ethylene glycol-based antifreeze and water
Carburetor choke shaft	Mopar combustion chamber conditioner (no. 2933500, 438001 or equivalent)
Transaxle shift linkage	NLGI no. 2 chassis grease
Clutch linkage	NLGI no. 2 chassis grease
Combustion chamber conditioner (Canadian models)	Autopar combustion chamber conditioner (no. VU788 or equivalent)
Parking brake mechanism	White lithium-based grease NLGI no. 2
Chassis lubrication	NLGI no. 2 EP grease
Steering shaft seal	NLGI no. 2 EP grease
Wheel bearings (front and rear)	NLGI no. 2 EP high-temperature wheel bearing grease
Steering gear	API GL-4 SAE 90W gear oil
Hood and door hinges/liftgate hinges	Engine oil
Door hinge half and check spring	NLGI no. 2 multi-purpose grease
Key lock cylinders	Graphite spray
Hood latch assembly	Mopar Lubriplate or equivalent
Door latch striker	Mopar Door Ease (no. 3744859 or equivalent)

Capacities

Engine oil (including filter)	
1.7L engine	4.0 qts (3.8 liters)
2.2L engine	
Non-turbo	4.0 qts (3.8 liters)
Turbo	5.0 qts (4.8 liters)
Fuel tank	14 gals (53.0 liters)
Automatic transaxle	
Drain and refill (approximate)	
1978 through 1982	3.0 qts (2.8 liters)
1983 on	4.0 qts (3.0 liters)
From dry (including torque converter)	
1978 through 1982	
Transaxle	7.5 qts (6.9 liters)
Differential	1.2 qts (1.1 liters)
1983 on	8.9 qts (8.4 liters)
Manual transaxle (approximate)	
4-speed	2.0 qts (1.8 liters)
5-speed	2.3 qts (2.1 liters)
Cooling system (approximate)	
1978 through 1982	
1.7L engine	6.0 qts (5.7 liters)
2.2L engine	7.0 qts (6.6 liters)
1983 on (all)	9.0 qts (8.5 liters)

Radiator cap pressure rating .... 4 to 17 psi

0755H

Brakes

Disc brake pad wear limit	5/16 in (7.94 mm)
Drum brake shoe wear limit	1/8 in (3.17 mm)

Ignition system

Spark plug type	Champion RN12Y
Spark plug gap	0.035 in (0.88 mm)
Spark plug wire resistance	
Minimum	3000 ohms per foot
Maximum	7200 ohms per foot
Ignition timing	See Emission Control Information label in engine compartment
Firing order	1-3-4-2

Cylinder location and distributor rotation

Drivebelt deflection

Alternator	
1.7L engine	
New	3/16 in (4 mm)
Used	1/4 in (6 mm)
2.2L engine	
New	1/8 in (3 mm)
Used	1/4 in (6 mm)

Power steering pump
  1.7L engine
    New . . . . 1/4 in (6 mm)
    Used . . . . 3/8 in (9 mm)
  2.2L engine
    New . . . . 1/4 in (6 mm)
    Used . . . . 7/16 in (11 mm)
Water Pump
  1.7L engine
    New . . . . 5/16 in (8 mm)
    Used . . . . 3/8 in (9 mm)
  2.2L engine
    New . . . . 1/8 in (3 mm)
    Used . . . . 1/4 in (6 mm)
Air pump (2.2L engine)
  New . . . . 3/16 in (5 mm)
  Used . . . . 1/4 in (6 mm)
Air conditioning compressor
  1.7L engine
    New . . . . 1/4 in (6 mm)
    Used . . . . 5/16 in (8 mm)
  2.2L engine
    New . . . . 5/16 in (8 mm)
    Used . . . . 3/8 in (9 mm)

Valve clearances (engine cold)*

Intake . . . . 0.006 to 0.010 in (0.15 to 0.25 mm)
Exhaust . . . . 0.014 to 0.018 in (0.35 to 0.45 mm)

The valve clearances must be rechecked and adjusted to the clearance specified on the Vehicle Emission Control Information label (in the engine compartment) after the engine is warmed up (the coolant temperature must be approximately 95-degrees F)

Automatic transaxle band adjustment

1978 through 1981 (A404 transaxle)
  Kickdown (front) . . . . Tighten to 72 in-lbs, then back off 3 turns
  Low-Reverse . . . . Non-adjustable
1982 and 1983
  Kickdown (front)
    A404 transaxle . . . . Tighten to 72 in-lbs, then back off 3 turns
    A413 and A470 transaxles . . . . Tighten to 72 in-lbs, then back off 2-3/4 turns
  Low-Reverse
    A404 transaxle . . . . Non-adjustable
    A413 and A470 transaxles . . . . Tighten to 41 in-lbs, then back off 3-1/2 turns
1984
  Kickdown (front)
    A415 transaxle . . . . Tighten to 72 in-lbs, then back off 3 turns
    A413 and A470 transaxles . . . . Tighten to 72 in-lbs, then back off 2-1/2 turns
  Low-Reverse
    A415 transaxle . . . . Non-adjustable
    A413 and A470 transaxles . . . . Tighten to 41 in-lbs, then back off 3-1/2 turns
1985 on
  Kickdown (front) . . . . Tighten to 72 in-lbs, then back off 2-1/2 turns
  Low-Reverse . . . . Tighten to 41 in-lbs, then back off 3-1/2 turns

Clutch

Pedal freeplay . . . . 1/2 in (3.1 mm)
Lever freeplay . . . . 1/4 in (6.3 mm)

Torque specifications

Ft-lbs *(unless otherwise indicated)*

Carburetor/throttle body mounting nuts 17
Spark plugs
  1.7L engine 20
  2.2L engine 26
Wheel lug nuts
  1978 through 1983 80
  1984 on 95
Differential cover bolts 14
Transaxle oil pan bolts 14
Filter-to-valve body screws . . . . 40 in-lbs

1

1 Dodge Omni/Plymouth Horizon Maintenance schedule

The following maintenance intervals are based on the assumption that the vehicle owner will be doing the maintenance or service work, as opposed to having a dealer service department do the work. Although the time/mileage intervals are loosely based on factory recommendations, most have been shortened to ensure, for example, that such items as lubricants and fluids are checked/changed at intervals that promote maximum engine/driveline service life. Also, subject to the preference of the individual owner interested in keeping his or her vehicle in peak condition at all times, and with the vehicle's ultimate resale in mind, many of the maintenance procedures may be performed more often than recommended in the following schedule. We encourage such owner initiative.

When the vehicle is new it should be serviced initially by a factory authorized dealer service department to protect the factory warranty. In many cases the initial maintenance check is done at no cost to the owner (check with your dealer service department for more information).

Every 250 miles or weekly, whichever comes first

Check the engine oil level; add oil as necessary (Section 4)
Check the engine coolant level; add water as necessary (Section 4)
Check the window washer fluid level (Section 4)
Check the battery electrolyte level (Section 4)
Check the brake fluid level (Section 4)
Check the tires and tire pressures (Section 5)
Check the automatic transaxle fluid level (Section 6)
Check the power steering fluid level (Section 7)
Check the wiper blade condition (Section 8)
Check the operation of all lights
Check the horn operation

Every 3000 miles or 3 months, whichever comes first

Change the engine oil and filter (all models) (Section 9)*

Every 7500 miles or 6 months, whichever comes first

Check the clutch pedal freeplay (1.7L engine only) (Section 11)
Check the fuel system hoses, lines and connections for leaks and damage (Section 27)
Add combustion chamber conditioner to the engine (Canadian models only) (Section 37)
Check the brake hoses and lines for leaks and damage (Section 33)
Check the suspension balljoint and steering linkage boots for damage and lubricant leaks (Section 30)*
Check the driveaxle boots for damage and lubricant leaks (Section 43)*
Check the manual transaxle lubricant level (Section 13)
Check the differential lubricant level (1978 through 1982 automatic transaxle equipped models only) (Section 14)

Every 15,000 miles or 12 months, whichevercomes first

Check/replace the wiper blade elements (Section 8)
Check and clean the battery (Section 10)
Check the drivebelts (Section 19)
Check the carburetor/fuel injection throttle body mounting nut torque (Section 24)

Check the cooling system hoses and connections for leaks and damage (Section 28)
Check the EGR system components for proper operation (Section 22)
Check the condition of all vacuum hoses and connections (Section 23)
Check the condition of the primary ignition wires and spark plug wires (Section 18)
Check the distributor cap and rotor (Section 18)
Replace the spark plugs (vehicles *without* catalytic converter) (Section 17)
Check the exhaust pipes and hangers (Section 29)
Check for freeplay in the steering linkage and balljoints (Section 30)
Check the fuel evaporative emission system hoses and connections (Section 44)
Rotate the tires (Section 12)
Check and adjust the valve clearances (1.7L engine only) (Section 38)

Every 22,500 miles or 18 months, whichever comes first

Replace the fuel filter (Section 15)
Check the front disc brake pads (Section 33)*
Check and service the rear wheel bearings (Section 32)*
Check the rear brake linings and drums (Section 33)*

Every 30,000 miles or 24 months, whichever comes first

Replace the air filter element (Section 20)*
Apply solvent to the carburetor choke shaft and sealing block (Section 25)
Check the PCV valve (Section 21)
Replace the spark plugs (vehicles *with* catalytic converter) (Section 17)
Check the choke for proper operation (Section 25)
Check the cylinder compression (Chapter 2, Part B)
Check the parking brake operation (Section 33)
Check the steering shaft seal; lubricate as necessary (Section 31)
Adjust the rear brake shoes (1978 through 1982 models only) (Chapter 9)
Lubricate the front suspension and steering balljoints (Section 16)*
Drain and replace the engine coolant (Section 34)
Change the automatic transaxle fluid andfilter (Section 41)*
Adjust the automatic transaxle bands (Section 42)*
Change the manual transaxle lubricant (Section 39)*

Every 50,000 miles or 60 months, whichever comes first

Replace the PCV valve (Section 21)
Replace the spark plug wires, distributor cap and
   rotor (Section 18)

This item is affected by "severe" operating conditions as described below. If the vehicle in question is operated under "severe" conditions, perform all maintenance procedures marked with an asterisk (*) at the following intervals . . .

Every 1,000 miles

Change the engine oil and filter (turbocharged models only)

Every 2,000 miles

Change the engine oil and filter (non-turbo charged models only)
Check the driveaxle, suspension and steering boots

Every 9,000 miles

Check the brakes
Service the rear wheel bearings

Every 15,000 miles

Replace the air filter element
Lubricate the tie-rod ends
Change the automatic transaxle fluid and filter
Adjust the automatic transaxle bands
Change the manual transaxle lubricant and clean
   the pan magnet

Consider the conditions "severe" if most driving is done . . .
in "stop-and-go" situations
in dusty areas
with extended periods of engine idling
as short trips
at sustained high speeds during hot weather (over
   90-degrees F)

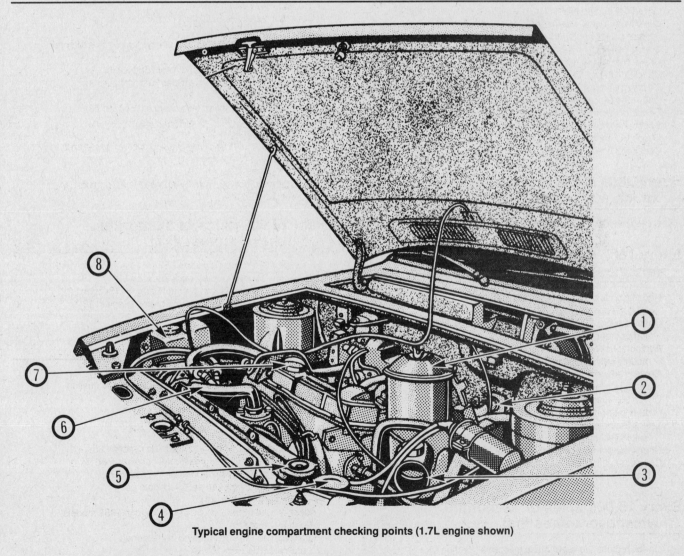

Typical engine compartment checking points (1.7L engine shown)

1	Air cleaner	4	Coolant reservoir	6	Upper radiator hose
2	Brake fluid reservoir	5	Radiator cap	7	Engine oil filler cap
3	Heated inlet air intake			8	Windshield washer fluid reservoir

Typical engine compartment under side components (2.2L engine shown)

1	Alternator	6	Left driveaxle	11	Suspension control arm
2	Fuel pump	7	Driveaxle outer CV joint boot	12	Suspension balljoint grease fitting
3	Oil filter	8	Swaybar	13	Driveaxle inner CV joint boot
4	Engine oil pan	9	Catalytic converter	14	Brake caliper
5	Transaxle fluid pan	10	Engine oil drain plug	15	Brake hose

2   Introduction

This Chapter is designed to help the home mechanic maintain the Dodge Omni/Plymouth Horizon with the goals of maximum performance, economy, safety and reliability in mind.

Included is a master maintenance schedule, followed by procedures dealing specifically with each item on the schedule. Visual checks, adjustments, component replacement and other helpful items are included. Refer to the accompanying illustrations of the engine compartment and the underside of the vehicle for the locations of various components.

Adhering to the mileage/time maintenance schedule and following the step-by-step procedures, which is simply a preventive maintenance program, will result in maximum reliability and vehicle service life. Keep in mind that it's a comprehensive program – maintaining some items but not others at the specified intervals will not produce the same results.

As you service the vehicle, you'll discover that many of the procedures can – and should – be grouped together because of the nature of the particular procedure you're performing or because of the close proximity of two otherwise unrelated components to one another.

For example, if the vehicle is raised, you should inspect the exhaust, suspension, steering and fuel systems while you're under the vehicle. When you're rotating the tires, it makes good sense to check the brakes, since the wheels are already removed. Finally, let's suppose you have to borrow or rent a torque wrench. Even if you only need it to tighten the spark plugs, you might as well check the torque of as many critical fasteners as time allows.

The first step in this maintenance program is to prepare yourself before the actual work begins. Read through all the procedures you're planning to do, then gather up all the parts and tools needed. If it looks like you might run into problems during a particular job, seek advice from a mechanic or an experienced do-it-yourselfer.

3   Tune-up general information

The term "tune-up" is used in this manual to represent a combination of individual operations rather than one specific procedure.

If, from the time the vehicle is new, the routine maintenance schedule is followed closely and frequent checks are made of fluid levels and high wear items, as suggested throughout this manual, the engine will be kept in relatively good running condition and the need for additional work will be minimized.

More likely than not, however, there will be times when the engine is running poorly due to lack of regular maintenance. This is even more likely if a used vehicle, which hasn't received regular and frequent maintenance checks, is purchased. In such cases, an engine tune-up will be needed outside of the regular routine maintenance intervals.

The first step in any tune-up or diagnostic procedure to help correct a poor running engine is a cylinder compression check. A compression check (see Chapter 2, Part B) will help determine the condition of internal engine components and should be used as a guide for tune-up and repair procedures. For instance, if a compression check indicates serious internal engine wear, a conventional tune-up will not improve the performance of the engine and would be a waste of time and money. Because of its importance, the compression check should be done by someone with the right equipment and the knowledge to use it properly.

The following procedures are those most often needed to bring a generally poor running engine back into a proper state of tune:

Minor tune-up

Check all engine related fluids (Section 4)
Clean, inspect and test the battery (Section 10)
Replace the spark plugs (Section 17)
Inspect the distributor cap and rotor (Section 18)
Inspect the spark plug and coil wires (Section 18)
Check and adjust the drivebelts (Section 19)
Check the air filter (Section 20)
Check the PCV valve (Section 21)
Check all underhood hoses (Section 23)
Check the cooling system (Section 28)
Check and adjust the idle speed (Section 35)
Check and adjust the ignition timing (Section 36)

Major tune-up

All items listed under Minor tune-up plus . . .
Replace the air filter (Section 20)
Replace the distributor cap and rotor (Section 18)
Replace the spark plug wires (Section 18)
Check the EGR system (Section 22)
Check the fuel system (Section 27)
Check the ignition system (Chapter 5)
Check the charging system (Chapter 5)

---

4   Fluid level checks

Note: *The following are fluid level checks to be done on a 250 mile or weekly basis. Additional fluid level checks can be found in specific maintenance procedures which follow. Regardless of the intervals, develop the habit of checking under the vehicle periodically for evidence of fluid leaks.*

1   Fluids are an essential part of the lubrication, cooling, brake and window washer systems. Because the fluids gradually become depleted and/or contaminated during normal operation of the vehicle, they must be replenished periodically. See *Recommended lubricants and fluids* at the beginning of this Chapter before adding fluid to any of the following components. **Note:** *The vehicle must be on level ground when fluid levels are checked.*

Engine oil

Refer to illustrations 4.4a, 4.4b and 4.5
2   The engine oil level is checked with a dipstick which is located on the front (radiator) side of the engine block. The dipstick extends through a tube and into the oil pan at the bottom of the engine.
3   The oil level should be checked before the vehicle has been driven, or about 15 minutes after the engine has been shut off. If the oil is checked immediately after driving the vehicle, some of the oil will remain in the upper engine components, resulting in an inaccurate reading on the dipstick.
4   Pull the dipstick out of the tube **(see illustration)** and wipe all the oil off the end with a clean rag or paper towel. Insert the clean dipstick all the way back into the tube, then pull it out again. Note the oil level at the end of the dipstick. Add oil as necessary to keep the level at the Full mark **(see illustration)**.
5   Oil is added to the engine after removing a twist-off cap located on the camshaft cover **(see illustration)**. The cap will be marked "Engine oil" or something similar. A funnel may help reduce spills as the oil is poured in.

4.4a   The engine oil dipstick is located on the front (radiator) side of the engine

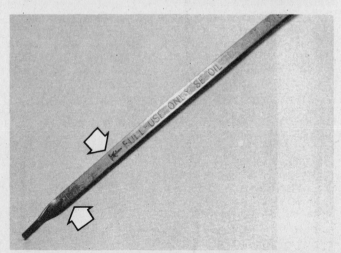

4.4b   The oil level should be between the ADD and FULL marks on the dipstick – if it isn't, add enough oil to bring the level up to or near the FULL mark (it takes one quart to raise the level from the ADD to the FULL mark)

4.5   Oil is added to the engine after removing the cap from the camshaft cover – always make sure the area around the opening is clean before unscrewing the cap

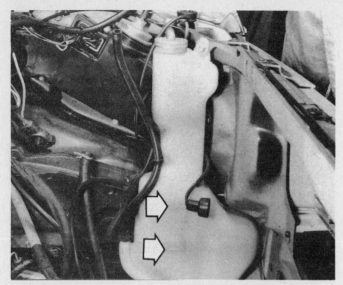

4.8   Make sure the coolant level in the reservoir is between the MIN and MAX marks – if it's below the MIN mark, add more coolant mixture or water

4.10   After the engine is completely cool, remove the radiator cap to check the condition of the coolant in the radiator – inspect the cap gasket at the same time

6   Don't allow the level to drop below the Add mark or engine damage may occur. On the other hand, don't overfill the engine by adding too much oil – it may result in oil fouled spark plugs, oil leaks or seal failures.

7   Checking the oil level is an important preventive maintenance step. A consistently low oil level indicates oil leakage through damaged seals, defective gaskets or past worn rings or valve guides. If the oil looks milky in color or has water droplets in it, the block may be cracked. The engine should be checked immediately. The condition of the oil should also be checked. Each time you check the oil level, slide your thumb and index finger up the dipstick before wiping off the oil. If you see small dirt or metal particles clinging to the dipstick, the oil should be changed (see Section 9).

Engine coolant

Refer to illustrations 4.8, 4.10 and 4.12

Warning: *Do not allow antifreeze to come in contact with your skin or painted surfaces of the vehicle. Flush contaminated areas immediately with plenty of water. Don't store new coolant or leave old coolant lying around where it's accessible to children or pets – they're attracted by its sweet taste. Ingestion of even a small amount of coolant can be fatal! Wipe up garage floor and drip pan spills immediately. Keep antifreeze containers covered and repair cooling system leaks as soon as they're noticed.*

8   All vehicles covered by this manual are equipped with a pressurized coolant recovery system, which makes coolant level checks very easy. A coolant reservoir attached to the inner fender panel is connected by a hose to the radiator filler neck **(see illustration)**. As the engine warms up, some coolant escapes through a valve in the radiator cap and travels through the hose into the reservoir. As the engine cools, the coolant is automatically drawn back into the cooling system to maintain the correct level.

9   The coolant level should be checked when the engine is at normal operating temperature. Simply note the fluid level in the reservoir – it should be at or near the Max mark.

10   The coolant level can also be checked by removing the radiator cap **(see illustration)**. **Warning:** *Don't remove the cap to check the coolant level when the engine is warm! Wait until the engine has cooled, then wrap a thick cloth around the cap and turn it to the first stop. If any steam escapes from the cap, allow the engine to cool further, then remove the cap and check the level in the radiator.*

11   If only a small amount of coolant is required to bring the system up to the proper level, regular water can be used. However, to maintain the proper antifreeze/water mixture in the system, both should be mixed together to replenish a low level. High-quality antifreeze/coolant should be mixed with water in the proportion specified on the antifreeze container.

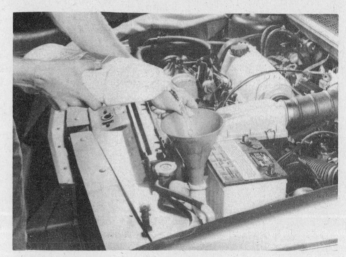

4.12   Use a funnel to prevent spills when adding coolant to the reservoir

12   Coolant should be added to the reservoir after removing the cap **(see illustration)**.

13   As the coolant level is checked, note the condition of the coolant as well. It should be relatively clear. If it's brown or rust colored, the system should be drained, flushed and refilled (see Section 34).

14   If the coolant level drops consistently, there may be a leak in the system. Check the radiator, hoses, filler cap, drain plugs and water pump (see Section 28). If no leaks are noted, have the radiator filler cap pressure tested by a service station.

Windshield and rear window washer fluid

Refer to illustrations 4.15a and 4.15b

15   The fluid for the windshield and rear window washer systems (if equipped) is stored in plastic reservoirs. The level inside each reservoir should be maintained about one inch below the filler cap. The reservoir is accessible after opening the hood or rear hatch **(see illustrations)**.

16   In milder climates, plain water can be used in the reservoir, but it should be kept no more than two-thirds full to allow for expansion if the water freezes. In colder climates, use windshield washer system antifreeze, available at any auto parts store, to lower the freezing point of the fluid. Mix

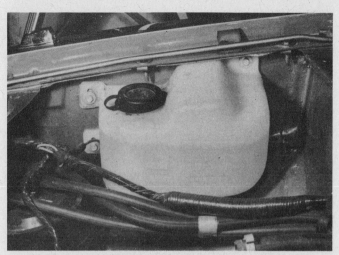

4.15a The windshield washer reservoir is mounted on the right-side inner fender panel

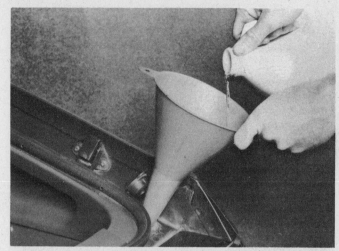

4.15b To prevent spilling on the carpet or body, it's a good idea to use a funnel when adding fluid to the rear window washer reservoir

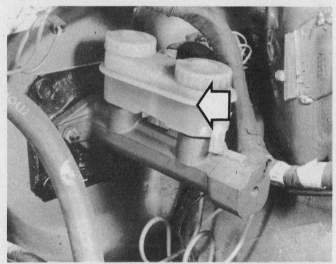

4.21 The brake fluid level must be maintained about 1/4-inch below the top of each reservoir – if it's above the ridge (arrow), it's fine

the antifreeze with water in accordance with the manufacturer's directions on the container. **Caution:** *Don't use cooling system antifreeze – it'll damage the vehicle's paint. To help prevent icing in cold weather, warm the windshield with the defroster before using the washer.*

Battery electrolyte

Warning: *Certain precautions must be followed when checking or servicing a battery. Hydrogen gas, which is highly flammable, is produced in the cells, so keep lighted tobacco, open flames, bare light bulbs and sparks away from the battery. The electrolyte inside the battery is dilute sulfuric acid, which can burn skin and cause serious injury if splashed in your eyes (wear safety glasses). It'll also ruin clothes and painted surfaces. Remove all metal jewelry which could contact the positive battery terminal and a grounded metal source, causing a direct short.*

17   Vehicles equipped with a maintenance-free battery require no maintenance – the battery case is sealed and has no removable caps for adding water.

18   If a maintenance-type battery is installed, the caps on top of the battery should be removed periodically to check for a low electrolyte level. This check is more critical during warm summer months.

19   Remove each of the caps and add distilled water to bring the level in each cell to the split ring in the filler opening.

20   At the same time the battery water level is checked, the overall condition of the battery and related components should be noted. See Section 10 for complete battery check and maintenance procedures.

Brake fluid

Refer to illustration 4.21

21   The brake master cylinder is located on the driver's side of the engine compartment firewall. The reservoir is translucent, so the fluid inside is readily visible without removing the caps. The level should be maintained above the molded-in ridge near the top of the reservoir (there are actually two separate reservoirs, so be sure to check both of them) **(see illustration)**.

22   Before removing the cap(s) to add fluid, use a rag to clean all dirt off the top of the reservoir. If any foreign matter enters the master cylinder when the caps are removed, blockage in the brake system lines can occur. Also, make sure all painted surfaces around the master cylinder are covered, since brake fluid will ruin paint.

23   If additional fluid is necessary to bring the level up, carefully pour new, clean brake fluid into the master cylinder. Be careful not to spill the fluid on painted surfaces. Be sure the specified fluid is used; mixing different types of brake fluid can cause damage to the system. See *Recommended lubricants and fluids* at the beginning of this Chapter or your owner's manual.

24   At this time the fluid and the master cylinder can be inspected for contamination. Normally the brake hydraulic system won't need periodic draining and refilling, but if rust deposits, dirt particles or water droplets are seen in the fluid, the system should be dismantled, cleaned and refilled with fresh fluid.

25   Reinstall the master cylinder caps.

26   The brake fluid in the master cylinder will drop slightly as the brake shoes or pads at each wheel wear down during normal operation. If the master cylinder requires repeated replenishing to keep the level up, it's an indication of leaks in the brake system which should be corrected immediately. Check all brake lines and connections, along with the wheel cylinders and booster (see Chapter 9 for more information).

27   If you discover one or both reservoirs empty or nearly empty, the brake system should be bled (see Chapter 9).

5   Tire and tire pressure checks

Refer to illustrations 5.2, 5.3, 5.4a, 5.4b and 5.8

1   Periodic inspection of the tires may spare you the inconvenience of being stranded with a flat tire. It can also provide you with vital information regarding possible problems in the steering and suspension systems before major damage occurs.

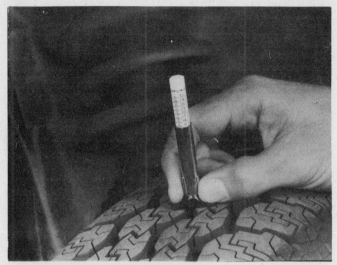

5.2   Use a tire tread depth indicator to monitor tire wear – they are available at auto parts stores and service stations and cost very little

2   The original tires on this vehicle are equipped with 1/2-inch wide bands that will appear when tread depth reaches 1/16-inch, but they don't appear until the tires are worn out. Tread wear can be monitored with a simple, inexpensive device known as a tread depth indicator **(see illustration)**.

3   Note any abnormal tread wear **(see illustration)**. Tread pattern irregularities such as cupping, flat spots and more wear on one side than the other are indications of front end alignment and/or balance problems. If

any of these conditions are noted, take the vehicle to a tire shop or service station to correct the problem.

4   Look closely for cuts, punctures and embedded nails or tacks. Sometimes a tire will hold air pressure for a short time or leak down very slowly after a nail has embedded itself in the tread. If a slow leak persists, check the valve stem core to make sure it's tight **(see illustration)**. Examine the tread for an object that may have embedded itself in the tire or for a "plug" that may have begun to leak (radial tire punctures are repaired with a plug that's installed in a puncture). If a puncture is suspected, it can be easily verified by spraying a solution of soapy water onto the puncture area **(see illustration)**. The soapy solution will bubble if there's a leak. Unless the puncture is unusually large, a tire shop or service station can usually repair the tire.

5   Carefully inspect the inner sidewall of each tire for evidence of brake fluid leakage. If you see any, inspect the brakes immediately.

6   Correct air pressure adds miles to the lifespan of the tires, improves mileage and enhances overall ride quality. Tire pressure cannot be accurately estimated by looking at a tire, especially if it's a radial. A tire pressure gauge is essential. Keep an accurate gauge in the vehicle. The pressure gauges attached to the nozzles of air hoses at gas stations are often inaccurate.

7   Always check tire pressure when the tires are cold. Cold, in this case, means the vehicle has not been driven over a mile in the three hours preceding a tire pressure check. A pressure rise of four to eight pounds is not uncommon once the tires are warm.

8   Unscrew the valve cap protruding from the wheel or hubcap and push the gauge firmly onto the valve stem **(see illustration)**. Note the reading on the gauge and compare the figure to the recommended tire pressure shown on the placard on the driver's side door pillar. Be sure to reinstall the valve cap to keep dirt and moisture out of the valve stem mechanism. Check all four tires and, if necessary, add enough air to bring them up to the recommended pressure.

9   Don't forget to keep the spare tire inflated to the specified pressure

Condition	Probable cause	Corrective action	Condition	Probable cause	Corrective action
Shoulder wear	• Underinflation (both sides wear) • Incorrect wheel camber (one side wear) • Hard cornering • Lack of rotation	• Measure and adjust pressure. • Repair or replace axle and suspension parts. • Reduce speed. • Rotate tires.	Feathered edge Toe wear	• Incorrect toe	• Adjust toe-in.
Center wear	• Overinflation • Lack of rotation	• Measure and adjust pressure. • Rotate tires.	Uneven wear	• Incorrect camber or caster • Malfunctioning suspension • Unbalanced wheel • Out-of-round brake drum • Lack of rotation	• Repair or replace axle and suspension parts. • Repair or replace suspension parts. • Balance or replace. • Turn or replace. • Rotate tires.

5.3   This chart will help you determine the condition of the tires, the probable cause(s) of abnormal wear and the corrective action necessary

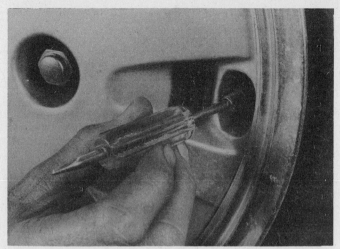

5.4a   If a tire loses air on a steady basis, check the valve core first to make sure it's snug (special inexpensive wrenches are commonly available at auto parts stores)

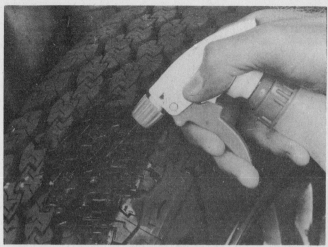

5.4b   If the valve core is tight, raise the corner of the vehicle with the low tire and spray a soapy water solution onto the tread as the tire is turned slowly – leaks will cause small bubbles to appear

5.8   To extend the life of the tires, check the air pressure at least once a week with an accurate gauge (don't forget the spare!)

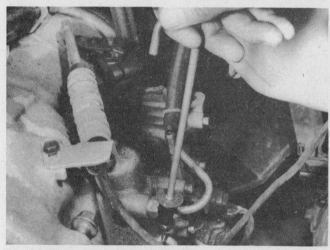

6.3   The automatic transaxle fluid level is checked by removing the dipstick don't confuse it with the engine oil dipstick

(refer to your owner's manual or the tire sidewall). Note that the pressure recommended for the compact spare is higher than for the tires on the vehicle.

6   Automatic transaxle fluid level check

Refer to illustrations 6.3, 6.4 and 6.5

1   The fluid inside the transaxle should be at normal operating temperature to get an accurate reading on the dipstick. This is done by driving the vehicle for several miles, making frequent starts and stops to allow the transaxle to shift through all gears.

2   Park the vehicle on a level surface, place the gear selector lever in Park and leave the engine running.

3   Remove the transaxle dipstick **(see illustration)** and wipe all the fluid from the end with a clean rag.

4   Push the dipstick back into the transaxle until the cap seats completely. Remove the dipstick again and note the fluid on the end. The level should be in the crosshatched area marked HOT (between the two upper holes in the dipstick) **(see illustration)**. If the fluid isn't hot (temperature about 100-degrees F), the level should be in the area marked WARM (between the two lower holes).

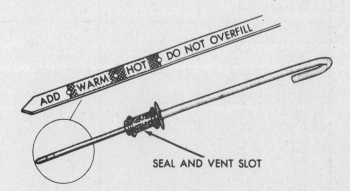

6.4   Check the fluid with the transaxle at normal operating temperature – the level should be kept in the HOT range (between the two upper holes)

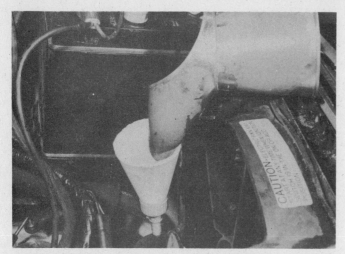

6.5   To avoid spills, use a funnel when adding fluid to the automatic transaxle

7.5a   The power steering fluid reservoir cap/dipstick is located on the right side of the engine compartment – unscrew the cap to check the level and/or add fluid

5   If the fluid level is at or below the ADD mark on the dipstick, add enough fluid to raise the level to within the marks indicated for the appropriate temperature. Fluid should be added directly into the dipstick hole, using a funnel to prevent spills **(see illustration)**.

6   Do not overfill the transaxle. Never allow the fluid level to go above the upper hole on the dipstick – it could cause internal transaxle damage. The best way to prevent overfilling is to add fluid a little at a time, driving the vehicle and checking the level between additions.

7   Use only the transaxle fluid specified by the manufacturer. This information can be found in the *Recommended lubricants and fluids* Section at the beginning of this Chapter.

8   The condition of the fluid should also be checked along with the level. If it's a dark reddish-brown color, or if it smells burned, it should be changed. If you're in doubt about the condition of the fluid, purchase some new fluid and compare the two for color and smell.

7.5b   On most models, the power steering fluid dipstick is marked on both sides so the level can be checked with the fluid cold . . .

7   Power steering fluid level check

Refer to illustrations 7.5a, 7.5b, 7.5c and 7.6

1   Unlike manual steering, the power steering system relies on fluid which may, over a period of time, require replenishing.

2   The reservoir for the power steering pump is located on the rear side of the engine.

3   The power steering fluid level can be checked with the engine cold.

4   With the engine off, use a rag to clean the reservoir cap and the area around the cap. This will help prevent foreign material from falling into the reservoir when the cap is removed.

5   Turn and pull out the reservoir cap **(see illustration)**, which has a dipstick attached to it. Remove the fluid at the bottom of the dipstick with a clean rag. Reinstall the cap to get a fluid level reading. Remove the cap

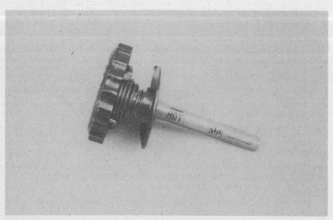

7.5c   . . . or hot

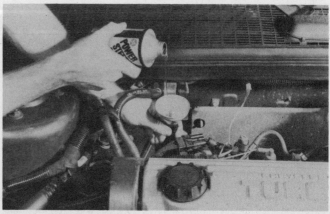

7.6   A funnel with a flexible spout can be used to add fluid to the power steering reservoir without spilling

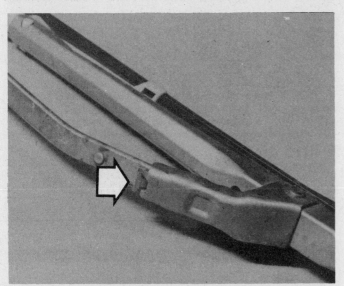

8.4 Lift up on the release lever (arrow) with a screwdriver and detach the blade assembly from the arm

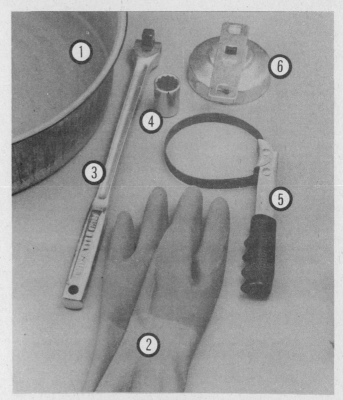

9.3 These tools are required when changing the engine oil and filter

1 *Drain pan* – *It should be fairly shallow in depth, but wide to prevent spills*
2 *Rubber gloves* – *When removing the drain plug and filter, you will get oil on your hands (the gloves will prevent burns)*
3 *Breaker bar* – *Sometimes the oil drain plug is tight and a long breaker bar is needed to loosen it*
4 *Socket* – *To be used with the breaker bar or a ratchet (must be the correct size to fit the drain plug – 6-point preferred)*
5 *Filter wrench* – *This is a metal band-type wrench, which requires clearance around the filter to be effective*
6 *Filter wrench* – *This type fits on the bottom of the filter and can be turned with a ratchet or breaker bar (different size wrenches are available for different types of filters)*

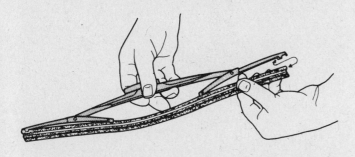

8.5 Bend the blade, slide the end out of the bridge, then slide the element out of the blade assembly

again and note the fluid level. It should be at the Full cold mark on the dipstick **(see illustration)**. If the engine is warm, the level can be checked on the other side of the dipstick **(see illustration)**.
6   If additional fluid is required, pour the specified type directly into the reservoir using a funnel to prevent spills **(see illustration)**.
7   If the reservoir requires frequent fluid additions, all power steering hoses, hose connections, the power steering pump and the steering box should be carefully checked for leaks.

8   Wiper blade inspection and replacement

Refer to illustrations 8.4 and 8.5
1   The windshield and rear window wiper blade elements should be checked periodically for cracks and deterioration.
2   To gain access to the wiper blades, turn on the ignition switch and cycle the wipers to a position on the windshield or rear window where the work can be performed, then turn off the ignition.
3   Lift the wiper blade assembly away from the glass.
4   Use a screwdriver to lift the release tab and remove the wiper blade assembly from the arm **(see illustration)**.
5   Push the blade element into a slight reverse bow, slide the end out of the bridge, then remove the element from the blade assembly **(see illustration)**.
6   Installation is the reverse of removal.

9   Engine oil and filter change

Refer to illustrations 9.3, 9.9, 9.14 and 9.19
1   Frequent oil changes are the most important preventive maintenance procedures that can be done by the home mechanic. When engine oil ages, it gets diluted and contaminated, which ultimately leads to premature engine wear.
2   Although some sources recommend oil filter changes every other oil change, a new filter should be installed every time the oil is changed.
3   Gather together all necessary tools and materials before beginning this procedure **(see illustration)**. **Note:** *To avoid rounding off the corners of the drain plug, use a six-point socket.*
4   In addition, you should have plenty of clean rags and newspapers handy to mop up any spills. Access to the underside of the vehicle is greatly improved if it can be lifted on a hoist, driven onto ramps or supported by jackstands. **Warning:** *Don't work under a vehicle which is supported only by a jack!*
5   If this is your first oil change on the vehicle, crawl underneath it and familiarize yourself with the locations of the oil drain plug and the oil filter. Since the engine and exhaust components will be warm during the actual work, it's a good idea to figure out any potential problems beforehand.

9.9   To avoid rounding off the corners, use the correct size box-end wrench or six-point socket to remove the engine oil drain plug

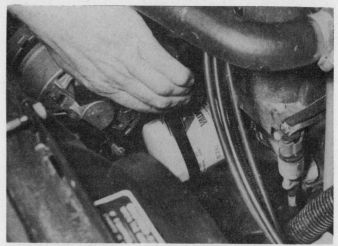

9.14   The oil filter is usually on very tight and normally will require a special wrench for removal – DO NOT use the wrench to tighten the new filter!

6   Allow the engine to warm up to normal operating temperature. If oil or tools are needed, use the warm-up time to gather everything necessary for the job. The correct type of oil to buy for your application can be found in the *Recommended lubricants and fluids* Section at the beginning of this Chapter.

7   With the engine oil warm (warm oil will drain better and more built-up sludge will be removed with it), raise the vehicle and support it securely on jackstands. They should be placed under the portions of the body designated as hoisting and jacking points (see *Jacking and towing* at the front of this manual).

8   Move all necessary tools, rags and newspapers under the vehicle. Place the drain pan under the drain plug. Keep in mind that the oil will initially flow from the engine with some force, so position the pan accordingly.

9   Being careful not to touch any of the hot exhaust components, use the breaker bar and socket to remove the drain plug near the bottom of the oil pan **(see illustration)**. Depending on how hot the oil is, you may want to wear gloves while unscrewing the plug the final few turns.

10   Allow the oil to drain into the pan. It may be necessary to move the pan further under the engine as the oil flow reduces to a trickle.

11   After all the oil has drained, clean the plug thoroughly with a rag. Small metal particles may cling to it and would immediately contaminate the new oil.

12   Clean the area around the oil pan opening and reinstall the plug. Tighten it securely.

13   Move the drain pan into position under the oil filter.

14   Now use the filter wrench to loosen the oil filter **(see illustration)**. Chain or metal band-type filter wrenches may distort the filter canister, but don't worry about it – the filter will be discarded anyway.

15   Sometimes the oil filter is on so tight it cannot be loosened, or it's positioned in an area inaccessible with a conventional filter wrench. Other type of tools, which fit over the end of the filter and turned with a ratchet/breaker bar, are available and may be better suited for removing the filter. If the filter is extremely tight, position the filter wrench near the threaded end of the filter, close to the engine.

16   Completely unscrew the old filter. Be careful, it's full of oil. Empty the old oil inside the filter into the drain pan.

17   Compare the old filter with the new one to make sure they're identical.

18   Use a clean rag to remove all oil, dirt and sludge from the area where the oil filter mounts on the engine. Check the old filter to make sure the rubber gasket isn't stuck to the engine mounting surface.

19   Apply a light coat of oil to the rubber gasket on the new oil filter **(see illustration)**.

20   Attach the new filter to the engine following the tightening directions printed on the filter canister or packing box. Most filter manufacturers recommend against using a filter wrench due to the possibility of overtightening and damaging the canister.

9.19   Lubricate the gasket with clean oil before installing the filter on the engine

21   Remove all tools and materials from under the vehicle, being careful not to spill the oil in the drain pan. Lower the vehicle off the jackstands.

22   Move to the engine compartment and locate the oil filler cap on the engine.

23   If the filler opening is obstructed, use a funnel when adding oil.

24   Pour the specified amount of new oil into the engine. Wait a few minutes to allow the oil to drain to the pan, then check the level on the dipstick (see Section 4 if necessary). If the oil level is at or above the Add mark, start the engine and allow the new oil to circulate.

25   Run the engine for only about a minute, then shut it off. Immediately look under the vehicle and check for leaks at the oil pan drain plug and around the oil filter. If either one is leaking, tighten with a bit more force.

26   With the new oil circulated and the filter now completely full, recheck the level on the dipstick. If necessary, add enough oil to bring the level to the Full mark on the dipstick.

27   During the first few trips after an oil change, make it a point to check for leaks and keep a close watch on the oil level.

28   The old oil drained from the engine cannot be reused in its present state and should be disposed of. Oil reclamation centers, auto repair shops and gas stations will normally accept the oil. After the oil has cooled, it should be drained into containers (plastic bottles with screw-on tops are preferred) for transport to a disposal site.

10.1   Tools and materials required for battery maintenance

1 *Face shield/safety goggles* – *When removing corrosion with a brush, the acidic particles can easily fly up into your eyes*
2 *Baking soda* – *A solution of baking soda and water can be used to neutralize corrosion*
3 *Petroleum jelly* – *A layer of this on the battery posts will help prevent corrosion*
4 *Battery post/cable cleaner* – *This wire brush cleaning tool will remove all traces of corrosion from the battery posts and cable clamps*
5 *Treated felt washers* – *Placing one of these on each post, directly under the cable clamps, will help prevent corrosion*
6 *Puller* – *Sometimes the cable clamps are very difficult to pull off the posts, even after the nut/bolt has been completely loosened. This tool pulls the clamp straight up and off the post without damage.*
7 *Battery post/cable cleaner* – *Here is another cleaning tool which is a slightly different version of number 4 above, but it does the same thing*
8 *Rubber gloves* – *Another safety item to consider when servicing the battery; remember that's acid inside the battery!*

10   Battery check and maintenance

Refer to illustrations 10.1, 10.2, 10.5a, 10.5b, 10.5c and 10.5d
Warning: *Certain precautions must be followed when checking or servicing a battery. Hydrogen gas, which is highly flammable, is produced in the cells, so keep lighted tobacco, open flames, bare light bulbs and sparks away from the battery. The electrolyte inside the battery is dilute sulfuric acid, which can burn skin and cause serious injury if splashed in your eyes (wear safety glasses). It'll also ruin clothes and painted surfaces. Remove all metal jewelry which could contact the positive battery terminal and a grounded metal source, causing a direct short.*
1   Tools and materials required for battery maintenance include eye and hand protection, baking soda, petroleum jelly, a battery cable puller and a

battery post/cable cleaning tool **(see illustration)**. In some cases where the cable clamp nuts are severely corroded and a wrench won't work to loosen them, a special battery terminal pliers may also be needed.
2   These models are equipped with a maintenance-free battery, which doesn't require the addition of water. These batteries have built-in test indicators which display different colors depending on battery condition. If the indicator is green, the battery is properly charged; if it's red or black, charging is required. A light yellow indicator means the battery must be replaced with a new one **(see illustration)**. **Warning:** *Don't charge, test or jump start a battery with a yellow indicator visible. If any doubt exists as to the battery state-of-charge, it should be tested by a dealer service department or a service station.*
3   The top of the battery should be kept clean and free of dirt and moisture so the battery doesn't become partially discharged. Clean the top and sides of the battery with a baking soda and water solution, but make sure that it doesn't enter the battery. After it's clean, check the case for cracks and other damage.
4   Make sure the cable clamps are tight to ensure good electrical connections and check the cables for cracked insulation, frayed wires and corrosion.
5   If the posts are corroded, remove the cables (negative first, then positive) and clean the clamps and battery posts with a battery terminal cleaning tool, then reinstall the cables (positive first, then negative) **(see illustrations)**. Apply petroleum jelly to the cable clamps and posts to keep corrosion to a minimum.

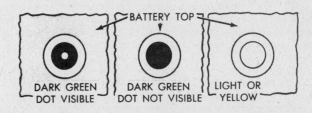

10.2   The original equipment battery installed in the vehicles covered by this manual are equipped with a built-in test indicator, which can be used to check the battery condition (state-of-charge)

10.5a   Battery terminal corrosion usually appears as light, fluffy powder

10.5b   Removing the cable from a battery post with a wrench – sometimes a special battery pliers is required for this procedure if corrosion has caused deterioration of the nut hex (always remove the ground cable first and hook it up last!)

10.5c   Regardless of the type of tool used on the battery posts, a clean, shiny surface should be the result

10.5d   When cleaning the cable clamps, all corrosion must be removed (the inside of the clamp is tapered to match the taper on the post, so don't remove too much material)

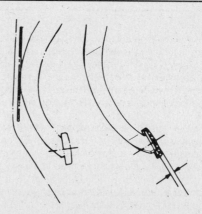

11.1   To check clutch pedal freeplay, measure the distance between the natural resting place of the pedal and the point at which resistance is felt

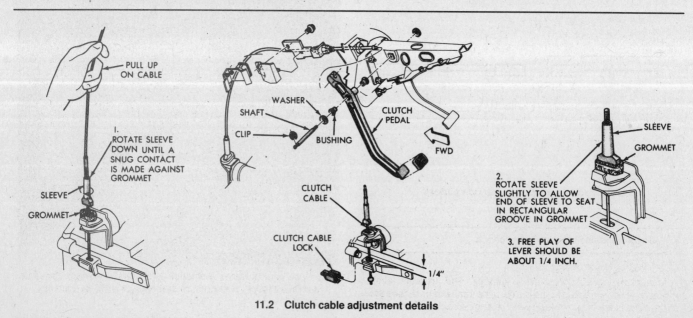

PULL UP ON CABLE

I. ROTATE SLEEVE DOWN UNTIL A SNUG CONTACT IS MADE AGAINST GROMMET

SLEEVE

GROMMET

SHAFT

WASHER

CLIP

BUSHING

CLUTCH PEDAL

FWD

CLUTCH CABLE

CLUTCH CABLE LOCK

1/4"

SLEEVE

GROMMET

2. ROTATE SLEEVE SLIGHTLY TO ALLOW END OF SLEEVE TO SEAT IN RECTANGULAR GROOVE IN GROMMET

3. FREE PLAY OF LEVER SHOULD BE ABOUT 1/4 INCH.

11.2   Clutch cable adjustment details

6   Make sure the battery carrier is in good condition and the hold-down clamp nut is tight. If the battery is removed, make sure no parts remain in the bottom of the carrier when it's reinstalled. When reinstalling the clamp nut, don't overtighten it.

7   Corrosion on the carrier and hold-down components can be removed with a solution of baking soda and water. Rinse the treated areas with clean water, dry them thoroughly and apply zinc-based primer and paint.

11   Clutch pedal freeplay check and adjustment (1.7L engine only)

Refer to illustrations 11.1 and 11.2

1   Push down on the clutch pedal and use a ruler to measure the distance it moves freely before the clutch resistance is felt **(see illustration)**. The freeplay should be within the limits listed in this Chapter's Specifications. If it isn't, it must be adjusted.

2   Working in the engine compartment, pull up on the clutch cable, rotate the sleeve down until it contacts the grommet, then rotate it slightly to allow the end to seat in the rectangular groove **(see illustration)**.

3   Recheck the freeplay. Repeat the adjustment as necessary.

12   Tire rotation

Refer to illustration 12.2

1   The tires should be rotated at the specified intervals and whenever uneven wear is noticed. Since the vehicle will be raised and the tires removed anyway, this is a good time to check the brakes (see Section 33) and/or repack the rear wheel bearings (see Section 32). Read over the appropriate Section if other work will be done at the same time.

2   The rotation pattern depends on whether or not the spare is included **(see illustration)**.

3   See the information in Jacking and towing at the front of this manual for the proper procedures to follow when raising the vehicle and changing a tire; however, if the brakes are to be checked, don't apply the parking brake as stated. Make sure the tires are blocked to prevent the vehicle from rolling.

4   Preferably, the entire vehicle should be raised at the same time. This can be done on a hoist or by jacking up each corner of the vehicle and lowering it onto jackstands. Always use four jackstands and make sure the vehicle is safely supported.

5   After the tire rotation, check and adjust the tire pressures as necessary and be sure to check wheel lug nut tightness.

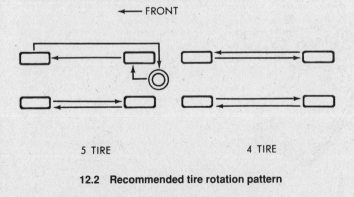

← FRONT

5 TIRE   4 TIRE

12.2   Recommended tire rotation pattern

13   Manual transaxle lubricant level check

Refer to illustrations 13.1 and 13.3

1   Manual transaxles don't have a dipstick. The lubricant level is checked by removing a plug from the side of the transaxle case **(see illustration)**. Check the lubricant level with the engine cold.

2   Locate the plug and use a rag to clean it and the surrounding area. It may be necessary to remove the left inner fender well cover for access to the plug.

3   Unscrew the plug. If oil immediately starts leaking out, thread the plug back into the transaxle – the oil level is alright. If oil doesn't leak out, completely remove the plug and use a finger to feel the oil level **(see illustration)**. The oil level should be even with the bottom of the plug hole.

4   If the transaxle requires additional lubricant, use a funnel with a rubber tube or a syringe to pour or squeeze the recommended lubricant into the plug hole to restore the level. **Caution:** *Use only the specified transaxle lubricant – see Recommended lubricants and fluids at the beginning of this Chapter.*

5   Thread the plug back into the transaxle and tighten it securely. Drive the vehicle and check for leaks around the plug.

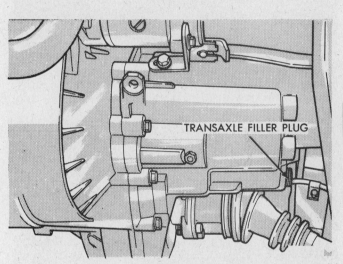

TRANSAXLE FILLER PLUG

13.1   The A-412 4-speed transaxle (which uses gear oil) installed in early models can be differentiated from other transaxles (which use other types of lubricants) by the location of the filler hole (under the clutch cable boss)

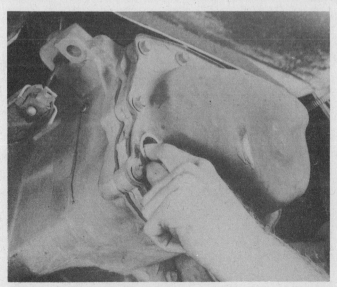

13.3   Use your finger as a dipstick to check the manual transaxle lubricant level – it should be at the lower edge of the hole

1

14.1   On 1978 through 1982 automatic transaxle models, the differential lubricant supply is separate from the transaxle and is checked after removing the fill plug (arrow)

14   Differential lubricant level check (1978 through1982 automatic transaxle equipped models only)

Refer to illustration 14.1

1   On these models the differential lubricant must be checked separately from the transaxle. Raise the vehicle, support it securely on jackstands and remove the differential fill plug **(see illustration)**.

2   The level must be within 3/8-inch of the bottom of the fill plug hole. If the level is low, add the specified lubricant with a syringe and reinstall the plug. See *Recommended lubricants and fluids* at the beginning of this Chapter for the type of lubricant to use.

15   Fuel filter replacement

Warning: *Gasoline is extremely flammable, so extra precautions must be taken when working on any part of the fuel system. DO NOT smoke or allow open flames or bare light bulbs near the vehicle. Also, don't work in a garage if a natural gas-type appliance with a pilot light is present. Have a fire extinguisher handy and make sure you know how to use it!*

Carburetor-equipped vehicles

1.7L engine

Refer to illustrations 15.6 and 15.8

1   The fuel filter is a disposable paper element type and is located inside the fuel inlet nut at the carburetor. It's made of pleated paper and cannot be cleaned or reused.

2   The job should be done with the engine cold (after sitting at least three hours) and the cable disconnected from the negative terminal of the battery. The necessary tools include open-end wrenches to fit the fuel line nuts. Flare nut wrenches (which wrap around the nut) should be used if available. In addition, you have to obtain the replacement filter (make sure it's for your specific vehicle and engine) and some clean rags.

3   Remove the air cleaner assembly. If vacuum hoses must be disconnected, be sure to note their positions and/or tag them to ensure they are reinstalled correctly.

4   Follow the fuel line to the point where it enters the carburetor. In most cases, the fuel line will be metal all the way from the fuel pump to the carburetor.

5   Place some rags under the fuel inlet fittings to catch spilled fuel as the fittings are disconnected.

6   Using diagonal cutting pliers, cut the hose clamp and disconnect the rubber fuel hose from the inlet fitting **(see illustration)**.

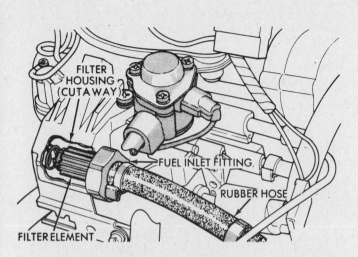

15.6   Detach the rubber fuel hose from the carburetor-mounted filter inlet fitting and discard the clamp (1.7L engine)

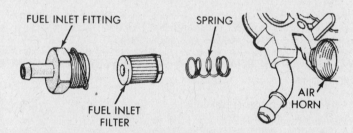

15.8   1.7L engine carburetor-mounted fuel filter components

7   Inspect the fuel hose for damage and deterioration – replace it if necessary.

8   Unscrew the fuel inlet fitting. As this fitting is drawn away from the carburetor body, be careful not to lose the thin washer-type gasket on the fitting, or the spring located behind the fuel filter. Also pay close attention to how the filter is installed **(see illustration)**.

9   Compare the old filter with the new one to make sure they're the same length and design.

10   Reinstall the spring in the carburetor body.

11   Place the filter in position (a gasket is usually supplied with the new filter) and tighten the fitting. Make sure it's not cross-threaded. Tighten it securely, but be careful not to overtighten it as the threads can strip easily, causing fuel leaks. Reconnect the fuel line to the fuel inlet fitting and install a new clamp.

12   Start the engine and check carefully for leaks.

2.2L engine

Refer to illustration 15.13

13   On these models, the fuel filter is located in the fuel line between the fuel pump and the carburetor **(see illustration)**.

14   This job should be done with the engine cold (after sitting at least three hours) and the negative battery cable disconnected.

You'll need a pair of pliers to loosen and slide back the fuel hose clamps, a replacement filter of the correct type and some clean rags.

15   Place rags under the fuel filter to catch any fuel that's spilled as the fuel hoses are disconnected.

16   Slide back the clamps, pull the hoses off the filter and remove the filter. If the hoses are damaged or deteriorated, install new ones.

17   Push the hoses onto the new filter and install the clamps. The new filter will probably be marked to indicate the direction of fuel flow (make sure the arrow points toward the carburetor).

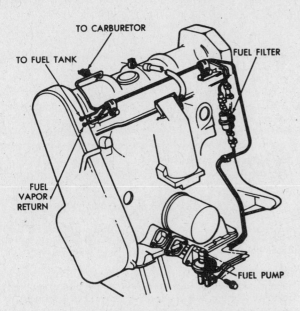

15.13   2.2L carburetor-equipped engine fuel filter location

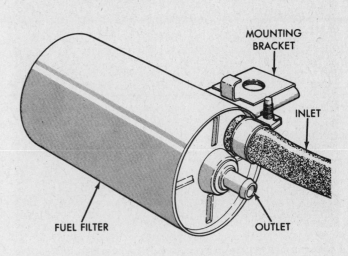

15.22   Fuel filter mounting details (fuel-injected vehicles)

1

18   Connect the negative cable to the battery, start the engine, check for leaks and make sure the filter is securely mounted.

19   A second fuel filter is attached to the end of the fuel suction tube in the gas tank. It doesn't require routine replacement, but it may be serviced if it gets clogged.

Fuel-injected vehicles

Refer to illustration 15.22

Warning: *Fuel-injected vehicles maintain pressure in the fuel system at all times, so the system must be depressurized BEFORE any lines are disconnected to avoid the possibility of spraying fuel. See Chapter 4 for the fuel pressure relief procedure.*

20   The fuel filter is a disposable canister type and is located in the fuel line under the rear of the vehicle, adjacent to the fuel tank.

21   Raise the rear of the vehicle and support it securely on jackstands.

22   Loosen the filter hose clamps **(see illustration)**.

23   Wrap a cloth around the fuel filter to catch the residual fuel (which may still be under slight pressure) and disconnect the hoses. It's a good idea to tie rags around your wrists to keep fuel from running down your arms.

24   Remove the bracket mounting bolt and detach the filter from the vehicle; hold your finger over the outlet to keep the residual fuel from running out.

25   Place the new filter in position, install the mounting bolt and tighten it securely. If the hoses are damaged or deteriorated, install new ones along with the new filter.

26   Install new clamps and attach the hoses to the filter. Tighten the clamps securely.

27   Start the engine and check carefully for leaks at the hose connections.

---

16   Chassis lubrication

Refer to illustrations 16.1 and 16.7

1   A grease gun and a cartridge filled with the proper grease (see Recommended lubricants and fluids), graphite spray and an oil can filled with engine oil will be required to lubricate the chassis components **(see illustration)**. Occasionally, on later model vehicles, plugs will be installed rather than grease fittings. If so, grease fittings will have to be purchased and installed.

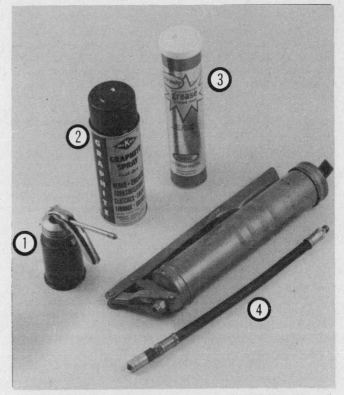

16.1   Materials required for chassis and body lubrication

1   **Engine oil** – *Light engine oil in a can like this can be used for door and hood hinges*

2   **Graphite spray** – *Used to lubricate lock cylinders*

3   **Grease** – *Grease, in a variety of types and weights, is available for use in a grease gun. Check the Specifications for your requirements.*

4   **Grease gun** – *A common grease gun, shown here with a detachable hose and nozzle, is needed for chassis lubrication. After use, clean it thoroughly!*

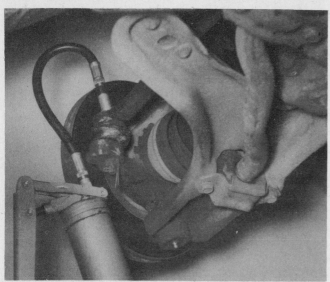

16.7   The steering system tie-rod end grease fittings are on the upper side of the steering arm and may be difficult to reach unless the grease gun is equipped with a flexible hose

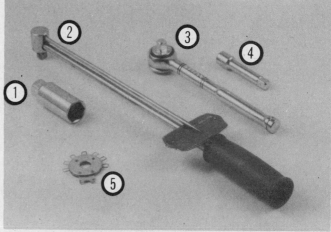

17.2   Tools required for changing spark plugs

1   **Spark plug socket** – *This will have special padding inside to protect the spark plug's porcelain insulator*
2   **Torque wrench** – *Although not mandatory, using this tool is the best way to ensure the plugs are tightened properly*
3   **Ratchet** – *Standard hand tool to fit the spark plug socket*
4   **Extension** – *Depending on model and accessories, you may need special extensions and universal joints to reach one or more of the plugs*
5   **Spark plug gap gauge** – *This gauge for checking the gap comes in a variety of styles. Make sure the gap for your engine is included.*

2   Look under the vehicle and see if grease fittings or plugs are installed. If there are plugs, remove them with a wrench and buy grease fittings which will thread into the component. A dealer parts department or auto parts store will be able to supply the correct fittings. Straight and angled fittings are available.

3   For easier access under the vehicle, raise it with a jack and place jack-stands under the portions of the body designated as hoisting and jacking points front and rear (see Jacking and towing at the front of this manual). Make sure it's securely supported by the stands.

4   Before beginning, force a little grease out of the nozzle to remove any dirt from the end of the gun. Wipe the nozzle clean with a rag.

5   With the grease gun and plenty of clean rags, crawl under the vehicle and begin lubricating the components.

6   Wipe the suspension balljoint grease fitting clean and push the nozzle firmly over it. Operate the lever on the grease gun to force grease into the component. The balljoints should be lubricated until the rubber seal is firm to the touch. Don't pump too much grease into the fitting as it could rupture the seal. For all other suspension and steering components, continue pumping grease into the fitting until it oozes out of the joint between the two components. If grease escapes around the grease gun nozzle, the fitting is clogged or the nozzle is not completely seated on the fitting. Resecure the gun nozzle to the fitting and try again. If necessary, replace the fitting with a new one.

7   Wipe the excess grease from the components and the grease fitting. Repeat the procedure for the remaining fittings **(see illustration)**.

8   Lubricate the sliding contact and pivot points of the manual transaxle shift linkage with the specified grease. While you're under the vehicle, clean and lubricate the parking brake cable along with the cable guides and levers. This can be done by smearing some of the chassis grease onto the cable and related parts with your fingers. Lubricate the clutch adjuster and cable, as well as the cable positioner, with a thin film of multi-purpose grease.

9   Lower the vehicle to the ground.

10   Open the hood and smear a little chassis grease on the hood latch mechanism. Have an assistant pull the hood release lever from inside the vehicle as you lubricate the cable at the latch.

11   Lubricate all the hinges (door, hood, etc.) with the recommended lubricant to keep them in proper working order.

12   The key lock cylinders can be lubricated with spray-on graphite or silicone lubricant which is available at auto parts stores.

13   Lubricate the door weatherstripping with silicone spray. This will reduce chafing and retard wear.

17   Spark plug replacement

Refer to illustrations 17.2, 17.5a, 17.5b, 17.7 and 17.11

1   The spark plugs are located on the front side of the engine, facing the radiator. **Caution:** *Before beginning work, disconnect the negative battery cable to prevent the electric cooling fan from coming on.*

2   In most cases the tools necessary for spark plug replacement include a plug wrench or spark plug socket which fits onto a ratchet (this special socket will be padded inside to protect the porcelain insulators on the new plugs), various extensions and a feeler gauge to check and adjust the spark plug gap **(see illustration)**. A special plug wire removal tool is available for separating the wire boot from the spark plug, but it isn't absolutely necessary. Since these engines are equipped with an aluminum cylinder head, a torque wrench should be used for tightening the spark plugs.

3   The best approach when replacing the spark plugs is to purchase the new spark plugs beforehand, adjust them to the proper gap and then replace each plug one at a time. When buying the new spark plugs, be sure to obtain the correct plug for your specific engine. This information can be found on the Emission Control Information label located under the hood, in the factory owner's manual or in the Specifications at the front of this Chapter. If differences exist between the sources, purchase the spark plug type specified on the VECI label as it was printed for your specific engine.

4   Allow the engine to cool completely before attempting to remove any of the plugs. During this cooling off time, each of the new spark plugs can be inspected for defects and the gaps can be checked.

5   The gap is checked by inserting the proper thickness gauge between the electrodes at the tip of the plug **(see illustration)**. The gap between the electrodes should be as specified on the VECI label in the engine compartment. The wire should touch each of the electrodes. If the gap is incorrect, use the adjuster on the thickness gauge body to bend the curved side electrode slightly until the proper gap is obtained **(see illustration)**. Also, at this time check for cracks in the spark plug body (if any are found, the plug should not be used). If the side electrode is not exactly over the center one, use the adjuster to align the two.

6   Cover the front of the vehicle to prevent damage to the paint.

17.5a   Spark plug manufacturers recommend using a wire type gauge when checking the gap – if the wire does not slide between the electrodes with a slight drag, adjustment is required

17.5b   To change the gap, bend the *side* electrode only, as indicated by the arrows, and be very careful not to crack or chip the porcelain insulator surrounding the center electrode

1

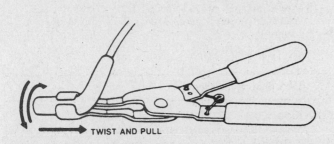

TWIST AND PULL

17.7   When removing the spark plug wires, pull only on the boot and twist it back-and-forth

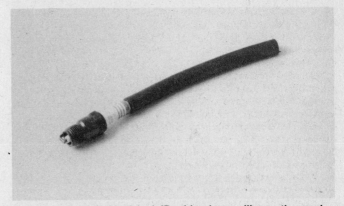

17.11   A length of 3/16-inch ID rubber hose will save time and prevent damaged threads when installing the spark plugs

7   With the engine cool, remove the spark plug wire from one spark plug. Pull only on the boot at the end of the wire; don't pull on the wire. Use a twisting motion to free the boot and wire from the plug. A plug wire removal tool (mentioned earlier) should be used if available **(see illustration)**.

8   If compressed air is available, use it to blow any dirt or foreign material away from the spark plug area. A common bicycle pump will also work. The idea here is to eliminate the possibility of material falling into the cylinder through the plug hole as the spark plug is removed.

9   Now place the spark plug socket over the plug and remove it from the engine by turning it in a counterclockwise direction.

10   Compare the spark plug with those shown in the accompanying photos to get an indication of the overall running condition of the engine.

11   Thread one of the new plugs into the hole, tightening it as much as possible by hand. **Caution:** *Be extremely careful – these engines have aluminum cylinder heads, which means the spark plug hole threads can be stripped easily.* It may be a good idea to slip a short length of rubber hose over the end of the plug to use as a tool to thread it into place. The hose will grip the plug well enough to turn it, but will start to slip on the plug if the plug begins to cross-thread in the hole – this will prevent damaged threads and the accompanying costs involved in repairing them **(see illustration)**.

12   Attach the plug wire to the new spark plug, again using a twisting motion on the boot until it's seated on the spark plug.

13   Repeat the above procedure for the remaining spark plugs, replacing them one at a time to prevent mixing up the spark plug wires.

18   Spark plug wire, distributor cap and rotor – check and replacement

Refer to illustrations 18.7, 18.9 and 18.10

1   The spark plug wires should be checked at the recommended intervals or whenever new spark plugs are installed.

2   The wires should be inspected one at a time to prevent mixing up the order which is essential for proper engine operation.

3   Disconnect the plug wire from the spark plug. A removal tool can be used for this, or you can grab the rubber boot, twist slightly and then pull the wire free. Don't pull on the wire itself, only on the rubber boot.

4   Check inside the boot for corrosion, which will look like a white, crusty powder (don't mistake the white dielectric grease used on some plug wire boots for corrosion).

5   Now push the wire and boot back onto the end of the spark plug. It should be a tight fit on the plug end. If not, remove the wire and use a pair of pliers to carefully crimp the metal connector inside the wire boot until the fit is snug.

6   Now, using a cloth, clean each wire along its entire length. Remove all built-up dirt and grease. As this is done, inspect for burned areas, cracks

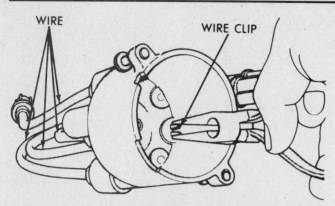

18.7   When replacing the spark plug wires, use a pair of pliers to compress the retaining clips inside the distributor cap before pulling the wire out

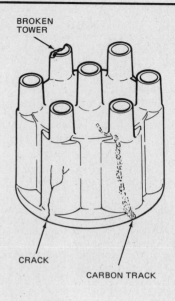

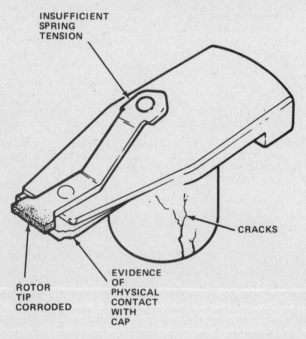

18.10   The ignition rotor should be checked for wear and corrosion as indicated here (if in doubt about its condition, buy a new one)

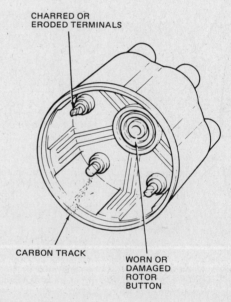

18.9   Shown here are some of the common defects to look for when inspecting the distributor cap (if in doubt about its condition, install a new one)

and any other form of damage. Bend the wires in several places to ensure that the conductive material inside hasn't hardened. Repeat the procedure for the remaining wires (don't forget the distributor cap-to-coil wire).

7   Remove the distributor cap splash shield and check the wires at the cap, making sure they aren't loose and that the wires and boots aren't cracked or damaged. **Note:** *Don't attempt to pull the wires off the cap – they're retained on the inside by wire clips. The manufacturer doesn't recommend removing the wires from the cap for inspection because this could damage the integrity of the boot seal.* If the wires appear to be damaged, replace them with new ones. Remove the distributor cap, release the wire clips with a pair of pliers and remove the wires **(see illustration)**. Insert the new wires into the cap while squeezing the boots to release any trapped air as you push them into place. Continue pushing until you feel the wire electrodes snap into position.

8   A visual check of the spark plug wires can also be made. In a darkened garage (make sure there is ventilation), start the engine and look at

each plug wire. Be careful not to come into contact with any moving engine parts. If there's a crack in the insulation, you'll see arcing or a small spark at the damaged area.

9   Remove the distributor cap with the wires attached and check the cap for cracks, carbon tracks and other damage. Examine the terminals inside the cap for corrosion (slight corrosion can be removed with a pocket knife) **(see illustration)**.

10   Check the rotor (now visible on the end of the distributor shaft) for cracks and a secure fit on the shaft. Make sure the terminals aren't burned, corroded or pitted excessively. A small fine file can be used to restore the rotor terminals **(see illustration)**.

11   If new spark plug wires are needed, purchase a complete pre-cut set for your particular engine. The terminals and rubber boots should already be installed on the wires. Replace the wires one at a time to avoid mixing up the firing order and make sure the terminals are securely seated in the distributor cap and on the spark plugs.

CARBON DEPOSITS

Symptoms: Dry sooty deposits indicate a rich mixture or weak ignition. Causes misfiring, hard starting and hesitation.

Recommendation: Check for a clogged air cleaner, high float level, sticky choke and worn ignition points. Use a spark plug with a longer core nose for greater anti-fouling protection.

OIL DEPOSITS

Symptoms: Oily coating caused by poor oil control. Oil is leaking past worn valve guides or piston rings into the combustion chamber. Causes hard starting, misfiring and hesition.

Recommendation: Correct the mechanical condition with necessary repairs and install new plugs.

TOO HOT

Symptoms: Blistered, white insulator, eroded electrode and absence of deposits. Results in shortened plug life.

Recommendation: Check for the correct plug heat range, over-advanced ignition timing, lean fuel mixture, intake manifold vacuum leaks and sticking valves. Check the coolant level and make sure the radiator is not clogged.

PREIGNITION

Symptoms: Melted electrodes. Insulators are white, but may be dirty due to misfiring or flying debris in the combustion chamber. Can lead to engine damage.

Recommendation: Check for the correct plug heat range, over-advanced ignition timing, lean fuel mixture, clogged cooling system and lack of lubrication.

HIGH SPEED GLAZING

Symptoms: Insulator has yellowish, glazed appearance. Indicates that combustion chamber temperatures have risen suddenly during hard acceleration. Normal deposits melt to form a conductive coating. Causes misfiring at high speeds.

Recommendation: Install new plugs. Consider using a colder plug if driving habits warrant.

GAP BRIDGING

Symptoms: Combustion deposits lodge between the electrodes. Heavy deposits accumulate and bridge the electrode gap. The plug ceases to fire, resulting in a dead cylinder.

Recommendation: Locate the faulty plug and remove the deposits from between the electrodes.

NORMAL

Symptoms: Brown to grayish-tan color and slight electrode wear. Correct heat range for engine and operating conditions.

Recommendation: When new spark plugs are installed, replace with plugs of the same heat range.

ASH DEPOSITS

Symptoms: Light brown deposits encrusted on the side or center electrodes or both. Derived from oil and/or fuel additives. Excessive amounts may mask the spark, causing misfiring and hesitation during acceleration.

Recommendation: If excessive deposits accumulate over a short time or low mileage, install new valve guide seals to prevent seepage of oil into the combustion chambers. Also try changing gasoline brands.

1

WORN

Symptoms: Rounded electrodes with a small amount of deposits on the firing end. Normal color. Causes hard starting in damp or cold weather and poor fuel economy.

Recommendation: Replace with new plugs of the same heat range.

DETONATION

Symptoms: Insulators may be cracked or chipped. Improper gap setting techniques can also result in a fractured insulator tip. Can lead to piston damage.

Recommendation: Make sure the fuel anti-knock values meet engine requirements. Use care when setting the gaps on new plugs. Avoid lugging the engine.

SPLASHED DEPOSITS

Symptoms: After long periods of misfiring, deposits can loosen when normal combustion temperature is restored by an overdue tune-up. At high speeds, deposits flake off the piston and are thrown against the hot insulator, causing misfiring.

Recommendation: Replace the plugs with new ones or clean and reinstall the originals.

MECHANICAL DAMAGE

Symptoms: May be caused by a foreign object in the combustion chamber or the piston striking an incorrect reach (too long) plug. Causes a dead cylinder and could result in piston damage.

Recommendation: Remove the foreign object from the engine and/or install the correct reach plug.

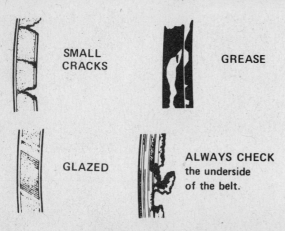

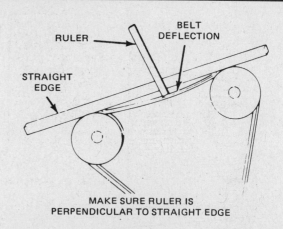

19.3   Here are some of the more common problems associated with drivebelts (check the belts very carefully to prevent an untimely breakdown)

19.4   Measuring drivebelt deflection with a straightedge and ruler

19   Drivebelt check, adjustment and replacement

Refer to illustrations 19.3, 19.4, 19.5a, 19.5b and 19.5c
Warning: *The electric cooling fan on some models can activate at any time, even when the ignition switch is in the Off position. Disconnect the negative battery cable when working in the vicinity of the fan.*

1   The drivebelts, or V-belts as they are sometimes called, at the front of the engine, play an important role in the overall operation of the vehicle and its components. Due to their function and material makeup, the belts are prone to failure after a period of time and should be inspected and adjusted periodically to prevent major damage.

2   The number of belts used on a particular engine depends on the accessories installed. Drivebelts are used to turn the alternator, AIR pump, power steering pump, water pump and air conditioning compressor. Depending on the pulley arrangement, a single belt may be used for more than one of these components.

3   With the engine off, open the hood and locate the various belts at the front of the engine. Using your fingers (and a flashlight if necessary), examine the belts. Check for cracks and separation of the plies. Look for contamination by grease or oil and glazed areas, which give the belt a shiny

appearance. Both sides of each belt should be inspected, which means you'll have to twist them to check the underside **(see illustration)**.

4   The tightness of each belt is checked by pushing on it at a distance halfway between the pulleys **(see illustration)**. Apply about 10 pounds of force with your thumb and see how much the belt moves down (deflects). Refer to this Chapter's Specifications for the amount of deflection allowed in each belt.

5   If adjustment is necessary, it's done by moving the belt-driven accessory on the bracket **(see illustrations)**.

6   For each component, there's a locking bolt and a pivot bolt or nut. Both must be loosened slightly to move the component.

7   After the two bolts have been loosened, move the component away from the engine (to tighten the belt) or toward the engine (to loosen the belt). Many accessories are equipped with a square hole designed to accept a 3/8-inch or 1/2-inch square drive breaker bar. The bar can be used to lever the component and tension the drivebelt. Hold the accessory in position and check the belt tension. If it's correct, tighten the two bolts until snug, then recheck the tension. If it's alright, tighten the two bolts completely.

8   To adjust the alternator drivebelt, loosen the pivot nut and the locking screw or T-bolt locknut, then turn the adjusting bolt to tension the belt.

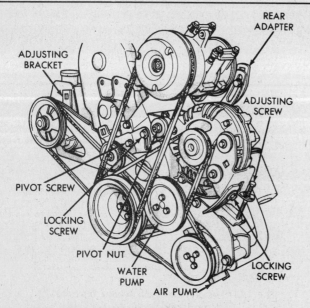

19.5a   Typical 1.7L engine drivebelt adjustment details

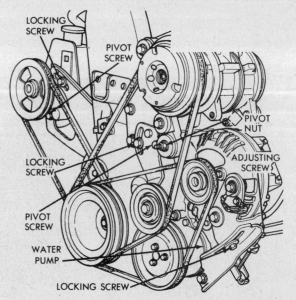

19.5b   Typical 2.2L engine drivebelt adjustment details

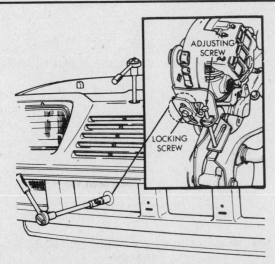

19.5c   On some two-door models, access to the alternator adjustment and locking screws is through the grille, using a ratchet with a long extension

9   It may be necessary to use some sort of pry bar to move a component while the belt is adjusted. If this must be done, be very careful not to damage the component being moved, or the part being pried against.

10   Run the engine for about 15 minutes, then recheck the belt tension.

20   Air filter replacement

1   At the specified intervals, the air filter element and (if equipped) crankcase ventilation filter should be replaced.

2   The air filter element is located in a housing adjacent to the engine.

Carburetor-equipped vehicles

Refer to illustrations 20.3a, 20.3b, 20.3c and 20.4

3   On the 1.7L engine, release the clips, remove the wingnut, detach the hose and lift the air cleaner top plate assembly (with the element attached) out of the housing **(see illustration)**. Remove the wingnut and detach the air filter element **(see illustrations)**.

4   On the 2.2L engine, release the hold-down bails, remove the wingnuts and lift off the cover. Lift the filter element out of the air cleaner body **(see illustration)**.

5   While the cover is off, be careful not to drop anything down into the carburetor or air cleaner housing. Clean the inside of the housing with a rag.

20.3a   Release the clips, remove the wingnut and lift the top plate and element out of the air cleaner housing (1.7L engine)

6   On the 1.7L engine, attach the new element to the top plate and secure it with the wingnut. Install the top plate, secure the clips, attach the hose and install the wingnuts.

20.3b   Remove the wingnut . . .

20.3c   . . . and withdraw the filter element

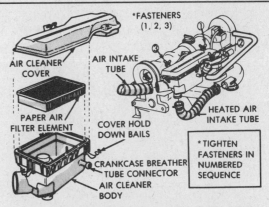

20.4   Air cleaner installation details (typical 2.2L carburetor-equipped engine)

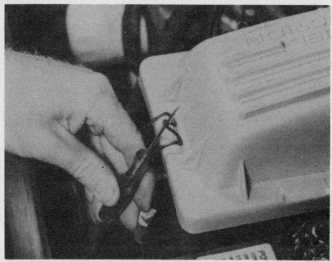

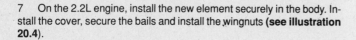

20.8a   Use a small screwdriver to release the air cleaner cover clips

20.8c   On some models, the cover can be rotated away from the air cleaner body after loosening the hose clamp (arrow)

7   On the 2.2L engine, install the new element securely in the body. Install the cover, secure the bails and install the wingnuts **(see illustration 20.4)**.

Fuel-injected vehicles

Refer to illustrations 20.8a, 20.8b, 20.8c, 20.9 and 20.11

8   Detach the clips or remove the threaded fasteners and lift the top cover off **(see illustrations)**. On some models it may be necessary to loosen the air output hose clamp so the cover can be rotated away from the air cleaner body **(see illustration)**.

9   Lift the element out **(see illustration)**.

10   Be careful not to drop anything down into the throttle body or air cleaner assembly. Clean the inside of the housing with a rag.

11   Pull the crankcase filter out of the housing **(see illustration)**. Wash the crankcase filter in solvent and oil it lightly before reinstalling.

12   Install the cover and secure it with the clips or threaded fasteners. Be sure to tighten any hose clamps which were loosened or removed.

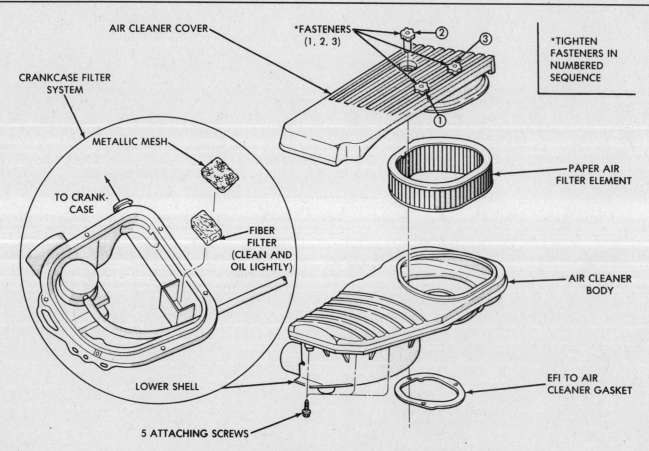

20.8b   Air cleaner installation details (typical fuel-injected vehicles)

20.9   Note the direction the filter element faces when lifting it out of the air cleaner body

20.11   Pull the crankcase filter out of the housing, wash it in solvent and oil it lightly before reinstalling it

---

21   Positive Crankcase Ventilation (PCV) valve check and replacement

Refer to illustrations 21.2a, 21.2b, 21.2c and 21.2d

1   The PCV valve is usually located in a vent module or rubber hoses connected to the camshaft cover.

2   With the engine idling at normal operating temperature, pull the valve (with the hose attached) from the rubber hose or grommet in the vent module **(see illustrations)**.

1

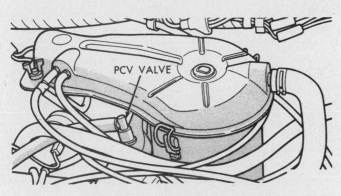

21.2a   PCV valve location (typical 1.7L engine)

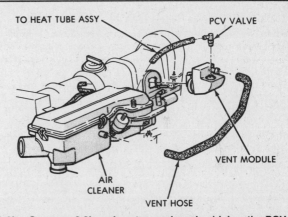

21.2b   On some 2.2L carburetor-equipped vehicles, the PCV valve is mounted in the vent module

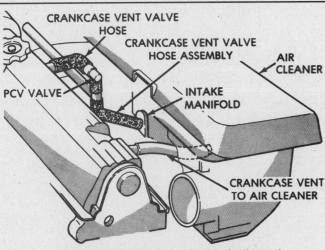

21.2c   PCV valve location (non-turbocharged, fuel-injected vehicles)

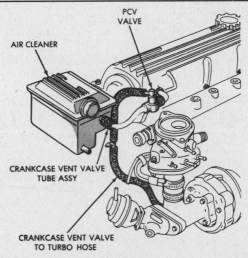

21.2d   PCV valve location (turbocharged vehicles)

3   Place your finger over the valve opening. If there's no vacuum at the valve, check for a plugged hose, manifold port or valve. Replace any plugged or deteriorated hoses.

4   Turn off the engine and shake the PCV valve, listening for a rattle. If the valve doesn't rattle, replace it with a new one.

5   To replace the valve, pull it from the end of the hose, noting its installed position and direction.

6   When purchasing a replacement PCV valve, make sure it's for your particular vehicle and engine size. Compare the old valve with the new one to make sure they're the same.

7   When replacing the PCV valve on a 2.2L engine (so equipped), inspect the vent module for cracks and damage and make sure the crankcase filter (see Section 20) is clean (**see illustration 21.2b**). Remove the vent module and wash it thoroughly with solvent. Prior to installation, invert the module and fill it up with engine oil. Allow the oil to drain out through the vent at the top into a container. With the interior of the module now coated with oil, it can be reinstalled.

8   Push the valve into the end of the hose until it's seated.

9   Inspect the rubber hose or grommet for damage and replace it with a new one if necessary.

10   Push the PCV valve and hose securely into position.

---

22   Exhaust Gas Recirculation (EGR) system check

---

1   The EGR valve is usually located on the intake manifold, adjacent to the carburetor or TBI unit. Most of the time when a problem develops, it's due to a stuck or corroded EGR valve.

2   With the engine cold to prevent burns, push on the EGR valve diaphragm. Using moderate pressure, you should be able to press the diaphragm in-and-out within the housing.

3   If the diaphragm doesn't move or moves only with much effort, replace the EGR valve with a new one. If in doubt about the condition of the valve, compare the free movement of the EGR valve with a new one.

4   See Chapter 6 for more information on the EGR system.

---

23   Underhood hose check and replacement

Caution: *Replacement of air conditioning hoses must be left to a dealer service department or air conditioning shop equipped to depressurize the system safely. Never remove air conditioning components or hoses until the system has been depressurized.*

General

1   High temperatures under the hood can cause the deterioration of the rubber and plastic hoses used for engine, accessory and emission systems operation. Periodic inspection should be made for cracks, loose clamps, material hardening and leaks.

2   Information specific to the cooling system hoses can be found in Section 28.

3   Some, but not all, hoses use clamps to secure the hoses to fittings. Where clamps are used, check to be sure they haven't lost their tension, allowing the hose to leak. Where clamps are not used, make sure the hose hasn't expanded and/or hardened where it slips over the fitting, allowing it to leak.

Vacuum hoses

4   It's quite common for vacuum hoses, especially those in the emissions system, to be color coded or identified by colored stripes molded into the hose. Various systems require hoses with different wall thicknesses, collapse resistance and temperature resistance. When replacing hoses, make sure the new ones are made of the same material.

5   Often the only effective way to check a hose is to remove it completely from the vehicle. Where more than one hose is removed, be sure to label the hoses and their attaching points to insure proper reattachment.

6   When checking vacuum hoses, be sure to include any plastic T-fittings in the check. Check the fittings for cracks and the hose where it fits over the fitting for enlargement, which could cause leakage.

7   A small piece of vacuum hose (1/4-inch inside diameter) can be used as a stethoscope to detect vacuum leaks. Hold one end of the hose to your ear and probe around vacuum hoses and fittings, listening for the "hissing" sound characteristic of a vacuum leak. **Warning:** *When probing with the vacuum hose stethoscope, be careful not to allow your body or the hose to come into contact with moving engine components such as the drivebelt, cooling fan, etc.*

Fuel hose

Warning: *There are certain precautions which must be taken when inspecting or servicing fuel system components. Work in a well ventilated area and don't allow open flames (cigarettes, appliance pilot lights, etc.) or bare light bulbs near the work area. Mop up any spills immediately and don't store fuel soaked rags where they could ignite. The fuel system is under pressure, so if any fuel lines are disconnected, the pressure in the system must be relieved first (see Chapter 4 for more information).*

8   Check all rubber fuel hoses for damage and deterioration. Check especially for cracks in areas where the hose bends and just before clamping points, such as where a hose attaches to the fuel filter, carburetor or fuel injection unit.

9   High quality fuel line, specifically designed for fuel injection systems, should be used for fuel line replacement on vehicles equipped with EFI. **Warning:** *Never use vacuum line, clear plastic tubing or water hose for fuel lines.*

10   Spring-type clamps are commonly used on fuel lines. These clamps often lose their tension over a period of time, and can be "sprung" during the removal process. Therefore it is recommended that all spring-type clamps be replaced with screw clamps whenever a hose is replaced.

Metal lines

11   Sections of metal line are often used for fuel line between the fuel pump and fuel injection unit or carburetor. Check carefully to be sure the line has not been bent and crimped and that cracks have not started in the line.

12   If a section of metal fuel line must be replaced, only seamless steel tubing should be used, since copper and aluminum tubing do not have the strength necessary to withstand normal engine operating vibration.

13   Check the metal brake lines where they enter the master cylinder and brake proportioning unit (if used) for cracks in the lines or loose fittings. Any sign of brake fluid leakage calls for an immediate thorough inspection of the brake system.

---

24   Carburetor/fuel injection throttle body mounting nut torque check

---

1   The carburetor or fuel injection throttle body is attached to the top of the intake manifold by nuts. The nuts can sometimes work loose during normal engine operation and cause a vacuum leak.

2   To properly tighten the mounting nuts, a torque wrench is necessary. If you do not own one, they can usually be rented on a daily basis.

3   Remove the air cleaner assembly-to-carburetor or throttle body hose.

4   Locate the mounting nuts at the base of the carburetor or throttle body. Decide what special tools or adaptors will be be necessary, if any, to tighten the nuts with a socket and the torque wrench.

5   Tighten the nuts to the torque listed in this Chapter's Specifications. Do not overtighten the nuts, as the threads may strip. On 2.2L engines, be careful not to bend the fast idle lever when tightening the nut next to it. Also, on turbocharged models, check the hoses and clamps between the throttle body and the turbocharger and the turbocharger and the intake manifold to make sure there are no leaks.

6   If you suspect a vacuum leak exists at the bottom of the carburetor or throttle body, obtain a short length of rubber hose. Start the engine and place one end of the hose next to your ear as you probe around the base of the carburetor or throttle body with the other end. You should hear a hissing sound if a leak exists.

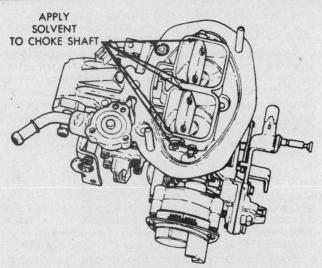

25.9a Work the choke linkage back-and-forth while spraying the solvent at the points where the shaft passes through the carburetor air horn, . . .

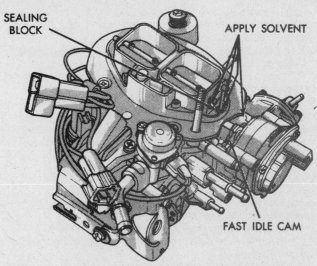

25.9b . . . at the link between the choke shaft and the choke heater and at the sealing block where the link passes through it

7   If, after the nuts are properly tightened, a vacuum leak still exists, the carburetor or throttle body must be removed and a new gasket installed. See Chapter 4 for more information.

8   After tightening the nuts, reinstall the air cleaner hose.

25   Carburetor choke check

Refer to illustrations 25.9a and 25.9b

1   The choke operates only when the engine is cold, so this check must be performed before the engine has been started for the day.

2   Open the hood and remove the top plate of the air cleaner assembly as described in Section 20. If any vacuum hoses must be disconnected, make sure you tag the hoses for reinstallation in their original positions.

3   Look at the top of the carburetor. You'll notice a flat plate in each of the carburetor throats.

4   Have an assistant press the accelerator pedal to the floor. The plates should close completely. Start the engine while you watch the plates at the carburetor. **Warning:** *Don't position your face directly over the carburetor – the engine could backfire, causing serious burns. When the engine starts, the choke plates should open slightly.*

5   Allow the engine to continue running at an idle speed. As the engine warms up to operating temperature, the plates should slowly open, allowing more air to enter through the top of the carburetor.

6   After a few minutes, the choke plates should be completely open to the vertical position.

7   You'll notice that the engine speed corresponds with the plate opening. With the plates closed, the engine should run at a fast idle speed. As the plates open, the engine speed will decrease.

8   If the choke doesn't operate as described, see Chapter 4 for specific information on adjusting and servicing the choke components.

9   At the recommended intervals, apply the solvent specified in Recommended lubricants and fluids at the beginning of this Chapter to the contact surfaces of the choke shaft to ensure free movement. Also, apply the solvent to the link connecting the choke shaft to the choke heater and the sealing block through which it passes **(see illustrations).**

26   Heated inlet air system check

Refer to illustration 26.3

1   All non-turbocharged models are equipped with a heated inlet air cleaner which draws air to the carburetor or fuel injection throttle body from

different locations, depending on engine temperature.

2   This is a simple visual check; however, the outside air duct must be removed.

3   Locate the vacuum air control valve in the air cleaner assembly. It's located inside the air cleaner snorkel **(see illustration)**. Make sure the flexible heat duct is securely attached and undamaged.

4   The check should be done when the engine and outside air are cold (less than 65-degrees F). Start the engine and look through the snorkel at the valve (which should move to the up or heat on position). With the valve up, air cannot enter through the end of the snorkel, but instead enters the air cleaner through the heat duct attached to the exhaust manifold.

5   As the engine warms up to operating temperature, the valve should move to the down or heat off position to allow air through the snorkel end. Depending on outside air temperature, this may take 10 to 15 minutes. To speed up the check you can reconnect the outside air duct, drive the vehicle and then check to see if the valve has moved down.

6   If the air cleaner isn't operating properly, see Chapter 6 for more information.

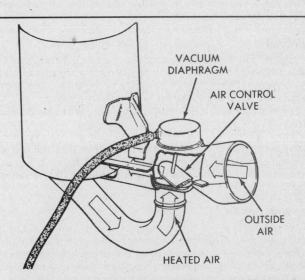

26.3   The vacuum diaphragm-controlled air control valve is located in the air cleaner housing (here it's just beginning to move from the down or heat off position to the up position)

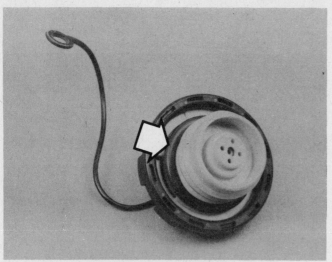

27.4   Check the fuel tank cap gasket (arrow) to make sure there's an even sealing imprint all the way around it

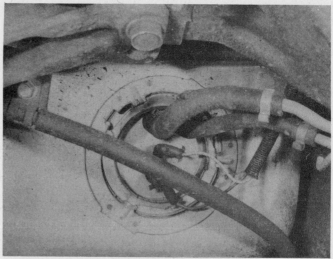

27.6   Check the fuel tank hoses for damage and deterioration

27   Fuel system check

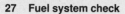

Refer to illustrations 27.4 and 27.6
Warning: *Gasoline is extremely flammable, so extra precautions must be taken when working on any part of the fuel system. DO NOT smoke or allow open flames or bare light bulbs near the vehicle. Also, don't work in a garage if a natural gas-type appliance with a pilot light is present. Have a fire extinguisher handy and make sure you know how to use it!*

1   The fuel system on models which are equipped with Electronic Fuel Injection (EFI) is under pressure even when the engine is off. Consequently, the EFI system must be depressurized (see Chapter 4) whenever the fuel system is worked on. Even after depressurization, if any fuel lines are disconnected for servicing, be prepared to catch some fuel as it spurts out. Plug all disconnected fuel lines immediately to prevent the tank from emptying itself.

2   The fuel system is most easily checked with the vehicle raised on a hoist where the components on the underside are readily visible and accessible.

3   If the smell of gasoline is noticed while driving, or after the vehicle has been parked in the sun, the fuel system should be thoroughly inspected immediately.

4   Remove the gas tank cap and check for damage, corrosion and a proper sealing imprint on the gasket **(see illustration)**. Replace the cap with a new one if necessary.

5   Inspect the gas tank and filler neck for punctures, cracks and other damage. The connection between the filler neck and the tank is especially critical. Sometimes a rubber filler neck will leak due to loose clamps or deteriorated rubber; problems a home mechanic can usually rectify. **Warning:** *Do not, under any circumstances, try to repair a fuel tank yourself (except to replace rubber components) unless you have considerable experience. A welding torch or any open flame can easily cause the fuel vapors to explode if the proper precautions are not taken.*

6   Carefully check all rubber hoses and metal lines leading away from the fuel tank. Check for loose connections, deteriorated hoses, crimped lines and damage of any kind **(see illustration)**. Follow the lines up to the front of the vehicle, carefully inspecting them all the way. Repair or replace damaged sections as necessary (see Chapter 4).

28   Cooling system check

Refer to illustration 28.4
Warning: *The electric cooling fan on some models can activate at any time, even when the ignition switch is in the Off position. Disconnect the*

fan motor or the negative battery cable when working in the vicinity of the fan.

1   Many major engine failures can be attributed to a faulty cooling system. If the vehicle is equipped with an automatic transaxle, the cooling system is also used to cool the transaxle fluid.

2   The cooling system should be checked with the engine cold. Do this before the vehicle is driven for the day or after it has been shut off for three or four hours.

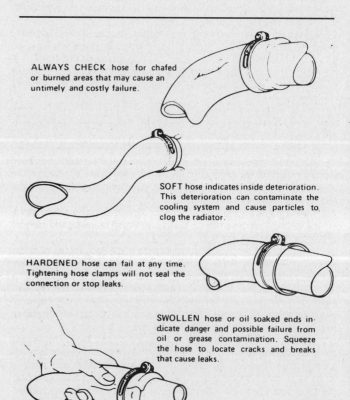

ALWAYS CHECK hose for chafed or burned areas that may cause an untimely and costly failure.

SOFT hose indicates inside deterioration. This deterioration can contaminate the cooling system and cause particles to clog the radiator.

HARDENED hose can fail at any time. Tightening hose clamps will not seal the connection or stop leaks.

SWOLLEN hose or oil soaked ends indicate danger and possible failure from oil or grease contamination. Squeeze the hose to locate cracks and breaks that cause leaks.

28.4   Hoses, like drivebelts, have a habit of failing at the worst possible time – to prevent the inconvenience of a blown radiator or heater hose, inspect them carefully as shown here

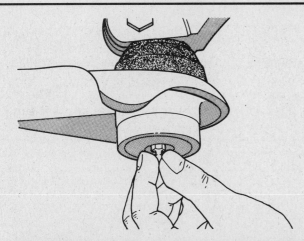

30.4   With the vehicle weight resting on the suspension, try to move the balljoint grease fittings with your fingers – if the fittings can be moved easily, the balljoints are worn and must be replaced

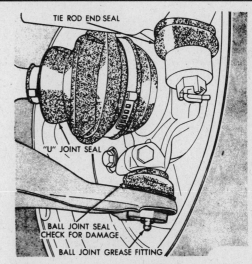

30.7a   Check the balljoint and tie-rod end seals for cracks and lubricant leaks

3   Remove the radiator cap and thoroughly clean the cap (inside and out) with water. Also clean the filler neck on the radiator. All traces of corrosion should be removed.

4   Carefully check the upper and lower radiator hoses along with the smaller diameter heater hoses. Inspect the entire length of each hose, replacing any that are cracked, swollen or deteriorated. Cracks may become more apparent when a hose is squeezed (see illustration).

5   Also check that all hose connections are tight. A leak in the cooling system will usually show up as white or rust-colored deposits on the areas adjoining the leak.

6   Use compressed air or a soft brush to remove bugs, leaves, and other debris from the front of the radiator or air conditioning condenser. Be careful not to damage the delicate cooling fins, or cut yourself on them.

7   Finally, have the cap and system pressure tested. If you do not have a pressure tester, most gas stations and repair shops will do this for a minimal charge.

29   Exhaust system check

1   With the engine cold (at least three hours after the vehicle has been driven), check the complete exhaust system from its starting point at the engine to the end of the tailpipe. This should be done on a hoist where unrestricted access is available.

2   Check the pipes and connections for signs of leakage and/or corrosion indicating a potential failure. Make sure that all brackets and hangers are in good condition and tight.

3   At the same time, inspect the underside of the body for holes, corrosion and open seams which may allow exhaust gases to enter the passenger compartment. Seal all body openings with silicone or body putty.

4   Rattles and other noises can often be traced to the exhaust system, especially the mounts and hangers. Try to move the pipes, muffler and catalytic converter. If the components can come into contact with the body, secure the exhaust system with new mounts.

5   This is also an ideal time to check the running condition of the engine by inspecting the very end of the tailpipe. The exhaust deposits here are an indication of engine state-of-tune. If the pipe is black and sooty or coated with white deposits, the engine may be in need of a tune-up (including a thorough carburetor or fuel injection system inspection and adjustment).

30   Steering and suspension check

Refer to illustrations 30.4, 30.7a and 30.7b

1   Whenever the front of the vehicle is raised for service it is a good idea

to visually check the suspension and steering components for wear and damage.

2   Indications of wear and damage include excessive play in the steering wheel before the front wheels react, excessive lean around corners, body movement over rough roads or binding at some point as the steering wheel is turned.

3   Before the vehicle is raised for inspection, test the shock absorbers by pushing down to rock the vehicle at each corner. If it does not come back to a level position within one or two bounces, the shocks are worn and should be replaced. As this is done, check for squeaks and unusual noises from the suspension components. Information on shock absorbers and suspension components can be found in Chapter 10.

4   Check the balljoints for wear on 1981 and later models by grasping the grease fittings securely and attempting to move them (see illustration). If the grease fittings move easily, the balljoints are worn and must be replaced with new ones. On 1978 through 1980 models, pry between the balljoint and the steering knuckle to check for wear (see Chapter 10).

5   Now raise the front end of the vehicle and support it securely with jackstands placed under the jacking and hoisting points (see *Jacking and towing* at the front of this manual). Because of the work to be done, the vehicle must be stable and safely supported.

6   Check the front wheel hub nuts for correct tightness and make sure they're properly crimped in place.

7   Crawl under the vehicle and check for loose bolts, broken or disconnected parts and deteriorated rubber bushings on all suspension and steering components (see illustration). Look for grease or fluid leaking from around the steering gear boots (see illustration). Check the shock

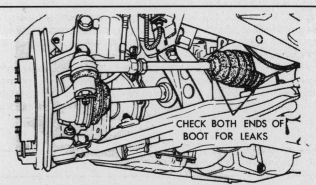

30.7b   Push on both ends of the steering gear boots to check for cracks and lubricant leaks

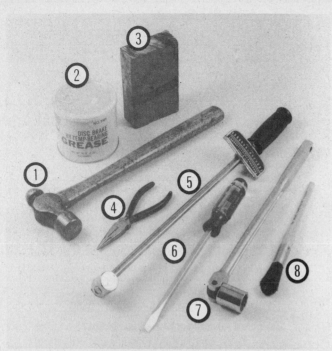

32.1   Tools and materials needed for rear wheel bearing maintenance

1 **Hammer** – A common hammer will do just fine
2 **Grease** – High-temperature grease which is formulated specially for front wheel bearings should be used
3 **Wood block** – If you have a scrap piece of 2x4, it can be used to drive the new seal into the hub
4 **Needle-nose pliers** – Used to straighten and remove the cotter pin in the spindle
5 **Torque wrench** – This is very important in this procedure; if the bearing is too tight, the wheel won't turn freely – if it's too loose, the wheel will "wobble" on the spindle. Either way, it could mean extensive damage.
6 **Screwdriver** – Used to remove the seal from the hub (a long screwdriver would be preferred)
7 **Socket/breaker bar** – Needed to loosen the nut on the spindle if it's extremely tight
8 **Brush** – Together with some clean solvent, this will be used to remove old grease from the hub and spindle

absorbers for signs of fluid leakage. Check the power steering hoses and connections for leaks. Check the steering joints for wear.
8   Have an assistant turn the steering wheel from side-to-side and check the steering components for free movement, chafing and binding. If the wheels don't respond to the movement of the steering wheel, try to determine where the slack is located.

31   Steering shaft seal lubrication

1   The steering shaft seal protects the steering shaft at the point where it passes through the firewall. Lubricate the inner circumference of the seal with the lubricant specified in Recommended lubricants and fluids if the shaft makes noise or sticks to the seal when it's turned.
2   Raise the vehicle and support it securely.
3   Peel back the upper edge of the seal and apply a light coat of grease all the way around the inner circumference where it contacts the steering shaft.
4   Lower the vehicle.

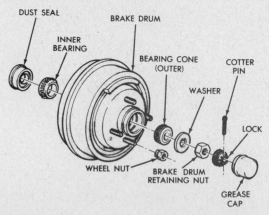

32.7   Exploded view of the rear hub and bearing components

32.8   Pull the brake drum/hub out slightly to dislodge the outer wheel bearing, then remove the washer and bearing

32   Rear wheel bearing check, repack and adjustment

Refer to illustrations 32.1, 32.7, 32.8, 32.14 and 32.26
1   In most cases the rear wheel bearings won't need servicing until the brake shoes are changed. However, the bearings should be checked whenever the rear of the vehicle is raised for any reason. Several items, including a torque wrench and special grease, are required for this procedure **(see illustration)**.
2   With the vehicle securely supported on jackstands, spin each wheel and check for noise, rolling resistance and free play.
3   Grasp the top of each tire with one hand and the bottom with the other. Move the wheel in-and-out on the spindle. If there's any noticeable movement, the bearings should be checked and then repacked with grease or replaced if necessary.
4   Remove the wheel.
5   Pry the grease cap out of the hub with a screwdriver or hammer and chisel.
6   Straighten the bent ends of the cotter pin, then pull the cotter pin out of the lock. Discard the cotter pin and use a new one during reassembly.
7   Remove the lock and brake drum retaining nut from the end of the spindle **(see illustration)**.
8   Pull the hub assembly out slightly, then push it back into its original position. This should force the outer bearing and washer off the spindle enough so they can be removed **(see illustration)**.

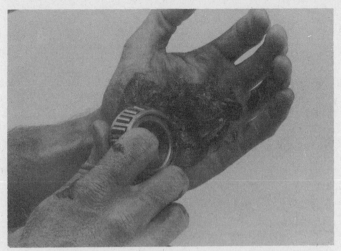

32.14   Work the grease into each bearing from the large diameter side until it's forced out the small diameter side

32.26   Tap the grease cap into place with a large punch and a hammer (work around the outer edge)

9   Pull the hub off the spindle.

10   Use a screwdriver to pry the dust seal out of the rear of the hub. As this is done, note how the seal is installed.

11   Remove the inner wheel bearing from the hub.

12   Use solvent to remove all traces of old grease from the bearings, hub and spindle. A small brush may prove helpful; however, make sure no bristles from the brush embed themselves inside the bearing rollers. Allow the parts to air dry.

13   Carefully inspect the bearings for cracks, heat discoloration, worn rollers, etc. Check the bearing races inside the hub for wear and damage. If the bearing races are defective, the hubs should be taken to a machine shop with the facilities to remove the old races and press new ones in. Note that the bearings and races come as matched sets - old bearings should never be installed on new races and vice-versa.

14   Use high-temperature wheel bearing grease to pack the bearings. Work the grease completely into the bearings, forcing it between the rollers, cone and cage from the back side **(see illustration)**.

15   Apply a thin coat of grease to the spindle at the outer bearing seat, inner bearing seat, shoulder and seal seat.

16   Put a small quantity of grease inboard of each bearing race inside the hub. Using your finger, form a dam at these points to provide extra grease availability and to keep thinned grease from flowing out of the bearing.

17   Place the grease-packed inner bearing into the rear of the hub and put a little more grease outboard of the bearing.

18   Place a new dust seal over the inner bearing and tap the seal evenly into place with a hammer and block of wood until it's flush with the hub.

19   Carefully place the hub assembly on the spindle and push the grease-packed outer bearing into position.

20   Install the washer and nut. Tighten the nut only slightly (no more than 12 ft-lbs of torque).

21   Spin the hub in a forward direction to seat the bearings and remove any grease or burrs which could cause excessive bearing play later.

22   Check to see that the tightness of the nut is still approximately 12 ft-lbs.

23   Loosen the nut until it's just loose, no more.

24   Using your hand (not a wrench of any kind), tighten the nut until it's snug. Install the lock and a new cotter pin through the hole in the spindle and lock. If the lock slots don't line up, take it off and rotate it to another position.

25   Bend the ends of the cotter pin until they're flat against the nut. Cut off any extra length which could interfere with the grease cap.

26   Install the grease cap, tapping it into place with a hammer **(see illustration)**.

27   Install the tire/wheel assembly on the hub and tighten the lug nuts.

28   Grasp the top and bottom of the tire and check the bearings in the manner described earlier in this Section.

29   Lower the vehicle.

---

33   Brake check

Refer to illustrations 33.5, 33.7, 33.14 and 33.16

1   The brakes should be inspected every time the wheels are removed or whenever a defect is suspected. Indications of a potential brake system problem include the vehicle pulling to one side when the brake pedal is depressed, noises coming from the brakes when they are applied, excessive brake pedal travel, pulsating pedal and leakage of fluid, usually seen on the inside of the tire or wheel.

Disc brakes (front)

2   Disc brakes can be visually checked without removing any parts except the wheels.

3   Raise the vehicle and place it securely on jackstands. Remove the front wheels (see *Jacking and towing* at the front of this manual if necessary).

4   Now visible is the disc brake caliper which contains the pads. There is an outer brake pad and an inner pad. Both should be checked for wear.

5   Note the pad thickness by looking at each end of the caliper and through the inspection hole in the caliper body **(see illustration)**. If the combined thickness of the pad lining and metal shoe is 5/16-inch or less, the pads should be replaced.

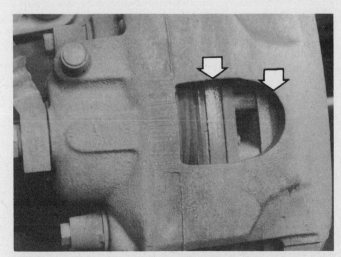

33.5   There's an inspection hole like this in each caliper – by looking through the hole, you can determine the thickness of the remaining pad material on both the inner and outer pads (arrows)

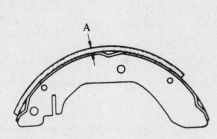

33.14   The lining thickness of the rear brake shoe (A) is measured from the outer surface of the lining to the metal shoe

33.7   Check the front brake hoses and caliper connections for damage and leaks

33.16   Check the rear brake hoses and connections for leaks and damage by flexing them

6   Since it'll be difficult, if not impossible, to measure the exact thickness of the pad, if you're in doubt as to the pad quality, remove them for further inspection or replacement. See Chapter 9 for disc brake pad replacement.
7   Before installing the wheels, check for leakage around the brake hose connections leading to the caliper and for damaged brake hoses (cracks, leaks, chafed areas, etc.) **(see illustration)**. Replace the hoses or fittings as necessary (see Chapter 9).
8   Also check the disc for score marks, wear and burned spots. If these conditions exist, the hub/disc assembly should be removed for servicing (see Chapter 9).

Drum brakes (rear)

9   Raise the vehicle and support it securely on jackstands. Block the front tires to prevent the vehicle from rolling; however, don't apply the parking brake or it'll lock the drums in place.
10   Remove the wheels, referring to *Jacking and towing* at the front of this manual if necessary.
11   Mark the hub so it can be reinstalled in the same position. Use a scribe, chalk, etc. on the drum, hub and backing plate.
12   Remove the brake drum as described in Chapter 10.
13   With the drum removed, carefully brush away any accumulations of dirt and dust. **Warning:** *Don't blow the dust out with compressed air and don't inhale any of it (it contains asbestos, which is harmful to your health).*
14   Note the thickness of the lining material on both front and rear brake shoes. If the material has worn away to within 1/8-inch of the recessed rivets or metal backing, the shoes should be replaced **(see illustration)**. The shoes should also be replaced if they're cracked, glazed (shiny areas), or covered with brake fluid.
15   Make sure all the brake assembly springs are connected and in good condition.
16   Check the brake components for signs of fluid leakage. With your finger, carefully pry back the rubber cups on the wheel cylinder located at the top of the brake shoes. Any leakage here is an indication that the wheel cylinders should be overhauled immediately (see Chapter 9). Also check all hoses and connections for signs of leakage **(see illustration)**.
17   Wipe the inside of the drum with a clean rag and denatured alcohol or brake cleaner. Again, be careful not to breathe the dangerous asbestos dust.
18   Check the inside of the drum for cracks, score marks, deep scratches and "hard spots" which will appear as small discolored areas. If imperfections cannot be removed with fine emery cloth, the drum must be taken to an automotive machine shop for resurfacing.
19   Repeat the procedure for the remaining wheel. If the inspection reveals that all parts are in good condition, reinstall the brake drums. Install the wheels and lower the vehicle to the ground.
20   On 1978 through 1982 models, adjust the brake shoes (see Chapter 9).

Parking brake

21   The easiest way to check the operation of the parking brake is to park the vehicle on a steep hill with the parking brake set and the transmission in Neutral. If the parking brake can't keep the vehicle from rolling, it must be adjusted (see Chapter 9).

---

34   Cooling system servicing (draining, flushing and refilling)

Refer to illustration 34.6
Warning: *Do not allow antifreeze to come in contact with your skin or painted surfaces of the vehicle. Flush contaminated areas immediately with plenty of water. Don't store new coolant or leave old coolant lying around where it's accessible to children or pets – they're attracted by its sweet taste. Ingestion of even a small amount of coolant can be fatal! Wipe up garage floor and drip pan spills immediately. Keep antifreeze containers covered and repair cooling system leaks as soon as they're noticed.*
1   The cooling system should be periodically drained, flushed and refilled to replenish the antifreeze mixture and prevent rust and corrosion, which can impair the performance of the cooling system and ultimately cause engine damage.
2   At the same time the cooling system is serviced, all hoses and the radiator cap should be inspected and replaced if faulty (see Section 28).
3   Consult local authorities about the dumping of antifreeze before draining the cooling system. In many areas reclamation centers have been set up to collect automobile oil and coolant mixtures rather than allowing them to be added to the sewage system.
4   With the engine cold, remove the radiator cap and set the heater control to Heat (Max).
5   Move a large container under the radiator to catch the coolant mixture as it's drained.
6   Drain the radiator. Most models are equipped with a drain fitting at the bottom of the radiator **(see illustration)**. If the fitting has excessive corrosion and can't be turned easily, or the radiator isn't equipped with one, detach the lower radiator hose to allow the coolant to drain. Be careful that none of the solution is splashed on your skin or in your eyes. **Note:** *On 2.2L engines, remove the vacuum switch or plug from the top of the thermostat housing on the engine.*
7   Disconnect the coolant reservoir hose, remove the reservoir and flush it with clean water.
8   Place a hose (a common garden hose is fine) in the radiator filler neck at the top of the radiator and flush the system until the water runs clear at all drain points.
9   In severe cases of contamination or clogging of the radiator, remove it (see Chapter 3) and reverse flush it. This involves inserting the hose in the bottom radiator outlet to allow the clean water to run against the normal

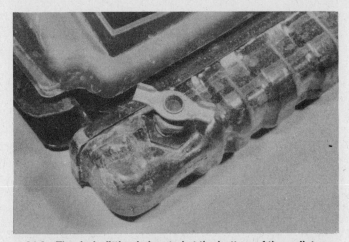

34.6   The drain fitting is located at the bottom of the radiator

flow, draining through the top. A radiator repair shop should be consulted if further cleaning or repair is necessary.

10   Where the coolant is regularly drained and the system refilled with the correct antifreeze mixture there should be no need to employ chemical cleaners or descalers.

11   Install the coolant reservoir, reconnect the hoses and close the drain fitting.

12   On 2.2L engines, add coolant to the radiator until it reaches the bottom of the threaded hole in the thermostat housing. Reinstall the vacuum switch or plug in the hole and tighten it to 15 ft-lbs. Continue adding coolant to the radiator until it reaches the radiator cap seat.

13   On all models add coolant to the reservoir until the level is between the Min and Max marks.

14   Run the engine until normal operating temperature is reached and, with the engine idling, add coolant up to the correct level.

15   Always refill the system with a mixture of antifreeze and water in the proportion called for on the antifreeze container or in your owner's manual. Chapter 3 also contains information on antifreeze mixtures.

16   Keep a close watch on the coolant level and the various cooling system hoses during the first few miles of driving. Tighten the hose clamps and add more coolant mixture as necessary.

35   Engine idle speed check and adjustment (carburetor equipped models only)

1   Engine idle speed is the speed at which the engine operates when no accelerator pedal pressure is applied. This speed is critical to the performance of the engine itself, as well as many other components.

2   A tachometer (other than the one in the vehicle) must be used when adjusting idle speed to get an accurate reading. The exact hook-up for these meters varies with the manufacturer, so follow the particular directions included.

3   The actual step-by-step idle speed adjusting procedure for each carburetor used on the vehicles covered by this manual is included in Chapter 4, along with specifications and illustrations. Each vehicle covered in this manual also has a Vehicle Emission Control Information label in the engine compartment. Printed instructions for setting idle speed on your particular engine can be found on the label (the instructions supersede any information included here or in Chapter 4).

4   Basically, on most models, the idle speed is set by turning an adjustment screw located at the side of the carburetor. The screw opens or closes the throttle plate, depending on how much it is turned and in which direction. The screw may be on the linkage itself or may be part of the idle stop solenoid. Refer to the emissions label or Chapter 4.

5   Once you have found the idle speed screw, experiment with different length screwdrivers until the adjustments can be made easily, without coming into contact with hot or moving engine components.

6   Follow the instructions on the emissions label or in Chapter 4, which will probably include disconnecting certain vacuum or electrical connec-

tions. To plug a vacuum hose after disconnecting it, insert a golf tee or metal rod, or thoroughly wrap the open end with tape to prevent any vacuum loss through the hose.

7   Make sure the parking brake is set and the wheels blocked to prevent the vehicle from rolling. This is particularly important if the transaxle must be in Drive. An assistant inside the vehicle, pushing on the brake pedal, is the safest method.

8   For all applications, the engine must be completely warmed-up to operating temperature, which will automatically render the choke fast idle inoperative.

36   Ignition timing check and adjustment

Refer to illustrations 36.2, 36.4, 36.6, 36.8, 36.11 and 36.13

1   All vehicles are equipped with an Emissions Control Information label inside the engine compartment. The label contains important ignition timing specifications and the proper timing procedure for your specific vehicle. If the information on the emissions label is different from the information included in this Section, follow the procedure on the label.

2   At the specified intervals, or when the distributor has been removed, the ignition timing must be checked and adjusted if necessary. Tools required for this procedure include an inductive pick-up timing light, a tachometer, a distributor wrench and, in some cases, a means of plugging vacuum hoses **(see illustration)**.

3   Before you check the timing, make sure the idle speed is correct (carburetor equipped models only – Section 35) and the engine is at normal operating temperature.

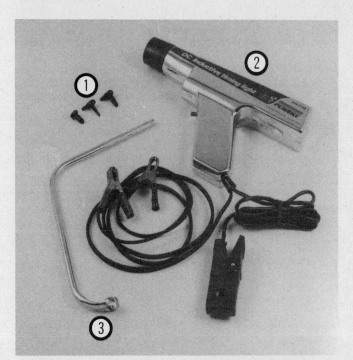

36.2   Tools needed to check and adjust the ignition timing

*1   **Vacuum plugs** – Vacuum hoses will, in most cases, have to be disconnected and plugged. Molded plugs in various shapes and sizes are available for this.*

*2   **Inductive pick-up timing light** – Flashes a bright concentrated beam of light when the number one spark plug fires. Connect the leads according to the instructions supplied with the light.*

*3   **Distributor wrench** – On some models, the hold-down bolt for the distributor is difficult to reach and turn with conventional wrenches or sockets. A special wrench like this must be used.*

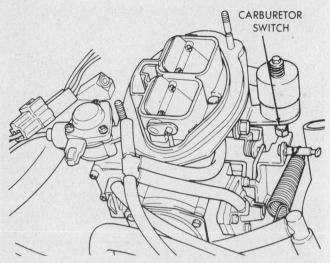

36.4   On models so equipped, locate the carburetor switch and ground it before checking the ignition timing

36.6   Use needle-nose pliers to pull out the rubber timing window plug

4   On vehicles with a carburetor switch, connect a jumper wire between the switch and a good ground (see illustration). Disconnect and plug the vacuum hose at the Spark Control Computer (2.2L engine only). If the engine is already idling at or below the specified speed, proceed to the next Step. If the idle is too high, turn the idle speed adjusting screw until the specified curb idle is attained.

5   Connect a timing light in accordance with the manufacturer's instructions. Usually, the light must be connected to the battery and the number one spark plug in some fashion. The number one spark plug wire or terminal should be marked at the distributor; trace it back to the spark plug and attach the timing light lead near the plug. Caution: *If an inductive pick-up timing light isn't available, don't puncture the spark plug wire to attach the timing light pick-up lead. Instead, use an adapter between the spark plug and plug wire. If the insulation on the plug wire is damaged, the secondary voltage will jump to ground at the damaged point and the engine will misfire.*

6   Locate the timing marks at the window in the transaxle bellhousing (see illustration).

7   Locate the notched groove across the flywheel. It may be necessary to have an assistant temporarily turn the ignition on and off in short bursts without starting the engine in order to bring the groove into a position where it can easily be cleaned and marked. Warning: *Stay clear of all moving engine components when the engine is turned over in this manner.*

8   Use white chalk or paint to mark the groove in the flywheel (see illustration). Also, mark the number corresponding to the number of degrees specified on the Emission Control Information label in the engine compartment.

9   On fuel injected engines, connect a tachometer to the engine, setting the selector to the correct cylinder position.

10   Make sure the wiring for the timing light is clear of all moving engine components, then start the engine.

11   On fuel injected engines, disconnect the coolant temperature sensor connector (located on the thermostat housing) (see illustration).

12   Aim the timing light at the marks, again being careful not to come into contact with moving parts. The marks you made should appear stationary. If the marks are in alignment, the timing is correct. If the marks are not

36.8   Mark the Flywheel/driveplate notch (arrow) to make it easier to see during the timing adjustment procedure

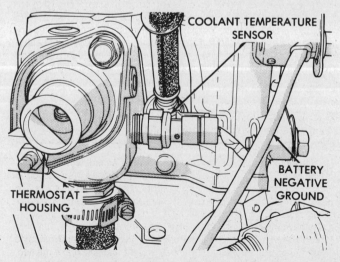

36.11   On fuel-injected vehicles, the coolant temperature sensor is located in the thermostat housing

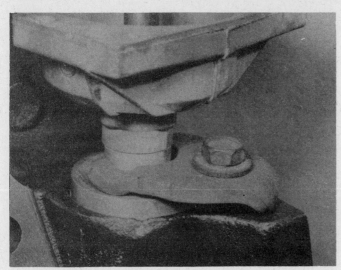

36.13 Loosen the hold-down bolt or nut and rotate the distributor housing to adjust the timing

38.5 Check the valve clearances with feeler gauges – if the gauge is the correct size, there should be a slight drag as it's inserted between the heel of the cam lobe and the shim in the follower (note that the lobes must be pointing up, away from the followers)

aligned, turn off the engine.

13 Loosen the hold-down bolt or nut at the base of the distributor **(see illustration)**. Loosen the bolt/nut only slightly, just enough to turn the distributor (see Chapter 5).

14 Now restart the engine and turn the distributor very slowly until the timing marks are aligned.

15 Shut off the engine and tighten the distributor bolt/nut, being careful not to move the distributor.

16 Start the engine and recheck the timing to make sure the marks are still in alignment. On fuel injected models, reconnect the water temperature sensor.

17 On carburetor equipped models, remove the jumper wire from the carburetor switch (if equipped). Disconnect the timing light, unplug the vacuum hose and connect the hose to the distributor or computer port.

18 On carburetor equipped models, drive the vehicle and listen for "pinging" noises. They will be most noticeable when the engine is hot and under load (climbing a hill, accelerating from a stop). If you hear pinging, the ignition timing is advanced too much. Reconnect the timing light and turn the distributor to move the mark 1 or 2 degrees in the retard direction. Road test the vehicle again to check for proper operation.

19 On fuel injected models, turn the engine off, then disconnect and reconnect the positive battery cable quick disconnect. Start the vehicle and verify that the Power Loss/Power Limited light is off.

20 On fuel injected models, shut the engine off and turn the ignition on, off, on, off, on. The fault codes should clear.

21 On all models, to keep "pinging" at a minimum, yet still allow the engine to operate at the specified timing setting, use gasoline of the same octane at all times. Switching fuel brands and octane levels can decrease performance and economy and may possibly damage the engine.

37 Combustion chamber conditioner application (Canadian models only)

1 At the intervals specified in the Maintenance schedule at the beginning of this Chapter, combustion chamber conditioner (see *Recommended lubricants and fluids*) must be sprayed into the carburetor or fuel injection throttle body to help prevent the buildup of deposits in the combustion chamber and on the valves.

2 Remove the carburetor or throttle body air inlet hose.

3 With the engine idling at normal operating temperature, the transaxle in Park (automatic) or Neutral (manual) and the parking brake applied, spray a can of the specified conditioner into the carburetor or throttle body opening.

4 Reattach the hose to the air inlet.

38 Valve clearance check and adjustment (1.7L engine only)

Refer to illustrations 38.5, 38.9 and 38.10

Note: *The 1.7L engine is equipped with a valvetrain design which requires changing shims located on top of the followers to vary the valve clearances. As a result, special tools, shims and a rather complicated procedure are involved. If you don't have access to the necessary tools, or if you don't want to tackle the procedure, take the vehicle to a dealer service department or a repair shop. If you plan to do the job yourself, read through the entire procedure before starting work. This will enable you to plan ahead, anticipate what's coming and avoid problems.*

Warning: *The electric cooling fan on some models can activate at any time, even when the ignition is in the Off position. To prevent injury, disconnect the fan motor or negative battery cable when working in the vicinity of the fan.*

1 The valve clearances are checked and adjusted with the engine cold, but they must be rechecked with the engine coolant temperature at approximately 95-degrees F.

2 Remove the air cleaner assembly (see Chapter 4).

3 Remove the camshaft cover (see Chapter 2).

4 Position the number one piston at TDC on the compression stroke (see Chapter 2, Part A). The number one cylinder cam lobes should be pointing up, away from the followers. **Caution:** *Don't turn the camshaft pulley to position the lobes – it will damage the timing belt.*

5 Use feeler gauges to determine the clearance between the number one cylinder camshaft lobes and the shims in the followers **(see illustration)**. The feeler gauge representing the clearance will just slide between the cam lobe and shim with a slight amount of drag. **Note:** *Since the shim sizes are in millimeters, the use of metric feeler gauges will make the job easier.*

6 Record the clearances for the number one cylinder valves, then position the number three piston at TDC on the compression stroke and repeat the procedure. Follow the instructions in Chapter 2 for finding TDC for various pistons following the firing order.

7 Do the same for the remaining cylinders.

8 Compare the measured clearances to the Specifications at the front of this Chapter. If the clearances are within the specified range, no action is required. If any of the clearances are outside the specified range (which is probably the case), the shims must be replaced with thicker or thinner ones to obtain the correct clearances.

38.9   Each shim size is marked on the back side (this one is 3.70 mm thick)

38.10   Depress the follower with the special tool and remove the adjusting shim with a needle-nose pliers

9   The next step is to record the shim sizes installed in the followers for the valves that require adjustment. This is done by removing them and noting the size etched on the back side **(see illustration)** or measuring the thickness with a micrometer.

10   To remove a shim, first make sure the cam lobes are facing away from the followers. Use the special tool (Chrysler no. L-4417) to depress the follower, then dislodge the shim with a small screwdriver and lift it out with needle-nose pliers **(see illustration)**. Note the size, or measure the shim thickness, and record it, then reinstall the shim. Never turn the crankshaft without shims in all of the followers – damage to the camshaft and followers will result if you do!

11   Next, use the following example to determine what shim sizes are needed to correct the clearances that are currently out of the specified range:

	Intake valve	Exhaust valve
Specified clearance:	0.15 to 0.25 mm	0.35 to 0.45 mm
Measured clearance:	0.09 mm	0.55 mm
Insert a shim:	0.10 mm THINNER	0.15 mm THICKER

12   New shims are available in 0.05 mm increments from 3.00 mm to 4.25 mm. **Note:** *Through careful analysis of the shim sizes needed to bring the clearances within the specified range, it's often possible to simply move a shim that has to come out anyway to another follower requiring a shim of that particular size, which will reduce the number of shims that must be purchased. Also, keep a record of the shim sizes installed to make the next valve adjustment easier.*

13   Install each new shim with the numbered side against the follower and double-check the clearance.

14   When all of the clearances are correct, reinstall the camshaft cover and air cleaner components.

15   Start the engine and allow it to run until the coolant temperature is approximately 95-degrees F, then recheck the clearances.

39   Manual transaxle lubricant change

Refer to illustrations 39.2 and 39.4

1   Raise the front of the vehicle and support it securely on jackstands. Apply the parking brake.

2   Remove the cover from the side of the differential **(see illustration)** and allow the lubricant to drain into a container.

3   Attached to the inside of the cover is a small magnet, installed to trap metal particles before they can damage the transaxle bearings. Clean the magnet and the inside surface of the cover thoroughly.

4   Use RTV sealant to form a new gasket for the cover and install the cover on the differential **(see illustration)**. Tighten the bolts evenly and securely in a criss-cross pattern.

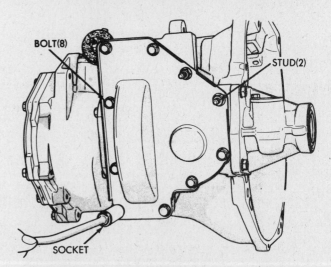

39.2   To drain the manual transaxle lubricant, remove the differential cover

5   Fill the transaxle with the recommended lubricant (see Recommended lubricants and fluids at the beginning of this Chapter) until the level is at the bottom edge of the filler plug. Drive the vehicle and check the cover for leaks.

40   Differential lubricant change (1978 through 1982 automatic transaxle equipped models only)

1   It's necessary to remove the cover plate on the differential housing to drain the lubricant on these models. As an alternative, a hand suction pump can be used to remove the differential lubricant through the filler hole. If there's no drain plug and a suction pump isn't available, be sure to obtain a new gasket at the same time the gear lubricant is purchased.

2   Raise the front of the vehicle and support it securely on jackstands. Apply the parking brake. Move a drain pan, rags, newspapers and wrenches under the vehicle.

3   Remove the fill plug from the differential.

4   If a suction pump is being used, insert the flexible hose. Work the hose down to the bottom of the differential housing and pump the oil out.

5   If the differential is being drained by removing the cover plate, remove

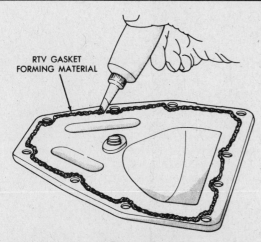

39.4   Apply a bead of RTV sealant to the differential cover-to-transaxle surface

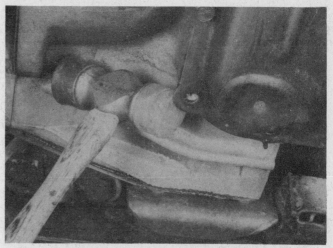

41.3   Use a soft-face hammer to break the gasket seal at the corner of the pan so the fluid will drain out

the bolts on the lower half of the plate. Loosen the bolts on the upper half and use them to keep the cover loosely attached. Allow the oil to drain into the pan, then completely detach the cover **(see illustration 39.2)**.

6   Using a lint-free rag, clean the inside of the cover and the accessible areas of the differential housing. As this is done, check for chipped gears and metal particles in the lubricant, indicating the differential should be more thoroughly inspected and/or repaired.

7   Thoroughly clean the gasket mating surfaces of the differential housing and the cover plate. Use a gasket scraper or putty knife to remove all traces of the old gasket.

8   Apply a thin layer of RTV sealant to the cover flange and install the cover while the sealant is still wet **(see illustration 39.4)**.

9   Place the cover on the differential housing and install the bolts. Tighten the bolts securely.

10   On all models, use a hand pump, syringe or funnel to fill the differential housing with the lubricant specified in Recommended lubricants and fluids until it's level with the bottom of the plug hole.

11   Install the filler plug and tighten it securely.

41   Automatic transaxle fluid and filter change

Refer to illustrations 41.3, 41.4 and 41.8

1   The automatic transaxle fluid and filter should be changed, the magnet cleaned and the bands adjusted at the recommended intervals.

2   Raise the front of the vehicle and support it securely on jackstands. Apply the parking brake.

3   Position a container under the transaxle fluid pan. Loosen the pan bolts. Completely remove the bolts along the rear of the pan. Tap the cor

ner of the pan **(see illustration)** to break the seal and allow the fluid to drain into the container (the remaining bolts will prevent the pan from separating from the transaxle). Remove the remaining bolts and detach the pan.

4   Remove the filter screws and detach the filter (a special Torx bit may be required for the screws) **(see illustration)**.

5   Refer to Section 42 and adjust the bands before proceeding with the fluid change.

6   Install the new gasket and filter. Tighten the filter screws securely.

7   Carefully remove all traces of old sealant from the pan and transaxle body (don't nick or gouge the sealing surfaces). Clean the magnet in the pan with a clean, lint-free cloth. On some models, the magnet is located in the differential cover. Remove the differential cover, take the magnet out of the recess and clean it.

8   Apply a 1/8-inch bead of RTV sealant to the oil pan sealing surface and position it on the transaxle **(see illustration)**. Install the bolts and tighten them to the torque listed in this Chapter's Specifications following a criss-cross pattern. Work up to the final torque in three or four steps. On models so equipped, install the magnet in the differential cover, apply a 1/8-inch bead of RTV sealant to the mating surface and install it following the same procedure.

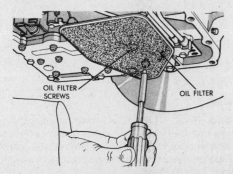

41.4   On most models, the transaxle filter is held in place with Allen or Torx head screws, both of which will require a special tool

41.8   Apply a 1/8-inch diameter bead of RTV sealant and install the pan before the sealant dries

42.7   Hold the screw so it won't turn and tighten the locknut with a box-end wrench

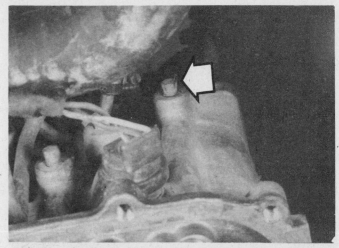

42.9   Low-Reverse band pressure plug location (arrow)

9   Lower the vehicle and add three quarts of the specified fluid (see *Recommended lubricants and fluids* at the beginning of this Chapter) to the transaxle. Start the engine and allow it to idle for at least two minutes, then move the shift lever through each of the gear positions, ending in Park or Neutral. Check for fluid leakage around the oil pan and differential cover.
10   Add more fluid until the level is at the Add mark on the dipstick.
11   Drive the vehicle until the fluid is hot, then recheck the level (see Section 6). If the level isn't between the Add and Full marks, add fluid, a little at a time, until it is (be careful not to overfill it).
12   Make sure the dipstick is seated completely or dirt could get into the transaxle.

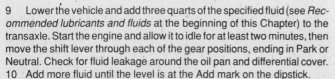

42   Automatic transaxle band adjustment

Refer to illustrations 42.7, 42.9, 42.10, 42.11a, 42.11b, 42.12a, 42.12b and 42.15

1   The transaxle bands should be adjusted when specified in the maintenance schedule or at the time of a fluid and filter change (Section 41).

Kickdown band

2   The kickdown band adjustment screw is located at the top left side of the transaxle case.
3   On some models the throttle cable may interfere with band adjustment. If so, mark its position and then remove the throttle cable adjustment bolt. Move the cable away from the band adjustment screw.
4   Loosen the locknut approximately five turns and make sure the adjusting screw turns freely.
5   Tighten the adjusting screw to the torque listed in this Chapter's Specifications.
6   Back the adjusting screw off the specified number of turns (see the Specifications Section at the beginning of this Chapter).
7   Hold the screw in position and tighten the locknut securely **(see illustration)**.

Low-Reverse band (1981 on)

8   To gain access to the low-Reverse band, the transaxle pan must be removed (Section 41).
9   To determine if the band is worn excessively, remove the Low-Reverse pressure plug from the transaxle case **(see illustration)** and apply 30 psi of air pressure to the port.
10   Measure the gap between the band ends **(see illustration)**. It should be 0.080-inch minimum. If it's less than that, the band should be replaced with a new one.
11   To proceed with adjustment, pry off the parking rod E-clip and remove the rod **(see illustrations)**.

42.10   Insert feeler gauges between the Low-Reverse band ends to measure wear – if the gap is less than 0.080-inch, a new band is needed

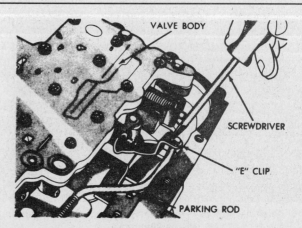

42.11a   Use a screwdriver to pry off the parking rod E-clip, . . .

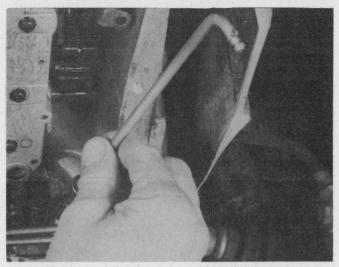

42.11b   . . . then lower the rod from the transaxle

42.12a   Location of the Low-Reverse band locknut and adjusting screw

12   Loosen the locknut approximately five turns **(see illustration)**. Use an in-lb torque wrench to tighten the adjusting screw to the torque listed in this Chapter's Specifications **(see illustration)**.
13   Back the screw off the specified number of turns (see the Specifications Section at the beginning of this Chapter).
14   Hold the adjusting screw in position and tighten the locknut securely.
15   Push the shift pawl in the transaxle case to the rear and reinstall the parking rod **(see illustration)**.
16   Install the pan and refill the transaxle (Section 41).

43   Driveaxle boot check

Refer to illustration 43.3
1   If the driveaxle rubber boots are damaged or deteriorated, serious and costly damage can occur to the CV joints the rubber boots are designed to protect. The boots should be inspected very carefully at the recommended intervals.
2   Raise the front of the vehicle and support it securely on jackstands (see *Jacking and towing* at the front of this manual if necessary).
3   Crawl under the vehicle and check the four driveaxle boots (two on each driveaxle) very carefully for cracks, tears, holes, deteriorated rubber and loose or missing clamps **(see illustration)**. If the boots are dirty, wipe them clean before beginning the inspection.

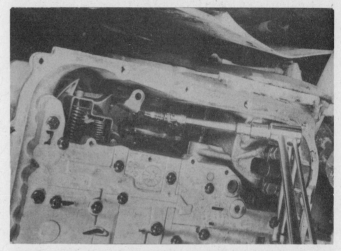

42.12b   It may be necessary to use a universal joint between the socket and extension when tightening the Low-Reverse band adjusting screw

42.15   Push the shift pawl back with your finger before inserting the parking rod

43.3   Flex the driveaxle boots by hand to check for damage and deterioration (this boot is cracked at the bottom of one of the folds)

4   If damage or deterioration is evident, replace the boots with new ones and check the CV joints for damage (see Chapter 8).

44   Evaporative emissions control system check

Refer to illustration 44.2

1   The function of the evaporative emissions control system is to draw fuel vapors from the gas tank and fuel system, store them in a charcoal canister and route them to the intake manifold during normal engine operation.

2   The most common symptom of a fault in the evaporative emissions system is a strong fuel odor in the engine compartment. If a fuel odor is detected, inspect the charcoal canister, located in the engine compartment **(see illustration)**. Check the canister and all hoses for damage and deterioration.

3   The evaporative emissions control system is explained in more detail in Chapter 6.

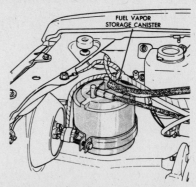

44.2 The evaporative emissions control system charcoal canister is located in the right front corner of the engine compartment – check the hoses for cracks and other damage – disconnect the hoses and loosen the clamp bolt to remove the canister

Chapter 2 Part A   Engine

Contents

Specifications

1.7L engine

General
Firing order 1-3-4-2
Cylinder numbers (drivebelt end-to-transaxle end) 1–2–3–4

0755H

Camshaft
Endplay .... 0.006 in (0.15 mm)
Runout .... 0.0004 in (0.01 mm)
Bearing oil clearance .... 0.0008 to 0.002 in (0.02 to 0.05 mm)

**Cylinder location and
distributor rotation**

Cylinder head
Warpage limit .... 0.004 in (0.1 mm)

Intake/exhaust manifolds
Warpage limit .... 0.008 in (0.2 mm) per foot of manifold length

1.7L engine (continued)

Oil pump gears
Backlash clearance .... 0.002 to 0.008 in (.105 to 0.20 mm)
Endplay .... 0.006 in (0.15 mm) max.

Torque specifications   Ft-lbs
Camshaft bearing cap nuts 14
Camshaft cover bolts/nuts 7
Timing belt tensioner bolt 32
Camshaft sprocket bolt 58
Crankshaft pulley Allen bolts 14
Crankshaft sprocket bolt 58
Cylinder head bolts (engine cold)
  Hex head bolts 54
  12-point bolts .... 43 plus 1/2-turn
Driveplate-to-crankshaft bolts 50
Pressure plate-to-crankshaft bolts 55
Front crankshaft oil seal housing bolts 14
Intake/exhaust manifold nuts/bolts 18
Intermediate shaft oil seal housing bolts 18
Intermediate shaft sprocket bolt 58
Oil pan-to-engine block fasteners
  Allen screws 7
  6 mm bolt 14
Oil pick-up tube-to-oil pump housing bolt 7
Oil pump mounting bolts 14
Rear crankshaft oil seal housing bolts 7
Water pump hub bolt 14

2.2L engine

General
Firing order 1-3-4-2
Cylinder numbers (drivebelt end-to-transaxle end) 1–2–3–4

Camshaft
Bearing oil clearance .... 0.004 in (0.10 mm) max.
Endplay
  Standard .... 0.005 to 0.013 in (0.13 to 0.33 mm)
  Service limit .... 0.020 in (0.50 mm)
Lobe wear limit .... 0.010 in (.25 mm)
Runout limit .... 0.0004 in (0.01 mm)

Intake/exhaust manifolds
Warpage limit .... 0.006 in (0.15 mm) per foot of manifold length

Oil Pump
Inner and outer rotor endplay
  Standard .... 0.001 to 0.003 in (0.03 to 0.08 mm)
  Service limit .... 0.004 in (0.10 mm)
Inner rotor-to-outer rotor tip clearance
  1982 through 1985 .... 0.010 in (0.25 mm)
  1986 on
    Standard .... 0.008 in (0.20 mm)
    Service limit .... 0.010 in (0.25 mm)
Outer rotor thickness
  1982 through 1985
    Standard .... 0.826 to 0.827 in (20.98 to 21.00 mm)
    Service limit .... 0.825 in (20.96 mm)
  1986 on
    Standard .... 0.944 to 0.946 in (23.97 to 24.00 mm)
    Service limit .... 0.944 in (23.97 mm)
Outer rotor-to-pump body clearance
  Standard .... 0.010 in (0.25 mm)
  Service limit .... 0.014 in (0.35 mm)
Pump cover warpage
  Standard .... 0.010 in (0.25 mm)
  Service limit .... 0.015 in (0.38 mm)
Relief spring free length .... 1.95 in (49.5 mm)

Torque specifications

	Ft-lbs
Camshaft bearing cap bolts	14
Camshaft cover bolts	9
Camshaft sprocket bolt	65
Crankshaft sprocket bolt	50
Cylinder head bolts	
1982 through 1985	
Step 1	30
Step 2	45
Step 3	45
Step 4	Tighten an additional 1/4-turn
1986 on	
Step 1	45
Step 2	65
Step 3	65
Step 4	Tighten an additional 1/4-turn
Flywheel or driveplate-to-crankshaft bolts	
1981 through 1983	60
1984 and 1985	65
1986 on	70
Front crankshaft oil seal housing bolts	9
Intake/exhaust manifold nuts/bolts	17
Intermediate shaft oil seal housing bolts	9
Intermediate shaft sprocket bolt	65
Oil pan-to-engine block bolts	
6 mm	9
8 mm	17
Oil pump cover bolts	9
Oil pump mounting bolts	17
Oil pump pick-up tube bolts	19
Rear crankshaft oil seal housing bolts	9

2A

1 General information

This Part of Chapter 2 is devoted to in-vehicle repair procedures for the engine. All information concerning engine removal and installation and engine block and cylinder head overhaul can be found in Part B of this Chapter.

The following repair procedures are based on the assumption that the engine is installed in the vehicle. If the engine has been removed from the vehicle and mounted on a stand, many of the steps outlined in this Part of Chapter 2 will not apply.

The Specifications included in this Part of Chapter 2 apply only to the procedures contained in this Part. Part B of Chapter 2 contains the Specifications necessary for cylinder head and engine block rebuilding.

2 Repair operations possible with the engine in the vehicle

Many major repair operations can be accomplished without removing the engine from the vehicle.

Clean the engine compartment and the exterior of the engine with some type of degreaser before any work is done. It will make the job easier and help keep dirt out of the internal areas of the engine.

Depending on the components involved, it may be helpful to remove the hood to improve access to the engine as repairs are performed (refer to Chapter 11 if necessary). Cover the fenders to prevent damage to the paint. Special pads are available, but an old bedspread or blanket will also work.

If vacuum, exhaust, oil or coolant leaks develop, indicating a need for gasket or seal replacement, the repairs can generally be made with the engine in the vehicle. The intake and exhaust manifold gaskets, oil pan gasket, crankshaft oil seals and cylinder head gasket are all accessible with the engine in place.

Exterior engine components, such as the intake and exhaust manifolds, the oil pan (and the oil pump), the water pump, the starter motor, the alternator, the distributor and the fuel system components can be removed for repair with the engine in place.

Since the cylinder head can be removed without pulling the engine, camshaft and valve component servicing can also be accomplished with the engine in the vehicle. Replacement of the timing belt and sprockets is also possible with the engine in the vehicle.

In extreme cases caused by a lack of necessary equipment, repair or replacement of piston rings, pistons, connecting rods and rod bearings is possible with the engine in the vehicle. However, this practice is not recommended because of the cleaning and preparation work that must be done to the components involved.

3 Top Dead Center (TDC) for number one piston – locating

Refer to illustrations 3.6 and 3.8

Note: *The following procedure is based on the assumption that the spark plug wires and distributor are correctly installed. If you are trying to locate TDC to install the distributor correctly, piston position must be determined by feeling for compression at the number one spark plug hole, then aligning the ignition timing marks as described in step 8.*

1   Top Dead Center (TDC) is the highest point in the cylinder that each piston reaches as it travels up-and-down when the crankshaft turns. Each piston reaches TDC on the compression stroke and again on the exhaust stroke, but TDC generally refers to piston position on the compression stroke.

2   Positioning the piston(s) at TDC is an essential part of many procedures such as camshaft and timing belt/sprocket removal and distributor removal.

3   Before beginning this procedure, be sure to place the transmission in Neutral and apply the parking brake or block the rear wheels. Also, disable the ignition system by detaching the coil wire from the center terminal of the distributor cap and grounding it on the block with a jumper wire. Remove the spark plugs (see Chapter 1).

4   In order to bring any piston to TDC, the crankshaft must be turned using one of the methods outlined below. When looking at the front of the engine, normal crankshaft rotation is clockwise.

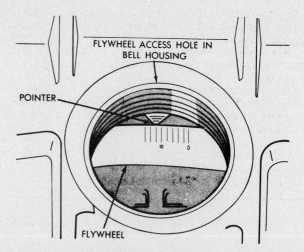

3.6   Use paint, a felt-tip permanent marker or chalk to mark the distributor housing directly beneath the number one spark plug wire terminal

a) The preferred method is to turn the crankshaft with a socket and ratchet attached to the bolt threaded into the front of the crankshaft.

b) A remote starter switch, which may save some time, can also be used. Follow the instructions included with the switch. Once the piston is close to TDC, use a socket and ratchet as described in the previous paragraph.

c) If an assistant is available to turn the ignition switch to the Start position in short bursts, you can get the piston close to TDC without a remote starter switch. Make sure your assistant is out of the vehicle, away from the ignition switch, then use a socket and ratchet as described in Paragraph a) to complete the procedure.

5   Note the position of the terminal for the number one spark plug wire on the distributor cap. If the terminal isn't marked, follow the plug wire from the number one cylinder spark plug to the cap.

3.8   When you're bringing the number one piston to TDC, look at the timing marks on the edge of the flywheel/driveplate through the opening in the bellhousing – you may have to remove a plug from the bellhousing to see the flywheel

6   Use a,felt-tip pen or chalk to make a mark on the distributor body directly under the terminal **(see illustration)**.

7   Detach the cap from the distributor and set it aside (see Chapter 1 if necessary).

8   Locate the round window in the bellhousing. You'll see a stationary pointer at the edge of the window. Turn the crankshaft (see Paragraph 3 above) until the TDC mark (zero) on the edge of the flywheel is aligned with the stationary pointer **(see illustration)**.

9   Look at the distributor rotor – it should be pointing directly at the mark you made on the distributor body. If the rotor is pointing at the mark, go to Step 12. If it isn't, go to Step 10.

10   If the rotor is 180-degrees off, the number one piston is at TDC on the exhaust stroke.

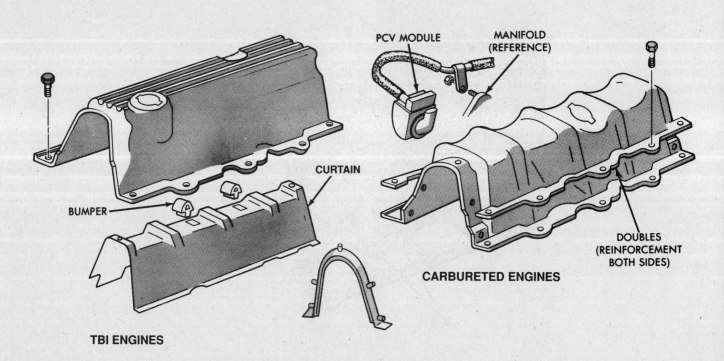

4.5a   Typical 2.2L engine camshaft covers and related components – exploded view

11   To get the piston to TDC on the compression stroke, turn the crankshaft one complete turn (360-degrees) clockwise. The rotor should now be pointing at the mark on the distributor. When the rotor is pointing at the number one spark plug wire terminal in the distributor cap and the ignition timing marks are aligned, the number one piston is at TDC on the compression stroke.

12   After the number one piston has been positioned at TDC on the compression stroke, TDC for any of the remaining pistons can be located by turning the crankshaft and following the firing order. Mark the remaining spark plug wire terminal locations on the distributor body just like you did for the number one terminal, then number the marks to correspond with the cylinder numbers. As you turn the crankshaft, the rotor will also turn. When it's pointing directly at one of the marks on the distributor, the piston for that particular cylinder is at TDC on the compression stroke.

4   Camshaft cover – removal and installation

Removal

Refer to illustrations 4.5a and 4.5b

1   Detach the cable from the negative battery terminal.

2   Detach the accelerator cable from the cable bracket.

3   Wipe off the camshaft cover thoroughly to prevent debris from falling onto the exposed cylinder head or camshaft/valve train assembly.

4   Detach the PCV valve and hose assembly from the camshaft cover (see Chapter 1).

5   Remove the camshaft cover bolts and, if equipped, the "doubles" strips which reinforce the cover flanges **(see illustrations)**.

2A

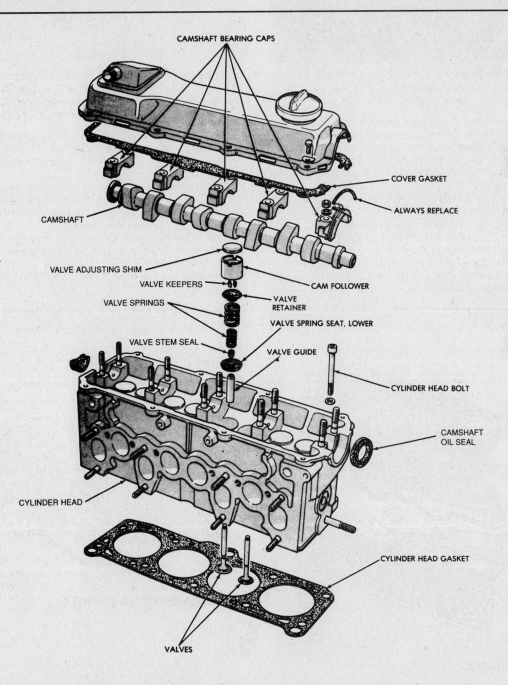

4.5b   Typical 1.7L engine camshaft cover and cylinder head components – exploded view

4.11a   On the 1.7L engine, use RTV sealant to tack down the ends of the camshaft cover front seal, . . .

4.11b . . . then install the rear seal, applying RTV sealant at the edges

6   Carefully lift off the camshaft cover and gasket. If the gasket is stuck to the cylinder head, use a putty knife to remove it. Set the cover aside.

7   If the vehicle is equipped with a 1.7L engine, remove and discard the front and rear rubber seals.

8   If the vehicle is fuel-injected or turbocharged, you'll note a "curtain" (baffle for enhancing air/oil separation) under the camshaft cover. If you're simply replacing a leaking camshaft cover gasket, you don't need to remove the curtain. If you want to adjust the valves or service the camshaft assembly or cylinder head, remove the curtain. Don't lose the two small rubber "bumpers" which act as cushions between the curtain and the camshaft cover.

Installation

Refer to illustrations 4.11a, 4.11b, 4.11c and 4.12

9   Make sure the gasket mating surfaces of the cylinder head and the camshaft cover are clean.

10   If the engine is equipped with a curtain (and its been removed), install it now, manifold side first, with the cutouts over the cam towers and contacting the cylinder head floor, then press the opposite (distributor) side into position below the gasket mating surface. Be sure to install the rubber bumpers on top of the curtain.

11   If the vehicle is equipped with a 1.7L engine, install new front and rear seals (**see illustrations**). Tack them in place with gasket sealant. Then carefully lay the new gasket in place (**see illustration**) and install the cam

cover, "doubles" strips (if equipped) and bolts. Tighten the bolts to the torque listed in this Chapter's Specifications.

12   If the vehicle is equipped with an earlier 2.2L engine, apply a 1/8-inch wide bead of RTV sealant to the cylinder head rail (**see illustration**), then install the cover and bolts and tighten them to the torque listed in this Chapter's Specifications.

13   If the vehicle is equipped with a newer non-turbo 2.2L engine, install a new molded one-piece rubber gasket on the camshaft cover by pushing the tabs through the slots in the cover. Install the cover and bolts and tighten the bolts to the torque listed in this Chapter's Specifications.

14   Turbocharged versions of the newer 2.2L engine also use a molded one-piece rubber gasket, but the gasket is attached differently. A continuous slot molded into the camshaft cover retains the gasket. Install the gasket by pressing the gasket rail section into the slot. Install the cover and bolts and tighten the bolts to the torque listed in this Chapter's Specifications.

15   The remainder of installation is the reverse of removal. Be sure to check the PCV valve (see Chapter 1) before you install it.

5   Intake/exhaust manifold – removal and installation

Warning: *Gasoline is extremely flammable, so take extra precautions when working on any part of the fuel system. Don't smoke or allow open flames or bare light bulbs in or near the work area. And don't work in a garage where a natural gas-type appliance (such as a water heater or clothes dryer) with a pilot light is present. If you spill any fuel on your skin, wash it off immediately with soap and plenty of water.*

4.11c   Make sure the gasket lays flat, especially around the front seal, or it can be easily damaged during installation of the camshaft cover

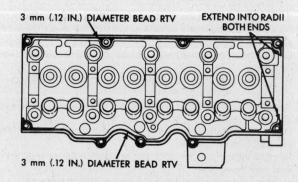

3 mm (.12 IN.) DIAMETER BEAD RTV   EXTEND INTO RADII BOTH ENDS

3 mm (.12 IN.) DIAMETER BEAD RTV

4.12   If the vehicle is equipped with a 2.2L engine and the camshaft cover has RTV sealant instead of a conventional gasket, apply a 1/8-inch diameter bead of RTV to the gasket sealing surface on the cylinder head

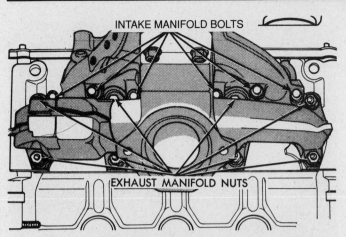

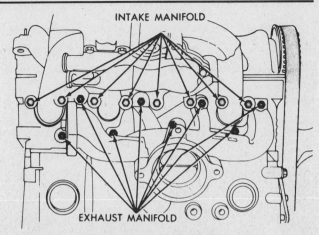

5.15a   Intake/exhaust manifold fasteners (1.7L engine)

5.15b   Intake/exhaust manifold fasteners (2.2L non-turbo engine)

1.7L engine and non-turbo 2.2L engine

Removal

Refer to illustrations 5.15a and 5.15b

1   Relieve the fuel system pressure (see Chapter 4).
2   Detach the cable from the negative battery terminal.
3   Drain the cooling system (see Chapter 1).
4   Remove the air cleaner (see Chapter 4).
5   Clearly label, then detach all vacuum lines, electrical wiring and fuel lines.
6   Detach the accelerator cable from the throttle linkage (see Chapter 4).
7   Loosen the power steering pump (if equipped) and remove the drivebelt (see Chapter 1).
8   Detach the power brake vacuum hose from the intake manifold.
9   If you're working on a Canadian model with a 2.2L engine, you may have to remove the coupling hose from the air injection tube.
10   If you're working on a 2.2L engine, detach the coolant crossover hoses.
11   Raise the front of the vehicle and support it securely on jackstands. Detach the exhaust pipe from the exhaust manifold (see Chapter 4).
12   Remove the power steering pump (if equipped) and set it aside (see Chapter 10).
13   If you're working on a 2.2L engine, remove the intake manifold support bracket and detach the EGR tube from the exhaust manifold.
14   If you're working on a Canadian model with a 2.2L engine, you may have to remove the air injection tube assembly.
15   Remove the intake manifold fasteners **(see illustrations)**.
16   Lower the vehicle.
17   If you're working on a 1.7L engine:
  a) Remove the exhaust manifold nuts **(see illustration 5.15a)**.
  b) Remove the carburetor and intake/exhaust manifold as a single assembly.
  c) Detach the carburetor and gasket from the intake manifold (see Chapter 4).
  d) Remove the nuts, then separate the intake and exhaust manifolds.
18   If you're working on a 2.2L engine:
  a) Remove the carburetor or throttle body and the intake manifold as a single assembly.
  b) Detach the carburetor or throttle body and gasket from the intake manifold (see Chapter 4).
  c) Remove the exhaust manifold nuts and detach the exhaust manifold from the engine.
19   Discard the old gaskets and clean all gasket mating surfaces.
20   Clean the manifolds with solvent and dry them with compressed air.
21   Check the mating surfaces of the manifolds for flatness with a precision straightedge and feeler gauges. Refer to this Chapter's Specifications for the warpage limit.

22   Inspect the manifolds for cracks and distortion.
23   If the manifolds are cracked or warped, replace them or see if they can be resurfaced/repaired at an automotive machine shop.

Installation

24   If you're replacing either manifold, transfer the studs from the old manifold to the new one.
25   If you're working on a 1.7L engine:
  a) Attach the intake manifold to the exhaust manifold. DO NOT tighten the nuts at this time.
  b) Install the carburetor on the manifold (see Chapter 4) and attach the manifold (with a new gasket) to the cylinder head.
  c) Tighten all intake and exhaust manifold nuts and bolts until they're just snug (about 10 to 15 in-lbs).
  d) Gradually tighten the inner and outer intake manifold-to-exhaust manifold nuts. Alternate between the inner and outer nuts until the torque listed in this Chapter's Specifications is reached. Don't overtighten them.
  e) Starting at the center and working out in both directions, gradually tighten the intake and exhaust manifold-to-cylinder head nuts and bolts to the torque listed in this Chapter's Specifications.
26   If you're working on a 2.2L engine:
  a) Apply a thin coat of gasket sealant to the manifold sides of the new gaskets and place them in position on the manifolds.
  b) Place the exhaust manifold in position on the cylinder head and install the nuts. Starting at the center, tighten the nuts in a criss-cross pattern until the torque listed in this Chapter's Specifications is reached.
  c) Position the intake manifold on the head.
  d) Raise the vehicle and support it securely on jackstands.
  e) Working under the vehicle, install the intake manifold bolts finger tight. Starting at the center and working out in both directions, tighten the bolts in a criss-cross pattern until the torque listed in this Chapter's Specifications is reached.
27   The remainder of the installation procedure is the reverse of removal.

Turbocharged 2.2L engine

Removal

Refer to illustration 5.46

   On these models the cylinder head, complete with turbocharger assembly and intake and exhaust manifolds, must be removed as a unit before the manifolds can be removed.
28   Disconnect the negative cable from the battery.
29   Drain the cooling system (see Chapter 1).
30   Raise the front of the vehicle and support it securely on jackstands.
31   Working under the vehicle, disconnect the exhaust pipe from the manifold and unplug the oxygen sensor wire harness connector.

2A

32   Remove the turbocharger-to-engine block support bracket (**see illustration 30.5** in Chapter 4).

33   Loosen the hose clamps on the oil drain back tube and push the tube down on the engine block fitting.

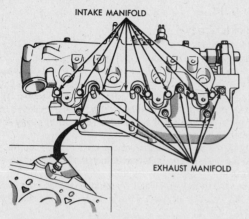

5.46   Intake/exhaust manifold fasteners (2.2L turbo engine)

34   Disconnect the turbocharger coolant inlet tube at the engine block and remove the bracket support.

35   Lower the vehicle.

36   Working in the engine compartment, remove the air cleaner assembly along with the throttle body adapter, hose and air cleaner box and bracket.

37   Disconnect the throttle linkage and throttle body electrical connector and vacuum hoses.

38   Locate the fuel rail out of the way (complete with injectors, wiring harness and fuel line) by removing the hose retainer bracket screw, the four bracket screws from the intake manifold and the two retaining clips.

39   Disconnect the upper radiator hose from the thermostat housing.

40   Remove the cylinder head with manifolds and turbocharger as an assembly (see Section 11).

41   Place the head on a clean working surface. Loosen the upper turbocharger discharge hose end clamp. **Note:** *Don't disturb the center deswirler retaining clamp.*

42   Remove the bolts and detach the throttle body assembly.

43   Disconnect the turbocharger coolant return tube at the water box along with the retaining bracket on the cylinder head.

44   Remove the heat shield.

45   Remove the turbocharger assembly.

46   Remove the bolts and detach the intake manifold. Remove the nuts and detach the exhaust manifold (**see illustration**).

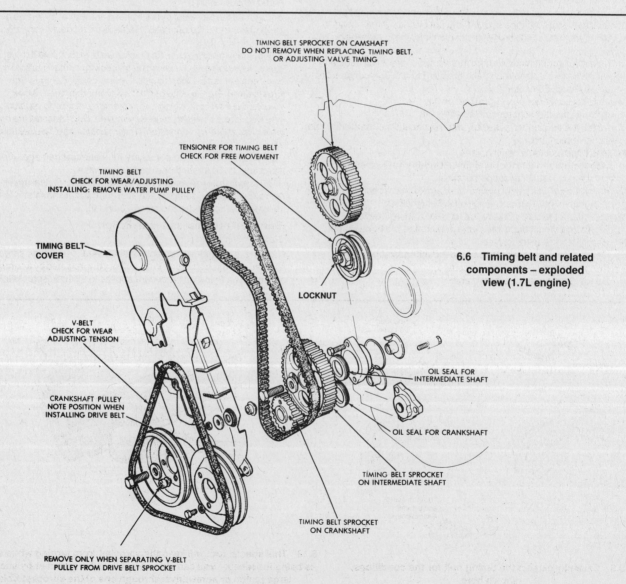

6.6   Timing belt and related components – exploded view (1.7L engine)

47   Discard the gasket and clean the cylinder head and manifold gasket surfaces.
48   Check the gasket mating surfaces of the manifolds for flatness with a precision straightedge and feeler gauges. Refer to this Chapter's Specifications for the warpage limit.
49   Inspect the manifolds for cracks, corrosion and damage. If they're warped or cracked, an automotive machine shop may be able to resurface/repair them.

Installation

50   Install a new gasket. **Note:** *Don't use sealant on the manifold gasket.*
51   Place the exhaust manifold in position. Apply anti-seize compound to the threads and install the mounting nuts. Working from the center out in both directions, tighten the nuts in 1/4-turn increments to the torque listed in this Chapter's Specifications.
52   Place the intake manifold in position and install the bolts and washers. Working from the center out in both directions, tighten the bolts in 1/4-turn increments until all bolts are at the torque listed in this Chapter's specifications.
53   Connect the turbocharger outlet-to-intake manifold tube and place the turbocharger in position on the exhaust manifold. Apply anti-seize compound to the threads and install the retaining nuts. Tighten the nuts to the torque listed in this Chapter's specifications. Tighten the connector tube clamps securely.
54   Install the coolant return tube in the water box connector, tighten the tube nut and install the tube support bracket on the cylinder head.
55   Install the heat shield on the intake manifold and tighten the bolts securely.
56   Install the throttle body air horn in the turbocharger inlet tube and install the three throttle body-to-intake manifold bolts. Tighten the bolts to the torque listed in Chapter 4.
57   Install the cylinder head (see Section 11).
58   Connect the turbocharger oil feed line.
59   Install the air cleaner assembly and reconnect the throttle linkage, wires and vacuum hoses.
60   Install the fuel rail (see Chapter 4).
61   Connect the turbocharger inlet coolant tube to the engine block. Tighten the tube nut. Install the support bracket.
62   Install the turbocharger housing-to-engine block support bracket with the bolts finger tight. Tighten the bolt on the engine block first, followed by the turbocharger housing bolt, to the torque listed in Chapter 4.
63   Reposition the oil drain back tube and tighten the hose clamps.
64   Reconnect the exhaust pipe.
65   Connect the upper radiator hose to the thermostat housing.
66   Fill the cooling system (see Chapter 1).
67   Connect the negative battery cable.

6   Timing belt and sprockets – removal, inspection and installation

1.7L engine

Timing belt removal

Refer to illustration 6.6

1   Detach the cable from the negative battery terminal.
2 . Remove the air cleaner assembly and air ducts (see Chapter 4).
3   Remove the air injection pump drivebelt, if equipped, alternator drivebelt and power steering drivebelt, if equipped (see Chapter 1).
4   Remove the four bolts that retain the crankshaft pulley to crankshaft sprocket and the three bolts that retain the water pump pulley to the water pump **(refer to illustration 6.6)**.
5   Remove the right engine mount and bolts (see Section 16).
6   Remove the nuts and bolts and detach the timing belt cover **(see illustration)**.
7   Loosen the tensioner locknut. To remove tension from the belt, turn the tensioner counterclockwise with a wrench. Slide the timing belt off the sprockets.

Timing belt, tensioner and sprocket inspection

Refer to illustration 6.9

8   Rotate the tensioner pulley by hand and move it side-to-side to detect roughness and excessive play. Replace it if it doesn't turn smoothly or if play is noted.
9   Inspect the timing belt for cracks, wear, signs of stretching, ply separation and damaged or missing teeth. Look for contamination by oil, gasoline, coolant and other liquids, which could damage the belt **(see illustration)**. Replace the belt if it's worn or damaged. **Note:** *Unless the engine has very low mileage, it's common practice to replace the timing belt with a new one every time it's removed. Don't reinstall the original belt unless it's in like-new condition. Never reinstall a belt in questionable condition.*
10   Visually inspect the sprockets for wear and damage. If any of the sprockets are damaged or worn, replace them.
11   Inspect the area directly below each sprocket for leaking engine oil. If there is oil below a sprocket, the seal behind that sprocket is leaking and must be replaced (see Sections 7, 8 and 9).

Sprocket removal and installation

Refer to illustration 6.13

12   The camshaft, intermediate shaft and crankshaft sprockets are aligned with each shaft by a Woodruff key and retained by a center bolt and washer. The following procedure applies to all three sprockets.

2A

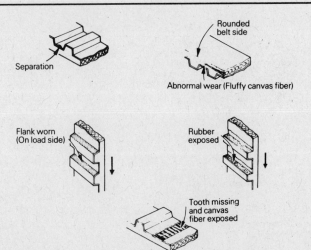

6.9   Carefully inspect the timing belt for the conditions shown here

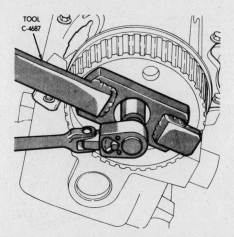

6.13   This special tool will keep the sprocket from turning while the bolt is being loosened – you can also immobilize the sprocket by sticking a large punch or screwdriver through one of the sprocket holes

6.16   On the 1.7L engine, align the dimple (arrow) on the camshaft sprocket with the camshaft cover mounting flange on the front (spark plug) side of the engine

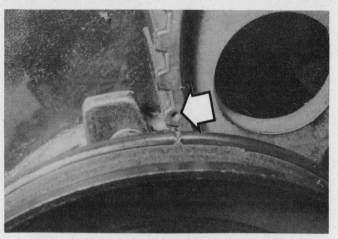

6.17   On the 1.7L engine, align the dimple (arrow) on the intermediate shaft sprocket with the V-notch on the crankshaft pulley

13   If the factory special tool is available, immobilize the sprocket and loosen the center bolt with a socket and ratchet or breaker bar **(see illus tration)**. If you don't have the special tool, you can prevent the sprocket from turning by inserting a large drift punch through a hole in the sprocket.
14   Pull off the sprocket. Don't lose the Woodruff key.
15   To install a sprocket, place the Woodruff key in the slot, align the slot in the sprocket bore with the key, push the sprocket onto the shaft, install the bolt and washer and tighten the bolt to the torque listed in this Chapter's Specifications.

Timing belt installation

Refer to illustrations 6.16, 6.17 and 6.19
16   Turn the camshaft sprocket by hand until the dimple on the back side is aligned with the upper side of the camshaft cover mounting flange **(see illustration)**.
17   Turn the crankshaft and intermediate shaft by hand until the dimple on the intermediate shaft sprocket is aligned with the V-notch in the crank- shaft pulley **(see illustration)**.
18   Install the timing belt on the crankshaft sprocket first, then on the cam- shaft sprocket. Don't allow any slack between the crankshaft and interme-

diate shaft sprockets or between the intermediate shaft and camshaft sprockets. In other words, make sure all the slack in the timing belt is at the tensioner, between the crankshaft and the camshaft sprockets.
19   Using a wrench on the tensioner, tighten the belt until you can just barely twist it 90-degrees with your thumb and finger at a point halfway be- tween the camshaft and intermediate shaft sprockets **(see illustration)**.
20   Tighten the tensioner locknut securely, then check the timing marks on the crankshaft pulley and the intermediate shaft sprocket. If they have moved out of alignment, remove the timing belt and repeat the installation procedure.
21   The remainder of installation is the reverse of removal. Be sure to ad- just the drivebelt tension when reassembly is complete (see Chapter 1).

2.2L engine

Timing belt removal

Refer to illustrations 6.24, 6.26, 6.27, 6.28 and 6.29
22   Detach the cable from the negative battery terminal.
23   Remove all accessory drivebelts (see Chapter 1).
24   Remove the bolts and detach the water pump pulley **(see illustra- tion)**.

6.19   Using one wrench on the locknut and another on the tension adjuster, turn the tension adjuster until the belt is tight – when the belt is properly adjusted, you should be able to turn it 90-degrees with your thumb and index finger

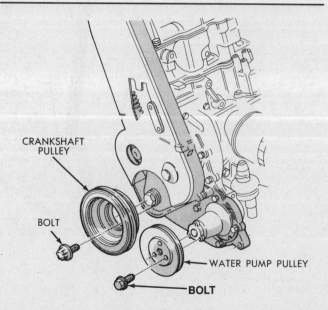

6.24   Crankshaft and water pump pulleys – exploded view (2.2L engine)

25 Remove the crankshaft pulley bolts.
26 Raise the vehicle, support it securely on jackstands and remove the right inner splash shield (see illustration). Remove the crankshaft pulley.
27 Remove the screws and nuts holding the timing belt cover to the cylinder head and block (see illustration). Remove both halves of the timing belt cover.
28 Position the number one piston at top dead center on the compression stroke (see Section 3). The marks on the crankshaft and intermediate shaft sprocket will be aligned (see illustration) and the arrows on the camshaft sprocket will line up with the bearing cap parting line (see illustration 6.40)
29 Use one wrench to hold the offset tensioner bolt while using another wrench or socket to loosen the center bolt, releasing the tension from the timing belt. Remove the belt (see illustration). Remove the tensioner.

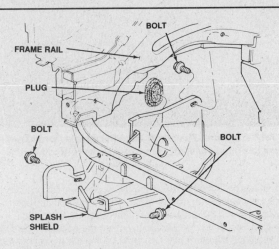

6.26 On the 2.2L engine, you'll have to raise the vehicle and detach the right inner splash shield to remove the crankshaft pulley

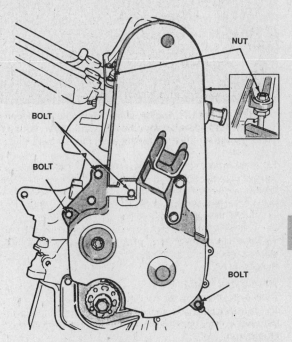

6.27 On the 2.2L engine, remove the fasteners and detach the two timing cover halves

2A

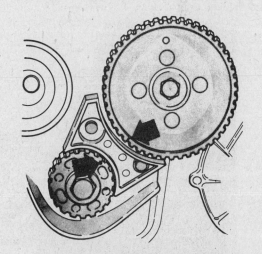

6.28 If you have correctly positioned the number one piston at TDC, the marks on the crankshaft and intermediate shaft sprockets will be aligned (2.2L engine)

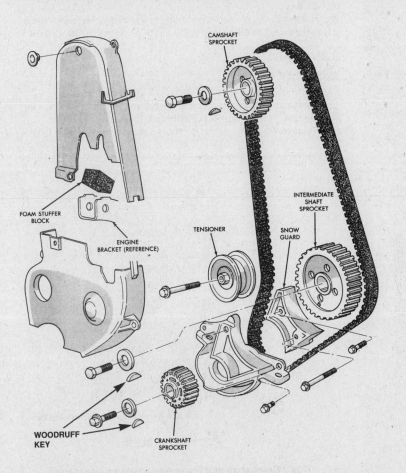

6.29 Timing belt and related components – exploded view (2.2L engine)

6.31   A pin spanner (or homemade substitute like the one shown here) will hold the intermediate shaft sprocket while the bolt is loosened (2.2L engine)

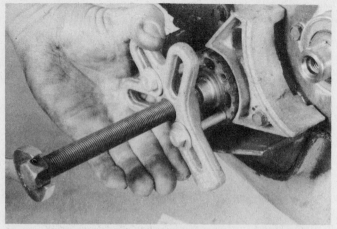

6.32   On the 2.2L engine, you'll have to use a puller to get the crankshaft sprocket off

Timing belt, tensioner and sprocket inspection

30   Refer to Steps 8 through 11 for the inspection procedures (they're the same for both engines).

6.34   On the 2.2L engine, use a straightedge to make sure the marks (dimples) line up with the centers of the sprocket bolt holes

Sprocket removal and installation

Refer to illustrations 6.31, 6.32, 6.34, 6.35 and 6.37

31   Remove the intermediate shaft sprocket bolt while holding the sprocket with a pin spanner or a homemade substitute **(see illustration)**. Pull the sprocket off the shaft.

32   Remove the bolt and use a puller to remove the crankshaft sprocket **(see illustration)**.

33   Hold the camshaft sprocket as described in Step 31 and remove the bolt, then detach the sprocket from the cam.

34   Make sure the Woodruff keys are in place, then install the crankshaft and intermediate shaft sprockets. Turn the shafts until the marks are aligned **(see illustration)**.

35   Install the crankshaft sprocket bolt, lock the crankshaft to keep it from rotating and tighten the bolt to the torque listed in this Chapter's specifications **(see illustration)**.

36   Install the intermediate shaft sprocket bolt and tighten it to the torque listed in this chapter's specifications. Double-check to make sure the marks are aligned as shown in illustration 6.34.

37   Install the camshaft sprocket and bolt. Tighten the bolt to the torque listed in this Chapter's specifications. The triangles on the sprocket hub must align with the camshaft bearing cap parting line **(see illustration)**.

Timing belt installation

Refer to illustrations 6.41 and 6.43

38   When installing the timing belt, the marks on the sprockets MUST BE ALIGNED as described in Steps 34 and 37.

39   Install the timing belt without turning any of the sprockets.

40   Install the tensioner pulley with the bolt finger tight.

6.35   Install and tighten the crankshaft sprocket bolt (2.2L engine)

6.37   On the 2.2L engine, the small hole must be at the top (arrow) and the triangles on the camshaft sprocket must be aligned with the bearing cap parting line (arrows)

6.41 Use a ruler to measure timing belt deflection (2.2L engine)

41   With the help of an assistant, apply tension to the timing belt and temporarily tighten the tensioner bolt. Measure the deflection of the belt halfway between the camshaft sprocket and tensioner pulley. Adjust the tensioner until belt deflection is approximately 5/16-inch **(see illustration)**.
42   Turn the crankshaft two complete revolutions in a clockwise direction (viewed from the front). This will align the belt on the pulleys. Recheck the belt deflection and tighten the tensioner pulley.
43   Recheck the camshaft timing mark with the timing belt cover installed and the number one piston at TDC on the compression stroke. The small hole in the camshaft sprocket must be centered in the timing belt cover hole **(see illustration)**.
44   The remainder of installation is the reverse of removal.

---

7   Camshaft oil seal – replacement

Refer to illustration 7.5
Note: *The following procedure applies to the camshaft oil seal on both 1.7L and 2.2L engines.*
1   Remove the timing belt and camshaft sprocket (see Section 6).
2   Wrap the tip of a small screwdriver with tape and use it to carefully pry out the seal. Don't nick or scratch the camshaft journal or the new seal will leak.
3   Thoroughly clean and inspect the seal bore and the seal journal on the camshaft. Both must be clean and smooth. Use emery cloth or 400 grit sandpaper to remove small burrs.

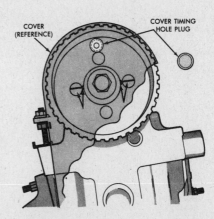

6.43 To check the camshaft timing when the timing belt cover is installed, bring the number one piston to TDC on the compression stroke and verify the small hole in the camshaft sprocket is aligned with the hole in the cover (2.2L engine) – DO NOT start the engine unless the marks are correctly aligned!

4   If a groove has been worn into the journal on the camshaft (from contact with the seal lip), installing a new seal probably won't stop the leak. Such wear normally indicates the camshaft or the bearing surfaces in the caps are worn. It's probably time to overhaul the cylinder head (see Chapter 2, Part B) or replace the head or camshaft.
5   Coat the lip of the new seal with clean engine oil or moly-base grease and carefully tap the seal into place with a large socket or piece of pipe and a hammer. If you don't have a socket as large in diameter as the seal, tap around the outer edge of the seal with the large end of a punch **(see illustration)**.
6   Install the camshaft sprocket and timing belt (see Section 6).
7   Start the engine and check for oil leaks.

---

8   Intermediate shaft oil seal – replacement

Refer to illustrations 8.3 and 8.7
Note: *The following procedure applies to the intermediate shaft oil seal on both 1.7L and 2.2L engines*
1   Drain the engine oil (see Chapter 1).
2   Remove the timing belt and intermediate shaft sprocket (see Section 6).
3   Remove the oil seal housing **(see illustration)**.

7.5 If you don't have a socket large enough to drive in the new seal, tap around the outer edge with the large end of a punch

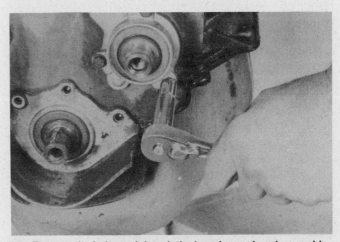

8.3 Remove the bolts and detach the housing and seal assembly (intermediate shaft housing for 2.2L engine shown, 1.7L similar, but it only has two bolts)

2A

8.7   Using a soft-face hammer, carefully tap the new seal into the housing

4   Pry the old seal out of the housing with a screwdriver (wrap the tip of the screwdriver with tape). Make sure you don't scratch the seal bore.
5   Thoroughly clean and inspect the seal bore and the seal journal on the intermediate shaft. Both must be clean and smooth. Remove small burrs with emery cloth or 400 grit sandpaper.
6   If a groove has been worn in the seal journal (from contact with the seal lip), installing a new seal probably won't stop the leak. Such wear normally indicates the intermediate shaft or shaft bearing surfaces in the engine block are worn. It's probably time to overhaul the engine (see Chapter 2, Part B).
7   Using a soft-face hammer, carefully tap the new seal into the housing **(see illustration)**.
8   Coat the lip of the seal with clean engine oil or moly-base grease and install the housing and seal on the front of the engine block. Make sure you don't damage the seal lip. Install the housing bolts and tighten them to the torque listed in this Chapter's specifications.
9   Install the intermediate shaft sprocket and the timing belt (see Section 6).
10   Check the engine oil level and add oil, if necessary (see Chapter 1).
11   Start the engine and check for oil leaks.

---

9   Front crankshaft oil seal – replacement

Refer to illustrations 9.5 and 9.9
Note: *The following procedure applies to the crankshaft oil seal on both 1.7L and 2.2L engines.*
1   Drain the engine oil (see Chapter 1).
2   Remove the timing belt and crankshaft sprocket (see Section 6).
3   Raise the front of the vehicle and support it securely on jackstands.
4   On models with a 2.2L engine, remove the oil pan (see Section 12).
5   Working underneath the vehicle, remove the bolts and detach the oil seal housing **(see illustration)**.
6   Use a punch and hammer to drive the old seal out of the housing. Make sure you don't damage the seal bore. To prevent this, wrap the tip of the punch with tape.
7   Thoroughly clean the seal bore in the housing and the seal journal on the end of the crankshaft. Remove small burrs with emery cloth or 400 grit sandpaper.
8   If a groove has been worn in the seal journal on the crankshaft (from contact with the seal lip), installing a new seal probably won't stop the leak. Such wear normally indicates the crankshaft and/or the main bearings are excessively worn. It's probably time to overhaul the engine (see Chapter 2, Part B).

9   Apply a thin coat of RTV sealant to the surface of the seal bore, lay the housing on a clean, flat work surface, position the new seal in the bore and tap it into place with a soft-face hammer **(see illustration)**.
10   Lubricate the seal lip with moly-base grease and apply a 1 mm wide bead of anaerobic gasket sealant to the engine block mating surface of the seal housing. Position the housing on the engine. Install the retaining bolts and tighten them to the torque listed in this Chapter's specifications.
11   Reinstall the crankshaft sprocket, timing belt and related components.
12   On models with a 2.2L engine, install the oil pan (see Section 12).
13   Check the engine oil level and add oil, if necessary (see Chapter 1).
14   Start the engine, let it warm up and check for leaks.

---

10   Camshaft and cam followers/rocker arms – removal, inspection and installation

---

Note: *The following procedure applies to both the 1.7L and 2.2L engines.*

Removal
Refer to illustrations 10.3 and 10.5
1   Remove the camshaft cover (see Section 4).
2   Remove the timing belt cover, timing belt and camshaft sprocket (see Section 6). **Note:** *If you want to save time by not removing and installing the timing belt, you can unfasten the camshaft sprocket and suspend it out of the way – with the belt still attached – on a piece of wire. Be sure the wire maintains tension on the belt so it won't disengage any of the sprockets.*

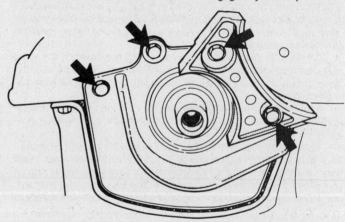

9.5   Remove the bolts and detach the housing/seal assembly (2.2L engine shown, 1.7L similar)

9.9   Tap the new crankshaft oil seal into the housing with a soft-face hammer (2.2L engine shown, 1.7L similar)

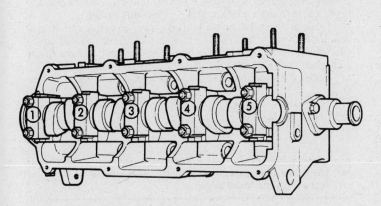

10.3 The camshaft bearing caps on some engines are numbered from 1 to 5 so they don't get mixed up – if the caps aren't numbered, mark them (they must be reinstalled in their original locations)

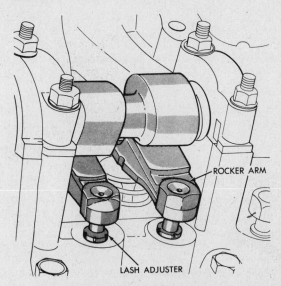

10.5 On the 2.2L engine, mark the rocker arms and lash adjusters before removing them

3 The camshaft rides on five bearings. Each bearing cap is held by two fasteners (nuts on 1.7L engines and bolts on 2.2L engines). On some engines, the bearing caps are numbered from 1 to 5, beginning at the drive-belt end of the engine **(see illustration)**. **Note:** *All numbers face either the spark plug or manifold side of the engine. This is to ensure you install the caps facing the right direction.*

4 On some engines, the bearing caps aren't numbered. If this is the case, you must mark them before removal. Be sure to put the marks on the same ends of all the caps to prevent incorrect orientation of the caps during installation.

5 If the vehicle has a 2.2L engine, also mark the rocker arms **(see illustration)** to ensure they're installed in the same position during reassembly.

6 Remove the nuts and washers (1.7L engine) or bolts (2.2L engine) from all bearing caps except numbers 2 and 4. Next, loosen each of the four fasteners on 2 and 4 a little at a time to relieve valve spring tension evenly until the caps are loose. If any of the caps stick, gently tap them with a soft-face hammer. **Caution:** *Failure to follow this procedure exactly as described could tilt the camshaft in the bearings, which could damage the bearings or bend the camshaft.*

7 Lift out the camshaft, wipe it off with a clean shop towel and set it aside.

8 If you're working on a 1.7L engine, wipe off each valve adjustment shim with a clean shop towel and number it with a felt-tip marker. Remove each cam follower/valve adjustment shim set and set them aside in labelled plastic bags or an egg carton to keep them from getting mixed up.

9 If the vehicle has a 2.2L engine, lift out each rocker arm and hydraulic lash adjuster set, wipe them off and set them aside in labelled plastic bags or an egg carton.

Inspection

Refer to illustrations 10.10 and 10.13

10 To check camshaft endplay:
 a) Install the camshaft and secure it with caps 1 and 5.
 b) Mount a dial indicator on the head **(see illustration)**.
 c) Using a large screwdriver as a lever at the opposite end, move the camshaft forward-and-backward and note the dial indicator reading.
 d) Compare the reading with the endplay listed in this Chapter's Specifications.
 e) If the indicated reading is higher, either the camshaft or the head is worn. Replace parts as necessary.

11 To check camshaft runout:

 a) Mount the camshaft between a pair of V-blocks and attach a dial indicator with the stem resting against the center bearing journal on the camshaft.
 b) Rotate the camshaft and note the indicated runout.
 c) Compare the results to the camshaft runout listed in this Chapter's Specifications.
 d) If the indicated runout exceeds the specified runout, replace the camshaft.

12 To check the camshaft bearing oil clearance, refer to Section 22 in Part B of Chapter 2. If the clearance at any of the journals exceeds the specified limit, replace the head.

13 Check the cam lobes for wear:
 a) Check the toe and ramp areas of each cam lobe for score marks and uneven wear. Also check for flaking and pitting.
 b) If there's wear on the toe or the ramp, replace the camshaft, but first try to find the cause of the wear. Check the valve clearances (see Chapter 1), look for abrasive substances in the oil and inspect the oil pump and oil passages for blockage. Lobe wear is usually caused by inadequate lubrication or dirty oil.

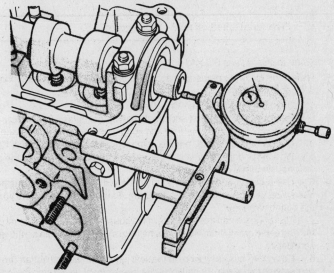

10.10 To check camshaft endplay, set up a dial indicator like this, with the gauge stem touching the nose of the camshaft (1.7L engine shown)

2A

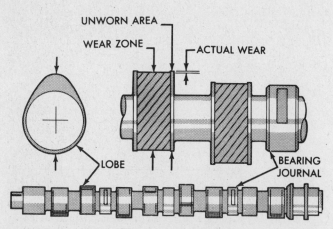

10.13   Measure the height of the camshaft lobes at the wear zone and unworn area, then subtract the wear zone measurement from the unworn area measurement to get the actual wear – compare the wear to the limit listed in this Chapter's specifications

10.21   Install the camshaft with the lobes pointing away from the number one cylinder intake and exhaust valves (1.7L shown, 2.2L similar)

c) If you're working on a 2.2L engine, calculate the lobe wear and compare it to the limit listed in this Chapter's Specifications **(see illustration)**. If the lobe wear is greater than specified, replace the camshaft.

14   If you're working on a 1.7L engine, check the valve adjustment shims. They're usually worn too if the camshaft lobes are worn. If the shims are worn, replace them.

15   If you're working on a 1.7L engine, inspect the cam followers for galling and signs of seizure. If aluminum from the cylinder head is adhering to cam followers, replace them. If any of the cam follower bores are rough, scored or worn, replace the cylinder head.

16   If you're working on a 2.2L engine, inspect the rocker arms and hydraulic lash adjusters for wear, galling and pitting of the contact surfaces.

17   If any of the conditions described above are noted, the cylinder head is probably getting insufficient lubrication or dirty oil, so make sure you track down the cause of this problem (low oil level, low oil pump capacity, clogged oil passage, etc.) before installing a new head, camshaft or followers.

Installation

Refer to illustrations 10.21 and 10.24

18   Thoroughly clean the camshaft, the bearing surfaces in the head and caps, the cam followers and shims (1.7L engine) or the rocker arms and hydraulic lash adjusters (2.2L engine). Remove all sludge and dirt. Wipe off all components with a clean, lint-free cloth.

19   If you're working on a 1.7L engine, lightly lubricate the cam follower bores with assembly lube or moly-base grease. Refer to the numbers marked on the shims and install the cam followers and valve adjustment shims in the head. Lubricate the upper side of the shims with assembly lube or moly-base grease.

20   If you're working on a 2.2L engine, install the hydraulic lash adjusters and rocker arms. Make sure you put them in their original locations. Lubricate the contact surfaces on the top of the rocker arms with assembly lube or moly-base grease.

21   Lubricate the camshaft bearing surfaces in the head and the bearing journals and lobes on the camshaft with assembly lube or moly-base grease. Carefully lower the camshaft into position with the lobes for the number one cylinder pointing away from the cam followers or rocker arms **(see illustration)**. **Caution:** *Failure to adequately lubricate the camshaft and related components can cause serious damage to bearing and friction surfaces during the first few seconds after engine start-up, when the oil pressure is low or nonexistent.*

22   Apply a thin coat of assembly lube or moly-base grease to the bearing surfaces of the camshaft bearing caps and install the caps in their original locations.

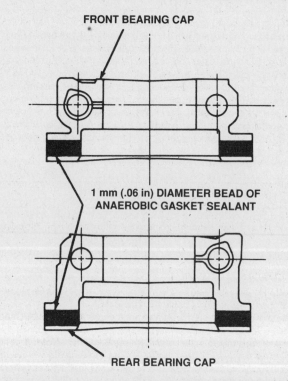

10.24   On the 2.2L engine, apply anaerobic-type gasket sealant to the dark areas only on the front and rear camshaft bearing caps

23   Install the nuts/bolts for bearing caps 2 and 4. Gradually tighten all four fasteners – 1/4-turn at a time – until the camshaft is drawn down and seated in the bearing saddles. Don't tighten the fasteners completely at this time.

24   On the 2.2L engine, apply anaerobic-type sealant to the contact surfaces of bearing caps 1 and 5 **(see illustration)**.

25   Install bearing caps 3 and 5 and tighten the fasteners the same way you did for caps 2 and 4.

26   Install a new oil seal on the front of the camshaft, then install bearing cap 1. Don't tighten the fasteners completely at this time.

27   Remove any excess sealant from the two end bearing caps (2.2L engine).

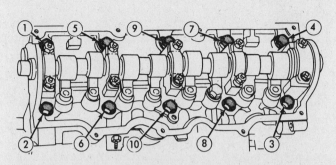

11.9   On the 2.2L engine, loosen the head bolts 1/4-turn at a time, in the sequence shown, until they can be removed by hand – on the 1.7L engine, loosen the bolts by reversing the sequence shown in illustration 11.17a

28   Working in a criss-cross pattern, tighten the fasteners for bearing caps 2 and 4 to the torque listed in this Chapter's Specifications. Then torque the fasteners for bearing caps 3 and 5 the same way. Finally, tighten the fasteners for bearing cap 1.

29   Install the camshaft sprocket, timing belt, timing belt cover and related components (see Section 6). If you suspended the camshaft sprocket out of the way and didn't disturb the timing belt or sprockets, the valve timing should still be correct. Rotate the camshaft as necessary to reattach the sprocket to the camshaft. If the valve timing was disturbed, align the sprockets and install the belt as described in Section 6.

30   Remove the spark plugs and rotate the crankshaft by hand to make sure the valve timing is correct. After two revolutions, the timing marks on the sprockets should still be aligned. If they're not, reindex the timing belt to the sprockets (see Section 6). **Note:** *If you feel resistance while rotating the crankshaft, stop immediately and check the valve timing by referring to Section 6.*

---

11   Cylinder head – removal and installation

Caution: *Allow the engine to cool completely before beginning this procedure.*

Removal

Refer to illustration 11.9

1   Position the number one piston at Top Dead Center (see Section 3).
2   Disconnect the negative cable from the battery.
3   Drain the cooling system and remove the spark plugs (see Chapter 1).
4   Remove the intake/exhaust manifold (see Section 5). **Note:** *If you're only replacing the cylinder head gasket, it's not necessary to remove the manifold. If you leave the manifold attached, you may need an assistant to help lift the head off the engine.*
5   Remove the distributor (see Chapter 5), including the cap and wires.
6   If the engine is equipped with a carburetor, remove the fuel pump (see Chapter 4).
7   Remove the timing belt (see Section 6).
8   Remove the camshaft cover (see Section 4).
9   Loosen the head bolts in 1/4-turn increments until they can be removed by hand. Follow the recommended sequence to avoid warping the head (**see illustration**). **Note:** *Although it isn't required by the manufacturer, the head bolts on 1985 through 1988 2.2L engines should be discarded and new bolts/washers should be used when the head is installed. If the original bolts are used, the head gasket may fail prematurely.*
10   Lift the head off the engine. If resistance is felt, don't pry between the head and block – damage to the mating surfaces will result. To dislodge the head, place a block of wood against the end and strike the wood block with a hammer. Store the head on blocks of wood to prevent damage to the gasket sealing surfaces.

11.16   When you put the new head gasket in position on the engine block, be sure it's right side up and facing the right direction – the holes in the gasket must match the passages in the block for coolant and oil to circulate properly

11   Cylinder head disassembly and inspection procedures are covered in detail in Chapter 2, Part B. It's a good idea to have the head checked for warpage, even if you're just replacing the gasket.

Installation

Refer to illustrations 11.16, 11.17a and 11.17b

12   The mating surfaces of the cylinder head and block must be perfectly clean when the head is installed.
13   Use a gasket scraper to remove all traces of carbon and old gasket material, then clean the mating surfaces with lacquer thinner or acetone. If there's oil on the mating surfaces when the head is installed, the gasket may not seal correctly and leaks may develop. When working on the block, stuff the cylinders with clean shop rags to keep out debris. Use a vacuum cleaner to remove material that falls into the cylinders. Since the head is made of aluminum, aggressive scraping can cause damage. Be extra careful not to nick or gouge the mating surfaces with the scraper.
14   Check the block and head mating surfaces for nicks, deep scratches and other damage. If damage is slight, it can be removed with a file; if it's excessive, machining may be the only alternative.
15   Use a tap of the correct size to chase the threads in the head bolt holes. Mount each bolt in a vise and run a die down the threads to remove corrosion and restore the threads. Dirt, corrosion, sealant and damaged threads will affect torque readings.
16   Place a new gasket on the block (**see illustration**) and set the cylinder head in position.
17   Install the bolts. They must be tightened in four steps, following a specific sequence (**see illustrations**), to the torque listed in this Chapter's Specifications.

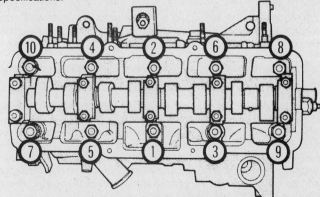

11.17a   Cylinder head bolt TIGHTENING sequence – 1.7L engine (when loosening the bolts, reverse this sequence)

2A

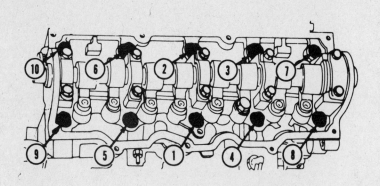

11.17b   Cylinder head bolt TIGHTENING sequence – 2.2L engine

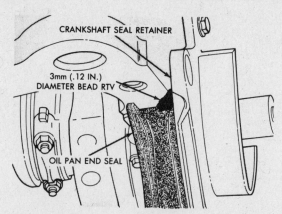

12.9a   On the 2.2L engine, install new oil pan and seals and hold them in place with a bead of RTV sealant as shown here

18   Reinstall the timing belt (see Section 6).
19   Reinstall the remaining parts in the reverse order of removal.
20   Be sure to refill the cooling system and check all fluid levels.
21   Rotate the crankshaft clockwise slowly by hand through two complete revolutions. Recheck the camshaft timing marks (see Section 6).
22   Start the engine and check the ignition timing (see Chapter 1).
23   Run the engine until normal operating temperature is reached. Check for leaks and proper operation.

12   Oil pan – removal and installation

Refer to illustrations 12.9a and 12.9b
Note: The following procedure is based on the assumption the engine is in the vehicle. If you're working on a 1.7L engine that's out of the vehicle, mounted on a stand, it's not necessary to use sealant to hold the gasket in place on the engine block. Just turn the engine upside-down.
1   Warm up the engine, then drain the oil and replace the oil filter (see Chapter 1).
2   Detach the cable from the negative battery terminal.
3   Raise the vehicle and support it securely on jackstands.
4   Remove the bolts securing the oil pan to the engine block.
5   Tap on the pan with a soft-face hammer to break the gasket seal, then detach the oil pan from the engine.
6   Using a gasket scraper, remove all traces of old gasket and/or sealant from the engine block and oil pan. If you're working on a 2.2L engine, remove the seals from each end of the engine block or oil pan. Clean the mating surfaces with lacquer thinner or acetone. Make sure the threaded bolt holes in the block are clean.

7   Clean the oil pan with solvent and dry it thoroughly. Check the gasket flanges for distortion, particularly around the bolt holes. If necessary, place the pan on a block of wood and use a hammer to flatten and restore the gasket surfaces.
8   If you're working on a 1.7L engine, attach the new gasket to the engine block with a few dabs of sealant to hold it in place.
9   If you're working on a 2.2L engine, install new seals in the retainers at the front and rear of the engine block **(see illustration)**. Apply a 1/8-inch wide bead of RTV sealant to the oil pan gasket surfaces. Continue the bead across the end seals. Make sure the sealant is applied to the inside of the bolt holes **(see illustration)**.
10   Carefully place the oil pan in position.
11   Install the bolts and tighten them in 1/4-turn increments to the torque listed in this Chapter's Specifications. Start with the bolts closest to the center of the pan and work out in a spiral pattern. Don't overtighten them or leakage may occur. Note that some 2.2L engines have bolts with different diameters, which require different torques.
12   Add oil, run the engine and check for oil leaks.

13   Oil pump – removal, inspection and installation

Removal
Refer to illustrations 13.2a and 13.2b
1   Remove the oil pan (see Section 12).
2   Remove the oil pump mounting bolts. If you're working on a 2.2L engine, also remove the brace bolt **(see illustrations)**.
3   Remove the oil pump assembly.

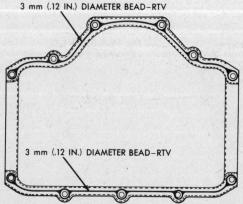

12.9b   On the 2.2L engine, apply a continuous 1/8-inch wide bead of RTV sealant to the oil pan, then install the pan

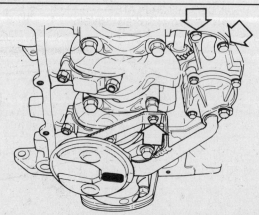

13.2a   2.2L engine oil pump mounting and brace bolt locations (arrows)

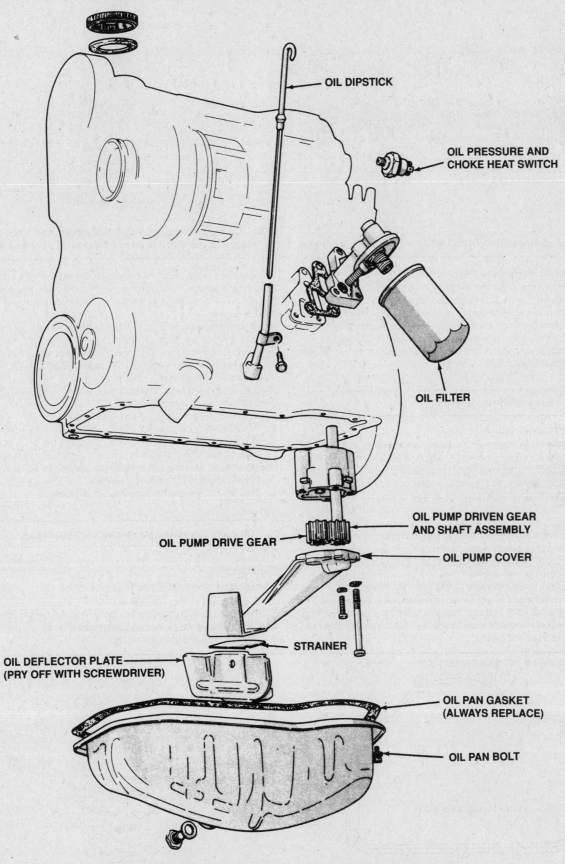

OIL DIPSTICK

OIL PRESSURE AND
CHOKE HEAT SWITCH

OIL FILTER

OIL PUMP DRIVEN GEAR
AND SHAFT ASSEMBLY

OIL PUMP DRIVE GEAR

OIL PUMP COVER

STRAINER

OIL DEFLECTOR PLATE
(PRY OFF WITH SCREWDRIVER)

OIL PAN GASKET
(ALWAYS REPLACE)

OIL PAN BOLT

13.2b   Oil pump and related components – exploded view (1.7L engine)

13.4   Check the face of the oil pump cover for score marks (1.7L engine)

13.7   To check gear backlash, insert a feeler gauge between the gear teeth (1.7L engine)

Inspection

1.7L engine

Refer to illustrations 13.4, 13.7 and 13.8

4   Pry off the oil deflector plate with a screwdriver and set the plate aside. Remove the strainer. Wash the plate and strainer in clean solvent. Unbolt the oil pump cover and wash it in clean solvent. Check the face of the pump cover for score marks **(see illustration)**. If it's worn or damaged, replace the pump.

5   Look inside the pump body at the two gears. If any of the gear teeth are broken, replace the pump. You should consider an engine overhaul too, because metal particles have probably caused damage elsewhere in the engine.

6   Turn the main shaft of the pump and see if the gears rotate smoothly inside the pump body. If they don't, replace the pump.

7   To measure gear backlash, remove the gears, clean them and the inside of the pump body, reinstall them and try to slide various sizes of feeler gauges between the gear teeth **(see illustration)**. The feeler gauge size that slides between the gears with a slight drag should be within the range listed in this Chapter's Specifications. If it isn't, replace the pump.

8   To measure gear endplay, place a straightedge across the gear faces and try to stick a 0.006-inch feeler gauge between the gear faces and the straightedge **(see illustration)**. It shouldn't fit. If it does, try a 0.007-inch gauge. If it fits, replace the pump.

9   If you replace the pump, swap the strainer and deflector plate from the old pump to the new one.

10   Reassemble the pump and tighten the housing bolts (the shorter ones) securely. Make sure the deflector plate and strainer are properly assembled.

2.2L engine

Refer to illustrations 13.12, 13.13, 13.14, 13.15, 13.16 and 13.17

11   Remove the bolts and lift off the oil pump cover.

12   Check the rotor endplay with feeler gauges and a straightedge **(see illustration)**.

13   Remove the outer rotor and measure its thickness **(see illustration)**.

14   Check the clearance between the inner and outer rotor tips with feeler gauges **(see illustration)**.

15   Measure the outer rotor-to-pump body clearance **(see illustration)**.

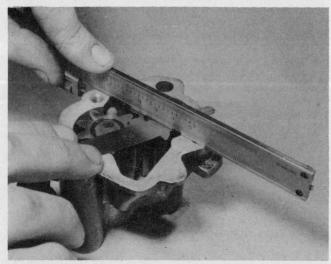

13.8   Check the gear endplay by placing a precision straightedge across the pump housing like this and inserting feeler gauges between the gear faces and the straightedge (1.7L engine)

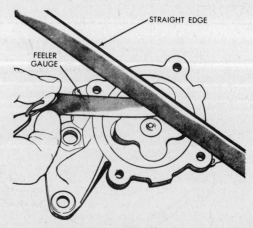

13.12   Check the rotor endplay by placing a precision straightedge across the pump housing like this and inserting feeler gauges between the rotor face and the straightedge (2.2L engine)

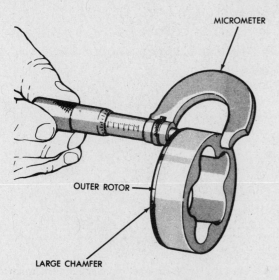

13.13 Measure the thickness of the oil pump rotor with a micrometer (2.2L engine)

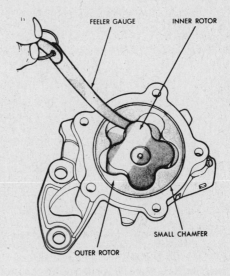

13.14 Check the inner rotor-to-outer rotor tip clearance with feeler gauges (2.2L engine)

16 Check the oil pump cover for warpage with feeler gauges and a straightedge **(see illustration)**.

17 Remove the cotter key and cup, then extract the spring and oil pump relief valve from the pump housing. Measure the free length of the oil pressure relief valve spring **(see illustration)**.

18 Compare the measurements to the oil pump Specifications at the beginning of this Chapter. If any of them are outside the limits, replace the pump.

19 Install the rotor with the large chamfered edge facing toward the pump body. Install the oil pressure relief valve and spring assembly. Install the pump cover and tighten the bolts to the torque listed in this Chapter's Specifications.

Installation

1.7L engine

20 Put a small dab of assembly lube or moly-base grease on the tip of the oil pump driveshaft. Install the pump and tighten the mounting bolts to the torque listed in this Chapter's specifications. Check the strainer one more time to make sure it's properly seated in the end of the oil pump cover. If it's loose, use a pair of locking pliers to crimp the edges tighter.

21 Install the oil pan (see Section 12).

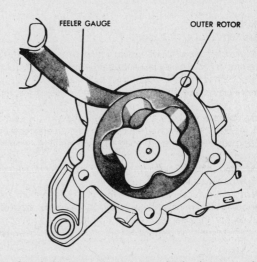

13.15 Check the outer rotor-to-pump body clearance with feeler gauges (2.2L engine)

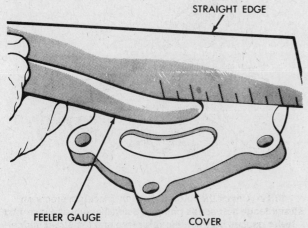

13.16 Check the oil pump cover for warpage with a straightedge and feeler gauges (2.2L engine)

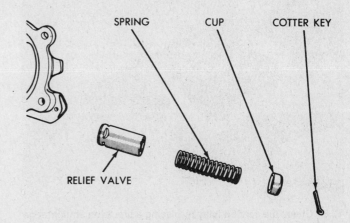

13.17 Oil pressure relief valve components – exploded view (2.2L engine)

13.24   Before attaching the oil pick-up tube assembly, lubricate the new O-ring and install it in the oil pump (2.2L engine)

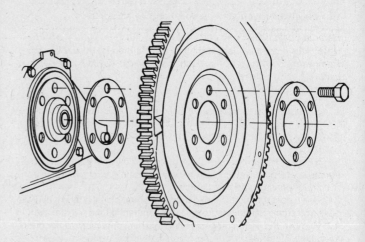

14.4a   Driveplate and related components (1.7L engine)

2.2L engine

Refer to illustration 13.24

22   Apply a thin coat of RTV sealant to the mating surface of the pump and place the pump in position. Rotate it back-and-forth a little to ensure there's positive contact between the pump and the engine block.

23   Coat the threads of the mounting bolts with sealant and, while holding the pump securely in place, install the bolts. Tighten them to the torque listed in this Chapter's Specifications.

24   Install a new O-ring in the oil pump pick-up opening **(see illustration)**.

25   Carefully work the pick-up tube into the pump, install the retaining bolt and tighten it to the torque listed in this Chapter's Specifications.

26   Install the brace bolt and tighten it securely.

27   Install the oil pan (see Section 12).

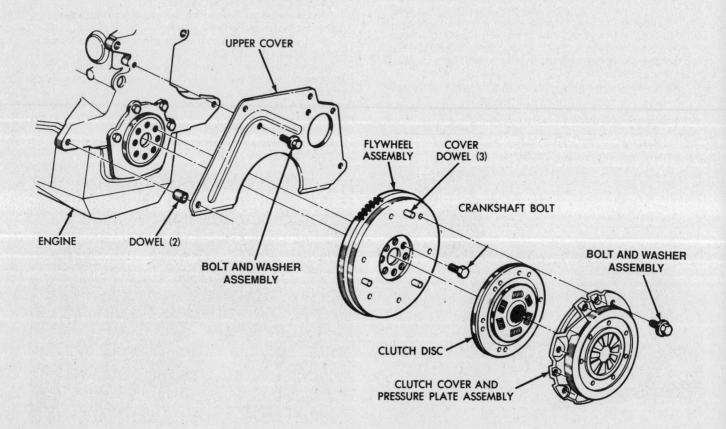

14.4b   Flywheel and related components (2.2L engine)

14 Flywheel/driveplate – removal and installation

Refer to illustrations 14.4a and 14.4b
Note: *This procedure does not apply to 1.7L manual transaxle models. Removing the flywheel on these models is part of the clutch removal procedure (see Chapter 8).*

Removal

1   Raise the vehicle and support it securely on jackstands, then refer to Chapter 7 and remove the transaxle. If it's leaking, now would be a very good time to replace the front pump seal/O-ring (automatic transaxle only).
2   Remove the pressure plate and clutch disc (Chapter 8) (manual transaxle equipped vehicles). Now is a good time to check/replace the clutch components and pilot bearing.
3   Use a center punch to make alignment marks on the flywheel/driveplate and crankshaft to ensure correct alignment during reinstallation.
4   Remove the bolts that secure the flywheel/driveplate to the crankshaft **(see illustrations)**. If the crankshaft turns, wedge a screwdriver through the starter opening to jam the flywheel.
5   Remove the flywheel/driveplate from the crankshaft. Since the flywheel is fairly heavy, be sure to support it while removing the last bolt.
6   Clean the flywheel to remove grease and oil. Inspect the surface for cracks, rivet grooves, burned areas and score marks. Light scoring can be removed with emery cloth. Check for cracked and broken ring gear teeth. Lay the flywheel on a flat surface and use a straightedge to check for warpage.
7   Clean and inspect the mating surfaces of the flywheel/driveplate and the crankshaft. If the crankshaft rear seal is leaking, replace it before reinstalling the flywheel/driveplate.

Installation

8   Position the flywheel/driveplate against the crankshaft. Be sure to align the marks made during removal. Note that some engines have an alignment dowel or staggered bolt holes to ensure correct installation. Before installing the bolts, apply thread locking compound to the threads.
9   Wedge a screwdriver through the starter motor opening to keep the flywheel/driveplate from turning as you tighten the bolts to the torque listed in this Chapter's Specifications.
10   The remainder of installation is the reverse of the removal procedure.

15 Rear crankshaft oil seal – replacement

Refer to illustrations 15.5, 15.8 and 15.9
1   Remove the transaxle (See Chapter 7).

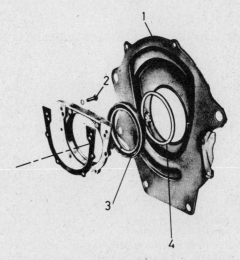

15.5   Typical rear crankshaft oil seal and housing – exploded view

1	Intermediate plate	3	Oil seal
2	Bolt	4	Sealing ring (not used on all models)

2   If the vehicle has a manual transaxle, remove the clutch and flywheel (see Chapter 8 and Section 14 of this Chapter).
3   If the vehicle has an automatic transaxle, remove the driveplate (see Section 14).
4   Remove the oil pan (see Section 12).
5   Remove the rear oil seal housing and gasket **(see illustration)**.
6   Remove the old seal from the housing.
7   Thoroughly clean the seal bore in the seal housing with a shop towel. Remove all traces of oil and dirt.
8   Carefully tap the new seal into the housing with a soft-face hammer **(see illustration)**. Coat the seal lip with moly-base grease so it will slide onto the crankshaft easily.
9   Install a new gasket **(see illustration)** (the dowel pins will hold it in place). Install the housing/seal assembly and tighten the bolts to the torque listed in this Chapter's Specifications.
10   Install the driveplate or flywheel and clutch (if equipped).
11   Install the transaxle.

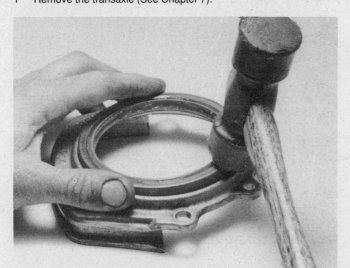

15.8   Use a soft-face hammer to tap the new seal into the housing (2.2L engine shown, 1.7L similar)

15.9   Make sure the new gasket is correctly positioned on the block before installing the seal housing assembly (1.7L engine shown, 2.2L similar)

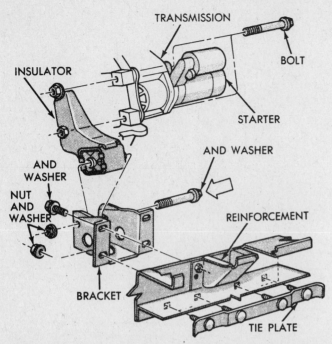

16.4a   An exploded view of the front engine mount (1.7L engine)

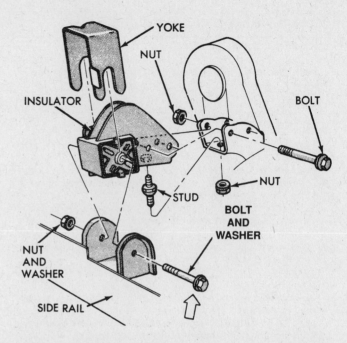

16.4b   An exploded view of the right engine mount (1.7L engine)

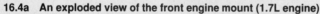

16   Engine mounts – check, replacement and adjustment

Refer to illustrations 16.4a, 16.4b, 16.4c, 16.4d, 16.4e, 16.4f, 16.4g and 16.15

1   Engine mounts seldom require attention, but broken or deteriorated mounts should be replaced immediately or the added strain placed on the driveline components may cause damage or wear.

Check

2   During the check, the engine must be raised slightly to remove the weight from the mounts.

3   Raise the vehicle and support it securely on jackstands, then position a jack under the engine oil pan. Place a large block of wood between the jack head and the oil pan, then carefully raise the engine just enough to take the weight off the mounts. **Warning:** *DO NOT place any part of your body under the engine when it's supported only by a jack!*

4   Check the mount insulators **(see illustrations)** to see if the rubber is cracked, hardened or separated from the metal plates. Sometimes the rubber will split right down the center.

5   Check for relative movement between the mount plates and the engine or frame (use a large screwdriver or prybar to attempt to move the mounts). If movement is noted, lower the engine and tighten the mount fasteners.

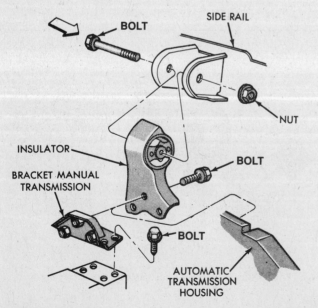

16.4c   An exploded view of the left engine mount (1.7L engine)

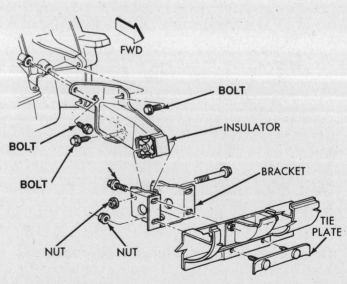

16.4d   An exploded view of the front engine mount (2.2L engine)

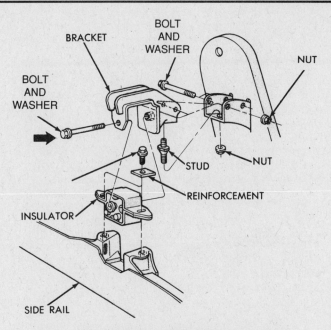

16.4e   An exploded view of the right engine mount (early 2.2L engine)

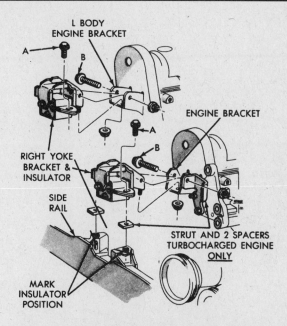

16.4f   An exploded view of the right engine mount (later 2.2L engine)

2A

6   Rubber preservative should be applied to the insulators to slow deterioration.

Replacement

7   Disconnect the negative battery cable from the battery, then raise the vehicle and support it securely on jackstands (if not already done).

8   Remove the fasteners and detach the insulator from the frame bracket.

9   Raise the engine slightly with a jack or hoist. Remove the insulator-to-engine bolts and detach the insulator.

10   Installation is the reverse of removal. Use thread locking compound on the mount bolts and be sure to tighten them securely.

Adjustment

11   The right and left engine mounts are adjustable to allow drivetrain movement in relation to driveaxle assembly length (see Chapter 8).

12   Always adjust the insulators when:
   a)   You service the driveaxles.
   b)   The vehicle sustains front end structural damage.
   c)   You replace an insulator.

13   Remove the load on the engine mounts by carefully supporting the engine and transaxle assembly with a floor jack.

14   Loosen the right insulator vertical fasteners and the front engine mount bracket-to-front crossmember bolts and nuts.

15   The left engine mount insulator is sleeved over the shaft and long support bolt **(see illustration)** to provide lateral movement adjustment.

16   Pry the engine right or left as required to achieve the proper driveaxle assembly length (see Chapter 8).

17   Tighten the right engine mount insulator vertical bolts securely, tighten the front engine mount bolts and nuts securely and center the left engine mount insulator.

18   Recheck the driveaxle length.

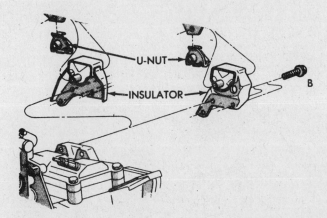

16.4g   An exploded view of the left engine mount (2.2L engine)

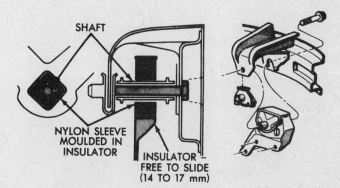

16.15   Cutaway of the left insulator sleeve assembly

Chapter 2 Part B
General engine overhaul procedures

Contents

Specifications

1.7L engine

General

Displacement	105 cu in (1.7 liters)
Cylinder compression pressure	142 to 184 psi
Oil pressure (at 2000 rpm)	28 psi

Cylinder head

Warpage limit	0.004 in (0.10 mm)

Valves

Stem diameter	0.314 in (7.97 mm)
Stem-to-guide clearance	
Intake	0.020 in (0.5 mm)
Exhaust	0.027 in (0.7 mm)
Valve margin width (minimum)	0.020 in (0.5 mm)
Seat angle	45-degrees
Spring	
Free length	Not available
Installed height	Not available

Camshaft

Maximum endplay	0.006 in (0.15 mm)

1.7L engine (continued)
Crankshaft
Maximum endplay	0.015 in (0.37 mm)
Main bearing journal diameter	2.124 to 2.155 in (53.96 to 53.98 mm)
Connecting rod journal diameter	1.809 to 1.810 in (45.96 to 45.98 mm)
Journal out-of-round/taper limits	0.0012 in (0.03 mm)
Main bearing oil clearance	
Standard	0.0008 to 0.003 in (0.02 to 0.08 mm)
Service limit	0.005 in (0.13 mm)
Connecting rod bearing oil clearance	0.001 to 0.003 in (0.30 to 0.75 mm)
Connecting rod endplay (side clearance) limit	0.014 in (0.37 mm)

Engine block
Cylinder out-of-round limit	0.0016 in (0.04 mm)
Cylinder taper limit	0.005 in (0.125 mm)
Block deck warpage limit	0.004 in (0.10 mm)

Pistons and piston rings
Piston-to-bore clearance	
Standard	0.0004 to 0.0015 in (0.011 to 0.039 mm)
Service limit	0.0027 in (0.07 mm)
Piston ring side clearance limit (all rings)	0.004 in (0.10 mm)
Piston ring end gap	0.012 to 0.018 in (0.30 to 0.45 mm)

Torque specifications*
	Ft-lbs
Main bearing cap bolts	47
Connecting rod bearing cap nuts	35

* Note: Refer to Part A for additional torque specifications.

2.2L engine
General
Displacement	135 cu in (2.2 liters)
Cylinder compression pressure	130 to 150 psi at 250 rpm
Oil pressure	
1982 through 1984 (at 2000 rpm)	40 psi
1985 (at 3000 rpm)	25 to 90 psi
1986 on (at 3000 rpm)	25 to 80 psi

Engine block
Cylinder taper limit	
1982 through 1984	0.010 in (0.25 mm)
1985 on	0.005 in (0.125 mm)
Cylinder out-of-round limit	
1982 through 1984	0.005 in (0.125 mm)
1985 on	0.002 in (0.050 mm)

Pistons and rings
Piston diameter	
Non-turbocharged engine	3.443 to 3.445 in (87.442 to 87.507 mm)
Turbocharged engine	3.4416 to 3.4441 in (87.416 to 87.481 mm)
Piston-to-bore clearance	0.001 to 0.003 in (0.30 to 0.75 mm)
Piston ring side clearance	
Top compression ring	
Standard	0.0015 to 0.0031 in (0.038 to 0.078 mm)
Service limit	0.004 in (0.10 mm)
Second compression ring	
Standard	0.0015 to 0.0037 in (0.038 to 0.093 mm)
Service limit	0.004 in (0.10 mm)
Oil ring	0.008 in (0.20 mm)

Piston ring end gap
Non-turbocharged engine	
Compression rings	0.011 to 0.021 in (0.28 to 0.53 mm)
Oil ring	
Standard	0.015 to 0.055 in (0.38 to 1.40 mm)
Service limit	0.074 in (1.88 mm)
Turbocharged engine	
Top compression ring	0.010 to 0.020 in (0.25 to 0.51 mm)
Second compression ring	0.009 to 0.019 in (0.23 to 0.48 mm)
Oil ring	
Standard	0.015 to 0.055 in (0.38 to 1.40 mm)
Service limit	0.074 in (1.88 mm)

2B

2.2L engine (continued)

Crankshaft
Endplay
  Standard .... 0.002 to 0.007 in (0.05 to 0.18 mm)
  Service limit .... 0.014 in (0.35 mm)
Main bearing journal
  Diameter
    Non-turbocharged engine .... 2.362 to 2.363 in (59.987 to 60.013 mm)
    Turbocharged engine .... 2.3622 to 2.3627 in (60.000 to 60.013 mm)
  Taper limit .... 0.0004 in (0.010 mm)
  Out-of-round limit .... 0.0012 in (0.03 mm)
Connecting rod journal
  Diameter .... 1.968 to 1.969 in (49.979 to 50.005 mm)
  Out-of-round/taper limits .... 0.0012 in (0.15 mm)
Main bearing oil clearance
  Non-turbocharged engine
    Standard .... 0.0003 to 0.0031 in (0.007 to 0.080 mm)
    Service limit .... 0.004 in (0.10 mm)
  Turbocharged engine .... 0.0004 to 0.0023 in (0.011 to 0.54 mm)
Connecting rod bearing oil clearance
  Non-turbocharged engine
    Standard .... 0.0008 to 0.0034 in (0.019 to 0.087 mm)
    Service limit .... 0.004 in (0.10 mm)
  Turbocharged engine .... 0.0008 to 0.0031 in (0.019 to 0.079 mm)
Connecting rod endplay (side clearance) .... 0.005 to 0.013 in (0.13 to 0.32 mm)

Camshaft
Endplay
  Standard .... 0.005 to 0.013 in (0.13 to 0.33 mm)
  Service limit .... 0.020 in (0.50 mm)

Cylinder head and valves
Head warpage limit .... 0.004 in (0.1 mm)
Valve seat angle 45-degrees
Valve face angle 45-degrees
Valve margin width
  Intake
    Standard .... 0.06 in (1.5 mm)
    Service limit .... 0.03 in (0.793 mm)
  Exhaust
    Standard .... 0.06 in (1.5 mm)
    Service limit .... 0.05 in (1.19 mm)
Valve stem diameter
  Intake .... 0.3124 in (7.935 mm)
  Exhaust .... 0.3103 in (7.881 mm)
Valve stem-to-guide clearance
  Intake .... 0.0009 to 0.0026 in (0.022 to 0.065 mm)
  Exhaust .... 0.003 to 0.0047 in (0.076 to 0.119 mm)
Valve spring free length
  1982 through 1984 .... 2.28 in (57.9 mm)
  1985 on
    Non-turbocharged engine .... 2.39 in (60.8 mm)
    Turbocharged engine .... 2.28 in (57.9 mm)
Valve spring installed height (both valves) .... 1.62 to 1.68 in (41.2 to 42.7 mm)

Torque specifications*
                                                      Ft-lbs
Main bearing cap bolts .... 30 plus 1/4-turn
Connecting rod bearing cap nuts .... 40 plus 1/4-turn

Note: Refer to Part A for additional torque specifications.

---

1   General information

Included in this portion of Chapter 2 are the general overhaul procedures for the cylinder head and internal engine components.

The information ranges from advice concerning preparation for an overhaul and the purchase of replacement parts to detailed, step-by-step procedures covering removal and installation of internal engine components and the inspection of parts.

The following Sections have been written based on the assumption that the engine has been removed from the vehicle. For information concerning in-vehicle engine repair, as well as removal and installation of the external components necessary for the overhaul, see Part A of this Chapter and Section 7 of this Part.

The Specifications included in this Part are only those necessary for the inspection and overhaul procedures which follow. Refer to Part A for additional Specifications.

2.4   Remove the oil pressure sending unit and install a pressure gauge in its place

2   Engine overhaul – general information

Refer to illustration 2.4

It's not always easy to determine when, or if, an engine should be completely overhauled, as a number of factors must be considered.

High mileage is not necessarily an indication that an overhaul is needed, while low mileage doesn't preclude the need for an overhaul. Frequency of servicing is probably the most important consideration. An engine that's had regular and frequent oil and filter changes, as well as other required maintenance, will most likely give many thousands of miles of reliable service. Conversely, a neglected engine may require an overhaul very early in its life.

Excessive oil consumption is an indication that piston rings, valve seals and/or valve guides are in need of attention. Make sure oil leaks aren't responsible before deciding the rings and/or guides are bad. Perform a cylinder compression check to determine the extent of the work required (see Section 3).

Check the oil pressure with a gauge installed in place of the oil pressure sending unit **(see illustration)** and compare it to this Chapter's Specifications. If it's extremely low, the bearings and/or oil pump are probably worn out.

Loss of power, rough running, knocking or metallic engine noises, excessive valve train noise and high fuel consumption rates may also point to the need for an overhaul, especially if they're all present at the same time. If a complete tune-up doesn't remedy the situation, major mechanical work is the only solution.

An engine overhaul involves restoring the internal parts to the specifications of a new engine. During an overhaul, the piston rings are replaced and the cylinder walls are reconditioned (rebored and/or honed). If a rebore is done by an automotive machine shop, new oversize pistons will also be installed. The main bearings and connecting rod bearings are generally replaced with new ones and, if necessary, the crankshaft may be reground to restore the journals. Generally, the valves are serviced as well, since they're usually in less-than-perfect condition at this point. While the engine is being overhauled, other components, such as the distributor, starter and alternator, can be rebuilt as well. The end result should be a like new engine that will give many trouble free miles. **Note:** *Critical cooling system components such as the hoses, drivebelts, thermostat and water pump MUST be replaced with new parts when an engine is overhauled. The radiator should be checked carefully to ensure that it isn't clogged or leaking (see Chapter 3). Also, we don't recommend overhauling the oil pump – always install a new one when an engine is rebuilt.*

Before beginning the engine overhaul, read through the entire procedure to familiarize yourself with the scope and requirements of the job. Overhauling an engine isn't difficult, if you follow all of the instructions carefully, have the necessary tools and equipment and pay close attention to all specifications; however, it can be time consuming. Plan on the vehicle being tied up for a minimum of two weeks, especially if parts must be taken to an automotive machine shop for repair or reconditioning. Check on availability of parts and make sure any necessary special tools and equipment are obtained in advance. Most work can be done with typical hand tools, although a number of precision measuring tools are required for inspecting parts to determine if they must be replaced. Often an automotive machine shop will handle the inspection of parts and offer advice concerning reconditioning and replacement. **Note:** *Always wait until the engine has been completely disassembled and all components, especially the engine block, have been inspected before deciding what service and repair operations must be performed by an automotive machine shop. Since the block's condition will be the major factor to consider when determining whether to overhaul the original engine or buy a rebuilt one, never purchase parts or have machine work done on other components until the block has been thoroughly inspected. As a general rule, time is the primary cost of an overhaul, so it doesn't pay to install worn or substandard parts.*

As a final note, to ensure maximum life and minimum trouble from a rebuilt engine, everything must be assembled with care in a spotlessly clean environment.

3   Cylinder compression check

Refer to illustration 3.6

1   A compression check will tell you what mechanical condition the upper end (pistons, rings, valves, head gaskets) of an engine is in. Specifically, it can tell you if the compression is down due to leakage caused by worn piston rings, defective valves and seats or a blown head gasket. **Note:** *The engine must be at normal operating temperature and the battery must be fully charged for this check. Also, if the engine is equipped with a carburetor, the choke valve must be all the way open to get an accurate compression reading (if the engine's warm, the choke should be open).*

2   Begin by cleaning the area around the spark plugs before you remove them (compressed air should be used, if available, otherwise a small brush or even a bicycle tire pump will work). The idea is to prevent dirt from getting into the cylinders as the compression check is being done.

3   Remove all of the spark plugs from the engine (see Chapter 1).

4   Block the throttle wide open.

5   Detach the coil wire from the center of the distributor cap and ground it on the engine block. Use a jumper wire with alligator clips on each end to ensure a good ground. On fuel-injected vehicles, the fuel pump circuit should also be disabled (see Chapter 4).

6   Install the compression gauge in the number one spark plug hole **(see illustration)**.

3.6   A compression gauge with a threaded fitting for the spark plug hole is preferred over the type that requires hand pressure to maintain the seal

7   Crank the engine over at least seven compression strokes and watch the gauge. The compression should build up quickly in a healthy engine. Low compression on the first stroke, followed by gradually increasing pressure on successive strokes, indicates worn piston rings. A low compression reading on the first stroke, which doesn't build up during successive strokes, indicates leaking valves or a blown head gasket (a cracked head could also be the cause). Deposits on the undersides of the valve heads can also cause low compression. Record the highest gauge reading obtained.

8   Repeat the procedure for the remaining cylinders and compare the results to this Chapter's Specifications.

9   Add some engine oil (about three squirts from a plunger-type oil can) to each cylinder, through the spark plug hole, and repeat the test.

10   If the compression increases after the oil is added, the piston rings are definitely worn. If the compression doesn't increase significantly, the leakage is occurring at the valves or head gasket. Leakage past the valves may be caused by burned valve seats and/or faces or warped, cracked or bent valves.

11   If two adjacent cylinders have equally low compression, there's a strong possibility that the head gasket between them is blown. The appearance of coolant in the combustion chambers or the crankcase would verify this condition.

12   If one cylinder is 20 percent lower than the others, and the engine has a slightly rough idle, a worn exhaust lobe on the camshaft could be the cause.

13   If the compression is unusually high, the combustion chambers are probably coated with carbon deposits. If that's the case, the cylinder head should be removed and decarbonized.

14   If compression is way down or varies greatly between cylinders, it would be a good idea to have a leak-down test performed by an automotive repair shop. This test will pinpoint exactly where the leakage is occurring and how severe it is.

4   Engine removal – methods and precautions

If you've decided an engine must be removed for overhaul or major repair work, several preliminary steps should be taken.

Locating a suitable place to work is extremely important. Adequate work space, along with storage space for the vehicle, will be needed. If a shop or garage isn't available, at the very least a flat, level, clean work surface made of concrete or asphalt is required.

Cleaning the engine compartment and engine before beginning the removal procedure will help keep tools clean and organized.

An engine hoist or A-frame will also be necessary. Make sure the equipment is rated in excess of the combined weight of the engine and accessories. **Note:** *On vehicles with a 1.7L engine and manual transaxle, the hoist's rating must be in excess of the combined weight of the engine and transaxle. Safety is of primary importance, considering the potential hazards involved in lifting the engine out of the vehicle.*

If the engine is being removed by a novice, a helper should be available. Advice and aid from someone more experienced would also be helpful. There are many instances when one person cannot simultaneously perform all of the operations required when lifting the engine out of the vehicle.

Plan the operation ahead of time. Arrange for or obtain all of the tools and equipment you'll need prior to beginning the job. Some of the equipment necessary to perform engine removal and installation safely and with relative ease are (in addition to an engine hoist) a heavy duty floor jack, complete sets of wrenches and sockets as described in the front of this manual, wooden blocks and plenty of rags and cleaning solvent for mopping up spilled oil, coolant and gasoline. If the hoist must be rented, be sure to arrange for it in advance and perform all of the operations possible without it beforehand. This will save you money and time.

Plan for the vehicle to be out of use for quite a while. A machine shop will be required to perform some of the work which the do-it-yourselfer can't accomplish without special equipment. These shops often have a busy schedule, so it would be a good idea to consult them before removing

the engine in order to accurately estimate the amount of time required to rebuild or repair components that may need work.

Always be extremely careful when removing and installing the engine. Serious injury can result from careless actions. Plan ahead, take your time and a job of this nature, although major, can be accomplished successfully.

5   Engine – removal and installation

Warning: *Gasoline is extremely flammable, so take extra precautions when disconnecting any part of the fuel system. Don't smoke or allow open flames or bare light bulbs near the work area and don't work in a garage where a natural gas-type appliance (such as a water heater or clothes dryer) with a pilot light is present. If you spill any fuel on your skin, rinse it off immediately with soap and water. Have a fire extinguisher handy and know how to use it!*

Note: *Read through the entire Section before beginning this procedure. Note that the 1.7L engine with a manual transaxle must be removed as a single assembly – then separated after removal from the vehicle – while the 1.7L engine with an automatic transaxle and any 2.2L engine can be removed with the transaxle still in the vehicle.*

Removal

Refer to illustration 5.9

1   If the vehicle is air conditioned, have the system discharged by a dealer service department or a service station.

2   Start the engine, warm it up, turn it off, allow it to cool for awhile, drain the oil and remove the oil filter (see Chapter 1).

3   If the vehicle is fuel-injected, relieve the fuel system pressure (see Chapter 4).

4   Place protective covers on the fenders.

5   Remove the battery (see Chapter 5).

6   Remove the hood (see Chapter 11).

7   Remove the air cleaner assembly (see Chapter 4).

8   Make sure the engine is cool, then drain the cooling system (see Chapter 1).

9   Carefully label, then disconnect all vacuum lines, coolant and emission hoses, heater hoses and wire harness connectors. **Note:** *Not all the coolant and emissions hoses can be detached from above. Some can only be reached from underneath the vehicle, after you raise it.* Masking tape and felt-tip pens work well for marking items **(see illustration)**. If necessary, take instant photos or sketch the locations to ensure correct reinstallation.

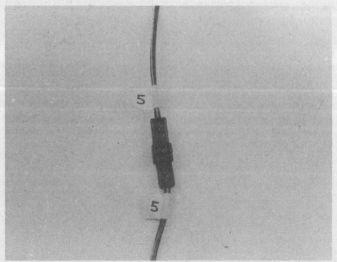

5.9   One way to ensure proper reattachment of connectors is to label each side of the connection with bits of masking tape and number them with a felt-tip pen – another way is to use matching colors of electrical tape

5.24 To lift the engine out of the engine compartment, attach a short section of heavy chain to the lifting brackets on the head, then hook up the engine hoist to the chain

10 Detach the fuel lines from the carburetor, throttle body or fuel rail (see Chapter 4).

11 If the vehicle is equipped with an automatic transaxle, drain the transaxle fluid (see Chapter 1) and detach the transaxle cooler lines (see Chapter 7, Part B).

12 Remove the accessory drivebelts (see Chapter 1).

13 Remove the radiator and cooling fan assembly (see Chapter 3).

14 Remove the alternator (see Chapter 5).

15 If the vehicle is air conditioned, remove the air conditioning compressor mounting bolts and set the compressor aside (see Chapter 3). **Note:** *It may be necessary to restrain the compressor with a piece of wire to make sure it remains clear of the engine during removal.*

16 If the vehicle is equipped with power steering, remove the power steering pump mounting bolts and set the pump aside (see Chapter 10).

Note: *You won't be able to actually remove the pump until you've raised the vehicle and removed the right inner splash shield (see Step 38).*

Vehicles with a 1.7L engine and manual transaxle
Refer to illustration 5.24

17 Disconnect the clutch cable and speedometer cable from the transaxle (see Chapter 7, Part A).

18 Raise the vehicle and place it securely on jackstands.

19 Detach the exhaust pipe from the exhaust manifold (see Chapter 4).

20 Label, then detach any remaining air pump hoses and lines, if equipped. Remove the air pump (see Chapter 6).

21 Detach the transaxle linkage (see Chapter 7, Part A).

22 Remove the driveaxles (see Chapter 8).

23 Lower the vehicle.

24 Attach a short length of heavy duty chain to the engine lifting brackets and hook up an engine hoist **(see illustration)**.

25 Raise the engine/transaxle assembly slightly and remove the front engine mounting bolt (see Chapter 2, Part A).

26 Remove the right engine mounting bolt (see Chapter 2, Part A).

27 Remove the left engine mounting bolt (see Chapter 2, Part A).

28 Lift the engine and transmission assembly out of the vehicle.

29 Remove the engine-to-transaxle bolts and separate the engine from the transaxle.

Vehicles with a 1.7L engine and automatic transaxle/all vehicles with a 2.2L engine
Refer to illustrations 5.36, 5.38, 5.43a and 5.43b

30 Remove the upper bellhousing bolts (see Chapter 7, Part B).

31 Loosen, but don't remove, the front wheel lug nuts (see Chapter 1).

32 Raise the vehicle and place it securely on jackstands.

33 Detach the exhaust pipe from the exhaust manifold (see Chapter 4).

34 Label, then detach any remaining air pump hoses and lines, if equipped. Remove the air pump (see Chapter 6).

35 Remove the left front wheel.

36 Remove the left inner splash shield **(see illustration)**.

37 Remove the right front wheel.

38 Remove the right inner splash shield **(see illustration)**.

39 Remove the power steering pump drivebelt and pump (see Chapter 10).

40 Detach the lower radiator hose from the water pump (see Chapter 3).

41 Remove the water pump pulley (see Chapter 3) and crankshaft pulley (see Chaper 2, Part A).

42 Remove the front engine mounting bolt (see Chapter 2, Part A).

2B

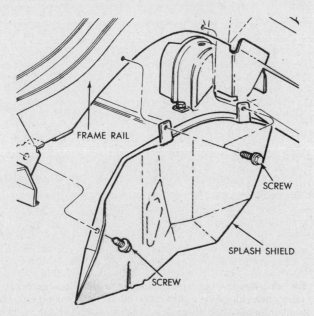

5.36 Left inner splash shield mounting details

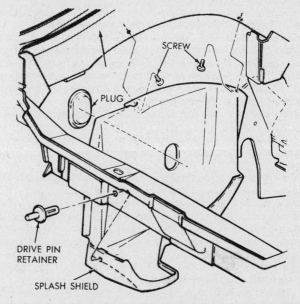

5.38 Right inner splash shield mounting details (1.7L engine shown, 2.2L engine similar)

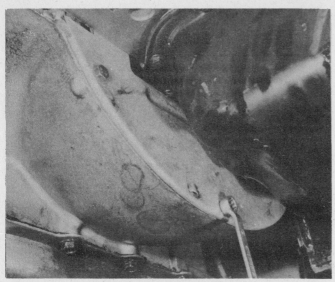

5.43a   Remove the bolts and detach the inspection cover from the transaxle, . . .

5.43b   . . . then remove the driveplate-to-torque converter bolts (arrow) – you'll have to turn the crankshaft to bring the other bolts into view

43   Detach the inspection cover from the transaxle and remove the drive-plate bolts **(see illustrations)**.
44   Remove the starter (see Chapter 5).
45   Remove the remaining lower bellhousing bolts (see Chapter 7, Part B).
46   Lower the vehicle.
47   Place a floor jack under the transaxle.
48   Attach a short length of heavy duty chain to the engine lifting brackets and hook up an engine hoist **(see illustration 5.24)**.
49   Remove the right engine mount (see Chapter 2, Part A).
50   Lift the engine out of the vehicle. **Caution:** *If the vehicle has an automatic transaxle, don't let the torque converter fall out of the bellhousing after the engine is lifted clear. Have an assistant hold it in place until you can secure it with a piece of wire or rope.*

Installation

51   Check the engine/transaxle mounts. If they're worn or damaged, replace them.
52   On manual transaxle equipped vehicles, inspect the clutch components (see Chapter 8) and apply a very small amount of high-temperature grease to the transaxle mainshaft (input shaft) splines.

Vehicles with a 1.7L engine and manual transaxle

53   Carefully rejoin the transaxle and engine following the procedure outlined in Chapter 7. **Caution:** *Do not use the bolts to force the engine and transaxle into alignment. It may crack or damage major components.*
54   Install the transaxle-to-engine bolts and tighten them securely.
55   Attach the hoist to the engine and carefully lower the engine/transaxle assembly into the vehicle.
56   Install the mount bolts and tighten them securely. **Note:** *Don't tighten any bolts until you've installed all of them.*

Vehicles with a 1.7L engine and automatic transaxle/all vehicles with a 2.2L engine

57   Attach the hoist to the engine and lower the engine into the engine compartment.
58   Align the engine with the engine mounts and install the mounting bolts. **Note:** *Don't tighten any bolts until you've installed all of them.*

All vehicles

59   Reinstall the remaining components and fasteners in the reverse order of removal.
60   Add coolant, oil, power steering and transmission fluid/lubricant as needed (see Chapter 1).

61   Run the engine and check for proper operation and leaks. Shut off the engine and recheck the fluid levels.

6   Engine rebuilding alternatives

The do-it-yourselfer is faced with a number of options when performing an engine overhaul. The decision to replace the engine block, piston/connecting rod assemblies and crankshaft depends on a number of factors, with the number one consideration being the condition of the block. Other considerations are cost, access to machine shop facilities, parts availability, time required to complete the project and the extent of prior mechanical experience on the part of the do-it-yourselfer.
Some of the rebuilding alternatives include:
Individual parts – If the inspection procedures reveal the engine block and most engine components are in reusable condition, purchasing individual parts may be the most economical alternative. The block, crankshaft and piston/connecting rod assemblies should all be inspected carefully. Even if the block shows little wear, the cylinder bores should be surface honed.
Short block – A short block consists of an engine block with a crankshaft and piston/connecting rod assemblies already installed. All new bearings are incorporated and all clearances will be correct. The existing camshaft, valve train components, cylinder head and external parts can be bolted to the short block with little or no machine shop work necessary.
Long block – A long block consists of a short block plus an oil pump, oil pan, cylinder head, camshaft cover, camshaft and valve train components and timing belt/sprockets. All components are installed with new bearings, seals and gaskets incorporated throughout. The installation of manifolds and external parts is all that's necessary.
Give careful thought to which alternative is best for you and discuss the situation with local automotive machine shops, auto parts dealers and experienced rebuilders before ordering or purchasing replacement parts.

7   Engine overhaul – disassembly sequence

Refer to illustrations 7.5a, 7.5b, 7.5c and 7.5d
1   It's much easier to disassemble and work on the engine if it's mounted on a portable engine stand. A stand can often be rented quite cheaply from an equipment rental yard. Before the engine is mounted on a stand, the flywheel/driveplate should be removed from the engine.

2   If a stand isn't available, it's possible to disassemble the engine with it blocked up on the floor. Be extra careful not to tip or drop the engine when working without a stand.

3   If you're going to obtain a rebuilt engine, all external components must come off first, to be transferred to the replacement engine, just as they will if you're doing a complete engine overhaul yourself. These include:

Alternator and brackets
Emissions control components
Distributor, spark plug wires and spark plugs
Thermostat and housing cover
Water pump
Carburetor or EFI components
Intake/exhaust manifolds
Oil filter
Engine mounts
Clutch and flywheel/driveplate
Engine rear plate (2.2L engine only)

Note: When removing the external components from the engine, pay close attention to details that may be helpful or important during installation. Note the installed position of gaskets, seals, spacers, pins, brackets, washers, bolts and other small items.

4   If you're obtaining a short block, which consists of the engine block, crankshaft, pistons and connecting rods all assembled, then the cylinder head, oil pan and oil pump will have to be removed as well. See Engine rebuilding alternatives for additional information regarding the different possibilities to be considered.

5   If you're planning a complete overhaul, the engine must be disassembled and the internal components removed in the following order **(see illustrations)**:

Camshaft cover
Timing belt cover
Timing belt and sprockets
Intake and exhaust manifolds
Camshaft
Rocker arms and lash adjusters (2.2L engine only)
Cam followers (1.7L engine only)
Cylinder head
Oil pan
Oil pump
Piston/connecting rod assemblies
Rear main oil seal/housing
Crankshaft and main bearings

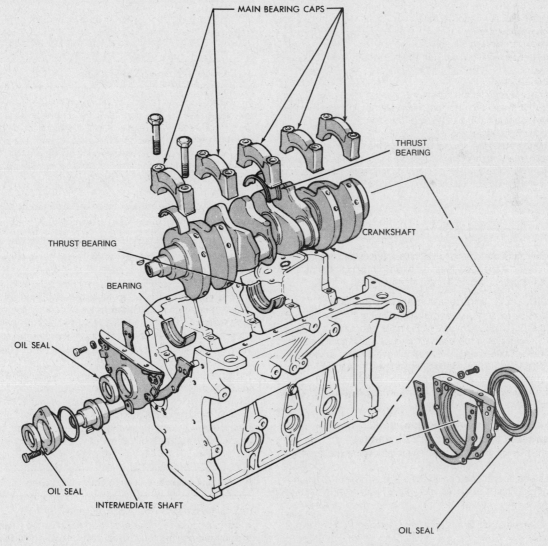

7.5a   Engine block components – exploded view (1.7L engine)

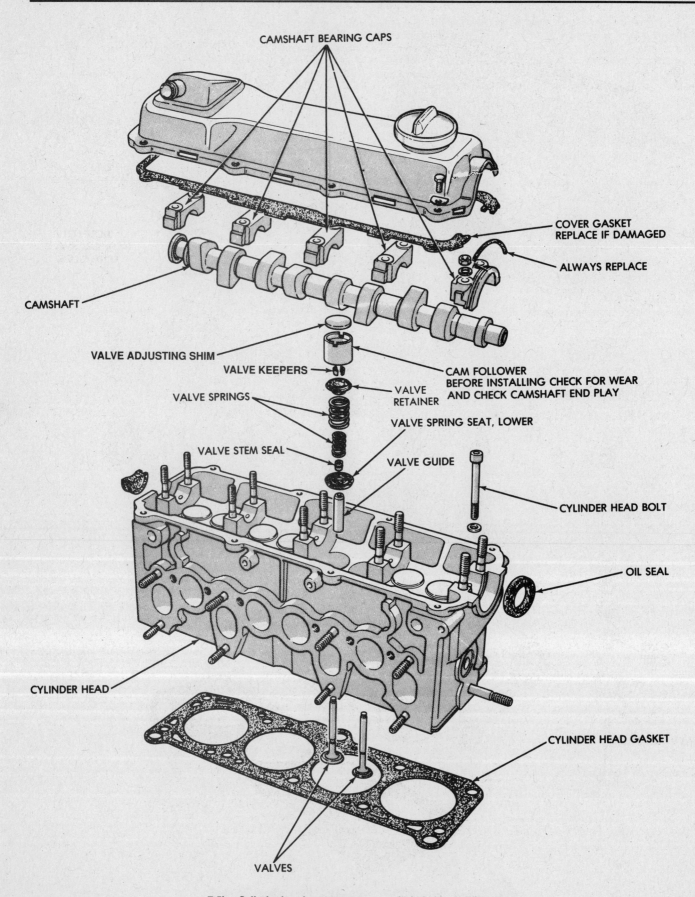

CAMSHAFT BEARING CAPS

COVER GASKET
REPLACE IF DAMAGED

ALWAYS REPLACE

CAMSHAFT

VALVE ADJUSTING SHIM

VALVE KEEPERS

CAM FOLLOWER
BEFORE INSTALLING CHECK FOR WEAR
AND CHECK CAMSHAFT END PLAY

VALVE SPRINGS

VALVE
RETAINER

VALVE SPRING SEAT, LOWER

VALVE STEM SEAL

VALVE GUIDE

CYLINDER HEAD BOLT

OIL SEAL

CYLINDER HEAD

CYLINDER HEAD GASKET

VALVES

7.5b Cylinder head components – exploded view (1.7L engine)

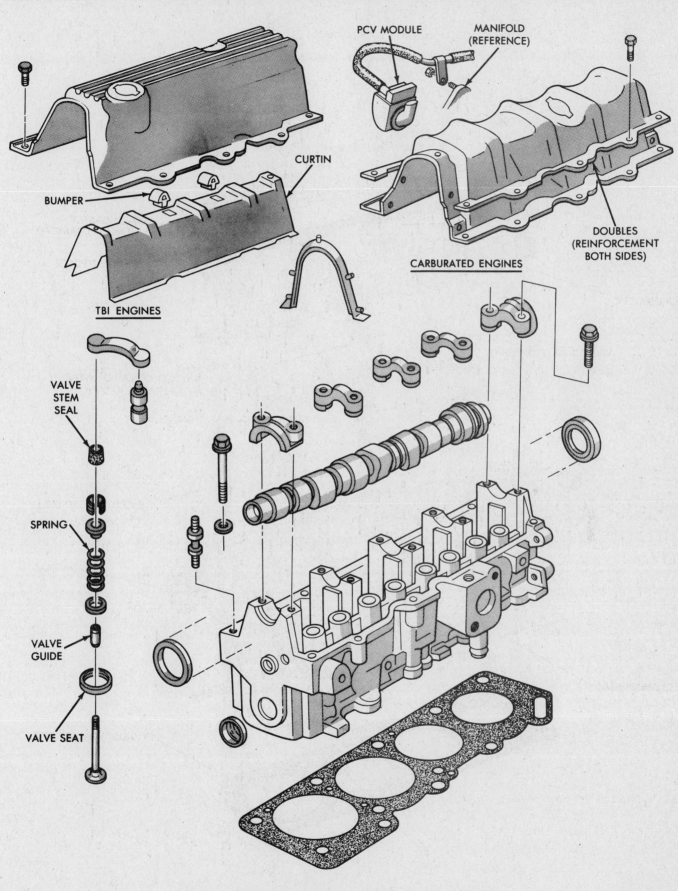

PCV MODULE

MANIFOLD (REFERENCE)

CURTIN

BUMPER

DOUBLES (REINFORCEMENT BOTH SIDES)

TBI ENGINES

CARBURATED ENGINES

VALVE STEM SEAL

SPRING

VALVE GUIDE

VALVE SEAT

2B

7.5c Cylinder head components – exploded view (2.2L engine)

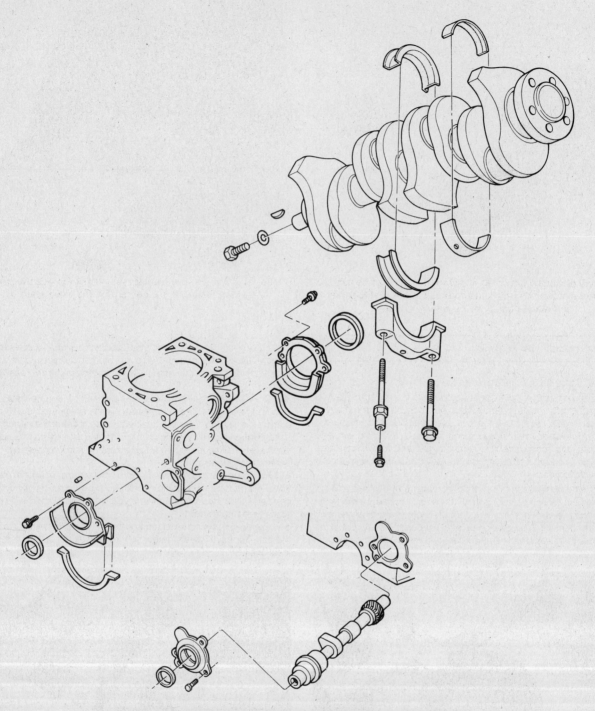

7.5d   Engine block components – exploded view (2.2L engine)

6   Before beginning the disassembly and overhaul procedures, make sure the following items are available. Also, refer to Engine overhaul - reassembly sequence for a list of tools and materials needed for engine reassembly.

Common hand tools
Small cardboard boxes or plastic bags for storing parts
Gasket scraper
Ridge reamer
Gear puller
Micrometers

Telescoping gauges
Dial indicator set
Valve spring compressor
Cylinder surfacing hone
Piston ring groove cleaning tool
Electric drill motor
Tap and die set
Wire brushes
Oil gallery brushes
Cleaning solvent

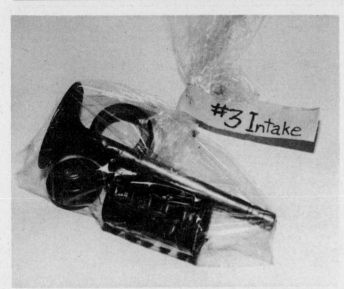

8.2 A small plastic bag, with an appropriate label, can be used to store the valve train components so they can be kept together and reinstalled in the original location

8.3a Use a valve spring compressor to compress the spring, then remove the keepers from the valve stem

8 Cylinder head – disassembly

Refer to illustrations 8.2, 8.3a, 8.3b and 8.4

Note: *New and rebuilt cylinder heads are commonly available for most engines at dealerships and auto parts stores. Due to the fact that some specialized tools are necessary for the disassembly and inspection procedures, and replacement parts may not be readily available, it may be more practical and economical for the home mechanic to purchase a replacement head rather than taking the time to disassemble, inspect and recondition the original.*

1   Cylinder head disassembly involves removal of the intake and exhaust valves and related components. If they're still in place, remove the camshaft, rocker arms and lash adjusters (2.2L engine only) or the cam followers and shims (1.7L engine only) (see Chapter 2, Part A). Label the parts or store them separately so they can be reinstalled in their original locations.

2   Before the valves are removed, arrange to label and store them, along with their related components, so they can be kept separate and reinstalled in the same valve guides they're removed from **(see illustration)**.

3   Compress the springs on the first valve with a spring compressor and remove the keepers **(see illustration)**. Carefully release the valve spring compressor and remove the retainer, the spring and the spring seat (if used). **Note:** *If you're working on a 1.7L engine, be very careful not to nick or otherwise damage the cam follower bores when compressing the valve springs* **(see illustration)**.

4   Pull the valve out of the head, then remove the oil seal from the guide. If the valve binds in the guide (won't pull through), push it back into the head and deburr the area around the keeper groove with a fine file or whetstone **(see illustration)**.

5   Repeat the procedure for the remaining valves. Remember to keep all the parts for each valve together so they can be reinstalled in the same locations.

2B

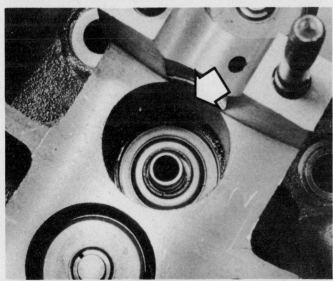

8.3b If you're working on a 1.7L engine, be very careful not to nick or gouge the cam follower bores in the cylinder head with the valve spring compressor

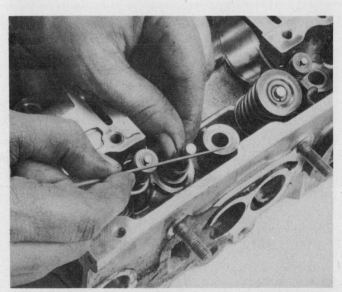

8.4 If the valve won't pull through the guide, deburr the edge of the stem end and the area around the top of the keeper groove with a file or whetstone

9.11   Check the cylinder head gasket surface for warpage by trying to slip a feeler gauge under the straightedge (see this Chapter's specifications for the maximum warpage allowed and use a feeler gauge of that thickness)

6   Once the valves and related components have been removed and stored in an organized manner, the head should be thoroughly cleaned and inspected. If a complete engine overhaul is being done, finish the engine disassembly procedures before beginning the cylinder head cleaning and inspection process.

---

9   Cylinder head – cleaning and inspection

Refer to illustrations 9.11, 9.13, 9.16, 9.17 and 9.18

1   Thorough cleaning of the cylinder head and related valve train components, followed by a detailed inspection, will enable you to decide how much valve service work must be done during the engine overhaul. **Note:** *If the engine was severely overheated, the cylinder head is probably warped (see Step 11).*

Cleaning

2   Scrape all traces of old gasket material and sealing compound off the head gasket, intake manifold and exhaust manifold sealing surfaces. Be very careful not to gouge the cylinder head. Special gasket removal solvents that soften gaskets and make removal much easier are available at auto parts stores.
3   Remove all built up scale from the coolant passages.
4   Run a stiff wire brush through the various holes to remove deposits that may have formed in them.
5   Run an appropriate size tap into each of the threaded holes to remove corrosion and thread sealant that may be present. If compressed air is available, use it to clear the holes of debris produced by this operation. **Warning:** *Wear eye protection when using compressed air!*
6   Clean the cylinder head with solvent and dry it thoroughly. Compressed air will speed the drying process and ensure that all holes and recessed areas are clean. **Note:** *Decarbonizing chemicals are available and may prove very useful when cleaning the cylinder head and valve train components. They're very caustic and should be used with caution. Be sure to follow the instructions on the container.*
7   Clean the rocker arms (2.2L engine only) or cam followers and shims (1.7L engine only) with solvent and dry them thoroughly (don't mix them up during the cleaning process). Don't submerge the lash adjusters (2.2L engine) in solvent! Compressed air will speed the drying process and can be used to clean out any oil passages.
8   Clean all the valve springs, spring seats, keepers and retainers with solvent and dry them thoroughly. Do the components from one valve at a time to avoid mixing up the parts.

9.13   A dial indicator can be used to determine the valve stem-to-guide clearance (move the valve stem as indicated by the arrows)

---

9   Scrape off any heavy deposits that may have formed on the valves, then use a motorized wire brush to remove deposits from the valve heads and stems. Again, make sure the valves don't get mixed up.

Inspection

Note: *Be sure to perform all of the following inspection procedures before concluding that machine shop work is required. Make a list of the items that need attention.*

Cylinder head

10   Inspect the head very carefully for cracks, evidence of coolant leakage and other damage. If cracks are found, check with an automotive machine shop concerning repair. If repair isn't possible, a new cylinder head should be obtained.
11   Using a straightedge and feeler gauge, check the head gasket mating surface for warpage **(see illustration)**. If the warpage exceeds the limit listed in this Chapter's Specifications, it can be resurfaced at an automotive machine shop.
12   Examine the valve seats in each of the combustion chambers. If they're pitted, cracked or burned, the head will require valve service that's beyond the scope of the home mechanic.
13   Check the valve stem-to-guide clearance by measuring the lateral movement of the valve stem with a dial indicator attached securely to the head **(see illustration)**. The valve must be in the guide and approximately 1/16-inch off the seat. The total valve stem movement indicated by the gauge needle must be divided by two to obtain the actual clearance. After this is done, if there's still some doubt regarding the condition of the valve guides they should be checked by an automotive machine shop (the cost should be minimal).

Valves

14   Carefully inspect each valve face for uneven wear, deformation, cracks, pits and burned areas.
15   Check the valve stem for scuffing and galling and the neck for cracks. Rotate the valve and check for any obvious indication that it's bent. Look for pits and excessive wear on the end of the stem. The presence of any of these conditions indicates the need for valve service by an automotive machine shop.
16   Measure the margin width on each valve **(see illustration)**. Any valve with a margin narrower than specified will have to be replaced with a new one.

Valve components

17   Check each valve spring for wear (on the ends) and pits. Measure the free length and compare it to this Chapter's Specifications **(see illustration)**. Any springs that are shorter than specified have sagged and should not be reused. The tension of all springs should be checked with a special fixture before deciding that they're suitable for use in a rebuilt engine (take the springs to an automotive machine shop for this check).
18   Stand each spring on a flat surface and check it for squareness **(see illustration)**. If any of the springs are distorted or sagged, replace all of them with new parts.

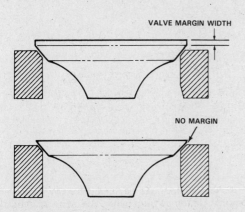

9.16 The margin width on each valve must be as specified (if no margin exists, the valve cannot be reused)

19 Check the spring retainers and keepers for obvious wear and cracks. Any questionable parts should be replaced with new ones, as extensive damage will occur if they fail during engine operation.

Camshaft, rocker arms, lash adjusters and camshaft followers

20 Refer to Part a for the inspection procedures for these components.
21 If the inspection process indicates that the valve components are in generally poor condition and worn beyond the limits specified, which is usually the case in an engine that's being overhauled, reassemble the valves in the cylinder head and refer to Section 10 for valve servicing recommendations.

---

10 Valves – servicing

1 Because of the complex nature of the job and the special tools and equipment needed, servicing of the valves, the valve seats and the valve guides, commonly known as a valve job, should be done by a professional.
2 The home mechanic can remove and disassemble the head, do the initial cleaning and inspection, then reassemble and deliver it to a dealer service department or an automotive machine shop for the actual service work. Doing the inspection will enable you to see what condition the head and valvetrain components are in and will ensure that you know what work and new parts are required when dealing with an automotive machine shop.
3 The dealer service department, or automotive machine shop, will remove the valves and springs, recondition or replace the valves and valve seats, recondition the valve guides, check and replace the valve springs, spring retainers and keepers (as necessary), replace the valve seals with new ones, reassemble the valve components and make sure the installed spring height is correct. The cylinder head gasket surface will also be resurfaced if it's warped.
4 After the valve job has been performed by a professional, the head will be in like new condition. When the head is returned, be sure to clean it again before installation on the engine to remove any metal particles and abrasive grit that may still be present from the valve service or head resurfacing operations. Use compressed air, if available, to blow out all the oil holes and passages.

---

11 Cylinder head – reassembly

Refer to illustrations 11.3, 11.6 and 11.8
1 Regardless of whether or not the head was sent to an automotive repair shop for valve servicing, make sure it's clean before beginning reassembly.
2 If the head was sent out for valve servicing, the valves and related components will already be in place. Begin the reassembly procedure with Step 8.

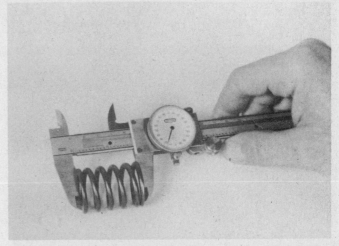

9.17 Measure the free length of each valve spring with a dial or vernier caliper

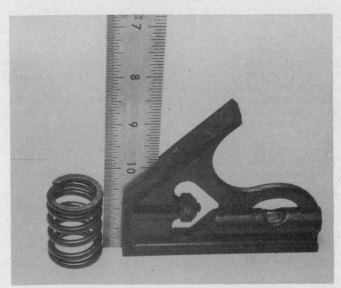

9.18 Check each valve spring for squareness

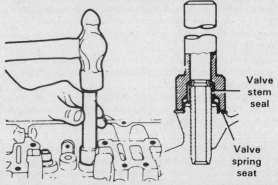

Valve stem seal

Valve spring seat

11.3 Using a deep socket and hammer (or the special seal installation tool shown here, if you've got one), gently tap each seal into place until it's completely seated on the guide – don't twist or cock the seal during installation or it won't seal properly

---

3 Install new seals on each of the intake valve guides. Using a hammer and a deep socket or seal installation tool, gently tap each seal into place until it's completely seated on the guide **(see illustration)**. Don't twist or cock the seals during installation or they won't seal properly on the valve stems.

2B

4   Beginning at one end of the head, lubricate and install the first valve. Apply moly-based grease or clean engine oil to the valve stem.
5   Drop the spring seat (if used) over the valve guide and set the valve spring and retainer in place.

11.6   Apply a small dab of grease to each keeper as shown here before installation – it will hold them in place on the valve stem as the spring is released

11.8   After you've reassembled the head, be sure to check the valve spring installed height for each valve

6   Compress the spring with a valve spring compressor and carefully install the keepers in the groove, then slowly release the compressor and make sure the keepers seat properly. Apply a small dab of grease to each keeper to hold it in place if necessary **(see illustration)**.
7   Repeat the procedure for the remaining valves. Be sure to return the components to their original locations – don't mix them up!
8   Check the installed valve spring height with a ruler graduated in 1/32-inch increments or a dial caliper. If the head was sent out for service work, the installed height should be correct (but don't automatically assume it is). The measurement is taken from the top of each spring seat or shim(s) (if used) to the bottom of the retainer **(see illustration)**. If the height is greater than specified, shims can be added under the springs to correct it. **Caution:** *Don't, under any circumstances, shim the springs to the point where the installed height is less than specified.*
9   Refer to Part A and install the cam followers and shims (1.7L engine only), the lash adjusters and rocker arms (2.2L engine only) and the camshaft.

12   Pistons/connecting rods – removal

Refer to illustrations 12.1, 12.3 and 12.6
Note: *Prior to removing the piston/connecting rod assemblies, remove the cylinder head, the oil pan and the oil pump by referring to the appropriate Sections in Chapter 2, Part A.*
1   Use your fingernail to feel if a ridge has formed at the upper limit of ring travel (about 1/4-inch down from the top of each cylinder). If carbon deposits or cylinder wear have produced ridges, they must be completely removed with a special tool **(see illustration)**. Follow the manufacturer's instructions provided with the tool. Failure to remove the ridges before attempting to remove the piston/connecting rod assemblies may result in piston damage.
2   After the cylinder ridges have been removed, turn the engine upside-down so the crankshaft is facing up.
3   Before the connecting rods are removed, check the endplay with feeler gauges. Slide them between the first connecting rod and the crankshaft throw until the play is removed **(see illustration)**. The endplay is equal to the thickness of the feeler gauge(s). If the endplay exceeds the limit listed in this Chapter's Specifications, new connecting rods will be required. If new rods (or a new crankshaft) are installed, the endplay may fall under the specified minimum (if it does, the rods will have to be machined to restore it – consult an automotive machine shop for advice if necessary). Repeat the procedure for the remaining connecting rods.
4   Check the connecting rods and caps for identification marks. If they aren't plainly marked, use a small center punch to make the appropriate

12.1   A ridge reamer is required to remove the ridge from the top of each cylinder – do this before removing the pistons!

12.3   Check the connecting rod side clearance with a feeler gauge as shown

number of indentations on each rod and cap (1, 2, 3 or 4, depending on the cylinder they're associated with).

5 Loosen each of the connecting rod cap nuts 1/2-turn at a time until they can be removed by hand. Remove the number one connecting rod cap and bearing insert. Don't drop the bearing insert out of the cap.

6 Slip a short length of plastic or rubber hose over each connecting rod cap bolt to protect the crankshaft journal and cylinder wall as the piston is removed **(see illustration)**.

7 Remove the bearing insert and push the connecting rod/piston assembly out through the top of the engine. Use a wooden hammer handle to push on the upper bearing surface in the connecting rod. If resistance is felt, double-check to make sure all of the ridge was removed from the cylinder.

8 Repeat the procedure for the remaining cylinders.

9 After removal, reassemble the connecting rod caps and bearing inserts in their respective connecting rods and install the cap nuts finger tight. Leaving the old bearing inserts in place until reassembly will help prevent the connecting rod bearing surfaces from being accidentally nicked or gouged.

10 Don't separate the pistons from the connecting rods (see Section 17 for additional information).

---

13 Crankshaft – removal

Refer to illustrations 13.1, 13.3, 13.4a, 13.4b, 13.4c and 13.4d

Note: *The crankshaft can be removed only after the engine has been removed from the vehicle. It's assumed the flywheel or driveplate, timing belt, oil pan, oil pump and piston/connecting rod assemblies have already been removed. Since the engine is equipped with a one-piece rear main oil seal, the seal housing must also be unbolted and separated from the block before proceeding with crankshaft removal.*

1 Before the crankshaft is removed, check the endplay. Mount a dial indicator with the stem in line with the crankshaft and just touching one of the crank throws **(see illustration)**.

2 Push the crankshaft all the way to the rear and zero the dial indicator. Next, pry the crankshaft to the front as far as possible and check the reading on the dial indicator. The distance that it moves is the endplay. If it's greater than specified, check the crankshaft thrust surfaces for wear. If no wear is evident, new main bearings should correct the play.

3 If a dial indicator isn't available, feeler gauges can be used. Gently pry or push the crankshaft all the way to the front of the engine. Slip feeler gauges between the crankshaft and the front face of the thrust main bearing to determine the clearance **(see illustration)**.

4 Check the main bearing caps to see if they're marked to indicate their locations. They should be numbered consecutively from the front of the engine to the rear. If they aren't, mark them with number stamping dies or a center punch **(see illustrations)**. Main bearing caps either have a cast-in

12.6 To prevent damage to the crankshaft journals and cylinder walls, slip sections of rubber or plastic hose over the rod bolts before removing the pistons

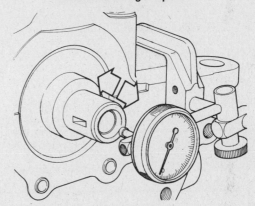

13.1 Checking crankshaft endplay with a dial indicator

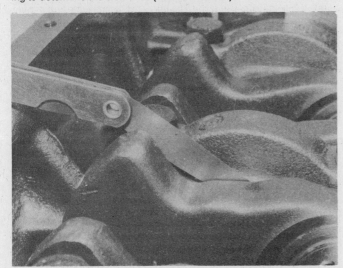

13.3 Checking crankshaft endplay with a feeler gauge

13.4a Use a center punch or number stamping dies to mark the main bearing caps to ensure installation in their original locations on the block (make the punch marks near one of the bolt heads)

2B

13.4b   Mark the caps in order from the front of the engine to the rear (one mark for the front cap, two for the second one and so on)

13.4c   The arrow on the main bearing cap indicates the front of the engine

arrow, which points to the front of the engine **(see illustration)** or an offset number **(see illustration)** which, when installed opposite the oil pump, insures correct orientation of the cap.

5   Loosen the main bearing cap bolts 1/4-turn at a time each, until they can be removed by hand. Note if any stud bolts are used and make sure they're returned to their original locations when the crankshaft is reinstalled.

6   Gently tap the caps with a soft-face hammer, then separate them from the engine block. If necessary, use the bolts as levers to remove the caps. Try not to drop the bearing inserts if they come out with the caps.

7   Carefully lift the crankshaft out of the engine. It may be a good idea to have an assistant available, since the crankshaft is quite heavy. With the bearing inserts in place in the engine block and main bearing caps, return the caps to their respective locations on the engine block and tighten the bolts finger tight.

14   Engine block – cleaning

Refer to illustrations 14.1, 14.8 and 14.10

Caution: *The core plugs (also known as freeze or soft plugs) may be difficult or impossible to retrieve if they're driven into the block coolant passages.*

1   Drill a small hole in the center of each core plug and pull them out with an auto body type dent puller **(see illustration)**.

2   Using a gasket scraper, remove all traces of gasket material from the engine block. Be very careful not to nick or gouge the gasket sealing surfaces.

3   Remove the main bearing caps and separate the bearing inserts from the caps and the engine block. Tag the bearings, indicating which location they were removed from and whether they were in the cap or the block, then set them aside.

13.4d   If there are offset numbers already stamped on the bearing caps, make sure the number is on the side opposite the oil pump (1.7L engine)

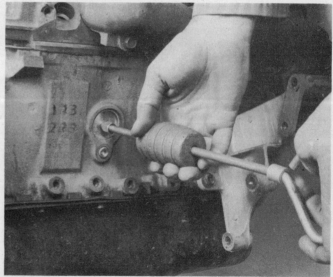

14.1   The core plugs should be removed with a puller – if they're driven into the block, they may be impossible to retrieve

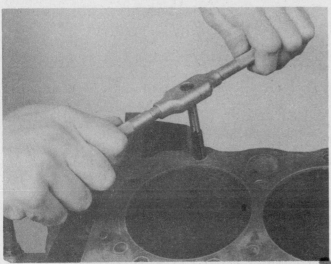

14.8   All bolt holes in the block – particularly the main bearing cap and head bolt holes – should be cleaned and restored with a tap (be sure to remove debris from the holes after this is done)

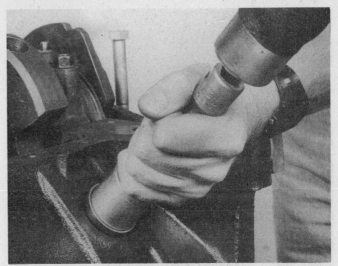

14.10   A large socket on an extension can be used to drive the new core plugs into the bores

4   Remove all of the threaded oil gallery plugs from the block. The plugs are usually very tight – they may have to be drilled out and the holes re-tapped. Use new plugs when the engine is reassembled.

5   If the engine is extremely dirty it should be taken to an automotive machine shop to be steam cleaned or hot tanked.

6   After the block is returned, clean all oil holes and oil galleries one more time. Brushes specifically designed for this purpose are available at most auto parts stores. Flush the passages with warm water until the water runs clear, dry the block thoroughly and wipe all machined surfaces with a light, rust preventive oil. If you have access to compressed air, use it to speed the drying process and to blow out all the oil holes and galleries. **Warning:** *Wear eye protection when using compressed air!*

7   If the block isn't extremely dirty or sludged up, you can do an adequate cleaning job with hot soapy water and a stiff brush. Take plenty of time and do a thorough job. Regardless of the cleaning method used, be sure to clean all oil holes and galleries very thoroughly, dry the block completely and coat all machined surfaces with light oil.

8   The threaded holes in the block must be clean to ensure accurate torque readings during reassembly. Run the proper size tap into each of the holes to remove rust, corrosion, thread sealant or sludge and restore damaged threads **(see illustration)**. If possible, use compressed air to clear the holes of debris produced by this operation. Now is a good time to clean the threads on the head bolts and the main bearing cap bolts as well.

9   Reinstall the main bearing caps and tighten the bolts finger tight.

10   After coating the sealing surfaces of the new core plugs with Permatex no. 2 sealant, install them in the engine block **(see illustration)**. Make sure they're driven in straight and seated properly or leakage could result. Special tools are available for this purpose, but a large socket, with an outside diameter that will just slip into the core plug, a 1/2-inch drive extension and a hammer will work just as well.

11   Apply non-hardening sealant (such as Permatex no. 2 or Teflon pipe sealant) to the new oil gallery plugs and thread them into the holes in the block. Make sure they're tightened securely.

12   If the engine isn't going to be reassembled right away, cover it with a large plastic trash bag to keep it clean.

15   Engine block – inspection

Refer to illustrations 15.4a, 15.4b and 15.4c

1   Before the block is inspected, it should be cleaned as described in Section 14.

2   Visually check the block for cracks, rust and corrosion. Look for stripped threads in the threaded holes. It's also a good idea to have the block checked for hidden cracks by an automotive machine shop that has

the special equipment to do this type of work. If defects are found, have the block repaired, if possible, or replaced.

3   Check the cylinder bores for scuffing and scoring.

4   Measure the diameter of each cylinder at the top (just under the ridge area), center and bottom of the cylinder bore, parallel to the crankshaft axis **(see illustrations)**.

2B

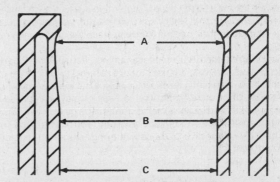

15.4a   Measure the diameter of each cylinder just under the wear ridge (A), at the center (B) and at the bottom (C)

15.4b   The ability to "feel" when the telescoping gauge is at the correct point will be developed over time, so work slowly and repeat the check until you're satisfied the bore measurement is accurate

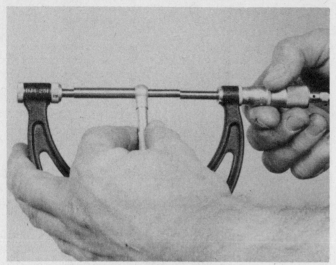

15.4c   The gauge is then measured with a micrometer to determine the bore size

16.3a   A "bottle brush" hone will produce better results if you've never honed cylinders before

5   Next, measure each cylinder's diameter at the same three locations across the crankshaft axis. Compare the results to the figures listed in this Chapter's Specifications.

6   If the required precision measuring tools aren't available, the piston-to-cylinder clearances can be obtained, though not quite as accurately, using feeler gauge stock. Feeler gauge stock comes in 12-inch lengths and various thicknesses and is generally available at auto parts stores.

7   To check the clearance, select a feeler gauge and slip it into the cylinder along with the matching piston. The piston must be positioned exactly as it normally would be. The feeler gauge must be between the piston and cylinder on one of the thrust faces (90-degrees to the piston pin bore).

8   The piston should slip through the cylinder (with the feeler gauge in place) with moderate pressure.

9   If it falls through or slides through easily, the clearance is excessive and a new piston will be required. If the piston binds at the lower end of the cylinder and is loose toward the top, the cylinder is tapered. If tight spots are encountered as the piston/feeler gauge is rotated in the cylinder, the cylinder is out-of-round.

10   Repeat the procedure for the remaining pistons and cylinders.

11   If the cylinder walls are badly scuffed or scored, or if they're out-of-round or tapered beyond the limits given in this Chapter's Specifications, have the engine block rebored and honed at an automotive machine shop. If a rebore is done, oversize pistons and rings will be required.

12   If the cylinders are in reasonably good condition and not worn to the outside of the limits, and if the piston-to-cylinder clearances can be maintained properly, then they don't have to be rebored. Honing is all that's necessary (see Section 16).

16   Cylinder honing

Refer to illustrations 16.3a and 16.3b

1   Prior to engine reassembly, the cylinder bores must be honed so the new piston rings will seat correctly and provide the best possible combustion chamber seal. **Note:** *If you don't have the tools or don't want to tackle the honing operation, most automotive machine shops will do it for a reasonable fee.*

2   Before honing the cylinders, install the main bearing caps and tighten the bolts to the specified torque.

3   Two types of cylinder hones are commonly available – the flex hone or "bottle brush" type and the more traditional surfacing hone with spring-loaded stones. Both will do the job, but for the less experienced mechanic the "bottle brush" hone will probably be easier to use. You'll also need some kerosene or honing oil, rags and an electric drill motor. Proceed as follows:

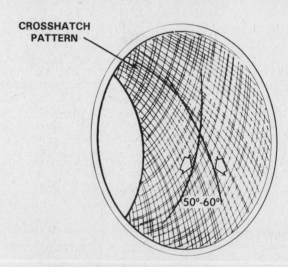

CROSSHATCH PATTERN

50°-60°

16.3b   The cylinder hone should leave a smooth, crosshatch pattern with the lines intersecting at approximately a 60-degree angle

a)   Mount the hone in the drill motor, compress the stones and slip it into the first cylinder **(see illustration)**. Be sure to wear safety goggles or a face shield!

b)   Lubricate the cylinder with plenty of honing oil, turn on the drill and move the hone up-and-down in the cylinder at a pace that will produce a fine crosshatch pattern on the cylinder walls. Ideally, the crosshatch lines should intersect at approximately a 60-degree angle **(see illustration)**. Be sure to use plenty of lubricant and don't take off any more material than absolutely necessary to produce the desired finish. **Note:** *Piston ring manufacturers may specify a smaller crosshatch angle than the traditional 60-degrees – read and follow any instructions included with the new rings.*

c)   Don't withdraw the hone from the cylinder while it's running. Instead, shut off the drill and continue moving the hone up-and-down in the cylinder until it comes to a complete stop, then compress the stones and withdraw the hone. If you're using a "bottle brush" type hone, stop the drill motor, then turn the chuck in the normal direction of rotation while withdrawing the hone from the cylinder.

d)   Wipe the oil out of the cylinder and repeat the procedure for the remaining cylinders.

17.4a The piston ring grooves can be cleaned with a special tool, as shown here, . . .

17.4b . . . or a section of a broken ring

4   After the honing job is complete, chamfer the top edges of the cylinder bores with a small file so the rings won't catch when the pistons are installed. Be very careful not to nick the cylinder walls with the end of the file.
5   The entire engine block must be washed again very thoroughly with warm, soapy water to remove all traces of the abrasive grit produced during the honing operation. **Note:** *The bores can be considered clean when a lint-free white cloth – dampened with clean engine oil – used to wipe them out doesn't pick up any more honing residue, which will show up as gray areas on the cloth. Be sure to run a brush through all oil holes and galleries and flush them with running water.*
6   After rinsing, dry the block and apply a coat of light rust preventive oil to all machined surfaces. Wrap the block in a plastic trash bag to keep it clean and set it aside until reassembly.

17 Pistons/connecting rods – inspection

Refer to illustrations 17.4a, 17.4b, 17.10 and 17.11

1   Before the inspection process can be carried out, the piston/connecting rod assemblies must be cleaned and the original piston rings removed from the pistons. **Note:** *Always use new piston rings when the engine is reassembled.*
2   Using a piston ring installation tool, carefully remove the rings from the pistons. Be careful not to nick or gouge the pistons in the process.
3   Scrape all traces of carbon from the top of the piston. A hand-held wire brush or a piece of fine emery cloth can be used once the majority of the deposits have been scraped away. Do not, under any circumstances, use a wire brush mounted in a drill motor to remove deposits from the pistons. The piston material is soft and may be eroded away by the wire brush.
4   Use a piston ring groove cleaning tool to remove carbon deposits from the ring grooves. If a tool isn't available, a piece broken off the old ring will do the job. Be very careful to remove only the carbon deposits – don't remove any metal and don't nick or scratch the sides of the ring grooves **(see illustrations)**.
5   Once the deposits have been removed, clean the piston/rod assemblies with solvent and dry them with compressed air (if available). Make sure the oil return holes in the back sides of the ring grooves are clear.
6   If the pistons and cylinder walls aren't damaged or worn excessively, and if the engine block is not rebored, new pistons won't be necessary. Normal piston wear appears as even vertical wear on the piston thrust surfaces and slight looseness of the top ring in its groove. New piston rings, however, should always be used when an engine is rebuilt.
7   Carefully inspect each piston for cracks around the skirt, at the pin bosses and at the ring lands.

8   Look for scoring and scuffing on the thrust faces of the skirt, holes in the piston crown and burned areas at the edge of the crown. If the skirt is scored or scuffed, the engine may have been suffering from overheating and/or abnormal combustion, which caused excessively high operating temperatures. The cooling and lubrication systems should be checked thoroughly. A hole in the piston crown is an indication that abnormal combustion (preignition) was occurring. Burned areas at the edge of the piston crown are usually evidence of spark knock (detonation). If any of the above problems exist, the causes must be corrected or the damage will occur again. The causes may include intake air leaks, incorrect fuel/air mixture, incorrect ignition timing and EGR system malfunctions.
9   Corrosion of the piston, in the form of small pits, indicates that coolant is leaking into the combustion chamber and/or the crankcase. Again, the cause must be corrected or the problem may persist in the rebuilt engine.
10   Measure the piston ring side clearance by laying a new piston ring in each ring groove and slipping a feeler gauge in beside it **(see illustration)**. Check the clearance at three or four locations around each groove. Be sure to use the correct ring for each groove – they are different. If the side clearance is greater than the limit listed in this Chapter's Specifications, new pistons will have to be used.

2B

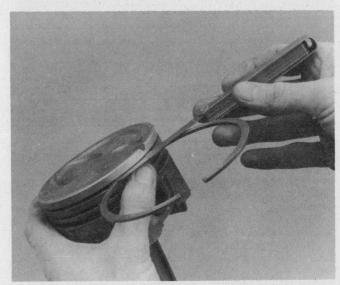

17.10 Check the ring side clearance with a feeler gauge at several points around the groove

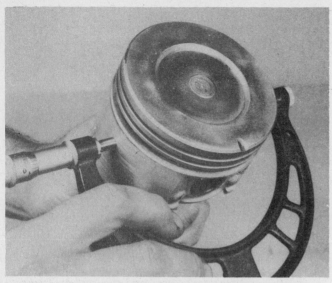

17.11   Measure the piston diameter at a 90-degree angle to the piston pin and in line with it

18.1   Use a wire or stiff plastic bristle brush to clean the oil passages in the crankshaft

11   Check the piston-to-bore clearance by measuring the bore (see Section 15) and the piston diameter. Make sure the pistons and bores are correctly matched. Measure the piston across the skirt, at a 90-degree angle to and in line with the piston pin **(see illustration)**. Subtract the piston diameter from the bore diameter to obtain the clearance. If it's greater than the limit listed in this Chapter's Specifications, the block will have to be rebored and new pistons and rings installed.

12   Check the piston-to-rod clearance by twisting the piston and rod in opposite directions. Any noticeable play indicates excessive wear, which must be corrected. The piston/connecting rod assemblies should be taken to an automotive machine shop to have the pistons and rods resized and new pins installed.

13   If the pistons must be removed from the connecting rods for any reason, they should be taken to an automotive machine shop. While they are there, have the connecting rods checked for bend and twist, since automotive machine shops have special equipment for this purpose. **Note:** *Unless new pistons and/or connecting rods must be installed, do not disassemble the pistons and connecting rods.*

14   Check the connecting rods for cracks and other damage. Temporarily remove the rod caps, lift out the old bearing inserts, wipe the rod and cap bearing surfaces clean and inspect them for nicks, gouges and scratches. After checking the rods, replace the old bearings, slip the caps into place and tighten the nuts finger tight. **Note:** *If the engine is being rebuilt because of a connecting rod knock, be sure to install new rods.*

18   Crankshaft – inspection

Refer to illustrations 18.1, 18.3, 18.4, 18.6 and 18.8

1   Clean the crankshaft with solvent and dry it with compressed air (if available). Be sure to clean the oil holes with a stiff brush **(see illustration)** and flush them with solvent.

2   Check the main and connecting rod bearing journals for uneven wear, scoring, pits and cracks.

3   Rub a penny across each journal several times **(see illustration)**. If a

18.3   Rubbing a penny lengthwise on each journal will reveal its condition – if copper rubs off and is embedded in the crankshaft, the journals should be reground

18.4   The oil holes should be chamfered so sharp edges don't gouge or scratch the new bearings

18.6 Measure the diameter of each crankshaft journal at several points to detect taper and out-of-round conditions

18.8 If the seals have worn grooves in the crankshaft journals, or if the seal contact surfaces are nicked or scratched, the new seals will leak

journal picks up copper from the penny, it's too rough and must be reground.

4 Remove all burrs from the crankshaft oil holes with a stone, file or scraper (see illustration).

5 Check the rest of the crankshaft for cracks and other damage. It should be magnafluxed to reveal hidden cracks – an automotive machine shop will handle the procedure.

6 Using a micrometer, measure the diameter of the main and connecting rod journals and compare the results to the figures listed in this Chapter's Specifications (see illustration). By measuring the diameter at a number of points around each journal's circumference, you'll be able to determine whether or not the journal is out-of-round. Take the measurement at each end of the journal, near the crank throws, to determine if the journal is tapered.

7 If the crankshaft journals are damaged, tapered, out-of-round or worn beyond the limits given in the Specifications, have the crankshaft reground by an automotive machine shop. Be sure to use the correct size bearing inserts if the crankshaft is reconditioned.

8 Check the oil seal journals at each end of the crankshaft for wear and damage. If the seal has worn a groove in the journal, or if it's nicked or scratched (see illustration), the new seal may leak when the engine is reassembled. In some cases, an automotive machine shop may be able to repair the journal by pressing on a thin sleeve. If repair isn't feasible, a new or different crankshaft should be installed.

9 Refer to Section 19 and examine the main and rod bearing inserts.

19 Main and connecting rod bearings – inspection

Refer to illustration 19.1

1 Even though the main and connecting rod bearings should be replaced with new ones during the engine overhaul, the old bearings should be retained for close examination, as they may reveal valuable information about the condition of the engine (see illustration). **Note:** *On turbocharger-equipped vehicles, the turbocharger must be flushed with clean oil whenever a rod or main bearing is replaced.*

2 Bearing failure occurs because of lack of lubrication, the presence of dirt or other foreign particles, overloading the engine and corrosion. Regardless of the cause of bearing failure, it must be corrected before the engine is reassembled to prevent it from happening again.

3 When examining the bearings, remove them from the engine block, the main bearing caps, the connecting rods and the rod caps and lay them out on a clean surface in the same general position as their location in the engine. This will enable you to match any bearing problems with the corresponding crankshaft journal.

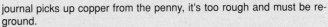

19.1 Typical bearing failures

4 Dirt and other foreign particles get into the engine in a variety of ways. It may be left in the engine during assembly, or it may pass through filters or the PCV system. It may get into the oil, and from there into the bearings. Metal chips from machining operations and normal engine wear are often present. Abrasives are sometimes left in engine components after reconditioning, especially when parts aren't thoroughly cleaned using the proper methods. Whatever the source, these foreign objects often end up embedded in the soft bearing material and are easily recognized. Large particles will not embed in the bearing and will score or gouge the bearing and journal. The best prevention for this cause of bearing failure is to clean all parts thoroughly and keep everything spotlessly clean during engine assembly. Frequent and regular engine oil and filter changes are also recommended.

5   Lack of lubrication (or lubrication breakdown) has a number of interrelated causes. Excessive heat (which thins the oil), overloading (which squeezes the oil from the bearing face) and oil leakage or throw off (from excessive bearing clearances, worn oil pump or high engine speeds) all contribute to lubrication breakdown. Blocked oil passages, which usually are the result of misaligned oil holes in a bearing shell, will also oil starve a bearing and destroy it. When lack of lubrication is the cause of bearing failure, the bearing material is wiped or extruded from the steel backing of the bearing. Temperatures may increase to the point where the steel backing turns blue from overheating.

6   Driving habits can have a definite effect on bearing life. Full throttle, low speed operation (lugging the engine) puts very high loads on bearings, which tends to squeeze out the oil film. These loads cause the bearings to flex, which produces fine cracks in the bearing face (fatigue failure). Eventually the bearing material will loosen in pieces and tear away from the steel backing. Short trip driving leads to corrosion of bearings because insufficient engine heat is produced to drive off the condensed water and corrosive gases. These products collect in the engine oil, forming acid and sludge. As the oil is carried to the engine bearings, the acid attacks and corrodes the bearing material.

7   Incorrect bearing installation during engine assembly will lead to bearing failure as well. Tight fitting bearings leave insufficient bearing oil clearance and will result in oil starvation. Dirt or foreign particles trapped behind a bearing insert result in high spots on the bearing which lead to failure.

20   Engine overhaul – reassembly sequence

1 Before beginning engine reassembly, make sure you have all the necessary new parts, gaskets and seals as well as the following items on hand:
Common hand tools
A 1/2-inch drive torque wrench
Piston ring installation tool
Piston ring compressor
Short lengths of rubber or plastic hose to fit over connecting rod bolts
Plastigage
Feeler gauges
A fine-tooth file
New engine oil
Engine assembly lube or moly-based grease

Gasket sealant
Thread locking compound
2   To save time and avoid problems, engine reassembly must be done in the following general order:
Piston rings
Crankshaft and main bearings
Rear main oil seal/housing
Piston/connecting rod assemblies
Oil pump
Rocker arms and lash adjusters (2.2L engine only)
Cam followers and shims (1.7L engine only)
Camshaft
Cylinder head
Oil pan
Timing belt and sprockets
Timing cover
Intake and exhaust manifolds
Camshaft cover
Engine rear plate (2.2L engine only)
Flywheel/driveplate

21   Piston rings – installation

Refer to illustrations 21.3, 21.4, 21.5, 21.9a, 21.9b and 21.12
1   Before installing the new piston rings, the ring end gaps must be checked. It's assumed the piston ring side clearance has been checked and verified correct (see Section 17).
2   Lay out the piston/connecting rod assemblies and the new ring sets so the ring sets will be matched with the same piston and cylinder during the end gap measurement and engine assembly.
3   Insert the top (number one) ring into the first cylinder and square it up with the cylinder walls by pushing it in with the top of the piston **(see illustration)**. The ring should be near the bottom of the cylinder, at the lower limit of ring travel.
4   To measure the end gap, slip feeler gauges between the ends of the ring until a gauge equal to the gap width is found **(see illustration)**. The feeler gauge should slide between the ring ends with a slight amount of drag. Compare the measurement to this Chapter's Specifications. If the gap is larger or smaller than specified, double-check to make sure you have the correct rings before proceeding.

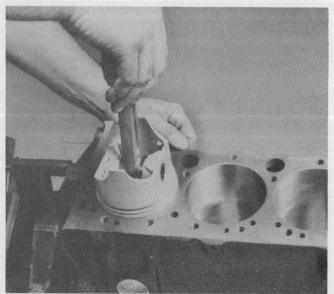

21.3   When checking piston ring end gap, the ring must be square in the cylinder bore (this is done by pushing the ring down with the top of a piston as shown)

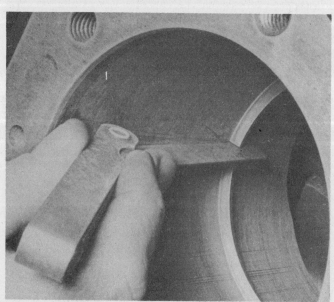

21.4   With the ring square in the cylinder, measure the end gap with a feeler gauge

21.5 If the end gap is too small, clamp a file in a vise and file the ring ends (from the outside in only) to enlarge the gap slightly

21.9a Installing the spacer/expander in the oil control ring groove

2B

5   If the gap is too small, it must be enlarged or the ring ends may come in contact with each other during engine operation, which can cause serious damage to the engine. The end gap can be increased by filing the ring ends very carefully with a fine file. Mount the file in a vise equipped with soft jaws, slip the ring over the file with the ends contacting the file face and slowly move the ring to remove material from the ends. When performing this operation, file only from the outside in **(see illustration)**.

6   Excess end gap isn't critical unless it's greater than 0.040-inch. Again, double-check to make sure you have the correct rings for the engine.

7   Repeat the procedure for each ring that will be installed in the first cylinder and for each ring in the remaining cylinders. Remember to keep rings, pistons and cylinders matched up.

8   Once the ring end gaps have been checked/corrected, the rings can be installed on the pistons.

9   The oil control ring (lowest one on the piston) is usually installed first. It's composed of three separate components. Slip the spacer/expander into the groove **(see illustration)**. If an anti-rotation tang is used, make sure it's inserted into the drilled hole in the ring groove. Next, install the

lower side rail. Don't use a piston ring installation tool on the oil ring side rails, as they may be damaged. Instead, place one end of the side rail into the groove between the spacer/expander and the ring land, hold it firmly in place and slide a finger around the piston while pushing the rail into the groove **(see illustration)**. Next, install the upper side rail in the same manner.

10   After the three oil ring components have been installed, check to make sure both the upper and lower side rails can be turned smoothly in the ring groove.

11   The number two (middle) ring is installed next. It's usually stamped with a mark which must face up, toward the top of the piston. **Note:** *Always follow the instructions printed on the ring package or box – different manufacturers may require different approaches. Don't mix up the top and middle rings, as they have different cross sections.*

12   Use a piston ring installation tool and make sure the identification mark is facing the top of the piston, then slip the ring into the middle groove on the piston **(see illustration)**. Don't expand the ring any more than necessary to slide it over the piston.

13   Install the number one (top) ring in the same manner. Make sure the

21.9b DO NOT use a piston ring installation tool when installing the oil ring side rails

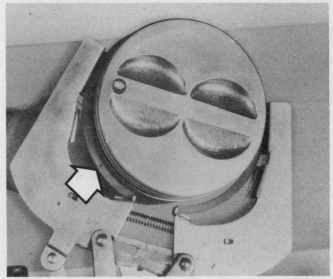

21.12 Installing the compression rings with a ring expander – the mark (arrow) must face up

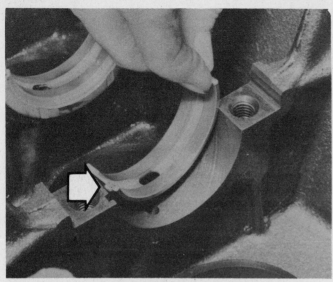

22.5   Make sure the tab on the bearing insert (arrow) fits into the recess in the block and the oil hole lines up with the oil passage in the block

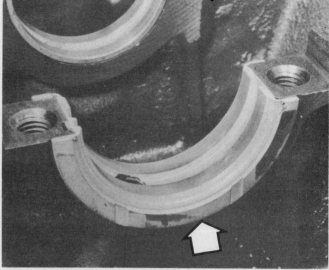

22.6   The thrust bearing (identified by the flange on each side – arrow) must be installed in the number three (center) cap and saddle

mark is facing up. Be careful not to confuse the number one and number two rings.

14   Repeat the procedure for the remaining pistons and rings.

22   Crankshaft – installation and main bearing oil clearance check

Refer to illustrations 22.5, 22.6, 22.11 and 22.15

1   Crankshaft installation is the first step in engine reassembly. It's assumed at this point that the engine block and crankshaft have been cleaned, inspected and repaired or reconditioned.

2   Position the engine with the bottom facing up.

3   Remove the main bearing cap bolts and lift out the caps. Lay them out in the proper order to ensure correct installation.

4   If they're still in place, remove the original bearing inserts from the block and the main bearing caps. Wipe the bearing surfaces of the block and caps with a clean, lint-free cloth. They must be kept spotlessly clean.

Main bearing oil clearance check

5   Clean the back sides of the new main bearing inserts and lay one in each main bearing saddle in the block. If one of the bearing inserts from each set has a large groove in it, make sure the grooved insert is installed in the block. Lay the other bearing from each set in the corresponding main bearing cap. Make sure the tab on the bearing insert fits into the recess in the block or cap. **Caution:** *The oil holes in the block must line up with the oil holes in the bearing insert* **(see illustration).** Do not hammer the bearing into place and don't nick or gouge the bearing faces. No lubrication should be used at this time.

6   The flanged thrust bearing must be installed in the number three (center) cap and saddle **(see illustration).**

7   Clean the faces of the bearings in the block and the crankshaft main bearing journals with a clean, lint-free cloth.

8   Check or clean the oil holes in the crankshaft, as any dirt here can go only one way – straight through the new bearings. Also check the rear seal contact surface very carefully for scratches and nicks that could damage the new seal lip and cause oil leaks. If the crankshaft is damaged, the only alternative is a new or different crankshaft.

9   Once you're certain the crankshaft is clean, carefully lay it in position in the main bearings.

10   Before the crankshaft can be permanently installed, the main bearing oil clearance must be checked.

11   Cut several pieces of the appropriate size Plastigage (they must be slightly shorter than the width of the main bearings) and place one piece on each crankshaft main bearing journal, parallel with the journal axis **(see illustration).**

12   Clean the faces of the bearings in the caps and install the caps in their respective positions (don't mix them up) with the arrows pointing toward the front of the engine. Don't disturb the Plastigage.

13   Starting with the center main and working out toward the ends, tighten the main bearing cap bolts, in three steps, to the torque listed in this Chapter's Specifications. Don't rotate the crankshaft at any time during this operation.

14   Remove the bolts and carefully lift off the main bearing caps. Keep them in order. Don't disturb the Plastigage or rotate the crankshaft. If any of the main bearing caps are difficult to remove, tap them gently from side-to-side with a soft-face hammer to loosen them.

15   Compare the width of the crushed Plastigage on each journal to the scale printed on the Plastigage envelope to obtain the main bearing oil clearance **(see illustration).** Check the Specifications to make sure it's correct.

22.11   Lay the Plastigage strips (arrow) on the main bearing journals, parallel to the crankshaft centerline

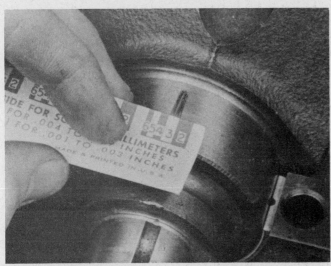

22.15   Compare the width of the crushed Plastigage to the scale on the envelope to determine the main bearing oil clearance (always take the measurement at the widest point of the Plastigage); be sure to use the correct scale – standard and metric ones are included

23.1   To remove the old crankshaft rear seal, support the housing on a pair of wood blocks and drive out the seal with a punch or screwdriver and hammer – make sure you don't damage the seal bore

16   If the clearance is not as specified, the bearing inserts may be the wrong size (which means different ones will be required). Before deciding that different inserts are needed, make sure no dirt or oil was between the bearing inserts and the caps or block when the clearance was measured. If the Plastigage was wider at one end than the other, the journal may be tapered (refer to Section 18).

17   Carefully scrape all traces of the Plastigage material off the main bearing journals and/or the bearing faces. Use your fingernail or the edge of a credit card – don't nick or scratch the bearing faces.

Final crankshaft installation

18   Carefully lift the crankshaft out of the engine.

19   Clean the bearing faces in the block, then apply a thin, uniform layer of moly-based grease or engine assembly lube to each of the bearing surfaces. Be sure to coat the thrust faces as well as the journal face of the thrust bearing.

20   Make sure the crankshaft journals are clean, then lay the crankshaft back in place in the block.

21   Clean the faces of the bearings in the caps, then apply lubricant to them.

22   Install the caps in their respective positions with the arrows pointing toward the front of the engine or with the bearing cap numbers aligned with each other (all on the side opposite the oil pump).

23   Install the bolts.

24   Tighten the bolts to the torque listed in this Chapter's Specifications. Work from the center out and approach the final torque in three steps.

25   Tap the ends of the crankshaft forward and backward with a lead or brass hammer to line up the main bearing and crankshaft thrust surfaces.

26   Retighten all main bearing cap bolts to the specified torque, starting with the center main and working out toward the ends.

27   Rotate the crankshaft a number of times by hand to check for any obvious binding.

28   Check the crankshaft endplay with a feeler gauge or a dial indicator as described in Section 13. The endplay should be correct if the crankshaft thrust faces aren't worn or damaged and new bearings have been installed.

29   Refer to Section 23 and install the new crankshaft rear seal, then bolt the housing to the block.

23   Rear main oil seal – installation

Refer to illustrations 23.1, 23.2 and 23.3

Note: *The crankshaft must be installed and the main bearing caps bolted in place before the new seal and housing assembly can be bolted to the block.*

1   Remove the old seal from the housing with a hammer and punch by driving it out from the back side **(see illustration)**. Be sure to note how far it's recessed into the housing bore before removing it; the new seal will have to be recessed an equal amount. Be very careful not to scratch or otherwise damage the bore in the housing or oil leaks could develop.

2   Make sure the housing is clean, then apply a thin coat of engine oil to the outer edge of the new seal. The seal must be pressed squarely into the housing bore, so hammering it into place isn't recommended. If you don't have access to a press, sandwich the housing and seal between two smooth pieces of wood and press the seal into place with the jaws of a large vise. If you don't have a vise big enough, lay the housing on a workbench and drive the seal into place with a block of wood and hammer **(see illustration)**. The pieces of wood must be thick enough to distribute the force evenly around the entire circumference of the seal. Work slowly and make sure the seal enters the bore squarely.

23.2   To install the new crankshaft rear seal in the housing, simply lay the housing on a clean, flat workbench, lay a block of wood on the seal and carefully tap it into place with a hammer

2B

23.3 Align the dowel pins with the holes (arrows) and gently push the seal onto the end of the crankshaft

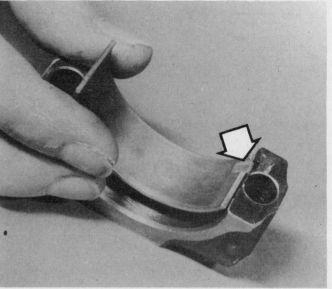

24.4 The tab on the bearing (arrow) must fit into the cap recess so the bearing will seat properly

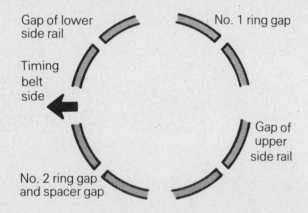

24.5 Position the ring gaps as shown here before installing the piston/connecting rod assemblies in the engine

3   Lubricate the seal lips with moly-based grease or engine assembly lube before you slip the seal/housing over the crankshaft and bolt it to the block. Use a new gasket – no sealant is required – and make sure the dowel pins are in place before installing the housing **(see illustration)**.
4   Tighten the housing bolts a little at a time until they're all snug.

24 Pistons/connecting rods – installation and rod bearing oil clearance check

Refer to illustrations 24.4, 24.5, 24.9a, 24.9b, 24.9c, 24.11, 24.13, 24.14 and 24.17
1   Before installing the piston/connecting rod assemblies, the cylinder walls must be perfectly clean, the top edge of each cylinder must be chamfered, and the crankshaft must be in place.
2   Remove the cap from the end of the number one connecting rod (refer to the marks made during removal). Remove the original bearing inserts and wipe the bearing surfaces of the connecting rod and cap with a clean, lint-free cloth. They must be kept spotlessly clean.

Connecting rod bearing oil clearance check
3   Clean the back side of the new upper bearing insert, then lay it in place in the connecting rod. Make sure the tab on the bearing fits into the recess in the rod. Don't hammer the bearing insert into place and be very careful not to nick or gouge the bearing face. Don't lubricate the bearing at this time.
4   Clean the back side of the other bearing insert and install it in the rod cap. Again, make sure the tab on the bearing fits into the recess in the cap **(see illustration)**, and don't apply any lubricant. It's critically important that the mating surfaces of the bearing and connecting rod are perfectly clean and oil free when they're assembled.
5   Position the piston ring gaps at the proper locations around the piston **(see illustration)**.
6   Slip a section of plastic or rubber hose over each connecting rod cap bolt.
7   Lubricate the piston and rings with clean engine oil and attach a piston ring compressor to the piston. Leave the skirt protruding about 1/4-inch to guide the piston into the cylinder. The rings must be compressed until they're flush with the piston.
8   Rotate the crankshaft until the number one connecting rod journal is at bottom dead center and apply a coat of engine oil to the cylinder walls.
9   Gently insert the piston/connecting rod assembly into the number one cylinder bore and rest the bottom edge of the ring compressor on the en-

24.9a On 1.7L engines, the arrow on the top of the piston must point to the front (timing belt) end of the engine

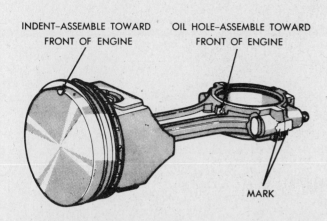

INDENT–ASSEMBLE TOWARD FRONT OF ENGINE

OIL HOLE–ASSEMBLE TOWARD FRONT OF ENGINE

MARK

24.9b   On 1982 through 1985 2.2L engines, the indent on the piston and the oil hole in the rod must face the front of the engine

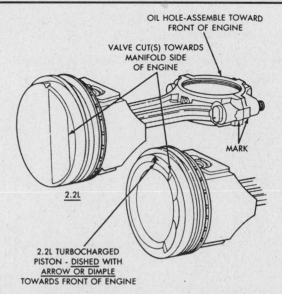

OIL HOLE–ASSEMBLE TOWARD FRONT OF ENGINE

VALVE CUT(S) TOWARDS MANIFOLD SIDE OF ENGINE

MARK

2.2L

2.2L TURBOCHARGED PISTON – DISHED WITH ARROW OR DIMPLE TOWARDS FRONT OF ENGINE

24.9c   On 1986 and later 2.2L engines, make sure the valve cuts face toward the manifold side of the engine

24.11   Drive the piston gently into the cylinder bore with the end of a wooden or plastic hammer handle

24.13   Lay the Plastigage strips on each rod bearing journal, parallel to the crankshaft centerline

2B

gine block. On 1.7L engines, make sure the mark (arrow) on the top of the piston faces the front of the engine (**see illustration**). On 2.2L engines, make sure the mark and oil holes in the rod face the appropriate direction (**see illustrations**).

10   Tap the top edge of the ring compressor to make sure it's contacting the block around its entire circumference.

11   Gently tap on the top of the piston with the end of a wooden hammer handle (**see illustration**) while guiding the end of the connecting rod into place on the crankshaft journal. The piston rings may try to pop out of the ring compressor just before entering the cylinder bore, so keep some downward pressure on the ring compressor. Work slowly, and if any resistance is felt as the piston enters the cylinder, stop immediately. Find out what's hanging up and fix it before proceeding. Do not, for any reason, force the piston into the cylinder – you might break a ring and/or the piston.

12   Once the piston/connecting rod assembly is installed, the connecting rod bearing oil clearance must be checked before the rod cap is permanently bolted in place.

13   Cut a piece of the appropriate size Plastigage slightly shorter than the width of the connecting rod bearing and lay it in place on the number one connecting rod journal, parallel with the journal axis (**see illustration**).

14   Clean the connecting rod cap bearing face, remove the protective hoses from the connecting rod bolts and install the rod cap. Make sure the mating mark on the cap is on the same side as the mark on the connecting rod (**see illustration**).

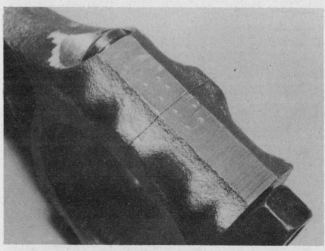

24.14   Make sure the marks on the rod and cap are matched up when the cap is installed (the marks shown here are center punch indentations made when the rod cap was removed)

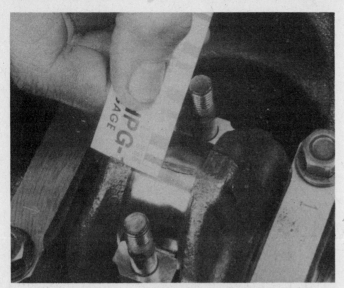

24.17 Measuring the width of the crushed Plastigage to determine the rod bearing oil clearance (be sure to use the correct scale – standard and metric ones are included)

15 Install the nuts and tighten them to the torque listed in this Chapter's Specifications, working up to it in three steps. **Note:** *Use a thin-wall socket to avoid erroneous torque readings that can result if the socket is wedged between the rod cap and nut. If the socket tends to wedge itself between the nut and the cap, lift up on it slightly until it no longer contacts the cap. Do not rotate the crankshaft at any time during this operation.*

16 Remove the nuts and detach the rod cap, being very careful not to disturb the Plastigage.

17 Compare the width of the crushed Plastigage to the scale printed on the Plastigage envelope to obtain the oil clearance **(see illustration)**. Compare it to the Specifications to make sure the clearance is correct.

18 If the clearance is not as specified, the bearing inserts may be the wrong size (which means different ones will be required). Before deciding that different inserts are needed, make sure no dirt or oil was between the bearing inserts and the connecting rod or cap when the clearance was measured. Also, recheck the journal diameter. If the Plastigage was wider at one end than the other, the journal may be tapered (refer to Section 18).

Final connecting rod installation

19 Carefully scrape all traces of the Plastigage material off the rod journal and/or bearing face. Be very careful not to scratch the bearing – use your fingernail or the edge of a credit card.

20 Make sure the bearing faces are perfectly clean, then apply a uniform layer of clean moly-based grease or engine assembly lube to both of them. You'll have to push the piston into the cylinder to expose the face of the bearing insert in the connecting rod – be sure to slip the protective hoses over the rod bolts first.

21 Slide the connecting rod back into place on the journal, remove the protective hoses from the rod cap bolts, install the rod cap and tighten the nuts to the specified torque. Again, work up to the torque in three steps.

22 Repeat the entire procedure for the remaining pistons/connecting rods.

23 The important points to remember are . . .
   a) Keep the back sides of the bearing inserts and the insides of the connecting rods and caps perfectly clean when assembling them.
   b) Make sure you have the correct piston/rod assembly for each cylinder.
   c) The marks on the top of the piston and the oil holes in the rods must face the appropriate directions **(see illustrations 24.9a and 24.9b)**.
   d) Lubricate the cylinder walls with clean oil.
   e) Lubricate the bearing faces when installing the rod caps after the oil clearance has been checked.

24 After all the piston/connecting rod assemblies have been properly installed, rotate the crankshaft a number of times by hand to check for any obvious binding.

25 As a final step, the connecting rod endplay must be checked. Refer to Section 12 for this procedure.

26 Compare the measured endplay to this Chapter's Specifications to make sure it's correct. If it was correct before disassembly and the original crankshaft and rods were reinstalled, it should still be right. If new rods or a new crankshaft were installed, the endplay may be inadequate. If so, the rods will have to be removed and taken to an automotive machine shop for resizing.

---

25   Initial start-up and break-in after overhaul

Warning: *Have a fire extinguisher handy when starting the engine for the first time.*

1   Once the engine has been installed in the vehicle, double-check the engine oil and coolant levels.

2   With the spark plugs out of the engine and the ignition system disabled (see Section 3), crank the engine until oil pressure registers on the gauge or the light goes out.

3   Install the spark plugs, hook up the plug wires and restore the ignition system functions (see Section 3).

4   Start the engine. It may take a few moments for the fuel system to build up pressure, but the engine should start without a great deal of effort. **Note:** *If backfiring occurs through the carburetor or throttle body, recheck the valve timing and ignition timing.*

5   After the engine starts, it should be allowed to warm up to normal operating temperature. While the engine is warming up, make a thorough check for fuel, oil and coolant leaks.

6   Shut the engine off and recheck the engine oil and coolant levels.

7   Drive the vehicle to an area with minimum traffic, accelerate at full throttle from 30 to 50 mph, then allow the vehicle to slow to 30 mph with the throttle closed. Repeat the procedure 10 or 12 times. This will load the piston rings and cause them to seat properly against the cylinder walls. Check again for oil and coolant leaks.

8   Drive the vehicle gently for the first 500 miles (no sustained high speeds) and keep a constant check on the oil level. It isn't unusual for an engine to use oil during the break-in period.

9   At approximately 500 to 600 miles, change the oil and filter.

10   For the next few hundred miles, drive the vehicle normally. Don't pamper it or abuse it.

11   After 2000 miles, change the oil and filter again and consider the engine broken in.

Chapter 3   Cooling, heating and air conditioning systems

Contents

3

Specifications

General

Radiator cap pressure rating	See Chapter 1
Thermostat rating (opening temperature)	195-degrees F (90-degrees C)
Cooling system capacity	See Chapter 1
Refrigerant capacity	33 to 34 ounces

Torque specifications

Ft-lbs (unless otherwise indicated)

1.7L engine

Water box-to-block bolts	84 in-lbs
Thermostat housing-to-water box bolts	108 in-lbs
Water pump pulley bolts	120 in-lbs
Water pump-to-housing bolts	21
Water pump housing-to-block	
6 mm bolts	100 in-lbs
8 mm bolts	21
10 mm bolts	40

2.2L engine

Water outlet bolts (1982 through 1984)	15
Thermostat housing-to-water box bolt/stud (1985 on)	17
Water pump pulley bolts	
1982 through 1984	132 in-lbs
1985 on	108 in-lbs
Water pump-to-housing bolts	21
Water pump housing-to-block	
Upper three bolts	21
Lower bolt	
1982 through 1987	50
1988 on	40

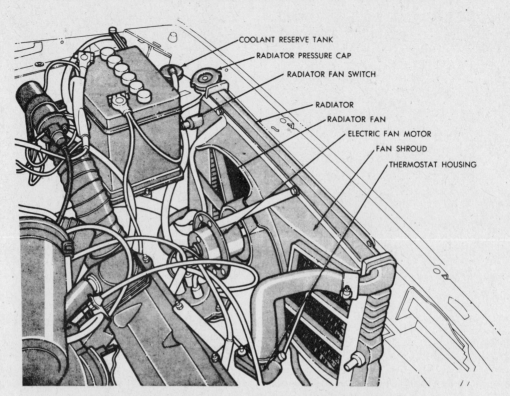

1.1   Cooling system component locations (1.7L engine shown, 2.2L similar)

1   General information

Refer to illustration 1.1

Engine cooling system

All vehicles covered by this manual employ a pressurized engine cooling system with thermostatically controlled coolant circulation **(see illustration)**. An impeller type water pump mounted on the front of the block pumps coolant through the engine. The coolant flows around the combustion chambers and toward the rear of the engine. Cast-in coolant passages direct coolant near the intake ports, exhaust ports, and spark plug areas.

A wax pellet type thermostat is located in a housing near the front of the engine. During warm-up, the closed thermostat prevents coolant from circulating through the radiator. As the engine nears normal operating temperature, the thermostat opens and allows hot coolant to travel through the radiator, where it's cooled before returning to the engine.

The cooling system is sealed by a pressure type radiator cap, which raises the boiling point of the coolant and increases the cooling efficiency of the radiator. If the system pressure exceeds the cap pressure relief value, the excess pressure in the system forces the spring-loaded valve inside the cap off its seat and allows the coolant to escape through the overflow tube into a coolant reservoir. When the system cools the excess coolant is automatically drawn from the reservoir back into the radiator.

The coolant reservoir does double duty as both the point at which fresh coolant is added to the cooling system to maintain the proper fluid level and as a holding tank for overheated coolant.

This type of cooling system is known as a closed design because coolant that escapes past the pressure cap is saved and reused.

Heating system

The heating system consists of a blower fan and heater core located in the heater box, the hoses connecting the heater core to the engine cooling system and the heater/air conditioning control head on the dashboard.

Hot engine coolant is circulated through the heater core. When the heater mode is activated, a flap door opens to expose the heater box to the passenger compartment. A fan switch on the control head activates the blower motor, which forces air through the core, heating the air.

Air conditioning system

The air conditioning system consists of a condenser mounted in front of the radiator, an evaporator mounted adjacent to the heater core, a compressor mounted on the engine, a filter-drier or receiver-drier (accumulator) which contains a high pressure relief valve and the plumbing connecting all of the above components.

A blower fan forces the warmer air of the passenger compartment through the evaporator core (sort of a radiator-in-reverse), transferring the heat from the air to the refrigerant. The liquid refrigerant boils off into low pressure vapor, taking the heat with it when it leaves the evaporator.

2   Antifreeze – general information

Warning: *Do not allow antifreeze to come in contact with your skin or painted surfaces of the vehicle. Rinse off spills immediately with plenty of water. Never leave antifreeze lying around in an open container or in a puddle in the driveway or on the garage floor. Children and animals are attracted by it's sweet smell. Antifreeze is toxic, so use common sense when disposing of it. Some communities maintain toxic material disposal sites and/or offer regular pick-up of hazardous materials. Antifreeze is also flammable, so don't store or use it near open flames.*

The cooling system should be filled with a water/ethylene glycol based antifreeze solution, which will prevent freezing down to at least -20-degrees F, or lower if local climate requires it. It also provides protection against corrosion and increases the coolant boiling point.

The cooling system should be drained, flushed and refilled at the specified intervals (see Chapter 1). Old or contaminated antifreeze solutions are likely to cause damage and encourage the formation of rust and scale in the system. Use distilled water with the antifreeze.

3.10 The thermostat is accessible after removing the bolts and detaching the housing cover (1.7L engine shown)

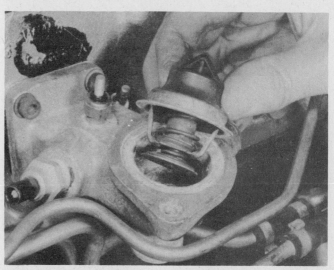

3.13a Make sure the thermostat is installed correctly – the spring end must be directed into the engine (1.7L engine shown)

Before adding antifreeze, check all hose connections, because antifreeze tends to search out and leak through very minute openings. Engines don't normally consume coolant, so if the level goes down, find the cause and correct it.

The exact mixture of antifreeze-to-water which you should use depends on the relative weather conditions. The mixture should contain at least 50 percent antifreeze, but should never contain more than 70 percent antifreeze. Consult the mixture ratio chart on the antifreeze container before adding coolant. Hydrometers are available at most auto parts stores to test the coolant. Use antifreeze which meets the vehicle manufacturer's specifications.

3 Thermostat – check and replacement

Warning: *Do not remove the radiator cap, drain the coolant or replace the thermostat until the engine has cooled completely.*

Check

1 Before assuming the thermostat is to blame for a cooling system problem, check the coolant level, drivebelt tension (see Chapter 1) and temperature gauge operation.
2 If the engine seems to be taking a long time to warm up (based on heater output or temperature gauge operation), the thermostat is probably stuck open. Replace the thermostat with a new one.
3 If the engine runs hot, use your hand to check the temperature of the upper radiator hose. If the hose isn't hot, but the engine is, the thermostat is probably stuck closed, preventing the coolant inside the engine from escaping to the radiator. Replace the thermostat. **Caution:** *Don't drive the vehicle without a thermostat. The computer may stay in open loop and emissions and fuel economy will suffer.*
4 If the upper radiator hose is hot, it means that the coolant is flowing and the thermostat is open. Consult the Troubleshooting Section at the front of this manual for cooling system diagnosis.

Replacement

Refer to illustrations 3.10, 3.13a and 3.13b
5 Disconnect the negative battery cable from the battery.
6 Drain the cooling system (see Chapter 1). If the coolant is relatively new or in good condition, save it and reuse it.
7 Follow the upper radiator hose to the engine to locate the thermostat housing.
8 Loosen the hose clamp, then detach the hose from the fitting. If it's stuck, grasp it near the end with a pair of adjustable pliers and twist it to break the seal, then pull it off. If the hose is old or deteriorated, cut it off and install a new one.

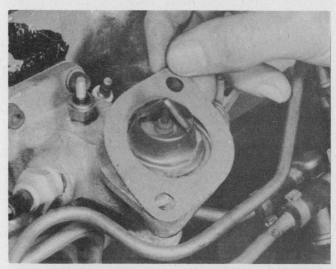

3.13b Be sure to apply sealant to both sides of the new gasket before installing it – remember, the gasket goes on after the thermostat on the 1.7L engine, before the thermostat on the 2.2L engine (1.7L engine shown)

9 If the outer surface of the large fitting that mates with the hose is deteriorated (corroded, pitted, etc.) it may be damaged further by hose removal. If it is, the thermostat housing cover will have to be replaced.
10 Remove the bolts and detach the housing cover **(see illustration)**. If the cover is stuck, tap it with a soft-face hammer to jar it loose. Be prepared for some coolant to spill as the gasket seal is broken.
11 Note how it's installed (which end is facing up), then remove the thermostat **(see illustration 3.10)**.
12 Stuff a rag into the engine opening, then remove all traces of old gasket material and sealant from the housing and cover with a gasket scraper. Remove the rag from the opening and clean the gasket mating surfaces with lacquer thinner or acetone.
13 If the vehicle has a 1.7L engine, install the new thermostat in the housing. Make sure the correct end faces up (the spring end should be directed into the engine) **(see illustration)**. Apply a thin, uniform layer of RTV sealant to both sides of the new gasket and position it on the housing **(see illustration)**.
14 If the vehicle has a 2.2L engine, install the gasket first, then the new thermostat.
15 Install the cover and bolts. Tighten the bolts to the torque listed in this Chapter's Specifications.

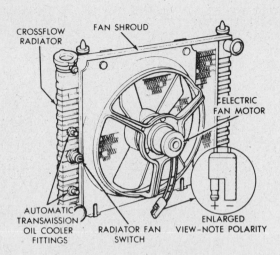

4.1   **You'll find the electrical connector for the cooling fan motor on the end of a short harness**

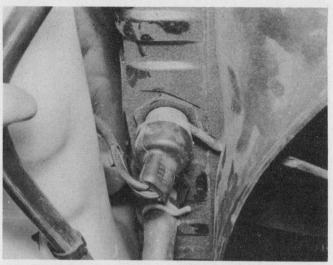

4.2   **The radiator fan switch is located in the lower left corner of the radiator (1.7L engine shown, 2.2L similar)**

16   Reattach the hose to the fitting and tighten the hose clamp securely.
17   Refill the cooling system (see Chapter 1).
18   Start the engine and allow it to reach normal operating temperature, then check for leaks and proper thermostat operation (as described in Steps 2 through 4).

4   Engine cooling fan – check and replacement

Warning: *To avoid possible injury or damage, DO NOT operate the engine with a damaged fan. Do not attempt to repair fan blades – replace a damaged fan with a new one.*

Check
Refer to Illustrations 4.1 and 4.2

1   If the engine is overheating and the cooling fan is not coming on, unplug the electrical connector at the motor **(see illustration)** and use jumper wires to connect the fan directly to the battery. If the fan still doesn't work, replace the motor.
2   If the motor is OK, but the cooling fan still doesn't come on when the engine gets hot, the fault lies in the radiator fan switch **(see illustration)** or

the wiring which connects the components. Bridge the terminals on the switch. If the fan operates, the switch is defective. If the fan still doesn't come on, use a voltmeter or test light to check the fan circuit (wiring diagrams are included at the end of Chapter 12). Carefully check all wiring and connections. If no obvious problems are found, further diagnosis should be done by a dealer service department or repair shop.

Replacement

Fan
Refer to illustrations 4.6, 4.7 and 4.8

3   Disconnect the negative battery cable from the battery.
4   Remove the fan wire harness from the clips.
5   Insert a small screwdriver into the connector to lift the lock tab and unplug the fan wire harness.
6   Unbolt the fan bracket assembly (see illustrations in Section 5), then carefully lift it out of the engine compartment. If the shroud assembly is secured by clips, you may have to rock the shroud back-and-forth to work it loose from the radiator **(see illustration)**.
7   To detach the fan from the motor, remove the clip from the motor shaft **(see illustration)**.

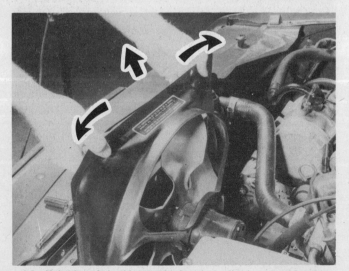

4.6   **If the fan shroud is attached to the radiator assembly with clips, rock it from side-to-side as you pull up on it**

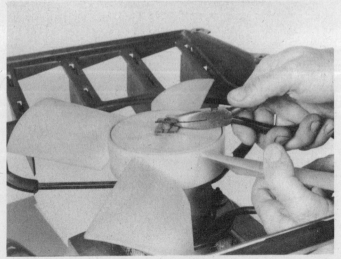

4.7   **You'll have to switch the fan blades to the new motor – to get the blades off the old motor, pull the retaining clip off the shaft with needle-nose pliers**

4.8   To separate the motor from the shroud, remove the mounting nuts

5.3a   After you've drained the cooling system, loosen the hose clamps and detach the upper hose . . .

8   To remove the fan motor from the shroud, remove the mounting nuts **(see illustration)**.
9   Installation is the reverse of removal.

Radiator fan switch

10 · Drain the coolant.
11   Unplug the electrical connector from the switch.
12   Unscrew the switch from the radiator **(see illustration 4.2).**
13   Wrap the threads of the new switch with teflon tape to prevent leaks.
14   Install the switch and tighten it securely.
15   Plug in the electrical connector.
16   Fill the cooling system (see Chapter 1).
17   Start the engine and check for leaks.

5   Radiator/transmission oil cooler – removal and installation

Warning: *Wait until the engine is completely cool before beginning this procedure.*

Radiator

Refer to illustrations 5.3a, 5.3b, 5.4, 5.8a, 5.8b, 5.8c, 5.8d, 5.8e, 5.13a and 5.13b

1   Disconnect the negative battery cable from the battery.
2   Drain the cooling system (see Chapter 1). If the coolant is relatively new and in good condition, save it and reuse it.
3   Loosen the hose clamps, then detach the radiator hoses from the fittings **(see illustrations)**. If they're stuck, grasp each hose near the end with a pair of adjustable pliers and twist it to break the seal, then pull it off - be careful not to distort the radiator fittings! If the hoses are old or deteriorated, cut them off and install new ones.
4   Disconnect the reservoir hose from the radiator filler neck **(see illustration)**.
5   Remove the screws and clips that attach the shroud to the radiator and slide the shroud toward the engine (see Section 4).
6   If the vehicle is equipped with an automatic transmission, disconnect the cooler lines from the radiator (see Step 18).

3

5.3b   . . . and lower hose from the radiator fittings (1.7L engine shown, 2.2L similar) – if you have to disconnect a shield (arrow) or hose bracket, be sure to note how and where it's attached to facilitate reassembly

5.4   When you detach the overflow hose at the filler neck, use a screwdriver to pry it off the fitting – don't try to pull it off or you'll rip the hose

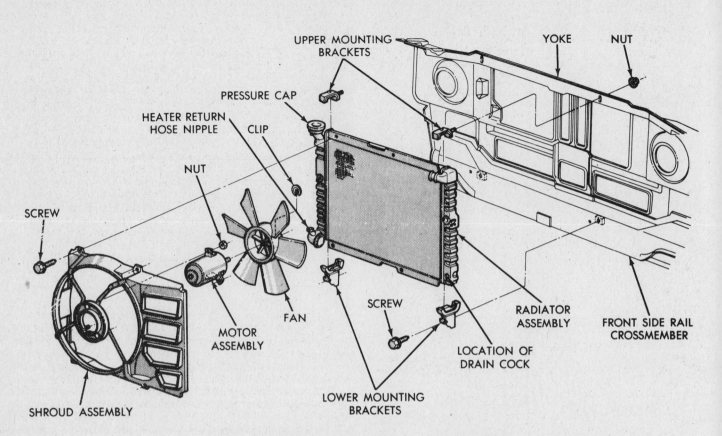

5.8a   1.7L radiator and related components – exploded view

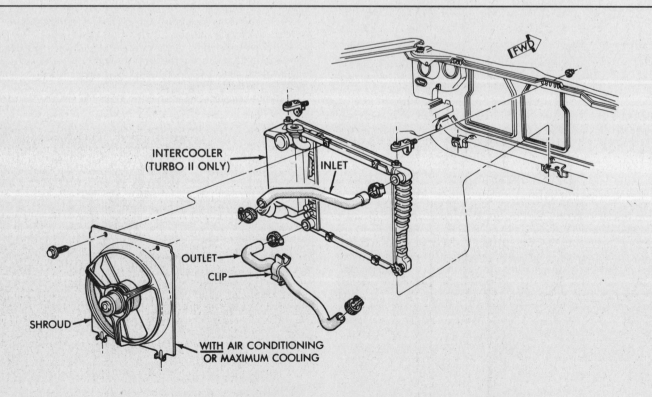

5.8b   2.2L radiator and related components – exploded view (with air conditioning)

7   Unplug the electrical connector from the radiator fan switch (see Section 4).
8   Remove the radiator mounting bolts (see illustrations).
9   Carefully lift out the radiator. Don't spill coolant on the vehicle or scratch the paint.
10   Check the radiator for leaks and damage. If it needs repair, have a radiator shop or dealer service department perform the work as special techniques are required.
11   Remove bugs and dirt from the radiator with compressed air and a soft brush (don't bend the cooling fins).
12   Inspect the radiator mounts for deterioration and make sure there's no dirt or gravel in them when the radiator is installed.

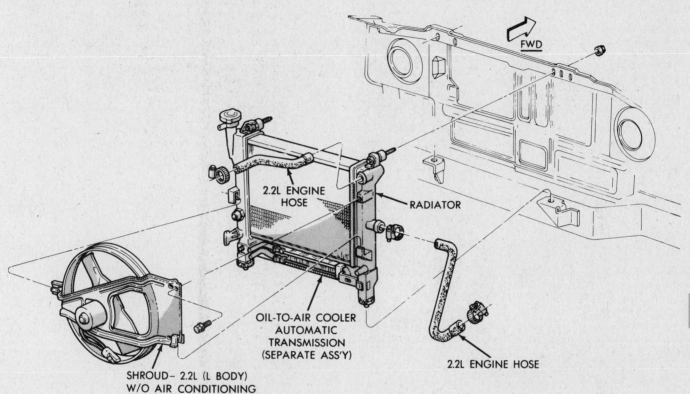

5.8c   2.2L radiator and related components – exploded view (w/o air conditioning)

5.8d   The top of the radiator is secured to the upper crossmember by a pair of brackets – to remove them, simply remove the nuts (arrows) . . .

5.8e   . . . and rotate the brackets up and out of the mounts

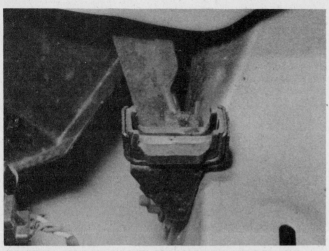

5.13a   Always check the bottom mounting brackets for deterioration and debris before installing the radiator – and make sure the radiator seats properly in the bottom brackets before fastening the clamps/brackets on top

5.13b   On 2.2L models, make sure the radiator tab seats securely in the rubber grommet when installing the radiator

13   Installation is the reverse of the removal procedure. Make sure the radiator seats properly in the bottom mounting brackets before fastening the top brackets **(see illustrations)**.
14   After installation, fill the cooling system with the proper mixture of antifreeze and water. See Chapter 1 if necessary.
15   Start the engine and check for leaks. Allow the engine to reach normal operating temperature, indicated by the upper radiator hose becoming hot. Recheck the coolant level and add more if required.
16   If you're working on an automatic transmission equipped vehicle, check and add fluid as needed.

Transmission oil cooler
Refer to Illustrations 5.18 and 5.19

17   If the vehicle is equipped with an automatic transaxle, it also has an oil cooler.
18   On vehicles with a 1.7L engine, the oil cooler is located inside the left radiator tank **(see illustration)**. One fitting is located above the radiator fan switch and one is located just below it.
19   On vehicles with a 2.2L engine, the oil cooler is located below the radiator **(see illustration)**.

20   To replace the oil cooler, place a drip pan under the line fittings, detach the fittings and plug the lines.
21   Remove the radiator (see above).
22   If the oil cooler is inside the radiator tank, take the radiator to a radiator repair shop to have the tank opened and the cooler replaced.
23   If the oil cooler is below the radiator, remove the screws and separate the cooler from the radiator.
24   Installation is the reverse of removal. Fill the cooling system with the proper mixture of antifreeze and water and top up the automatic transmission with the recommended fluid (see Chapter 1).

---

6   Coolant reservoir – removal and installation

Refer to illustration 6.2

1   Detach the overflow hose at the radiator filler neck **(see illustration 5.4).** Plug the hose so you don't spill any coolant out of the reservoir during removal.
2   Remove the mounting fasteners **(see illustration)** and lift the reservoir straight up.
3   Installation is the reverse of removal.

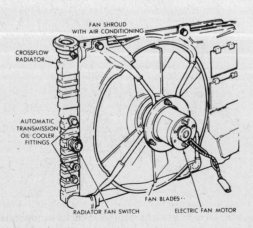

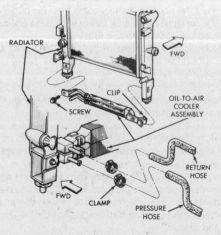

5.18   On 1.7L models with an automatic transaxle, the auxiliary oil cooler is located inside the left radiator tank

5.19   On 2.2L models with an automatic transaxle, the oil cooler is located under the radiator

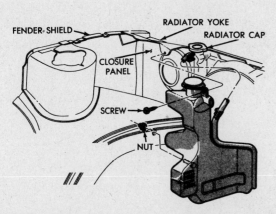

6.2 A typical coolant reservoir (1.7L model shown, 2.2L similar)

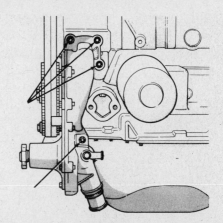

8.8 Water pump mounting bolt locations (2.2L engine shown, 1.7L similar)

7 Water pump – check

1 A failure in the water pump can cause serious engine damage due to overheating.

2 There are three ways to check the operation of the water pump while it's installed on the engine. If the pump is defective, it should be replaced with a new or rebuilt unit.

3 With the engine running at normal operating temperature, squeeze the upper radiator hose. If the water pump is working properly, a pressure surge should be felt as the hose is released. **Warning:** *Keep your hands away from the fan blades!*

4 Water pumps are equipped with weep or vent holes. If a failure occurs in the pump seal, coolant will leak from the hole. In most cases you'll need a flashlight to find the hole on the water pump from underneath to check for leaks.

5 If the water pump shaft bearings fail there may be a howling sound at the front of the engine while it's running. Shaft wear can be felt if the water pump pulley is rocked up-and-down. Don't mistake drivebelt slippage, which causes a squealing sound, for water pump bearing failure.

8 Water pump – replacement

Refer to illustrations 8.8, 8.10, 8.11a, 8.11b and 8.14
Warning: *Wait until the engine is completely cool before beginning this procedure.*

1 Disconnect the negative battery cable from the battery.

2 Drain the cooling system (see Chapter 1). If the coolant is relatively new or in good condition, save and reuse it.

3 Remove the cooling fan and shroud (see Section 4).

4 Remove the drivebelts (see Chapter 1) and the pulley at the end of the water pump shaft.

5 On air-conditioned models, remove the compressor (see Section 15). **Note:** *Simply set the compressor aside – don't disconnect the lines.*

6 Remove the alternator (see Chapter 5).

7 Loosen the clamps and detach the hoses from the water pump. If they're stuck, grasp each hose near the end with a pair of adjustable pliers and twist it to break the seal, then pull it off. If the hoses are deteriorated, cut them off and install new ones.

8 Remove the bolts **(see illustration)** and detach the water pump and housing from the engine. Note the locations of the various lengths and different types of bolts as they're removed to ensure correct installation.

9 Clean the bolt threads and the threaded holes in the engine to remove corrosion and sealant.

10 Remove all traces of old gasket material from the engine and pump housing with a gasket scraper **(see illustration)**.

11 Separate the water pump from the housing **(see illustrations)**.

8.10 Scrape the old sealant material off the engine block and the water pump housing (2.2L engine shown, 1.7L similar)

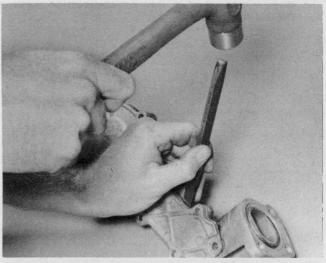

8.11a You may have to use a hammer and chisel to separate the water pump from the housing, but be extremely careful – don't damage the mating surface of the housing (2.2L engine shown, 1.7L similar)

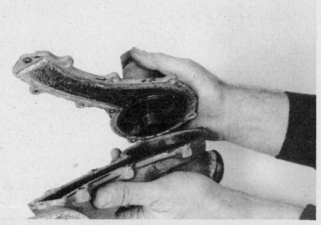

8.11b   Once the bond has been broken, separate the pump from the housing (2.2L engine shown, 1.7L similar)

12   If you're installing a new pump, compare the new pump to the old pump to make sure they're identical.

13   Clean the mating surfaces of the housing. Remove all old sealant material. Remove the old O-ring from the housing groove.

14   Apply a bead of RTV sealant to the mating surface of the housing **(see illustration)**. Install a new O-ring in the housing groove.

15   Attach the new pump to the housing and tighten the bolts to the torque listed in this Chapter's Specifications.

16   Install the pump/housing assembly on the engine (make sure a new gasket is used) and tighten the bolts to the torque listed in this Chapter's Specifications.

17   Reinstall all parts removed for access to the pump.

18   Refill the cooling system and check the drivebelt tension (see Chapter 1). Run the engine and check for leaks.

---

9   Coolant temperature sending unit – check and replacement

Refer to illustrations 9.1a and 9.1b

Warning: *Wait until the engine is completely cool before beginning this procedure.*

1   The coolant temperature indicator system is composed of a light or temperature gauge mounted in the instrument panel and a coolant temperature sending unit mounted on the thermostat housing or water box **(see illustrations).** Most of the vehicles covered by this book have more than one sending unit on the housing, but only one is used for the indicator system. **Warning:** *If the vehicle is equipped with an electric cooling fan, stay clear of the fan blades, which can come on at any time.*

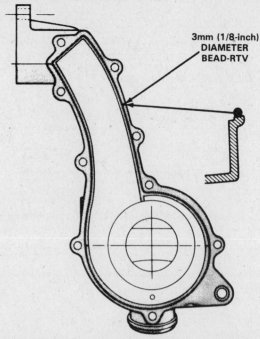

8.14   Apply a continuous bead of RTV-type sealant between the bolt holes and the inner edge of the housing (2.2L engine shown, 1.7L similar)

2   If an overheating indication occurs, check the coolant level in the system and then make sure the wiring between the light or gauge and the sending unit is secure and all fuses are intact.

3   When the ignition switch is turned on and the starter motor is turning, the indicator light should be on (overheated engine indication).

4   If the light is not on, the bulb may be burned out, the ignition switch may be faulty or the circuit may be open. Test the circuit by grounding the wire to the sending unit while the ignition is on (engine not running for safety). If the gauge deflects full scale or the light comes on, replace the sending unit.

5   As soon as the engine starts, the light should go out and remain out unless the engine overheats. Failure of the light to go out may be due to a grounded wire between the light and the sending unit, a defective sending unit or a faulty ignition switch. Check the coolant to make sure it's the proper type. Plain water may have too low a boiling point to activate the sending unit.

6   If the sending unit must be replaced, simply unscrew it from the engine and install the replacement. Use sealant on the threads. Make sure the engine is cool before removing the defective sending unit. There will be some coolant loss as the unit is removed, so be prepared to catch it. Check the level after the replacement has been installed.

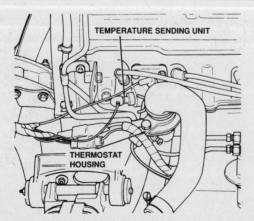

9.1a   Coolant temperature sending unit location (1.7L engine)

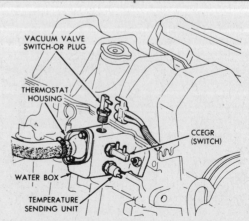

9.1b   Coolant temperature sending unit location (2.2L engine)

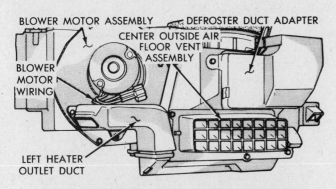

10.3   Heater blower motor and related components

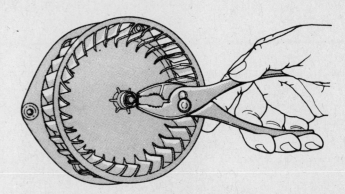

10.6   To detach the fan from the motor shaft, remove the retainer with pliers

10   Heater and air conditioner blower motor – removal and installation

Refer to illustrations 10.3 and 10.6

1   Detach the cable from the negative terminal of the battery.
2   Unplug the electrical connector from the blower motor.

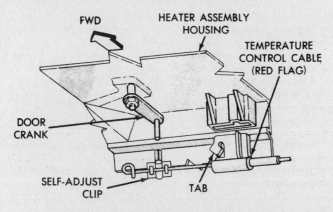

11.5   Depress the tab on the temperature control cable and pull the cable out of the heater assembly receiver

3   Remove the screws from the left-side heater outlet duct **(see illustration)**.
4   Remove the screws retaining the blower mounting plate to the heater assembly.
5   Detach the blower assembly.
6   Switch the fan to the new blower unit. To detach it from the motor shaft, remove the retainer from the hub **(see illustration)** and slide the fan off the shaft.
7   Installation is the reverse of removal.

11   Heater core – removal and installation

Heater core only

Refer to illustrations 11.5, 11.7a, 11.7b, 11.8, 11.12, 11.14, 11.16, 11.17, 11.18, 11.19 and 11.20

1   Detach the cable from the negative terminal of the battery.
2   Drain the engine coolant (see Chapter 1).
3   Unplug the electrical connector from the blower motor (see Section 10).
4   Remove the ash tray and receptacle.
5   Depress the tab on the temperature control cable and pull the cable out of the receiver on the heater assembly **(see illustration)**.
6   Remove the glove box and door assembly.
7   Detach the heater hoses at the firewall **(see illustrations)** and seal the heater core openings to prevent coolant spills.

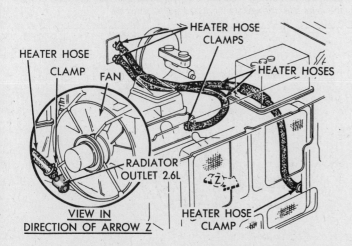

11.7a   Typical heater hose routing (1.7L engine)

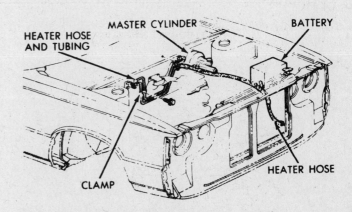

11.7b   Typical heater hose routing (2.2L engine)

8   Remove the two nuts that fasten the heater assembly to the dash **(see illustration)**.
9   Detach the electrical connector from the blower motor resistor block.
10   Remove the screw that attaches the heater support brace to the instrument panel.

11   Remove the heater support bracket nut. Detach the strap from the plenum stud and lower the heater assembly from under the instrument panel.
12   Depress the tab on the flag and pull the mode door control cable out of the heater assembly receiver **(see illustration)**.

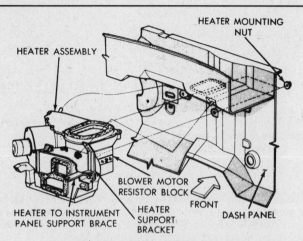

11.8   **Heater assembly installation details (non-air conditioned models)**

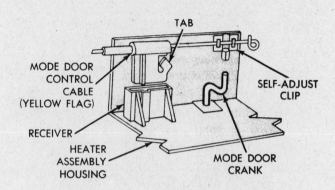

11.12   **Depress the tab on the flag and pull the mode door control cable out of the heater assembly receiver (non-air conditioned models)**

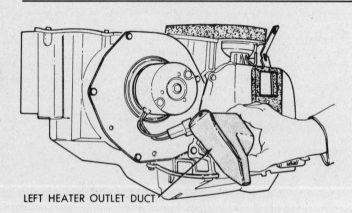

11.14   **Remove the left heater outlet duct (non-air conditioned models)**

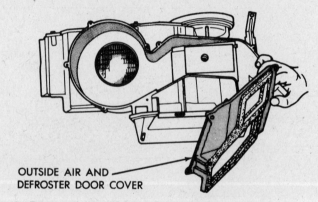

11.16   **Remove the four screws that attach the outside air and defroster door cover, then remove the cover (non-air conditioned models)**

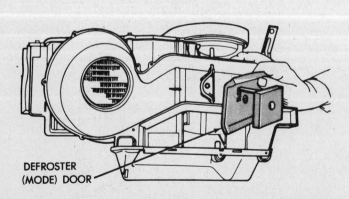

11.17   **Remove the screw from the center of the defroster door and remove the door, screw and screw retaining plate (non-air conditioned models)**

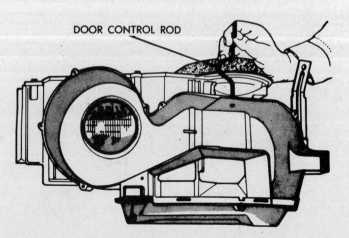

11.18   **Lift the defroster door control rod out of the heater unit (non-air conditioned models)**

13   Move the heater unit toward the passenger side of the vehicle and then pull it out from under the instrument panel.
14   Remove the left heater outlet duct (see illustration).
15   Remove the blower motor assembly (see Section 10).
16   Remove the four screws and detach the outside air and defroster door cover (see illustration).

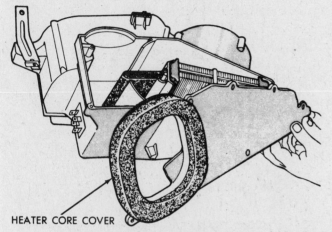

HEATER CORE COVER

11.19   Remove the screws from the heater core cover, then lift off the cover (non-air conditioned models)

17   Remove the screw from the center of the defroster door and remove the door, screw and screw retaining plate (see illustration).
18   Lift the defroster door control rod out of the unit (see illustration).
19   Remove the screws and detach the heater core cover (see illustration).
20   Slide the heater core out of the unit (see illustration).
21   Installation is the reverse of removal.

Heater/evaporator assembly (air conditioned vehicles)

Refer to illustrations 11.27, 11.28, 11.31, 11.37, 11.42, 11.44 and 11.47

22   Have the air conditioning system discharged by a service station before beginning this procedure.
23   Detach the cable from the negative terminal of the battery.
24   Detach the blend air door cable and disengage it from the clip on the heated air duct (see illustration 11.5).
25   Remove the glove box.
26   Disconnect and remove the center bezel (see Chapter 12).
27   Remove the center distribution duct (see illustration).
28   Remove the defroster duct adapter (see illustration).
29   Detach the heater hoses and air conditioner lines at the dash panel. Plug the heater hoses to prevent coolant from leaking when the unit is tipped forward during removal. Plug the air conditioner lines to prevent moisture from contaminating the air conditioning system.
30   Detach the vacuum lines at the engine and the heater valve.
31   Remove the four nuts that attach the heater/evaporator assembly to the dash (see illustration).

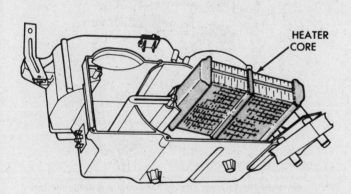

HEATER CORE

11.20   Slide the heater core up and out of the heater unit (non-air conditioned models)

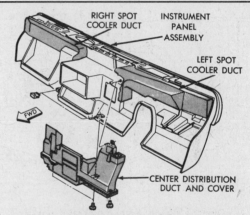

RIGHT SPOT COOLER DUCT   INSTRUMENT PANEL ASSEMBLY

LEFT SPOT COOLER DUCT

FWD

CENTER DISTRIBUTION DUCT AND COVER

11.27   Remove the center distribution duct (air conditioned models)

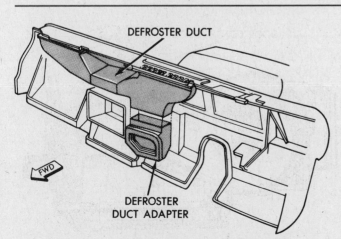

DEFROSTER DUCT

FWD

DEFROSTER DUCT ADAPTER

11.28   Remove the defroster duct adapter (air conditioned models)

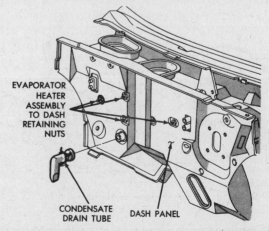

EVAPORATOR HEATER ASSEMBLY TO DASH RETAINING NUTS

CONDENSATE DRAIN TUBE   DASH PANEL

11.31   Remove the four nuts that attach the heater/evaporator assembly to the dash (air conditioned models)

3

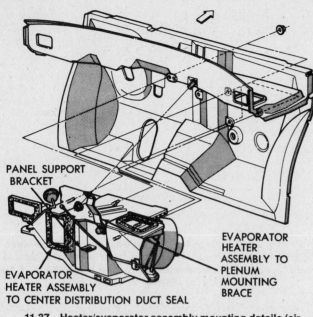

11.37   Heater/evaporator assembly mounting details (air conditioned models)

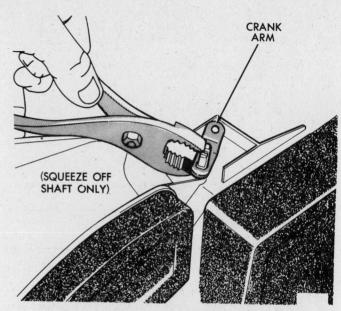

11.42   Press the crank arm off the pivot shaft (air conditioned models)

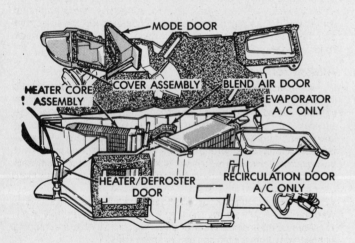

11.44   Carefully lift the cover off the unit after all the screws have been removed (air conditioned models)

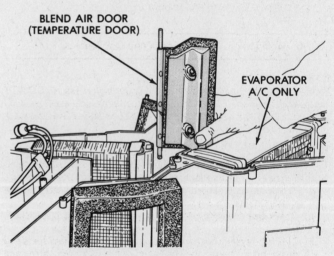

11.47   Installing the blend air door pivot shaft in the socket (air conditioned models)

32   Remove the pivot bracket screw from the right-hand side of the instrument panel (see Chapter 12).

33   Remove the two screws that secure the lower instrument panel at the steering column (see Chapter 12).

34   Remove the instrument panel top cover (see Chapter 12).

35   Remove all but the left panel-to-fenceline attaching screw.

36   Pull back the carpet from under the air conditioning unit and move it to the rear as far as possible.

37   While supporting the heater/evaporator unit, remove the support strap nut and the blower motor ground cable, then remove the support strap **(see illustration)**.

38   You'll need a helper for this step. While your assistant pulls the panel to the rear to provide sufficient clearance, lift the unit out, pulling it back as far as possible to clear the dash panel and liner.

39   Slowly lower the unit, taking care to prevent the dash attachment studs from hanging up in the dash liner.

40   When the unit reaches the floor, slide it back until it's out from under the panel.

41   Place the heater/air conditioning unit on a clean working surface.

42   Remove the retaining nut from the pivot shaft of the blend air door and use a pair of pliers to force the crank off the pivot shaft **(see illustration)**.

43   Detach the vacuum lines from the defrost and panel mode vacuum actuators and position them out of the way.

44   Remove the three heater/evaporator unit cover screws pointing up at the defroster outlet chamber, the two screws pointing up at the air inlet plenum and the 11 screws pointing down. Detach the cover from the heater/evaporator unit **(see illustration)**.

45   Detach the heater core-to-dash panel seal from the core tubes and remove the heater core from the heater/evaporator unit.

46   Install the new heater core.

47   When installing the heater/evaporator cover, be sure to guide the pivot shaft of the blend air door into the socket **(see illustration)**.

48   Installation is otherwise the reverse of removal.

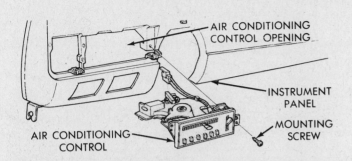

12.4   Heater/air conditioner control assembly mounting details

12   Heater or heater/air conditioner control assembly – removal and installation

Refer to illustration 12.4

1   Detach the cable from the negative terminal of the battery.
2   Remove the headlight switch knob (see Chapter 12).
3   Remove the bezel that surrounds the headlight switch and heater/air conditioner assembly (see Chapter 12).
4   Remove the two control mounting screws **(see illustration)**.
5   Slide the control assembly back, detach the cables, wires and vacuum hoses, then remove the control unit.
6   Installation is the reverse of removal.

13   Air conditioning system – check and maintenance

Refer to illustration 13.7
Warning: *The air conditioning system is under high pressure. DO NOT disassemble any part of the system (hose, compressor, line fittings, etc.) until after the system has been depressurized by a dealer service department or service station.*

Check

1   The following maintenance checks should be performed on a regular basis to ensure the air conditioner continues to operate at peak efficiency.
   a) Check the compressor drivebelt. If it's worn or deteriorated, replace it (see Chapter 1).
   b) Check the drivebelt tension and, if necessary, adjust it (see Chapter 1).
   c) Check the system hoses. Look for cracks, bubbles, hard spots and deterioration. Inspect the hoses and all fittings for oil bubbles and seepage. If there's any evidence of wear, damage or leaks, replace the hose(s).
   d) Inspect the condenser fins for leaves, bugs and other debris. Use a "fin comb" or compressed air to clean the condenser.
   e) Make sure the system has the correct refrigerant charge.
2   It's a good idea to operate the system for about 10 minutes at least once a month, particularly during the winter. Long term non-use can cause hardening, and subsequent failure, of the seals.
3   Because of the complexity of the air conditioning system and the special equipment necessary to service it, in-depth troubleshooting and repairs are not included in this manual (refer to the Haynes Automotive Heating and Air Conditioning Manual). However, simple checks and component replacement procedures are provided in this Chapter.
4   The most common cause of poor cooling is simply a low system refrigerant charge. If a noticeable drop in cool air output occurs, the following quick check will help you determine if the refrigerant level is low.
5   Warm the engine up to normal operating temperature.
6   Place the air conditioning temperature selector at the coldest setting and put the blower at the highest setting. Open the doors (to make sure the air conditioning system doesn't cycle off as soon as it cools the passenger compartment).

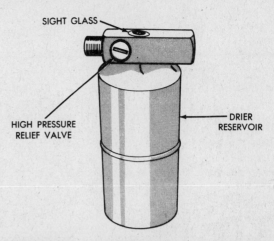

13.7   The sight glass on top of the filter-drier, or receiver-drier, assembly enables you to view the condition of the refrigerant in the air conditioning system while the system is operating – if the refrigerant looks foamy, the charge is low

7   With the compressor engaged - the clutch will make an audible click and the center of the clutch will rotate - inspect the sight glass, if equipped **(see illustration)**. If the refrigerant looks foamy, it's low. Charge the system as described later in this Section.
8   If there's no sight glass, feel the inlet and outlet pipes at the compressor. One side should be cold and one hot. If there's no perceptible difference between the two pipes, there's something wrong with the compressor or the system. It might be a low charge – it might be something else. Take the vehicle to a dealer service department or an automotive air conditioning shop.

Adding refrigerant

9   Buy an automotive charging kit at an auto parts store. A charging kit includes a 14-ounce can of refrigerant, a tap valve and a short section of hose that can be attached between the tap valve and the system low side service valve. Because one can of refrigerant may not be sufficient to bring the system charge up to the proper level, it's a good idea to buy a few additional cans. Make sure that one of the cans contains red refrigerant dye. If the system is leaking, the red dye will leak out with the refrigerant and help you pinpoint the location of the leak. **Warning:** *Never add more than three cans of refrigerant to the system.*
10   Hook up the charging kit by following the manufacturer's instructions. **Warning:** *DO NOT hook the charging kit hose to the system high side!*
11   Warm up the engine and turn on the air conditioner. Keep the charging kit hose away from the fan and other moving parts.
12   If the system in your vehicle is an accumulator type:
   a) Add refrigerant to the low side of the system until both the accumulator surface and the evaporator inlet pipe feel about the same temperature. Allow stabilization time between each addition.
   b) Once the accumulator surface and the evaporator inlet pipe feel about the same temperature, add the contents remaining in the can.
13   Place a thermometer in the dashboard vent nearest the evaporator and add refrigerant until the indicated temperature is around 40 to 45-degrees F.

14   Air conditioning filter-drier/receiver-drier – removal and installation

Refer to illustration 14.5
Warning: *The air conditioning system is under high pressure. DO NOT disassemble any part of the system (hose, compressor, line fittings, etc.) until after the system has been depressurized by a dealer service department or service station.*

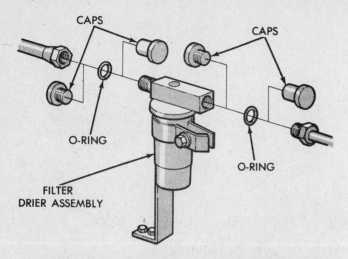

14.5   **Typical filter-drier/receiver-drier installation details – if you plan to reinstall the same unit, be sure to plug the openings immediately after detaching the refrigerant lines**

Caution: *Replacement filter-drier/receiver-drier units are so effective at absorbing moisture that they can quickly saturate upon exposure to the atmosphere. When installing a new unit, have all tools and supplies ready for quick reassembly to avoid having the system open any longer than necessary.*

1   The filter-drier, or receiver-drier, acts as a reservoir for the system refrigerant. It's located near the radiator.

2   Have the system discharged (see Warning above).
3   Disconnect the cable from the negative terminal of the battery.
4   Unplug any electrical connectors from the filter-drier/receiver-drier.
5   Disconnect the refrigerant lines from the filter-drier/receiver drier **(see illustration)**. Use a back-up wrench to prevent twisting the tubing.
6   Plug the open fittings to prevent entry of dirt and moisture.
7   Loosen the mounting bracket bolts and lift the filter-drier/receiver-drier out.
8   Installation is the reverse of removal.
9   Take the vehicle back to the shop that discharged it. Have the system evacuated, recharged and leak tested.

---

15   Air conditioning compressor – removal and installation

Refer to illustrations 15.6a and 15.6b

Warning: *The air conditioning system is under high pressure. DO NOT disassemble any part of the system (hoses, compressor, line fittings, etc.) until after the system has been depressurized by a dealer service department or service station.*

Note: *The filter-drier/receiver-drier (Section 14) should be replaced whenever the compressor is replaced.*

1   Have the system discharged (see Warning above).
2   Disconnect the negative cable from the battery.
3   Disconnect the compressor clutch wiring harness.
4   Remove the drivebelt (see Chapter 1).
5   Disconnect the refrigerant lines from the rear of the compressor. Plug the open fittings to prevent entry of dirt and moisture.
6   Unbolt the compressor from the mounting brackets **(see illustrations)** and lift it out of the vehicle.

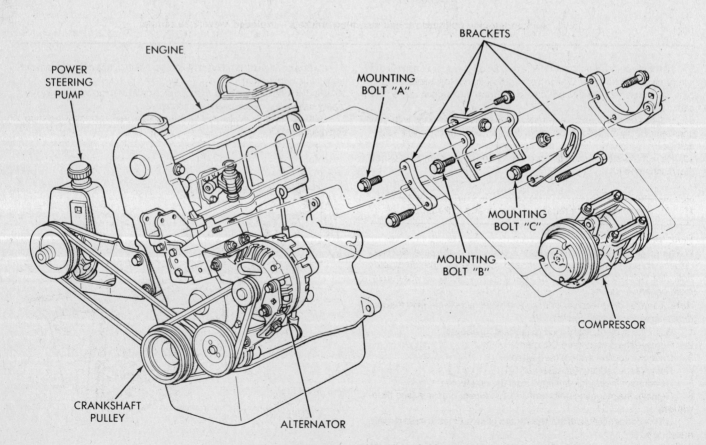

15.6a   **Air conditioning compressor and mounting brackets – exploded view (1.7L engine)**

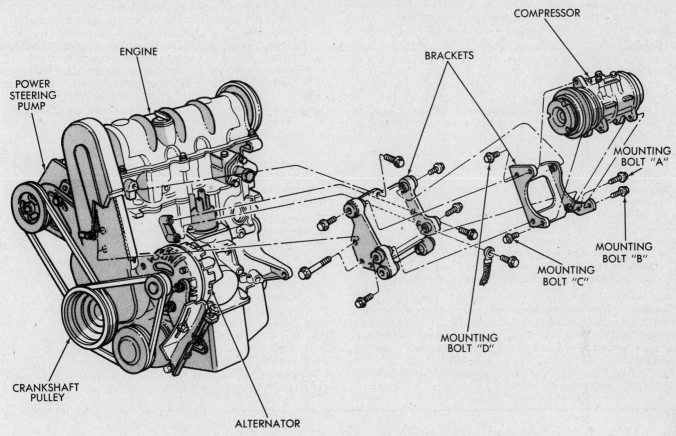

15.6b Air conditioning compressor and mounting brackets – exploded view (2.2L engine)

7   If a new compressor is being installed, follow the directions with the compressor regarding the draining of excess oil prior to installation.

8   The clutch may have to be transferred from the original to the new compressor.

9   Installation is the reverse of removal. Replace all O-rings with new ones specifically made for A/C system use and lubricate them with refrigerant oil.

10   Have the system evacuated, recharged and leak tested by the shop that discharged it.

16   Air conditioning condenser – removal and installation

Refer to illustration 16.6

Warning: *The air conditioning system is under high pressure. DO NOT disassemble any part of the system (hoses, compressor, line fittings, etc.) until after the system has been depressurized by a dealer service department or service station.*

Note: *The filter-drier/receiver-drier should be replaced whenever the condenser is replaced (see Section 14).*

1   Have the system discharged (see Warning above).

2   Remove the battery (see Chapter 5).

3   Drain the cooling system (see Chapter 1).

4   Remove the radiator (see Section 5).

5   Disconnect the refrigerant lines from the condenser.

6   Remove the mounting bolts from the condenser brackets (**see illustration**).

7   Lift the condenser out of the vehicle and plug the lines to keep dirt and moisture out.

8   If the original condenser will be reinstalled, store it with the line fittings on top to prevent oil from draining out.

9   If a new condenser is being installed, pour one ounce of refrigerant oil into it prior to installation.

10   Reinstall the components in the reverse order of removal. Be sure the rubber pads are in place under the condenser.

11   Have the system evacuated, recharged and leak tested by the shop that discharged it.

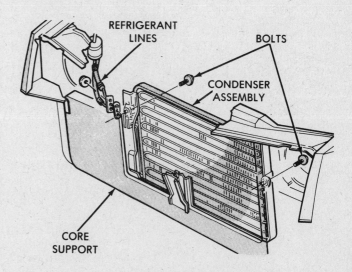

16.6 Condenser mounting details

17   Air conditioning evaporator – removal and installation

Refer to illustration 17.5

Warning: *The air conditioning system is under high pressure. DO NOT disassemble any part of the system (hoses, compressor, line fittings, etc.) until after the system has been depressurized by a dealer service department or service station.*

1   Have the air conditioning system discharged by a dealer service department or a service station.

2   Detach the refrigerant lines where they go through the firewall into the evaporator.

3   Refer to Section 11 and remove the heater/air conditioner unit top cover (Steps 22 through 44).

4   Remove the expansion valve sealing plate seal and seal retaining screw from under the sealing plate.

5   Lift the evaporator coil **(see illustration)** from the heater/evaporator unit.

6   Installation is the reverse of removal.

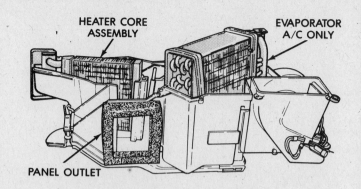

17.5   Evaporator mounting details

Chapter 4 Fuel and exhaust systems

Contents

4

Specifications

Carburetor-equipped vehicles

1.7L engine

Accelerator pump setting	No. 2 hole
Float drop	1.875 in (47.6 mm)
Float Level	0.480 in (12.2 mm)
Choke setting	2 notches rich
Choke vacuum kick	
1979 vehicles with manual transaxle	0.070 in (1.8 mm)
All others	0.040 in (1.0 mm)
Curb idle speed	900 rpm
Fast idle speed	
1978	1100 rpm
1979	1400 rpm
Throttle position transducer	0.55 in (14 mm)

Carburetor-equipped vehicles (continued)
2.2L engine
Curb idle speed .... Refer to VECI label
Fast idle speed .... Refer to VECI label
Float drop .... 1-7/8 in (47.6 mm)
Dry float level .... 0.480 in (12.2 mm)
Choke vacuum kick adjustment

Carburetor number	Gauge size
1981	
R9060A, R9065A, R9123A and R9126A	0.030 in (0.76 mm)
R9602A, R9603A, R9604A and R9605A	0.065 in (1.65 mm)
R9054A and R9055A	0.040 in (1.0 mm)
R9052A and R9053A	0.070 in (1.8 mm)
1982	
R9582A, R9583A, R9584A and R9585A	0.060 in (1.5 mm)
R9824A	0.065 in (1.65 mm)
R9503A, R9504A, R9750A and R9751A	0.085 in (2.15 mm)
R9822A and R9823A	0.080 in (2.05 mm)
R9505A, R9506A, R9752A and R9753A	0.100 in (2.55 mm)
R9513A and R9514A	0.120 in (3.05 mm)
R9499A, R9511A and R9512A	0.130 in (3.30 mm)
1983	
R40003A, R40007A, R40008A, R40012A, R40023A, R40024A, R40025A, R40026A, R40141A, R40003A, R40007A, R40008A and R40012A	0.070 in (1.80 mm)
R40004A, R40005A, R40006A, R40010A and R40014A	0.080 in (2.00 mm)
R40080A and R40081A	0.045 in (1.20 mm)
R400203A and R40022A	0.055 in (1.35 mm)
1984	
R40060A	0.055 in (1.35 mm)
R400851A	0.040 in (1.05 mm)
R40170A and R40171A	0.060 in (1.5 mm)
R400671A, R40068A and R400581A	0.070 in (1.8 mm)
R400641A, R400651A, R400811A, R400821A, R40071A and R40122A	0.080 in (2.00 mm)
1985	
R40058A	0.070 in (1.8 mm)
R40060A	0.055 in (1.4 mm)
R40116A and R40117A	0.095 in (2.4 mm)
R40134A, R40135A, R40138A and R40139A	0.075 in (1.9 mm)
1986	
R400581A	0.070 in (1.7 mm)
R400602A	0.055 in (1.4 mm)
R40138A, R401341A, R401351A, R401381A and R401391A	0.075 in (1.9 mm)
R401161A and R401171A	0.095 in (2.4 mm)

Single-point EFI system
Fuel pressure .... 34 to 38 psi

Torque specifications
Ft-lbs (unless otherwise indicated)
General
Carburetor mounting nuts 17
EFI fuel filter screw 6
EFI fuel line fittings 15
EFI hose clamp screws .... 10 in-lbs

Single-point EFI
AIS motor-to-throttle body screws .... 20 in-lbs
Throttle body-to-intake manifold bolts 17
Pressure regulator mounting screws 4
Throttle position sensor mounting screws .... 20 in-lbs
Fuel injector cap Torx screws .... 40 in-lbs

Multi-point EFI

Fuel rail bolts	19
Throttle body-to-intake manifold bolts	40
Throttle position sensor mounting bolts	17 in-lbs

Turbocharger

Air cleaner box support bracket bolts	40
Exhaust manifold flange nut	20
Exhaust pipe-to-manifold bolt and nut	20
Throttle body-to-intake manifold bolt	40
Turbocharger discharge hose clamp screw	3
Turbocharger-to-exhaust manifold nuts	40
Turbocharger heat shield bolts	9
Turbocharger fuel rail bolts	20
Turbocharger support bracket-to-engine block bolts	40
Turbocharger support bracket-to-turbocharger bolts	20

1   General information

Fuel system

The fuel system consists of the fuel tank, a mechanical or electric fuel pump, an air cleaner, either a carburetor or a fuel injection system and the hoses and lines which connect these components.

Earlier models are carburetor equipped. Vehicles with the 1.7L engine use a Holley 5220. Vehicles with the 2.2L engine use a Holley 6520 carburetor. Both models have a mechanical fuel pump mounted on the engine block. The pump is driven by an eccentric cam off the intermediate shaft.

Later models are fuel-injected. Two different fuel injection systems are used. A Single-point (one injector) Electronic Fuel Injection (EFI) system is standard. A Multi-point (four injectors) EFI system is used on turbocharged models. Fuel injected models use an in-tank electric fuel pump.

Exhaust system

The exhaust system consists of the exhaust manifold, exhaust pipes, catalytic converter and muffler. For information regarding the removal and installation of the exhaust manifold, refer to Chapter 2, Part A. For information regarding exhaust system and catalytic converter servicing, refer to the last Section in this Chapter. For further information regarding the catalytic converter, refer to Chapter 6.

2   Fuel pressure relief procedure

Refer to illustration 2.5
Warning: *Gasoline is extremely flammable, so extra precautions must be taken when working on any part of the fuel system. Don't smoke or allow open flames or bare light bulbs near the work area. Also, don't work in a garage if a natural gas-type appliance with a pilot light is present. Have a fire extinguisher handy and know how to use it!*

1   The fuel system of fuel injected models is pressurized, even when the engine is off. Consequently any time the fuel system is worked on (such as when the fuel filter is replaced) the system must be depressurized to avoid the spraying of fuel when a component is disconnected.
2   Loosen the fuel tank cap to release any pressure in the tank.
3   Unplug the harness connector at the throttle body (single-point) or one of the fuel injectors (multi-point).
4   Ground one of the injector terminals.
5   Connect a jumper wire between the other terminal and the positive (+) post of the battery. Touch the end of the jumper wire to the terminal for no longer than five seconds to depressurize the fuel system **(see illustration)**. Do not energize the injector for more than five seconds to avoid damage to the fuel injector. It's recommended that the pressure be bled in several spurts of one to two seconds to make sure the injector system isn't damaged. The fuel pressure can be heard escaping into the throttle body or combustion chamber. When the sound is no longer heard, the system is depressurized.

3   Fuel pump – check

Mechanical pump

Refer to illustration 3.1
1   Disconnect the fuel line from the carburetor and install a T-fitting **(see illustration)**. Connect a fuel pressure gauge to the T-fitting with a section of fuel hose that's no longer than six inches.

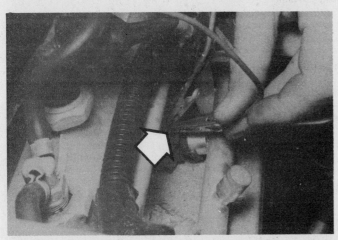

2.5   Bleed the fuel pressure in short bursts by touching the fuel injector terminal (arrow) with the jumper wire clip (multi-point fuel injection system shown, single-point similar)

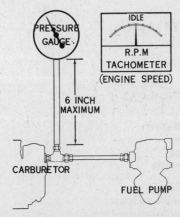

3.1   Attach the T-fitting as close to the carburetor as possible and use a six-inch (maximum) length of hose when hooking up the pressure gauge to check the fuel pump pressure

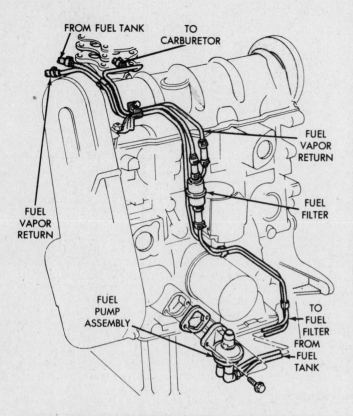

4.1   Mechanical fuel pump location (2.2L engine shown, 1.7L similar)

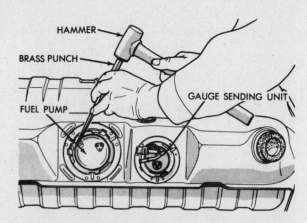

4.9   Use a hammer and BRASS punch (to prevent sparks) to unscrew the fuel pump lock ring

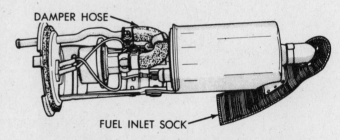

4.11   Inspect the fuel pump damper hose and the fuel inlet sock for damage

2   Disconnect the gauge from the end of the fuel hose and direct the end of the hose into an approved gasoline container. Operate the starter for a few seconds, until fuel spurts out of the hose, to vent the pump (this eliminates any air in the fuel chamber, which could affect the pressure reading). Reattach the gauge to the fuel hose.
3   Start the engine and allow it to idle. The pressure on the gauge should be about 4.5 to 6 psi, remain constant and return to zero slowly when the engine is shut off.
4   An instant pressure drop indicates a faulty outlet valve. If this occurs, or if the pressure is too high or low, replace the fuel pump with a new one. **Note:** *if the pressure is too high, check the air vent to see if it's plugged before replacing the pump.*

Electric in-tank pump

5   Remove the fuel tank cap and place your ear close to the filler neck. Have an assistant turn the ignition key to On while you listen for the sound of the in-tank pump. It should make a whirring sound. If you don't hear the pump, make the following quick checks.
6   Relieve the fuel system pressure (see Section 2).
7   Raise the rear of the vehicle and place it securely on jackstands.
8   Lower the fuel tank slightly (see Section 5) and locate the wire harness to the fuel pump.
9   Using a voltmeter, verify that there's voltage to the pump when the key is turned to On and Start.
   a) If there is voltage to the pump, replace it.
   b) If there is no voltage to the pump, locate the fuel pump relay or fuse, check it and replace as necessary.
10   If the pump still doesn't work, have it checked by a dealer service department or a repair shop. Further testing requires special equipment.

4   Fuel pump – removal and installation

Warning: *Gasoline is extremely flammable, so extra precautions must be taken when working on any part of the fuel system. Don't smoke or allow open flames or bare light bulbs near the work area. Also, don't work in a garage if a natural gas-type appliance with a pilot light is present. Have a fire extinguisher handy and know how to use it!*

Mechanical pump

Refer to illustration 4.1

1   The fuel pump is bolted to the engine block adjacent to the oil filter **(see illustration).**
2   Place clean rags or newspaper under the fuel pump to catch any gasoline spilled during removal.
3   Carefully unscrew the fuel line fittings and detach the lines from the pump. A flare-nut wrench should be used to prevent damage to the fittings.
4   Unbolt and remove the fuel pump.
5   Before installation, coat both sides of the spacer block with RTV sealant, hold the fuel pump and spacer in place and install the bolts.
6   Attach the lines to the pump and tighten the fittings securely (use a flare-nut wrench, if available, to prevent damage to the fittings).
7   Run the engine and check for leaks.

Electric in-tank pump

Refer to illustrations 4.9 and 4.11

8   Remove the fuel tank (see Section 5).
9   Use a hammer and a BRASS punch (a steel punch may cause a spark, which could be extremely dangerous when working on the fuel tank!) to remove the fuel pump lock ring. Drive it in a counterclockwise direction until it can be unscrewed **(see illustration).**

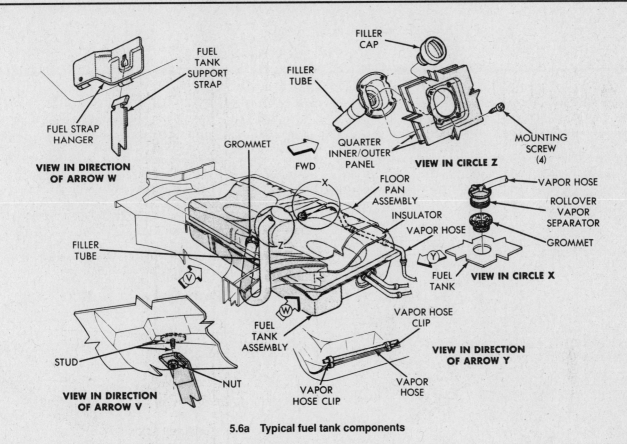

5.6a   Typical fuel tank components

10   Lift the fuel pump and O-ring out of the fuel tank.
11   Clean the sealing area of the fuel tank and install a new O-ring on the fuel pump. Prior to installation, inspect the fuel inlet sock filter on the fuel pump suction tube for damage and contamination. Replace it with a new one if necessary (see illustration).
12   Place the fuel pump in position in the tank, install the locking ring and use a hammer and a BRASS punch to lock the pump in place.
13   Install the fuel tank.

5 Fuel tank – removal and installation

Refer to illustrations 5.6a, 5.6b and 5.6c
Warning: *Gasoline is extremely flammable, so extra precautions must be taken when working on any part of the fuel system. Don't smoke or allow open flames or bare light bulbs near the work area. Also, don't work in a garage if a natural gas-type appliance with a pilot light is present. Have a fire extinguisher handy and know how to use it!*
Note: *The following procedure is much easier if the tank is empty. Some tanks have a drain plug – if it doesn't, simply run the engine until the tank is empty.*

1   Remove the filler cap to relieve the tank pressure.
2   If the vehicle is fuel-injected, relieve the fuel system pressure (see Section 2).
3   Detach the cable from the negative terminal of the battery.
4   If the tank still has fuel in it, you can drain it at the fuel feed line after raising the vehicle. If the tank has a drain plug,
remove it and allow the fuel to collect in an approved gasoline container.
5   Raise the vehicle and place it securely on jackstands.
6   Disconnect the fuel lines and the fuel filler tube (see illustrations).
Note: *The fuel lines are different diameters, so reattachment is simplified. If you have any doubts, however, clearly label the lines and the fittings. Be sure to plug the hoses to prevent leakage and contamination of the fuel system.*

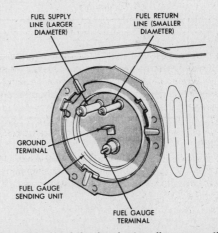

5.6b   Typical fuel tank feed and return line connections on a carburetor-equipped vehicle (1.7L engine shown, 2.2L similar)

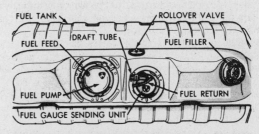

5.6c   Typical fuel tank feed and return line connections on a fuel-injected vehicle

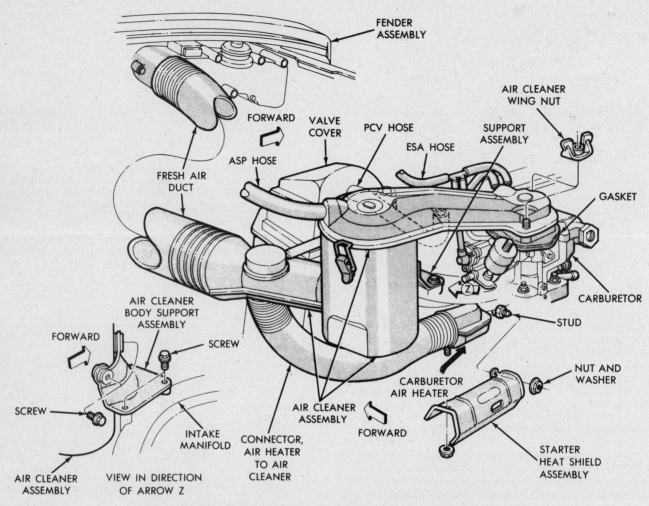

FENDER ASSEMBLY

AIR CLEANER WING NUT

FORWARD

VALVE COVER

PCV HOSE

SUPPORT ASSEMBLY

ESA HOSE

ASP HOSE

FRESH AIR DUCT

GASKET

CARBURETOR

STUD

AIR CLEANER BODY SUPPORT ASSEMBLY

FORWARD

SCREW

NUT AND WASHER

SCREW

CARBURETOR AIR HEATER

AIR CLEANER ASSEMBLY

FORWARD

INTAKE MANIFOLD

CONNECTOR, AIR HEATER TO AIR CLEANER

STARTER HEAT SHIELD ASSEMBLY

AIR CLEANER ASSEMBLY

VIEW IN DIRECTION OF ARROW Z

7.3a   Typical 1.7L engine air cleaner assembly components – exploded view

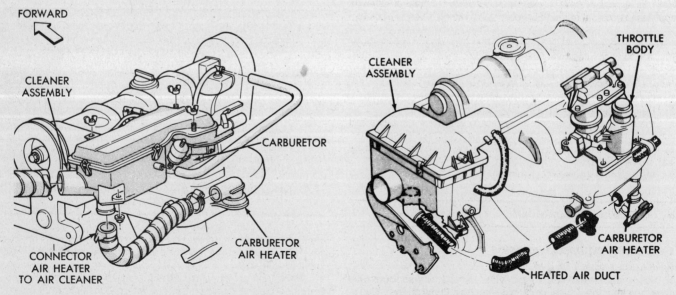

FORWARD

CLEANER ASSEMBLY

CARBURETOR

CLEANER ASSEMBLY

THROTTLE BODY

CARBURETOR AIR HEATER

CONNECTOR AIR HEATER TO AIR CLEANER

CARBURETOR AIR HEATER

HEATED AIR DUCT

7.3b   Typical carburetor-equipped 2.2L engine air cleaner assembly components – exploded view

7.3c   Typical fuel-injected, non-turbocharged 2.2L engine air cleaner assembly components – exploded view

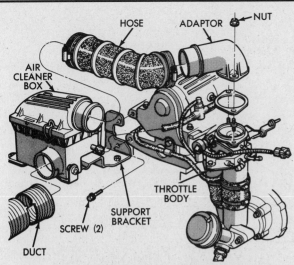

7.3d   Typical turbocharged 2.2L engine air cleaner assembly components – exploded view

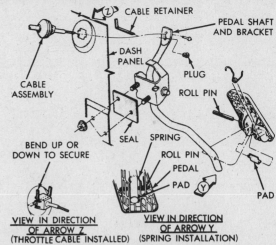

8.1a   Typical throttle cable installation details (1.7L engine) – to detach the cable, lift up the pedal and remove the plug and cable from the upper end of the pedal shaft

7   Siphon the fuel from the tank at the fuel feed – not the return – line.

8   Support the tank with a jack or jackstands. Position a piece of wood between the jack head and the tank to protect the tank.

9   Disconnect both fuel tank retaining straps and pivot them down until they're hanging out of the way.

10   Lower the tank enough to disconnect the electrical wires from the fuel gauge and ground terminals **(see illustration 5.6b)**, if you haven't already done so.

11   Remove the tank from the vehicle.

12   Installation is the reverse of removal.

6   Fuel tank cleaning and repair – general information

1   All repairs to the fuel tank or filler neck should be carried out by a professional who has experience in this critical and potentially dangerous work. Even after cleaning and flushing of the fuel system, explosive fumes can remain and ignite during repair of the tank.

2   If the fuel tank is removed from the vehicle, it shouldn't be placed in an area where sparks or open flames could ignite the fumes coming out of the tank. Be especially careful inside garages where a natural gas-type appliance is located, because the pilot light could cause an explosion.

7   Air cleaner – removal and installation

Refer to illustrations 7.3a, 7.3b, 7.3c and 7.3d

1   Detach the cable from the negative battery terminal.

2   Remove the air filter element (see Chapter 1).

3   Clearly label, then detach all remaining vacuum lines, tubes and hoses from the lower half of the air cleaner assembly **(see illustrations)**.

4   Remove the fasteners from the air cleaner mounting brackets and detach the air cleaner.

5   Installation is the reverse of removal.

8   Throttle cable – replacement

Carburetor equipped vehicles

Refer to illustrations 8.1a, 8.1b and 8.2

1   Working inside the vehicle, remove the retainer or plug and detach the cable end from the accelerator pedal shaft **(see illustrations)**. On vehicles with a 1.7L engine, bend down the metal tabs of the firewall clip, remove the clip, compress the plastic tabs with pliers and push the cable

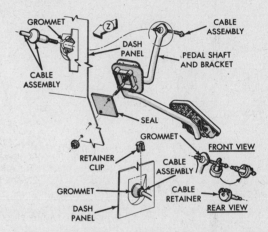

8.1b   Typical throttle cable installation details (2.2L engine) – to detach the cable, remove the retainer and disengage the cable from the pedal shaft

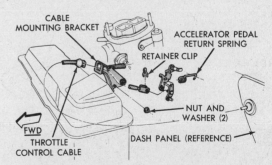

8.2   Typical throttle cable-to-carburetor mounting details (1.7L engine shown, 2.2L similar)

through the firewall. On vehicles with a 2.2L engine, remove the retainer clip from the cable assembly housing at the grommet and push the cable through the firewall.

2   Working in the engine compartment, remove the retainer clip and separate the cable from the pin or stud, then detach the cable from the mounting bracket **(see illustration)**. Compress the cable-to-bracket fitting with a pair of pliers that has wide jaws.

8.7a   Pull the throttle cable retainer clip off with a pair of needle-nose pliers

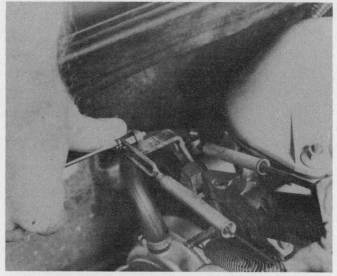

8.7b   Use a small screwdriver to pry off the cruise control cable clip

3   Pull the cable assembly into the engine compartment and remove it from the vehicle. Make sure the grommet remains in place in the firewall.
4   Installation is the reverse of removal.

Fuel-injected vehicles

Refer to illustrations 8.7a, 8.7b, 8.7c and 8.7d

5   Working inside the vehicle, disconnect the throttle cable from the pedal shaft, then disconnect the cable from the firewall **(see illustrations 8.1a and 8.1b)**.
6   Working in the engine compartment, pull the cable housing end fitting out of the dash panel grommet, making sure the grommet remains in place.
7   Remove the retainer clips and disconnect the throttle cable and cruise control cable (if equipped) from the throttle body **(see illustrations)**. Use a pair of pliers to compress the end fitting tabs so the cable can be separated from the mounting bracket.
8   To install the cable, insert the housing into the cable mounting bracket on the engine and attach the clevis to the throttle body with the retainer

clip. Insert the cable through the firewall grommet and connect it to the throttle pedal.

9   Carburetor – description

Refer to illustrations 9.1a and 9.1b

Holley models 5220 and 6520 **(see illustrations)** are staged dual venturi carburetors. The primary bore is smaller than the secondary bore.

The secondary stage is mechanically operated by a linkage connecting the primary and secondary throttle levers.

The primary stage includes a curb idle and transfer system, diaphragm type accelerator pump system, main metering system and power enrichment system. On model 6520 carburetors, there's also an oxygen feedback solenoid that responds to input from the oxygen sensor.

The secondary stage includes a main metering system and power system. Both the primary and secondary venturi draw fuel from a common float bowl.

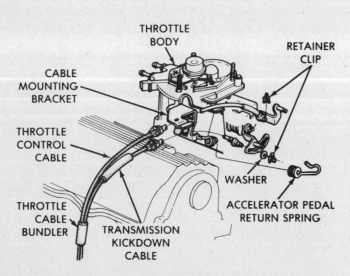

8.7c   Typical throttle cable-to-throttle body mounting details (single-point EFI)

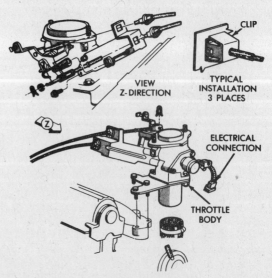

8.7d   Typical throttle cable-to-throttle body mounting details (multi-point EFI)

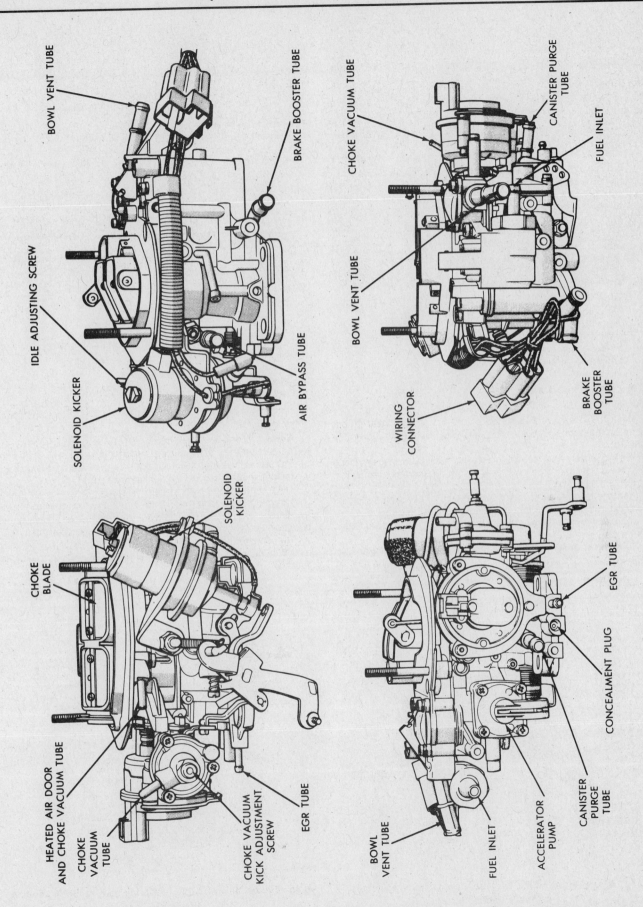

9.1a   Holley Model 5220 carburetor

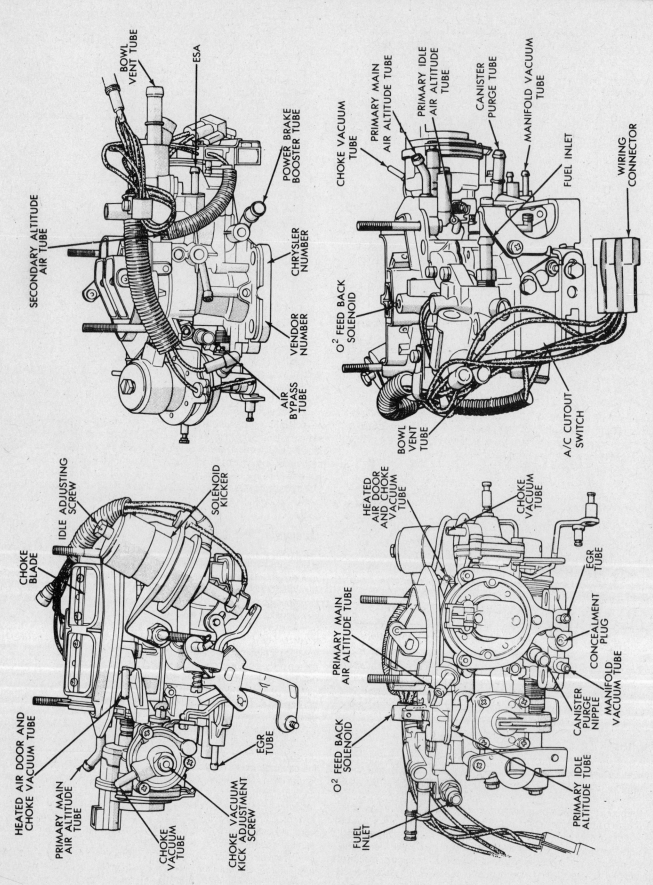

9.1b Holley Model 6520 carburetor

The electric automatic choke has a bimetal two-stage heating element. In normal service, the idle mixture shouldn't require adjustment. The idle set rpm can be checked without removing the tamper resistant plug.

10 Carburetor – removal and installation

Warning: *Gasoline is extremely flammable, so extra precautions must be taken when working on any part of the fuel system. Don't smoke or allow open flames or bare light bulbs near the work area. Also, don't work in a garage if a natural gas-type appliance with a pilot light is present. Have a fire extinguisher handy and know how to use it!*

Removal

1   Remove the fuel tank cap to relieve the tank pressure.
2   Remove the air cleaner from the carburetor. Be sure to label all vacuum hoses attached to the air cleaner housing.
3   Disconnect the throttle cable from the throttle lever (see Section 8).
4   If the vehicle is equipped with an automatic transmission, disconnect the TV cable from the throttle lever.
5   Clearly label all vacuum hoses and fittings, then disconnect the hoses.
6   Disconnect the fuel line from the carburetor.
7   Label the wires and terminals, then unplug all wire harness connectors.
8   Remove the mounting fasteners and detach the carburetor from the intake manifold. Remove the carburetor mounting gasket. Stuff a shop rag into the intake manifold openings.

Installation

9   Use a gasket scraper to remove all traces of gasket material and sealant from the intake manifold (and the carburetor, if it's being reinstalled), then remove the shop rag from the manifold openings. Clean the mating surfaces with lacquer thinner or acetone.
10   Place a new gasket on the intake manifold.
11   Position the carburetor on the gasket and install the mounting fasteners.
12   To prevent carburetor distortion or damage, tighten the fasteners, in a criss-cross pattern, 1/4-turn at a time, to the torque listed in this Chapter's Specifications.
13   The remaining installation steps are the reverse of removal.
14   Check and, if necessary, adjust the idle speed (see Chapter 1).
15   If the vehicle is equipped with an automatic transmission, refer to Chapter 7, Part B, for the TV cable adjustment procedure.
16   Start the engine and check carefully for fuel leaks.

11 Carburetor diagnosis and overhaul – general information

Warning: *Gasoline is extremely flammable, so extra precautions must be taken when working on any part of the fuel system. Don't smoke or allow open flames or bare light bulbs near the work area. Also, don't work in a garage if a natural gas-type appliance with a pilot light is present. Have a fire extinguisher handy and know how to use it!*

Diagnosis

1   A thorough road test and check of carburetor adjustments should be done before any major carburetor service work. Specifications for some adjustments are listed on the Vehicle Emissions Control Information (VECI) label found in the engine compartment.
2   Carburetor problems usually show up as flooding, hard starting, stalling, severe backfiring and poor acceleration. A carburetor that's leaking fuel and/or covered with wet looking deposits definitely needs attention.
3   Some performance complaints directed at the carburetor are actually a result of loose, out-of-adjustment or malfunctioning engine or electrical components. Others develop when vacuum hoses leak, are disconnected or are incorrectly routed. The proper approach to analyzing carburetor problems should include the following items:

a)   Inspect all vacuum hoses and actuators for leaks and correct installation (see Chapters 1 and 6).
b)   Tighten the intake manifold and carburetor mounting nuts/bolts evenly and securely.
c)   Perform a cylinder compression test (see Chapter 2).
d)   Clean or replace the spark plugs as necessary (see Chapter1).
e)   Check the spark plug wires (see Chapter 1).
f)   Inspect the ignition primary wires.
g)   Check the ignition timing (follow the instructions printed on the Emissions Control Information label).
h)   Check the fuel pump pressure/volume (see Section 3).
i)   Check the heat control valve in the air cleaner for proper operation (see Chapter 1).
j)   Check/replace the air filter element (see Chapter 1).
k)   Check the PCV system (see Chapters 1 and 6).
l)   Check/replace the fuel filter (see Chapter 1). Also, the strainer in the tank could be restricted.
m)   Check for a plugged exhaust system.
n)   Check EGR valve operation (see Chapter 6).
o)   Check the choke – it should be completely open at normal engine operating temperature (see Chapter 1).
p)   Check for fuel leaks and kinked or dented fuel lines (see Chapters 1 and 4)
q)   Check accelerator pump operation with the engine off (remove the air cleaner cover and operate the throttle as you look into the carburetor throat – you should see a stream of gasoline enter the carburetor).
r)   Check for incorrect fuel or bad gasoline.
s)   Check the valve clearances (if applicable) and camshaft lobe lift (see Chapters 1 and 2)
t)   Have a dealer service department or repair shop check the electronic engine and carburetor controls.

4   Diagnosing carburetor problems may require that the engine be started and run with the air cleaner off. While running the engine without the air cleaner, backfires are possible. This situation is likely to occur if the carburetor is malfunctioning, but just the removal of the air cleaner can lean the fuel/air mixture enough to produce an engine backfire. **Warning:** *Don't position any part of your body, especially your face, directly over the carburetor during inspection and servicing procedures. Wear eye protection!*

Overhaul

5   Once it's determined that the carburetor needs an overhaul, several options are available. If you're going to attempt to overhaul the carburetor yourself, first obtain a good quality carburetor rebuild kit (which will include all necessary gaskets, internal parts, instructions and a parts list). You'll also need some special solvent and a means of blowing out the internal passages of the carburetor with air.
6   An alternative is to obtain a new or rebuilt carburetor. They're readily available from dealers and auto parts stores. Make absolutely sure the exchange carburetor is identical to the original. A tag is usually attached to the top of the carburetor or a number is stamped on the float bowl. It'll help determine the exact type of carburetor you have. When obtaining a rebuilt carburetor or a rebuild kit, make sure the kit or carburetor matches your application exactly. Seemingly insignificant differences can make a large difference in engine performance.
7   If you choose to overhaul your own carburetor, allow enough time to disassemble it carefully, soak the necessary parts in the cleaning solvent (usually for at least one-half day or according to the instructions listed on the carburetor cleaner) and reassemble it, which will usually take much longer than disassembly. When disassembling the carburetor, match each part with the illustration in the carburetor kit and lay the parts out in order on a clean work surface. Overhauls by inexperienced mechanics can result in an engine which runs poorly or not at all. To avoid this, use care and patience when disassembling the carburetor so you can reassemble it correctly.
8   Because carburetor designs are constantly modified by the manufacturer in order to meet increasingly more stringent emissions regulations, the overhaul procedures in this Chapter may not apply exactly to your vehicle. You'll receive a detailed, well illustrated set of instructions with any

4

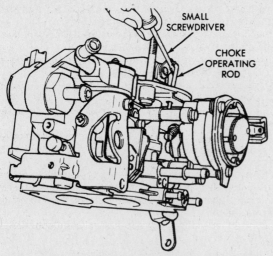

12.2   Detach the choke operating rod (1.7L engine)

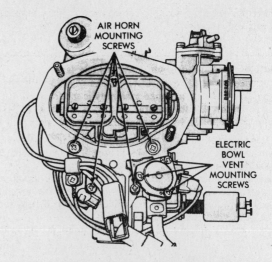

12.3   Location of air horn and electric bowl vent mounting screws (1.7L engine)

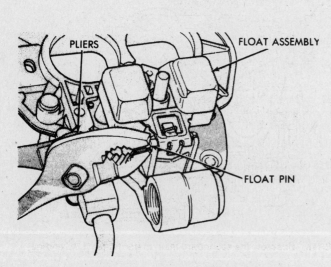

12.5   Withdraw the float pivot pin (1.7L engine)

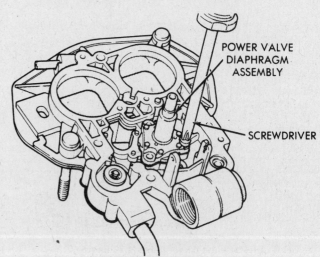

12.6   Remove the power valve diaphragm assembly screws (1.7L engine)

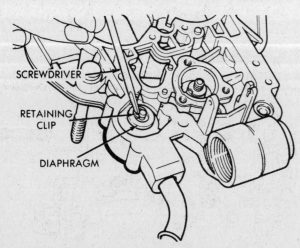

12.7   Remove the bowl vent solenoid retaining clip (1.7L engine)

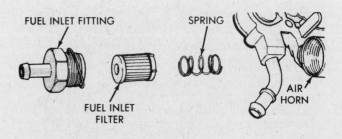

12.8   Exploded view of the fuel inlet fitting, filter and spring (1.7L engine)

carburetor overhaul kit; they'll apply in a more specific manner to the carburetor on your vehicle.

12   Carburetor – overhaul (1.7L engine)

Refer to illustrations 12.2, 12.3, 12.5, 12.6, 12.7, 12.8, 12.9, 12.11a, 12.11b, 12.12a, 12.12b, 12.13, 12.15, 12.16, 12.18, 12.19, 12.20, 12.26, 12.27, 12.37 and 12.38

1   Before disassembling the carburetor, clean off all the external dirt.

2   Disconnect the choke operating rod, then remove the rod and the choke rod seal **(see illustration)**.

3   Remove the three screws securing the electric bowl vent cover and detach the cover **(see illustration)**. Remove the harness retaining screw.

4   Remove the five screws securing the air horn to the main body, then separate the air horn from the carburetor.

5   Carefully remove the float pivot pin **(see illustration)** and lift out the float assembly, followed by the needle valve. Using a socket wrench, remove the fuel inlet needle valve seat and gasket.

6   Remove the three screws that secure the power valve diaphragm, then detach it from the air horn **(see illustration)**.

7   Remove the bowl vent diaphragm assembly retaining clip and lift out the vent assembly **(see illustration)**.

8   Unscrew the fuel inlet fitting and remove the fuel filter and spring **(see illustration)**.

9   Remove the power valve from the bottom of the float bowl **(see illustration)**.

10   Next remove the jets. To prevent damaging the jets during removal, make sure the screwdriver is the correct size and the end of the blade is in good condition.

11   Remove the secondary main metering jet **(see illustration)** and the primary main metering jet **(see illustration)**. Record the respective size and location of each jet so they can be installed in their original locations during reassembly.

12   Unscrew the secondary high speed bleed **(see illustration)** and the

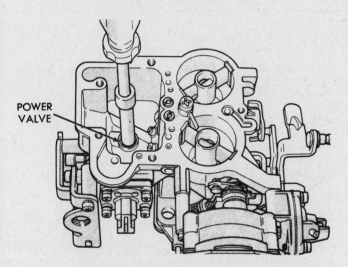

12.9   Unscrew the power valve (1.7L engine)

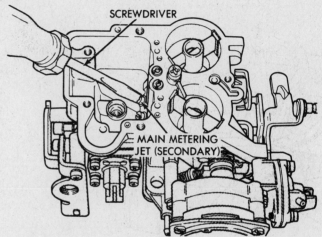

12.11a   Unscrew the secondary main metering jet (1.7L engine)

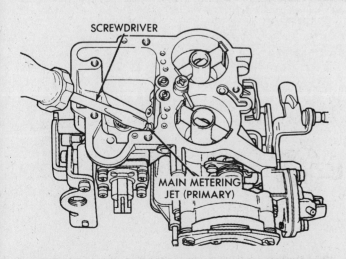

12.11b   Unscrew the primary main metering jet (1.7L engine)

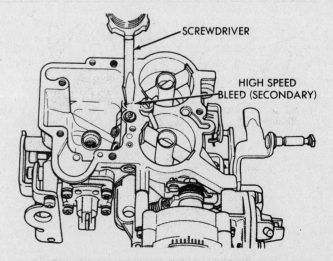

12.12a   Remove the secondary high speed bleed (1.7L engine)

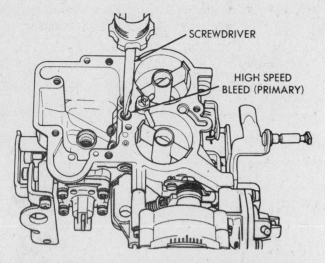

12.12b   Remove the primary high speed bleed (1.7L engine)

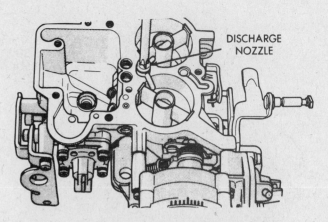

12.13   Remove the discharge nozzle (1.7L engine)

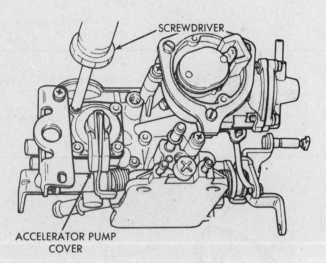

**12.15   Remove the four accelerator pump cover screws
(1.7L engine)**

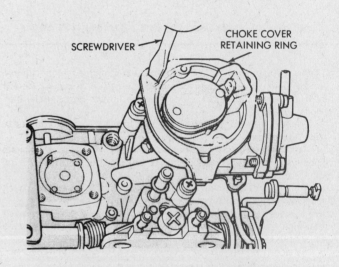

12.16   Remove the choke cover screws (1.7L engine)

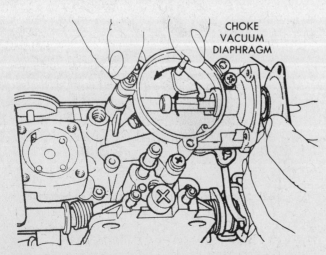

**12.18   Rotate the choke lever, then remove the choke vacuum
diaphragm (1.7L engine)**

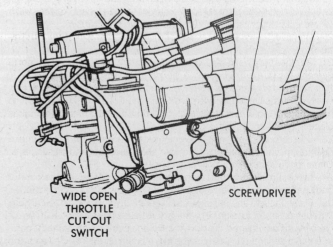

**12.19   If the vehicle is air-conditioned, remove the wide open
throttle cut-out switch (1.7L engine)**

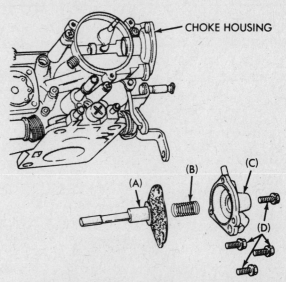

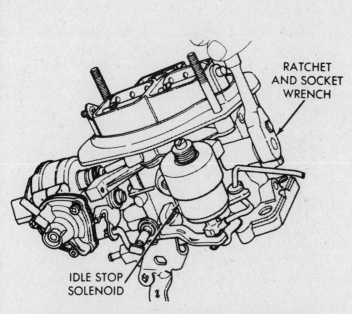

12.20   Remove the idle stop solenoid screws (1.7L engine)

12.26   Exploded view of the choke diaphragm assembly (1.7L engine)

A	Diaphragm	C	Diaphragm cover
B	Spring	D	Screws

primary high speed bleed **(see illustration)**. Remove the primary and secondary main well tubes located under the high speed bleeds. Identify the high speed bleeds and main well tubes so they can be installed in their original locations.

13   Remove the discharge nozzle screw. Detach the nozzle and gasket **(see illustration)**.

14   Turn the carburetor body upside down. Collect the accelerator pump discharge weight ball and check ball as they drop out. Both balls are the same size.

15   Remove the four accelerator pump cover screws. Remove the cover, accelerator pump diaphragm and spring **(see illustration)**.

16   Remove the three choke mounting screws. Remove the choke cover retaining ring, choke coil heating element and cover assembly, ground ring, choke lever sleeve and choke housing **(see illustration)**.

17   Remove the three screws securing the choke diaphragm cover and lift off the cover and spring.

18   Remove the choke diaphragm by rotating the choke shaft and lever assembly counterclockwise **(see illustration)**. Then rotate the choke diaphragm assembly clockwise and pull it out of the housing.

19   Remove the two screws and detach the wide open throttle cut-out switch (vehicles with air conditioning only). Mark the location of the switch for correct positioning during reassembly **(see illustration)**.

20   Remove the two screws and lift off the idle stop solenoid **(see illustration)**.

21   Remove the plastic cap from the idle mixture screw, taking care not to damage the screw. Then remove the idle mixture screw and spring.

22   Further disassembly isn't recommended. If the throttle shaft is excessively worn, the carburetor body assembly should be replaced. There's no point in installing a new shaft in an old body, as most of the wear takes place in the body.

23   Use carburetor cleaning solvent to wash the parts, except the choke diaphragm, choke heater nylon choke shaft bushings and plastic parts. Clean those parts with a cloth or soft brush.

24   Make sure all sediment is removed from the float bowl and carburetor body passages. Remove all traces of old gaskets with a sharp knife.

25   Clean the jets and passages with clean, dry compressed air. Check the float assembly for signs of damage and leaks (shake it to see if there's gasoline inside). Inspect the power valve and pump diaphragms for damage and deterioration. Examine the idle mixture screw, needle valve and seat for wear. Replace parts as necessary. Obtain a carburetor repair kit.

26   To reassemble the choke diaphragm assembly, rotate the choke shaft counterclockwise. Then insert the choke diaphragm into the housing with a clockwise motion. Install the diaphragm spring, cover and screws **(see illustration)**. Position the choke cover two notches rich.

27   Install the accelerator pump spring, diaphragm, cover and four screws **(see illustration)**.

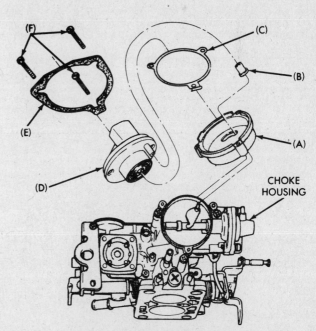

12.27   Exploded view of the electric choke assembly (1.7L engine)

A	Choke housing	D	Heating element
B	Choke lever sleeve	E	Retaining ring
C	Ground ring	F	Screws

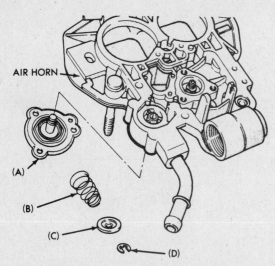

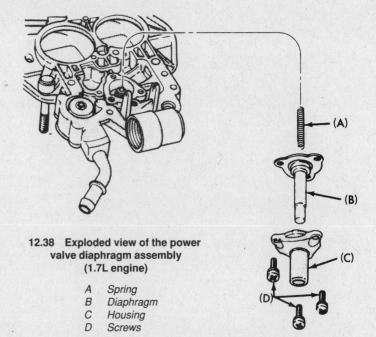

**12.37   Exploded view of float bowl vent solenoid
(1.7L engine)**

A	Diaphragm assembly	C	Retainer
B	Spring	D	Clip

**12.38   Exploded view of the power
valve diaphragm assembly
(1.7L engine)**

A   Spring
B   Diaphragm
C   Housing
D   Screws

28   Insert the accelerator pump discharge check ball into the discharge passage. Fill the float bowl with clean gasoline and check for leakage by holding the check ball down, using a piece of brass rod, and operating the pump plunger by hand.

29   If the check ball and seat are leaking, no resistance will be felt when operating the plunger. If there's leakage, stake the check ball against the seat with a small pin punch. Don't damage the bore.

30   After staking the seat, remove the old check ball and discard it. Insert a new check ball, from the repair kit, and recheck for leakage. If there's still leakage, the carburetor body assembly must be replaced.

31   Insert the pump discharge weight ball on top of the check ball.

32   Install the discharge nozzle and screw. Use new gaskets.

33   Install the primary and secondary main well tubes (both tubes are the same size) and the primary and secondary high speed bleeds (the number stamped on the secondary bleed is larger than the one stamped on the primary bleed).

34   Install the primary and secondary main metering jets. The primary main jet has a larger number than the secondary main jet.

35   Screw in the power valve.

36   Install the fuel filter spring, fuel filter and fuel inlet fitting.

37   To install the electric bowl vent assembly, insert the diaphragm shaft into the housing within the air horn. Follow this with the spring, the retainer and retaining clip **(see illustration)**.

38   Install the power valve diaphragm spring, followed by the diaphragm, the diaphragm housing and the three screws **(see illustration)**.

39   Install the fuel inlet seat and a new gasket.

40   Install the fuel inlet needle valve, float and float pivot pin. Carry out the float level and float drop adjustments as described in Section 13.

41   Install the choke rod seal and choke operating rod.

42   Install a new gasket on the air horn and carefully assemble the air horn to the carburetor body. Install new choke operating rod retainers on the choke shaft lever and fast idle cam pickup lever. Then connect the choke operating rod to the levers.

43   Install the five air horn-to-carburetor body screws and tighten them a little at a time in a criss-cross pattern.

44   Install and tighten the three screws securing the electric bowl vent cover.

45   Install the idle stop solenoid and tighten the two screws.

46   Install the wide open throttle cut-out switch (vehicles equipped with air conditioning). Position the switch as marked during disassembly and tighten the two screws.

47   Install and tighten the wiring harness screw.

48   Install the carburetor on the engine and carry out the carburetor adjustments as described in Section 13.

13   Carburetor – adjustments (1.7L engine)

Float level and float drop adjustment

Refer to illustrations 13.7 and 13.8

1   Remove the air cleaner (see Section 7).

2   Disconnect the fuel line at the fuel inlet fitting and plug the end to prevent the entry of dirt.

3   Remove the wiring harness screw and disconnect the wiring.

4   Remove the five air horn screws and lift the air horn off the carburetor body.

5   Carefully examine the float for damage (particularly holes). This can be done by immersing the float in warm water and checking for air bubbles.

6   Examine the float for cracks and other damage.

7   Hold the air horn upside down and insert a 0.480-inch diameter drill bit between the air horn and the float as shown **(see illustration)**. Adjust the float level, if necessary, by bending the tang which rests against the needle valve, to obtain the correct float level.

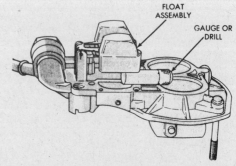

**13.7   Check the float level with a float gauge or drill bit
(1.7L engine)**

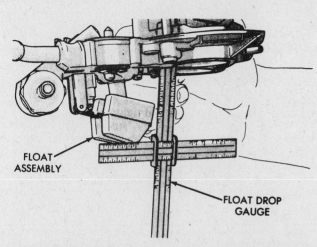

13.8   Check the float drop with a float drop gauge (1.7L engine)

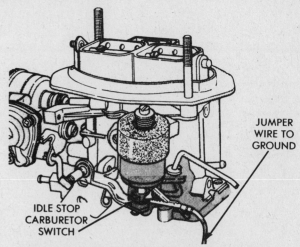

13.14   Ground the idle stop switch (1.7L engine)

8   Now hold the air horn upright and allow the float to hang down (see illustration).

9   Using a float drop gauge, measure the distance from the air horn to the lowest point of the float.

10   Compare the measurement with the figure listed in this Chapter's specifications. If necessary, bend the tang on the back of the float to obtain the correct float drop.

11   Install the air horn on the carburetor body by reversing the removal procedure. Install the air cleaner assembly (see Section 7.

Curb idle speed adjustment

12   To conform to emission control specifications, the idle speed adjustment should be done using an artificial idle enrichment gas (propane) to determine the best idle speed. Since this requires a tachometer, propane metering valve and container of propane gas, it must be done by a dealer service department or a repair shop.

Fast idle adjustment

Refer to illustrations 13.14 and 13.16

13   Remove the air cleaner (see Section 7).

14   Disconnect the EGR valve and plug all the disconnected vacuum ports. Don't disconnect the hose to the vacuum transducer on the spark control computer. Use a jumper wire to ground the idle stop carburetor switch (see Illustration).

15   Disconnect the wiring from the engine cooling fan thermoswitch on the radiator and, using a jumper wire at the connector to complete the circuit, energize the fan. **Note:** *A short to ground will damage the wiring system.*

16   Open the throttle slightly and position the slowest speed step of the fast idle cam under the adjusting screw (see illustration).

17   Start the engine and allow the speed to stabilize (choke valve completely open). If the engine speed continues to rise slowly, the idle stop switch isn't properly grounded.

18   Adjust the fast idle speed by turning the adjusting screw as necessary to obtain the specified engine speed.

Choke vacuum kick adjustment

Refer to Illustration 13.22

19   Open the throttle, close the choke, then close the throttle to set the fast idle at the closed choke position.

20   Disconnect the vacuum hose from the carburetor and apply a vacuum (15 in-Hg) with a hand-held pump.

21   Apply sufficient force to position the choke valve at the smallest opening possible without distorting the linkage.

22   Insert a drill bit, the size listed in this Chapter's Specifications, into the center of the area between the top of the choke valve and the air horn wall at the primary throttle end of the carburetor (see illustration).

4

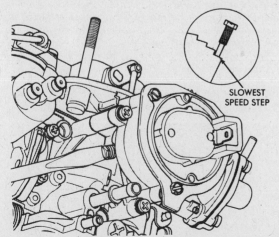

13.16   Position the adjusting screw on the slowest step of the fast idle cam (1.7L engine)

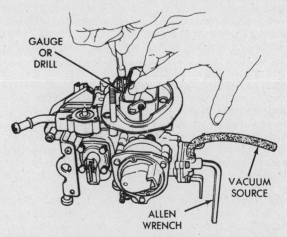

13.22   Adjusting the choke vacuum kick (1.7L engine)

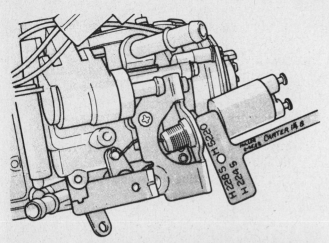

13.26   If the vehicle has a manual transaxle, adjust the throttle position transducer (1.7L engine)

14.1a   Remove the fuel inlet (2.2L engine)

14.1b   Detach the choke rod (2.2L engine)

14.1c   Remove the feedback solenoid screws (2.2L engine)

14.1d   Remove the feedback solenoid (2.2L engine)

23   Using an Allen wrench, adjust the screw in the center of the diaphragm housing to obtain the correct setting.
24   Reconnect the vacuum hose to the carburetor.

Throttle position transducer adjustment (vehicles with a manual transaxle)

Refer to Illustration 13.26

25   Disconnect the wiring from the throttle position transducer and loosen the locknut.
26   Measure the distance between the transducer casing and the mounting bracket. It should be 0.55-inch. Use Chrysler tool no. C-4522 to check the setting **(see illustration)**. Adjust by screwing the transducer in or out as necessary.
27   Tighten the locknut and reconnect the wiring.
28   Install the air cleaner (see Section 7).

14   Carburetor – overhaul (2.2L engine)

Disassembly

Refer to illustrations 14.1a through 14.1v

1   With the carburetor removed from the vehicle (see Section 10), disassembly can begin (make sure you have a rebuild kit available before proceeding). Carburetor disassembly is illustrated in a step-by-step fashion with photos. Follow the photos in the alphabetical sequence, beginning with 14.1a. Have a large, clean work area available to lay out the parts as

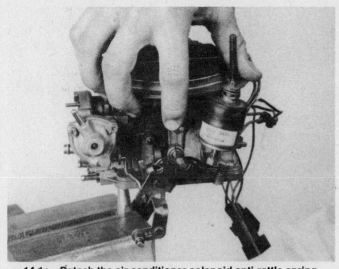

14.1e Detach the air conditioner solenoid anti-rattle spring (2.2L engine)

14.1f Remove the air conditioner solenoid (2.2L engine)

14.1g Remove the wide open throttle cut-out switch (2.2L engine)

14.1h Remove the air horn screws (2.2L engine)

14.1i Carefully pry the air horn off the carburetor (2.2L engine)

14.1j Detach the choke lever and lift off the air horn (2.2L engine)

14.1k   Remove the pin and detach the float (2.2L engine)

14.1l   Remove the fuel inlet needle and seat (2.2L engine)

14.1m   Remove the secondary (S) and primary (P) main metering jets – note their sizes to ensure proper reassembly (2.2L engine)

14.1n   Remove the primary (P) and secondary (S) bleeds and main well tubes – note their sizes to ensure proper reassembly (2.2L engine)

14.1o   Remove the accelerator discharge pump assembly (2.2L engine)

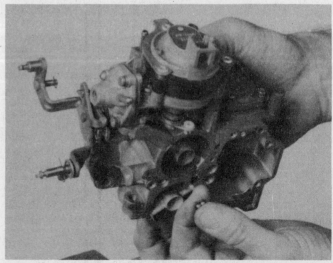

14.1p   Invert the carburetor and catch the accelerator pump discharge weight and check balls (2.2L engine)

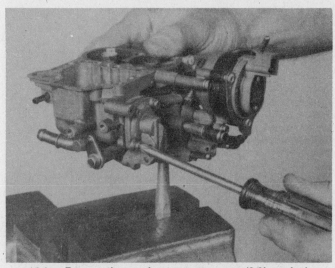

14.1q Remove the accelerator pump cover (2.2L engine)

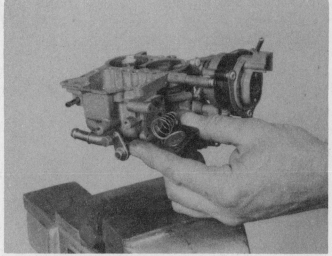

14.1r Remove the pump diaphragm and spring (2.2L engine)

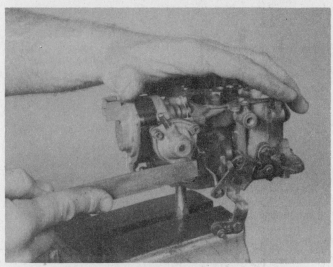

14.1s File the head off the choke diaphragm cover rivet
(2.2L engine)

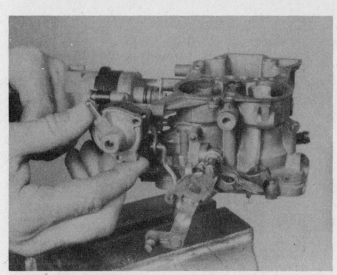

14.1t Remove the screws and lift the cover off (2.2L engine)

4

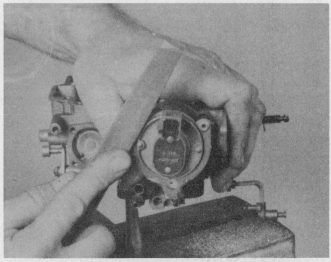

14.1u File the heads off the choke retainer ring rivets and
remove the ring (2.2L engine)

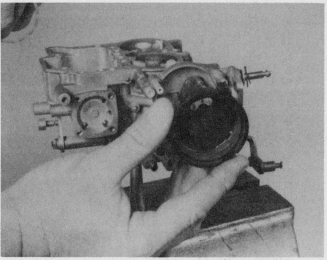

14.1v Remove the choke housing (2.2L engine)

14.10   Rotate the choke diaphragm in a clockwise direction when installing it (2.2L engine)

14.11   Install the breakaway screw in the bottom hole (2.2L engine)

14.13   Hold the screws in place when installing the accelerator pump cover (2.2L engine)

14.14   Install the check ball in the accelerator pump discharge passage (2.2L engine)

they're removed from the carburetor. Many of the parts are very small and can be easily lost if the area is cluttered. Take your time during disassembly. Sketch the relationship of the various components of any assembly which appears complicated or tag the various parts for ease of reassembly. Care taken during disassembly will pay off with an easier job during reassembly.

Cleaning

2   After disassembly, clean the carburetor components with carburetor cleaner/solvent. Make sure you keep track of primary and secondary main metering jet and bleed assemblies (they must be reinstalled in their original locations).

3   The choke, vacuum diaphragms, O-rings, feedback solenoid, floats and seals shouldn't be placed in the solvent – they could be damaged.

4   Clean the external surfaces of the carburetor with a soft brush and wash all of the parts thoroughly in the solvent. If the instructions on the solvent or cleaner recommend the use of water for rinsing, hot water will produce the best results. After rinsing, all traces of water must be blown out of the passages with compressed air. Never clean jets with a wire, drill bit or other objects. The orifices may be enlarged, making the mixture too rich for proper performance.

5   When checking parts removed from the carburetor, it's often difficult to be sure if they're serviceable. As a result, new parts should be installed, if available, when the carburetor is reassembled. The required parts should be included in the rebuild kit.

6   After the parts have been cleaned and dried, check the throttle shaft for excessive wear. Inspect the idle mixture screw for a ridge or groove on the tapered portion.

7   Check the jets to make sure they're not clogged. Replace them if damage is evident.

8   Check for freeness of movement of the choke mechanism in the air horn. It should move freely for proper operation.

9   Replace any worn or damaged components with new ones.

Reassembly

Refer to illustrations 14.10, 14.11, 14.13, 14.14, 14.23, 14.24, 14.25, 14.26, 14.27, 14.28, 14.29, 14.31, 14.34, 14.35, 14.38a and 14.38b

10   Press down on the choke lever, insert the choke diaphragm and rotate it into position **(see illustration)**.

11   Position the spring and cover. Install the two top screws snugly, followed by the breakaway screw in the bottom hole **(see illustration)**.

12   Tighten the breakaway screw until the head breaks off. Tighten the top screws evenly and securely.

13   Install the accelerator pump, spring (small end first), cover and screws **(see illustration)**.

14.23   To determine the dry float level, measure the distance between the bottom of the float and the air horn (2.2L engine)

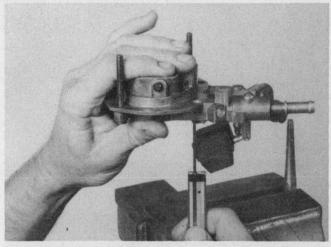

14.24   To determine float drop, measure the distance from the air horn surface to the top of the float (2.2L engine)

14   Fill the float bowl with fuel to a depth of one inch and drop the check ball into the accelerator pump discharge passage (see illustration).

15   Use a small brass punch to hold the check ball in place and push the throttle lever to make sure resistance is felt (which means no leakage is occurring). If there's leakage, drain the fuel and stake the ball in place with one or two taps on the punch. Remove the old ball and install the new one from the rebuild kit. Install the weight ball and repeat the test.

16   Install the accelerator pump discharge nozzle assembly.

17   Install the primary main well tube and high speed bleed.

18   Install the secondary main well tube and high speed bleed.

19   Install the primary main metering jets.

20   Install the secondary main metering jets.

21   Install the fuel inlet needle and seat assembly.

22   Hook the new needle onto the float tang and lower the assembly into place. Install the float retaining pin.

23   Measure the dry float level (see illustration) and compare the measurement with the figure listed in this Chapter's Specifications.

24   Invert the air horn and measure the float drop (see illustration). Compare the measurement with the figure listed in this Chapter's Specifications.

25   Adjust the dry float level by carefully bending the inner adjustment tang until the level is within the range listed in this Chapter's Specifications (see illustration).

26   Bend the outer adjustment tang to bring the float drop to the figure listed in this Chapter's Specifications (see illustration).

27   Install the choke seal and link and squeeze the link retainer bushing into place (see illustration).

14.25   Bend the tang carefully up or down to adjust the dry float level (2.2L engine)

14.26   Be sure to support the pivot when bending the float drop adjustment tang (2.2L engine)

14.27   Install the choke link retainer bushing (2.2L engine)

14.28   Be careful not to bend the float tangs when lowering the
air horn assembly onto the carburetor body (2.2L engine)

14.29   Tighten the screws evenly in a criss-cross pattern
(2.2L engine)

14.31   Adjust the solenoid switch with a screwdriver
(2.2L engine)

14.34   Place the O-ring in the groove and work it over the end of
the solenoid (2.2L engine)

14.35   Rock the solenoid gently from side-to-side to seat the
O-ring (2.2L engine)

28   Position the gasket, engage the choke link and lower the air horn assembly into place **(see illustration)**.
29   Install the screws and tighten them securely **(see illustration)**.
30   Install the wide open throttle cut-out switch with the two screws and
one bolt (just snug them up, don't tighten them completely).
31   Adjust the solenoid switch by loosening the bolt and using a screwdriver to rotate the switch until a click is felt **(see illustration)**.
32   Tighten the bolt and screws and install the anti-rattle spring.
33   Install the idle speed solenoid.
34   Lubricate the feedback solenoid tip lightly with petroleum jelly and install a new O-ring **(see illustration)**.
35   Install a new gasket and insert the solenoid into position **(see illustration)**.
36   Install the solenoid screws and tighten them evenly and securely.
37   Wrap a piece of teflon tape around the threads and install the fuel inlet.
38   Install the choke inner housing lever bushing, followed by the spacer
and outer housing with the spring end loop over the lever **(see illustrations)**.
39   Install the choke housing rivets. The shorter rivet goes in the bottom
hole.
40   Install the air cleaner gasket.

14.38a Install the choke inner housing lever bushing
(2.2L engine)

14.38b Rotate the outer housing about 1/8-turn clockwise to
align the rivet holes

15 Carburetor – adjustments (2.2L Engine)

Idle speed adjustment

Vehicles without air conditioning

Refer to illustration 15.8

1   Start the engine and run it until normal operating temperature is reached.

2   Check the ignition timing and adjust as necessary (see Chapter 1), then shut off the engine.

3   Disconnect and plug the vacuum hose at the EGR valve.

4   Unplug the fan wire connector and install a jumper wire so the fan will run continuously.

5   Remove the PCV valve from the vent module so the valve will draw air from the engine compartment. Plug the control hose at the module.

6   Leave the air cleaner in place and connect a tachometer. On 1983 and later models, ground the carburetor switch with a jumper wire.

7   Start the engine.

8   Check the idle speed reading on the tachometer and compare it to the Vehicle Emissions Control Information label in the engine compartment. Turn the idle speed adjusting screw **(see illustration)** as necessary to achieve the idle speed listed on the label.

9   Shut off the engine and remove the tachometer.

10   Remove the carburetor switch jumper wire, plug in the fan connector, install the PCV valve and reinstall any vacuum hoses that were disconnected.

Vehicles with air conditioning

11   Air conditioned vehicles are equipped with solenoids or kickers to increase idle speed when the air conditioning compressor engages, putting a greater load on the engine. Before checking the air conditioning idle speed, check the curb idle and ignition timing to make sure they're correct. The checks should be made with the engine at normal operating temperature.

12   When the air conditioner is engaged, the idle speed on these models is increased by either a vacuum or solenoid-type kicker.

13   Kicker operation can be checked by running the engine (at normal operating temperature) and moving the temperature control to the coldest setting, then turning the air conditioner on. The kicker plunger should move in and out as the compressor clutch engages and disengages. Remove the air cleaner for better visual access to the kicker, if necessary.

14   No adjustment of the kicker is possible, although the adjusting screw on the top is used for normal curb idle speed adjustment.

15   Check the kicker and vacuum hose for leaks. If no leaks are found and the kicker doesn't work right, install a new one.

Fast idle adjustment

Refer to illustration 15.18

16   Perform Steps 1 through 6 above.

17   On 1981 and 1982 models, unplug the wiring connector with the red and tan wires at the carburetor. On 1983 and later models, unplug the oxygen sensor test connector located at the left shock tower.

18   Start the engine, open the throttle slightly and set the fast idle screw on the slowest speed step of the fast idle cam **(see illustration)**.

4

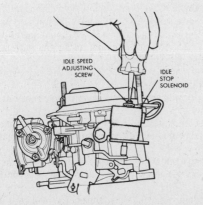

15.8 Turn the idle speed adjusting screw as necessary to adjust
the idle speed to the rpm specified on the VECI label (2.2L engine)

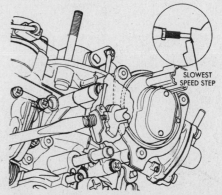

15.18 Start the engine, open the throttle slightly and set the fast
idle screw on the slowest speed step of the fast idle cam
(2.2L engine)

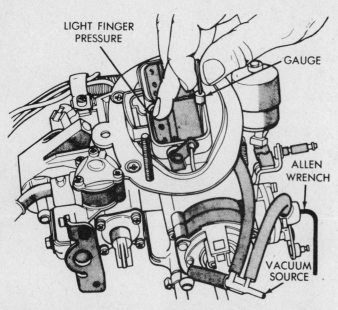

15.25   Close the choke with light finger pressure until the choke plates are at their smallest opening, then insert a gauge or drill bit of the correct size (listed in the Specifications at the beginning of this Chapter) between the plate and the air horn wall at the primary throttle end of the carburetor and adjust as necessary (2.2L engine)

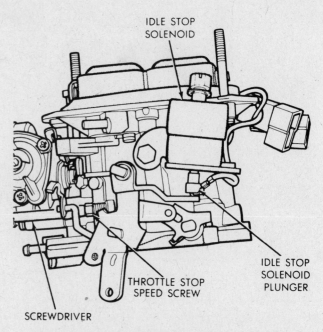

15.31   Adjust the idle speed to the specified rpm with the throttle stop screw (2.2L engine)

19   With the choke valve all the way open, adjust the fast idle speed to the specification on the Emissions Control Information label by turning the adjustment screw.

20   Return the engine to idle and place the fast idle screw on the slowest speed step of the fast idle cam to verify the fast idle speed. Adjust as necessary.

21   Turn off the engine, remove the tachometer and reconnect all components removed for the adjustment procedure.

Choke vacuum kick adjustment

Refer to illustration 15.25

22   Remove the air cleaner (see Section 7).

23   Open the throttle, close the choke and then the throttle so the fast idle system is trapped at the closed choke position.

24   Disconnect the carburetor vacuum hose, connect a vacuum pump and apply 15 in-Hg of vacuum.

25   Push the choke lightly closed so the plates are at their smallest opening **(see illustration)**. The choke system internal spring will now be compressed.

26   Insert a drill bit or gauge between the plate and the air horn wall at the primary throttle end of the carburetor. Check the clearance against this Chapter's Specifications and adjust as necessary using an Allen wrench inserted into the diaphragm.

27   After adjustment, replace the vacuum hose and the air cleaner assembly.

Anti-diesel adjustment

Refer to illustration 15.31

28   Warm up the engine to operating temperature, then shut it off.

29   Connect a tachometer.

30   With the transaxle in Neutral, the parking brake set securely, the carburetor idle stop switch grounded with a jumper wire, the idle stop carburetor unplugged and the headlights off, start the engine.

31   Adjust the throttle stop speed screw **(see illustration)** to achieve an idle of 700 rpm.

32   Shut off the engine, remove the tachometer, remove the jumper wire and connect the carburetor idle stop switch.

---

16   Fuel injection system – general information

Two types of Electronic Fuel Injection (EFI) are used on these models; single-point and multi-point. Single-point EFI is used on non-turbocharged models and multi-point on turbocharged models.

Both types are similar in operation and are controlled by the logic module and power module in combination with a variety of sensors and switches. On both the single and multi-point EFI, the conventional carburetor is replaced by a throttle body and injector (single point) or throttle body, fuel rail and injectors (multi-point). On single-point EFI, the fuel is mixed with air in the throttle body and sprayed into the intake manifold, which directs it to the intake ports and cylinders. On multi-port EFI, the fuel is sprayed directly into the ports by the fuel injectors, with the intake manifold supplying only the air.

The EFI system consists of a throttle body, fuel rail (multi-point), fuel injector(s), pressure regulator, throttle position sensor (TPS), automatic idle speed (AIS) motor and throttle body temperature sensor, all of which interact with the power module and the logic module.

Because of the complexity of the EFI system, the home mechanic can do very little in the way of diagnosis because of the special expertise and equipment required. However, checking of the EFI system components and electrical and vacuum connections to make sure they're secure and not obviously damaged is one thing the home mechanic can do which can often detect a potential or current problem. Since the logic and power modules are completely dependent on the information provided by the many sensors and vacuum connections, a simple visual check and tightening of loose connections can save diagnostic time and a possibly unnecessary trip to a dealer service department.

Damaged or faulty EFI components can be replaced using the procedures in the following Sections.

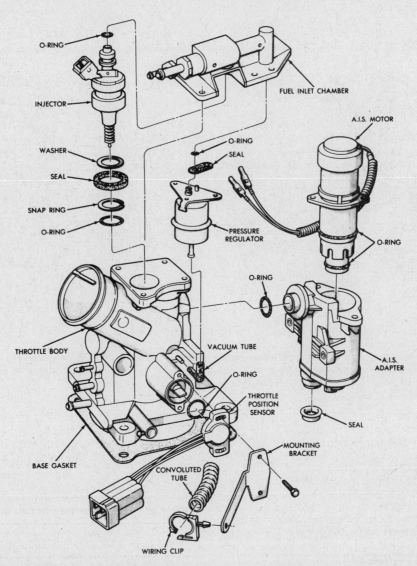

O-RING

INJECTOR

WASHER

SEAL

SNAP RING

O-RING

THROTTLE BODY

BASE GASKET

FUEL INLET CHAMBER

O-RING

SEAL

PRESSURE
REGULATOR

A.I.S. MOTOR

O-RING

O-RING

VACUUM TUBE

O-RING

THROTTLE
POSITION
SENSOR

A.I.S.
ADAPTER

SEAL

MOUNTING
BRACKET

CONVOLUTED
TUBE

WIRING CLIP

18.4a   Typical single-point EFI throttle body components (1984 and 1985) – exploded view

17   Fuel lines and fittings – replacement

Warning: *Gasoline is extremely flammable, so extra precautions must be taken when working on any part of the fuel system. Don't smoke or allow open flames or bare light bulbs near the work area. Also, don't work in a garage if a natural gas-type appliance with a pilot light is present. Have a fire extinguisher handy and know how to use it!*

Note: *Since the EFI system is under considerable pressure, always replace all clamps released or removed with new ones.*

1   Remove the air cleaner assembly.
2   Relieve the fuel system pressure (see Section 2).
3   Disconnect the negative cable from the battery.
4   Loosen the hose clamps, wrap a cloth around each end of the hose to catch the residual fuel and twist and pull to remove the hose.
5   Remove the fuel fittings. Note the inlet diameter and remove the copper washers.
6   When installing fuel fittings, make sure the inlet diameters match and always use new copper washers. Tighten the fittings to the specified torque.
7   When replacing hoses, always use hoses marked EFI/EFM and new original equipment-type clamps only.

8   Connect the negative battery cable, start the engine and check for leaks.
9   Install the air cleaner assembly.

18   Single-point EFI throttle body – removal and installation

Refer to illustrations 18.4a, 18.4b and 18.4c
Warning: *Gasoline is extremely flammable, so extra precautions must be taken when working on any part of the fuel system. Don't smoke or allow open flames or bare light bulbs near the work area. Also, don't work in a garage if a natural gas-type appliance with a pilot light is present. Have a fire extinguisher handy and know how to use it!*

Removal

1   Remove the air cleaner assembly.
2   Relieve the fuel system pressure (see Section 2).
3   Disconnect the negative cable from the battery.
4   Disconnect the vacuum hoses and electrical connectors (**see illustrations**).

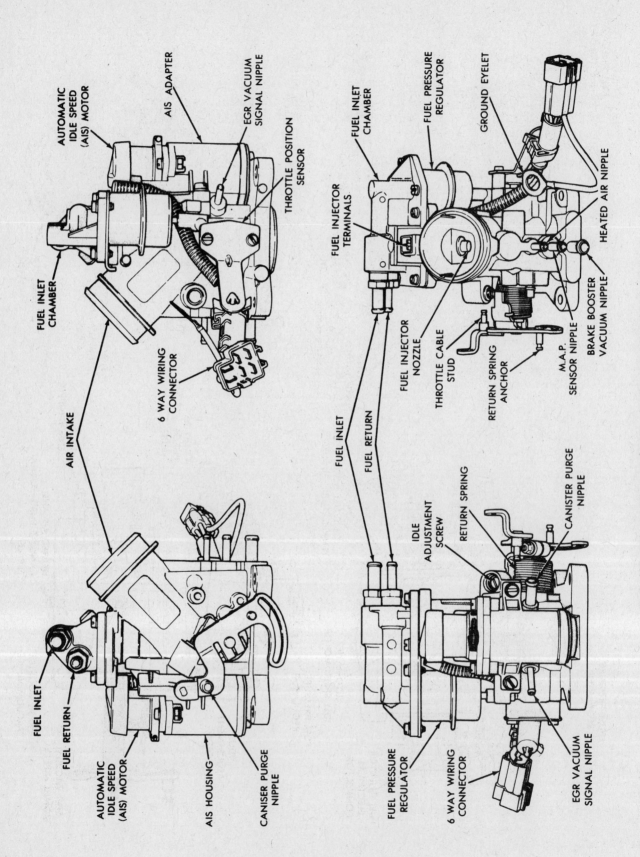

18.4b   Single-point EFI throttle body external details (1984 and 1985)

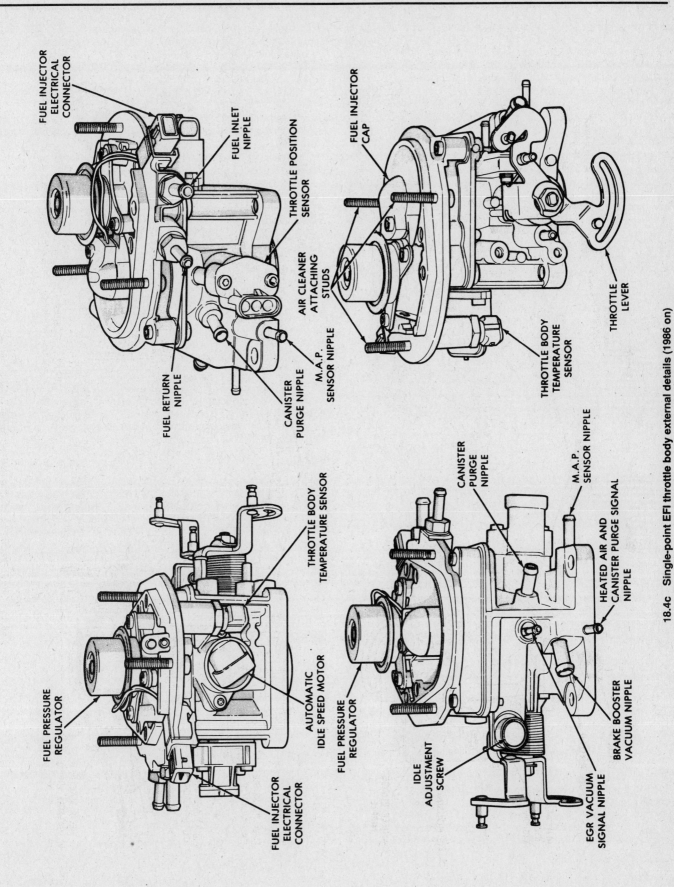

FUEL INJECTOR ELECTRICAL CONNECTOR

FUEL INLET NIPPLE

THROTTLE POSITION SENSOR

FUEL RETURN NIPPLE

CANISTER PURGE NIPPLE

M.A.P. SENSOR NIPPLE

AIR CLEANER ATTACHING STUDS

FUEL INJECTOR CAP

THROTTLE BODY TEMPERATURE SENSOR

THROTTLE LEVER

FUEL PRESSURE REGULATOR

THROTTLE BODY TEMPERATURE SENSOR

AUTOMATIC IDLE SPEED MOTOR

FUEL INJECTOR ELECTRICAL CONNECTOR

CANISTER PURGE NIPPLE

M.A.P. SENSOR NIPPLE

HEATED AIR AND CANISTER PURGE SIGNAL NIPPLE

FUEL PRESSURE REGULATOR

IDLE ADJUSTMENT SCREW

EGR VACUUM SIGNAL NIPPLE

BRAKE BOOSTER VACUUM NIPPLE

18.4c Single-point EFI throttle body external details (1986 on)

4

5　Disconnect the throttle linkage and (if equipped) the cruise control and transaxle kickdown cable.
6　Remove the throttle return spring.
7　Place rags or newspapers under the fuel hoses to catch the residual fuel. Loosen the clamps, wrap a cloth around each fuel hose and pull them off. Remove the copper washers from the hoses, noting their locations.
8　Remove the mounting bolts or nuts and lift the throttle body off the manifold.

Installation

9　Inspect the mating surfaces of the throttle body and the manifold for nicks, burrs and debris that could cause air leaks.
10　Using a new gasket, place the throttle body in position and install the mounting bolts or nuts.
11　Tighten the bolts or nuts to the torque listed in this Chapter's Specifications, following a criss-cross pattern. Work up to the final torque in three or four steps.
12　Check all of the vacuum hoses and electrical connectors for damage, replacing them with new parts if necessary, and install them.
13　Connect the throttle linkage and (if equipped) cruise control and kickdown cable.
14　Connect the throttle return spring.
15　Using new clamps and washers, install the fuel hoses.
16　Check the operation of the throttle linkage.
17　Install the air cleaner assembly.
18　Connect the negative battery cable.
19　Start the engine and check for fuel leaks.

19　Single-point EFI pressure regulator – check, removal and installation

Warning: *Gasoline is extremely flammable, so extra precautions must be taken when working on any part of the fuel system. Don't smoke or allow open flames or bare light bulbs near the work area. Also, don't work in a garage if a natural gas-type appliance with a pilot light is present. Have a fire extinguisher handy and know how to use it!*

Check

1　Relieve the fuel system pressure (see Section 2).
2　Detach the fuel hose at the throttle body. Using a T-fitting so you don't disturb normal fuel flow, attach a fuel injection system fuel pressure gauge between the fuel filter and the throttle body.
3　Start the engine. If the gauge reads within the pressure range listed in this Chapter's Specifications, the pressure is correct and no further testing is required. Detach the gauge and T-fitting, reattach the fuel hose to the throttle body and tighten the clamp securely (it's a good idea to use a new clamp).
4　If the gauge indicates low fuel pressure, install the test gauge and T-fitting between the fuel filter hose and the fuel inlet line. Start the engine and note the indicated pressure reading.
　a)　If the pressure is now correct, replace the fuel filter.
　b)　If the pressure is still low, squeeze the fuel return hose and note the indicated pressure reading. If the pressure increases, replace the pressure regulator. If the pressure is still low, the problem is either a plugged pump filter sock or a defective fuel pump (see Section 3).
5　If the gauge indicates high fuel pressure, detach the fuel return hose from the throttle body. Attach a short section of test hose in its place and place the other end of the hose in an approved gasoline container. Be prepared for fuel to spurt out of the end of the hose. Start the engine.
　a)　If the pressure is now correct, check for a restricted fuel return line.
　b)　If the pressure is still high, replace the fuel pressure regulator.

Removal

6　Remove the air cleaner assembly (see Section 7).
7　Relieve the fuel system pressure (see Section 2).
8　Disconnect the negative cable from the battery.

9　On 1984 and 1985 models, remove the fuel inlet chamber **(see illustrations 18.4a and 18.4b)**, then remove the vacuum tube from the regulator and throttle body.
10　On 1984 and 1985 models, remove the vacuum tube from the regulator and throttle body.
11　Wrap a cloth around the fuel inlet chamber to catch any residual fuel, which is under pressure.
12　Withdraw the pressure regulator from the throttle body.
13　Carefully remove the O-ring from the pressure regulator, followed by the gasket.

Installation

14　Place a new gasket in position on the pressure regulator and carefully install a new O-ring.
15　On 1986 and later models, place the pressure regulator in position on the throttle body, press it into position and install the three mounting screws. Tighten the screws to the torque listed in this Chapter's Specifications.
16　On 1984 and 1985 models, install the vacuum tube.
17　On 1984 and 1985 models, install the fuel inlet chamber.
18　Connect the negative battery cable.
19　Install the air cleaner assembly (see Section 7).

20　Single-point EFI fuel injector – check, removal and installation

Warning: *Gasoline is extremely flammable, so extra precautions must be taken when working on any part of the fuel system. Don't smoke or allow open flames or bare light bulbs near the work area. Also, don't work in a garage if a natural gas-type appliance with a pilot light is present. Have a fire extinguisher handy and know how to use it!*

Check

1　With the engine running, or cranking, listen to the sound from the injector with an automotive stethoscope and verify that the injector sounds as if it's operating normally. If you don't have a stethoscope, touch the area of the throttle body immediately above the fuel injector with your finger and try to determine whether the injector feels like it's operating smoothly. It should sound/feel smooth and uniform and its sound/feel should rise and fall with engine rpm. If the injector isn't operating, or sounds/feels erratic, check the injector electrical connector and the wire harness connector. If the connectors are snug, check for voltage to the injector. If there's voltage to the injector and it isn't operating or operating erratically, replace it.

Removal

All models

2　Remove the air cleaner assembly.
3　Relieve the fuel system pressure (See Section 2).
4　Disconnect the negative cable from the battery.

1984 and 1985 models

5　Remove the four Torx screws retaining the fuel inlet chamber to the throttle body **(see illustration 18.4a)**.
6　Remove the fuel pressure regulator-to-throttle body vacuum tube.
7　Wrap a cloth around the fuel inlet chamber to catch the residual fuel and lift the inlet chamber and injector off the throttle body.
8　Withdraw the injector from the inlet chamber **(see illustration 18.4a)**.
9　Peel the upper and lower O-rings off the fuel injector.
10　Remove the snap-ring retaining the seal and washer on the injector, followed by the seal and washer.

1986 and later models

11　Remove the Torx screw(s) retaining the injector cap and pry the cap off the injector using two screwdrivers inserted in the slots provided for this purpose **(see illustration 18.4c)**.
12　Pry the injector out of the pod using a screwdriver inserted in the holes in the side of the electrical connector. After removal, make sure the lower injector O-ring is removed from the pod.

Installation

1984 and 1985 models

13 Install a new O-ring, washer and seal on the injector, retaining them with the snap-ring.

14 Insert the injector into the fuel inlet chamber.

15 Place the injector/fuel inlet chamber in position on the throttle body and install the pressure regulator-to-throttle body vacuum tube.

16 Place the assembly in the throttle body and install the Torx retaining screws. Tighten the screws securely.

1986 and later models

17 Install new O-rings on the injector and injector cap (a new injector should already have the upper O-ring installed).

18 Place the injector in the pod and position it so the cap (which is keyed to the injector) can be installed without interference.

19 Rotate the cap and injector so they line up with the mounting holes, push down to ensure a good seal and install the Torx retaining screws. Tighten the screws to the torque listed in this Chapter's Specifications.

All models

20 Connect the negative battery cable, start the engine and check for leaks.

21 Turn off the engine and install the air cleaner assembly.

---

21 Single-point EFI Throttle Position Sensor (TPS) – check, removal and installation

---

Warning: *Gasoline is extremely flammable, so extra precautions must be taken when working on any part of the fuel system. Don't smoke or allow open flames or bare light bulbs near the work area. Also, don't work in a garage if a natural gas-type appliance with a pilot light is present. Have a fire extinguisher handy and know how to use it!*

Check

1 The Throttle Position Sensor (TPS) is monitored by the logic module (computer) located inside the passenger compartment. If the TPS malfunctions, a trouble code is stored in the logic module's memory. To get the module to display any stored trouble codes, refer to the appropriate Section in Chapter 6. If a Code 24 is displayed, replace the TPS.

Removal

All models

2 Disconnect the negative cable from the battery.

1984 and 1985 models

3 Unplug the six-way wiring connector (see illustrations 18.4a and 18.4b).

4 Remove the two TPS-to-throttle body screws, detach the wiring clip from the convoluted tube and remove the mounting bracket.

5 Separate the TPS from the throttle shaft and remove the O-ring.

6 Pull the three TPS wires from the convoluted tube.

7 Look inside the six-way connector and use a small screwdriver to lift the locking tab for each of the TPS wire blade terminals. Disconnect each TPS blade (noting their positions to simplify reinstallation).

1986 and later models

8 Disconnect the throttle cable and unplug the electrical connector.

9 Remove the two TPS-to-throttle body screws.

10 Lift the TPS off the throttle shaft.

11 Remove the O-ring.

Installation

1984 and 1985 models

12 Making sure they go into the proper locations, insert the wire blade terminals into the throttle body connector.

13 Insert the TPS wires into the convoluted tube.

14 Place the TPS and new O-ring in position with the mounting bracket on the throttle body and install the retaining screws. Tighten the screws to the torque listed in this Chapter's Specifications.

15 Attach the wiring clips to the convoluted tube and connect the six-way connector.

1986 and later models

16 Install the TPS with a new O-ring on the throttle body and install the retaining screws. Tighten the screws to the torque listed in this Chapter's Specifications.

17 Plug in the electrical connector and connect the throttle cable.

All models

18 Install the air cleaner.

19 Connect the negative battery cable.

---

22 Single-point EFI Automatic Idle Speed (AIS) motor – check, removal and installation

---

Warning: *Gasoline is extremely flammable, so extra precautions must be taken when working on any part of the fuel system. Don't smoke or allow open flames or bare light bulbs near the work area. Also, don't work in a garage if a natural gas-type appliance with a pilot light is present. Have a fire extinguisher handy and know how to use it!*

Check

1 The Automatic Idle Speed (AIS) motor is monitored by the logic module (computer). If the AIS malfunctions, a trouble code is stored in the logic module's memory. To get the module to display any stored trouble codes, refer to the appropriate Section in Chapter 6. If a Code 25 is displayed, replace the AIS.

Removal

All models

2 Disconnect the negative cable from the battery.

3 Remove the air cleaner assembly (see Section 7).

1984 and 1985 models

4 Remove the two screws retaining the AIS adapter to the throttle body (see illustration 18.4a).

5 Remove the wiring clips, followed by the two AIS wires from the throttle body connector. Use a small screwdriver to lift each locking tab (noting the position of each wire to simplify reinstallation) and disconnect each blade terminal.

6 Carefully withdraw the assembly from the rear of the throttle body. Note that the O-ring at the top and the seal at the bottom may fall off the adapter, so keep track of them.

7 Remove the O-ring and seal.

8 To separate the motor from the adapter, remove the two retaining screws (but not the clamp), lift the motor out and remove the O-ring.

1986 and later models

9 Unplug the four-pin connector on the AIS.

10 Remove the throttle body temperature sensor (see Section 23).

11 Remove the two retaining screws.

12 Withdraw the AIS from the throttle body. Make sure the O-ring doesn't fall into the throttle body opening.

Installation

1984 and 1985 models

13 If the AIS motor has been removed from the adapter, install new O-rings and carefully work the motor into the adaptor and install the retaining screws.

14 To install the AIS motor/adaptor assembly, first install a new O-ring and seal on the adaptor.

15 Place the assembly carefully in position on the back of the throttle body, making sure the O-ring and seal are in place and install the retaining screws. Tighten the screws to the torque listed in this Chapter's Specifications.

1986 and later models

16 Prior to installation, make sure the pintle is in the retracted position. If the retracted pintle measurement is more than 1.26-inches, the AIS must be taken to a dealer service department to be retracted.

4

17   Install a new O-ring and insert the AIS into the housing, making sure the O-ring isn't dislodged.
18   Install the two retaining screws. Tighten the screws to the torque listed in this Chapter's Specifications.
19   Plug the four-pin connector into the AIS.
20   Install the throttle body temperature sending unit (see Section 23).

All models

21   Install the air cleaner assembly and connect the negative battery cable.

23   Single-point EFI throttle body temperature sensor (1986 on) – check and replacement

Warning: *Gasoline is extremely flammable, so extra precautions must be taken when working on any part of the fuel system. Don't smoke or allow open flames or bare light bulbs near the work area. Also, don't work in a garage if a natural gas-type appliance with a pilot light is present. Have a fire extinguisher handy and know how to use it!*

Check

1   The throttle body temperature sensor is monitored by the logic module (computer). If the sensor malfunctions, a trouble code is stored in the logic module's memory. To get the module to display any stored trouble codes, refer to the appropriate section in Chapter 6. If a Code 23 is displayed, replace the sensor.

Removal

2   Disconnect the negative cable from the battery.
3   Remove the air cleaner assembly (see Section 7).
4   Disconnect the throttle cable from the throttle body, remove the two cable bracket screws and lay the bracket aside.
5   Unplug the wiring connector by pulling down on it.
6   Remove the sensor by unscrewing it **(see illustration 18.4c)**.

Installation

7   Apply a thin coat of heat transfer compound to the tip of the new sensor.
8   Screw the sensor into the throttle body and tighten it securely.
9   Plug in the wiring connector.
10   Connect the throttle cable.
11   Install the air cleaner and connect the negative battery cable.

24   Multi-point EFI throttle body – removal and installation

Refer to illustrations 24.2, 24.4, 24.5, 24.8 and 24.11
Warning: *Gasoline is extremely flammable, so extra precautions must be taken when working on any part of the fuel system. Don't smoke or allow open flames or bare light bulbs near the work area. Also, don't work in a garage if a natural gas-type appliance with a pilot light is present. Have a fire extinguisher handy and know how to use it!*

Removal

1   Disconnect the negative cable from the battery.
2   Remove the air cleaner hose and adapter **(see illustration)**.
3   Remove the return spring, disconnect the throttle cable and remove (if equipped) the cruise control and automatic transaxle kickdown cable.
4   Unbolt the throttle cable bracket **(see illustration)**.
5   Unplug the electrical connector **(see illustration)**.
6   Disconnect the vacuum hoses from the throttle body.
7   Loosen the turbocharger-to-throttle body hose clamp.

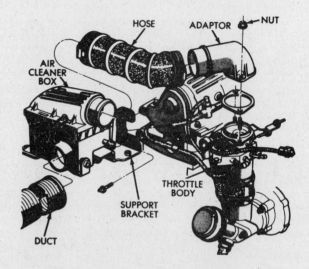

24.2   Multi-point EFI air cleaner hose and adapter details

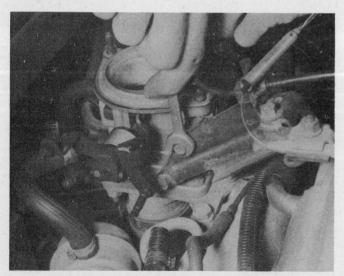

24.4   Remove the two throttle cable bracket bolts

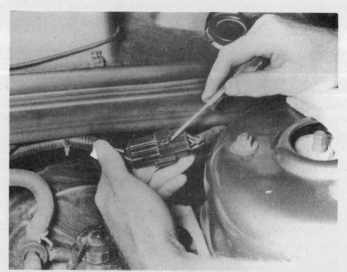

24.5   Bend the clip up with a small screwdriver before separating the electrical connector

8   Remove the bolts and detach the throttle body from the intake manifold **(see illustration)**.

Installation

9   Place the throttle body in position and install the mounting bolts. Tighten them in a criss-cross pattern to the torque listed in this Chapter's Specifications.
10   Tighten the turbocharger hose clamp.
11   Connect the vacuum hoses **(see illustration)**.
12   Plug in the electrical connector.
13   Install the bracket and connect the throttle cable, return spring and (if equipped) cruise control and automatic transaxle kickdown cable.
14   Install the air cleaner hose and adapter.
15   Connect the negative battery cable.

---

25   Multi-point EFI Throttle Position Sensor (TPS) – check, removal and installation

Check

1   The Throttle Position Sensor (TPS) is monitored by the logic module (computer). If the TPS malfunctions, a trouble code is stored in the logic

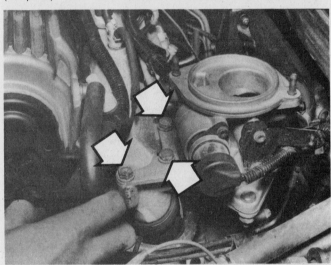

24.8   Multi-point throttle body mounting bolt locations (arrows)

module's memory. To get the module to display any stored trouble codes, refer to the appropriate section in Chapter 6. If a Code 24 is displayed, replace the TPS.

Removal

Refer to illustration 25.3

2   Disconnect the negative cable from the battery.
3   Unplug the six-way electrical connector **(see illustration)**.
4   Remove the TPS-to-throttle body screws.
5   Unclip the convoluted plastic wiring tube and remove the mounting bracket.
6   Withdraw the TPS from the throttle shaft and remove the O-ring.
7   Look inside the six-way connector and locate the TPS wire blade terminals. Noting their locations for installation in the same positions, use a small screwdriver to lift each locking tab and disconnect the TPS.

Installation

8   Insert the TPS blade terminals into the six-way connector.
9   Push the TPS wires into the convoluted plastic wiring tube.
10   Install the TPS and new O-ring with the mounting bracket on the throttle body. Tighten the screws to the torque listed in this Chapter's Specifications.
11   Install the clips on the convoluted plastic wiring tube.
12   Plug in the six-way connector and connect the negative battery cable.

---

26   Multi-point EFI Automatic Idle Speed (AIS) motor – check, removal and installation

Check

1   The Automatic Idle Speed (AIS) motor is monitored by the logic module (computer). If the AIS motor malfunctions, a trouble code is stored in the logic module's memory. To get the module to display any stored trouble codes, refer to the appropriate Section in Chapter 6. If a Code 25 is displayed, replace the TPS.

Removal

2   Disconnect the negative cable from the battery.
3   Unplug the six-way electrical connector.
4   Remove the wiring clips, then detach the two AIS wires from the six-way connector. Using a small screwdriver, lift each locking tab and, noting their locations to simplify reassembly, remove each blade terminal.

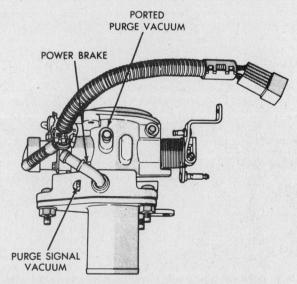

24.11   Multi-point EFI throttle body vacuum connections

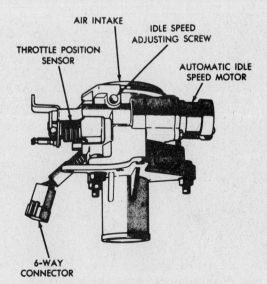

25.3   Multi-point EFI throttle body external details

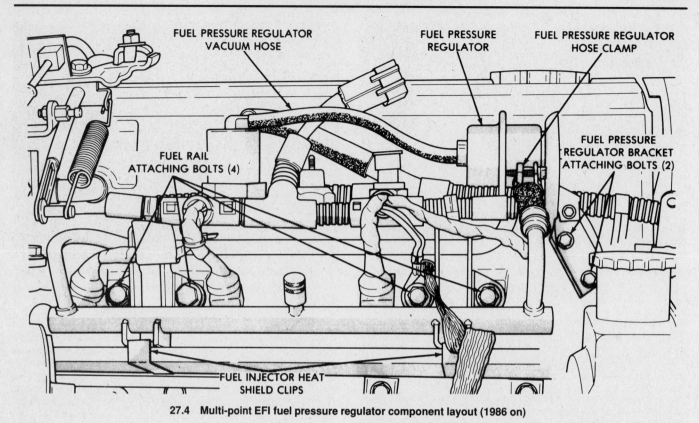

FUEL PRESSURE REGULATOR
VACUUM HOSE

FUEL PRESSURE
REGULATOR

FUEL PRESSURE REGULATOR
HOSE CLAMP

FUEL RAIL
ATTACHING BOLTS (4)

FUEL PRESSURE
REGULATOR BRACKET
ATTACHING BOLTS (2)

FUEL INJECTOR HEAT
SHIELD CLIPS

27.4   Multi-point EFI fuel pressure regulator component layout (1986 on)

5   Remove the two AIS motor-to-throttle body screws. Don't remove the clamp **(see illustration 25.3)**.
6   Remove the AIS motor from the throttle body. Make sure both O-rings remain on the motor.

Installation

7   Carefully position the AIS motor (using new O-rings – new motors should be already equipped with O-rings) on the throttle body.
8   Install the screws and tighten them securely.
9   Route the AIS wiring to the connector and plug in the blade terminals in the correct positions.
10   Connect the wiring clips and plug in the six-way connector.
11   Connect the negative battery cable.

27.7   A small screwdriver can be used to pry off the heat shield clips

27   Multi-point EFI fuel rail assembly – removal and installation

Refer to illustrations 27.4, 27.7, 27.9 and 27.10
Warning: *Gasoline is extremely flammable, so extra precautions must be taken when working on any part of the fuel system. Don't smoke or allow open flames or bare light bulbs near the work area. Also, don't work in a garage if a natural gas-type appliance with a pilot light is present. Have a fire extinguisher handy and know how to use it!*

Removal

1   Relieve the fuel system pressure (see Section 2).
2   Disconnect the negative cable from the battery.
3   Loosen the supply hose clamp at the fuel rail inlet and pull the hose off.
4   Disconnect the fuel pressure regulator vacuum hose, remove the two bracket bolts, loosen the regulator hose clamp at the end of the rail and detach the hose and regulator **(see illustration)**.
5   Remove the fuel rail-to-camshaft cover bracket bolt.
6   Unplug the fuel injector wiring connector.
7   Remove the fuel injector heat shield clips with a small screwdriver **(see illustration)**.
8   Remove the four fuel rail mounting bolts.
9   Grasp the fuel rail and injector assembly securely and pull the injectors straight out of the ports. Working carefully, to avoid damaging the injector O-rings, remove the rail assembly from the vehicle **(see illustration)**. The fuel injectors must not be removed until the fuel rail is detached from the vehicle.
10   Support the fuel rail and disconnect the remaining fuel hoses **(see illustration)**.

Installation

11   Prior to installation, make sure the injectors are securely seated in the receiver cup with the lock rings in place.
12   Inspect the injector holes to make sure they're clean.
13   Lubricate the injector O-rings with clean engine oil.

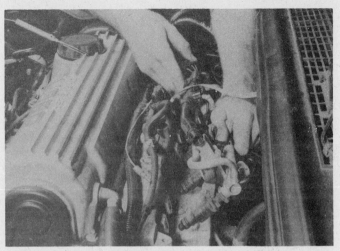

27.9   Grasp the fuel rail securely and pull the injectors out of the intake manifold

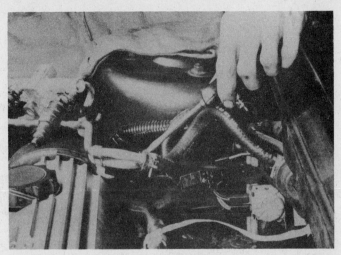

27.10   With the fuel rail supported out of the way, loosen the fuel hose clamps

14   Insert the injector assemblies carefully into the holes and install the bolts and ground straps. Tighten the bolts evenly in a criss-cross pattern so the injectors are drawn evenly into place. Once the injectors are seated, tighten the bolts to the torque listed in this Chapter's Specifications.

15   Connect the injector wiring harness to the injectors and fasten it in the wiring clips.

16   Install the heat shield clips and connect the wiring harness.

17   Install the fuel rail-to-camshaft cover bracket bolt.

18   Connect the fuel pressure regulator vacuum hose.

19   Install the fuel supply hose and clamp on the rail and tighten the clamp securely.

20   Check to make sure the ground straps, hoses and wiring harnesses and connectors are securely installed in their original locations.

21   Connect the negative battery cable.

---

28   Multi-point EFI fuel injector – check, removal and installation

Refer to illustrations 28.3a, 28.3b, 28.4a, 28.4b, 28.4c, 28.4d and 28.6

Check

1   With the engine running or cranking, listen to the sound from each injector with an automotive stethoscope and verify the injectors sound as if they're operating normally. If you don't have a stethoscope, touch each injector with your finger and try to determine whether the injector feels like it's operating smoothly. It should sound/feel smooth and uniform and its sound/feel should rise and fall with engine RPM. If an injector isn't operating, or sounds/feels erratic, check the injector connector and the wire harness connector. If the connectors are snug, check for voltage to the injector. If there's voltage to the injector and the injector isn't operating or sounds/feels erratic, replace the injector.

Removal

2   Remove the fuel rail assembly (see Section 27) and place the fuel rail assembly on a clean work surface so the fuel injectors are accessible.

3   Remove the injector clip from the fuel rail and injector by prying it off with a small screwdriver. Pull the injector straight out of the receiver cup **(see illustrations)**.

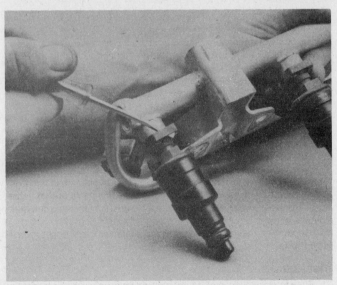

28.3a   Insert a small screwdriver under the injector clip and pry it off

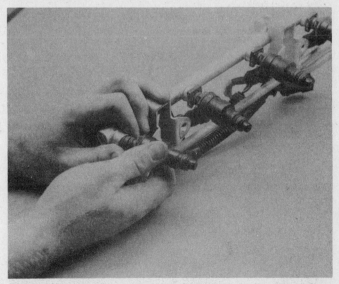

28.3b   Pull the injector straight out of the fuel rail receiver clip

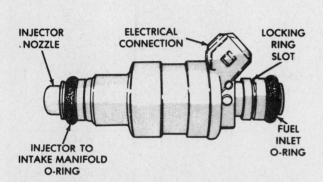

28.4a   The fuel injector has two different size O-rings

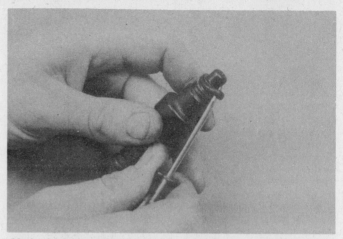

28.4b   Insert a small screwdriver under the O-ring and pry if off –
be careful not to damage the injector tip

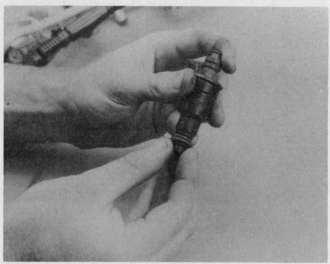

28.4c   Push the new O-ring over the tip of the injector and into
the groove

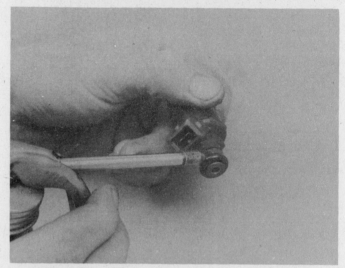

28.4d   A drop of clean engine oil will allow the injector to
seat easily

4   Inspect the injector O-rings for damage. Replace them with new ones if necessary **(see illustration)**. Use a small screwdriver to remove the old O-ring, roll the new one into the groove and apply a drop of engine oil to the O-ring **(see illustrations)**.

28.6   Insert the injector carefully so it goes straight into the
receiver cup

Installation

5   Prior to installation, lubricate the O-ring with a drop of clean engine oil (if you haven't already).
6   Install the top of the injector carefully in the fuel rail receiver cup, taking care not to damage the O-ring **(see illustration)**.
7   Slide the open end of the injector clip into the top slot of the injector, onto the receiver cup ridge and into the side slots of the clip **(see illustrations 28.3a and 28.3b)**.
8   Install the fuel rail (see Section 27).

29   Turbocharger – check

1   The turbocharger increases power by using an exhaust gas-driven turbine to pressurize the fuel/air mixture as it enters the combustion chambers. The amount of boost (intake manifold pressure) is controlled by the wastegate (exhaust bypass valve). This is operated by a spring-loaded actuator assembly which controls the maximum boost level by allowing some of the exhaust gas to bypass the turbine. The wastegate is controlled by the logic module. While a comparatively simple design, the turbocharger is a precision device which can be severely damaged by an interrupted oil or coolant supply or loose or damaged ducting.
2   Due to the special techniques and equipment required, any checks or diagnosis of suspected problems should be left to a dealer service department. The home mechanic can, however, check the connections and linkages for security, damage and obvious problems.

3   Because each turbocharger has its own distinctive sound, a change in the noise level can be a sign of potential problems.

4   A high-pitched or whistling sound is a symptom of an inlet air or exhaust gas leak.

5   If an unusual sound emanates from the turbine, the turbocharger can be removed and the turbine wheel inspected. **Warning:** *All checks must be made with the engine off and cool to the touch and the turbocharger stopped or injury could result. Operating the turbocharger without all the ducts and filters installed is dangerous and can result in damage to the turbine wheel blades.*

6   Reach inside the housing and turn the turbine wheel to make sure it turns freely. If it doesn't, it could be a sign the oil has sludged or coked from overheating. Push in on the shaft wheels and check for binding. The wheels should rotate freely with no binding or rubbing on the housing.

7   Inspect the exhaust manifold for cracks and loose connections.

8   Because the turbine wheel rotates at speeds up to 140,000 rpm, severe damage can result from the interruption of coolant or contamination of the oil supply to the turbine bearings. Check for leaks in the coolant and oil inlet lines or obstructions in the oil drain back line, as this can cause severe oil loss through the turbocharger seals. Burned oil on the turbine housing is a sign of this. **Caution:** *Any time a major engine bearing such as a main or connecting rod bearing is replaced, the turbocharger should be flushed with clean oil.*

30   Turbocharger – removal and installation

Refer to illustrations 30.4, 30.5, 30.6 and 30.13

Removal

1   Disconnect the negative cable from the battery.

2   Drain the cooling system (see Chapter 1).

3   Raise the front of the vehicle and support it securely on jackstands. Apply the parking brake and block the rear wheels to keep the vehicle from rolling.

4   Working under the vehicle, disconnect the exhaust pipe and unplug the oxygen sensor connector **(see illustration)**.

5   Remove the turbocharger housing-to-engine block bracket support at the block **(see illustration)**.

30.4   Exhaust pipe bolts and oxygen sensor connector locations (arrows) – turbocharged models

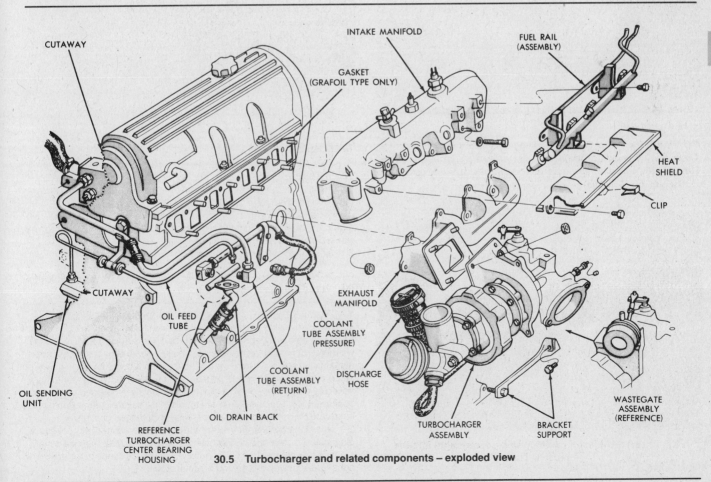

30.5   Turbocharger and related components – exploded view

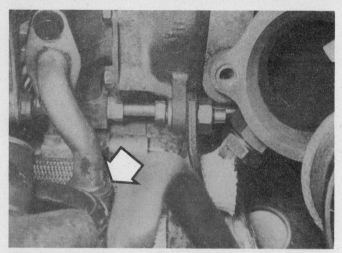

30.6   Detach the turbocharger oil drain return hose at the block fitting (arrow) and push it down with a screwdriver

30.13   Loosen only the two turbocharger discharge hose clamps (arrows)

6   Loosen the oil drain return hose clamps and push the hose down on the block fitting with a screwdriver **(see illustration)**.
7   Disconnect the turbocharger coolant tube nut at the block outlet (located below the power steering pump bracket) and the tube support bracket at the block.
8   Lower the vehicle.
9   Working in the engine compartment, remove the air cleaner assembly, along with the throttle body adapter, hose and air cleaner box and support.
10   Disconnect the throttle linkage, electrical connections and vacuum hoses from the throttle body.
11   Loosen the turbocharger-to-throttle body inlet hose clamps. Because the clamps are difficult to reach, a small wrench or socket will make the job easier.
12   Remove the three bolts and lift the throttle body off.
13   Loosen only the turbocharger-to-intake manifold discharge hose clamps **(see illustration)**.
14   Locate the fuel rail out of the way (complete with injectors, wiring harness and fuel lines) by removing the hose retainer bracket screw, the four bracket screws from the intake manifold and the two bracket retaining clips.
15   Disconnect the oil line at the turbocharger bearing housing.
16   Remove the three screws and detach the heat shield.
17   Disconnect the coolant return tube and hose assembly from the turbocharger and water box and remove the tube support bracket.
18   Remove the four turbocharger-to-exhaust manifold nuts. To make this job easier, apply penetrating oil to the exposed threads and allow it to soak in for a few minutes.
19   To remove the turbocharger, lift the assembly off the exhaust manifold studs and push it down toward the passenger side, then up and out of the engine compartment.

Installation

20   Carefully clean the mating surfaces of the turbocharger and manifold.
21   Place the turbocharger in position on the manifold studs, making sure the discharge tube is in place between the intake manifold and turbocharger.
22   Apply anti-seize compound to the studs and install the nuts. Tighten the nuts to the torque listed in this Chapter's Specifications.
23   Connect the oil line and tighten the tube nut securely.
24   Install the support bracket on the turbocharger and tighten the bolt securely.
25   Install the heat shield.
26   Connect the coolant tube and tighten the tube nut securely.
27   Install the bracket-to-engine block bolt. Tighten it to the torque listed in this Chapter's Specifications.
28   Install the fuel rail (See Section 27).
29   Tighten the turbocharger discharge hose clamp securely.

30   Place the throttle body in position and install the bolts. Tighten the bolts to the torque listed in this Chapter's Specifications.
31   Connect the throttle body hose and tighten the clamp screw securely.
32   Connect the throttle linkage, electrical and vacuum connections to the throttle body.
33   Install the throttle body adapter, hose and air cleaner box, support and the air cleaner assembly.
34   Raise the front of the vehicle and support it securely on jackstands.
35   Working under the vehicle, connect the coolant tube and install the tube nut. Tighten the nut securely.
36   Connect the oil drain return hose.
37   Connect the exhaust pipe and install the exhaust pipe articulated joint shoulder bolts.
38   Connect the oxygen sensor wire.
39   Lower the vehicle.
40   Fill the cooling system and connect the negative battery cable.

31   Exhaust system servicing – general information

Refer to illustrations 31.1a, 31.1b, 31.1c, 31.1d, 31.1e and 31.4
Warning: *Inspection and repair of exhaust system components should be done only with the engine and exhaust components completely cool. Also, when working under the vehicle, make sure it's securely supported on jackstands.*

1   The exhaust system **(see illustrations)** consists of the exhaust manifold(s), the catalytic converter, the muffler, the tailpipe and all connecting pipes, brackets, hangers and clamps. The exhaust system is attached to the body with mounting brackets and rubber hangers **(see illustrations)**. If any of the parts are improperly installed, excessive noise and vibration will be transmitted to the body.
2   Conduct regular inspections of the exhaust system to keep it safe and quiet. Look for any damaged or bent parts, open seams, holes, loose connections, excessive corrosion or other defects which could allow exhaust fumes to enter the vehicle. Deteriorated exhaust system components shouldn't be repaired; they should be replaced with new parts.
3   If the exhaust system components are extremely corroded or rusted together, welding equipment will probably be required to remove them. The convenient way to accomplish this is to have a muffler repair shop remove the corroded sections with a cutting torch. If, however, you want to save money by doing it yourself (and you don't have a welding outfit with a cutting torch), simply cut off the old components with a hacksaw. If you have compressed air, special pneumatic cutting chisels can also be used. If you do decide to tackle the job at home, be sure to wear safety goggles to protect your eyes from metal chips and work gloves to protect your hands.

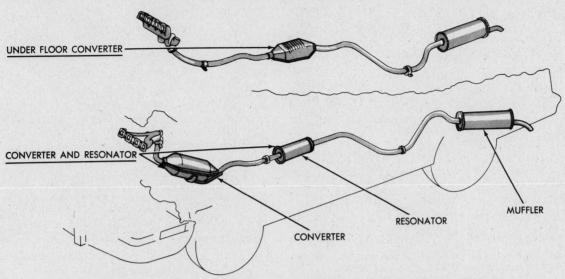

UNDER FLOOR CONVERTER

CONVERTER AND RESONATOR

MUFFLER

RESONATOR

CONVERTER

31.1a   Typical exhaust system components (top – turbocharged models; bottom – all others)

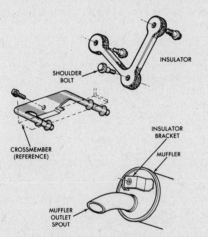

INSULATOR

SHOULDER BOLT

INSULATOR BRACKET

MUFFLER

CROSSMEMBER (REFERENCE)

MUFFLER OUTLET SPOUT

31.1b   Typical tailpipe and muffler support/insulator assembly – exploded view

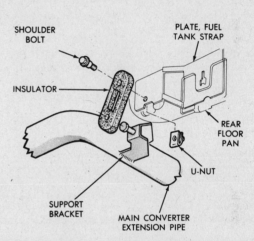

SHOULDER BOLT

PLATE, FUEL TANK STRAP

INSULATOR

REAR FLOOR PAN

U-NUT

SUPPORT BRACKET

MAIN CONVERTER EXTENSION PIPE

31.1c   Typical under floor converter or extension pipe support assembly – exploded view

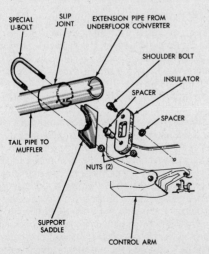

SPECIAL U-BOLT

SLIP JOINT

EXTENSION PIPE FROM UNDERFLOOR CONVERTER

SHOULDER BOLT

INSULATOR

SPACER

SPACER

TAIL PIPE TO MUFFLER

NUTS (2)

SUPPORT SADDLE

CONTROL ARM

31.1d   Typical front (exhaust extension/tailpipe) support assembly – exploded view

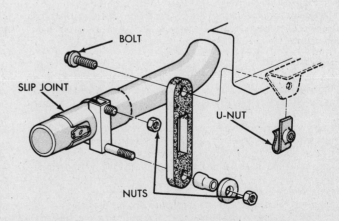

BOLT

SLIP JOINT

U-NUT

NUTS

31.1e   Typical front tailpipe support assembly – exploded view

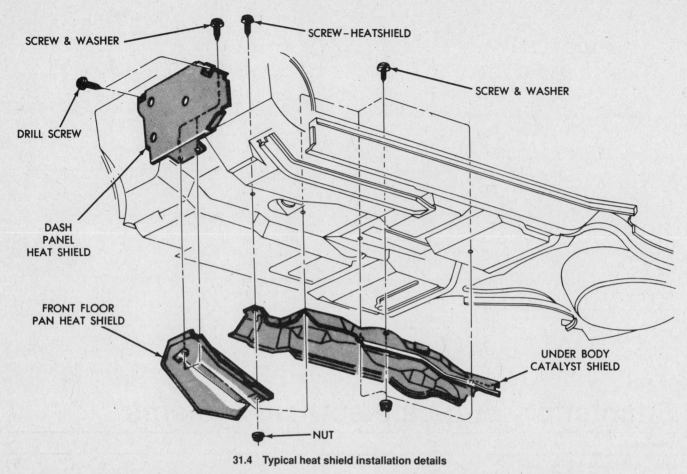

SCREW & WASHER

SCREW–HEATSHIELD

SCREW & WASHER

DRILL SCREW

DASH
PANEL
HEAT SHIELD

FRONT FLOOR
PAN HEAT SHIELD

UNDER BODY
CATALYST SHIELD

NUT

31.4   Typical heat shield installation details

4   Here are some simple guidelines to follow when repairing the exhaust system:

a) Work from the back to the front when removing exhaust system components.

b) Apply penetrating oil to the component fasteners to make them easier to remove.

c) Use new gaskets, hangers and clamps when installing exhaust system components.

d) Apply anti-seize compound to the threads of all exhaust system fasteners during reassembly.

e) Be sure to allow sufficient clearance between newly installed parts and all points on the underbody to avoid overheating the floor pan and possibly damaging the interior carpet and insulation. Pay particularly close attention to the catalytic converter and heat shield **(see illustration)**.

Chapter 5   Engine electrical systems

Contents

Specifications

Ignition coil resistance

1978 through 1985
  Primary
    Echlin or Essex .... 1.41 to 1.62 ohms
    Prestolite .... 1.60 to 1.79 ohms
  Secondary
    Echlin or Essex .... 8 to 11.2 k-ohms
    Prestolite .... 9.4 to 11.7 k-ohms
1986 on
  Primary
    Essex .... 1.34 to 1.55 ohms
    Prestolite .... 1.34 to 1.55 ohms
  Secondary
    Essex .... 9 to 12.2 k-ohms
    Prestolite .... 9.4 to 11.7 k-ohms

Ballast resistor resistance .... 0.5 to 0.6 ohms

1   General information

The engine electrical systems include all ignition, charging and starting components. Because of their engine-related functions, these components are discussed separately from chassis electrical devices such as the lights, the instruments, etc. (which are included in Chapter 12).

Always observe the following precautions when working on the electrical systems:

a) Be extremely careful when servicing engine electrical components. They are easily damaged if checked, connected or handled improperly.

b) Never leave the ignition switch on for long periods of time with the engine off.

c) Don't disconnect the battery cables while the engine is running.

d) Maintain correct polarity when connecting a battery cable from another vehicle during jump starting.

e) Always disconnect the negative cable first and hook it up last or the battery may be shorted by the tool being used to loosen the cable clamps.

It's also a good idea to review the safety-related information regarding the engine electrical systems located in the *Safety First* section near the front of this manual before beginning any operation included in this Chapter.

2   Battery – emergency jump starting

Refer to the *Booster battery (jump) starting* procedure at the front of this manual.

3   Battery – removal and installation

Refer to illustrations 3.1 and 3.2

1   **Caution:** *Always disconnect the negative cable first and hook it up last or the battery may be shorted by the tool being used to loosen the cable clamps.* Disconnect both cables from the battery terminals **(see illustration).**

2   Remove the battery hold-down clamp or strap **(see illustration).**

3   Lift out the battery. Be careful – it's heavy.

4   While the battery is out, inspect the carrier (tray) for corrosion (see Chapter 1).

5   If you're replacing the battery, make sure you purchase one that's identical, with the same dimensions, amperage rating, cold cranking rating, etc.

6   Installation is the reverse of removal.

4   Battery cables – check and replacement

1   Periodically inspect the entire length of each battery cable for damage, cracked or burned insulation and corrosion. Poor battery cable connections can cause starting problems and decreased engine performance.

2   Check the cable-to-terminal connections at the ends of the cables for cracks, loose wire strands and corrosion. The presence of white, fluffy deposits under the insulation at the cable terminal connection is a sign that the cable is corroded and should be replaced. Check the terminals for distortion, missing mounting bolts and corrosion.

3   When removing the cables, **always disconnect the negative cable first and hook it up last** or the battery may be shorted by the tool used to loosen the cable clamps. Even if only the positive cable is being replaced, be sure to disconnect the negative cable from the battery first (see Chapter 1 for further information regarding battery cable removal).

4   Disconnect the old cables from the battery, then trace each of them to their opposite ends and detach them from the starter solenoid and ground terminals. Note the routing of each cable to ensure correct installation.

5   If you're replacing either or both of the old cables, take them with you when buying new cables. It's very important to replace the cables with identical parts. Cables have characteristics that make them easy to identify: Positive cables are usually red, larger in cross-section and have a larger diameter battery post clamp; ground cables are usually black, smaller in cross-section and have a slightly smaller diameter clamp for the negative post.

6   Clean the threads of the solenoid or ground connection with a wire brush to remove rust and corrosion. Apply a light coat of battery terminal corrosion inhibitor, or petroleum jelly, to the threads to prevent future corrosion.

7   Attach the cable to the solenoid or ground connection and tighten the mounting nut/bolt securely.

8   Before connecting a new cable to the battery, make sure it reaches the battery post without having to be stretched.

9   Connect the positive cable first, followed by the negative cable.

5   Ignition system – general information

The ignition system includes the ignition switch, the battery, the coil, the primary (low voltage) and secondary (high voltage) wiring circuits, the distributor and the spark plugs. The ignition system on carbureted vehicles is controlled by the spark control computer; the ignition system on fuel-injected vehicles is controlled by the logic module (computer). Both the spark control computer and the logic module monitor various engine operating parameters – such as rpm, intake air volume, engine tempera-

3.1   Always detach the cable from the negative terminal
(A – smaller diameter post) first, then detach the positive cable
(B – larger diameter post)

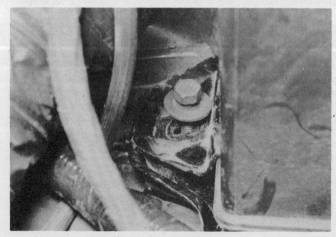

3.2   To remove the battery, unscrew the bolt and detach
the hold-down clamp

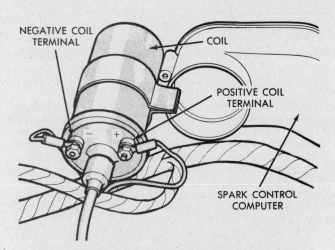

7.1   To check the coil primary resistance, touch the ohmmeter leads to the positive and negative terminals – check the secondary resistance by touching one of the ohmmeter leads to one of the primary terminals and the other to the large center terminal

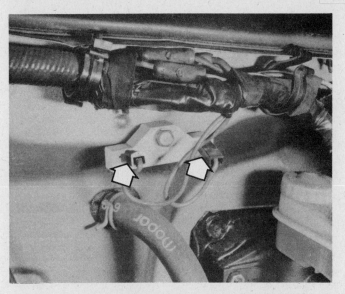

7.9   To check the ballast resistor, unplug the wires and touch the ohmmeter leads to the resistor terminals

ture, etc. – to ensure a perfectly timed spark under all driving conditions. For more information regarding the spark control computer or the logic module, refer to Chapter 6.

6   Ignition system – check

1   Attach an inductive timing light to each plug wire, one at a time, and crank the engine.
   a) If the light flashes, voltage is reaching the plug.
   b) If the light doesn't flash, proceed to the next Step.
2   Inspect the spark plug wire(s), distributor cap, rotor and spark plug(s) (see Chapter 1).
3   If the engine still won't start, check the ignition coil (see Section 7).

7   Ignition coil and ballast resistor – check and replacement

Ignition coil

Refer to illustration 7.1
1   Mark the wires and terminals with pieces of numbered tape, then remove the primary wires and the high-tension lead from the coil **(see illustration)**.
2   Remove the coil from the mount, clean the outer case and check it for cracks and other damage.
3   Clean the coil primary terminals and check the coil tower terminal for corrosion. Clean it with a wire brush if any corrosion is found.
4   Check the coil primary resistance by attaching the leads of an ohmmeter to the positive and negative terminals. Compare your readings to the primary resistance listed in this Chapter's Specifications.
5   Check the coil secondary resistance by hooking one of the ohmmeter leads to one of the primary terminals and the other ohmmeter lead to the large center terminal. Compare your readings to the secondary resistance listed in this Chapter's Specifications.
6   If the measured resistances are not as specified, the coil is probably defective and should be replaced with a new one.
7   For proper ignition system operation, all coil terminals and wire leads must be kept clean and dry.
8   Install the coil in the vehicle and hook up the wires.

Ballast resistor

Refer to illustration 7.9
9   Some earlier models use a ballast resistor **(see illustration)** to pro-

tect the coil from excessive voltage during low speed operation.
10   To check the ballast resistor, detach it from the firewall, unplug the leads, touch the probes of an ohmmeter to the terminals of the resistor and compare your readings to the resistance listed in this Chapter's Specifications. If the resistance is not as specified, replace the resistor.

8   Distributor – removal and installation

Refer to illustrations 8.3a, 8.3b, 8.6, 8.7 and 8.9

Removal
1   Disconnect the cable from the negative terminal of the battery.
2   Detach the primary lead from the coil.
3   Unplug the electrical connector for the Hall Effect pick-up **(see illustration)**. Follow the wires as they exit the distributor to find the connector. On some models, it may be necessary to detach the connector from a mounting bracket on the distributor **(see illustration)**.

5

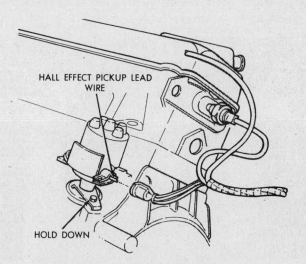

8.3a   The first step in distributor removal is to unplug the electrical connector for the Hall Effect pick-up assembly (1.7L engine shown, 2.2L similar)

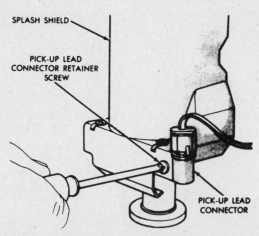

8.3b On some models, the connector for the Hall Effect pick-up lead will have to be disconnected from the mounting bracket (which is part of the distributor base) (2.2L engine shown)

8.6 Using white paint, mark the relationship of the rotor to the distributor body and the position of the distributor body in relation to the block (2.2L engine shown)

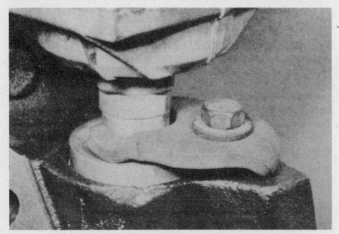

8.7 Typical distributor hold-down clamp and bolt (1.7L engine shown, 2.2L similar)

8.9 When installing the distributor, make sure the helical gear meshes with the gear on the intermediate shaft and the slot in the distributor shaft mates with the tang on the tip of the oil pump drive shaft

4   Look for a raised "1" on the distributor cap. This marks the location for the number one cylinder spark plug wire terminal. If the cap doesn't have a mark for the number one terminal, locate the number one spark plug and trace the wire back to the terminal on the cap.

5   Remove the distributor cap (see Chapter 1) and turn the engine over until the rotor is pointing toward the number one spark plug wire terminal (see locating TDC procedure in Chapter 2 if necessary).

6   Make a mark on the edge of the distributor base directly below the rotor tip and in line with it (if the rotor has more than one tip, use the center one for reference). Also, mark the distributor base and the engine block to ensure that the distributor will be reinstalled correctly **(see illustration)**.

7   Remove the distributor hold down-bolt and clamp **(see illustration)**, then pull the distributor straight up to remove it. **Caution:** *DO NOT turn the crankshaft while the distributor is out of the engine, or the alignment marks will be useless.*

Installation

Note: *If the crankshaft has been moved while the distributor is out, the number one piston must be repositioned at TDC. This can be done by feeling for compression pressure at the number one plug hole as the crankshaft is turned. Once compression is felt, align the ignition timing zero mark with the pointer.*

8   Insert the distributor into the engine in exactly the same relationship to the block that it was when removed.

9   To mesh the helical gears on the intermediate shaft and the distributor, it may be necessary to turn the rotor slightly. Also, make sure the slot in the bottom of the distributor shaft **(see illustration)** fits over the tang on the upper end of the oil pump shaft. If it isn't, the distributor won't seat completely. Recheck the alignment marks between the distributor base and block to verify the distributor is in the same position it was before removal. Also check the rotor to see if it's aligned with the mark you made on the edge of the distributor base.

10   Place the hold-down clamp in position and loosely install the bolt.

11   Install the distributor cap.

12   Plug in the Hall Effect pick-up electrical connector.

13   Reattach the spark plug wires to the plugs (if removed).

14   Connect the cable to the negative terminal of the battery.

15   Check the ignition timing (see Chapter 1) and tighten the distributor hold-down bolt securely.

9   Distributor – overhaul (1.7L engine only)

Refer to illustrations 9.3, 9.6 and 9.7

1   Remove the distributor as described in Section 8, then pull the rotor off the distributor shaft.

2   Remove the screw securing the Hall Effect pick-up lead.

3   Withdraw the lock springs securing the pick-up assembly in the distributor housing and remove the pick-up **(see illustration)**.

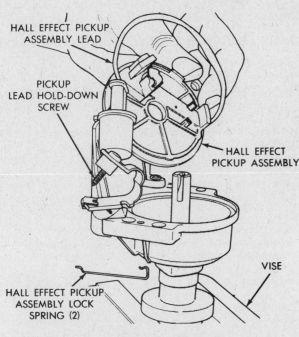

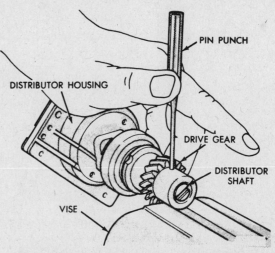

9.6   Use a pin punch to drive out the roll pin that secures the drive gear to the shaft (1.7L engine)

9.3   Remove the lock springs and detach the pick-up assembly (1.7L engine)

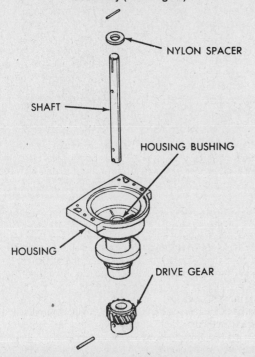

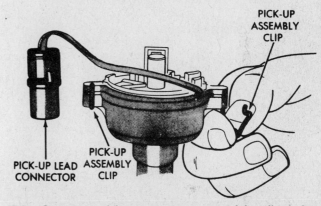

10.4a   On some models, you must remove retaining clips before you can detach the pick-up assembly (2.2L engine)

11   Check the fit of the distributor shaft in the housing. If there's excessive side movement, try to obtain replacement bushings.
12   Reassembly is the reverse of disassembly, with the following exceptions:
   a) Lubricate the distributor shaft with a light film of engine oil. Don't use too much oil.
   b) When installing the distributor shaft, make sure the nylon spacer contacts the housing bushing.
   c) Use a new roll pin when installing the drive gear on the distributor shaft.

9.7   Distributor components – exploded view (1.7L engine)

4   Remove the two screws securing the shield to the distributor and detach the shield.
5   Mark the location of the drive gear on the distributor shaft so it can be installed in the same position during reassembly.
6   Using a pin punch, drive out the roll pin securing the gear to the shaft **(see illustration)**.
7   Remove the gear and withdraw the distributor shaft from the housing **(see illustration)**.
8   Remove the nylon spacer from the distributor shaft.
9   Clean all the parts and inspect them for wear and damage.
10   Check the distributor cap and rotor as described in Chapter 1.

10   Hall Effect pick-up assembly – replacement (2.2L engine only)

Refer to illustrations 10.4a and 10.4b
Note: *The Hall Effect pick-up assembly, which is located inside the distributor, supplies the basic ignition timing signal to the computer. The check for the Hall Effect pick-up assembly is part of a larger diagnostic procedure for the entire electronic spark advance system, and is beyond the scope of the average home mechanic. However, if the part is known to be defective and you elect to install a new one, the replacement procedure itself is easy.*

1   Disconnect the cable from the negative terminal of the battery.
2   Remove the distributor splash shield and cap.
3   Detach the rotor.
4   Remove the clips (if equipped) and lift the pick-up assembly off the distributor shaft **(see illustrations)**.

5

10.4b Lift the Hall Effect pick-up assembly off the distributor shaft (2.2L engine)

5   To install the pick-up, place it in position, making sure the electrical lead retainer is in the locating hole. Install the retaining clips (if equipped) and the rotor.
6   Install the distributor cap and splash shield and connect the negative battery cable.

11   Charging system – general information and precautions

The charging system includes the alternator, either an internal or external voltage regulator, a charge indicator, the battery, a fusible link and the wiring between all the components. The charging system supplies electrical power for the ignition system, the lights, the radio, etc. The alternator is driven by a drivebelt at the front of the engine.

The purpose of the voltage regulator is to limit the alternator's voltage to a preset value. This prevents power surges, circuit overloads, etc., during peak voltage output.

The fusible link is a short length of insulated wire integral with the engine compartment wiring harness. The link is four wire gauges smaller in diameter than the circuit it protects. Production fusible links and their identification flags are identified by the flag color. See Chapter 12 for additional information regarding fusible links.

The charging system doesn't ordinarily require periodic maintenance. However, the drivebelt, battery and wires and connections should be inspected at the intervals outlined in Chapter 1.

The dashboard warning light should come on when the ignition key is turned to Start, then go off immediately. If it remains on, there is a malfunction in the charging system (see Section 12). Some vehicles are also equipped with a voltmeter. If the voltmeter indicates abnormally high or low voltage, check the charging system (see Section 12).

Be very careful when making electrical circuit connections to a vehicle equipped with an alternator and note the following:

a) When reconnecting wires to the alternator from the battery, be sure to note the polarity.
b) Before using arc welding equipment to repair any part of the vehicle, disconnect the wires from the alternator and the battery terminals.
c) Never start the engine with a battery charger connected.
d) Always disconnect both battery leads before using a battery charger.
e) The alternator is turned by an engine drivebelt which could cause serious injury if your hands, hair or clothes become entangled in it with the engine running.
f) Because the alternator is connected directly to the battery, it could arc or cause a fire if overloaded or shorted out.

g) Wrap a plastic bag over the alternator and secure it with rubber bands before steam cleaning the engine.

12   Charging system – check

1   If a malfunction occurs in the charging circuit, don't automatically assume the alternator is causing the problem. First check the following items:

a) Check the drivebelt tension and condition (Chapter 1). Replace it if it's worn or deteriorated.
b) Make sure the alternator mounting and adjustment bolts are tight.
c) Inspect the alternator wiring harness and the connectors at the alternator and voltage regulator. They must be in good condition and tight.
d) Check the fusible link (if equipped) located between the starter solenoid and the alternator. If it's burned, determine the cause, repair the circuit and replace the link (the vehicle won't start and/or the accessories won't work if the fusible link blows). Sometimes a fusible link may look good, but still be bad. If in doubt, remove it and check it for continuity.
e) Start the engine and check the alternator for abnormal noises (a shrieking or squealing sound indicates a bad bearing).
f) Check the specific gravity of the battery electrolyte. If it's low, charge the battery (doesn't apply to maintenance free batteries).
g) Make sure the battery is fully charged (one bad cell in a battery can cause overcharging by the alternator).
h) Disconnect the battery cables (negative first, then positive). Inspect the battery posts and the cable clamps for corrosion. Clean them thoroughly if necessary (see Chapter 1). Reconnect the cable to the negative terminal.
i) With the key off, connect a test light between the negative battery post and the disconnected negative cable clamp.
   1) If the test light does not come on, reattach the clamp and proceed to the next Step.
   2) If the test light comes on, there is a short (drain) in the electrical system of the vehicle. The short must be repaired before the charging system can be checked.
   3) Disconnect the alternator wiring harness.
      (a) If the light goes out, the alternator is bad.
      (b) If the light stays on, pull each fuse until the light goes out (this will tell you which component is shorted).

2   Using a voltmeter, check the battery voltage with the engine off. If should be approximately 12-volts.
3   Start the engine and check the battery voltage again. It should now be approximately 14-to-15 volts.
4   Turn on the headlights. The voltage should drop, and then come back up, if the charging system is working properly.
5   If the voltage reading is more than the specified charging voltage, replace the voltage regulator (see Section 15). If the voltage is less, the alternator diode(s), stator or rectifier may be bad or the voltage regulator may be malfunctioning.

13   Alternator – removal and installation

Refer to illustrations 13.2, 13.3a and 13.3b
1   Detach the cable from the negative terminal of the battery.
2   Detach the electrical connectors from the alternator **(see illustration)**.
3   Loosen the alternator adjustment and pivot bolts and detach the drivebelt **(see illustrations)**.
4   Remove the adjustment and pivot bolts and separate the alternator from the engine.
5   If you're replacing the alternator, take the old one with you when purchasing a replacement unit. Make sure the new/rebuilt unit looks identical to the old alternator. Look at the terminals – they should be the same in number, size and location as the terminals on the old alternator. Finally,

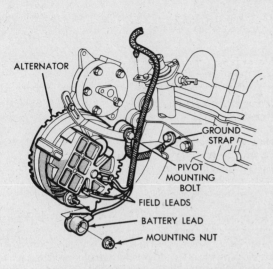

13.2 Typical alternator wiring connections

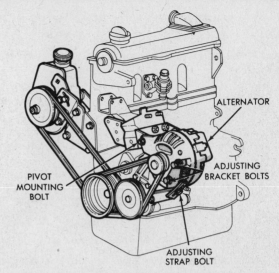

13.3a Typical alternator mounting details (1.7L engine)

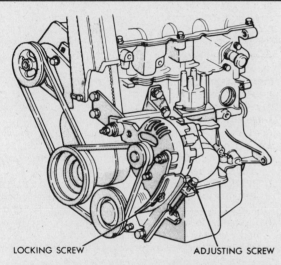

13.3b Typical alternator mounting details (2.2L engine)

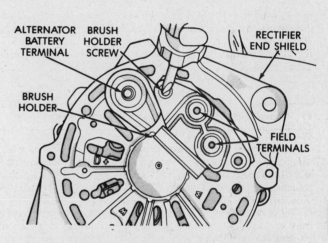

14.2 On Bosch alternators, loosen the screws in small increments, moving from screw-to-screw, so the holder won't be damaged, . . .

look at the identification numbers – they will be stamped into the housing or printed on a tag attached to the housing. Make sure the numbers are the same on both alternators.

6   Many new/rebuilt alternators DO NOT have a pulley installed, so you may have to switch the pulley from the old unit to the new/rebuilt one. When buying an alternator, find out the shop's policy regarding pulleys - some shops will perform this service free of charge.

7   Installation is the reverse of removal.

8   After the alternator is installed, adjust the drivebelt tension (see Chapter 1).

9   Check the charging voltage to verify proper operation of the alternator (see Section 12).

14   Alternator brushes – replacement

1   Disconnect the negative cable at the battery. Label the wires and detach them from the alternator terminals.

Bosch alternator

Refer to illustrations 14.2, 14.3, 14.5 and 14.6

2   Loosen the brush holder mounting screws a little at a time to prevent distortion of the holder, then remove them **(see illustration)**.

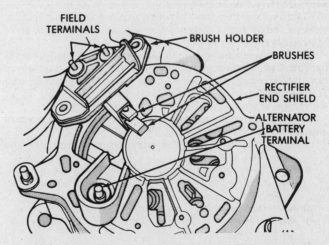

14.3   . . . then rotate the brush holder out of the alternator housing

3   Rotate the brush holder and separate it from the rear of the alternator **(see illustration)**.

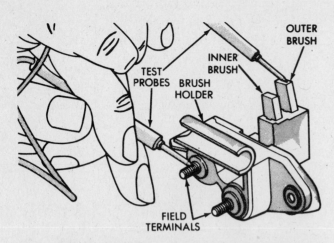

14.5   Using an ohmmeter, check for continuity between each brush and the appropriate field terminal (Bosch alternator shown)

14.6   Push the brush holder into place, making sure the brushes (which are spring loaded) seat properly (Bosch alternator shown)

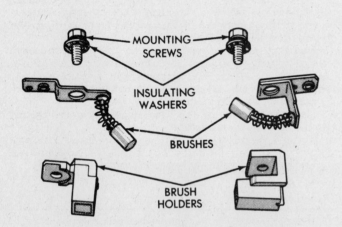

14.11   On Chrysler 60, 65 and 78 amp alternators, the brushes are held in the holders with screws – when installing the brushes, the insulating washers must be in place

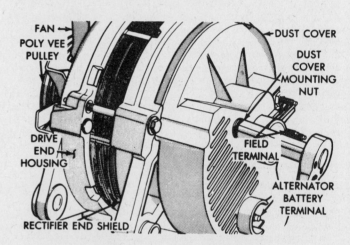

14.16   Remove the nut and detach the dust cover

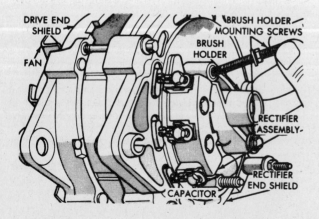

14.17a   Remove the brush holder mounting screws . . .

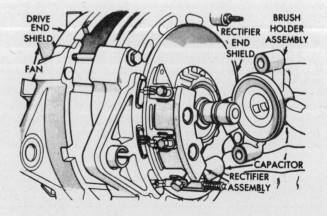

14.17b   . . . and detach the brush holder to service the brushes on 40 and 90 amp alternators

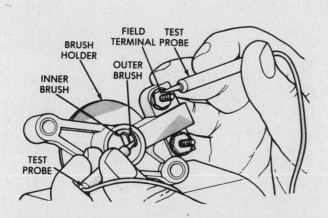

14.18   Using an ohmmeter, check for continuity between each brush and the appropriate field terminal before installing the brush holder assembly on 40 and 90 amp alternators

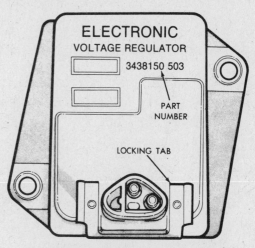

15.3   Typical external type voltage regulator (1.7L unit shown, 2.2L similar)

4   If the brushes appear to be significantly worn, or if they don't move smoothly in the brush holder, replace the brush holder assembly with a new one.

5   Before installing the brush holder assembly, check for continuity between each brush and the appropriate field terminal **(see illustration)**.

6   Insert the holder into position, making sure the brushes seat correctly **(see illustration)**.

7   Hold the brush holder securely in place and install the screws. Tighten them evenly, a little at a time, so the holder isn't distorted. Once the screws are snug, tighten them securely.

8   Reconnect the negative battery cable.

Chrysler 60, 65 and 78 amp alternators

Refer to illustration 14.11

9   Remove the alternator.

10   The brushes are mounted in plastic holders which locate them in the proper position.

11   Remove the brush mounting screws and insulating washers and separate the brush assemblies from the rectifier end shield **(see illustration)**.

12   If the brushes appear to be significantly worn or are oil soaked or damaged, replace them with new ones.

13   Make sure the brushes move smoothly in the holders.

14   Insert the brush assemblies into the rectifier end shield and install the screws and washers. Tighten the screws securely. Make sure the brushes aren't grounded.

15   Install the alternator.

Chrysler 40 and 90 amp alternators

Refer to illustrations 14.16, 14.17a, 14.17b and 14.18

16   Remove the nut and detach the dust cover from the rear of the alternator **(see illustration)**.

17   Remove the brush holder mounting screws and separate the brush holder from the end shield **(see illustrations)**.

18   Before installing the new brush holder assembly, check for continuity between each brush and the appropriate field terminal **(see illustration)**.

19   Installation is the reverse of removal. Be careful when sliding the brushes over the slip rings and don't overtighten the brush holder screws.

15   Voltage regulator – general information

Refer to illustration 15.3

1   The voltage regulator controls the charging system voltage by limiting the alternator output. The regulator is a sealed unit and isn't adjustable.

2   If the ammeter fails to register a charge rate or the red warning light on the dash comes on and the alternator, battery, drivebelt tension and electrical connections seem to be fine, have the regulator checked by a dealer service department or a repair shop.

3   The voltage regulator **(see illustration)** on 1.7L and 2.2L carburetor-equipped vehicles is located on the left-hand inner fender panel (under a cover on some models) in the engine compartment. To replace the regulator, unplug the wiring connector, remove the mounting screws and detach it. Installation is the reverse of removal.

4   Some Bosch alternators incorporate an integral voltage regulator which is part of the brush assembly.

5   On fuel-injected models, the voltage regulator is incorporated into the logic and power module/EFI system and consequently all diagnosis and repair must be left to a dealer service department or repair shop.

16   Starting system – general information and precautions

The sole function of the starting system is to turn over the engine quickly enough to allow it to start.

The starting system consists of the battery, the starter motor, the starter solenoid, the switch and the wires connecting them. The solenoid is mounted directly on the starter motor.

The solenoid/starter motor assembly is installed on the lower part of the engine, next to the transmission bellhousing.

When the ignition key is turned to the Start position, the starter solenoid is actuated through the starter control circuit. The starter solenoid then connects the battery to the starter. The battery supplies the electrical energy to the starter motor, which does the actual work of cranking the engine.

The starter motor on a vehicle equipped with a manual transmission can only be operated when the clutch pedal is depressed; the starter on a vehicle equipped with an automatic transmission can only be operated when the transmission selector lever is in Park or Neutral.

Always observe the following precautions when working on the starting system:

a) Excessive cranking of the starter motor can overheat it and cause serious damage. Never operate the starter motor for more than 30 seconds at a time without pausing to allow it to cool for at least two minutes.

b) The starter is connected directly to the battery and could arc or cause a fire if mishandled, overloaded or shorted out.

c) Always detach the cable from the negative terminal of the battery before working on the starting system.

5

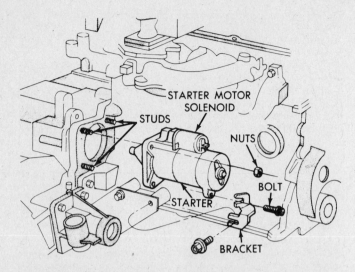

18.5a   Typical starter motor installation details (early unit for 2.2L engine shown) – note the three studs in the bellhousing flange, with nuts on the starter motor side of the bellhousing

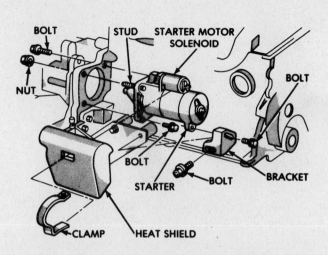

18.5b   Typical starter motor installation details (later unit for 2.2L engine shown) – note the combination of studs, nuts and bolts, which go through the bellhousing flange from both sides

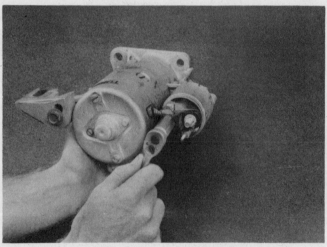

19.3   Remove the nut securing the field coil strap to the solenoid, then detach the strap

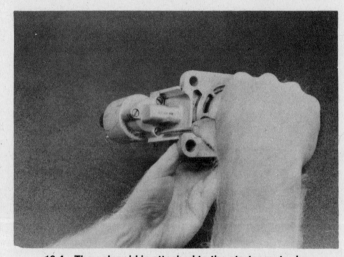

19.4   The solenoid is attached to the starter motor by two or three screws, depending on the unit

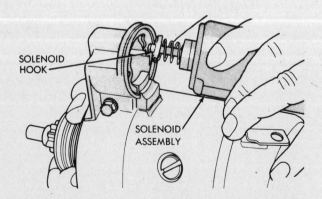

19.5a   If the starter motor is a Bosch unit on a vehicle with a manual transaxle, carefully work the solenoid off the shift fork to detach it

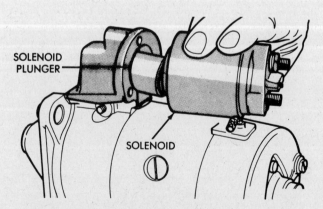

19.5b   If the starter motor is a Bosch unit on a vehicle with an automatic transaxle, slide the solenoid off the plunger to detach it

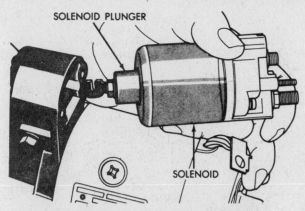

19.5c   If the starter motor is a Nippondenso unit, unhook the solenoid from the shift fork to detach it

---

17   Starter motor – in-vehicle check

Note: *Before diagnosing starter problems, make sure the battery is fully charged.*

1   If the starter motor doesn't turn at all when the switch is operated, make sure the shift lever is in Neutral or Park (automatic transmission) or the clutch pedal is depressed (manual transmission).

2   Make sure the battery is charged and all cables, both at the battery and starter solenoid terminals, are clean and secure.

3   If the starter motor spins but the engine isn't cranking, the overrunning clutch in the starter motor is slipping and the starter motor must be replaced.

4   If, when the switch is actuated, the starter motor doesn't operate at all but the solenoid clicks, then the problem lies with either the battery, the main solenoid contacts or the starter motor itself (or the engine is seized).

5   If the solenoid plunger can't be heard when the switch is actuated, the battery is bad, the fusible link is burned (the circuit is open) or the solenoid itself is defective.

6   To check the solenoid, connect a jumper lead between the battery (+) and the ignition switch wire terminal (the small terminal) on the solenoid. If the starter motor now operates, the solenoid is OK and the problem is in the ignition switch, neutral start switch or the wiring.

7   If the starter motor still doesn't operate, remove the starter/solenoid assembly for disassembly, testing and repair.

8   If the starter motor cranks the engine at an abnormally slow speed, first make sure the battery is fully charged and all terminal connections are tight. If the engine is partially seized, or has the wrong viscosity oil in it, it will crank slowly.

9   Run the engine until normal operating temperature is reached, then disconnect the coil wire from the distributor cap and ground it on the engine.

10   Connect a voltmeter positive lead to the positive battery post and connect the negative lead to the negative post.

11   Crank the engine and take the voltmeter readings as soon as a steady figure is indicated. Don't allow the starter motor to turn for more than 30 seconds at a time. A reading of 9-volts or more, with the starter motor turning at normal cranking speed, is normal. If the reading is 9-volts or more but the cranking speed is slow, the motor is faulty. If the reading is less than 9-volts and the cranking speed is slow, the solenoid contacts are probably burned, the starter motor is bad, the battery is discharged or there's a bad connection.

---

18   Starter motor – removal and installation

Refer to illustrations 18.5a and 18.5b

Note: *On some vehicles, it may be necessary to remove the exhaust pipe(s) or frame crossmember to gain access to the starter motor. In extreme cases it may even be necessary to unbolt the mounts and raise the engine slightly to get the starter out.*

1   Detach the cable from the negative terminal of the battery.

2   Raise the vehicle and support it securely on jackstands.

3   If the starter motor is equipped with a heat shield, remove it **(see illustration)**.

4   Clearly label, then disconnect the wires from the terminals on the starter motor and solenoid.

5   Remove the mounting fasteners **(see illustrations)** and detach the starter.

6   Installation is the reverse of removal.

---

19   Starter solenoid – removal and installation

Refer to illustrations 19.3, 19.4, 19.5a, 19.5b and 19.5c

1   Disconnect the cable from the negative terminal of the battery.

2   Remove the starter motor (see Section 18).

3   Disconnect the field coil strap from the solenoid terminal **(see illustration)**.

4   Remove the screws that secure the solenoid to the starter motor **(see illustration)**.

5   If the starter motor is a Bosch unit on a vehicle with a manual transaxle, carefully work the solenoid off the shift fork to detach it **(see illustration)**. If it's a Bosch on an automatic transaxle, slide the solenoid off the plunger to detach it **(see illustration)**. If the starter motor is a Nippondenso unit, unhook the solenoid from the shift fork **(see illustration)** to detach it.

6   Installation is the reverse of removal.

5

Chapter 6   Emissions control systems

Contents

---

1   General information

Refer to illustrations 1.1 and 1.6

To prevent pollution of the atmosphere from incompletely burned and evaporating gases, and to maintain good driveability and fuel economy, a number of emission control systems are incorporated. The principal systems are **(see illustration)** . . .

Positive Crankcase Ventilation (PCV) system
Fuel evaporative emission control system
*Heated inlet air system (thermostatically
    controlled air cleaner)*
Exhaust Gas Recirculation (EGR) system
Air injection system
Air aspirator system
Electronic feedback carburetor emission system
Throttle kickers
Automatic choke system
Oxygen sensor
Catalytic converter
Spark control computer/Logic module and sensors

The Sections in this Chapter include general descriptions, checking procedures within the scope of the home mechanic and component replacement procedures (when possible) for each of the systems listed above.

Before assuming an emissions control system is malfunctioning, check the fuel and ignition systems carefully. The diagnosis of some emission control devices requires specialized tools, equipment and training. If checking and servicing become too difficult or if a procedure is beyond your ability, consult a dealer service department. Remember, the most frequent cause of emissions problems is simply a loose or broken vacuum hose or wire, so always check the hose and wiring connections first.

This doesn't mean, however, that emission control systems are particularly difficult to maintain and repair. You can quickly and easily perform many checks and do most of the regular maintenance at home with common tune-up and hand tools. **Note:** *Because of a Federally mandated extended warranty which covers the emission control system components, check with your dealer about warranty coverage before working on any emissions-related systems. Once the warranty has expired, you may wish to perform some of the component checks and/or replacement procedures in this Chapter to save money.*

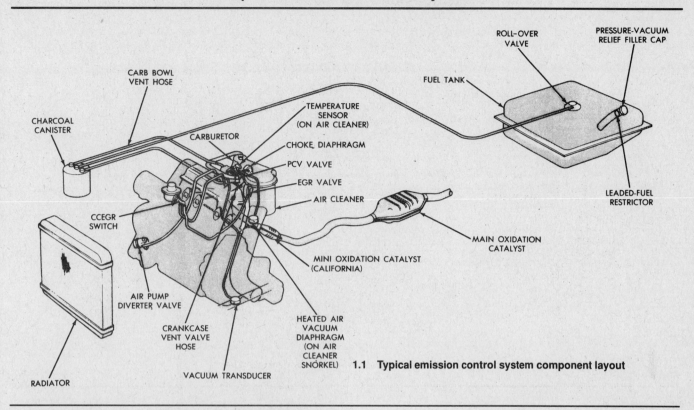

1.1   Typical emission control system component layout

Pay close attention to any special precautions outlined in this Chapter. It should be noted that the illustrations of the various systems may not exactly match the system installed on your vehicle because of changes made by the manufacturer during production or from year-to-year.

A Vehicle Emissions Control Information label is located in the engine compartment (see illustration). This label contains important emissions specifications and adjustment information. When servicing the engine or emissions systems, the VECI label in your particular vehicle should always be checked for up-to-date information.

2   Positive Crankcase Ventilation (PCV) system

1   The Positive Crankcase Ventilation (PCV) system reduces hydrocarbon emissions by scavenging crankcase vapors. It does this by circulating fresh air from the air cleaner through the crankcase, where it mixes with blow-by gases and is then rerouted through a PCV valve to the intake manifold.
2   The main components of the PCV system are the PCV valve, a fresh air filtered inlet and the vacuum hoses connecting these two components with the engine.
3   To maintain idle quality, the PCV valve restricts the flow when the intake manifold vacuum is high. If abnormal operating conditions (such as piston ring problems) arise, the system is designed to allow excessive amounts of blow-by gases to flow back through the crankcase vent tube into the air cleaner to be consumed by normal combustion.
4   Checking and replacement of the PCV valve and filter is covered in Chapter 1.

3   Evaporative emissions control system

Refer to illustrations 3.6, 3.8, 3.9, 3.12, 3.13 and 3.14

General description

1   This system is designed to trap and store fuel that evaporates from the fuel system that would normally enter the atmosphere in the form of hydrocarbon (HC) emissions.

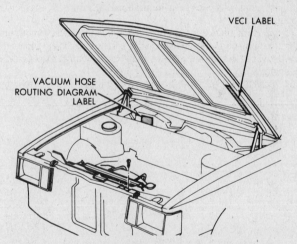

1.6   There are two helpful labels to look for in the engine compartment – on the right (passenger) side of the firewall, you'll find the vacuum hose routing diagram; on the left (driver's) under side of the hood, you'll find the Vehicle Emissions Control Information (VECI) label

2   The system is very simple and consists of a charcoal-filled canister, a damping canister, a purge solenoid (some models), a combination rollover/separator valve and connecting lines and hoses. Later models may also have a valve in the fuel tank vent line which retains vapor until it can be drawn into the canister when the engine is running.
3   When the engine is off and pressure begins to build up in the fuel tank (caused by fuel evaporation), the charcoal in the canister absorbs the fuel vapor. When the engine is started (cold), the charcoal continues to absorb and store fuel vapor. As the engine warms up, the stored fuel vapors are routed to the intake manifold or air cleaner and combustion chambers where they are burned during normal engine operation.
4   The canister is purged using air from the air injection pump delay or purge valve (carburetor-equipped models) or engine vacuum by the purge solenoid which is controlled by the logic module (EFI models). On EFI

models, when the engine coolant temperature is below 70-degrees F the logic module energizes the solenoid by grounding it so vacuum won't flow through it to the vacuum canister. Once the coolant temperature rises above 70-degrees F the solenoid is de-energized and vacuum then acts on the canister.

5   The relief valve, which is mounted in the fuel tank filler cap, is calibrated to open when the fuel tank vacuum or pressure reaches a certain level. This vents the fuel tank and relieves the high vacuum or pressure.

Checking

Canister, lines, hoses, fuel filler cap and relief valve

6   Check the canister, hoses and lines for cracks and other damage **(see illustration)**.
7   To check the filler cap, look for a damaged or deformed gasket as described in Chapter 1.

Canister delay valve (carburetor-equipped models)

8   A symptom of a failed delay valve is difficulty in starting the engine when it's hot. Disconnect the top vacuum hose **(see illustration)** and con-

nect a vacuum pump to it. Apply ten inches of vacuum to the valve – if the valve can't hold the vacuum, replace the canister with a new one.

Component replacement

Canister

9   The canister is located in the right front corner of the engine compartment, behind the headlight **(see illustration)**.
10   To replace the canister, disconnect the vacuum hoses, remove the mounting nuts and lower the canister, removing it from beneath the vehicle.
11   Installation is the reverse of removal.

Canister filter

12   Some older canisters have a replaceable filter. Simply turn the canister upside down, peel the old filter out and install a new one **(see illustration)**.

Canister purge/EGR solenoid (EFI models)

13   The canister purge solenoid is located under a cover in the engine compartment on the right inner fender panel. On models equipped with an EGR solenoid, this solenoid is mounted together with the canister purge solenoid **(see illustration)**.

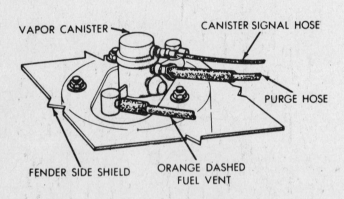

3.6   Check the charcoal canister hoses – make sure they're in good condition and connected securely

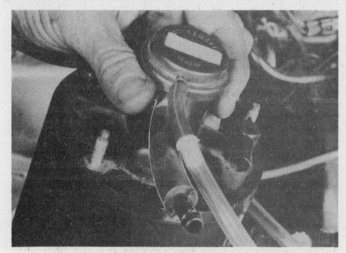

3.8   Apply vacuum with a hand pump to check the canister delay valve

3.9   On most models, you'll find the canister in the right front corner of the engine compartment, right behind the headlight (1.7L engine shown, 2.2L similar)

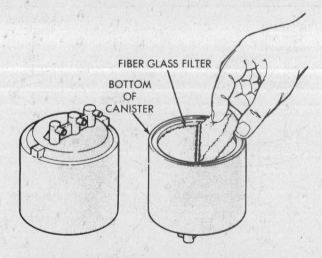

3.12   On older units, the charcoal canister filter is easily replaced – simply turn the canister upside down, peel out the old filter and install the new one

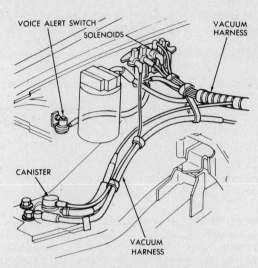

3.13 On some fuel-injected models, the canister purge and EGR solenoids are located on the same bracket

3.14 The solenoid cover on early models is secured by clips and can be removed by pulling it straight off the inner fender panel

14 To gain access to the solenoid(s), remove the cover. On early models this is accomplished by grasping it securely and pulling it off **(see illustration)**. On later models the cover is retained by a nut.

15 Disconnect the vacuum hose(s), unplug the electrical connector(s), remove the mounting bolt and detach the solenoid(s) and bracket assembly from the fender panel.

16 Installation is the reverse of removal.

4 Heated inlet air system

Refer to illustrations 4.1a, 4.1b, 4.1c and 4.8

General description

1 The heated inlet air (temperature control) system **(see illustrations)** provides heated intake air during warm-up, then maintains the inlet air temperature within a 70 to 105-degrees F operating range by mixing warm and cool air. This allows leaner fuel/air mixture settings for the carburetor, which reduces emissions and improves driveability.

2 Two fresh air inlets – one warm and one cold – are used. The balance between the two is controlled by intake manifold vacuum. A vacuum diaphragm, which operates a heat duct valve in the air cleaner, is actuated by intake vacuum.

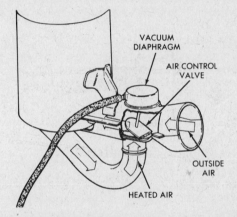

4.1a A typical heated inlet air system on an older model (1.7L engine shown) – note the externally mounted vacuum diaphragm (on all other units, the diaphragm is located inside the air cleaner housing)

6

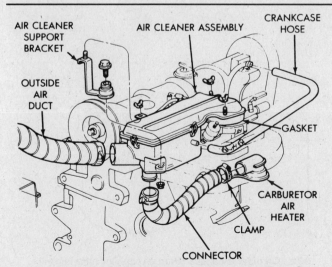

4.1b A typical heated inlet air system on a later model (carburetor-equipped 2.2L engine shown)

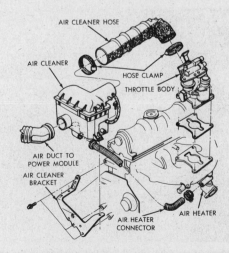

4.1c A typical heated inlet air system on a newer model (fuel-injected 2.2L engine shown)

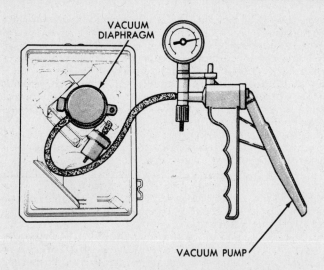

VACUUM
DIAPHRAGM

VACUUM PUMP

4.8   To check the vacuum diaphragm, unplug the vacuum source hose from the delay valve and attach a hand operated vacuum pump like this – when vacuum is applied, the diaphragm should open the door and it should also hold the applied vacuum without leaking down – if the diaphragm fails to open the door, or leaks, replace it

3   When the underhood temperature is cold, warm air radiating off the exhaust manifold is routed by a shroud which fits over the manifold up through a hot air inlet tube and into the air cleaner. This provides warm air for the carburetor, resulting in better driveability and faster warm-up. As the temperature inside the air cleaner rises, the heat duct valve is gradually closed by the vacuum diaphragm (which, in turn is controlled by a bi-metal temperature sensor inside the air cleaner) and the air cleaner draws air through a cold air duct instead. The result is a consistent intake air temperature.

Checking

Note: *Refer to Chapter 1 for the initial system check. If the system doesn't operate as described in Chapter 1, proceed as described below.*

4   Always check the vacuum source and the integrity of all vacuum hoses between the source and the vacuum diaphragm before beginning the following test. Don't proceed until you're sure they're okay.

5   Apply the parking brake and block the wheels.
6   Detach, but do not remove, the air cleaner housing and element (see Chapter 4).
7   Turn the air cleaner housing upside down so the vacuum diaphragm door is visible. The door should be open. If it isn't, it might be binding or sticking. Make sure it's not rusted in an open or closed position by attempting to move it by hand. If it's rusted, it can usually be freed by cleaning and oiling the hinge. If it fails to work properly after servicing, replace it.
8   If the vacuum diaphragm door is okay but the diaphragm still fails to operate correctly, check carefully for a leak in the hose leading to it. Check the vacuum source to and from the diaphragm, and the operation of the diaphragm itself **(see illustration)** with a hand vacuum pump. If no leak is found, replace the vacuum diaphragm. If the diaphragm is okay, check the vacuum delay valve.

Component replacement

9   On some models, the vacuum diaphragm is secured with a rivet, which must be removed with a drill. Use a self-tapping screw to install the new diaphragm.
10   To replace the vacuum delay valve, disconnect the hoses from each end of the valve, then install the new valve facing the same direction as the old one.

---

5   Exhaust Gas Recirculation (EGR) system

General description

Refer to illustrations 5.2a and 5.2b

1   This system recirculates a portion of the exhaust gases into the intake manifold or carburetor to reduce the combustion temperatures and decrease the amount of oxides of nitrogen (NOx) produced.
2   The main component in the system is the EGR valve **(see illustration)**. On carburetor-equipped models, it operates in conjunction with the Coolant Control Exhaust Gas Recirculation (CCEGR) valve (1.7L engines) **(see illustration)** or the Coolant Vacuum Switch Cold Closed (CVSCC) valve (2.2L engines). On EFI models it works with the backpressure transducer and (on some models) the EGR solenoid.
3   On carburetor-equipped engines, the coolant valve and the EGR valves remain shut at low engine temperatures. At higher engine temperatures the coolant valve opens, allowing vacuum to be applied to the EGR valve so the exhaust gas can recirculate.

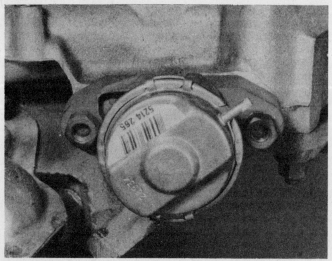

5.2a   A typical EGR valve (1.7L engine shown, 2.2L similar) – you'll find the EGR valve on the exhaust manifold on some models, on the intake manifold on others and on the turbo inlet on turbocharged models

5.2b   The coolant valve is installed in the thermostat housing (CCEGR valve shown, CVSCC valve similar)

4   On EFI models, the EGR valve is a backpressure type. The amount of exhaust gas admitted is regulated by engine vacuum and the backpressure transducer in the signal line. This transducer uses exhaust system backpressure to control the EGR valve vacuum, bleeding the vacuum off to the atmosphere whenever the backpressure at the valve itself drops below the calibrated level. The EGR valve and transducer are controlled by the EGR solenoid (operated by the logic module) which controls the vacuum flow to the EGR valve body in accordance with engine temperature and driving conditions. Symptoms of problems associated with the EGR system on EFI models are rough idling or stalling when at idle, rough engine performance during light throttle application and stalling during deceleration.

Checking

Refer to illustrations 5.5a, 5.5b, 5.5c, 5.5d and 5.17

5   Check all hoses for cracks, kinks, broken sections and proper connection **(see illustrations)**. Inspect all system connections for damage, cracks and leaks.

Carburetor-equipped engines

6   To check the EGR valve operation, bring the engine up to operating temperature and, with the transmission in Neutral (tires blocked to prevent movement), allow it to idle for 70 seconds. Open the throttle abruptly so the engine speed is between 2000 and 3000 rpm and then allow it to close. The EGR valve stem should move if the control system is working properly. The test should be repeated several times. Movement of the stem indicates the control system is functioning correctly.

7   If the EGR valve stem doesn't move, check all hose connections to make sure they aren't leaking or clogged. Disconnect the vacuum hose and apply vacuum with a hand pump. If the stem still doesn't move, replace the EGR valve with a new one.

8   Apply vacuum with the pump and then clamp the hose shut. The valve should stay open for 30 seconds or longer. If it doesn't, the diaphragm is leaking and the valve should be replaced with a new one.

9   To check the coolant valve (CCEGR/CVSCC) located in the thermostat housing, bypass it with a length of 3/16-inch hose. If the EGR valve didn't operate under the conditions described in Step 6, but does operate properly with the CCEGR/CVSCC bypassed, the CCEGR/CVSCC is defective and should be replaced.

10   If the EGR valve doesn't operate with the CCEGR/CVSCC bypassed, the carburetor must be removed to check and clean the slotted port in the throttle bore and the vacuum passages and orifices in the throttle body. Use solvent to remove deposits and check for flow with light air pressure.

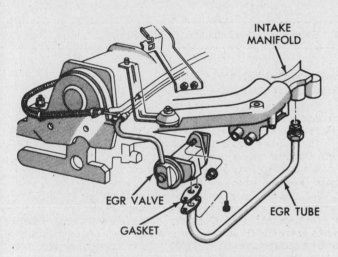

5.5a   Exploded view of a typical EGR system used on 2.2L carburetor-equipped engines (1.7L engine similar)

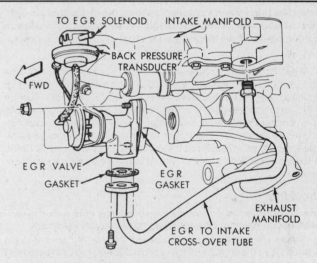

5.5b   Exploded view of a typical EGR system used on a fuel-injected (non-turbocharged) engine

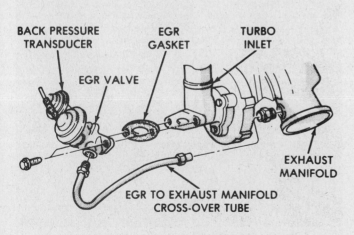

5.5c   Exploded view of a typical EGR system used on a turbocharged engine

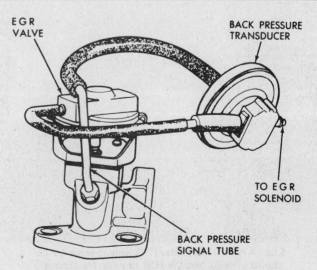

5.5d   Typical EGR valve and backpressure transducer assembly on a fuel-injected engine

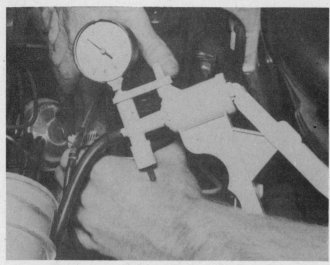

5.17   With the engine cold, detach the vacuum hose from the EGR valve, connect a vacuum pump, apply vacuum and make sure the valve holds vacuum – if it doesn't, replace it

11   Remove the EGR valve and inspect the poppet and seat area for deposits. If the deposits are more than a thin film of carbon, the valve should be cleaned. To clean the valve, apply solvent and allow it to penetrate and soften the deposits, making sure none gets on the valve diaphragm, as it could be damaged. Use a vacuum pump to hold the valve open and carefully scrape the deposits from the seat and poppet area with a tool. Inspect the poppet and stem for wear and replace the valve with a new one if wear is found.

Fuel-injected engines (non-turbocharged)

12   To check the EGR valve operation, bring the engine up to operating temperature with the transaxle in Neutral (tires blocked to prevent movement).
13   Disconnect the hose from the transducer **(see illustration 5.5d)** and connect a vacuum pump. Start the engine, raise the engine speed to approximately 2000 rpm, hold it there and apply ten inches of vacuum with the pump. The EGR valve stem should move and stay open for at least 30 seconds if the control system is working properly.
14   If the stem moves but won't stay open, the EGR valve/backpressure transducer assembly is faulty and must be replaced with a new one.
15   If the EGR valve stem doesn't move except when vacuum from the pump is applied, remove the EFI throttle body (see Chapter 4) and clean the EGR ports in the throttle bore and body with solvent.
16   If the engine exhibits rough idle, dies when returned to idle or the idle is both rough and slow, the EGR valve is leaking in the closed position. Inspect the EGR tube for leaks at the connection to the manifold. Loosen the tube connection and then tighten it securely. Remove the EGR valve and transducer assembly and inspect the poppet to make sure it's seated. If it isn't, replace the EGR valve transducer assembly with a new one; don't attempt to clean the EGR valve.

Fuel-injected engines (turbocharged)

17   With the engine cold, disconnect the vacuum hose from the EGR valve and connect a vacuum pump, apply vacuum and make sure the valve holds vacuum **(see illustration)**. If the valve doesn't hold vacuum, replace it with a new one.
18   Disconnect the vacuum pump and connect a vacuum gauge in line with the EGR valve. Start the engine and verify the gauge reading is zero.
19   With the engine still cold, increase the speed to approximately 2000 rpm and hold it there. If the gauge shows an unsteady vacuum reading above zero, the EGR solenoid is faulty and should be replaced with a new one.
20   Disconnect the vacuum hose between the EGR backpressure solenoid and the EGR solenoid. Connect the vacuum gauge, start the engine

and make sure the reading is at least five inches of vacuum, indicating the system is working properly and holding vacuum.
21   Warm the engine up to normal operating temperature (the EGR solenoid will now be open), increase the engine speed to approximately 2000 rpm and make sure the vacuum reading is still at least five inches of vacuum. If the reading is less, there's a vacuum leak between the EGR solenoid and the EFI throttle body.
22   Remove the vacuum gauge and recollect the vacuum line.
23   Disconnect the EGR valve-to-backpressure transducer vacuum hose and connect the vacuum gauge to the hose. The gauge should still read approximately five inches of vacuum with the engine off. If it doesn't, replace the EGR valve and backpressure transducer assembly with a new one.
24   Start the engine and raise the engine speed to approximately 2000 rpm. Connect a vacuum pump to the EGR valve and slowly apply vacuum. If the system is operating properly, the engine speed will begin to drop when 2 to 3.5-inches of vacuum is applied.
25   Release the vacuum and allow the engine to slow to idle speed. Apply vacuum with the pump to make sure the engine speed again drops when 2 to 3.5-inches of vacuum is applied. If the speed doesn't drop, check the EGR supply tube and passages to make sure they aren't blocked. Clear them if necessary. If they're open, then the EGR valve/backpressure transducer and tube are faulty and must be replaced with new parts.
26   Apply ten inches of vacuum to the EGR valve. The system should hold the vacuum for at least ten seconds if it's operating properly. If it doesn't hold vacuum, the EGR valve/backpressure transducer assembly is faulty and must be replaced with a new unit.

Component replacement

Carburetor-equipped engine

27   The CCEGR/CVSCC should only be replaced when the engine is cold, by removing the vacuum hoses and unscrewing the valve. Have the new part ready (wrap the threads with teflon tape), as there will be some coolant leakage when the old part is removed.
28   To replace the EGR valve, remove the air cleaner, air injection pump and shield. Disconnect the metal tube and vacuum hose, remove the two mounting nuts and detach the valve. Clean off all old gasket material from the mating surfaces of the valve and manifold, and be sure to use a new gasket when installing the valve.

Fuel-injected engines

29   To remove the EGR valve/backpressure transducer, disconnect the vacuum hose from the backpressure transducer assembly, then pull the assembly out of the mounting clip.
30   Remove the bolts or unscrew the tube nut and disconnect the crossover tube from the EGR valve.
31   Remove the mounting bolts and detach the EGR valve/backpressure transducer assembly from the engine. Clean off all old gasket material from the mating surfaces of the valve and manifold, and be sure to use a new gasket when installing the valve.
32   The EGR solenoid is located under a cover at the right front corner of the engine compartment, adjacent to the canister purge solenoid. The cover is held in place by clips on 1984 models and by the solenoid bracket retaining nut on later models.

---

6   Air injection system (carburetor-equipped models)

General description

Refer to illustrations 6.2a and 6.2b

1   This system supplies air under pressure to the exhaust ports to promote the combustion of unburned hydrocarbons and carbon monoxide before they're allowed to exit the exhaust.
2   The air injection system consists of an air pump (driven by a belt from the crankshaft pulley on 1.7L models or from the rear of the camshaft on 2.2L models), a relief valve and associated hoses and check valves, which protect the system from hot exhaust gases **(see illustrations)**.

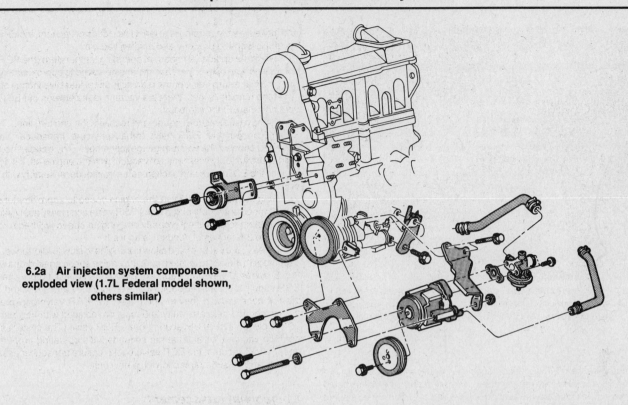

**6.2a   Air injection system components –
exploded view (1.7L Federal model shown,
others similar)**

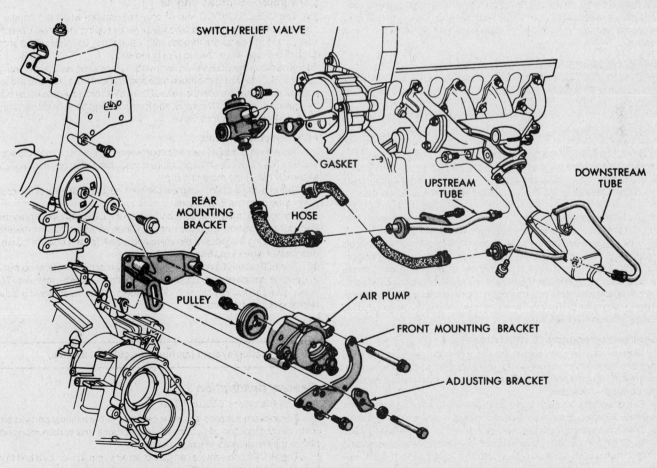

6.2b   Air injection system components – exploded view (2.2L California model shown, others similar)

Checking

General

3   Visually check the hoses, tubes and connections for cracks, loose fittings and separated parts. Use soapy water to locate a suspected leak.
4   Check the drivebelt condition and tension (Chapter 1).

Air pump

5   The air pump can only be checked using special equipment. Noise from the pump can be due to improper drivebelt tension, faulty relief or check valves, loose mounting bolts and leaking hoses or connections. If these conditions have been corrected and the pump still makes excessive noise, there's a good chance that it's faulty.

Switch/relief valve

6   If air can be heard escaping from the switch/relief valve with the engine at idle, the valve is faulty and must be replaced with a new one.

Check valve

7   Remove the hose from the inlet tube. If exhaust gas escapes past the inlet tube, the check valve is faulty and must be replaced.

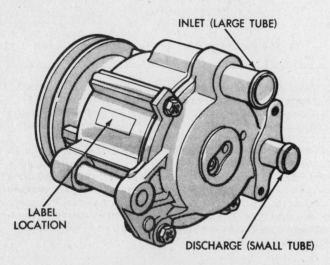

6.13   Make sure the part numbers on the old and new air pump labels are exactly the same

Component replacement

Refer to illustrations 6.13, 6.15 and 6.16

Air pump

Caution: *Disconnect the cable from the negative terminal of the battery before removing the pump.*

8   Remove the air hoses from the pump and switch/relief valve.
9   Remove the air pump drivebelt pulley shield (2.2L engines) **(see illustration 6.2b)**.
10   Loosen the pump pivot and adjustment bolts and remove the drivebelt **(see illustrations 6.2a or 6.2b)**.
11   Remove the bolts and detach the pump from the engine.
12   Remove the switch/relief valve from the pump and clean all gasket material from the valve mating surface.
13   Compare the old pump to the new unit. Make sure they have the same part number on the ID label **(see illustration)**.
14   Attach the switch/relief valve to the new air pump, using a new gasket. Transfer the pulley from the old pump to the new one.
15   With the drivebelt over the air pump and camshaft or crankshaft pulleys, place the pump in position **(see illustration)** and loosely install the bolts.
16   Adjust the air pump drivebelt. On 2.2L engines, use a breaker bar to exert pressure on the bracket (not the pump housing) and adjust the belt until the tension is correct (see Chapter 1 Specifications). Tighten the locking bolt, followed by the pivot bolt **(see illustration)**. On 1.7L engines, the belt tension is adjusted by moving the idler pulley **(see illustration 6.2a)**.
17   Tighten the air pump bracket bolts securely, install the pulley shield (2.2L engines) and reconnect the hoses to the pump and relief valve.

Switch/relief valve

18   Disconnect the hoses from the switch/relief valve, remove the two bolts and detach the valve from the pump. Carefully remove any gasket material from the valve and pump mating surfaces.
19   Place a new gasket in position and install the valve. Tighten the bolts securely and reconnect the hoses.

Check valve (2.2L engines)

20   Disconnect the hose from the valve inlet and remove the nut securing the tube to the exhaust manifold or converter. Loosen the starter motor bolt and remove the check valve from the engine.
21   Attach the new valve to the exhaust manifold or converter, tighten the starter motor bolt and connect the air hose.

6.15   Rotate the air pump into position and make sure the drivebelt is seated in the pulley grooves (2.2L engine)

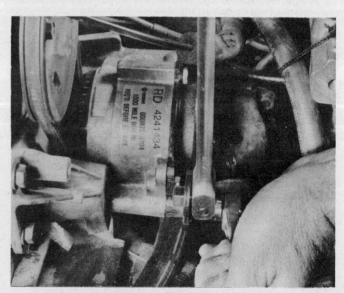

6.16   Use a breaker bar to apply leverage to the air pump bracket as the bolts are tightened

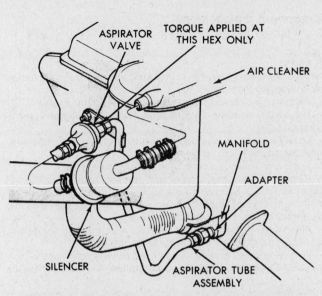

7.1a   A typical aspirator system on an older (1.7L) model

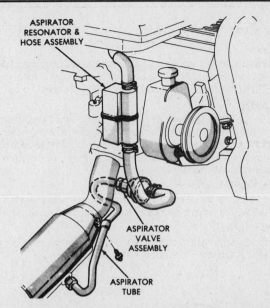

7.1b   A typical aspirator system on a newer (2.2L) model

7   Air aspirator system

General description

Refer to illustrations 7.1a and 7.1b

1   The air aspirator system **(see illustrations)** uses exhaust pulsations to draw fresh air from the air cleaner into the exhaust system. This reduces carbon monoxide (CO) and, to a lesser degree, hydrocarbon (HC) emissions.

2   The system is composed of a valve, hoses and tubes between the air cleaner assembly and the exhaust system.

3   The aspirator valve works most efficiently at idle and slightly off idle, where the negative exhaust pulses are strongest. The valve remains closed at higher engine speeds.

Checking

Refer to illustration 7.6

4   Aspirator valve failure results in excessive exhaust system noise from under the hood and hardening of the rubber hose from the valve to the air cleaner.

5   If exhaust noise is excessive, check the aspirator tube-to-exhaust manifold joint and the valve and air cleaner hose connections for leaks. If the manifold joint is leaking, retighten the tube fitting. If the hose connections are leaking, install new hose clamps (if the hose hasn't hardened). If the hose has hardened, replace it with a new one as well.

6   To determine if the valve has failed, disconnect the hose from the inlet. With the engine idling (transmission in Neutral), hold a strip of paper in front of the inlet – the paper should be sucked against the opening of the valve if it's working properly. If a steady stream of exhaust gas is escaping from the inlet (which will blow the paper away from the valve), the valve is defective and should be replaced with a new one **(see illustration)**. **Warning:** *Don't use your hand to feel for the exhaust pulses – the exhaust gas can be very hot!*

Component replacement

7   The valve can be replaced by removing the hose clamp, detaching the hose and unscrewing it from the tube.

8   The aspirator tube can be replaced by removing the valve, unscrewing the fitting at the manifold and removing the bracket bolt.

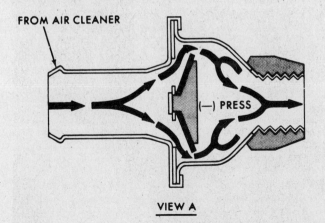

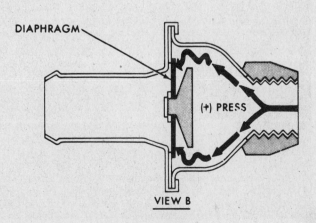

7.6   When the negative exhaust pulses are strong, air is drawn through the valve and into the exhaust manifold (view A) – when exhaust backpressure increases, the valve closes (view B)

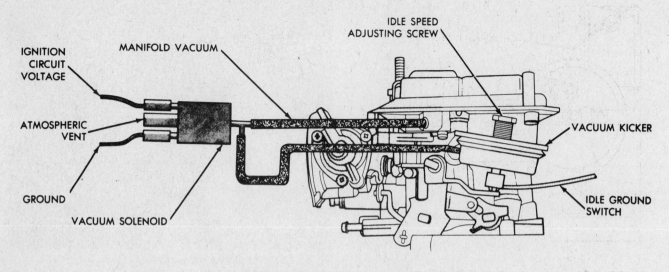

8.1a   Vacuum-type throttle kicker system (2.2L engine)

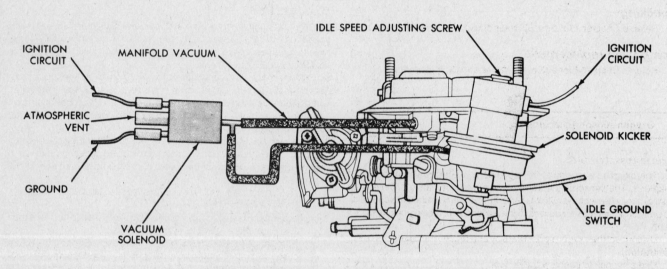

8.1b   Solenoid-type throttle kicker system (2.2L engine)

8   Throttle kickers (2.2L carburetor-equipped models)

Refer to illustrations 8.1a and 8.1b

General description

1   Solenoid and vacuum kickers (see illustrations) are used on some models to maintain idle speed when additional loads, such as the air conditioning, are put on the engine.
2   The vacuum kicker opens the throttle a fixed amount above idle when an electrical signal activates the kicker by supplying the necessary manifold vacuum. The idle speed is adjusted by a screw located at the top of the kicker.
3   When the engine is running, the solenoid kicker extends to hold the engine at the proper curb idle. The kicker retracts when the engine is turned off and manifold vacuum is no long supplied. This allows the throttle to close so fuel is cut off, reducing the possibility of dieseling.

Checking

4   Checking consists of inspecting the kickers, wires and associated hoses for damage, wear and secure connections. Operation of the vacuum kicker can be checked with a hand vacuum pump.

Component replacement

5   The throttle kickers can be replaced by removing the hoses and separating the electrical connectors, then unscrewing the mounting fasteners from the carburetor body.

9   Automatic choke system (carburetor-equipped models)

Refer to illustration 9.2

General description

1   The automatic choke system temporarily supplies a rich fuel/air mixture to the engine by closing the choke plate(s) during cold engine starting.
2   An electric signal from the oil pressure switch operates the choke control switch and activates the choke heater so it slowly opens the choke plates as the engine warms up (see illustration). This progressively leans out the mixture until the engine is warmed up.

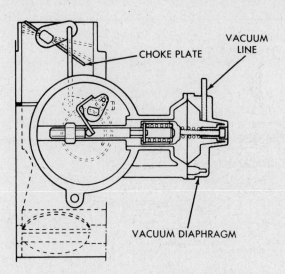

9.2   Typical automatic choke (2.2L engine)

10.2   The oxygen sensor (arrow) is installed in the exhaust manifold – on some models, it's accessible only from underneath the vehicle

Checking

3   Refer to Chapter 1 for the automatic choke checking procedure.

Component replacement

4   Refer to Chapter 4 for automatic choke servicing procedures.

10   Oxygen sensor replacement

Refer to illustration 10.2

1   The oxygen sensor must be replaced at the intervals specified in Chapter 1. The sensor is threaded into the exhaust manifold. On some models it may be necessary to raise the front of the vehicle and support it securely on jackstands for access to the underside of the engine compartment.
2   Disconnect the oxygen sensor wire by unplugging the connector **(see illustration)**.
3   Use a wrench to unscrew the sensor.
4   Use a tap to clean the threads in the exhaust manifold.
5   If the original sensor is being installed, apply anti-seize compound to the threads. New sensors will already have the anti-seize compound on the threads.
6   Install the sensor, tighten it securely and plug in the electrical connector.

11   Catalytic converter

Note: *Because of a Federally mandated extended warranty which covers emissions-related components such as the catalytic converter, check with a dealer service department before replacing the converter at your own expense.*

General description

1   The catalytic converter is an emission control device added to the exhaust system to reduce pollutants in the exhaust gas stream. There are two types of converters. The conventional oxidation catalyst reduces the levels of hydrocarbon (HC) and carbon monoxide (CO). The three-way catalyst lowers the levels of oxides of nitrogen (NOx) as well as hydrocarbons (HC) and carbon monoxide (CO).

Checking

2   The test equipment for a catalytic converter is expensive and highly sophisticated. If you suspect the converter is malfunctioning, take the vehicle to a dealer service department or authorized emissions inspection facility for diagnosis and repair.
3   Whenever the vehicle is raised for servicing of underbody components, check the converter for leaks, corrosion, dents and other damage. Check the welds/flange bolts that attach the front and rear ends of the converter to the exhaust system. If damage is discovered, the converter should be replaced.
4   Although catalytic converters don't break too often, they can become plugged. The easiest way to check for a restricted converter is to use a vacuum gauge to diagnose the effect of a blocked exhaust on intake vacuum.
   a) Open the throttle until the engine speed is about 2000 rpm.
   b) Release the throttle quickly.
   c) If there's no restriction, the gauge will quickly drop to not more than 2 in-Hg or more above its normal reading.
   d) If the gauge doesn't show 5 in-Hg or more above its normal reading, or seems to momentarily hover around its highest reading for a moment before it returns, the exhaust system, or the converter, is plugged (or an exhaust pipe is bent or dented, or the core inside the muffler has shifted).
5   Refer to the exhaust system servicing procedures in Chapter 4.

12   Spark Control Computer and sensors (carburetor-equipped models)

General description

Refer to illustrations 12.1 and 12.3

1   To enable the engine to burn a lean fuel/air mixture to improve exhaust emission control, a Chrysler Electronic Lean Burn system is used instead of the conventional ignition system. The system consists of a spark control computer **(see illustration)**, a breakerless, transistorized distributor and ignition coil, four engine sensors (five on some manual transaxle equipped vehicles) and a specially calibrated carburetor.
2   The system is controlled by the Spark Control Computer (SCC). The computer receives the signals from the sensors, analyzes them and then advances or retards the ignition timing to obtain optimum engine performance.
3   The sensors which transmit the necessary information to the spark control computer, and their functions, are as follows:

6

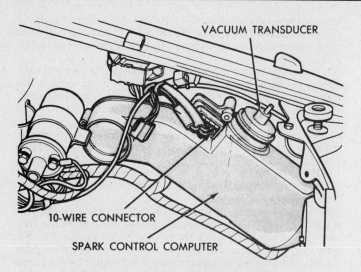

12.1 The spark control computer and vacuum transducer are located on the left inner fender panel

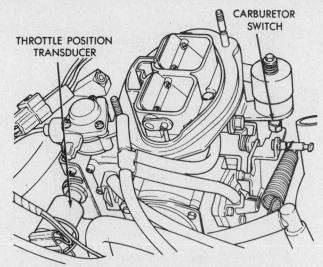

12.3 The throttle position transducer (manual transaxle only) and the carburetor switch are mounted on the carburetor

a) The vacuum transducer: Mounted on the spark control computer **(see illustration 12.1)**, it monitors the amount of intake manifold vacuum.

b) The Hall Effect Pickup assembly: Located in the distributor (see Chapter 5), it provides the computer with information on the engine speed and the position of the crankshaft.

c) The coolant temperature sending unit: This sensor signals the computer when the coolant temperature is below 150-degrees F. It's located on the thermostat housing (see Chapter 3).

d) The throttle position transducer: Located on the carburetor **(see illustration)**, it transmits the position and rate of change of the throttle plates to the spark control computer. The ignition will then be advanced after 30-degrees of throttle opening (and in every position to full throttle on some vehicles with a manual transaxle).

e) The carburetor switch: Located on the idle stop solenoid (or air conditioning solenoid, if so equipped) it tells the spark control computer whether the engine is at idle or off idle **(see illustration 12.3)**.

4   The spark control computer has two separate functional modes, Start and Run. The Start mode is in operation during engine cranking and starting. The Run mode operates only after engine starts and controls the system while the engine is running. The two modes are never in operation at the same time.

5   During cranking and starting, the Run mode is bypassed and a set amount of ignition advance is provided because of the permanent position of the Hall Effect Pickup assembly. In this mode the amount of ignition advance is determined by the position of the distributor.

6   After the engine starts, the Hall Effect Pickup assembly signal continues to feed into the computer. Now that the Start mode is bypassed and the Run mode is operating, the amount of ignition advance is determined by the spark control computer according to the information it receives from the sensors. If there's a failure of the Run mode, the Start mode will take over and keep the engine running. But, because the Start mode timing setting is fixed, very poor engine performance and fuel economy will result.

7   After the engine starts, the computer provides additional advance, which is slowly eliminated during a period of approximately one minute. With the engine running and the engine coolant temperature below 150-degrees F, the coolant temperature switch signals this information to the computer to prevent any further spark advance. After the engine reaches operating temperature, normal system operation will begin. The higher the vacuum the more the spark is advanced, the lower the vacuum the less spark advance. To obtain the maximum amount of advance at any given amount of vacuum, the carburetor switch must remain open for a specified period. During that period the ignition will not advance quickly, but will build up at a slow rate. If the carburetor switch closes before the predetermined specified period, the state of advance at that time will be

cancelled in the ignition system. However, the spark control computer will store it in its memory, and slowly return it to zero. If the switch is reopened before the advance is returned to zero, the build up of advance starts at the point where the computer still has it in memory. If the switch is reopened after the advance is returned to zero, the build up of advance must start all over again.

8   When the Hall Effect Pickup assembly signal is received by the computer, the maximum amount of timing advance is available and, according to the information received from all the sensors, the computer determines how much advance is needed.

9   If there's a failure of the Start mode of the computer or the Hall Effect Pickup assembly, the engine won't start until the problem is corrected.

Checking

Refer to illustrations 12.11, 12.17, 12.20 and 12.25

10   Prior to testing the spark control computer, check the coil and battery to make sure they're in good condition. Inspect the electrical harness and wires for shorts, broken or worn insulation and all connectors for security. Check the vacuum hose for kinks, damage and secure connection.

11   Fabricate a pair of jumper wires and hook them up as shown **(see illustration)** to the negative terminal of the coil. Ground the other end. Pull the coil wire from the distributor and, holding it with an insulated tool, place it 1/4-inch from a good ground and have an assistant turn the ignition switch to the On position. A spark should be seen arcing from the coil wire to ground.

12   If there is a spark, proceed to Step 17.

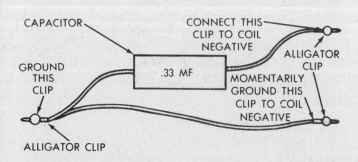

12.11 Using three alligator clips and a 0.33 microfarad capacitor (available at any electronics store), fabricate a pair of jumper wires like this and hook them up as indicated

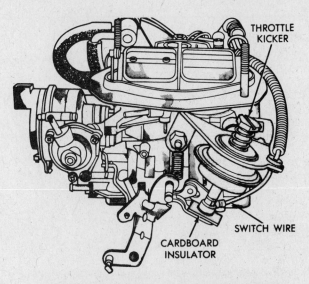

12.17   Use a thin piece of cardboard to hold the carburetor switch open and measure the voltage at the switch – the reading should be at least five volts

13   If there is no spark, turn off the ignition switch, disconnect the 10-wire harness connector (see illustration 12.1) and repeat the test. If a spark is now obtained, the computer output is shorted and the spark control computer assembly must be replaced with a new one.

14   If there was no spark, check the voltage at the coil positive terminal to make sure it's within one volt of battery output.

15   If there was no voltage reading, check the wiring between the battery and the positive terminal of the coil.

16   If there was a proper voltage reading, check the voltage at the coil negative terminal. This reading should also be within one volt of battery voltage. If there is no voltage or there is voltage but no spark was obtained when performing the test in Step 11, replace the coil with a new one.

17   If there is a voltage reading but the engine will not start, use a thin piece of cardboard to hold the carburetor switch open (see illustration), reconnect the 10-wire connector and measure the voltage at the switch. The reading should be at least five volts.

18   If the voltage reading is correct, go to Step 25.

19   If there is no voltage, turn off the ignition switch and unplug the SCC 10-wire connector (see illustration 12.1).

20   Turn the switch on and check the voltage at cavity two (2) of the connector (see illustration) – it should be within one volt of the battery.

21   If there is no voltage reading, check for continuity between cavity two (2) and the battery. Correct any fault and repeat the test in Step 20.

22   If there is voltage present, turn off the ignition switch and check for

continuity between cavity seven (7) of the SCC electrical connector and the carburetor switch (see illustration 12.20). If no continuity is present, check for an open wire between cavity seven (7) and the carburetor switch and correct the fault.

23   If continuity exists, check for continuity between cavity ten (10) and a good ground (see illustration 12.20). If there is continuity, you'll have to replace the computer with a new one as power is going into it but not out. Repeat the test in Step 17.

24   If continuity is not present, check for an open wire.

25   If the wiring is alright and the engine won't start, plug the connector into the computer and turn on the ignition switch. Using an insulated tool, hold the coil secondary wire near a good ground, unplug the distributor harness connector and connect a jumper wire between cavities two (2) and three (3) (see illustration). A spark should now jump between the coil wire and ground.

26   If spark is present but the engine still doesn't start, make sure the rotor is completely seated on the distributor shaft. This can be verified by connecting one lead of the ohmmeter to a shutter blade on the rotor and the other to a good ground and checking for continuity. If there is none, push the rotor down on the shaft until continuity is achieved. If there is still no continuity, replace the rotor and distributor pickup (Hall Effect) assembly (see Chapter 5).

27   Repeat the test in Step 25 and if there is no spark present, measure the voltage at cavity one (1) of the distributor connector (see illustration 12.25). This should be within one volt of battery voltage.

28   If the voltage isn't correct, turn off the ignition, unplug the connector from the computer and check between cavity two (2) of the distributor harness and cavity nine (9) of the computer connector (see illustrations 12.20 and 12.25). Follow this by checking cavity three (3) of the distributor harness and cavity five (5) of the computer connector. If there is no continuity, find and repair the fault in the harness. If there is continuity, replace the computer with a new one as power is going into it but not coming out.

29   Repeat the test in Step 25.

30   If no voltage is present when making the check in Step 27, turn off the ignition, unplug the computer connector and check for continuity between cavity one (1) of the distributor harness connector and cavity ten (10) of the computer connector (see illustrations 12.20 and 12.25). If there is no continuity, repair any opens or shorts and repeat the test in Step 25.

31   If there is no voltage, check for continuity between cavity one (1) of the distributor harness connector and cavity three (3) of the computer connector (see illustrations 12.20 and 12.25). If there is no continuity between these terminals, find and repair any harness wiring defects and repeat the test in Step 25.

32   If there is continuity, turn on the ignition switch and check for voltage between cavities two (2) and ten (10) of the computer connector (see illustration 12.20). If there is voltage, the computer is defective and must be replaced with a new one. Repeat the test in Step 25.

33   If there is no voltage between cavities two (2) and ten (10), check and repair the ground wire as the computer isn't grounded. Repeat the Step 25 test.

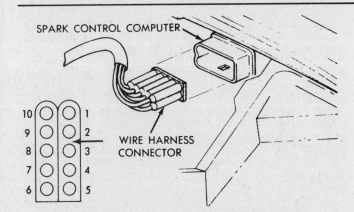

12.20   Terminal locations (SCC 10-wire electrical connector)

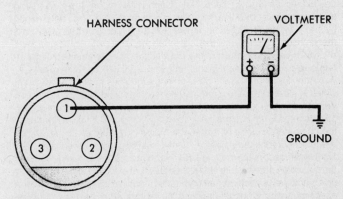

12.25   Distributor harness electrical connector terminal locations

6

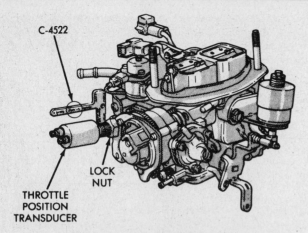

12.34   Measure the distance between the transducer body and the locknut – it should be 9/16-inch – if it isn't, adjust it accordingly

Throttle position transducer adjustment (1978 vehicles with a manual transaxle only)

Refer to illustration 12.34

34   Disconnect the electrical connector from the throttle position transducer **(see illustration)**.

35   Loosen the locknut. Measure the distance between the transducer case and the locknut. Adjustment is accomplished by screwing the transducer in or out, as required, to achieve a dimension of 9/16-inch.

36   Hold the transducer to keep it from turning and tighten the locknut.

37   Recheck the distance between the case and the locknut to make sure it hasn't changed. Reconnect the electrical connector.

Component replacement

Spark control computer

38   Remove the battery (see Chapter 5).

39   Disconnect the 10-wire connector from the computer **(see illustration 12.1)**. **Note:** *Don't remove the grease from the connector or the socket in the computer. The grease prevents corrosion of the terminals. Make sure there's always at least 1/4-inch of grease in the bottom of the computer connector socket. Use Mopar multi-purpose grease (no. 2932524) or equivalent.*

40   Pull the vacuum hose off the vacuum transducer, mounted on the spark control computer, and disconnect the air duct from the computer.

41   Remove the three screws securing the spark control computer to the left-side inner fender panel. Lift the computer out of the engine compartment.

42   Installation is the reverse of the removal procedure.

Vacuum transducer

43   If the vacuum transducer is defective, the spark control computer must be replaced as described above.

Hall Effect Pickup assembly

44   Removal and installation of the Hall Effect Pickup is described in Chapter 5.

Coolant sensor

Refer to illustration 12.45

45   Removal and installation of the coolant sensor **(see illustration)** is the same procedure described for the coolant temperature sending unit (see Chapter 3).

Carburetor switch

46   Disconnect the wiring at the connector.

47   Remove the screws securing the carburetor switch mounting bracket to the carburetor and lift away the switch and bracket assembly **(see illustration 12.3)**.

48   Installation is the reverse of the removal procedure.

12.45   Coolant sensor location (2.2L engine)

Throttle position transducer

49   Disconnect the wiring connector from the transducer **(see illustration 12.34)**.

50   Loosen the locknut and unscrew the transducer from the mounting bracket on the carburetor.

51   Disconnect the core of the transducer from the carburetor linkage.

52   Installation is the reverse of the removal procedure. Make sure the transducer core snaps into position when connecting it to the linkage.

53   If the vehicle is a 1978 model, adjust the throttle position transducer as described in Steps 34 through 37.

13   Power Loss or Power Limited light (EFI models) – general information

On EFI-equipped models, the Power Loss/Power Limited light, located in the instrument panel, ordinarily flashes on briefly and then goes out when the engine is started. The light comes on and stays on when there's a problem in the EFI system and can also be used to diagnose problems in the EFI system (see Section 14).

14   Logic module and power module/Single Module Engine Controller (SMEC) (EFI models) – description and check

1   The logic module, located in the passenger compartment behind the right kick panel, is a digital computer containing a microprocessor. The power module is located in the left front corner of the engine compartment and works in conjunction with the logic module, handling the heavier electric currents, including the ground for the ignition coil and power for the fuel injection system. It directs the voltage to the logic module and the Hall Effect pickup assembly in the distributor (which then directs voltage to the spark plugs) and the automatic shutdown relay which energizes the fuel tank mounted electric fuel pump. The logic module receives the input signals from all of the sensors and switches which monitor the engine and then determines the fuel injector operation as well as the spark advance, ignition coil dwell, idle speed, canister purge solenoid, cooling fan operation and alternator charge rate. The electric fuel pump which delivers fuel to the injectors and maintains pressure in the system, is located in the fuel tank (see Chapter 4).

2   Four components which provide basic information so the logic module can operate the EFI system are the Manifold Absolute Pressure (MAP) sensor, Throttle Position Sensor (TPS), oxygen sensor and coolant temperature sensor. The MAP sensor is located on or adjacent to the logic module, is connected to the throttle body by a vacuum line and monitors the manifold vacuum. The TPS is located in the throttle body and monitors the actual position of the throttle lever which is connected to the throttle pedal. The oxygen sensor (located in the exhaust manifold) provides information on the exhaust gas makeup and the coolant temperature sensor (threaded into the water box) monitors engine operating temperature.

3   Because the EFI system is controlled by the logic module and power module or Single Module Engine Controller (SMEC) in combination with a

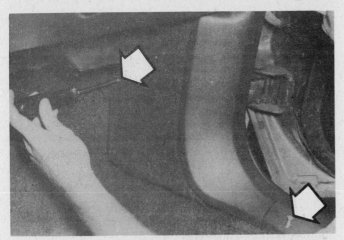

15.2   The kick panel covering the logic module is held in place by screws

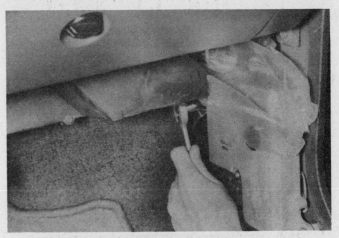

15.3   Use a ratchet and deep socket to remove the logic module mounting nuts

variety of sensors and switches, the home mechanic can do very little in the way of diagnosis without factory Diagnostic Read Out Tool number C-4805 or its equivalent. Consequently, diagnosis should be confined to inspection and checking of all electrical and vacuum connections to make sure they're secure and not obviously damaged.

4   The logic module is self-testing and a problem in the system will be indicated by the Power Loss/Limited light on the dash. The Power Loss/Limited light will come on when there's electrical system voltage fluctuation or a fault in the MAP, throttle position or coolant temperature sensor circuits. If the fault is severe enough to affect driveability, the logic module will go into a "limp-home" mode so the vehicle can still be driven.

5   The logic module stores trouble codes which can be checked using the Power Loss/Limited light. Within a five second period, turn the ignition key On-Off-On-Off-On. The Power Loss/Limited light will then flash fault codes indicating the area of the fault. The codes are two digit numbers and the start of test (88) for example, will be indicated by eight flashes, a pause and eight more flashes. If there's more than one code, the light will flash them in order, ending with the end of message code (55). Because the fault codes indicate the general location of a fault, simply checking and tightening a vacuum hose or electrical connector can often correct a problem. Any further checking of fault codes should be left to a dealer service department or properly equipped shop.

Fault codes

88	Start of test
11	Engine not cranked since battery disconnected
12	Memory standby power lost
13*	MAP sensor pneumatic circuit
14*	MAP sensor electrical circuit
15	Vehicle speed/distance sensor circuit
16	*Loss of battery voltage
17	Engine running too cold
21	Oxygen sensor circuit
22*	Coolant sensor circuit
23	Throttle body temperature circuit
24*	Throttle position circuit
25	Automatic Idle Speed (AIS) motor driver circuit
26	Peak injector circuit has not been reached
27	Logic module fuel circuit internal problem
31	Purge solenoid circuit
33	Air conditioning cutout relay circuit
35	Cooling fan relay circuit
37	Shift indicator light circuit
41	Charging system excess or lack of field current
42	Automatic shutdown relay driver circuit
43	Spark interface circuit
44	Battery temperature out of range
46*	Battery voltage too high
47	Battery voltage too low
51	Oxygen sensor stuck at lean position
52	Oxygen sensor stuck at rich position
53	Logic module internal problem
55	End of message

* Activates Power Loss/Limited light

15   Logic module (EFI models) – removal and installation

Refer to illustrations 15.2 and 15.3

1   Disconnect the cable from the negative terminal of the battery.
2   Remove the passenger's side kick panel **(see illustration)**.
3   Remove the nuts, lift the logic module off the studs, unplug the electrical connectors and remove the module from the vehicle **(see illustration)**.
4   Plug in the electrical connectors, place the logic module in position and install the mounting nuts. Tighten the nuts securely.
5   Install the kick panel and connect the negative battery cable.

16   Manifold Absolute Pressure (MAP) sensor (EFI models) – removal and installation

Refer to illustrations 16.3 and 16.6

1   Disconnect the cable from the negative terminal of the battery.

1984 models

2   Remove the glovebox for access to the MAP sensor.
3   Unplug the vacuum hose and wiring connector, remove the mounting bolts and withdraw the sensor from under the instrument panel **(see illustration)**.
4   To install the sensor, place it in position and install the bolts. Tighten the bolts securely and install the glovebox.

1985 and later models

5   Remove the logic module (Section 15).
6   Remove the two screws and detach the MAP sensor from the logic module **(see illustration)**.
7   To install the sensor, place it in position on the logic module and install the screws. Tighten them securely.

17   Automatic shutdown relay (EFI models) – removal and installation

1   Disconnect the cable from the negative terminal of the battery.

1984 models

2   Remove the glovebox.

6

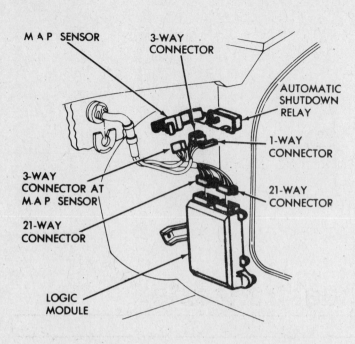

16.3   The MAP sensor and Automatic Shutdown Relay are mounted above the logic module on 1984 models

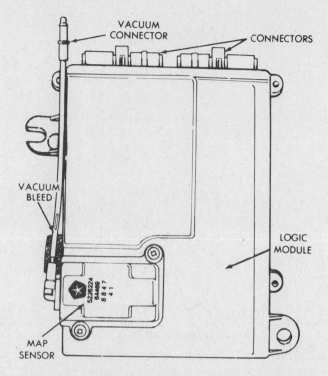

16.6   On 1985 and later models, the MAP sensor is located on the logic module

3   Unplug the wiring harness connector, remove the mounting bolt and lower the relay from under the dash **(see illustration 16.3)**.
4   Installation is the reverse of removal.

1985 and later models

5   The relay on these models is mounted behind the single module engine controller (SMEC – the same as the power module), next to the A/C clutch cutout relay in the engine compartment.
6   Remove the bolt and detach the relay and bracket, then unplug the wire harness.
7   Installation is the reverse of removal.

---

18   Power module/Single Module Engine Controller (SMEC) (EFI models) – removal and installation

Refer to illustration 18.4
1   Disconnect the battery cables (negative first, followed by the positive cable).
2   Disconnect the air cleaner duct from the module.
3   Remove the battery (See Chapter 5).
4   Remove the mounting bolts, unplug the connectors and remove the power module/SMEC from the engine compartment **(see illustration)**.
5   Hold the module in position, install the bolts and plug in the connectors.

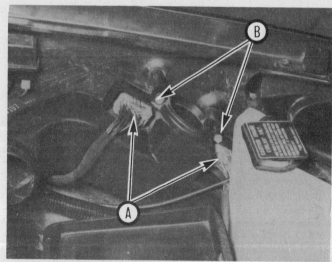

18.4   The power module can be removed after unplugging the electrical connectors (A) and removing the mounting bolts (B)

6   Connect the air cleaner duct.
7   Install the battery and connect the battery cables (positive first, then negative).

Chapter 7 Part A Manual transaxle

Contents

Specifications

General

Fluid type and capacity .... See Chapter 1

Torque specifications
Shift linkage lock pin 9
Shift linkage tube clamp bolt 19

Ft-lbs

---

1   General information

The vehicles covered by this manual are equipped with either a four or five-speed manual transaxle or a three-speed automatic transaxle. Information on the manual transaxle is included in this Part of Chapter 7. Service procedures for the automatic transaxle are contained in Chapter 7, Part B.

The manual transaxle is a compact, two-piece, lightweight aluminum alloy housing containing both the transmission and differential assemblies.

Because of the complexity, unavailability of replacement parts and special tools required, internal repair of the manual transaxle by the home mechanic is not recommended. The bulk of information in this Chapter is devoted to removal and installation procedures.

2   Shift linkage – adjustment

Vehicles with a 1.7L engine
Refer to illustrations 2.2 and 2.3

1   Place the shift lever in Neutral between Third and Fourth gears. Raise the vehicle and support it securely on jackstands.

2   Loosen the shift tube clamp and line up the mark on the slider with the mark on the blocker bracket **(see illustration)**.

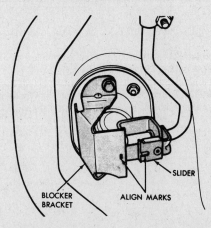

2.2   The marks on the slider and blocker bracket must be lined up (vehicles with a 1.7L engine)

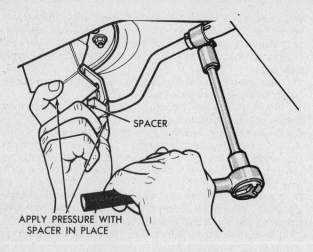

2.3   Push up on the spacer while tightening the clamp (vehicles with a 1.7L engine)

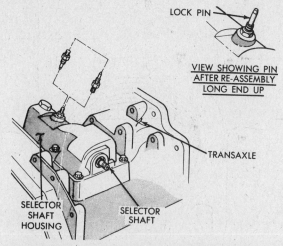

2.6   Use the lock pin to secure the transaxle selector shaft in the First/Neutral position (vehicles with a 2.2L engine)

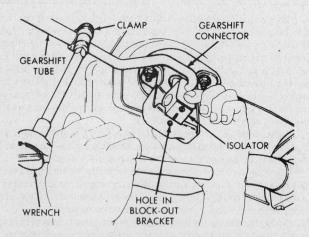

2.8   Make sure the ridge on the isolator is centered in the hole in the block-out bracket before tightening the clamp (vehicles with a 2.2L engine)

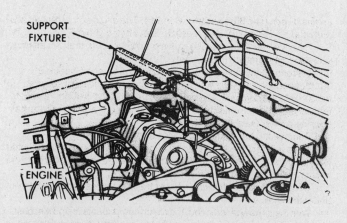

3.7   When removing the transaxle, support the engine from above with a fixture as shown here or with a jack from underneath

3   Insert a 3/4-inch spacer between the slider and blocker bar, apply pressure at the points shown and tighten the clamp **(see illustration)**.
4   Remove the spacer and check the operation of the shifter.

Vehicles with a 2.2L engine

Refer to illustrations 2.6 and 2.8

5   Raise the hood and place a pad or blanket over the left fender to protect it.
6   Remove the lock pin from the transaxle selector shaft housing. Reverse the lock pin so the longer end is down, reinstall it in the hole and move the selector shaft in. When the lock pin aligns with the hole in the selector shaft, thread it into place so the shaft is locked in Neutral between First and Second gear **(see illustration)**.
7   Raise the vehicle and support it securely on jackstands.
8   Working under the vehicle, loosen the gearshift connector clamp bolt **(see illustration)**. Make sure the connector moves freely within the gearshift tube.
9   Place the shifter mechanism in position with the isolator contacting the upright flange and the isolator rib aligned with the hole in the block-out bracket. With no pressure on the linkage, tighten the clamp bolt to the torque listed in this Chapter's Specifications.
10 Lower the vehicle.

11 Remove the lock pin, reverse it so the longer end is upright, screw it into place and then tighten it to the torque listed in this Chapter's specifications.
12 Check the shifter operation in First and Reverse and make sure the reverse lockout mechanism works properly.

3   Transaxle – removal and installation

Refer to illustrations 3.7 and 3.10

Removal

1   Disconnect the negative cable from the battery.
2   Raise the vehicle and support it securely on jackstands.
3   Drain the transaxle lubricant (see Chapter 1).
4   Disconnect the shift and clutch linkage from the transaxle.
5   Detach the speedometer cable and wire harness connectors from the transaxle. If you're working on a vehicle with a 1.7L engine, remove the starter.
6   Remove the exhaust system components as necessary for clearance.
7   Support the engine. This can be done from above with a support fixture or by placing a jack (with a block of wood as an insulator) under the

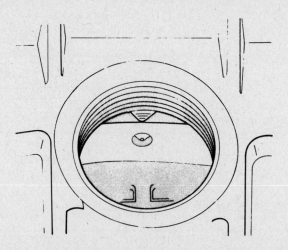

3.10   On vehicles with a 1.7L engine, the flywheel dimple must be aligned with the pointer on the bellhousing when the transaxle is separated from the engine – you may have to remove a plug to expose the dimple and pointer

engine oil pan **(see illustration). Caution:** *The engine must remain supported at all times while the transaxle is out of the vehicle!*

8   Remove any chassis or suspension components that will interfere with transaxle removal (see Chapter 10).

9   Disconnect the driveaxles from the transaxle (see Chapter 8).

10   Support the transaxle with a jack, then remove the bolts securing the transaxle to the engine. If you're working on a vehicle with a 1.7L engine, rotate the crankshaft until the dimple in the flywheel is aligned with the bellhousing pointer **(see illustration).**

11   Remove the transaxle mount nuts and bolts.

12   Make a final check that all wires and hoses have been disconnected from the transaxle, then carefully pull the transaxle and jack away from the engine.

13   Once the input shaft is clear, lower the transaxle and remove it from under the vehicle.

14   With the transaxle removed, the clutch components are now accessible and can be inspected. In most cases, new clutch components should be routinely installed when the transaxle is removed.

Installation

15   If removed, install the clutch components (see Chapter 8).

16   If you're working on a vehicle with a 1.7L engine, make sure the flywheel dimple and bellhousing pointer are still lined up. With the transaxle secured to the jack with a chain, raise it into position behind the engine,

then carefully slide it forward, engaging the input shaft with the clutch plate hub splines. Don't use excessive force to install the transaxle – if the input shaft doesn't slide into place, readjust the angle of the transaxle so it's level and/or turn the input shaft so the splines engage properly with the clutch plate hub.

17   Install the transaxle-to-engine bolts. Tighten the bolts securely.

18   Install the transaxle mount nuts or bolts.

19   Install the chassis and suspension components which were removed. Tighten all nuts and bolts securely.

20   Remove the jacks supporting the transaxle and engine.

21   Install the various items removed previously, referring to Chapter 8 for installation of the driveaxles and Chapter 4 for information regarding the exhaust system components. If you're working on a vehicle with a 1.7L engine, install the starter.

22   Make a final check that all wires, hoses, linkages and the speedometer cable have been connected and that the transaxle has been filled with lubricant to the proper level (see Chapter 1).

23   Connect the negative battery cable. Road test the vehicle for proper operation and check for leaks.

4   Manual transaxle overhaul – general information

Overhauling a manual transaxle is a difficult job for the do-it-yourselfer. It involves the disassembly and reassemble of many small parts. Numerous clearances must be precisely measured and, if necessary, changed with select fit spacers and snap-rings. As a result, if transaxle problems arise, it can be removed and installed by a competent do-it-yourselfer, but overhaul should be left to a transmission repair shop. Rebuilt transaxles may be available - check with your dealer parts department and auto parts stores. At any rate, the time and money involved in an overhaul is almost sure to exceed the cost of a rebuilt unit.

Nevertheless, it's not impossible for an inexperienced mechanic to rebuild a transaxle if the special tools are available and the job is done in a deliberate step-by-step manner so nothing is overlooked.

The tools necessary for an overhaul include internal and external snap-ring pliers, a bearing puller, a slide hammer, a set of pin punches, a dial indicator and possibly a hydraulic press. In addition, a large, sturdy workbench and a vise or transaxle stand will be required.

During disassembly of the transaxle, make careful notes of how each piece comes off, where it fits in relation to other pieces and what holds it in place.

Before taking the transaxle apart for repair, it will help if you have some idea what area of the transaxle is malfunctioning. Certain problems can be closely tied to specific areas in the transaxle, which can make component examination and replacement easier. Refer to the Troubleshooting section at the front of this manual for information regarding possible sources of trouble.

7A

Chapter 7 Part B Automatic transaxle

Contents

Specifications

General

Fluid type and capacity .... See Chapter 1

Torque specifications   **Ft-lbs**
Neutral start and back-up light switch 25
Throttle valve cable adjustment bracket lock bolt/screw 9
Torque converter-to-driveplate bolts
  1978 through 1985 40
  1986 on 55

---

1 General information

All vehicles covered in this manual come equipped with either a four or five-speed manual transaxle or a three-speed automatic transaxle. All information on the automatic transaxle is included in this Part of Chapter 7. Information on the manual transaxle can be found in Part A of this Chapter.

Due to the complexity of the automatic transaxle and the need for special equipment and expertise to perform most service operations, this Chapter contains only general diagnosis, seal replacement, adjustments and removal and installation procedures.

If the transaxle requires major repair work, it should be left to a dealer service department or an automotive or transmission repair shop. You can, however, remove and install the transaxle yourself and save the expense, even if the repair work is done by a transmission shop.

2 Diagnosis – general

Note: *Automatic transaxle malfunctions may be caused by four general conditions: Poor engine performance, improper adjustments, hydraulic malfunctions or mechanical malfunctions. Diagnosis of these problems should always begin with a check of the easily repaired items: Fluid level and condition (see Chapter 1), shift linkage adjustment and throttle linkage adjustment. Next, perform a road test to determine if the problem has been corrected or if more diagnosis is necessary. If the problem persists*

after the preliminary tests and corrections are completed, additional diagnosis should be done by a dealer service department or transmission repair shop. Refer to the Troubleshooting section at the front of this manual for transaxle problem diagnosis.

Preliminary checks

1   Drive the vehicle to warm the transaxle to normal operating temperature.
2   Check the fluid level as described in Chapter 1:
   a) If the fluid level is unusually low, add enough fluid to bring the level within the designated area on the dipstick, then check for external leaks.
   b) If the fluid level is abnormally high, drain off the excess, then check the drained fluid for contamination by coolant. The presence of engine coolant in the automatic transmission fluid indicates that a failure has occurred in the internal radiator walls that separate the coolant from the transmission fluid (see Chapter 3).
   c) If the fluid is foaming, drain it and refill the transaxle, then check for coolant in the fluid or a high fluid level.
3   Check the engine idle speed. **Note:** *If the engine is malfunctioning, don't proceed with the preliminary checks until it has been repaired and runs normally.*
4   Check the throttle valve cable for freedom of movement. Adjust it if necessary (see Section 5). **Note:** *The throttle valve cable may function properly when the engine is shut off and cold, but it may malfunction once the engine is hot. Check it cold and at normal engine operating temperature.*

5   Inspect the shift linkage (see Section 4). Make sure it's properly adjusted and operates smoothly.

Fluid leak diagnosis

6   Most fluid leaks are easy to locate visually. Repair usually consists of replacing a seal or gasket. If a leak is difficult to find, the following procedure may help.

7   Identify the fluid. Make sure it's transmission fluid and not engine oil or brake fluid (automatic transmission fluid is a deep red color).

8   Try to pinpoint the source of the leak. Drive the vehicle several miles, then park it over a large sheet of cardboard. After a minute or two, you should be able to locate the leak by determining the source of the fluid dripping onto the cardboard.

9   Make a careful visual inspection of the suspected component and the area immediately around it. Pay particular attention to gasket mating surfaces. A mirror is often helpful for finding leaks in areas that are hard to see.

10   If the leak still can't be found, clean the suspected area thoroughly with a degreaser or solvent, then dry it.

11   Drive the vehicle for several miles at normal operating temperature and varying speeds. After driving the vehicle, visually inspect the suspected component again.

12   Once the leak has been located, the cause must be determined before it can be properly repaired. If a gasket is replaced but the sealing flange is bent, the new gasket won't stop the leak. The bent flange must be straightened.

13   Before attempting to repair a leak, check to make sure the following conditions are corrected or they may cause another leak.

Note: *Some of the following conditions can't be fixed without highly specialized tools and expertise. Such problems must be referred to a transmission shop or a dealer service department.*

Gasket leaks

14   Check the pan periodically. Make sure the bolts are all in place (none missing) and tight, the gasket is in good condition and the pan is flat (dents in the pan may indicate damage to the valve body inside).

15   If the pan gasket is leaking, the fluid level or the fluid pressure may be too high, the vent may be plugged, the pan bolts may be too tight, the pan sealing flange may be warped, the sealing surface of the transaxle housing may be damaged, the gasket may be damaged or the transaxle casting may be cracked or porous. If sealant is used in place of a gasket, it may be the wrong sealant.

Seal leaks

16   If a transaxle seal is leaking, the fluid level or pressure may be too high, the vent may be plugged (these models are vented through the hollow dipstick), the seal bore may be damaged, the seal itself may be damaged or improperly installed, the surface of the shaft protruding through the seal may be damaged or a loose bearing may be causing excessive shaft movement.

17   Make sure the dipstick tube seal is in good condition and the tube is properly seated. Periodically check the area around the speedometer gear or sensor for leakage. If transmission fluid is evident, check the O-ring for damage. Also inspect the side gear shaft oil seals for leakage.

Case leaks

18   If the case itself appears to be leaking, the casting is porous and will have to be repaired or replaced.

19   Make sure the oil cooler hose fittings are tight and in good condition.

Fluid comes out the filler opening

20   If this condition occurs, the transaxle is overfilled, there is coolant in the fluid, the case is porous, the dipstick is incorrect, the vent is plugged or the drain back holes are plugged.

---

3   Oil seal replacement

Refer to illustrations 3.8a and 3.8b

1   Oil leaks frequently occur due to wear of the driveaxle oil seals and/or the speedometer drive gear oil seal and O-ring. Replacement of the seals is relatively easy, since the repairs can usually be performed without removing the transaxle from the vehicle.

2   The driveaxle oil seals are located at the sides of the transaxle, where the driveaxles are attached. If leakage at the seal is suspected, raise the vehicle and support it securely on jackstands. If the seal is leaking, lubricant will be found on the sides of the transaxle.

3   Refer to Chapter 8 and remove the driveaxle(s).

4   Using a screwdriver or pry bar, carefully pry the oil seal out of the transaxle bore.

5   If the oil seal can't be removed with a screwdriver or pry bar, a special oil seal removal tool (available at auto parts stores) will be required.

6   Using a large section of pipe or a large deep socket as a drift, install the new oil seal. Drive it into the bore squarely and make sure it's completely seated. Apply moly-base grease to the seal lip before installing the driveaxle.

7   Install the driveaxle(s). Be careful not to damage the lip of the new seal.

8   The speedometer cable and extension housing is located on the transaxle housing. Look for lubricant around the cable housing to determine if the O-ring or seals are leaking **(see illustrations)**.

7B

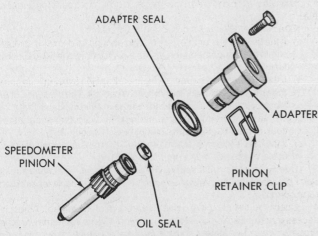

3.8a   Early model speedometer drive components – exploded view

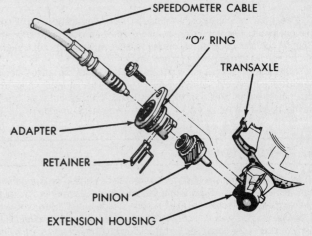

3.8b   Later model speedometer drive components – exploded view

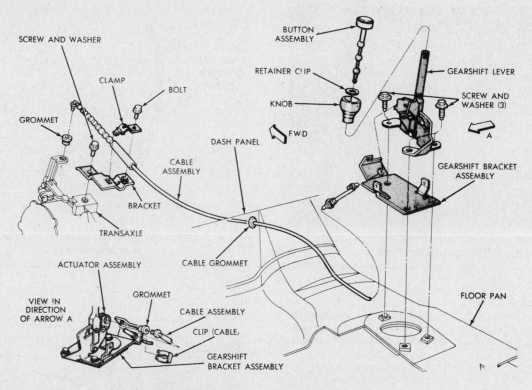

4.3   Automatic transaxle shift linkage – exploded view

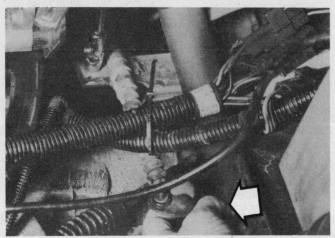

4.5   Keep pressure on the shift lever (arrow) while tightening the shift cable clamp bolt

9   Remove the bolt and detach the speedometer cable and adapter from the transaxle. Remove the retainer clip and separate the pinion from the adapter.
10   Using a hook, remove the seals or O-ring.
11   Install the new seals or O-ring, assemble the adapter and pinion, then reinstall the speedometer cable and adapter.

---

4   Shift linkage – check and adjustment

Check

1   Check the operation of the transaxle in each shift lever position (try to start the engine in each position – the starter should operate in the Park and Neutral positions only).

Adjustment

Refer to illustrations 4.3 and 4.5
2   Place the shift lever in Park.
3   Working in the engine compartment, loosen the shift cable clamp bolt on the transaxle bracket **(see illustration)**.
4   Pull the shift lever all the way to the front detent (Park position) by hand.
5   Keep pressure on the shift lever and tighten the cable clamp bolt **(see illustration)**.
6   Check the shift lever in the Neutral and Drive positions to make sure it's within the confines of the lever stops. The engine should start only when the lever is in the Park or Neutral position.

---

5   Throttle Valve (TV) cable – adjustment

1   The throttle valve cable controls a valve in the transaxle which governs shift quality and speed. If shifting is harsh or erratic, the throttle valve cable should be adjusted.
2   The adjustment must be made with the engine at normal operating temperature (or disconnect the choke to make sure the carburetor isn't on the fast idle cam).

1978 through 1985 models

Refer to illustration 5.3
3   Loosen the adjustment bracket lock bolt **(see illustration)**.
4   To ensure proper adjustment, the bracket must be free to slide back-and-forth. If necessary, remove it and clean the slot and sliding surfaces as well as the bolt.
5   Slide the bracket to the left (toward the engine) to the end of its travel. Release the bracket and move the throttle lever all the way to the right, against the internal stop, then tighten the adjustment bracket lock bolt to the torque listed in this Chapter's Specifications.

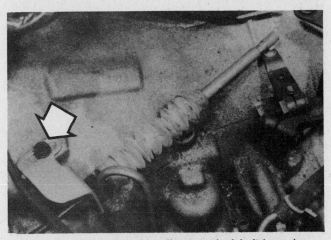

5.3   Throttle valve cable adjustment lock bolt (arrow) –
1978 through 1985 models

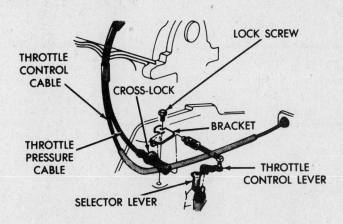

5.6   Throttle valve cable and related components – 1986
and later models

1986 and later models

Refer to illustration 5.6

6   Loosen the cable mounting bracket lock screw and position the bracket so the alignment tabs are in contact with the transaxle casting **(see illustration)**. Tighten the lock screw to the torque listed in this Chapter's Specifications.

7   Release the cross-lock on the cable assembly by pulling up on it. To ensure proper adjustment, the cable must be free to slide all the way toward the engine, against the stop, after the cross-lock is released.

8   Move the transaxle throttle control lever clockwise as far as possible (against the internal stop) and press the cross-lock down into the locked position.

9   It's a good idea to lubricate the TV linkage and cable components at this time. Don't lubricate any of the throttle linkage components.

All models

10   Connect the choke (if disconnected) and check the cable action. Move the transaxle throttle cable all the way forward, release it slowly and make sure it returns completely.

---

6   Neutral start and back-up light switch – check and replacement

Refer to illustration 6.6

1   The Neutral start and back-up light switch is located at the lower front edge of the transaxle. The switch controls the back-up lights and the center terminal of the switch grounds the starter solenoid circuit when the transaxle is in Park or Neutral, allowing the engine to start.

2   Prior to checking the switch, make sure the shift linkage is properly adjusted (see Section 4).

3   Unplug the connector and use an ohmmeter to check for continuity between the center terminal and the case. Continuity should exist only when the transaxle is in Park or Neutral.

4   Check for continuity between the two outer terminals. Continuity should exist only when the transaxle is in Reverse. No continuity should exist between either outer terminal and the case.

5   If the switch fails any of the tests, replace it with a new one.

6   Position a drain pan under the switch to catch the fluid released when the switch is removed. Unscrew the switch from the transaxle **(see illustration)**.

7   Move the shift lever from Park to Neutral and check to see if the switch operating fingers are centered in the opening.

8   Install the new switch, tighten it to the torque listed in this Chapter's Specifications and plug in the connector. Repeat the checks on the new switch.

9   Check the fluid level and add fluid as required (see Chapter 1).

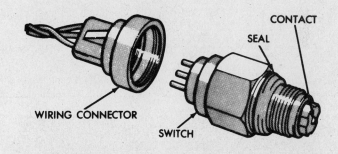

6.6   Neutral start and back-up light switch details

---

7   Automatic transaxle – removal and installation

Refer to illustrations 7.4, 7.5, 7.6, 7.10 and 7.19

Removal

1   Disconnect the negative cable from the battery.

2   Raise the vehicle and support it securely on jackstands.

3   Drain the transaxle fluid (see Chapter 1).

4   Remove the torque converter cover and the left splash shield **(see illustration)**.

5   Mark the torque converter and driveplate so they can be reinstalled in the same position **(see illustration)**.

6   Remove the torque converter-to-driveplate bolts **(see illustration)**. Turn the crankshaft to bring each bolt into view.

7   Remove the starter motor (see Chapter 5).

8   Remove the driveaxles from the transaxle (see Chapter 8).

9   Disconnect the speedometer cable.

10   Unplug the electrical connector from the Neutral start/back-up light switch **(see illustration)**.

11   On models so equipped, disconnect the vacuum hose(s).

12   Remove any exhaust components that will interfere with transaxle removal (see Chapter 4).

13   Disconnect the TV linkage cable.

14   Disconnect the shift linkage.

15   Support the engine with a hoist from above or a jack from below (position a block of wood between the jack and oil pan to spread the load).

16   Support the transaxle with a jack - preferably a special jack made for this purpose. Safety chains will help steady the transaxle on the jack.

7B

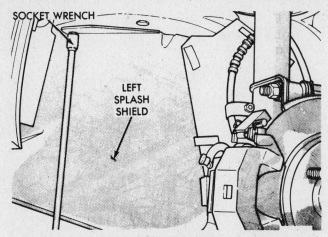

7.4   Remove the left splash shield mounting bolts with a socket on a long extension

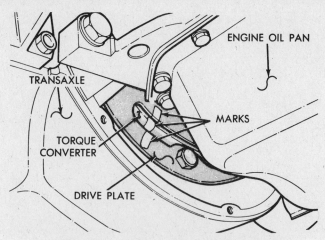

7.5   Use a scribe or felt-tip marker to make alignment marks on the driveplate and torque converter

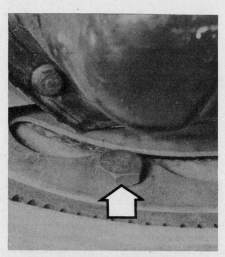

7.6   Remove the exposed driveplate-to-torque converter bolt (arrow), then rotate the crankshaft to expose the remaining ones (there are either three or four bolts total)

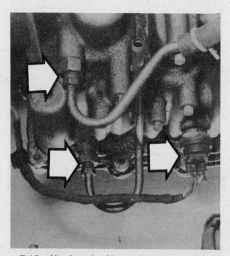

7.10   Unplug the Neutral start/back-up light switch wire harness connector and unscrew the transmission fluid cooler lines (arrows) – when detaching the fluid lines, use a flare-nut wrench to avoid rounding off the corners of the fittings

7.19   With the vehicle securely supported, remove the transaxle mount through-bolt (arrow)

17   Remove any chassis or suspension components that will interfere with transaxle removal.
18   Remove the bolts securing the transaxle to the engine.
19   Remove the transaxle mount through-bolt **(see illustration)**.
20   Lower the transaxle slightly and disconnect and plug the transaxle cooler lines **(see illustration 7.10)**.
21   Move the transaxle back to disengage it from the engine block dowel pins and make sure the torque converter is detached from the driveplate. Secure the torque converter to the transaxle so it won't fall out during removal. Lower the transaxle from the vehicle.

Installation

22   Prior to installation, make sure the torque converter hub is securely engaged in the pump.
23   With the transaxle secured to the jack, raise it into position. Be sure to keep it level so the torque converter doesn't slide out. Connect the fluid cooler lines.
24   Turn the torque converter to line up the bolts with the holes in the driveplate. The marks on the torque converter and driveplate must line up.
25   Move the transaxle forward carefully until the dowel pins and transaxle housing are engaged.

26   Install the transaxle housing-to-engine bolts. Tighten them securely.
27   Install the torque converter-to-driveplate bolts. Tighten the bolts to the torque listed in this Chapter's Specifications.
28   Install the transaxle and any suspension and chassis components that were removed. Tighten the bolts and nuts to the specified torque.
29   Remove the jacks supporting the transaxle and engine.
30   Install the starter motor (see Chapter 5).
31   Connect the vacuum hose(s) (if equipped).
32   Connect the shift and TV linkages.
33   Attach the electrical connector to the Neutral start/back-up light switch.
34   Install the torque converter cover and left splash shield.
35   Connect the driveaxles (see Chapter 8).
36   Connect the speedometer cable.
37   Adjust the shift linkage (see Section 4).
38   Install any exhaust system components that were removed or disconnected.
39   Lower the vehicle.
40   Fill the transaxle (see Chapter 1), run the vehicle and check for fluid leaks.

Chapter 8   Clutch and driveaxles

Contents

Specifications

8

Clutch

Release lever freeplay . . . .   See Chapter 1

Driveaxle length

1978 through 1983 models . . . .   Check with a dealer service department
1984 models
  GKN driveaxle
    Right . . . .   19.6 to 20.0 in (498 to 509 mm)
    Left . . . .   9.5 to 10.0 in (240 to 253 mm)
  ACI driveaxle
    Right . . . .   18.5 to 19.0 in (496 to 478 mm)
    Left . . . .   8.2 to 8.6 in (208 to 218 mm)
1985 models
  GKN driveaxle
    Right . . . .   19.6 to 20.0 in (498 to 509 mm)
    Left . . . .   9.5 to 10.0 in (240 to 253 mm)

Driveaxle length (continued)

1985 models (continued)
  ACI driveaxle
    GLH models
      Right .... 18.2 to 18.6 in (463 to 472 mm)
      Left .... 8.0 to 8.4 in (204 to 213 mm)
    All other models
      Right .... 18.5 to 19.0 in (496 to 478 mm)
      Left .... 8.2 to 8.6 in (208 to 218 mm)
  Citroen driveaxle
    Turbo models (right or left) .... 8.3 to 8.7 in (211 to 220 mm)
    GLH models
      Right .... 18.3 to 18.8 in (465 to 477 mm)
      Left .... 8.3 to 8.7 in (211 to 220 mm)
1986 models
  GKN driveaxle
    Right .... 19.6 to 20.0 in (498 to 509 mm)
    Left .... 9.5 to 10.0 in (240 to 253 mm)
  ACI driveaxle
    GLH models
      Right .... 18.2 to 18.6 in (463 to 472 mm)
      Left .... 8.0 to 8.4 in (204 to 213 mm)
    All other models
      Right .... 18.5 to 19.0 in (496 to 478 mm)
      Left .... 8.2 to 8.6 in (208 to 218 mm)
  Citroen driveaxle
    Turbo models (right or left) .... 8.3 to 8.7 in (211 to 220 mm)
    GLH models
      Right .... 18.3 to 18.8 in (465 to 477 mm)
      Left .... 8.3 to 8.7 in (211 to 220 mm)
1987 models
  GKN driveaxle (non-turbo models)
    Right .... 19.6 to 20.0 in (498 to 509 mm)
    Left
      Automatic transaxle .... 8.2 to 8.7 in (208 to 221 mm)
      Manual transaxle .... 9.4 to 10.0 in (240 to 253 mm)
  GKN driveaxle (turbo models)
    Right .... 8.3 to 8.7 in (211 to 220 mm)
    Left .... 8.3 to 8.7 in (211 to 220 mm)
  Citroen driveaxle (turbo models) (right or left) .... 8.9 to 9.1 in (227 to 232 mm)
1988 models
  Right .... 19.6 to 19.8 in (498 to 504 mm)
  Left
    Automatic transaxle .... 8.2 to 8.7 in (208 to 221 mm)
    Manual transaxle .... 9.4 to 10.0 in (240 to 253 mm)
1989 models
  ACI driveaxle (right only, automatic transaxle) .... 19.6 to 19.8 in (498 to 504 mm)
  GKN driveaxle
    Right .... 19.6 to 19.8 in (498 to 504 mm)
    Left
      Automatic transaxle .... 8.2 to 8.7 in (208 to 221 mm)
      Manual transaxle .... 9.4 to 10.0 in (240 to 253 mm)

Torque specifications

	Ft-lbs
Clutch	
Models with 1.7L engine	
Pressure plate-to-crankshaft bolts	55
Flywheel-to-clutch cover bolts	15
Models with 2.2L engine	
Pressure plate-to-flywheel bolts	21
Flywheel-to-crankshaft bolts	
1981 through 1983	60
1984 and 1985	65
1986 on	70
Driveaxle hub nut	180
Inner driveaxle CV joint-to-transaxle flange	
bolts (models with 1.7L engine)	36

Torque specifications (continued)

Ft-lbs

Steering knuckle-to-balljoint clamp bolt/nut

   1978 through 1983 50

   1984 on 70

Intermediate shaft mount-to-engine bolts 40

Wheel lug nuts .... See Chapter 1

---

1   General information

The information in this Chapter deals with the components from the rear of the engine to the front (drive) wheels (except for the transaxle, which is covered in the previous Chapter). In this Chapter, the components are grouped into two categories: Clutch and driveaxles. Separate Sections within this Chapter offer general information, checks and repair procedures for components in each of the two groups.

Warning: *Since nearly all the procedures included in this Chapter involve working under the vehicle, make sure it's securely supported on sturdy jackstands or on a hoist where it can be easily raised and lowered.*

---

2   Clutch – description and check

1   All vehicles with a manual transaxle have a single dry plate, diaphragm spring-type clutch. The clutch disc has a splined hub which allows it to slide along the splines of the transaxle input shaft or mainshaft. The clutch disc is held in place against the flywheel by the pressure plate springs. During disengagement (when shifting gears for example), the clutch pedal is depressed, which operates a cable, actuating the release lever so the release bearing or plate pushes on the pressure plate springs, disengaging the clutch.

2   On the A-412 four-speed transaxle used with 1.7L engines built through 1983, the release mechanism requires periodic adjustment (see Chapter 1). The release mechanism on 460/465/525 transaxles used on later models incorporates a self-adjusting device which compensates for clutch disc wear **(see illustration 5.8)**. A spring in the clutch pedal arm maintains tension on the cable and the adjuster pivot grabs the positioner adjuster when the pedal is depressed and the clutch is released. Consequently, the slack is always taken up in the cable, making adjustment unnecessary.

3   On vehicles with a 1.7L engine, when pressure is applied to the pedal to release the clutch, the cable pulls against the end of the clutch operating lever. The operating lever motion is transferred to the release bearing, which contacts a long pushrod. The pushrod, which runs through the hollow transaxle mainshaft, pushes on the release plate, disengaging the clutch. On vehicles with a 2.2L engine, when pressure is applied to the pedal to release the clutch, the cable pulls against the end of the release lever, which turns a shaft connected to the clutch release fork. As the fork pivots, the release bearing pushes against the fingers of the diaphragm springs in the pressure plate assembly, which in turn disengages the clutch plate.

4   Terminology can be a problem when discussing the clutch components because common names are in some cases different from those used by the manufacturer. For example, the clutch disc is also called the clutch plate or driven plate, the clutch release bearing is sometimes called a throwout bearing and the release fork is sometimes called the release lever.

5   Other than to replace components with obvious damage, some preliminary checks should be performed to diagnose clutch problems.

  a) The first check should be of the clutch cable adjustment (if applicable). If there's too much slack in the cable, the clutch won't release completely, making gear engagement difficult or impossible. Refer to Chapter 1 for the adjustment procedure.

  b) To check "clutch spin down time," run the engine at normal idle speed with the transaxle in Neutral (clutch pedal up – engaged). Disengage the clutch (pedal down), wait several seconds and shift the transaxle into Reverse. No grinding noise should be heard. A grinding noise would most likely indicate a problem in the pressure plate or the clutch disc.

  c) To check for complete clutch release, run the engine (with the parking brake applied to prevent vehicle movement) and hold the clutch pedal approximately 1/2-inch from the floor. Shift the transaxle between First and Reverse gear several times. If the shift is rough, component failure is indicated, or as stated above, the cable is out of adjustment.

  d) Visually inspect the pivot bushing at the top of the clutch pedal to make sure there's no binding or excessive play.

  e) A clutch pedal that's difficult to operate is most likely caused by a faulty clutch cable. Check the cable where it enters the housing for frayed wires, rust and other signs of corrosion. If it looks good, lubricate the cable with penetrating oil. If pedal operation improves, the cable is worn out and should be replaced.

---

3   Clutch components – removal, inspection and installation

Warning: *Dust produced by clutch wear and deposited on clutch components may contain asbestos, which is a health hazard. DO NOT blow it out with compressed air or inhale any of it. DO NOT use gasoline or petroleum-based solvents to clean off the dust. Brake system cleaner should be used to flush the dust into a drain pan. After the clutch components are wiped clean with rags, dispose of the contaminated rags and cleaner in a sealed, marked container.*

Removal

All vehicles

1   Access to the clutch components is normally accomplished by removing the transaxle, leaving the engine in the vehicle. Of course, if the engine is being removed for major overhaul, then check the clutch for wear and replace worn components as necessary. However, the relatively low cost of the clutch components, compared to the time and trouble spent gaining access to them, warrants their replacement anytime the engine or transaxle is removed (unless they're new or in near perfect condition). The following procedures are based on the assumption the engine will stay in place.

2   Referring to Chapter 7, Part A, remove the transaxle from the vehicle. Support the engine while the transaxle is out. Preferably, an engine hoist should be used to support it from above. However, if a jack is used underneath the engine, make sure a piece of wood is positioned between the jack and oil pan to spread the load. **Caution:** *The pick-up for the oil pump is very close to the bottom of the oil pan. If the pan is bent or distorted in any way, engine oil starvation could occur.*

3   On vehicles with a 2.2L engine, the clutch release fork and release bearing can remain attached to the transaxle housing (see Section 4 for the procedures to follow when checking and replacing the release bearing and related components).

4   To support the clutch disc during removal, install a clutch alignment tool through the clutch disc hub.

5   Carefully inspect the flywheel and pressure plate for indexing marks. The marks are usually an X, an O or a white letter. If they can't be found, scribe marks yourself so the pressure plate and flywheel will be in the same alignment during installation.

Vehicles with a 1.7L engine

Refer to illustration 3.6

6   On these models, the clutch cover/pressure plate assembly is bolted directly to the crankshaft and the flywheel is bolted to the clutch cover/

8

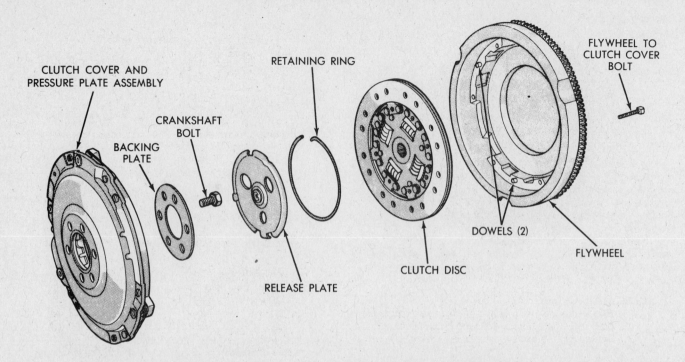

3.6   **An exploded view of the clutch components used on vehicles with a 1.7L engine – the clutch cover/pressure plate assembly is bolted to the crankshaft and the flywheel mounts on the clutch cover**

pressure plate **(see illustration)**. Loosen the flywheel-to-clutch cover bolts 1/4-turn at a time in a criss-cross sequence to avoid warping anything, then remove the flywheel and clutch disc.

7   Note where the ends of the retaining ring are positioned (make marks on the release plate if necessary), then use a screwdriver to detach the retaining ring **(see illustration 3.6)**. Remove the release plate from the

clutch assembly.

8   Mark the relationship of the clutch cover and pressure plate assembly to the crankshaft. Following a criss-cross pattern, loosen the bolts in 1/4-turn increments until they can be removed by hand. Remove the bolts and detach the clutch cover and pressure plate assembly, as well as the backing plate.

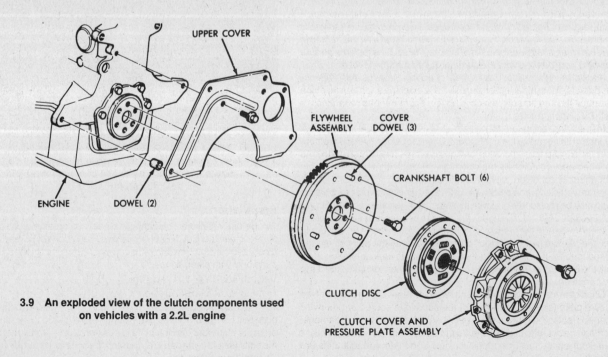

3.9   **An exploded view of the clutch components used on vehicles with a 2.2L engine**

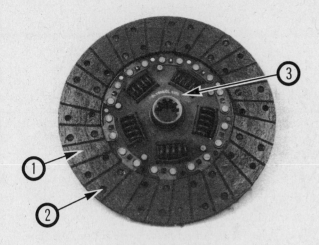

3.12 The clutch disc

1   Lining – will wear down in use
2   Rivets – secure the lining and will damage the pressure
     plate or flywheel surface if allowed to contact it
3   Marks – "flywheel side" or something similar

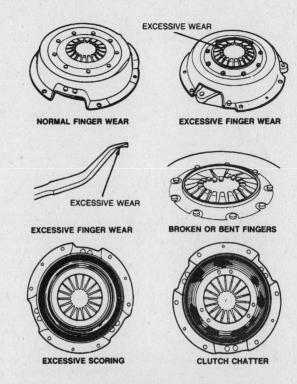

**3.14a   Replace the pressure plate if excessive wear or
damage is noted**

Vehicles with a 2.2L engine
Refer to illustration 3.9

9   Loosen the pressure plate-to-flywheel bolts 1/4-turn at a time, following a criss-cross pattern, until all spring pressure is relieved **(see illustration)**. Hold the pressure plate in place and remove the bolts, then detach the pressure plate and clutch disc. Refer to Chapter 2, Part A, for the flywheel removal and installation procedure.

Inspection
Refer to illustrations 3.12, 3.14a and 3.14b

10   Ordinarily, when a problem occurs in the clutch, it can be attributed to wear of the clutch disc. However, all components should be inspected at this time. **Note:** *If the clutch components are contaminated with oil, there will be shiny, black, glazed spots on the clutch disc lining, which will cause the clutch to slip. Replacing clutch components won't completely solve the problem – be sure to check the rear crankshaft oil seal and the transaxle input shaft/mainshaft seal for leaks. If it looks like a seal is leaking, be sure to install a new one to avoid the same problem with a new clutch.*
11   Inspect the flywheel for cracks, heat checking, grooves and other obvious defects. If the imperfections are slight, a machine shop can machine the surface flat and smooth, which is highly recommended regardless of the surface appearance.
12   Inspect the lining on the clutch disc. There should be at least 1/16-inch of lining above the rivet heads. Check for loose rivets, distortion, cracks, broken springs and other obvious damage **(see illustration)**. As mentioned above, ordinarily the clutch disc is routinely replaced, so if in doubt about its condition, replace it with a new one.
13   If the vehicle is equipped with a 2.2L engine, the release bearing should also be replaced along with the clutch disc (see Section 4). On vehicles equipped with a 1.7L engine, the release bearing is easier to replace with the transaxle in the vehicle, so it isn't as critical. However, be sure to check the release plate for distortion and for wear at the point where the pushrod touches it (wear greater than 0.010-inch is unacceptable). Also, check the pushrod seal inside the transaxle mainshaft to make sure it's in good condition.
14   Check the machined surfaces and the diaphragm spring fingers of the pressure plate **(see illustrations)**. If the surface is scored or otherwise damaged, replace the pressure plate. Also check for obvious damage, distortion, cracks, etc. Light glazing can be removed with emery cloth. If the pressure plate must be replaced, new and factory-rebuilt units are available.

**3.14b   Also examine the pressure plate friction surfaces for score
marks, cracks and evidence of overheating (blue
discolored areas)**

Installation

15   Before installation, clean the flywheel and pressure plate machined surfaces with lacquer thinner or acetone. It's important to keep these surfaces, and the clutch disc lining, clean and free of oil or grease. Handle the parts only with clean hands.

Vehicles with a 1.7L engine
Refer to illustrations 3.18a and 3.18b

16   Prior to installation, apply thread locking compound to the pressure plate bolts. Align the marks made during removal, place the clutch cover/ pressure plate and backing plate in position on the crankshaft and install the bolts **(see illustration 3.6)**. Tighten the bolts to the torque listed in this Chapter's specifications.

8

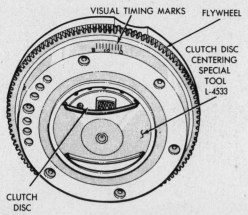

3.18a   On vehicles with a 1.7L engine, center the clutch disc with the special tool and install the flywheel and clutch disc – line up the radial V-groove hole on the outer flange of the clutch cover with the dowel in the flywheel located near the visual timing marks

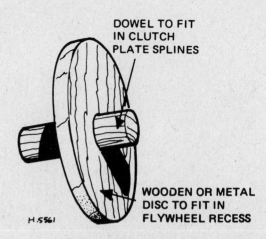

3.18b   A substitute clutch centering tool can be fabricated if the factory tool isn't available

17   Install the release plate and secure it with the retaining ring. Make sure the ends of the ring are positioned correctly.

18   Note the location of the dowel hole in the outer flange of the clutch cover. It's marked with a radial V-groove. Align the flywheel dowel near the visual timing marks with the dowel hole in the clutch cover. Using a centering tool (Chrysler tool no. L-4533 or a home-made substitute), install the new clutch disc and flywheel on the pressure plate **(see illustrations)**. **Note:** *Make sure the clutch disc is installed correctly – it should be marked to indicate which side faces the flywheel or pressure plate.*

19   Install the flywheel-to-clutch cover bolts finger tight, then tighten them in 1/4-turn increments, in a criss-cross pattern, to the torque listed in this Chapter's specifications.

20   Remove the centering tool, install the transaxle and adjust the clutch freeplay (see Chapter 1).

Vehicles with a 2.2L engine

Refer to illustration 3.21

21   Position the clutch disc and pressure plate against the flywheel with the clutch held in place with an alignment tool **(see illustration)**. Make sure it's installed properly (most replacement clutch plates will be marked "flywheel side" or something similar – if it's not marked, install the clutch disc with the damper springs toward the transaxle).

22   Tighten the pressure plate-to-flywheel bolts only finger tight, working around the pressure plate.

23   Center the clutch disc by ensuring the alignment tool extends through the splined hub and into the pocket in the crankshaft. Wiggle the tool up, down or side-to-side as needed to center the disc. Tighten the pressure plate-to-flywheel bolts a little at a time, working in a criss-cross pattern to prevent cover distortion. After all the bolts are snug, tighten them to the specified torque. Remove the alignment tool.

24   Using high-temperature grease, lubricate the release bearing (refer to Section 4). Also place grease on the release lever contact areas and the transaxle input shaft.

25   Install the clutch release bearing as described in Section 4.

All vehicles

26   Install the transaxle and all components removed previously. Tighten all fasteners to the proper torque specifications.

---

4   Clutch release bearing and related components – removal and installation

---

Warning: *Dust produced by clutch wear and deposited on clutch components may contain asbestos, which is a health hazard. DO NOT blow it out with compressed air or inhale any of it. DO NOT use gasoline or petroleum-based solvents to clean off the dust. Brake system cleaner*

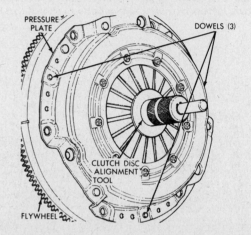

3.21   On vehicles with a 2.2L engine, use an alignment tool to center the clutch disc, then install the pressure plate on the flywheel dowels

should be used to flush the dust into a drain pan. After the clutch components are wiped clean with rags, dispose of the contaminated rags and cleaner in a sealed, marked container.

Vehicles with a 1.7L engine

Refer to illustrations 4.3, 4.4, 4.5 and 4.6

1   Raise the vehicle and support it securely on jackstands.

2   Detach the clutch cable from the operating lever (see Section 5).

3   Remove the bolts and detach the clutch release bearing end cover from the transaxle **(see illustration)**. **Note:** *You may be able to move the operating lever enough to position the release lever (the lever inside the housing) out of the way far enough to withdraw the release bearing at this point. However, if the release lever is in the way, or if the shaft seal must be replaced, proceed to Step 4.*

4   Pry out the circlips (one on each side of the release lever) **(see illustration)**.

5   Note how the spring is positioned, then pull out the operating lever shaft **(see illustration)**. Remove the release lever and return spring from the housing.

6   Lift out the release bearing and guide sleeve **(see illustration)**.

7   Hold the center of the bearing and turn the outer portion while applying pressure. If it doesn't turn smoothly or if it's noisy, install a new one.

8   Check the shaft seal in the transaxle housing. If it's worn or deteriorated, pry it out and drive a new one into place with a socket and hammer. Lubricate the seal lips with grease.

4.3   On vehicles with a 1.7L engine, the clutch release bearing is accessible after removing the end cover from the transaxle (the cover is held in place with four bolts as shown here)

4.4   Remove the circlips (arrow), . . .

4.5   . . . then support the release lever while pulling out the operating lever and shaft

4.6   The release bearing can now be pulled out of the bore in the transaxle housing

9   Installation is the reverse of removal. Note that the release lever will only slide onto the shaft in one position. The return spring must be installed with the center engaged with the release lever and the ends bearing against the housing.

Vehicles with a 2.2L engine
Refer to illustration 4.12

Note: *On these vehicles, the transaxle must be removed to gain access to the release bearing (see Chapter 7, Part A).*

10   Using needle-nose pliers, disengage the ends of the wire retainer and detach the release bearing from the fork.

11   Hold the center of the bearing and turn the outer portion while applying pressure. If it doesn't turn smoothly or if it's noisy, install a new one. It's a good idea to replace it anyway, when you consider the time and effort spent on removing the transaxle. However, if you elect to reinstall the old bearing, wipe it off with a clean rag. Don't immerse the bearing in solvent – it's sealed for life and would be ruined by the solvent.

12   Check the release fork ends for excessive wear. If the fork must be replaced, remove the E-clip from the clutch release shaft (**see illustration**). Slide the shaft out of the clutch housing and remove the fork.

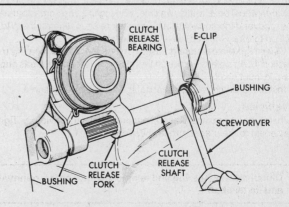

4.12   On vehicles with a 2.2L engine, the clutch release shaft is held in place by an E-clip – once the clip is removed, the release fork and bearing can be detached and the bushings can be replaced

8

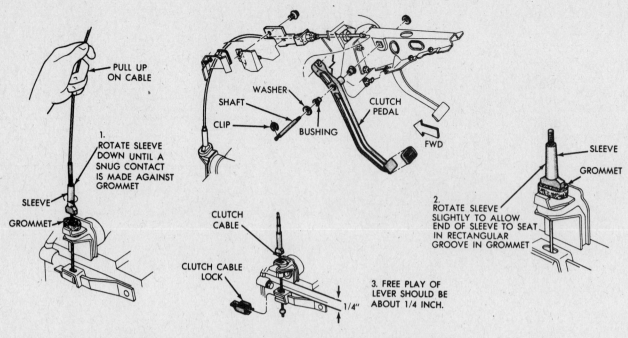

5.2   Clutch cable mounting details – 1.7L engine

13   If the shaft bushings **(see illustration 4.12)** are worn, they should be replaced.

14   Lubricate the release shaft bushings with high-temperature grease, slide the shaft part way into the housing and hold the fork in position. Continue to slide the shaft into place, through the fork, until it seats in the inner bushing.

15   Install the E-clip in the shaft groove. Make sure it's seated correctly.

16   Lubricate the release fork ends with a small amount of high-temperature grease (don't overdo it). Lubricate the release bearing bore with the same grease.

17   Install the release bearing on the fork. Make sure the wire retainer is properly engaged.

18   Install the transaxle.

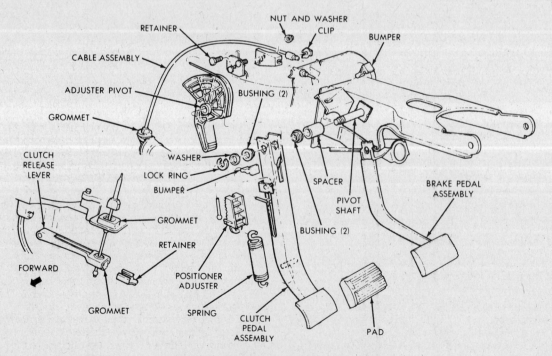

5.8   Clutch cable mounting details – 2.2L engine

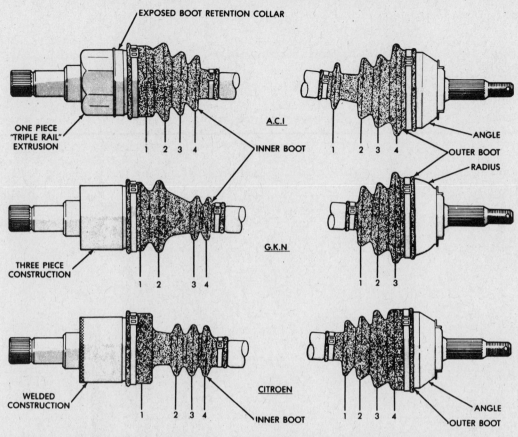

6.1   The four different driveaxles used in the vehicles covered by this manual differ slightly in several ways

5   Clutch cable – removal, installation and adjustment

1   Raise the front of the vehicle and support it securely on jackstands. Apply the parking brake and block the rear wheels so the vehicle can't roll off the stands.

Vehicles with a 1.7L engine

Refer to illustration 5.2

2   Push up on the transmission operating lever to release the cable tension, then remove the clutch cable lock and disengage the cable end from the lever **(see illustration)**.

3   Working inside the vehicle, disengage the cable end from the clutch pedal.

4   Remove the mounting bracket bolt, then pull the cable through the firewall and disengage it from the transmission mount.

5   Attach the new cable to the mounting bracket, then insert it through the firewall opening and connect the cable end to the pedal.

6   Install the mounting bracket bolt, then engage the lower end of the cable in the transmission mount and connect the cable end to the operating lever. Don't forget to install the cable lock.

7   Refer to Chapter 1 and adjust the clutch pedal freeplay.

Vehicles with a 2.2L engine

Refer to illustration 5.8

8   Remove the clip and disengage the cable housing from the retainer bracket **(see illustration)**.

9   Remove the clutch cable retainer and disengage the cable end from the clutch release lever on the transmission **(see illustration 5.8)**.

10   Pull the lower end of the cable out of the grommet in the transmission mount.

11   Working inside the vehicle, disengage the cable end from the clutch pedal.

12   Pull the cable through the firewall to remove it.

13   When installing the new cable, hook the ends to the pedal and transmission lever first, then pull on the housing and engage the cable in the retainer bracket. Don't forget to install the clip.

6   Driveaxles – general information and inspection

General information

Refer to illustrations 6.1 and 6.2

Power from the engine passes through the clutch and transaxle to the front wheels via two driveaxles **(see illustration)**. On non-turbocharged models, the driveaxles are unequal length. Turbocharged models are equipped with equal length driveaxles and feature an intermediate shaft incorporating a Cardan joint. Each driveaxle consists of three sections: An inner splined end which is held in the differential by clips or springs, two constant velocity (CV) joints and an outer splined end which is held in the hub by a nut. The CV joints are internally splined and contain ball bearings which allow them to operate at various lengths and angles as the driveaxles move through their full range of travel. The CV joints are lubricated with special grease and protected by rubber boots which must be inspected periodically for damage and deterioration that could lead to contamination of the joints and failure of the driveaxle.

The driveaxles are identified as "GKN", "ACI", or "Citroen" assemblies (depending on the manufacturer). Vehicles may be equipped with any of the three types. However, they should not be interchanged. The driveaxles on a particular vehicle can be identified by referring to the accompanying illustration.

8

6.2   Driveaxle and CV joint component layout

1	Right driveaxle	4	CV joint
2	Left driveaxle	5	Cardan joint
3	Intermediate shaft		

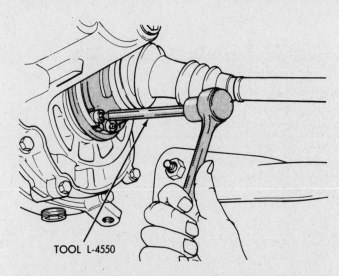

7.3a On vehicles with a 1.7L engine, remove the inner driveaxle CV joint-to-transaxle flange bolts with an Allen wrench or socket

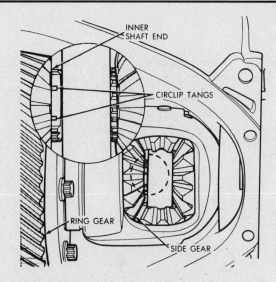

7.3b The circlip tangs that retain the driveaxle to the differential side gears can be difficult to locate

Inspection

The boots should be periodically inspected for leaks, damage and deterioration (see Chapter 1). Damaged CV joint boots must be replaced immediately or the joints can be damaged. Boot replacement involves removal of the driveaxle. **Note:** *Some auto parts stores carry "split" type replacement boots, which can be installed without removing the driveaxle from the vehicle – a convenient alternative. However, the driveaxle should be removed and the CV joint disassembled and cleaned to make sure the joint is free from contaminants such as moisture and dirt, which will accelerate CV joint wear.*

The most common symptom of worn or damaged CV joints, besides lubricant leaks, is a clicking noise in turns, a clunk when accelerating from a coasting condition or vibration at highway speeds.

To check for wear in the CV joints and driveaxle shafts, grasp each axle (one at a time) and rotate it in both directions while holding the CV joint housings. Watch for movement, indicating worn splines or sloppy CV joints. Also, check the driveaxle shafts for cracks and distortion.

7   Driveaxles – removal and installation

Removal

Refer to illustrations 7.3a, 7.3b, 7.3c, 7.5, 7.7, 7.8a and 7.8b

1   Remove the front hub dust cap, cotter pin, nut lock and wave washer, if equipped **(see illustration 9.4a or 9.4b,** if necessary). With the weight of the vehicle on the wheels and an assistant applying the brakes, loosen the hub nut.

2   Raise the front of the vehicle, support it securely on jackstands, apply the parking brake and block the rear wheels. Remove the front wheel, hub nut and washer.

3   If the vehicle is equipped with a 1.7L engine, pry off the plastic covers and remove the six Allen head screws retaining the inner CV joint to the transaxle flange **(see illustration)**. On 1978 through 1982 vehicles with a 2.2L engine, the driveaxle inner ends are retained in the differential side gears by circlips which must be released prior to driveaxle removal. Remove the differential cover (see Chapter 7) and rotate the driveaxle to expose the circlip tangs **(see illustration)**. Compress the circlip tangs with needle-nose pliers and use a screwdriver to push the axleshaft into the splined cavity of the side gear **(see illustration)**. Pull the axle out slightly.

4   On all vehicles, remove the speedometer drive gear prior to removing the right axle.

5   Remove the steering knuckle-to-balljoint clamp bolt **(see illustration)**.

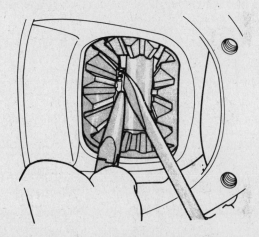

7.3c Compress the circlip tangs while pushing the driveaxle shaft into the differential side gear cavity with a screwdriver

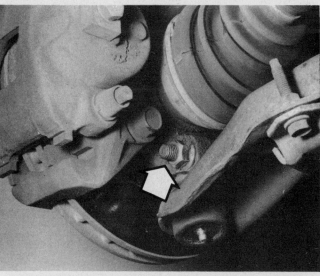

7.5 Remove the nut from the balljoint clamp bolt (arrow)

8

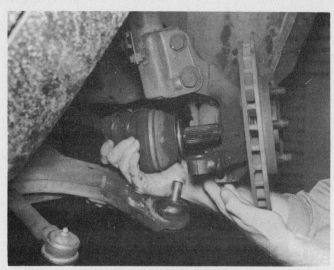

7.7   Grasp the outer CV joint and pull the steering knuckle out to separate it from the driveaxle splines

7.8a   Support both CV joints as the driveaxle is lowered from the vehicle

6   Pry the lower balljoint stud out of the steering knuckle. **Note:** *The sway bar must be disconnected from the suspension arm to allow enough movement to separate the balljoint (see Chapter 10).*

7   Grasp the outer CV joint and the steering knuckle and pull the steering knuckle out to separate the driveaxle from the hub **(see illustration)**. Be careful not to damage the CV joint boot. **Caution:** *Don't pry on or damage the wear sleeve on the CV joint when separating it from the hub.*

8   Grasp the CV joints so they'll be supported during removal and withdraw the driveaxle from the differential. **Caution:** *Don't pull on the shaft – pull only on the inner CV joint* **(see illustrations)**.

9   The driveaxles, when in place, secure the hub bearing assemblies. If the vehicle must be supported or moved on the front wheels while the driveaxles are out, install bolts through the hubs and thread nuts onto them to keep the bearings from loosening.

Installation

Refer to illustration 7.19

10   Prior to installation, clean the wear sleeve on the driveaxle outer CV joint and the seal in the hub. Lubricate the entire circumference of the seal lip and fill the seal cavity with grease. Apply a 1/4-inch bead of grease to the wear sleeve seal contact area as well.

11   On driveaxles equipped with circlips, install new circlips in the inner CV joint shaft grooves.

12   Apply a small amount of multi-purpose grease to the splines at each end of the driveaxle. Place the driveaxle in position and carefully insert the inner end of the shaft into the transaxle.

13   Push the steering knuckle out and insert the outer splined shaft of the CV joint into the hub.

14   Rejoin the balljoint stud to the steering knuckle, install the clamp bolt and tighten it to the torque listed in this Chapter's specifications. On vehicles equipped with a 1.7L engine, install the six Allen head screws that retain the inner CV joint to the flange, then tighten the screws to the torque listed in this Chapter's specifications.

15   Install the sway bar ends, if removed (see Chapter 10).

16   On models with circlip driveaxles, install the differential cover (see Chapter 7).

17   Install the speedometer drive gear.

18   Install the wheels, washers and axle hub nuts.

19   Tighten the driveaxle hub nuts to the torque listed in this Chapter's specifications and install the wave washers, nut locks and new cotter pins. On 1978 models, stake the hub nut in place **(see illustration)**.

Driveaxle position check

Refer to illustration 7.22

20   Later model vehicles have engine mounts with slotted holes that allow for side-to-side positioning of the engine. If the vertical bolts on the right or

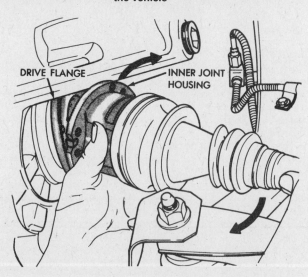

7.8b   On vehicles with a 2.2L engine, rotate the outer end of the driveaxle down while lifting the inner joint up and withdraw the axle – keep the inner joint level or the special lubricant inside will spill out

left upper engine mounts have been loosened for any reason, or if the vehicle has been damaged structurally at the front end, driveaxle length must be checked/corrected. A driveaxle that's shorter than required will result in objectionable noise, while a driveaxle that's longer than necessary may result in damage.

21   The vehicle must be completely assembled, the front wheels must be properly aligned and pointing straight ahead and the weight of the vehicle must be on all four wheels.

22   Using a tape measure, check the distance from the inner edge of the outboard boot to the inner edge of the inboard boot on both driveaxles. Take the measurement at the lower edge of the driveaxles (six o'clock position) **(see illustration)**. Compare the measurement with the length listed in this Chapter's Specifications. Note that the required dimension varies with transaxle type and driveaxle manufacturer (see illustration 6.2 to identify the driveaxle type).

23   If the dimensions aren't as specified, the mount bolts can be loosened and the engine repositioned to obtain the specified driveaxle lengths. If the engine can't be moved enough within the range of the slotted engine mounts, check for damaged or distorted support brackets and side rails.

24   If the engine is moved, see Chapter 7 and adjust the shift linkage.

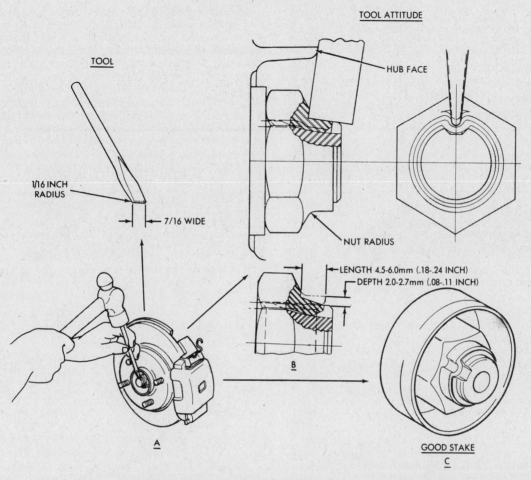

7.19   On 1978 models, the driveaxle hub nut must be securely staked in place

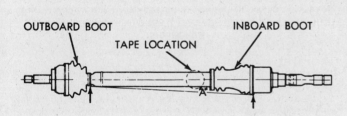

7.22   Measure the driveaxles between the points shown (arrows) to verify they are at the correct length when installed

8   Intermediate shaft (turbocharged models only) – removal and installation

Refer to illustrations 8.3 and 8.5

Removal

1   Remove the right driveaxle (see Section 7).
2   Remove the retaining bolt and push up on the speedometer cable to disengage the speedometer drive gear from the transaxle.

8.3   Use a socket to remove the intermediate shaft bearing mount bolts

3   Remove the bearing mount bolts (see illustration).
4   Have an assistant with a drain pan ready to catch the fluid that will pour out of the transaxle with considerable force when the shaft is removed. Grasp the intermediate shaft/bearing assembly securely with both hands and pull it out of the transaxle.

Installation

5   Place the intermediate shaft and bearing assembly in position and carefully insert the splined stub yoke into the transaxle extension housing **(see illustration)**.

6   Place the bearing mount in position and install the bolts. Tighten the mount-to-engine bolts to the torque listed in this Chapter's Specifications.

7   Lubricate the inside splines and the pilot bore of the intermediate shaft with a liberal amount of multi-purpose grease.

8   Install the right driveaxle.

9   Constant velocity (CV) joints – disassembly, inspection and reassembly

1   Obtain a CV joint rebuild or replacement kit.

2   Remove the driveaxles (see Section 7) and identify which types of CV joints are installed (see Section 6).

3   Place one of the driveaxles in a vise, using wood blocks to protect it from the vise jaws. If the CV joint has been operating properly with no noise or vibration, replace the boot as described in Section 10. If the CV joint is badly worn or has run for some time with no lubricant due to a damaged boot, it should be disassembled and inspected.

Inner CV joint

Refer to illustrations 9.4a, 9.4b, 9.6, 9.7, 9.8a, 9.8b, 9.10a, 9.10b, 9.14, 9.16, 9.21, 9.23a, 9.23b, 9.23c, 9.24a and 9.24b

4   Remove the clamps and slide the boot back to gain access to the tripod **(see illustrations)**.

5   Depending on the type of CV joint involved, separate the tripod from the housing as follows.

6   On GKN driveaxles, the retaining tabs are an integral part of the housing cover. Hold the housing and lightly compress the retention spring while bending the tabs back with a pair of pliers **(see illustration)**. Support the housing as the retention spring pushes it off the tripod. This will prevent the housing from reaching an unacceptable angle and keep the tripod rollers from being pulled from the tripod studs.

7   Citroen driveaxles utilize a tripod retainer ring which is rolled into a groove in the housing. Deform the retainer ring slightly at each roller with a screwdriver **(see illustration)**. The retention spring will push the housing off the tripod. The retainer ring can also be carefully cut off the housing. New rings are included in the rebuild kit and can be installed by rolling the edge into the machined groove in the housing with a hammer and punch.

8   On ACI driveaxles, the tripod retaining tabs are part of the boot retaining collar, which is staked in place. On 1984 models, place the housing in position so the three rollers are flush with the retaining tabs. Pull the housing while angling the joint slightly so the rollers can be snapped through the tabs, one at a time. Be careful not to angle the joint too far or the tripod rollers will be pulled off the studs **(see illustration)**. On 1985 and later models, compress the retaining spring lightly while bending the tabs back with a pair of pliers **(see illustration)**. Be sure to support the housing as the spring pushes it off the tripod.

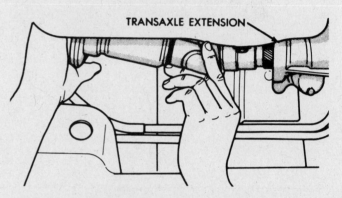

8.5   Support the intermediate shaft while inserting the splines into the transaxle extension

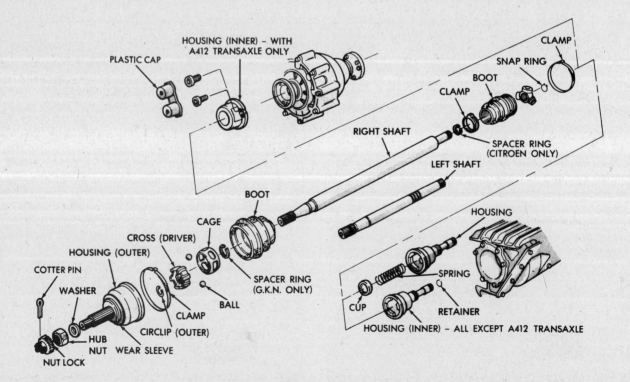

9.4a   1978 through 1983 driveaxle and CV joint components – exploded view

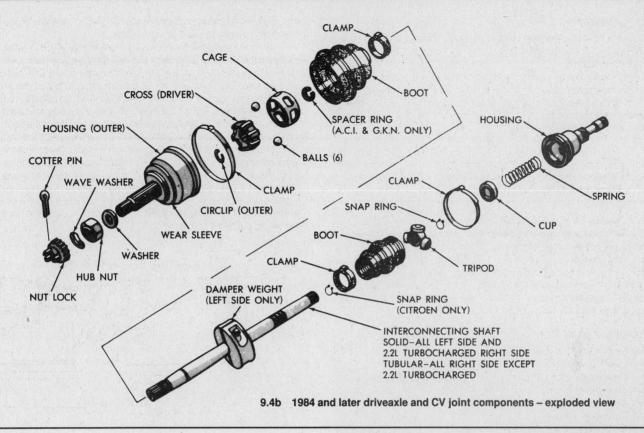

CLAMP

CAGE

CROSS (DRIVER)

BOOT

SPACER RING
(A.C.I. & G.K.N. ONLY)

HOUSING (OUTER)

HOUSING

COTTER PIN

BALLS (6)

CLAMP

SPRING

WAVE WASHER

CLAMP

SNAP RING

CLAMP

CUP

CIRCLIP (OUTER)

WEAR SLEEVE

BOOT

TRIPOD

WASHER

CLAMP

HUB NUT

NUT LOCK

DAMPER WEIGHT
(LEFT SIDE ONLY)

SNAP RING
(CITROEN ONLY)

INTERCONNECTING SHAFT
SOLID–ALL LEFT SIDE AND
2.2L TURBOCHARGED RIGHT SIDE
TUBULAR–ALL RIGHT SIDE EXCEPT
2.2L TURBOCHARGED

9.4b   1984 and later driveaxle and CV joint components – exploded view

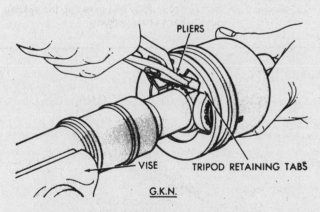

PLIERS

VISE

TRIPOD RETAINING TABS

G.K.N.

9.6   To separate the inner joint tripod from the housing on GKN driveaxles, the retaining tabs must be bent up with a pair of pliers

9.7   To disassemble Citroen inner CV joints, carefully pry up on the retainer at each bearing roller

8

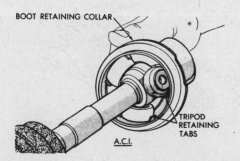

BOOT RETAINING COLLAR

TRIPOD RETAINING TABS

A.C.I.

9.8a   On 1984 ACI CV joints, align the rollers with the retaining tabs, then snap them out of the collar, one at a time

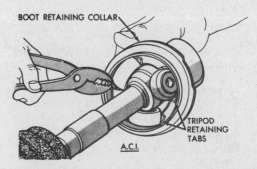

BOOT RETAINING COLLAR

TRIPOD RETAINING TABS

A.C.I.

9.8b   On 1985 and later ACI CV joints, compress the spring and bend each tab back with pliers to remove the tripod from the collar

9.10a   The tripod is held on the shaft by a snap-ring - remove it with a pair of snap-ring pliers

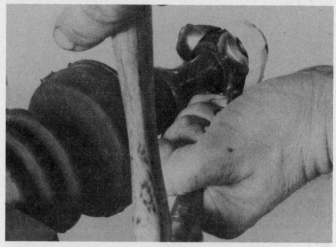

9.10b   Secure the bearings with tape and drive the tripod off the shaft with a brass punch and hammer

9.14   Detach the Citroen CV joint retainer ring with pliers

9   When removing the housing from the tripod, hold the rollers in place on the studs to prevent the rollers and needle bearings from falling. After the tripod is out of the housing, secure the rollers in place with tape.

10   Remove the snap-ring **(see illustration)** and use a brass punch to drive the bearing and tripod assembly off the splined shaft **(see illustration)**.

11   Clean the grease from the tripod assembly. Check for score marks, wear, corrosion and excessive play. Replace any damaged or worn components with new ones.

12   Inspect the inner splined area of the bearing tripod for wear and damage. Replace parts as necessary.

13   Remove all old grease from the housing. Inspect the housing splines, ball races, spring, spring cup and the spherical end of the shaft for wear, damage, nicks and corrosion. Replace parts as necessary.

14   Place the housing in a vise and remove the retainer ring with a pair of pliers **(see illustration)**.

15   Install the new boot on the axle.

16   On GKN and ACI driveaxles, slide the tripod onto the shaft with the non-chamfered end facing out (next to the snap-ring groove) **(see illustration)**.

17   Citroen driveaxles are equipped with tripods that can be installed with either end out (both ends are the same). Be sure to install the wire ring tripod retainer on the interconnecting shaft before sliding the tripod onto the shaft.

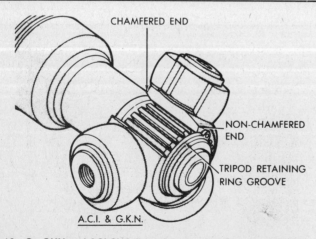

9.16   On GKN and ACI CV joints, the non-chamfered end of the tripod must face OUT when installed on the driveaxle splines

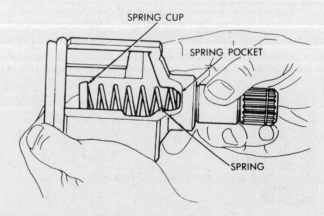

9.21   When assembling the inner CV joint, make sure the spring is seated securely in the spring pocket and the spring cup is installed on the outer end

9.23a   Make sure the bearing grooves in the housing have been greased, then slide the housing over the tripod until it bottoms (Citroen CV joint)

9.23b   Stake the new retainer ring in place with a hammer and punch (Citroen CV joint)

18   If necessary, use a section of pipe or a socket and hammer to carefully tap the tripod onto the shaft until it just clears the snap-ring groove.

19   Install a new snap-ring and make sure it's seated in the groove.

20   On GKN driveaxles, distribute two of the three or four packets of grease supplied with the kit in the boot and the remaining packet(s) in the housing. On ACI driveaxles, distribute one of the two supplied packets of grease in the boot and the remaining packet in the housing. On Citroen driveaxles, distribute two-thirds of the grease in the packet in the boot and the remaining amount in the housing. Make sure the grease is applied to the bearing grooves in the housing. On GKN driveaxles used with A-412 transaxles, add two more packets of grease to the joint housing after securing the boot to the housing (for a total of four packets).

21   Position the spring in the housing spring pocket with the cup attached to the exposed end of the spring (see illustration). Apply a small amount of grease to the concave surface of the spring cup.

22   On GKN driveaxles, slip the tripod into the housing and bend the retaining ring tabs down to their original positions. Make sure the tabs retain the tripod in the housing.

23   On Citroen driveaxles, slide the housing over the tripod until it bottoms (see illustration). Install a new retainer ring by rolling the edge into the machined groove in the housing with a hammer and punch (see illustration). If the retainer ring won't stay in place during this operation, hold it with two C-clamps (see illustration). Make sure the retainer ring secures the tripod in the housing.

24   On 1984 model ACI driveaxles, align the tripod rollers with the retaining tabs and housing tracks and snap one roller at a time through the retaining tabs (see illustrations). Make sure the retaining tab holds the tripod securely in the housing. On 1985 and later model ACI driveaxles,

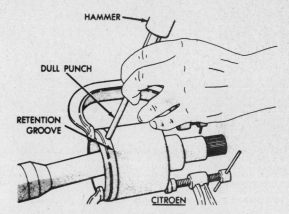

HAMMER

DULL PUNCH

RETENTION GROOVE

CITROEN

9.23c   If the retainer ring moves around while staking it, use C-clamps to hold it in place

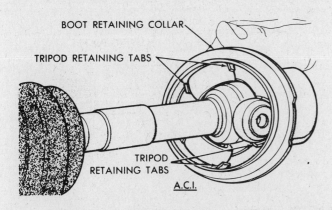

BOOT RETAINING COLLAR

TRIPOD RETAINING TABS

TRIPOD RETAINING TABS

A.C.I.

9.24a   On 1984 model ACI CV joints, snap each roller into place, one at a time

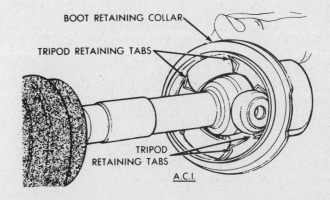

BOOT RETAINING COLLAR

TRIPOD RETAINING TABS

TRIPOD RETAINING TABS

A.C.I.

9.24b   On 1985 ACI CV joints, press the housing onto the tripod – don't try to snap the roller into the tabs

8

9.28a   The outer joint housing can be dislodged from the shaft circlip with a soft-face hammer . . .

9.28b   . . . and removed by hand

9.32   Mark the bearing cage, cross and housing relationship after removing the grease

9.33   With the cage and cross tilted, the balls can be removed one at a time

slip the tripod into the housing but don't bend the retaining tabs back to their original positions. Reattach the boot instead, which will hold the housing on the shaft. When the driveaxle is reinstalled on the vehicle, make sure the tripod is re-engaged in the housing.

25   Make sure the retention spring is centered in the housing spring pocket when the tripod is installed and seated in the spring cup.

26   Install the boot and retaining clamp (see Section 10).

Outer CV joint

Refer to illustrations 9.28a, 9.28b, 9.32, 9.33, 9.34, 9.35, 9.38, 9.40, 9.41, 9.42a, 9.42b and 9.46

27   Remove the boot clamps and push the boot back.

28   Wipe the grease out of the joint. Use a soft-face hammer to drive the housing off the axle **(see illustrations)**. Support the CV joint as this is done and rap the housing sharply on the outer edge to dislodge it from the internal circlip installed on the shaft. If the shaft is equipped with a damper weight **(see illustration 9.4b)**, loosen the damper weight bolts, mark its position and slide the weight and the boot toward the inner joint. Remove the circlip with snap-ring pliers and slide the inner joint off the axle.

29   Slide the boot off the driveaxle. If the CV joint was operating properly and the grease doesn't appear to be contaminated, just replace the boot

(see Section 10). Bypass the following disassembly procedure. If the CV joint was noisy or the grease was contaminated, proceed with the disassembly procedure to determine if it should be replaced with a new one.

30   Remove the circlip from the driveaxle groove and discard it (the rebuild kit will include a new circlip). GKN and ACI driveaxles are equipped with a large spacer ring, which must not be removed unless the driveaxle is being replaced with a new one.

31   Clean the axle spline area and check the splines for wear, damage and corrosion.

32   Clean the outer CV joint bearing assembly with a clean cloth to remove excess grease. Mark the relative position of the bearing cage, cross and housing **(see illustration)**.

33   Grip the housing shaft securely in the wood blocks in the vise. Push down one side of the cage and remove the ball bearing from the opposite side. Repeat the procedure in a criss-cross pattern until all of the balls are removed **(see illustration)**. If the joint is tight, tap on the cross (not the cage) with a hammer and brass punch.

34   Remove the bearing cage assembly from the housing by tilting it vertically and aligning two opposing elongated cage windows in the area between the ball grooves **(see illustration)**.

35   Turn the cross 90-degrees to the cage and align one of the spherical

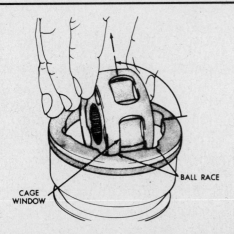

9.34   Tilt the inner race and cage 90-degrees, then align the windows in the cage with the lands and rotate the inner race up and out of the outer race

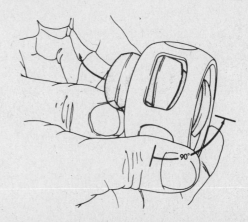

9.35   Turn the cross 90-degrees, align the cross lands with the cage windows and rotate the cross out of the cage

9.38   If the wear sleeve (on models so equipped) requires replacement, pry it off the housing with a large screwdriver

9.40   The bearing cross will slide into the cage by aligning one of the lands with the elongated window in the cage

lands with an elongated cage window. Raise the land into the window and swivel the cross out of the cage **(see illustration)**.

36   Clean all of the parts with solvent and dry them with compressed air (if available).

37   Inspect the housing, splines, balls and races for damage, corrosion, wear and cracks. Check the bearing cross for wear and scoring in the races. If any of the components are not serviceable, the entire CV joint assembly must be replaced with a new one.

38   Check the outer housing wear sleeve for damage and distortion. If it's damaged or worn, pry the sleeve off the housing **(see illustration)** and replace it with a new one. A special tool is available for installing the new sleeve, but a large section of pipe slightly smaller in diameter than the outer edge of the sleeve will work if care is exercised (don't nick or gouge the seal mating surface).

39   Apply a thin coat of oil to all CV joint components before beginning reassembly.

40   Align the marks and install the cross in the cage so one of the cross lands fits into the elongated window **(see illustration)**.

41   Rotate the cross into position in the cage and install the assembly in the CV joint housing, again using the elongated window for clearance **(see illustration)**.

9.41   Lower the cage and cross assembly into the housing with the elongated window aligned with the race

8

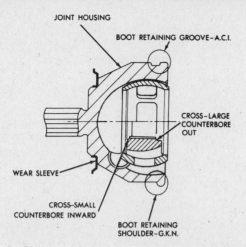

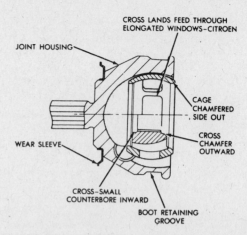

9.42a   On GKN and ACI CV joints, make sure the large cross counterbore faces out when the joint is reassembled

9.42b   On Citroen CV joints, make sure the large cross and cage chamfers face OUT when the joint is reassembled

42   Rotate the cage into position in the housing. On GKN and ACI driveaxles, the large cross counterbore must face out **(see illustration)**. On Citroen driveaxles, the cage and cross chamfers must face out **(see illustration)**. The marks made during disassembly should face out and be aligned.

43   Pack the lubricant from the kit into the ball races and grooves.

44   Install the balls into the elongated holes, one at a time, until they're all in position.

45   Place the driveaxle in the vise and slide the boot over it. Install a new circlip in the axle groove, taking care not to twist it.

46   Place the CV joint housing in position on the axle, align the splines and rap it sharply with a soft-face hammer **(see illustration)**. Make sure it's seated on the circlip by attempting to pull it off the shaft.

47   Install the boot (see Section 10).

48   Install the driveaxle (see Section 7).

10   Constant velocity (CV) joint boots – replacement

Note: *If the instructions supplied with the replacement boot kit differ from the instructions here, follow the ones with the new boots. A special tool is required to install the factory-supplied boot clamps, so it may be a good idea to leave the entire procedure to a dealer service department. Do-it-yourself kits which offer greatly simplified installation may be available for your vehicle. Consult an auto parts store or dealer parts department for more information on these kits.*

1   If the boot is cut, torn or leaking, it must be replaced and the CV joint inspected as soon as possible. Even a small amount of dirt in the joint can cause premature wear and failure. Obtain a replacement boot kit before beginning this procedure.

2   Remove the driveaxle (see Section 7).

3   Disassemble the CV joint and remove the boot as described in Section 9.

4   Inspect the CV joint to determine if its been damaged by contamination or running with too little lubricant. If you have any doubts about the condition of the joint components, perform the inspection procedures described in Section 9.

5   Clean the old grease out of the CV joint and repack it with the grease supplied with the kit.

6   Pack the interior of the new boot with the remaining grease.

7   Install the boot and clamps as follows:

GKN and ACI driveaxles

Refer to illustrations 10.9, 10.11 and 10.12

8   GKN units generally are equipped with metal ladder-type clamps. However, two alternative clamps are also used. They include a small rub-

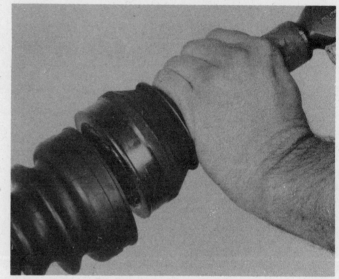

9.46   Strike the end of the housing shaft with a soft-face hammer to engage it with the shaft circlip

ber clamp at the shaft end of the inner CV joint and a large spring-type clamp on the housing.

9   If so equipped, slide the small rubber clamp over the shaft. Slide the small end of the boot over the shaft and position it as follows: On right inner joints, the small end of the boot lip must be aligned with the mark on the shaft. On left inner and all outer joints, position the small end of the boot in the groove in the shaft **(see illustration)**.

10   Place the rubber clamp in the boot groove (if so equipped) or install the metal clamp.

11   Make sure the boot is properly located on the shaft, then locate the metal clamp tangs in the slots, making the clamp as tight as possible by hand **(see illustration)**.

12   Squeeze the clamp bridge with tool number C-4124 to complete the tightening procedure **(see illustration)**. On 1988 and 1989 models, use tool C-4653. Don't cut through the clamp bridge or damage the rubber boot.

13   Reassemble the CV joints and driveaxle components (see Section 9).

14   Locate the large end of the boot over the shoulder or in the groove in the housing (make sure the boot isn't twisted).

15   Install the spring-type clamp or ladder-type clamp. If a ladder-type clamp is used, repeat the tightening procedure described in Steps 11 and 12.

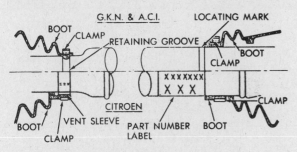

10.9 CV joint boot installation details

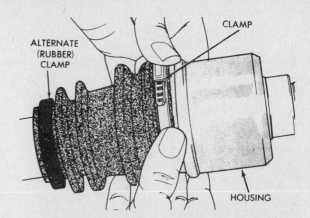

10.11 GKN ladder-type boot clamp installation details

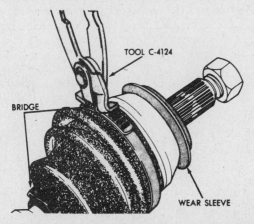

10.12 Use the special tool to squeeze the boot clamp bridge

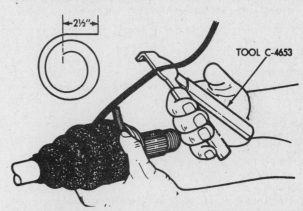

10.18 Wrap the clamp around the boot twice, leaving about 2-1/2 inches of extra material, then cut off the excess

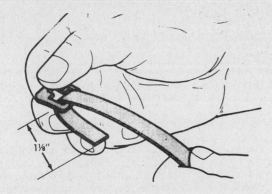

10.19 Pass the strap through the buckle and fold it back about 1-1/8 inch on the inside of the buckle

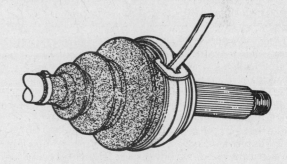

10.21a Install the strap on the boot and bend it back so it can't unwind

8

Citroen driveaxles

Refer to illustrations 10.18, 10.19, 10.21a, 10.21b, 10.22, 10.23a and 10.23b

16   Slide the boot over the shaft. If you're installing an outer CV joint boot, position the vent sleeve under the boot clamp groove.

17   On right inner joints, align the boot lip face with the inner edge of the part number label. If the label is missing, use the mark left by the original boot. On left inner and all outer joints, position the boot between the locating shoulders and align the edge of the lip with the mark made by the original boot. **Note:** *Clamping procedures are identical for attaching the boot to the shaft and the CV joint housing.*

18   Wrap the clamping strap around the boot twice, plus 2-1/2 inches, and cut it off **(see illustration)**.

19   Pass the end of the strap through the buckle opening and fold it back about 1-1/8 inch on the inside of the buckle **(see illustration)**.

20   Position the clamping strap around the boot, on the clamping surface, with the eye of the buckle facing you. Wrap the strap around the boot once and pass it through the buckle, then wrap it around a second time and pass it through the buckle again.

21   Fold the strap back slightly to prevent it from unwinding itself **(see illustration)**, then open the special tool (C-4653) and place the strap in the

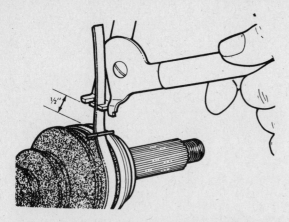

10.21b Attach the tool about 1/2-inch from the buckle, . . .

10.22 . . . then push the tool forward and up to engage the tool hook in the buckle eye

10.23a Close the tool handles slowly to tighten the clamp strap, . . .

10.23b . . . then rotate the tool down while releasing the pressure on the handles (allow the handles to open)

narrow slot, about 1/2-inch from the buckle **(see illustration)**.

22 Hold the strap with one hand and push the tool forward and up slightly, then fit the tool hook into the buckle eye **(see illustration)**.

23 Tighten the strap by closing the tool handles **(see illustration)**, then rotate the tool down slowly while releasing the pressure on the handles **(see illustration)**. Allow the handles to open progressively, then open the tool all the way and slide it sideways off the strap. **Caution:** *Never fold the strap back or rotate the tool down while squeezing the handles together (if this is done, the strap will break).*

24 If the strap isn't tight enough, repeat the procedure. Always engage the tool about 1/2-inch from the buckle. Make sure the strap moves smoothly as tightening force is applied and don't allow the buckle to fold over as the strap passes through it.

25 When the strap is tight, cut it off 1/8-inch above the buckle and fold it back neatly. It must not overlap the edge of the buckle.

26 Repeat the procedure for the remaining boot clamps.

Chapter 9   Brakes

Contents

Specifications

General

Brake fluid type	See Chapter 1

Disc brakes

Brake pad wear limit	See Chapter 1
Minimum disc thickness*	0.431 in (10.95 mm)
Disc runout (maximum)	0.005 in (0.13 mm)
Disc thickness (parallelism) variation limit	0.0005 in (0.013 mm)

* Refer to marks cast in the disc (they supercede information printed here)

Drum brakes

Brake shoe wear limit	See Chapter 1
Drum	
Standard diameter	7.87 in (200 mm)
Maximum diameter	See marks on drum
Out-of-round (maximum)	0.002 in (0.05 mm)

9

Torque specifications

	Ft-lbs (unless otherwise indicated)
Master cylinder-to-booster (or firewall) nuts	21
Power brake booster-to-firewall nuts	21
Caliper guide pin(s)	
ATE	
1978 through 1980	25 to 40
1981 on	18 to 26
Kelsey-Hayes	25 to 35
Caliper adapter-to-steering knuckle bolts	
1978 through 1982	70 to 100
1983 on	130 to 190
Brake hose-to-caliper inlet fitting bolt	19 to 29
Wheel cylinder-to-brake backing plate bolts	75 in-lbs
Brake backing plate-to-rear axle bolts	
1978 through 1986	35 to 55
1987 on	45 to 60

1   General information

All models are equipped with disc-type front and drum-type rear brakes which are hydraulically-operated.

The front brakes feature a single piston, floating caliper design. Disc brake calipers from two different manufacturers are used on these models: ATE and Kelsey-Hayes. The brakes differ in design and parts are not interchangeable. The easiest way to tell the difference between the ATE and Kelsey-Hayes caliper is to count the guide pins. ATE calipers have two guide pins, while Kelsey-Hayes calipers have only one.

The rear drum brakes are leading/trailing shoe type with a single pivot. Early model rear drum brakes (1978 through 1982) require adjustment at specified intervals. Later models feature automatic adjustment.

Front wheel drive vehicles tend to wear the front brake pads at a faster rate than rear drive vehicles. Consequently, it's very important to inspect the brake pads frequently to make sure they haven't worn to the point where the disc itself is scored or damaged. Note that the pad thickness limit on these models includes the metal portion of the brake pad, not just the lining material (see Chapter 1).

The hydraulic system consists of two separate circuits. the master cylinder has a separate section in the reservoir for each circuit – in the event of a leak or failure in one hydraulic circuit, the other circuit will remain operative.

All models are equipped with a cable-actuated parking brake, which operates the rear brakes.

2   Disc brake pads – replacement

Warning: *Disc brake pads must be replaced on both front wheels at the same time – never replace the pads on only one wheel. Also, the dust created by the brake system may contain asbestos, which is harmful to your health. Never blow it out with compressed air and don't inhale any of it. An approved filtering mask should be worn when working on the brakes. Do not, under any circumstances, use petroleum-based solvents to clean brake parts. Use brake system cleaner or clean brake fluid only!*

Note: *When servicing the disc brakes, use only high-quality, nationally-recognized, name-brand parts.*

1   Raise the front of the vehicle and support it securely on jackstands. Block the rear wheels and apply the parking brake, then remove the front wheels.

ATE caliper

1978 through 1983 models
Refer to illustrations 2.2, 2.3, 2.4 and 2.6

2   Unscrew the guide pins and detach the anti-rattle spring **(see illustration)**.

3   Slide the caliper carefully off the disc and adapter assembly. Hang the caliper out of the way with a piece of wire **(see illustration). Warning:** *Don't allow the caliper to hang by the brake hose!*

2.2   Unscrew the guide pins and lift the caliper out of the adapter to expose the brake pads (1978 through 1983 ATE caliper)

2.3   Hang the caliper out of the way on a piece of wire – DO NOT let it hang by the brake hose!

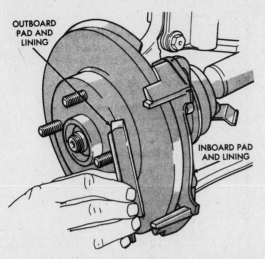

2.4 Slide the outboard pad out of the adapter (1978 through 1983 ATE caliper)

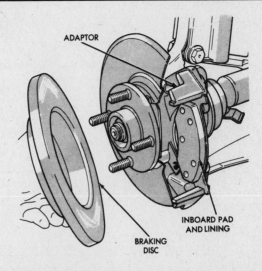

2.6 Once the disc has been removed, the inboard brake pad can be removed from the adapter (1978 through 1983 ATE caliper)

4 Slide the outboard brake pad out of the adapter (**see illustration**).
5 Inspect/remove the brake disc as described in Section 3.
6 Slide the inboard pad out of the adapter (**see illustration**).
7 Inspect the caliper and adapter for wear, damage, rust and evidence of brake fluid leaks. If the caliper-to-adapter mating surfaces are rusty, clean them thoroughly with a wire brush (the caliper must be free to move as the brakes are applied).
8 Apply a thin film of Mopar Lubricant (no. 2932524) or high-temperature brake grease to the adapter-to-brake pad and caliper mating surfaces. Remove the protective paper from the noise suppression gasket on both pads.
9 Slide the new inboard pad into position on the adapter and then install the brake disc over the studs.
10 Install the outboard brake pad in the adapter.
11 Before installing the caliper, it's a good idea to siphon a small amount of brake fluid out of the master cylinder reservoir or place rags or newspapers underneath it to catch the overflow that will occur when the piston is pushed back to make room for the new pads. Use a piece of wood to carefully push the piston back into the caliper to provide clearance for the new pads.
12 Hold the outboard pad in place on the adapter and carefully slide the caliper into position on the adapter.

13 Install the anti-rattle spring.
14 Carefully push the guide pins into place and screw them in finger tight – don't cross-thread them. Tighten the guide pins to the torque listed in this Chapter's Specifications.
15 Install the wheel. Tighten the lug nuts to the torque listed in the Chapter 1 Specifications.
16 Repeat the procedure for the other caliper.
17 Pump the brake pedal several times to bring the pads into contact with the disc. Check the brake fluid level (see Chapter 1). Drive the vehicle and make several stops to wear off any foreign material on the pads and seat them on the disc.

1984 and later models
Refer to illustrations 2.18, 2.21 and 2.22

18 Remove the hold-down retainer by pushing down at the center and prying it out with a screwdriver (**see illustration**).
19 Loosen the caliper guide pins enough to allow the caliper to be removed (**see illustration 2.2**).
20 Move the caliper forward and off the adapter and brake disc. The inner pad will remain with the caliper.
21 Remove the inner pad by pulling it away from the piston (**see illustration**).

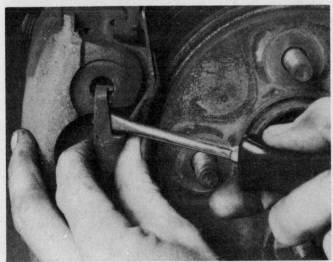

2.18 Push in on the hold-down spring, then pry it out of the caliper with a small screwdriver (1984 and later ATE calipers)

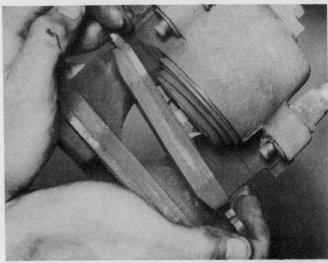

2.21 Pull the inboard pad straight out, disengaging the retainer spring from the piston (1984 and later ATE calipers)

9

2.22   If it's stuck, pry the outboard pad off the caliper (1984 and later ATE calipers)

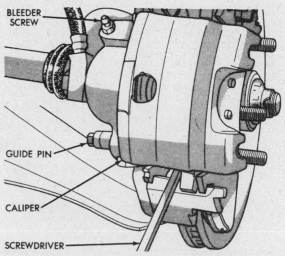

2.34   Unscrew the guide pin and pry the caliper up to detach it from the adapter and pads (Kelsey-Hayes caliper)

22   Remove the outer pad from the adapter. If the noise suppression gasket causes the pad to adhere to the caliper, pry it loose with a screwdriver **(see illustration)**.

23   Support the caliper out of the way with a wire hanger **(see illustration 2.3)**. **Warning:** *Don't allow the caliper to hang by the brake hose!*

24   Inspect and clean the caliper as described in Step 7, then lubricate the caliper and adapter mating surfaces as described in Step 8.

25   Push the caliper piston back into the bore to make room for the new pads (see Step 11).

26   Install the inner brake pad by pressing the retainer into the piston recess. **Caution:** *Don't get any grease on the pad lining material, gasket surface or brake disc.*

27   Place the outer pad in the adapter.

28   Install the caliper over the brake disc and adapter. ·

29   Install the guide pins by hand don't cross-thread them. Tighten the guide pins to the torque listed in this Chapter's Specifications.

30   Install the pad retainer.

31   Install the wheel. Tighten the lug nuts to the torque listed in the Chapter 1 Specifications.

32   Repeat the procedure for the remaining caliper.

33   Pump the brake pedal several times to bring the pads into contact with the disc. Check the brake fluid level (see Chapter 1). Drive the vehicle and make several stops to wear off any foreign material on the pads and seat them on the disc.

Kelsey-Hayes caliper

Refer to illustrations 2.34, 2.36 and 2.38

34   Remove the caliper guide pin and pry the bottom of the caliper away from the adapter, then remove it completely **(see illustration)**.

35   Support the caliper out of the way with a wire hanger **(see illustration 2.3)**. **Warning:** *Don't allow the caliper to hang by the brake hose!*

36   Disengage the anti-rattle clip and detach the outer brake pad from the adapter **(see illustration)**.

37   Remove the brake disc from the hub.

38   Disengage the anti-rattle clip and remove the inner brake pad **(see illustration)**.

39   Inspect the caliper and adapter for wear, damage, rust and evidence of fluid leaks. If the caliper-to-adapter mating surfaces are rusty, clean them thoroughly with a wire brush (the caliper must be free to move as the brakes are applied).

40   Push the caliper piston back into the bore to make room for the new pads (see Step 11).

41   Apply a thin film of Mopar Lubricant (no. 2932524) or high-temperature brake grease to the adapter-to-brake pad and caliper mating surfaces. Remove the protective paper from the noise suppression gasket on both pads.

42   Install the inner brake pad, making sure the anti-rattle spring is secure. **Caution:** *Don't get any grease on the pad lining material, gasket sur-*

2.36   After the caliper is detached, remove the outer brake pad and anti-rattle clip (Kelsey-Hayes caliper)

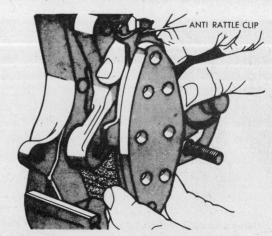

2.38   Note how the anti-rattle clips are positioned and remove the inner pad (Kelsey-Hayes caliper)

3.3   The brake pads on this vehicle were obviously neglected, as they wore down completely and cut deep grooves into the disc – wear this severe will require replacement of the disc

3.4a   Check the disc runout with a dial indicator (make sure the lug nuts are in place and tightened evenly)

face or brake disc.

43   Install the brake disc (see Section 3).

44   Place the outer pad in position in the adapter.

45   Slide the caliper into position over the pad and disc assembly.

46   Install the guide pin and tighten it to the torque listed in this Chapter's Specifications. Don't cross-thread the guide pin as it's installed.

47   Repeat the procedure for the remaining caliper.

48   Install the wheel. Tighten the lug nuts to the torque listed in the Chapter 1 Specifications.

49   Pump the brake pedal several times to bring the pads into contact with the disc. Check the brake fluid level (see Chapter 1). Drive the vehicle and make several stops to wear off any foreign material on the pads and seat them on the disc.

3   Brake disc – inspection, removal and installation

1   Loosen the wheel lug nuts, raise the vehicle and support it securely on jackstands. Remove the wheel and reinstall the lug nuts to hold the disc in place.

2   Remove the brake caliper as outlined in Section 2 (it's part of the brake pad replacement procedure). It's not necessary to disconnect the brake hose. After removing the caliper guide pin(s), suspend the caliper out of the way with a piece of wire. Don't let the caliper hang by the hose and don't stretch or twist the hose.

Inspection

Refer to illustrations 3.3, 3.4a, 3.4b, 3.5a and 3.5b

3   Visually inspect the disc surface for scoring and other damage. Light scratches and shallow grooves are normal after use and may not affect brake operation, but deep score marks – over 0.015-inch (0.38 mm) – require disc removal and refinishing by an automotive machine shop. Be sure to check both sides of the disc **(see illustration)**. If pulsating has been noticed during application of the brakes, suspect disc runout.

4   To check disc runout, mount a dial indicator with the stem resting about 1/2-inch from the outer edge of the disc **(see illustration)**. Set the indicator to zero and turn the disc. The indicator reading should not exceed the maximum allowable runout listed in this Chapter's Specifications. If it does, the disc should be refinished by an automotive machine shop. **Note:** *Professionals recommend resurfacing of brake discs regardless of the dial indicator reading (to produce a smooth, flat surface that will eliminate brake pedal pulsations and other undesirable symptoms related to questionable discs). At the very least, if you elect not to have the discs resurfaced, deglaze them with sandpaper or emery cloth (use a swirling motion to ensure a non-directional finish)* **(see illustration)**.

5   The disc must not be machined to a thickness less than the minimum listed in this Chapter's Specifications. The minimum wear (or discard) thickness is also cast into the inside of the disc **(see illustration)**. The disc thickness can be checked with a micrometer **(see illustration)**.

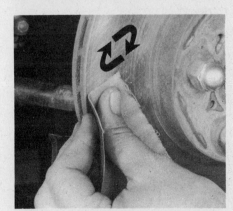

3.4b   Using a swirling motion, remove the glaze from the disc surface with sandpaper or emery cloth

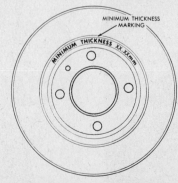

3.5a   The disc can be resurfaced by an automotive machine shop, providing the machining operation doesn't result in a disc thickness less than the minimum stamped on it

3.5b   Measure the disc thickness with a micrometer at several points around its circumference (1-inch from the outer edge)

9

4.6   With the caliper padded to catch the piston, use compressed air to force the piston out of the bore – make sure your hands or fingers aren't between the piston and caliper frame

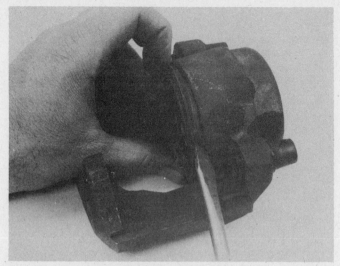

4.7   Use a screwdriver to pry the dust boot out of the caliper bore

Removal

6   Remove the lug nuts which were put on to hold the disc in place and slide the disc off the threaded studs.

Installation

7   Place the disc in position over the threaded studs.

8   Install the caliper and brake pads (see Section 2). Tighten the caliper guide pin(s) to the torque listed in this Chapter's Specifications.

9   Install the wheel and lug nuts, then lower the vehicle to the ground. Tighten the lug nuts to the torque listed in the Chapter 1 Specifications.

10   Depress the brake pedal a few times to bring the brake pads into contact with the disc. Bleeding of the system isn't necessary unless the brake hose was disconnected from the caliper. Check the operation of the brakes carefully before driving the vehicle in traffic.

---

4   Disc brake caliper – removal, overhaul and installation

Warning: *Dust created by the brake system may contain asbestos, which is harmful to your health. Never blow it out with compressed air and don't*
inhale any of it. An approved filtering mask should be worn when working on the brakes. Do not, under any circumstances, use petroleum-based solvents to clean brake parts. Use brake cleaner or clean brake fluid only!

Note: *If an overhaul is indicated (usually because of fluid leakage) explore all options before beginning the job. New and factory rebuilt calipers are available on an exchange basis, which makes this job quite easy. If it's decided to rebuild the calipers, make sure a rebuild kit is available before proceeding. Always rebuild the calipers in pairs – never rebuild just one of them.*

Removal

1   Loosen the wheel lug nuts, raise the front of the vehicle and support it securely on jackstands. Remove the front wheels.

2   **Note:** *Don't remove the brake hose from the caliper if you're only removing the caliper to gain access to other components.* Remove the brake hose inlet fitting bolt and detach the hose **(see illustration 2.2)**. Have a rag handy to catch spilled fluid and wrap a plastic bag tightly around the end of the hose to prevent fluid loss and contamination.

3   Remove the caliper guide pin(s) and detach the caliper from the vehicle (refer to Section 2 if necessary).

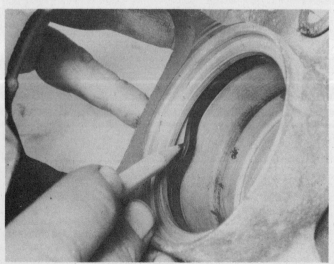

4.8   The piston seal should be removed with a wood or plastic tool to avoid damage to the bore and seal groove – a pencil will do the job

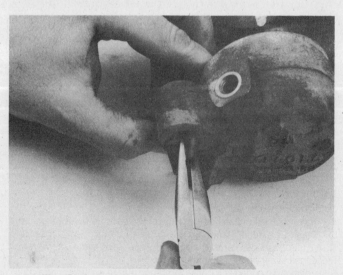

4.9a   Grab the ends of the mounting pin bushings with needle-nose pliers and push them through the caliper ears with a twisting motion

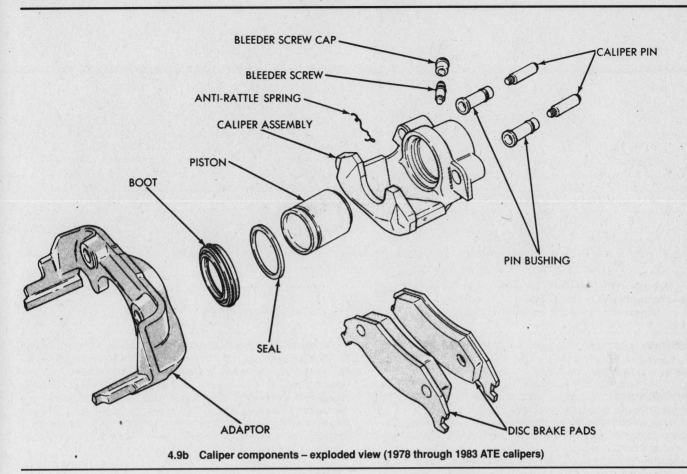

4.9b   Caliper components – exploded view (1978 through 1983 ATE calipers)

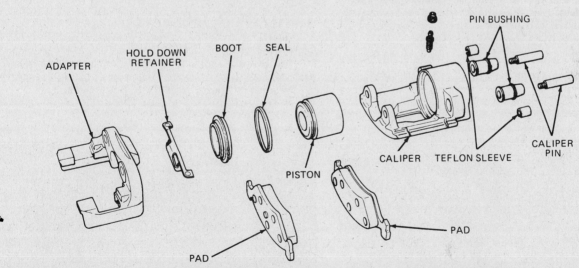

4.9c   Caliper components – exploded view (1984 and later ATE calipers)

9

Overhaul

Refer to illustrations 4.6, 4.7, 4.8, 4.9a, 4.9b, 4.9c, 4.9d, 4.14 and 4.15

4   Refer to Section 2 and remove the brake pads from the caliper.

5   Clean the exterior of the caliper with brake cleaner or new brake fluid. Never use gasoline, kerosene or petroleum-based cleaning solvents. Place the caliper on a clean workbench.

6   Position a wooden block or several shop rags in the caliper as a cushion, then use compressed air to remove the piston from the caliper **(see illustration)**. Use only enough air pressure to ease the piston out of the bore. If the piston is blown out, even with the cushion in place, it may be

damaged. **Warning:** *Never place your fingers in front of the piston in an attempt to catch or protect it when applying compressed air – serious injury could result!*

7   Carefully pry the dust boot out of the caliper bore **(see illustration)**.

8   Using a wood or plastic tool, remove the piston seal from the groove in the caliper bore **(see illustration)**. Metal tools may damage the bore.

9   Remove the caliper bleeder screw, then remove and discard the caliper (guide) pin bushings from the caliper ears. Discard all rubber parts **(see illustrations)**.

10   Clean the remaining parts with brake system cleaner or new brake

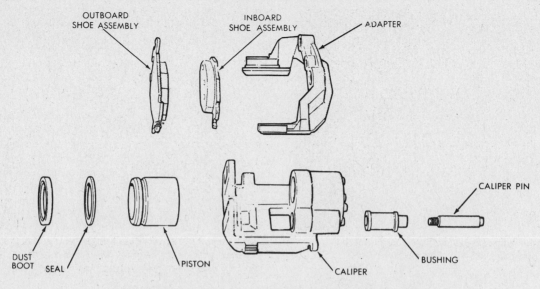

4.9d   Caliper components – exploded view (Kelsey-Hayes caliper)

fluid then blow them dry with compressed air.

11   Carefully examine the piston for nicks, burrs and excessive wear. If surface defects are present, the parts must be replaced.

12   Check the caliper bore in a similar way. Light polishing with crocus cloth is permissible to remove light corrosion and stains, but rust or pitting will require caliper replacement.

13   When reassembling the caliper, lubricate the bore and seal with clean brake fluid. Position the seal in the caliper bore groove – make sure it isn't twisted.

14   Lubricate the piston with clean brake fluid, install it squarely in the bore and apply pressure to bottom it in the caliper **(see illustration)**.

15   Stretch the dust boot over the groove in the piston, then carefully seat it in the caliper bore **(see illustration)**.

16   Install the bleeder screw.

17   Install new caliper pin bushings.

Installation

18   Inspect the caliper pins for excessive corrosion. Replace them if necessary.

19   Clean the caliper and adapter contact surfaces with a wire brush, then apply a thin film of high-temperature brake grease to them.

20   Install the brake pads and caliper as described in Section 2.

21   Install the brake hose and inlet fitting bolt, using new copper washers, then tighten the bolt to the torque listed in this Chapter's Specifications.

22   If the line was disconnected, be sure to bleed the brakes (see Section 11).

23   Install the wheels and lower the vehicle. Tighten the lug nuts to the torque listed in the Chapter 1 Specifications.

24   After the job has been completed, firmly depress the brake pedal a few times to bring the pads into contact with the disc.

25   Check brake operation before driving the vehicle in traffic.

5   Rear brake shoes (1978 through 1982) – adjustment

Refer to illustrations 5.3 and 5.5

1   The rear drum brakes on these models should be periodically adjusted to compensate for wear of the brake shoes.

2   Raise the vehicle and support it securely on jackstands.

3   Remove the rubber plug from the adjustment hole in the backing plate **(see illustration)**.

4   Release the parking brake and, if necessary, back off the cable adjustment so the cable is slack.

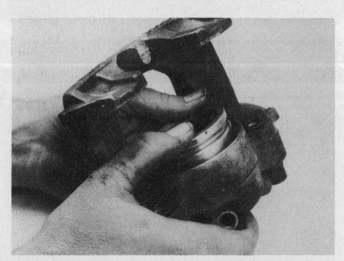

4.14   When installing the piston, make sure it doesn't become cocked in the caliper bore when pushing it down

4.15   If the correct seal driver tool isn't available, a drift punch can be used to tap around the edge until the dust boot is seated

5.3   Pry the rubber adjusting hole plug out of the backing plate with a screwdriver

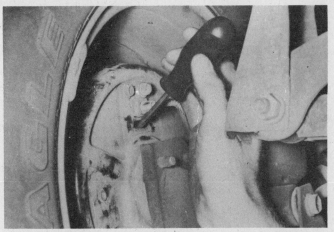

5.5   Insert the screwdriver into the hole and turn the star wheel until the brake shoes drag as the wheel is turned, then back off the star wheel until the wheel turns freely

5   Insert a narrow screwdriver through the hole in the backing plate and turn the star wheel until the brake drags slightly as the tire is turned **(see illustration)**.

6   Back off the star wheel until the tire turns freely.

7   Repeat the adjustment on the opposite wheel.

8   Install the plugs in the backing plate holes.

9   Adjust the parking brake (see Section 12).

10   Lower the vehicle and check the brake operation very carefully before driving the vehicle in traffic.

6   Rear brake shoes (1978 through 1982) – replacement

Refer to illustrations 6.4a, 6.4b, 6.5, 6.6 ,6.7a, 6.7b, 6.8, 6.9, 6.11, 6.12 and 6.14

Warning: *Drum brake shoes must be replaced on both rear wheels at the same time – never replace the shoes on only one wheel. Also, the dust created by the brake system may contain asbestos, which is harmful to your health. Never blow it out with compressed air and don't inhale any of it. An approved filtering mask should be worn when working on the brakes.*

Do not, under any circumstances, use petroleum-based solvents to clean brake parts. Use brake system cleaner or clean brake fluid only!

Caution: *Whenever the brake shoes are replaced, the return and hold-down springs should also be replaced. Due to the continuous heating/ cooling cycle the springs are subjected to, they lose tension over a period of time and may allow the shoes to drag on the drum and wear at a much faster rate than normal. When servicing the drum brakes, use only high-quality, nationally-recognized, name-brand parts. Disassemble one brake at a time so the remaining brake can be used as a guide if difficulties are encountered during reassembly.*

1   Loosen the rear wheel lug nuts. Raise the rear of the vehicle, support it securely on jackstands and block the front wheels. Remove the rear wheels.

2   Remove the hub/brake drum assembly (see Section 32 in Chapter 1).

3   Use brake system cleaner to remove dust and brake fluid from the shoe assembly components.

4   Disconnect the parking brake cable from the lever **(see illustrations)**.

5   Remove the two brake shoe-to-anchor springs **(see illustration)**.

6   Remove the shoe hold-down springs by depressing them and sliding them off the pins **(see illustration)**.

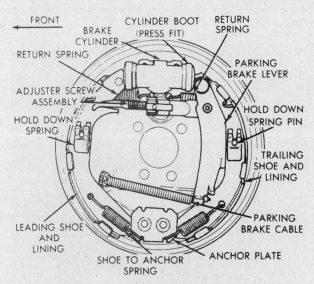

6.4a   Rear drum brake component layout – left side (1978 through 1983 models)

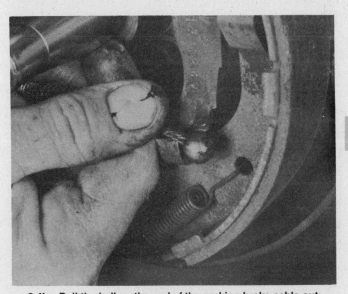

6.4b   Pull the ball on the end of the parking brake cable out of the lever to disengage it (1978 through 1983 models)

7   Back off the adjuster screw assembly and remove it **(see illustrations)**.

8   Rotate the trailing (rear) shoe forward and remove it, followed by the front (leading) shoe **(see illustration)**.

9   Check the drum for cracks, score marks and signs of overheating (which will appear as small discolored areas). If the discoloration can't be removed with fine emery cloth or sandpaper, the drum must be taken to an automotive machine shop to have it resurfaced. **Note:** *Professionals rec–*

ommend resurfacing the drums each time a brake job is done. Resurfacing will eliminate the possibility of out-of-round drums. If the drums are worn so much they can't be resurfaced without exceeding the maximum allowable diameter (cast into the drum) **(see illustration)**, *then new ones will be required. At the very least, if you elect not to have the drums resurfaced, remove the glazing from the surface with emery cloth or sandpaper (using a swirling motion).*

10   Check the adjuster screw assembly and threads for bent, corroded

6.5   Using a pair of pliers, stretch the lower ends of the shoe-to-anchor springs down to disconnect them (1978 through 1983 models)

6.6   Compress the hold-down springs and slide them off the pins (1978 through 1983 models)

6.7a   Hold the adjuster clip out of the way with a small pair of pliers, back the star wheel off, . . .

6.7b   . . . then disengage the adjuster clevis from the front shoe (1978 through 1983 models)

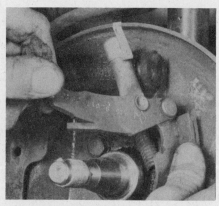

6.8   Rotate the rear shoe and parking brake lever assembly forward to remove it from the backing plate (1978 through 1983 models)

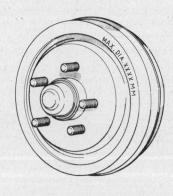

6.9   The maximum allowable diameter is cast into the brake drum

6.11   Carefully peel the wheel cylinder boots back to check for brake fluid leakage

6.12   Lubricate all of the shoe pivot and backing plate contact points with high-temperature grease

6.14   Rotate the rear shoe and parking brake lever assembly into position in the wheel cylinder piston

and damaged components. Replace the assembly if the screw threads are damaged or rusted. Clean the threads and lubricate them with white lithium-based grease.

11 Check the wheel cylinder boots for damage and signs of leakage **(see illustration)**. Rebuild or replace the wheel cylinder if necessary.

12 Lubricate the brake shoe contact points on the backing plate with high-temperature grease **(see illustration)**.

13 Insert the return spring into the backing plate and install the leading shoe. Be sure to seat the ends securely in the wheel cylinder piston and anchor plate.

14 Install the trailing shoe return spring, then rotate the shoe and parking brake lever assembly to the rear, into position **(see illustration)**. Seat the shoe ends in the anchor plate and wheel cylinder.

15 Insert the adjuster screw assembly into the shoe notch (make sure the forward facing clevis of the screw is pointed down). Turn the adjuster star wheel until the screw is secure in the support.

16 Lightly lubricate the hold-down springs with high-temperature grease and install them.

17 Install the shoe-to-anchor springs.

18 Pull the parking brake cable spring back to expose the cable and attach the cable end to to the lever.

19 Install the hub/drum assembly and adjust the wheel bearings (see Chapter 1). Install the wheel, tightening the lug nuts to the torque listed in the Chapter 1 Specifications.

20 Repeat the procedure for the other wheel.

21 Adjust the brakes (see Section 5).

22 Adjust the parking brake (see Section 12).

23 Lower the vehicle and check the brake operation very carefully before driving the vehicle in traffic.

---

7   Rear brake shoes (1983 on) – replacement

Refer to illustrations 7.4a, 7.4b, 7.4c, 7.5, 7.6, 7.7, 7.8a, 7.8b, 7.9a, 7.9b, 7.10, 7.11, 7.16a, 7.16b and 7.17

Warning: *Drum brake shoes must be replaced on both rear wheels at the same time – never replace the shoes on only one wheel. Also, the dust created by the brake system may contain asbestos, which is harmful to your health. Never blow it out with compressed air and don't inhale any of it. An approved filtering mask should be worn when working on the brakes. Do not, under any circumstances, use petroleum-based solvents to clean brake parts. Use brake system cleaner or clean brake fluid only!*

Caution: *Whenever the brake shoes are replaced, the return and hold-down springs should also be replaced. Due to the continuous heating/cooling cycle the springs are subjected to, they lose tension over a period of time and may allow the shoes to drag on the drum and wear at a much faster rate than normal. When servicing the drum brakes, use only high-quality, nationally-recognized, name-brand parts. Disassemble one brake*

at a time so the remaining brake can be used as a guide if difficulties are encountered during reassembly.

1   Loosen the wheel lug nuts. Raise the rear of the vehicle, support it securely on jackstands and block the front wheels. Remove the rear wheels.

2   Remove the hub/brake drum assembly (see Chapter 1, Section 32).

3   Use brake system cleaner to remove dust and brake fluid from the shoe assembly components.

4   Remove the adjuster lever spring and adjuster lever **(see illustrations)**.

5   Back off the adjuster screw star wheel **(see illustration)**.

6   Disconnect the parking brake cable from the parking brake lever with a pair of pliers **(see illustration)**.

7   Remove the hold-down springs by depressing them with a pair of pliers or a special tool and turning the retainer until the slot aligns with the flattened end of the pin, allowing removal **(see illustration)**.

8   Disengage the brake shoe assembly from the wheel cylinder at the top and the anchor plate at the bottom and remove it from the backing plate **(see illustrations)**.

9   Remove the springs **(see illustrations)**.

10   Separate the shoes from the adjuster **(see illustration)**.

11   Remove the parking brake lever retaining clip with a small screwdriver and transfer the lever to the new shoe **(see illustration)**.

12   Check the drum for cracks, score marks and signs of overheating (which will appear as small discolored areas). If the discoloration can't be removed with fine emery cloth or sandpaper, the drum must be taken to an automotive machine shop to have it resurfaced. **Note:** *Professionals rec-*

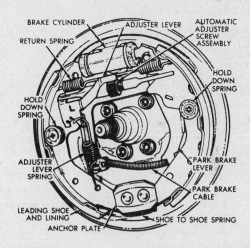

7.4a   Rear drum brake component layout – left side (1983 on)

7.4b   Detach the adjuster lever spring, . . .

7.4c . . . then unhook the lever from the adjuster screw clevis (1983 on)

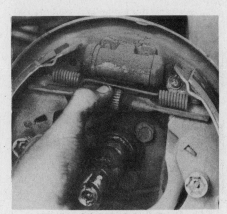

7.5   Back the adjuster screw star wheel off (1983 on)

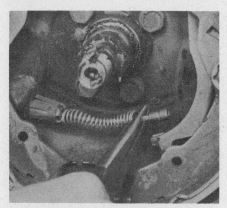

7.6   Detach the cable from the parking brake lever with needle-nose pliers (1983 on)

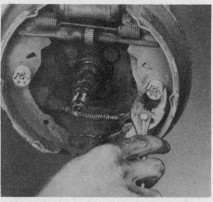

7.7   Use a pair of pliers or a brake tool to compress the hold-down springs and turn the retainer until the flattened end of the pin lines up with the slot in the retainer, releasing the spring (1983 on)

7.8a   Pull the ends of the brake shoes out of the slots in the wheel cylinders, . . .

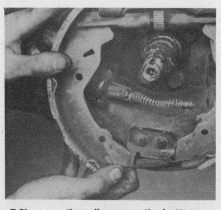

7.8b   . . . then disengage the bottoms of the shoes from the anchor plate (1983 on)

7.9a   Unhook the lower spring by hand . . .

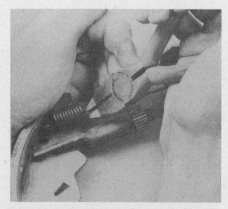

7.9b   . . . and use pliers to disengage the upper spring from the shoes (1983 on)

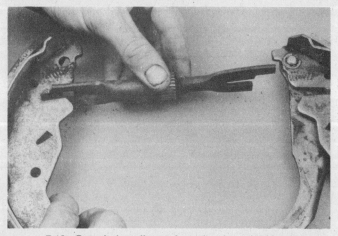

7.10   Detach the adjuster from the shoes (1983 on)

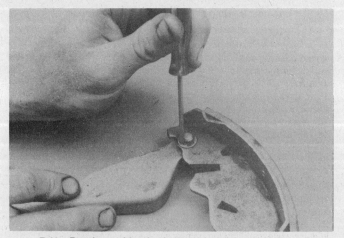

7.11   Pry the parking brake lever retaining clip off the post with a small screwdriver (1983 on)

ommend resurfacing the drums each time a brake job is done. Resurfacing will eliminate the possibility of out-of-round drums. If the drums are worn so much they can't be resurfaced without exceeding the maximum allowable diameter (cast into the drum) **(see illustration 6.9)**, then new ones will be required. At the very least, if you elect not to have the drums resurfaced, remove the glazing from the surface with emery cloth or sandpaper (using a swirling motion).

13   Check the adjuster screw assembly and threads for bent, corroded and damaged components. Replace the assembly if the screw threads are damaged or rusted. Clean the threads and lubricate them with white

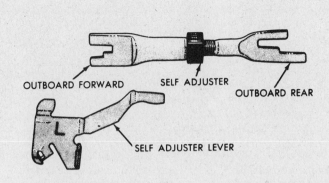

7.16a When connecting the adjuster to the brake shoes, make sure it's situated as shown

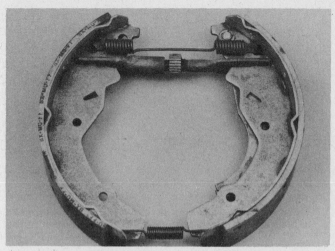

7.16b Assemble the shoes, adjuster and springs prior to installing them on the backing plate

7.17 Use needle-nose pliers to retract the spring and hold the cable, then insert the cable end into the lever

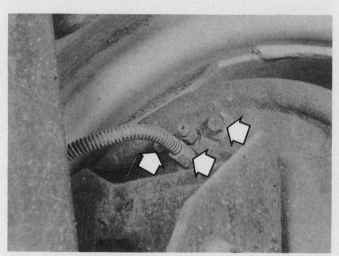

8.4 Completely loosen the brake line fitting, then remove the two wheel cylinder mounting bolts (arrows)

lithium-based grease.

14 Check the wheel cylinder boots for damage and signs of leakage **(see illustration 6.11)**. Rebuild or replace the wheel cylinder if necessary.

15 Lubricate the contact points with high-temperature grease **(see illustration 6.12)**.

16 Assemble the shoes over the adjuster and connect the springs **(see illustrations)**.

17 Place the assembly in position on the backing plate and insert the parking brake cable into the parking brake lever **(see illustration)**

18 Spread the lower ends of the shoes apart enough to allow them to be seated in the anchor plate.

19 Spread the tops of the shoes and seat them in the wheel cylinder pistons.

20 Insert the pins through the backing plate from the rear and hold them in place while installing the hold-down springs and retainers.

21 Install the adjuster lever and connect the spring to it.

22 Turn the adjuster until the shoes are retracted enough to allow the drum to be reinstalled.

23 Install hub/drum assembly (see Chapter 1). Install the wheel and tighten the lug nuts to the torque listed in the Chapter 1 Specifications.

24 Repeat the procedure for the other wheel.

25 Adjust the parking brake (see Section 12).

26 Lower the vehicle and check the brake operation very carefully before driving the vehicle in traffic.

8 Wheel cylinder – removal, overhaul and installation

Note: If an overhaul is indicated (usually because of fluid leakage or binding of the pistons) explore all options before beginning the job. New wheel cylinders are available, which makes this job quite easy. If it's decided to rebuild the wheel cylinder, make sure a rebuild kit is available before proceeding. Never overhaul only one wheel cylinder – always rebuild both of them at the same time.

Removal

Refer to illustration 8.4

1 Loosen the rear wheel lug nuts. Raise the rear of the vehicle and support it securely on jackstands. Block the front wheels to keep the vehicle from rolling. Remove the rear wheels.

2 Remove the brake shoe assembly (see Section 6 or 7).

3 Remove all dirt and foreign material from around the wheel cylinder.

4 Unscrew the brake line fitting **(see illustration)**. Use a flare-nut wrench if possible. Don't pull the brake line away from the wheel cylinder.

5 Remove the wheel cylinder mounting bolts.

6 Detach the wheel cylinder from the brake backing plate and immediately plug the brake line to prevent fluid loss and contamination. **Note:** *If the brake shoe linings are contaminated with brake fluid, install new brake shoes.*

9

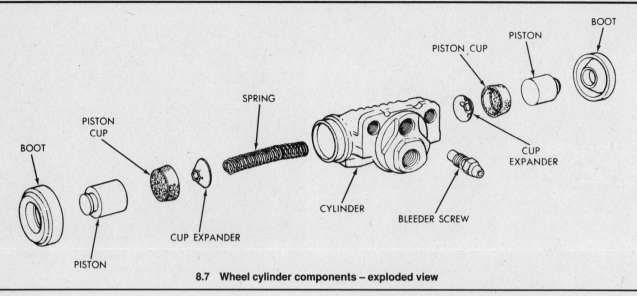

8.7   Wheel cylinder components – exploded view

Overhaul

Refer to illustration 8.7

7   Remove the bleeder screw, boots, pistons, cups, expanders and spring from the wheel cylinder body **(see illustration)**.
8   Clean the wheel cylinder with brake fluid, denatured alcohol or brake system cleaner. **Warning:** *Do not, under any circumstances, use petroleum-based solvents to clean brake parts!*
9   Use compressed air to remove excess fluid from the wheel cylinder and blow out the passages.
10   Check the bore for corrosion and score marks. Crocus cloth can be used to remove light corrosion and stains, but the cylinder must be replaced with a new one if the defects can't be removed easily, or if the bore is scored.
11   Lubricate the new cups with brake fluid.
12   Assemble the wheel cylinder components. Make sure the cup lips face in.

Installation

13   Place the wheel cylinder in position and install the bolts.
14   Connect the brake line and tighten the fitting.
15   Install the brake shoe assembly.
16   Bleed the brakes (see Section 11).
17   Check brake operation before driving the vehicle in traffic.

9   Master cylinder – removal, overhaul and installation

Removal

Refer to illustration 9.4

1   The master cylinder is located in the engine compartment, mounted on the power brake booster or firewall.
2   Remove as much fluid as possible from the reservoir with a syringe.
3   Place rags under the fittings and prepare caps or plastic bags to cover the ends of the lines once they're disconnected. **Caution:** *Brake fluid will damage paint. Cover all body parts and be careful not to spill fluid during this procedure.*
4   Loosen the fittings at the ends of the brake lines where they enter the master cylinder **(see illustration)**. To prevent rounding off the corners on the fittings, use a flare nut wrench.
5   Pull the brake lines slightly away from the master cylinder and plug the ends to prevent contamination.
6   On models without power brakes, disconnect the master cylinder pushrod at the brake pedal.
7   Detach the electrical connector from the master cylinder, then remove the nuts attaching the master cylinder to the power booster or fire-

wall. Pull the master cylinder off the studs and out of the engine compartment. Again, be careful not to spill the fluid as this is done.

Overhaul

Refer to illustrations 9.10, 9.11, 9.12a and 9.12b

8   Before attempting to overhaul the master cylinder, obtain the proper rebuild kit. It will contain the necessary replacement parts and all instructions specific to the vehicle.
9   Place the master cylinder in a vise, with the jaws of the vise clamping the mounting flange. Remove the reservoir, using a side-to-side rocking motion.
10   Depress the pistons with a punch or Phillips screwdriver until they bottom against the end of the master cylinder, then pull out the secondary piston retainer pin with a pair of needle-nose pliers **(see illustration)**.
11   With the pistons still depressed, remove the snap-ring from the end of the master cylinder **(see illustration)**.
12   The internal components can now be removed from the master cylinder bore **(see illustrations)**. Note the installed order of the components so they can be reinserted in the same order. **Note:** *The two springs are different – pay particular attention to their installed order. Also, note very carefully the way the cup lips face.*
13   Carefully inspect the bore of the master cylinder. Any scoring or other damage will mean a new master cylinder is required. **Warning:** *DO NOT attempt to hone the cylinder bore.*

9.4   If possible, use a flare-nut wrench to unscrew the brake line fitting – if one isn't available, use an open-end wrench (but be careful not to round off the fitting hex)

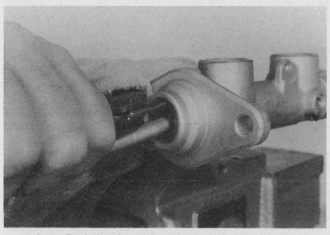

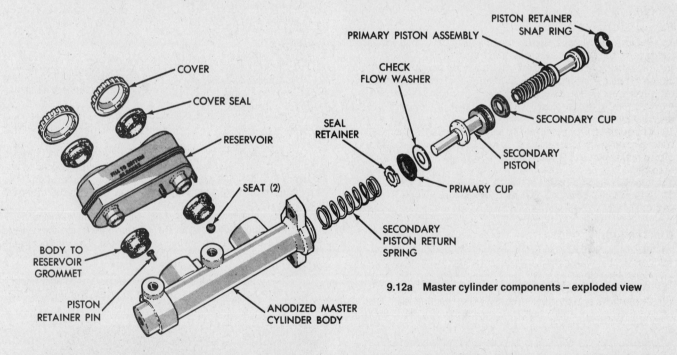

9.10 Depress the pistons in the bore and pull out the secondary piston retainer pin

9.11 Push the pistons in and use snap-ring pliers to remove the snap-ring

9.12a Master cylinder components – exploded view

14   Install all parts included in the rebuild kit, following the instructions with the kit. Clean all reused parts with brake cleaner or new brake fluid. **Warning:** *Do not use petroleum-based solvents to clean brake parts! During reassembly, lubricate all parts liberally with clean brake fluid. Use only your fingers when installing the new piston cups on the pistons and make sure the lips on the cups face in the proper direction.*

15   Lubricate the cylinder bore with clean brake fluid, then push the assembled components into the bore, bottoming them against the end of the master cylinder. Install the secondary piston stop pin.

16   On models without power brakes, lubricate the end of the master cylinder pushrod with multi-purpose grease and insert it in the end of the piston.

17   Install the snap-ring – make sure it's seated properly in the groove.

18   Install the new reservoir grommets, then push the reservoir onto the cylinder until it's completely seated.

19   Before installing the master cylinder, it should be bench bled. Since it's necessary to apply pressure to the master cylinder piston and at the same time control flow from the brake line outlets, the master cylinder

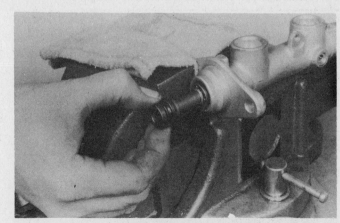

9.12b Remove the primary piston assembly from the master cylinder bore

9

should be mounted in a vise, with the jaws of the vise clamping on the mounting flange.

20   Insert threaded plugs into the brake line outlet holes and snug them down so no air can leak past them, but not so tight that they cannot be easily loosened.

21   Fill the reservoir with brake fluid of the recommended type (see Chapter 1).

22   Remove one plug and push the piston assembly into the master cylinder to expel the air from the bore. A large Phillips screwdriver can be used to push on the piston assembly.

23   To prevent air from being drawn back into the master cylinder, the plug must be replaced and snugged down before releasing the pressure on the piston.

24   Repeat the procedure until only brake fluid is expelled from the brake line outlet hole. When only brake fluid is expelled, repeat the procedure at the other outlet hole and plug. Be sure to keep the master cylinder reservoir filled with brake fluid to prevent the introduction of air into the bore.

25   Since high pressure isn't involved in the bench bleeding procedure, an alternative to the removal and replacement of the plugs with each stroke of the piston assembly is available. Before pushing in on the piston assembly, remove the plug as described in Step 22. Before releasing the piston, however, instead of replacing the plug, simply put your finger tightly over the hole to keep air from being drawn back into the master cylinder. Wait several seconds for brake fluid to be drawn from the reservoir into the piston bore, then depress the piston again, removing your finger as brake fluid is expelled. Be sure to put your finger back over the hole each time before releasing the piston. When the bleeding procedure is complete, replace the plug and tighten it before going on to the other port.

Installation

26   Install the master cylinder over the studs and tighten the nuts only finger tight at this time.

27   Thread the brake line fittings into the master cylinder. Since the master cylinder is still a bit loose, it can be moved slightly for the fittings to thread in easily. Don't strip the threads as the fittings are tightened.

28   Tighten the mounting nuts and the brake line fittings.

29   Fill the master cylinder reservoir with fluid, then bleed the master cylinder (only if it hasn't been bench bled) and the brake system as described in Section 11.

30   To bleed the master cylinder on the vehicle, have an assistant pump the brake pedal several times and hold it down. Loosen the fitting nut to allow air and fluid to escape. Repeat this procedure on both fittings until the fluid is free of air bubbles. Test the operation of the brake system carefully before driving the vehicle in traffic.

---

10   Brake hoses and lines – inspection and replacement

1   About every six months, the flexible hoses which connect the steel brake lines with the rear brakes and the front calipers should be inspected for cracks, chafing of the outer cover, leaks, blisters and other damage.

2   Replacement steel and flexible brake lines are commonly available from dealer parts departments and auto parts stores. Do not, under any circumstances, use anything other than steel lines or approved flexible brake hoses as replacement items.

3   When installing the brake line, leave at least 3/4-inch between the line and any moving or vibrating parts.

4   When disconnecting a hose and a line, hold the hose end with an open-end wrench and loosen the fitting with a flare-nut wrench. Once the fitting has been loosened, the spring clip can be removed.

5   When connecting two hoses, use open-end wrenches on the hose ends. When connecting two hoses, make sure they're not bent, twisted or strained in any way.

6   Steel brake lines are usually retained at several points with clips. Always remove the clips before detaching a steel brake line. Always reinstall the clips (or new ones if the old ones are damaged) when replacing a brake

line – they provide support and keep the lines from vibrating, which can eventually break them.

7   After installing a line or hose, bleed the brakes (see Section 11).

---

11   Brake hydraulic system – bleeding

Refer to illustration 11.8

Warning: *Wear eye protection when bleeding the brake system. If the fluid comes in contact with your eyes, immediately rinse them with water and seek medical attention.*

Note: *Bleeding the hydraulic system is necessary to remove air that manages to find its way into the system when it's been opened during removal and installation of a hose, line, caliper or master cylinder.*

1   It'll probably be necessary to bleed the system at all four brakes if air has entered the system due to low fluid level, or if the brake lines have been disconnected at the master cylinder.

2   If a brake line was disconnected only at a wheel, then only that caliper or wheel cylinder must be bled.

3   If a brake line is disconnected at a fitting located between the master cylinder and any of the brakes, that part of the system served by the disconnected line must be bled.

4   Remove any residual vacuum from the brake power booster by applying the brake several times with the engine off.

5   Remove the master cylinder reservoir cover and fill the reservoir with brake fluid. Reinstall the cover. **Note:** *Check the fluid level often during the bleeding operation and add fluid as necessary to prevent the fluid level from falling low enough to allow air into the master cylinder.*

6   Have an assistant on hand, as well as a supply of new brake fluid, a clear plastic container partially filled with clean brake fluid, a length of tubing (preferably clear) to fit over the bleeder screw and a wrench to open and close the bleeder screw.

7   Beginning at the right rear wheel, loosen the bleeder screw slightly, then tighten it to a point where it's snug but can still be loosened quickly and easily.

8   Place one end of the tubing over the bleeder screw and submerge the other end in brake fluid in the container **(see illustration)**.

9   Have your assistant pump the brakes slowly a few times to get pressure in the system, then hold the pedal down firmly.

10   While the pedal is held down, open the bleeder screw. Watch for air bubbles to exit the submerged end of the tube. When the fluid flow slows, tighten the screw and have your assistant release the pedal.

11   Repeat Steps 9 and 10 until no more air is seen leaving the tube, then tighten the bleeder screw and proceed to the left rear wheel, the right front

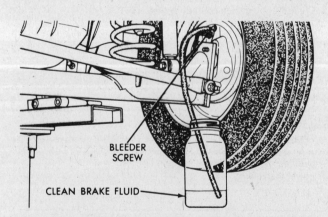

11.8   When bleeding the brakes, a tube is connected to the bleeder screw at the caliper or wheel cylinder and the other end is submerged in brake fluid – air will be seen as bubbles in the tube and container (all air must be expelled before moving to the next wheel)

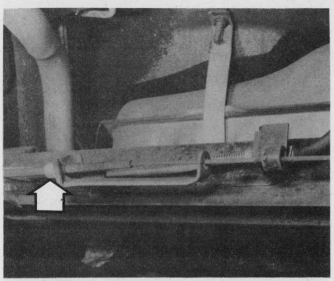

12.3 The parking brake adjuster is located on the rear axle beam – tighten the adjusting nut (arrow) until the brakes drag slightly as the tire is rotated, then back it off the amount specified in the text

wheel and the left front wheel, in that order, and perform the same procedure. Be sure to check the fluid in the master cylinder reservoir frequently.

12 Never use old brake fluid. It contains moisture which will deteriorate the brake system components and boil when the fluid gets hot.

13 Refill the master cylinder with fluid at the end of the operation.

14 Check the operation of the brakes. The pedal should feel solid when depressed, with no sponginess. If necessary, repeat the entire process. **Warning:** *Don't operate the vehicle if you're in doubt about the condition of the brake system.*

12 Parking brake – adjustment

Refer to illustration 12.3

1 The rear drum brakes must be in proper working order before adjusting the parking brake (see Sections 6 and 7).

2 Block the front wheels to prevent vehicle movement, raise the rear of the vehicle and support it securely on jackstands. Release the parking brake lever.

3 Clean the cable adjuster threads **(see illustration)** with a wire brush and lubricate them with multi-purpose grease.

4 Loosen the adjusting nut until there's slack in the cable.

5 Have an assistant rotate the rear wheels to make sure they turn easily.

6 Tighten the adjusting nut until a slight drag can be felt when the rear wheels are turned. You may have to keep the adjuster rod from turning by holding it with a wrench or pair of pliers.

7 Loosen the nut until the rear wheels turn freely, then back it off an additional two full turns.

8 Apply and release the parking brake several times to make sure it operates properly. It must lock the rear wheels when applied and the wheels must turn easily, without dragging, when it's released.

9 Lower the vehicle.

13 Parking brake cables – removal and installation

Refer to illustrations 13.2 and 13.15

Front cable

1 Raise the rear of the vehicle and support it securely on jackstands.

2 Working under the vehicle, remove the adjusting nut and detach the cable from the connectors **(see illustration)**.

3 Loosen the exhaust system heat shield for access and remove the cable housing-to-floor pan bracket and clips.

4 Working inside the vehicle, remove the parking brake lever cover and lift up the carpet for access.

5 Pull the cable forward to disconnect it from the clevis.

6 Remove the floor pan seal panel.

7 Compress the tangs on the cable housing retainer, then push the cable out of the floor pan.

8 To install the cable, insert the cable retainers into the floor pan opening, install the seal panel and feed the end through the opening and the seal, engaging it in the clevis.

9 Push the cable housing into the retainer until it seats. Install the carpet and parking brake lever cover.

10 Working under the vehicle, install the cable housing bracket and clips. Tighten the heat shield bolts. Slide the adjuster end of the cable through the connectors, install the adjusting nut and adjust the parking brake (see Section 12).

Rear cables

11 Remove the rear wheels and the hub/drum assemblies.

12 Back off the adjusting nut until the cable is slack.

13 Disconnect the rear brake cable from the connector.

14 Disconnect the cable at the parking brake lever on the brake shoe.

15 Use a screw-type hose clamp to compress the retainers so the cable can be removed from the brake backing plate **(see illustration)**. Remove the clamp when the retainer tangs have passed through the backing plate.

16 Pull the cable out of the backing plate and detach it from the rear axle.

17 To install the cable, insert the cable and the inner housing end through the suspension arm holes and the crossmember cable bracket.

18 Connect the chassis fitting to the bracket.

19 Insert the cable outer end through the hole in the backing plate and snap the retainer into place.

20 Attach the cable end to the parking brake lever on the brake shoe.

21 Install the hub/drum assemblies.

22 Attach the cable to the connector, then adjust the parking brake (Section 12).

14 Power brake booster – check, removal and installation

Operating check

1 Depress the brake pedal several times with the engine off and make sure there's no change in the pedal reserve distance.

2 Depress the pedal and start the engine. If the pedal goes down slightly, operation is normal.

Air tightness check

3 Start the engine and turn it off after one or two minutes. Slowly depress the brake pedal several times. If the pedal goes down farther the first time but gradually rises after the second or third depression, the booster is air tight.

4 Depress the brake pedal while the engine is running, then stop the engine with the pedal depressed. If there's no change in the pedal reserve travel (distance between the pedal and the floor) after holding the pedal for 30 seconds, the booster is air tight.

Removal

5 Power brake booster units should not be disassembled. They require special tools not normally found in most service stations or shops. They're fairly complex and because of their critical relationship to brake performance it's best to replace a defective booster unit with a new or rebuilt one.

6 To remove the booster, first remove the brake master cylinder as described in Section 9.

7 Working under the dash, disconnect the booster pushrod from the brake pedal.

9

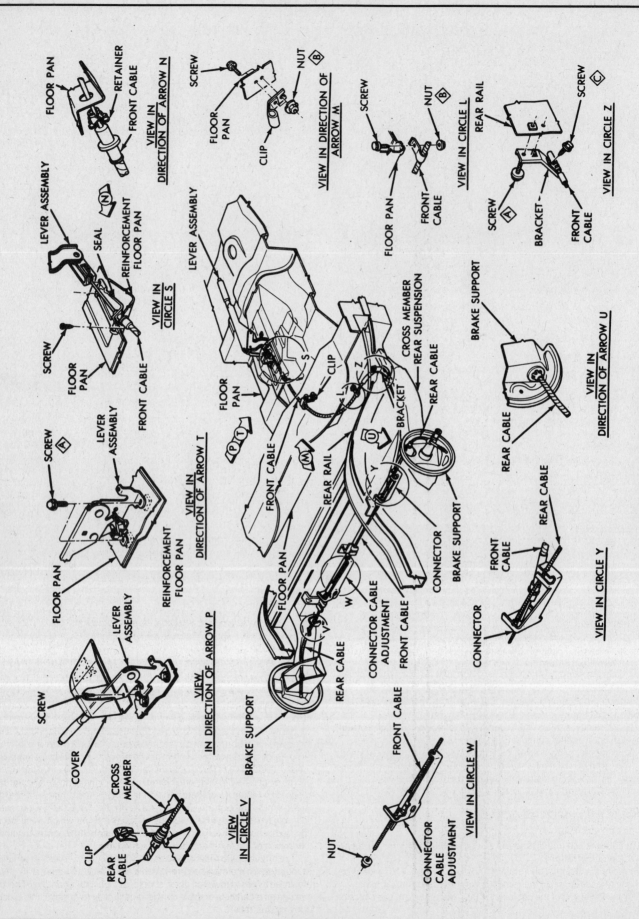

13.2   Parking brake component layout

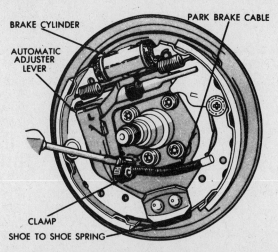

13.15   Use a small screw-type hose clamp to compress the tangs on the cable housing retainer so the cable can be removed from the backing plate

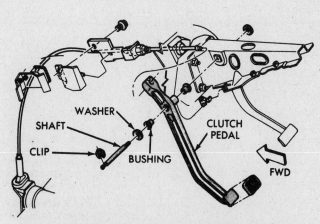

16.2   Brake and clutch pedal mounting details (models without a self adjusting clutch)

8   Disconnect the hose leading from the engine to the booster. Be careful not to damage the hose when removing it from the booster fitting.
9   Remove the nuts and washers holding the brake booster to the firewall. You may need a light to see them – they're up under the dash.
10   Slide the booster straight out until the studs clear the holes and lift it (along with any installed gaskets) out of the engine compartment.

Installation

11   Lubricate the tip of the master cylinder pushrod (booster output rod) with multi-purpose grease. The remainder of installation is the reverse of the removal procedure. Tighten the booster mounting nuts to the torque listed in this Chapter's Specifications.
12   Adjust the brake light switch as described in Section 15.

---

15   Brake light switch – adjustment

1   Loosen the screw securing the switch to the brake pedal bracket and slide the switch assembly away from the pedal.
2   Push the brake pedal down and allow it to return freely. Don't pull back on the pedal.
3   Position a 0.130-inch (3.275 mm) spacer between the pedal and the switch. Slide the switch towards the pedal until the switch plunger is completely depressed against the spacer, then tighten the screw.
4   Remove the spacer and check the operation of the brake lights.

---

16   Brake pedal – removal and installation

Refer to illustration 16.2

Non-self adjusting clutch-equipped models

1   Disconnect the clutch cable from the pedal. Remove the retaining clip and pin securing the master cylinder pushrod to the brake pedal.
2   Remove the retaining clips from the ends of the clutch and brake pedal pivot shaft **(see illustration)**.
3   Withdraw the shaft from the pedal support bracket mounted on the firewall. Remove the washers, clutch and brake pedals and bushings.
4   Inspect the shaft and bushings for wear and replace as necessary.
5   Installation is the reverse of the removal procedure. Check the clutch pedal freeplay (see Chapter 1). Also check the operation of the brake light switch (see Section 15).

Self adjusting clutch-equipped models

6   Disconnect the power brake pushrod from the brake pedal.
7   On manual transaxle equipped models, remove the lock ring from the pivot shaft and carefully withdraw the shaft. Remove the clutch pedal assembly, followed by the brake pedal.
8   On automatic transaxle equipped vehicles, remove the pivot shaft nut, withdraw the shaft and remove the brake pedal.
9   To install the pedal, place it in position and insert the pivot shaft.
10   On manual transaxle models, install the clutch pedal assembly and lock ring.
11   On automatic transaxle models, install the pivot shaft nut and tighten it securely.

9

Chapter 10
Suspension and steering systems

Contents

Specifications

General
Wheel bearing grease type .... See Chapter 1

Torque specifications   Ft-lbs (unless otherwise indicated)

Front suspension
Strut-to-steering knuckle nuts
  1978 through 1980 .... 90 plus 1/4-turn
  1981 on .... 45 plus 1/4-turn
Strut upper mounting nuts 20
Balljoint clamp bolt/nut
  1978 through 1983 50
  1984 on 70
Control arm pivot bolt
  1978 through 1985 105
  1986 on 95
Balljoint mounting bolt/nut (1978 through 1980 models) 60
Control arm stub strut nut 70
Sway bar bushing retainer nuts 25
Sway bar end-to-control arm nuts 22
Driveaxle hub nut .... See Chapter 8

Torque specifications (continued)

Ft-lbs (unless otherwise indicated)

Rear suspension

Trailing arm mounting nuts	40
Upper strut mounting nuts	20
Shock absorber mounting bolts	40 to 50
Spindle retaining bolts	
1978 through 1987	45
1988 and later	55

Steering system

Steering gear mounting bolts/nuts	21
Tie-rod end castle nut	35
Tie-rod jam nut	55
Crossmember mounting bolts	90
Steering wheel retaining nut	45
Column mounting nuts and bolts	105 in-lbs
Wheel lug nuts	See Chapter 1

1   General information

Front suspension is by MacPherson struts. Each steering knuckle is located by a control arm and both front control arms are connected by a sway bar.

The rear suspension is semi-independent with trailing arms connected by a crossmember which acts as a sway bar. The trailing arms are connected to the chassis by coil spring/shock absorber units.

The rack-and-pinion steering gear is located behind the engine and actuates the steering arms, which are integral with the steering knuckles. Power assist is optional. The steering column is designed to collapse in the event of an accident. **Note:** *These vehicles have a combination of standard and metric fasteners on the various suspension and steering components, so it would be a good idea to have both types of tools available when beginning work.*

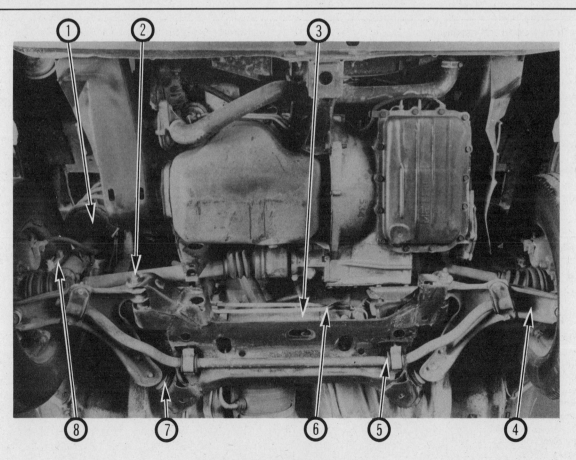

Typical front suspension components

1	Front strut/shock absorber and spring assembly	3	Crossmember	6	Steering gear
2	Control arm pivot bolt	4	Control arm	7	Control arm stub strut
		5	Sway bar	8	Steering knuckle

10

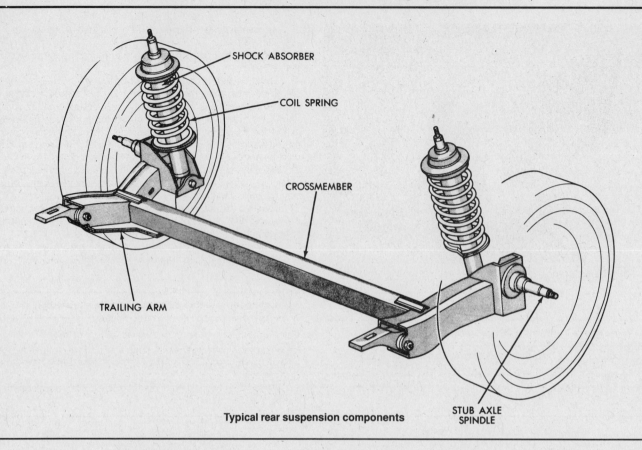

SHOCK ABSORBER

COIL SPRING

CROSSMEMBER

TRAILING ARM

STUB AXLE
SPINDLE

Typical rear suspension components

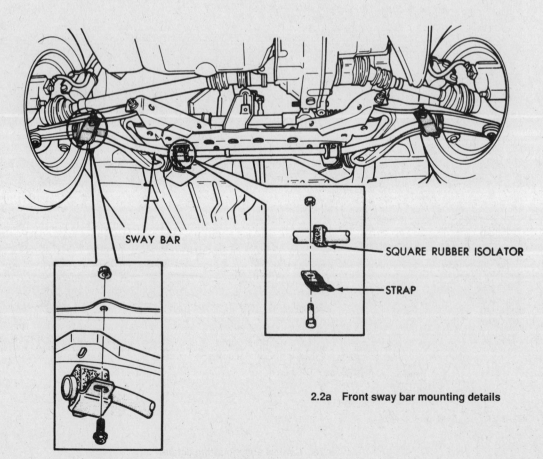

SWAY BAR

SQUARE RUBBER ISOLATOR

STRAP

2.2a   Front sway bar mounting details

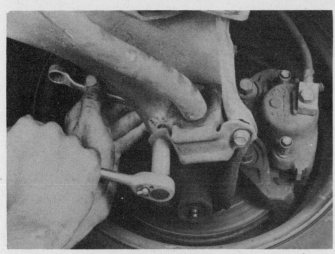

2.2b   Use a wrench to hold the nut when removing the sway bar bolts

2   Sway bar – removal and installation

Refer to illustrations 2.2a and 2.2b

1   Loosen the wheel lug nuts, raise the front of the vehicle and support it securely on jackstands. Apply the parking brake. Remove the front wheels.

2   Remove the sway bar nuts, bolts and retainers at the control arms **(see illustrations)**.
3   Unbolt the clamps at the crossmember and remove the sway bar from the vehicle.
4   Check the bar for damage, corrosion and distortion.
5   Check the clamps, bushings and retainers for distortion, damage and wear. Replace the inner bushings by prying them open at the split and removing them. Install the new bushings with the curved surface up and the split facing toward the front of the vehicle. The outer bushing can be removed by cutting it off or hammering it from the bar. Force the new bushing onto the end of the bar until 1/2-inch of the bar is protruding.
6   Place the upper bushing retainers in position on the crossmember bushings, attach the bar to the crossmember and then install the lower clamps, bolts and nuts.
7   Install the bushing retainers, nuts and bolts at the lower control arm.
8   Raise the lower control arms to normal ride height and tighten the nuts to the torque listed in this Chapter's Specifications.
9   Install the wheels and tighten the lug nuts snugly. Lower the vehicle and tighten the lug nuts to the torque specified in Chapter 1.

3   Control arm – removal, inspection and installation

Refer to illustrations 3.2a, 3.2b, 3.4 and 3.5

1   Raise the front of the vehicle, support it securely on jackstands and remove the front wheels. Apply the parking brake. Detach the sway bar (see Section 2).
2   Remove the nut and pivot bolt from the control arm **(see illustrations)**.

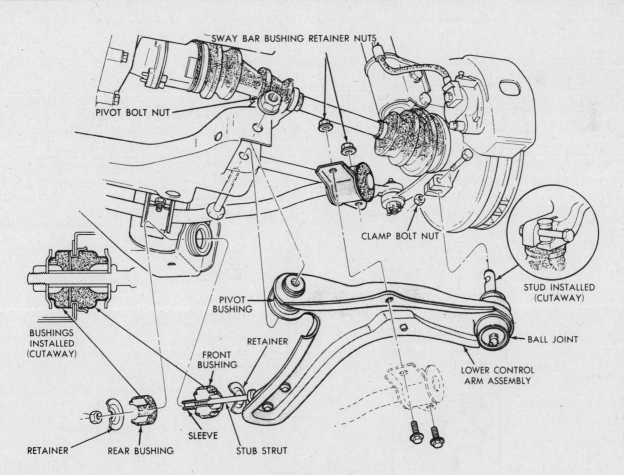

3.2a   Control arm mounting details

10

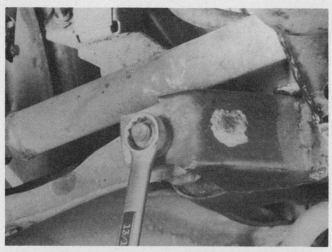

3.2b   Remove the nut and pull out the pivot bolt to detach the
front of the control arm

3.4   Use a back-up wrench on the nut when removing the
balljoint clamp bolt

3.5   Pull down sharply to disconnect the balljoint from the
steering knuckle (a pry bar may be required) – the knuckle will
tend to swing out, so be careful not to separate the inner CV joint
from the transaxle

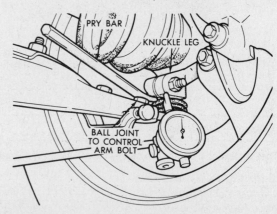

4.3   Pry between the steering knuckle and balljoint and measure
the movement to determine if the balljoint is worn (1978 through
1980 models)

3   Remove the rear stub strut nut, retainer and bushing.

4   Remove the balljoint clamp bolt and nut from the steering knuckle
(see illustration).

5   Disconnect the balljoint stud from the steering knuckle. Be careful not
to separate the inner CV joint (see illustration).

6   Remove the sway bar bolts and nuts (see illustration 2.2b). Separate the control arm and remove it from the vehicle.

7   Remove the rear stub strut bushing and sleeve assembly (see illustration 3.2a).

8   Inspect the lower control arm for distortion and the bushings for wear,
damage and deterioration. Replace a damaged or bent control arm with a
new one. If the inner pivot bushing or the balljoint are worn, take the control
arm assembly to a dealer service department or a repair shop, as special
tools are required to replace them. The strut bushings can be replaced by
sliding them off the strut.

9   Assemble the retainer, bushing and sleeve on the stub strut.

10   Place the control arm in position over the sway bar and attach the stub
strut and front pivot to the crossmember.

11   Install the pivot bolt and stub strut assembly in the crossmember, with
the nuts finger tight.

12   Attach the balljoint stud to the steering knuckle and tighten the clamp
bolt to the torque listed in this Chapter's Specifications.

13   Attach the sway bar end to the control arm and tighten the bolts and
nuts to the torque listed in this Chapter's Specifications.

14   Install the wheels and lower the vehicle. With the vehicle weight on
the suspension, tighten the pivot bolt and stub strut nuts to the torque listed
in this Chapter's Specifications.

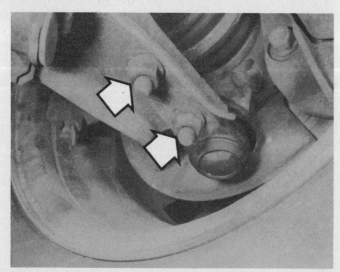

4.6   The balljoints are attached to the control arm with large nuts
and bolts on 1979 and 1980 models

CAM BOLT NUT

ADAPTOR SCREW AND WASHER

STRUT DAMPER
(REFERENCE)

WEAR SLEEVE

SEAL

BRAKE CALIPER

WASHER
PLATE

DRIVE SHAFT

BEARING

STEERING LINKAGE

RETAINER

HUB

WASHER

CLAMP BOLT

COTTER
PIN

GASKET

KNUCKLE

WHEEL BOLT

LOWER CONTROL ARM
(REFERENCE)

NUT LOCK   HUB NUT

5.1   Steering knuckle and related components – exploded view

---

4   Balljoints – check and replacement

1   The suspension balljoints are designed to operate without freeplay.

1978 through 1980 models
Refer to illustrations 4.3 and 4.6

2   Raise the vehicle and support it securely on jackstands.

3   Pry between the top of the balljoint housing and the steering knuckle and measure the movement of the knuckle leg in relation to the control arm **(see illustration)**. If the movement is more than 0.050-inch (1.2 mm) replace the balljoint with a new one.

4   On 1978 models, the balljoint is riveted to the control arm. Replacement should be done by a dealer service department or a repair shop.

5   On 1979 and 1980 models, the balljoint is bolted to the control arm. Remove the balljoint clamp bolt and disconnect the stud from the knuckle **(see illustrations 3.4 and 3.5)**.

6   Remove the two bolts and nuts and detach the balljoint from the control arm **(see illustration)**.

7   Place the new balljoint in position and install the bolts and nuts. Hold the bolts and tighten the nuts to the torque listed in this Chapter's Specifications.

8   Connect the balljoint to the steering knuckle. Tighten the clamp bolt nut to the torque listed in this Chapter's Specifications.

1981 and later models
9   Refer to Section 30 in Chapter 1.

---

5   Steering knuckle and hub – removal, inspection and installation

Removal
Refer to illustrations 5.1, 5.4, 5.9, 5.11, 5.13 and 5.14

1   Pry off the hub cap. On 1979 and later models, remove the cotter pin, nut lock and spring washer **(see illustration)**. With the vehicle weight resting on the front suspension, loosen, but don't remove, the front hub (axle) nut and wheel lug nuts.

2   Raise the front of the vehicle, support it securely on jackstands and apply the parking brake. Remove the front wheels.

3   Remove the hub nut and washer.

4   Push the driveaxle in until it clears the hub **(see illustration)**. You may have to tap on the axle end with a brass punch and hammer to dislodge the driveaxle from the hub.

5   Remove the cotter pin and nut and use a puller to disconnect the steering tie-rod from the hub (see Section 17).

6   Position the tie-rod out of the way and secure it with a piece of wire.

7   Disconnect the brake hose from the shock strut by removing the bolt and retainer.

8   Remove the caliper and brake pads (see Chapter 9), then remove the adapter from the steering knuckle. Being very careful not to twist the brake hose, hang the caliper out of the way in the wheel well with a piece of wire.

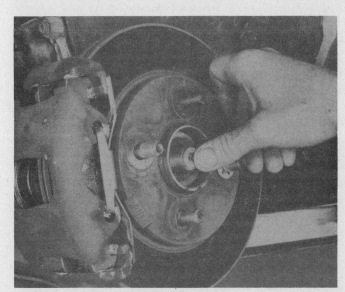

5.4   Push in on the driveaxle to detach it from the hub (be sure to support the outer CV joint)

10

5.9   Once the bushing bolts are loose, the sway bar can be pulled down out of the way

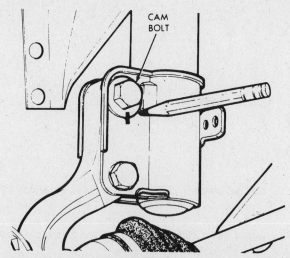

5.11   Mark the location of the cam bolt and washer on the steering knuckle

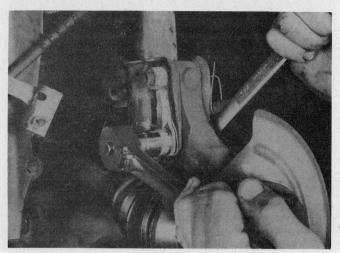

5.13   Use a socket and wrench to remove the knuckle-to-strut bolts and nuts

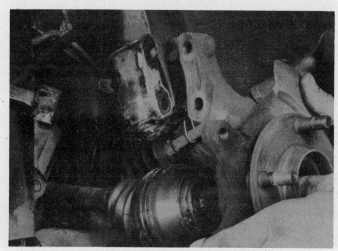

5.14   Pull the steering knuckle out, off the driveaxle splines

9   Loosen the sway bar bushing bolts, unbolt the ends from the control arm and pull the sway bar down and out of the way **(see illustration)**.
10   Remove the retainer from the wheel stud and pull the brake disc off.
11   Mark the cam bolt and washer location prior to removal. The cam bolt is the upper bolt **(see illustration)**.
12   Remove the balljoint pinch bolt and nut and disengage the balljoint from the hub.
13   Remove the steering knuckle-to-strut bolts, nuts and washer plate **(see illustration)**.
14   With the knuckle and hub assembly in the straight-ahead position, grasp it securely and pull it directly out and off the driveaxle splines **(see illustration)**.

Inspection

15   Place the assembly on a clean work surface and wipe it off with a lint-free cloth. Inspect the knuckle for corrosion and cracks. Check the bearings by rotating them to make sure they move freely and smoothly. The bearings should be packed with an adequate supply of clean grease. If there isn't enough grease, or if the grease is contaminated with dirt, clean the bearings and inspect them for wear and damage. Repack the bearings with NLGI no.2 EP wheel bearing grease. Inspect the grease seals to make sure they aren't damaged or leaking. Further disassembly will have to be done by a dealer service department or repair shop because of the special tools required.

Installation

Refer to illustrations 5.16 and 5.18

16   Prior to installation, clean the CV joint seal and the hub grease seal with solvent (don't get any solvent on the CV joint boot). Lubricate the en-

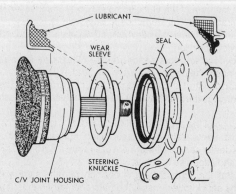

5.16   Lubricate the wear sleeve seal contact areas with multi-purpose grease before connecting the CV joint to the knuckle

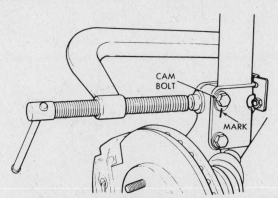

5.18   Use a C-clamp to pull the strut and steering knuckle into alignment

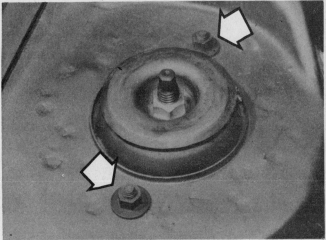

6.6   While supporting the strut, remove the two upper mounting nuts (arrows) – Warning: DO NOT remove the large nut in the center!

tire outer edge of the CV joint wear sleeve and seal contact surface with multi-purpose grease **(see illustration)**.

17   Carefully place the knuckle and hub assembly in position. Align the splines of the axle and hub and slide the hub into place.

18   Install the knuckle-to-strut bolts, nuts and washer plate, followed by the balljoint pinch bolt and nut. Adjust the knuckle so the mark made during removal is aligned with the cam bolt and washer. You may have to use a large C-clamp to pull the steering knuckle and strut together and line up the marks **(see illustration)**. Tighten the nuts to the torque listed in this Chapter's Specifications.

19   Install the tie-rod end, tighten the nut to the torque listed in this Chapter's Specifications and install the cotter pin.

20   Install the brake disc, pads and caliper/adapter assembly.

21   Connect the brake hose to the shock strut.

22   Attach the sway bar end to the control arm and tighten the fasteners to the torque listed in this Chapter's Specifications.

23   Push the CV joint completely into the hub to make sure it's seated and install the washer and hub nut finger tight.

24   Install the wheels and lower the vehicle.

25   With an assistant applying the brakes, tighten the hub nut to the torque listed in this Chapter's Specifications. On 1978 models, stake the hub nut in place (see Chapter 8). On 1979 and later models, install the spring washer, nut lock and a new cotter pin.

26   With the weight of the vehicle on the suspension, check the steering knuckle and balljoint nuts to make sure they're tight.

27   Have the vehicle front end alignment checked.

6   Front shock absorber strut and spring assembly – removal, inspection and installation

Refer to illustration 6.6

1   Loosen the front wheel lug nuts.

2   Raise the front of the vehicle and support it securely on jackstands. Apply the parking brake. Remove the front wheels.

3   Mark the location of the cam bolt and washer as described in Step 11 of the previous Section.

4   Remove the strut-to-steering knuckle nuts, bolts and washer plate.

5   Disconnect the brake hose from the strut.

6   Support the strut and remove the upper mounting nuts **(see illustration)**. Disengage the strut from the steering knuckle and detach it from the vehicle.

7   Checking of the strut and spring assembly is limited to inspection for leaking fluid, dents, damage and corrosion. Further disassembly should be left to a dealer service department or a repair shop because of the special tools and expertise required.

8   To install the strut, place it in position with the studs extending up through the shock tower. Install the nuts and tighten them to the torque listed in this Chapter's Specifications.

9   Attach the strut to the steering knuckle, then insert the mounting bolts and install the washer plate.

10   Use a large C-clamp to align the knuckle and strut so the cam bolt marks line up **(see illustration 5.18)**. Install the nuts on the bolts and tighten them to the torque listed in this Chapter's Specifications. Remove the clamp.

11   Attach the brake hose to the strut.

12   Install the wheels and lower the vehicle.

7   Rear axle assembly – removal and installation

Refer to illustrations 7.3 and 7.5

1   Raise the rear of the vehicle and support it securely on jackstands. Block the front wheels to keep the vehicle from rolling. Remove the rear wheels.

2   Disconnect and plug the brake lines at the connections on the axle crossmember.

3   Remove the parking brake cable adjusting nut. Release both parking brake cables from the bracket on the crossmember by slipping the ball-end of the cables through the brake connectors. Pull the parking brake cable through the bracket **(see illustration)**.

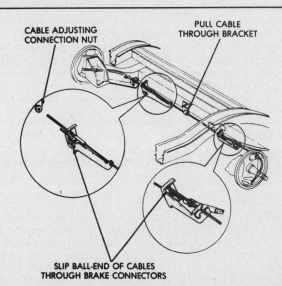

7.3   To disconnect the parking brake cable, loosen the cable adjusting connection nut and slip the ball end of the cables through the brake connectors

10

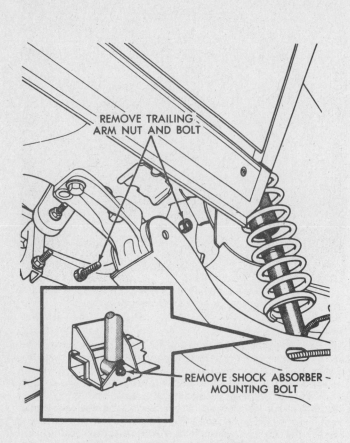

7.5   Rear suspension trailing arm mounting details

8.1   Pull off the protective cap for access to the upper strut retaining nut (arrow) (sedan)

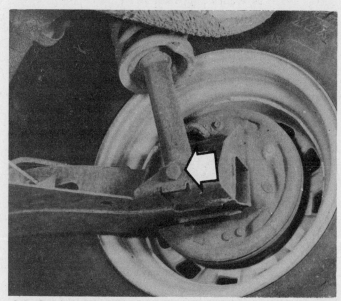

8.4   Support the trailing arm with a jack and remove the nut from the lower shock absorber bolt (arrow)

4   Support the rear suspension with jacks placed under the crossmember.

5 . Remove the lower mounting bolts from the shock absorbers **(see illustration)**.

6   Remove the trailing arm mounting bolts on both sides **(see illustration 7.5)**. Lower the jacks under the crossmember and pull the axle assembly out from under the vehicle.

7   Installation is the reverse of the removal procedure. Tighten all the nuts and bolts to the torque listed in this Chapter's Specifications. Tighten the trailing arm mounting bolts after the vehicle has been lowered to the ground. Bleed the brake hydraulic system as described in Chapter 9.

8   Rear shock absorber strut and spring assembly – removal, inspection and installation

Refer to illustrations 8.1 and 8.4

1   Open the liftgate and, on four-door models, remove the plastic cap for access to the upper strut retaining nut **(see illustration)**. On two-door models, you'll have to remove the rear quarter panel for access.

2   Hold the end of the strut shaft with a wrench so it can't turn, then remove the nut.

3   Raise the vehicle and support it securely on jackstands.

4   Support the trailing arm with a jack and remove the nut from the lower shock absorber bolt **(see illustration)**. If necessary, use a punch and hammer to drive the bolt out, then detach the shock absorber strut and spring assembly from the vehicle. Refer to Section 6 for the inspection procedure.

5   To install the shock, place the assembly in position and install the fasteners finger tight. Lower the vehicle weight onto the suspension before tightening the nuts to the torque listed in this Chapter's Specifications.

9   Rear spindle – inspection, removal and installation

Refer to illustration 9.6

Inspection and removal

1   Remove the rear hub/drum assembly (see Chapter 1, Section 32).

2   Clean the spindle and inspect the bearing contact surfaces for wear and damage.

3   The spindle should be replaced with a new one if it's worn or distorted.

4   Disconnect the parking brake cable (see Chapter 9, if necessary).

5   Disconnect and plug the rear brake line at the wheel cylinder (see Chapter 9, if necessary).

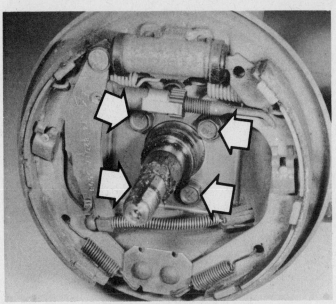

9.6   Remove the backing plate mounting bolts (arrows) to separate the spindle from the axle

11.3   Pull off the connector, then remove the three screws and detach the horn switch (arrows)

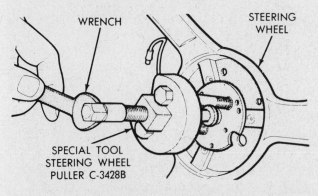

11.5   Use a puller to remove the steering wheel – DO NOT hammer on the end of the shaft to jar the wheel loose!

6   Remove the four backing plate mounting bolts and detach the brake assembly and spindle **(see illustration)**. The bolts on some models may have Torx-type heads, which require a special tool for removal. Be sure to mark the location of any spindle shims.

Installation

7   Place the shim(s) (if equipped), spindle and brake assembly in position, install the bolts and tighten them in a criss-cross pattern to the torque listed in this Chapter's Specifications.
8   Connect the brake line and parking brake cable.
9   Install the hub/drum assembly (see Chapter 1), bleed the brakes and adjust the parking brake (see Chapter 9).

10   Steering system – general information

All models are equipped with rack-and-pinion steering. The steering gear is attached directly behind the engine and operates the steering arms through tie-rods. The inner ends of the tie-rods are protected by rubber boots which should be inspected periodically for secure attachment, damage and leaking lubricant.

As an option, some models are equipped with power-assisted steer-

ing. The power assist system consists of a belt-driven pump and associated lines and hoses. The power steering system fluid level should be checked periodically (see Chapter 1).

The steering wheel operates the steering shaft, which actuates the steering gear through a universal joint. Looseness in the steering can be caused by wear in the steering shaft universal joint, the steering gear, the tie-rod ends and loose retaining bolts. Inadequate lubrication of the steering shaft seal can cause binding of the steering; the seal should be lubricated periodically (see Chapter 1).

11   Steering wheel – removal and installation

Warning: *Later models are equipped with a driver's side air bag installed in the center of the steering wheel. The air bag must be disarmed and removed before the steering wheel is removed (see Section 20).*
Refer to illustrations 11.3 and 11.5
1   Disconnect the negative cable from the battery.
2   Remove the steering wheel center pad by grasping it securely and pulling straight out, releasing the clips.
3   Unplug the connector and remove the horn switch **(see illustration)**.
4   Remove the steering wheel retaining nut and mark the relationship of the steering shaft and hub to simplify installation.
5   Use a puller to remove the steering wheel **(see illustration)**. **Caution:** *Don't hammer on the shaft to remove the steering wheel.*
6   To install the wheel, align the mark on the steering wheel hub with the mark made on the shaft during removal and slip the wheel onto the shaft. Install the retaining nut (and damper if removed) and tighten it to the torque listed in this Chapter's Specifications.
7   Install the horn switch.
8   Install the center pad assembly.
9   Connect the negative battery cable.

12   Steering column – removal and installation

Refer to illustrations 12.3 and 12.7
Removal
1   Disconnect the negative cable from the battery.
2   Disconnect all electrical connectors from the steering column.

10

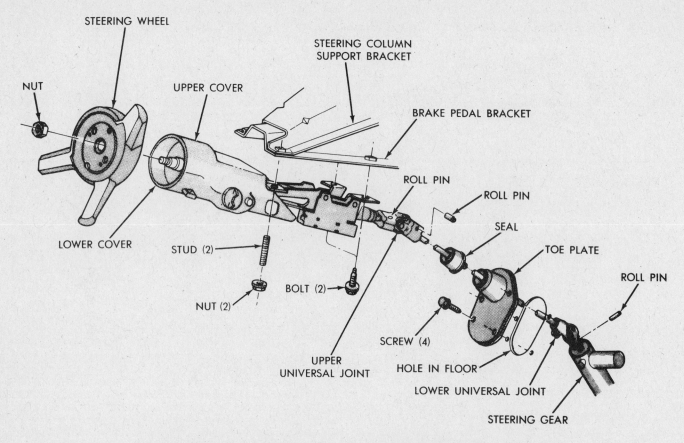

STEERING WHEEL

STEERING COLUMN
SUPPORT BRACKET

NUT

UPPER COVER

BRAKE PEDAL BRACKET

ROLL PIN

ROLL PIN

SEAL

LOWER COVER

TOE PLATE

STUD (2)

ROLL PIN

BOLT (2)

NUT (2)

SCREW (4)

UPPER
UNIVERSAL JOINT

HOLE IN FLOOR

LOWER UNIVERSAL JOINT

STEERING GEAR

12.3   Steering column components – exploded view (1978 through 1986 models shown)

3   Using a small diameter pin punch, drive the lower roll pin out of the upper universal joint (1978 through 1986 models) **(see illustration)**. Later models (1987 on) have a slip joint which doesn't require a roll pin.
4   Remove the two nuts securing the column assembly to the support bracket. Also remove the two bolts securing the column to the brake pedal bracket, then remove the assembly from the vehicle. On 1987 and later models, it may be necessary to pull back sharply on the column to disengage it from the slip joint.
5   Pull back the carpet and pad from the toe plate and remove the four toe plate screws **(see illustration 12.3)**.
6   Slide the toe plate and seal off the shaft and remove the seal from the plate.
7   Remove the lower universal joint. On 1978 through 1986 models, first drive out the roll pin **(see illustration)**.

Installation

8   Align the master serrations, install the lower universal joint assembly and drive in a new roll pin (if equipped).
9   Insert a new seal in the toe plate and lubricate the inside of the seal. Slide the toe plate over the lower shaft and secure the toe plate to the floor with the four screws. Replace the pad and carpet.
10   Place the column assembly in position and install the upper right mounting nut. Unlock the steering column with the ignition key and, aligning the shaft serrations, engage the lower shaft in the upper universal joint (1978 through 1986 models) or the slip joint (1987 and later models).
11   Loosely install the other mounting nut and two bolts. Insert a new roll pin in the upper universal joint and drive it in. When driving in the pin, use a wood block behind the universal joint to prevent damaging the lower bearing in the column.
12   Tighten the mounting nuts and bolts finger tight, loosen them two

turns, then tighten them completely, beginning with the bolts.
13   Reconnect the electrical wiring connectors and the negative battery cable.

12.7   On 1978 through 1986 models, you must drive out the lower universal joint roll pin (arrow) before you can remove the steering column or steering gear

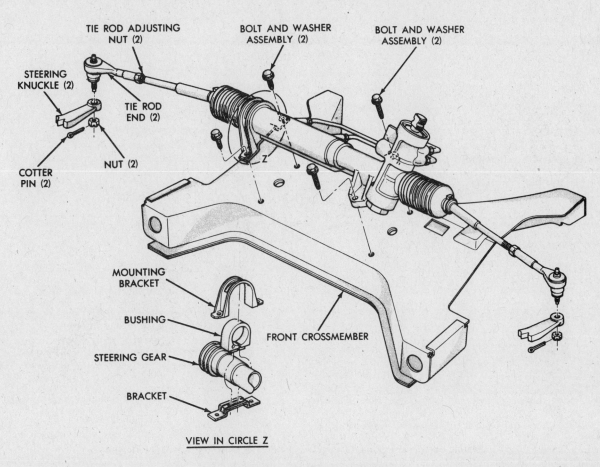

TIE ROD ADJUSTING NUT (2)

BOLT AND WASHER ASSEMBLY (2)

BOLT AND WASHER ASSEMBLY (2)

STEERING KNUCKLE (2)

TIE ROD END (2)

COTTER PIN (2)

NUT (2)

MOUNTING BRACKET

BUSHING

FRONT CROSSMEMBER

STEERING GEAR

BRACKET

VIEW IN CIRCLE Z

13.8   Steering gear mounting details

13   Steering gear – removal and installation

Refer to illustration 13.8

1   Raise the front of the vehicle, support it securely on jackstands and apply the parking brake. Remove the front wheels. Mark both shafts, where the steering column shaft attaches to the steering gear input shaft, so they can be reassembled in the same relative position. On 1978 through 1986 models, drive out the lower universal joint roll pin **(see illustration 12.7)**.

2   Disconnect the tie-rod ends from the steering knuckles (see Section 17).

3   Remove the anti-rotational link or damper (if equipped) from the front crossmember.

4   Support the front crossmember with a jack. Loosen the front crossmember bolts and remove the rear nuts.

5   Lower the crossmember with the jack to gain access to the steering gear.

6   Remove the boot seal and splash shields from the crossmember.

7   On power steering equipped models, disconnect the hoses and drain the fluid into a container.

8   Remove the four steering gear mounting bolts and separate it from the crossmember by pulling it out from the left side of the vehicle **(see illustration)**.

9   To install the steering gear, position it in the crossmember, install the bolts and tighten them securely.

10   Attach the tie-rod ends to the steering knuckles.

11   On power steering equipped models, reconnect the hoses, using new O-rings.

12   Align the marks you made on the steering column and input shafts. On manual steering equipped models, check to make sure the master serrations on the steering gear shaft are properly aligned so the steering shaft will be installed in the straight-ahead position.

13   Install the boot seal and splash shields.

14   Raise the crossmember and steering gear into position with the jack, install the crossmember bolts/nuts and tighten them securely. **Note:** *The right rear bolt is a pilot bolt and must be tightened first.*

15   On 1978 through 1986 models, install the steering shaft roll pin. Use a wood block to support the steering shaft as the pin is driven in.

16   Install the front wheels and lower the vehicle.

17   On power steering equipped models, start the engine and bleed the steering system (see Section 15). While the engine is running, check for leaks at the hose connections.

18   Have the front end alignment checked by a dealer service department or an alignment shop.

14   Power steering pump – removal and installation

Refer to illustrations 14.2 and 14.10

1   Disconnect the vapor separator hose from the carburetor. On air conditioned models, disconnect the two wires from the compressor clutch switch.

10

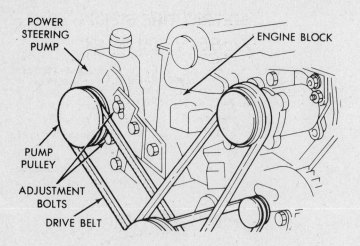

14.2   Loosen the adjustment bolts to remove the drivebelt

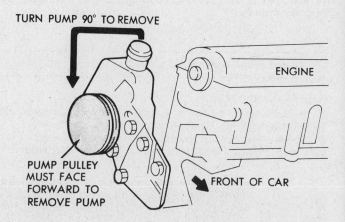

14.10   Power steering pump removal details

2   Loosen the two adjustment bolts and the nut on the engine side of the pump housing, then remove the drivebelt **(see illustration)**.
3   Raise the vehicle and support it securely on jackstands.
4   Remove the pressure hose locating bracket from the crossmember. Disconnect the hose from the steering gear housing and drain the fluid into a container.
5   While the fluid is draining, remove the right splash shield from the right inner fender.
6   Disconnect the hoses from the pump and plug all of the openings.
7   Remove the lower stud nut and pivot bolt from the pump.
8   Lower the vehicle and remove the adjustment bolts, then remove the nut on the engine side of the pump housing.
9   Move the pump away from the engine to clear the mounting bracket, then remove the adjustment bracket.
10 Turn the pump 90-degrees with the pulley facing forward and lift it out of the engine compartment **(see illustration)**.
11 Installation is the reverse of removal. Be sure to use new O-rings when attaching the hoses to the pump and tighten all fasteners securely.
12 After installation, fill the pump reservoir with the fluid specified in Chapter 1, then bleed the power steering system as described in Section 15.

15   Power steering system – bleeding

1   Following any operation where the power steering fluid lines have been disconnected, the power steering system must be bled to remove all air and obtain proper steering performance.
2   With the front wheels in the straight-ahead position, check the power steering fluid level (see Chapter 1). If it's low, add fluid.
3   Start the engine and allow it to run at fast idle. Recheck the fluid level and add more if necessary.
4   Bleed the system by turning the wheels from side-to-side, without hitting the stops. This will work the air out of the system. Keep the reservoir full of fluid as this is done.
5   When the air is worked out of the system, return the wheels to the straight-ahead position and leave the vehicle running for several more minutes before shutting it off.
6   Road test the vehicle to make sure the steering system is functioning normally and noise free.
7   Recheck the fluid level to make sure it's correct (see Chapter 1).

16   Steering gear boots – replacement

Refer to illustration 16.3

1   Raise the front of the vehicle and support it securely on jackstands. Apply the parking brake.
2   Remove the tie-rod end (see Section 17).
3   Remove the boot clamp(s) **(see illustration)**. Some TRW model steering gears have an outer boot clamp.
4   Mark the location of the breather tube, use a small screwdriver to lift the boot out of the groove in the steering gear and remove the boot **(see illustration 16.3)**.
5   Prior to installation, lubricate the boot groove in the steering tie-rod with silicone-type grease.
6   Slide the new boot into position on the steering gear until it seats in the groove and install a new inner clamp. Make sure the breather tube fits securely in the boot.

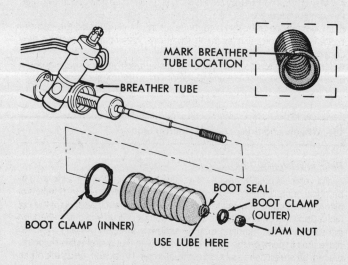

**16.3   Typical steering gear boot installation details
(TRW type shown)**

7   Install a new outer clamp, if equipped.
8   Install the tie-rod end.
9   Lower the vehicle.
10 Have the front end alignment checked by a dealer service department or an alignment shop.

17   Tie-rod ends – removal and installation

Refer to illustration 17.2

1   Raise the front of the vehicle, support it securely on jackstands and apply the parking brake. Remove the front wheel(s).
2   Remove the cotter pin, loosen the castle nut and disconnect the tie-rod from the steering knuckle with a two-jaw puller **(see illustration)**.

17.2   Separate the tie-rod end from the steering knuckle with a two-jaw puller

3   Loosen the jam nut enough to allow room for marking the position of the tie-rod end on the tie-rod. Unscrew the tie-rod.
4   Thread the tie-rod end onto the rod to the marked position and tighten the jam nut securely.
5   Connect the tie-rod end to the steering knuckle, install the nut and tighten it to the torque listed in this Chapter's Specifications. Install a new cotter pin.
6   If a new tie-rod end has been installed, have the front end alignment checked by a dealer service department or an alignment shop.

18   Wheels and tires – general information

Refer to illustration 18.1

All vehicles covered by this manual are equipped with metric-size fiberglass or steel-belted radial tires **(see illustration)**. The installation of different size or other type tires may affect the ride and handling of the vehicle. Don't mix different types of tires, such as radials and bias belted, on the same vehicle; handling may be seriously affected. Always try to replace tires in pairs on the same axle. However, if only one tire is being replaced, be sure it's the same size, structure and tread design as the other.

Because tire pressure has a substantial effect on handling and wear, the pressure in all tires should be checked at least once a month or before any extended trips (see Chapter 1).

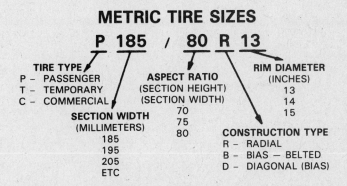

METRIC TIRE SIZES

P 185 / 80 R 13

TIRE TYPE
P – PASSENGER
T – TEMPORARY
C – COMMERCIAL

SECTION WIDTH
(MILLIMETERS)
185
195
205
ETC

ASPECT RATIO
(SECTION HEIGHT)
(SECTION WIDTH)
70
75
80

RIM DIAMETER
(INCHES)
13
14
15

CONSTRUCTION TYPE
R – RADIAL
B – BIAS – BELTED
D – DIAGONAL (BIAS)

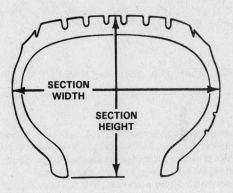

SECTION WIDTH

SECTION HEIGHT

18.1   Metric tire size code

Wheels must be replaced if they're bent, dented, leak air, have elongated bolt holes, are heavily rusted, out of vertical symmetry or if the lug nuts won't stay tight. Wheel repairs by welding or peening aren't recommended.

Tire and wheel balance is important to the overall handling, braking and performance of the vehicle. Unbalanced wheels can adversely affect handling and ride characteristics as well as tire life. Whenever a tire is installed on a wheel, the tire and wheel should be balanced by a shop with the proper equipment.

19   Front end alignment – general information

A front end alignment refers to the adjustments made to the front wheels so they're in proper angular relationship to the suspension and the ground. Front wheels that are out of proper alignment not only affect steering control, but also increase tire wear. The front end adjustments normally required are camber and toe-in.

Getting the proper front wheel alignment is a very exacting process in which complicated and expensive machines are necessary to perform the job properly. Because of this, you should have a technician with the proper equipment perform these tasks. We will, however, use this space to give you a basic idea of what's involved with front end alignment so you can better understand the process and deal intelligently with the shop that does the work.

Toe-in is the turning in of the front wheels. The purpose of a toe specification is to ensure parallel rolling of the front wheels. In a vehicle with zero toe-in, the distance between the front edges of the wheels will be the same as the distance between the rear edges of the wheels. The actual amount of toe-in is normally only a fraction of an inch. Toe-in adjustment is con-

10

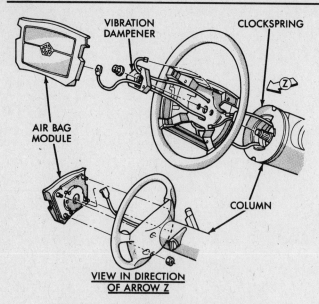

VIEW IN DIRECTION OF ARROW Z

20.3   Air bag module installation details

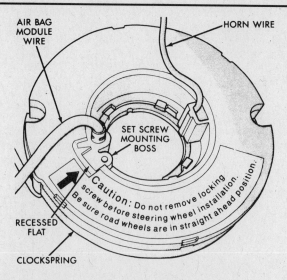

20.5   On models so equipped, install the tethered screw through the mounting boss to hold the clockspring in place if the steering wheel must be removed.

trolled by the positions of the tie-rod ends on the tie-rods. Incorrect toe-in will cause the tires to wear improperly by making them scrub against the road surface.

Camber is the tilting of the front wheels from vertical when viewed from the front of the vehicle. When the wheels tilt out at the top, the camber is said to be positive (+). When the wheels tilt in at the top the camber is negative (-). The amount of tilt is measured in degrees from vertical - this measurement is called the camber angle. This angle affects the amount of tire tread contacting the road and compensates for changes in the suspension geometry when the vehicle is cornering or travelling over an undulating surface.

Caster is the tilting of the top of the front steering axis from vertical. A tilt toward the rear is positive caster and a tilt toward the front is negative caster. Caster isn't adjustable on these vehicles.

20   Air bag module – removal and installation

Refer to illustrations 20.3 and 20.5
Warning: *Later model vehicles are equipped with a driver's side air bag installed in the center of the steering wheel. The air bag must be disarmed and removed before the steering wheel is removed!*

Caution: *The front wheels must be in the straight-ahead position during this procedure to ensure the clockspring in the steering hub is held in the proper position. The clockspring maintains electrical power to the air bag*

module during normal use and if not centered, could cause failure of the air bag system.

1   Removal of the air bag is necessary before the steering wheel can be removed for steering column switch replacement or other service procedures. **Warning:** *Always wear shatter-proof eye protection when servicing the air bag and never probe the air bag electrical connectors.*

Removal

2   The air bag is activated by battery power, so first disconnect the negative cable from the battery.
3   Use a thin-wall 10 mm socket to remove the four air bag module retaining nuts from the back side of the steering wheel **(see illustration)**. On some models, Chrysler tool no. 6239 may be required because tamper resistant nuts are used.
4   Detach the clockspring wiring connector and remove the air bag module.
5   If the steering wheel must be removed, make sure the clockspring will remain centered. Some models have autolocking tabs which center the clockspring, while others have a tethered screw which must be installed in the set screw mounting boss at this time **(see illustration)**. **Warning:** *Do not remove the set screw until after the steering wheel and nut have been installed.*

Installation

6   Attach the air bag module wiring connector to the clockspring.
7   Install the air bag module in the steering wheel and tighten the four nuts to 80 to 100 in-lbs.

Chapter 11   Body

Contents

1   General information

These models feature a "unibody" layout, using a floor pan with front and rear frame side rails which support the body components, front and rear suspension systems and other mechanical components.

Certain components are particularly vulnerable to accident damage and can be unbolted and repaired or replaced. Among these parts are the body moldings, bumpers, the hood and trunk lids and all glass.

Only general body maintenance practices and body panel repair procedures within the scope of the do-it-yourselfer are included in this Chapter.

2   Body – maintenance

1   The condition of your vehicle's body is very important, because the resale value depends a great deal on it. It's much more difficult to repair a neglected or damaged body than it is to repair mechanical components. The hidden areas of the body, such as the wheel wells, the frame and the engine compartment, are equally important, although they don't require as frequent attention as the rest of the body.

2   Once a year, or every 12,000 miles, it's a good idea to have the underside of the body steam cleaned. All traces of dirt and oil will be removed and the area can then be inspected carefully for rust, damaged brake lines, frayed electrical wires, damaged cables and other problems. The front suspension components should be greased after completion of this job.

3   At the same time, clean the engine and the engine compartment with a steam cleaner or water soluble degreaser.

4   The wheel wells should be given close attention, since undercoating can peel away and stones and dirt thrown up by the tires can cause the paint to chip and flake, allowing rust to set in. If rust is found, clean down to the bare metal and apply an anti-rust paint.

5   The body should be washed about once a week. Wet the vehicle thoroughly to soften the dirt, then wash it down with a soft sponge and plenty of clean soapy water. If the surplus dirt is not washed off very carefully, it can wear down the paint.

6   Spots of tar or asphalt thrown up from the road should be removed with a cloth soaked in solvent.

11

These photos illustrate a method of repairing simple dents. They are intended to supplement *Body repair - minor damage* in this Chapter and should not be used as the sole instructions for body repair on these vehicles.

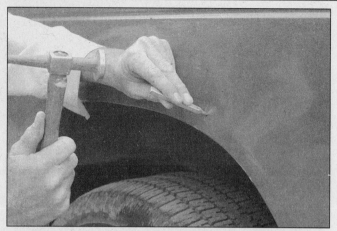

1   If you can't access the backside of the body panel to hammer out the dent, pull it out with a slide-hammer-type dent puller. In the deepest portion of the dent or along the crease line, drill or punch hole(s) at least one inch apart . . .

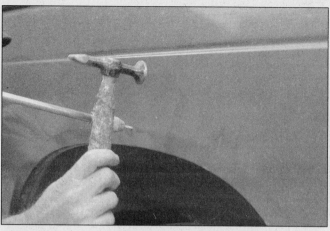

2   . . . then screw the slide-hammer into the hole and operate it. Tap with a hammer near the edge of the dent to help 'pop' the metal back to its original shape. When you're finished, the dent area should be close to its original contour and about 1/8-inch below the surface of the surrounding metal

3   Using coarse-grit sandpaper, remove the paint down to the bare metal. Hand sanding works fine, but the disc sander shown here makes the job faster. Use finer (about 320-grit) sandpaper to feather-edge the paint at least one inch around the dent area

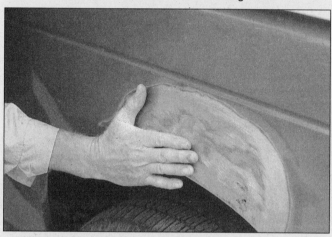

4   When the paint is removed, touch will probably be more helpful than sight for telling if the metal is straight. Hammer down the high spots or raise the low spots as necessary. Clean the repair area with wax/silicone remover

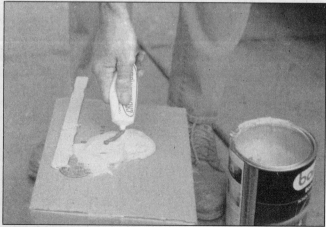

5   Following label instructions, mix up a batch of plastic filler and hardener. The ratio of filler to hardener is critical, and, if you mix it incorrectly, it will either not cure properly or cure too quickly (you won't have time to file and sand it into shape)

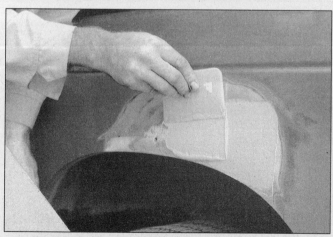

6   Working quickly so the filler doesn't harden, use a plastic applicator to press the body filler firmly into the metal, assuring it bonds completely. Work the filler until it matches the original contour and is slightly above the surrounding metal

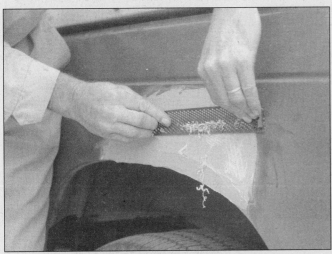

7 Let the filler harden until you can just dent it with your fingernail. Use a body file or Surform tool (shown here) to rough-shape the filler

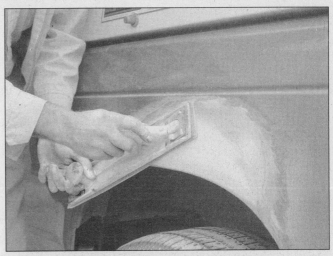

8 Use coarse-grit sandpaper and a sanding board or block to work the filler down until it's smooth and even. Work down to finer grits of sandpaper - always using a board or block - ending up with 360 or 400 grit

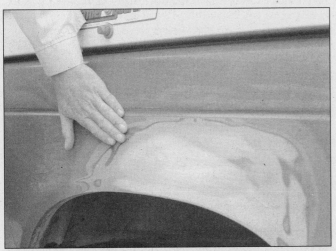

9 You shouldn't be able to feel any ridge at the transition from the filler to the bare metal or from the bare metal to the old paint. As soon as the repair is flat and uniform, remove the dust and mask off the adjacent panels or trim pieces

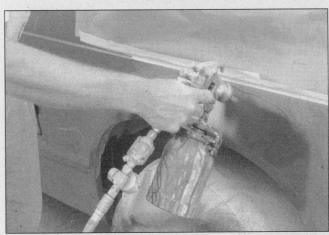

10 Apply several layers of primer to the area. Don't spray the primer on too heavy, so it sags or runs, and make sure each coat is dry before you spray on the next one. A professional-type spray gun is being used here, but aerosol spray primer is available inexpensively from auto parts stores

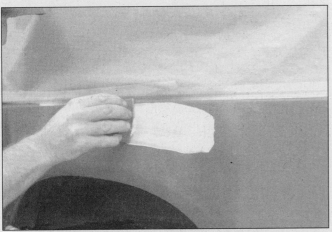

11 The primer will help reveal imperfections or scratches. Fill these with glazing compound. Follow the label instructions and sand it with 360 or 400-grit sandpaper until it's smooth. Repeat the glazing, sanding and respraying until the primer reveals a perfectly smooth surface

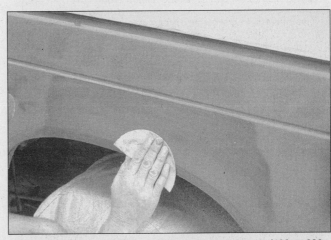

12 Finish sand the primer with very fine sandpaper (400 or 600-grit) to remove the primer overspray. Clean the area with water and allow it to dry. Use a tack rag to remove any dust, then apply the finish coat. Don't attempt to rub out or wax the repair area until the paint has dried completely (at least two weeks)

7   Once every six months, wax the body and chrome trim. If a chrome cleaner is used to remove rust from any of the vehicle's plated parts, remember that the cleaner also removes part of the chrome, so use it sparingly.

3   Vinyl trim – maintenance

Don't clean vinyl trim with detergents, caustic soap or petroleum-based cleaners. Plain soap and water works just fine, with a soft brush to clean dirt that may be ingrained. Wash the vinyl as frequently as the rest of the vehicle.

After cleaning, application of a high quality rubber and vinyl protectant will help prevent oxidation and cracks. The protectant can also be applied to weatherstripping, vacuum lines and rubber hoses, which often fail as a result of chemical degradation, and to the tires.

4   Upholstery and carpets – maintenance

1   Every three months remove the carpets or mats and clean the interior of the vehicle (more frequently if necessary). Vacuum the upholstery and carpets to remove loose dirt and dust.
2   Leather upholstery requires special care. Stains should be removed with warm water and a very mild soap solution. Use a clean, damp cloth to remove the soap, then wipe again with a dry cloth. Never use alcohol, gasoline, nail polish remover or thinner to clean leather upholstery.
3   After cleaning, regularly treat leather upholstery with a leather wax. Never use car wax on leather upholstery.
4   In areas where the interior of the vehicle is subject to bright sunlight, cover leather seats with a sheet if the vehicle is to be left out for any length of time.

5   Body repair – minor damage

Repair of scratches
1   If the scratch is superficial and does not penetrate to the metal of the body, repair is very simple. Lightly rub the scratched area with a fine rubbing compound to remove loose paint and built up wax. Rinse the area with clean water.
2   Apply touch-up paint to the scratch, using a small brush. Continue to apply thin layers of paint until the surface of the paint in the scratch is level with the surrounding paint. Allow the new paint at least two weeks to harden, then blend it into the surrounding paint by rubbing with a very fine rubbing compound. Finally, apply a coat of wax to the scratch area.
3   If the scratch has penetrated the paint and exposed the metal of the body, causing the metal to rust, a different repair technique is required. Remove all loose rust from the bottom of the scratch with a pocket knife, then apply rust inhibiting paint to prevent the formation of rust in the future. Using a rubber or nylon applicator, coat the scratched area with glaze-type filler. If required, the filler can be mixed with thinner to provide a very thin paste, which is ideal for filling narrow scratches. Before the glaze filler in the scratch hardens, wrap a piece of smooth cotton cloth around the tip of a finger. Dip the cloth in thinner and then quickly wipe it along the surface of the scratch. This will ensure that the surface of the filler is slightly hollow. The scratch can now be painted over as described earlier in this section.

Repair of dents
See photo sequence
4   When repairing dents, the first job is to pull the dent out until the affected area is as close as possible to its original shape. There is no point in trying to restore the original shape completely as the metal in the damaged area will have stretched on impact and cannot be restored to its original contours. It is better to bring the level of the dent up to a point which is about 1/8-inch below the level of the surrounding metal. In cases where the dent is very shallow, it is not worth trying to pull it out at all.

5   If the back side of the dent is accessible, it can be hammered out gently from behind using a soft-face hammer. While doing this, hold a block of wood firmly against the opposite side of the metal to absorb the hammer blows and prevent the metal from being stretched.
6   If the dent is in a section of the body which has double layers, or some other factor makes it inaccessible from behind, a different technique is required. Drill several small holes through the metal inside the damaged area, particularly in the deeper sections. Screw long, self tapping screws into the holes just enough for them to get a good grip in the metal. Now the dent can be pulled out by pulling on the protruding heads of the screws with locking pliers.
7   The next stage of repair is the removal of paint from the damaged area and from an inch or so of the surrounding metal. This is easily done with a wire brush or sanding disk in a drill motor, although it can be done just as effectively by hand with sandpaper. To complete the preparation for filling, score the surface of the bare metal with a screwdriver or the tang of a file or drill small holes in the affected area. This will provide a good grip for the filler material. To complete the repair, see the Section on filling and painting.

Repair of rust holes or gashes
8   Remove all paint from the affected area and from an inch or so of the surrounding metal using a sanding disk or wire brush mounted in a drill motor. If these are not available, a few sheets of sandpaper will do the job just as effectively.
9   With the paint removed, you will be able to determine the severity of the corrosion and decide whether to replace the whole panel, if possible, or repair the affected area. New body panels are not as expensive as most people think and it is often quicker to install a new panel than to repair large areas of rust.
10   Remove all trim pieces from the affected area except those which will act as a guide to the original shape of the damaged body, such as headlight shells, etc. Using metal snips or a hacksaw blade, remove all loose metal and any other metal that is badly affected by rust. Hammer the edges of the hole inward to create a slight depression for the filler material.
11   Wire brush the affected area to remove the powdery rust from the surface of the metal. If the back of the rusted area is accessible, treat it with rust inhibiting paint.
12   Before filling is done, block the hole in some way. This can be done with sheet metal riveted or screwed into place, or by stuffing the hole with wire mesh.
13   Once the hole is blocked off, the affected area can be filled and painted. See the following subsection on filling and painting.

Filling and painting
14   Many types of body fillers are available, but generally speaking, body repair kits which contain filler paste and a tube of resin hardener are best for this type of repair work. A wide, flexible plastic or nylon applicator will be necessary for imparting a smooth and contoured finish to the surface of the filler material. Mix up a small amount of filler on a clean piece of wood or cardboard (use the hardener sparingly). Follow the manufacturer's instructions on the package, otherwise the filler will set incorrectly.
15   Using the applicator, apply the filler paste to the prepared area. Draw the applicator across the surface of the filler to achieve the desired contour and to level the filler surface. As soon as a contour that approximates the original one is achieved, stop working the paste. If you continue, the paste will begin to stick to the applicator. Continue to add thin layers of paste at 20-minute intervals until the level of the filler is just above the surrounding metal.
16   Once the filler has hardened, the excess can be removed with a body file. From then on, progressively finer grades of sandpaper should be used, starting with a 180-grit paper and finishing with 600-grit wet-or-dry paper. Always wrap the sandpaper around a flat rubber or wooden block, otherwise the surface of the filler will not be completely flat. During the sanding of the filler surface, the wet-or-dry paper should be periodically rinsed in water. This will ensure that a very smooth finish is produced in the final stage.
17   At this point, the repair area should be surrounded by a ring of bare metal, which in turn should be encircled by the finely feathered edge of

good paint. Rinse the repair area with clean water until all of the dust produced by the sanding operation is gone.

18   Spray the entire area with a light coat of primer. This will reveal any imperfections in the surface of the filler. Repair the imperfections with fresh filler paste or glaze filler and once more smooth the surface with sandpaper. Repeat this spray-and-repair procedure until you are satisfied that the surface of the filler and the feathered edge of the paint are perfect. Rinse the area with clean water and allow it to dry completely.

19   The repair area is now ready for painting. Spray painting must be carried out in a warm, dry, windless and dust free atmosphere. These conditions can be created if you have access to a large indoor work area, but if you are forced to work in the open, you will have to pick the day very carefully. If you are working indoors, dousing the floor in the work area with water will help settle the dust which would otherwise be in the air. If the repair area is confined to one body panel, mask off the surrounding panels. This will help minimize the effects of a slight mismatch in paint color. Trim pieces such as chrome strips, door handles, etc., will also need to be masked off or removed. Use masking tape and several thicknesses of newspaper for the masking operations.

20   Before spraying, shake the paint can thoroughly, then spray a test area until the spray painting technique is mastered. Cover the repair area with a thick coat of primer. The thickness should be built up using several thin layers of primer rather than one thick one. Using 600-grit wet-or-dry sandpaper, rub down the surface of the primer until it is very smooth. While doing this, the work area should be thoroughly rinsed with water and the wet-or-dry sandpaper periodically rinsed as well. Allow the primer to dry before spraying additional coats.

21   Spray on the top coat, again building up the thickness by using several thin layers of paint. Begin spraying in the center of the repair area and then, using a circular motion, work out until the whole repair area and about two inches of the surrounding original paint is covered. Remove all masking material 10 to 15 minutes after spraying on the final coat of paint: Allow the new paint at least two weeks to harden, then use a very fine rubbing compound to blend the edges of the new paint into the existing paint. Finally, apply a coat of wax.

6   Body repair – major damage

1   Major damage must be repaired by an auto body shop specifically equipped to perform unibody repairs. These shops have the specialized equipment required to do the job properly.

2   If the damage is extensive, the body must be checked for proper alignment or the vehicle's handling characteristics may be adversely affected and other components may wear at an accelerated rate.

3   Due to the fact that all of the major body components (hood, fenders, etc.) are separate and replaceable units, any seriously damaged components should be replaced rather than repaired. Sometimes the components can be found in a wrecking yard that specializes in used vehicle components, often at considerable savings over the cost of new parts.

7   Hinges and locks – maintenance

Once every 3000 miles, or every three months, the hinges and latch assemblies on the doors, hood and trunk should be given a few drops of light oil or lock lubricant. The door latch strikers should also be lubricated with a thin coat of grease to reduce wear and ensure free movement. Lubricate the door and trunk locks with spray-on graphite lubricant.

8   Fixed glass – replacement

Replacement of the windshield and fixed glass requires the use of special fast-setting adhesive/caulk materials and some specialized tools and techniques. These operations should be left to a dealer service department or a shop specializing in glass work.

9   Hood – removal, installation and adjustment

Refer to illustration 9.4

Note: *The hood is heavy and somewhat awkward to remove and install – at least two people should perform this procedure.*

Removal and installation

1   Use blankets or pads to cover the cowl area of the body and the fenders. This will protect the body and paint as the hood is lifted off.

2   Scribe or paint alignment marks around the bolt heads to insure proper alignment during installation (a permanent-type felt tip marker also will work for this).

3   Disconnect any cables or wire harnesses which will interfere with removal.

4   Have an assistant support the weight of the hood. Remove the hinge-to-hood nuts or bolts **(see illustration)** .

5   Lift off the hood.

6   Installation is the reverse of removal.

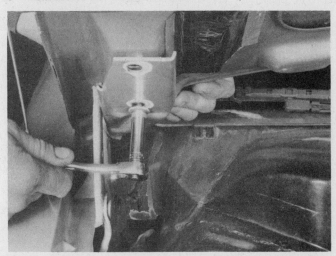

9.4   Support the hood while removing the bolts – note the white paint used to outline the bolt heads

Adjustment

7   Fore-and-aft and side-to-side adjustment of the hood is done by moving the hood in relation to the hinge plate after loosening the bolts or nuts.

8   Scribe or trace a line around the entire hinge plate so you can judge the amount of movement.

9   Loosen the bolts or nuts and move the hood into correct alignment. Move it only a little at a time. Tighten the hinge bolts or nuts and carefully lower the hood to check the alignment.

10   If necessary after installation, the entire hood latch assembly can be adjusted side-to-side on the radiator support so the hood closes securely and is flush with the fenders. To do this, scribe a line around the hood latch mounting bolts to provide a reference point. Then loosen the bolts and reposition the latch assembly as necessary. Following adjustment, retighten the mounting bolts. Up-and-down adjustment of the hood is accomplished by moving the position of the hood latch striker.

11   Finally, adjust the hood bumpers on the radiator support so the hood is flush with the fenders when closed.

12   The hood latch assembly, as well as the hinges, should be periodically lubricated with white lithium-base grease to prevent sticking and wear.

10   Radiator grille (4-door models) – removal and installation

Refer to illustration 10.2

1   Open the hood for access to the upper retaining rivets.

2   Use pliers or wire cutters to carefully pull up the center of each plastic

11

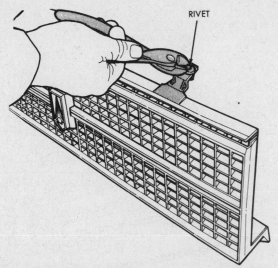

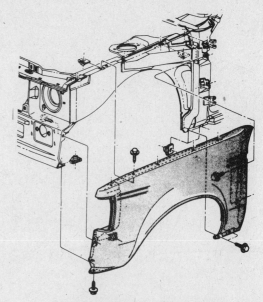

10.2 Use pliers or wire cutters to pull up the centers of the plastic retaining rivets so they can be removed (don't cut off the rivet heads!)

11.3 Front fender mounting details

retaining rivet (see illustration). Once the center of the rivet is pulled up, the rivet can be removed.

3   After the five rivets have been removed, detach the grille.

4   To install, place the grille in position and install the plastic rivets. Press the centers of the rivets in to lock the grille in place.

11 Front fender – removal and installation

Refer to illustration 11.3

1   Raise the vehicle, support it securely on jackstands and remove the front wheel.

2   Disconnect the antenna and all light bulb wiring harness connectors and other components that would interfere with fender removal.

3   Remove the fender mounting bolts (see illustration).

4   Detach the fender. It's a good idea to have an assistant support the fender while it's being moved away from the vehicle to prevent damage to the surrounding body panels.

5   Installation is the reverse of removal.

6   Tighten all nuts, bolts and screws securely.

12 Bumpers – removal and installation

Refer to illustrations 12.4a, 12.4b, 12.4c and 12.4d

1   Detach the bumper cover (if equipped).

2   Disconnect any wiring or other components that would interfere with bumper removal.

3   Support the bumper with a jack or jackstand or have an assistant support the bumper as the bolts are removed.

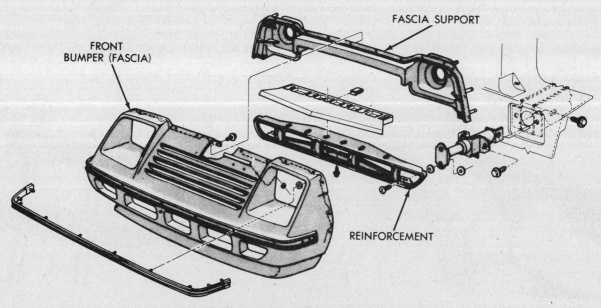

12.4a Front bumper mounting details (2-door models)

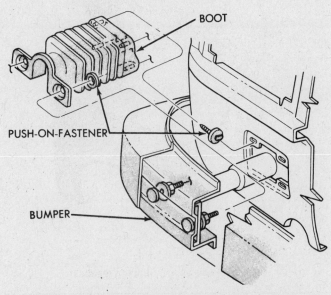

12.4b   Front bumper mounting details (4-door models)

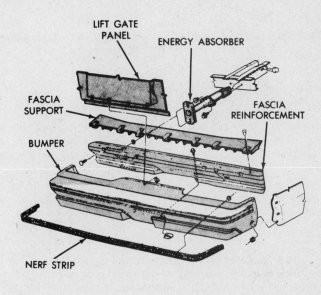

12.4c   Rear bumper mounting details (2-door models)

4   · Remove the mounting bolts and detach the bumper **(see illustrations)**.
5   Installation is the reverse of removal.
6   Tighten the mounting bolts securely.
7   Install the bumper cover and any other components that were removed.

13   Door trim panel – removal and installation

Refer to illustrations 13.2a, 13.2b and 13.3

1   Disconnect the negative cable from the battery.
2   Remove all door trim panel retaining screws and door pull/armrest assemblies **(see illustrations)**.

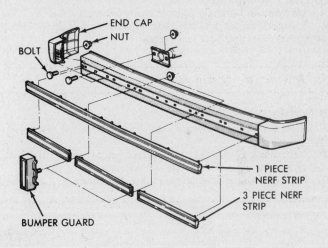

12.4d   Rear bumper mounting details (4-door models)

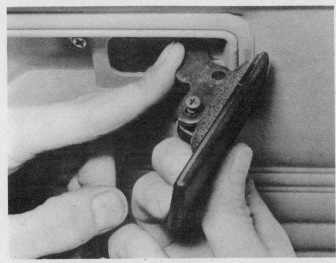

13.2a   Pull the door handle out for access to the mounting screw on the back side

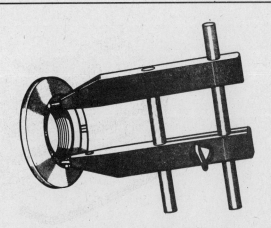

13.2b   A special tool such as this one may be required to remove the exterior mirror decorative retaining nut

11

13.3   Use an Allen wrench to remove the window crank screw

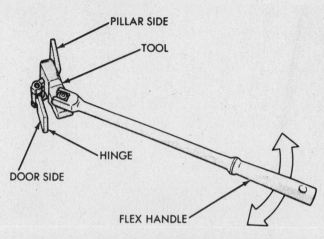

14.6   The door position can be adjusted by carefully bending the hinges with a special tool

3   Remove the window crank **(see illustration)**. Unscrew the door lock knob.
4   Insert a putty knife between the trim panel and the door and disengage the retaining clips. Work around the outer edge until the panel is free.
5   Once all of the clips are disengaged, detach the trim panel, unplug any wire harness connectors and remove the trim panel from the vehicle.
6   For access to the inner door, carefully peel back the plastic watershield.
7   Prior to installation of the door panel, be sure to reinstall any clips in the panel which may have come out during the removal procedure and remain in the door itself.
8   Plug in the wire harness connectors and place the panel in position in the door. Press the trim panel into place until the clips are seated.
9   Install the armrest/door pulls and the window crank.

14   Door – removal, installation and adjustment

Refer to illustration 14.6

1   Remove the door trim panel. Disconnect any wire harness connectors and push them through the door opening so they won't interfere with door removal.
2   Place a jack or jackstand under the door or have an assistant on hand to support it when the hinge bolts are removed. **Note:** *If a jack or jackstand is used, place a rag between it and the door to protect the door's painted surfaces.*

3   Remove the door stop bolts.
4   Remove the hinge-to-door bolts or drive out the pins and carefully lift off the door.
5   Installation is the reverse of removal.
6   Following installation of the door, check the alignment and adjust it if necessary as follows:
    a) Up-and-down and forward-and-backward adjustments are made by carefully bending the hinges slightly, using a special tool **(see illustration)**.
    b) The door lock striker can also be adjusted both up-and-down and sideways to provide positive engagement with the lock mechanism. This is done by loosening the mounting bolts and moving the striker as necessary.

15   Door latch and lock cylinder – removal and installation

Refer to illustrations 15.3, 15.4, 15.7 and 15.9

Latch

1   Close the window completely and remove the door trim panel and watershield (see Section 13).
2   Disconnect the link rods from the latch.
3   Remove the three mounting screws **(see illustration)**. It may be necessary to use an impact-type screwdriver to loosen them.
4   Pull the two halves of the latch out of the door **(see illustration)**.

15.3   The door latch is retained by three screws (arrows)

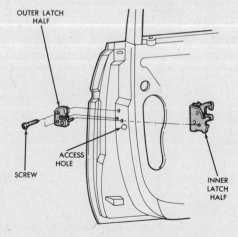

15.4   Door latch mounting details

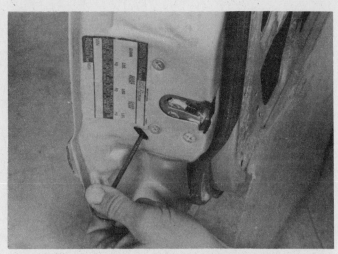

15.7   Insert the Allen wrench through the access hole into the latch adjusting screw

5   To install the latch, place the two halves in position and install the screws. Tighten the screws securely.

6   Connect the operating links to the latch.

7   Insert a 5/32-inch Allen wrench through the access hole in the door into the latch adjustment screw, then loosen the screw **(see illustration)**. Adjust the latch by moving the Allen wrench and screw up in the slot, then tighten the screw securely. Check the door handle position to make sure it's flush with the door surface.

8   Check the door to make sure it closes properly. Readjust the latch as necessary until the door closes smoothly (with the door handle flush with the door).

Lock cylinder

9   Disconnect the link, use a screwdriver to push the cylinder retainer off and withdraw the lock cylinder from the door **(see illustration)**.

10   Installation is the reverse of removal.

16   Door exterior handle – removal and installation

Refer to illustrations 16.2 and 16.3

1   Close the window completely and remove the door trim panel and watershield (see Section 13).

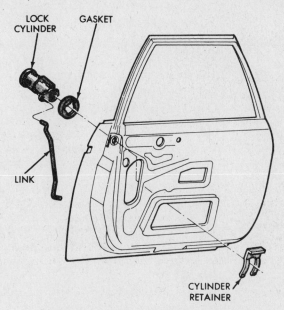

15.9   Lock cylinder mounting details

2   Disconnect the outside handle link from the latch, remove the mounting nuts and detach the handle from the door **(see illustration)**.

3   Prior to installation, lubricate the door handle hinge pivots with clean engine oil **(see illustration)**.

4   Place the handle in position, attach the link and install the nuts. Tighten the nuts securely.

5   Install the watershield and door trim panel.

17   Door window glass – removal, installation and adjustment

Front door

Removal

Refer to illustrations 17.2a and 17.2b

1   Remove the door trim panel and watershield (see Section 13).

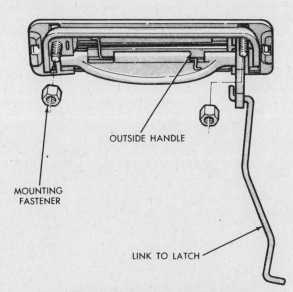

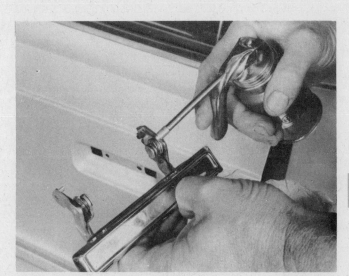

16.3   Lubricate the door handle hinge pivot prior to installation

16.2   Exterior door handle mounting details

11

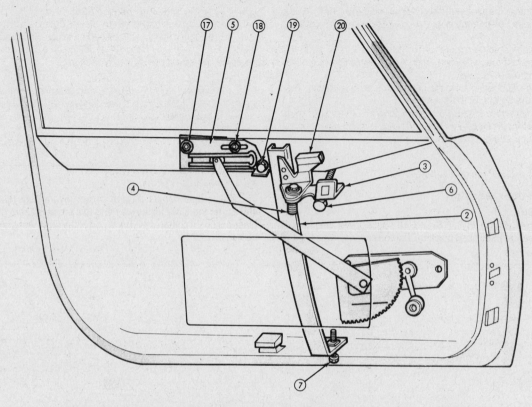

17.2a   Front door glass mechanism – 1978 thru 1981 models (see text for callouts)

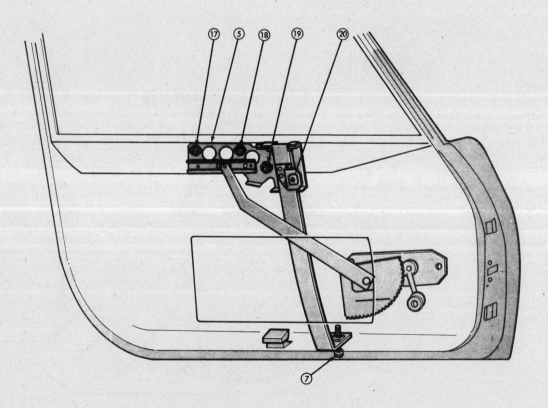

17.2b   Front door glass mechanism – 1982 and later models (see text for callouts)

2   Temporarily install the window crank and line up screws (17), (18) and (19) with the access holes in the door **(see illustrations)**. Remove the screws.
3   Lower the glass stabilizer (number 5 in the illustrations) so the lift channel is accessible through the inner door panel. On 1978 through 1981 models, loosen screw (4) as well.
4   Disengage the lift channel from the glass studs, then lower the glass and let it rest on the bottom of the door.
5   Use a small screwdriver and wood block to remove the outer glass channel weatherstripping by prying the spring clips out of the door panel.
6   Lift the glass up and out of the door channel.

Installation
7   Installation is the reverse of removal.

Adjustment (4-door models)
1978 through 1981
8   With screws (4), (6), (7), (17), (18) and (19) loose, lower the glass all the way, then raise it to the closed position. Tighten screws (18), (17) and

(19) in that order **(see illustration 17.2a)**.
9   Lightly tighten screw (6), push out on the glass track (20) so the stabilizer (20) is against the glass, then tighten screw (4). Loosen screw (6) so the bracket (3) can move freely, then lower the glass to the bottom of the door and tighten screws (6) and (7) securely.

1982 on
10   With screws (7), (17), (18), (19) and 20 loose, lower the glass all the way, then raise it to the closed position **(see illustration 17.2b)**. Tighten screws (17) and (19) securely.
11   Lightly tighten screw (20).
12   Lower the glass to the bottom of the door and tighten screws (7) and (20) securely.

Adjustment (2-door models)
Refer to illustration 17.13
13   Make sure screws (1), (2), (3), (4) and (5) are loose **(see illustration)**.
14   Lower the glass all the way and use the stabilizers (34) to push the glass out until it contacts the lower pad of the outer weatherstripping, then tighten screw (1).

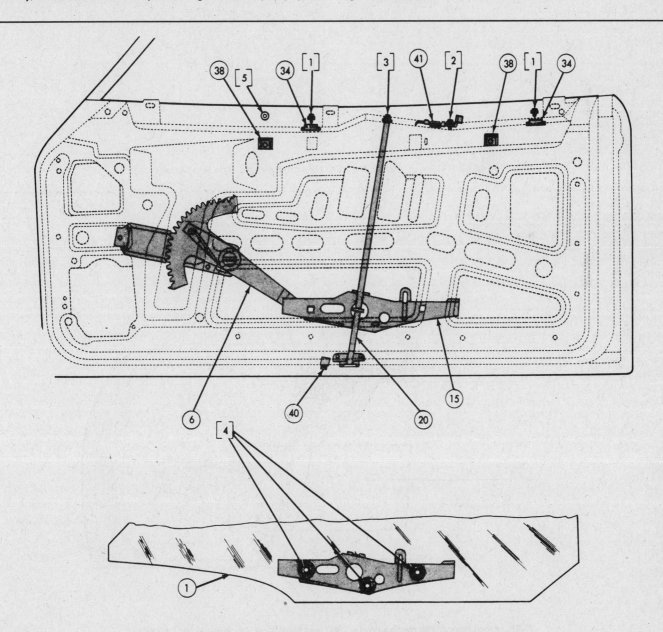

17.13   Front door glass adjustment details – 2-door models (see text for callouts)

11

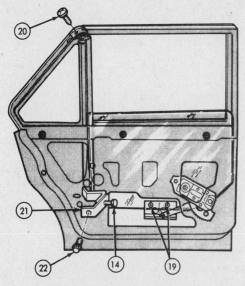

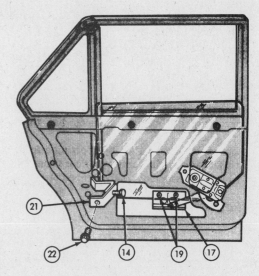

17.19   Rear door glass mounting details (see text for callouts)   **17.27   Rear door glass adjustment details (see text for callouts)**

15   Raise the glass to the closed position and adjust for correct alignment at the roof rails, A pillar and quarter window frame.
16   Tighten screws (4) and (3), in that order.
17   Adjust the up stops (38) until contact is made with the up stop flange of the lift plate (15), then tighten screw (5).
18   Pull the bracket and liner assembly (41) in until it contacts the hook on the glass lift plate (15), then tighten screw (2).

Rear door
Removal
Refer to illustration 17.19
19   Install the window crank and position the glass so the lift plate screws (19) are accessible through the inner door panel **(see illustration)**.
20   Support the door glass and remove the lift plate screws, then lower the glass to the bottom of the door.
21   Remove the upper division bar screw (20).
22   Remove the division bar bottom bracket screws, (14 and 22) and remove the bracket (21).
23   Detach the division bar and withdraw it through the access hole in the inner door panel.
24   Apply steady forward pressure to the fixed glass to disengage it from the door frame seal.
25   Lift the door glass up and out of the door.

Installation
26   Installation is the reverse of removal.

Adjustment
Refer to illustration 17.27
27   Make sure screws (14), (19) and (22) are loose **(see illustration)**.
28   Close the glass all the way and tighten the two lift channel screws (19).
29   Lower the glass all the way, make sure the division glass and bar are securely and squarely installed, then tighten screws (14) and (22).

---

18   Center console – removal and installation

Refer to illustrations 18.4a and 18.4b
1   Pull the parking brake handle all the way up. On manual transaxle models, remove the shift knob.
2   Remove the gearshift boot and parking brake cover.
3   Remove the mounting screws/bolts, detach the console and lift it up.
4   Unplug any electrical connectors and remove the console from the vehicle **(see illustrations)**.
5   Installation is the reverse of removal.

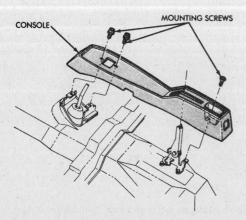

18.4a   Standard center console installation details

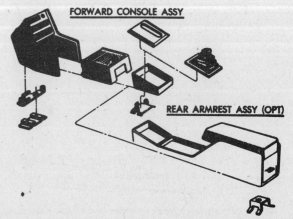

18.4b   Optional center console component layout

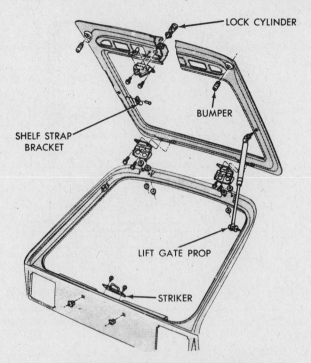

19.5a   Liftgate mounting details (4-door)

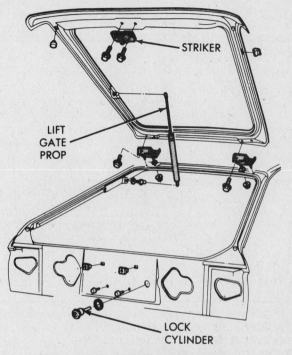

19.5b   Liftgate mounting details (2-door)

19   Liftgate – removal, installation and adjustment

Refer to illustrations 19.5a and 19.5b

1   Open the liftgate and cover the upper body area around the opening with an old blanket to protect the painted surfaces when the liftgate is removed.
2   Disconnect all cables and wire harness connectors that would interfere with removal of the liftgate.
3   Mark or scribe around the hinge flanges.
4   While an assistant supports the liftgate, detach the support props.
5   Remove the hinge bolts and detach the liftgate from the vehicle (see illustrations).
6   Installation is the reverse of removal.
7   After installation, close the liftgate and make sure it's in proper alignment with the surrounding body panels. Adjustments are made by chang-

ing the position of the hinge bolts in the slots. To adjust it, loosen the hinge bolts and reposition the hinges either side-to-side or fore-and-aft the desired amount and retighten the bolts.
8   The engagement of the liftgate can be adjusted by loosening the lock striker bolts, repositioning the striker and retightening the bolts.

20   Liftgate lock cylinder, latch and striker – removal and installation

Refer to illustrations 20.1a and 20.1b

Lock cylinder

1   Disconnect the link (2-door models), remove the retaining nut and detach the lock cylinder from the vehicle (see illustrations).
2   Installation is the reverse of removal.

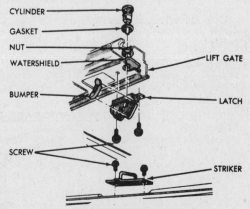

20.1a   Liftgate latch, lock cylinder and striker mounting details (4-door)

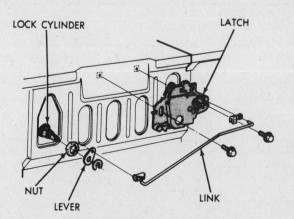

20.1b   Liftgate latch and lock cylinder mounting details (2-door)

11

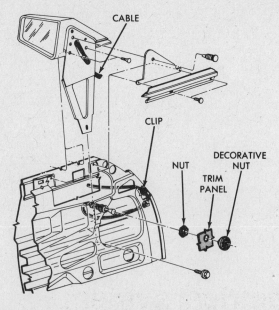

21.3a   Outside mirror and control cable installation details (later 2-door)

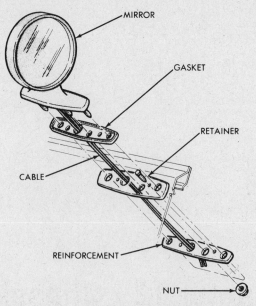

21.3b   Outside mirror and control cable installation details (early 2-door/all 4-door)

Latch

3   Disconnect the link (2-door models), remove the bolts and separate the latch from the vehicle.
4   Installation is the reverse of removal.

Striker

5   Unscrew the bolts and remove the striker.
6   To install the striker, place it in position and install the bolts. The position of the striker can be adjusted by loosening the bolts and moving it to achieve proper closing of the liftgate.

21   Outside mirror – removal and installation

Refer to illustrations 21.3a and 21.3b

1   Lower the window glass and remove the door trim panel and watershield (see Section 13).
2   On models so equipped, remove the armrest bracket.
3   On models with remote control mirrors, remove the retaining nut, detach the control from the bracket and the cable from the clip **(see illustrations)**.
4   Remove the nuts or bolts and detach the mirror from the door.
5   Installation is the reverse of removal.

22   Front fender inner splash panel – removal and installation

Refer to illustration 22.2

1   Loosen the wheel lug nuts, raise the front of the vehicle and support it securely on jackstands. Remove the wheel.
2   The splash panel is retained by plastic fasteners (rivets) **(see illustration)**. To remove them, carefully pull up on the center of each rivet with pliers or wire cutters (don't cut the rivet heads) **(see illustration 10.2)**. Once the center of each rivet is pulled up, the rivet can be removed.
3   After all the rivets have been removed, detach the splash shield.
4   To install the shield, hold it in position and install the plastic rivets. Press the centers of the rivets in to lock them (and the panel) in place.

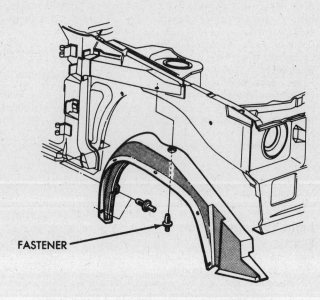

22.2   Fender splash panel mounting details

23   Seat belt check

1   Check the seat belts, buckles, latch plates and guide loops for obvious damage and signs of wear.
2   See if the seat belt reminder light comes on when the key is turned to the Run or Start positions. A chime should also sound.
3   The seat belts are designed to lock up during a sudden stop or impact, yet allow free movement during normal driving. Make sure the retractors return the belt against your chest while driving and rewind the belt fully when the buckle is unlatched.
4   If any of the above checks reveal problems with the seat belt system, replace parts as necessary.

Chapter 12 Chassis electrical system

Contents

Specifications

Light bulb application

Front	Type
Headlight	
Four-door and Shelby models	
Halogen	H6054
Standard	6052
Two-door models	H4656 and H4651
Park/turn signal light	1157
Side marker light	168

Interior

Speedometer and instrument cluster	168
Dome light	211-2
Map and courtesy light	562
Cargo area	
Four-door	912
Two-door	212-2

Rear

License plate light	168
Back-up light	1156
Brake/taillight	1157
High-mounted brake light	912
Turn signal light	1156
Side marker light	168

12

1   General information

The electrical system is a 12-volt, negative ground type. Power for the lights and all electrical accessories is supplied by a lead/acid-type battery which is charged by the alternator.

This Chapter covers repair and service procedures for the various electrical components not associated with the engine. Information on the battery, alternator, distributor and starter motor can be found in Chapter 5. **Caution:** *When working on the electrical system, disconnect the negative battery cable from the battery to prevent electrical shorts and/or fires.*

2   Electrical troubleshooting – general information

A typical electrical circuit consists of an electrical component, any switches, relays, motors, fuses, fusible links or circuit breakers related to the component and the wiring and connectors that link the component to both the battery and the chassis. To help pinpoint an electrical circuit problem, wiring diagrams are included at the end of this Chapter.

Before tackling any troublesome electrical circuit, first study the appropriate wiring diagrams to get a complete understanding of what makes up that individual circuit. Trouble spots, for instance, can often be narrowed down by noting if other components related to the circuit are operating properly. If several components or circuits fail at one time, chances are the problem is in a fuse or ground connection, because several circuits are often routed through the same fuse and ground connections.

Electrical problems usually stem from simple causes, such as loose or corroded connections, a blown fuse, a melted fusible link or a bad relay. Visually inspect the condition of all fuses, wires and connections in a problem circuit before troubleshooting it.

If testing instruments are going to be utilized, use the diagrams to plan ahead of time where to make the necessary connections to accurately pinpoint the trouble spot.

The basic tools needed for electrical troubleshooting include a circuit tester or voltmeter (a 12-volt bulb with a set of test leads can also be used), a continuity tester, which includes a bulb, battery and set of test leads, and a jumper wire, preferably with a circuit breaker incorporated, which can be used to bypass electrical components. Before attempting to locate a problem with test instruments, use the wiring diagram(s) to decide where to make the connections.

Voltage checks

Voltage checks should be performed if a circuit isn't functioning properly. Connect one lead of a circuit tester to either the negative battery terminal or a known good ground. Connect the other lead to a connector in the circuit being tested, preferably nearest to the battery or fuse. If the bulb of the tester lights, voltage is present, which means the part of the circuit between the connector and the battery is problem free. Continue checking the rest of the circuit in the same fashion. When you reach a point where no voltage is present, the problem lies between that point and the last test point with voltage. Most of the time the problem can be traced to a loose connection. **Note:** *Keep in mind that some circuits receive voltage only when the ignition key is in the Accessory or Run position.*

Finding a short

One method of finding a short in a circuit is to remove the fuse and connect a test light or voltmeter in its place to the fuse terminals. There should be no voltage present in the circuit. Move the wiring harness from side-to-side while watching the test light. If the bulb lights, there's a short to ground somewhere in that area, probably where the insulation has rubbed through. The same test can be performed on each component in the circuit, even a switch.

Ground check

Perform a ground test to check whether a component is properly grounded. Disconnect the battery and connect one lead of a self-powered test light, known as a continuity tester, to a known good ground. Connect the other lead to the wire or ground connection being tested. If the bulb lights, the ground is good. If the bulb doesn't light, the ground is no good.

Continuity check

A continuity check is done to determine if there are breaks in a circuit – if it's capable of passing electricity properly. With the circuit off (no power in the circuit), a self-powered continuity tester can be used to check it. Connect the test leads to both ends of the circuit (or to the "power" end and a good ground) – if the test light comes on the circuit is passing current properly. If the light doesn't come on, there's a break (open) somewhere in the circuit. The same procedure can be used to test a switch by connecting the continuity tester to the switch terminals. With the switch on, the test light should come on.

Finding an open circuit

When diagnosing for possible open circuits, it's often difficult to locate them by sight because oxidation or terminal misalignment are hidden by the connectors. Merely wiggling a connector on a sensor or in the wiring harness may correct the open circuit condition. Remember this when an open is indicated when troubleshooting a circuit. Intermittent problems may also be caused by oxidized or loose connections.

Electrical troubleshooting is simple if you keep in mind that all electrical circuits are basically electricity running from the battery, through the wires, switches, relays, fuses and fusible links to each electrical component (light bulb, motor, etc.) and to ground, where it's passed back to the battery. Any electrical problem is an interruption in the flow of electricity to and from the battery.

3   Fuses – general information

Refer to illustration 3.1

The electrical circuits of the vehicle are protected by a combination of fuses, circuit breakers and fusible links. The fuse block is located under the instrument panel on the left side of the dashboard **(see illustration)**.

Each of the fuses is designed to protect a specific circuit, and the various circuits are identified on the fuse panel itself. On 1979 and later models, miniaturized fuses are installed. These compact fuses allow fingertip removal and installation.

If an electrical component fails, always check the fuse first. A blown fuse is easily identified through the clear plastic body. Visually inspect the

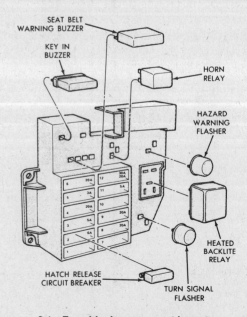

3.1   Fuse block component layout

element for evidence of damage. If a continuity check is called for, the blade terminal tips are exposed in the fuse body.

Be sure to replace blown fuses with the correct type. Fuses of different ratings are physically interchangeable, but only fuses of the proper rating should be used. Replacing a fuse with one of a higher or lower value than specified isn't recommended. Each electrical circuit needs a specific amount of protection. The amperage value of each fuse is molded into the fuse body.

If the replacement fuse immediately fails, don't replace it again until the cause of the problem is isolated and corrected. In most cases, the cause will be a short circuit in the wiring caused by a broken or deteriorated wire.

4   Fusible links – general information

Refer to illustration 4.3

Some circuits are protected by fusible links. The links are used in circuits which are not ordinarily fused, such as the ignition circuit.

Although the fusible links appear to be a heavier gauge than the wires they're protecting, the appearance is due to the thick insulation. All fusible links are four wire gauges smaller than the wire they're designed to protect.

Fusible links can't be repaired, but a new link of the same size wire can be installed. The procedure is as follows:

a) Disconnect the negative cable from the battery.
b) Disconnect the fusible link from the wiring harness.
c) Cut the damaged fusible link out of the wire just behind the connector.
d) Strip the insulation back approximately 1-inch **(see illustration)**.
e) Position the connector on the new fusible link and crimp it into place.
f) Use rosin core solder at each end of the new link to obtain a good connection.
g) Use plenty of electrical tape around the soldered joint. No wires should be exposed.
h) Connect the negative battery cable. Test the circuit for proper operation.

5   Circuit breakers – general information

Circuit breakers protect components such as power windows, power door locks and headlights. Some circuit breakers are located in the fuse box.

On some models the circuit breaker resets itself automatically, so an electrical overload in the circuit will cause it to fail momentarily, then come back on. If the circuit doesn't come back on, check it immediately. Once the condition is corrected, the circuit breaker will resume its normal function. Some circuit breakers must be reset manually.

6   Relays – general information

Several electrical accessories in the vehicle utilize relays to transmit current to the component. If the relay is defective, the component won't operate properly.

If a faulty relay is suspected, it can be removed and tested by a dealer service department or a repair shop. Defective relays must be replaced as a unit.

7   Turn signal and hazard flashers – check and replacement

Turn signal flasher

1   The turn signal flasher, a small canister-shaped unit located in the fuse block **(see illustration 3.1)**, flashes the turn signals.
2   When the flasher unit is functioning properly, an audible click can be heard during its operation. If the turn signals fail on one side or the other and the flasher unit doesn't make its characteristic clicking sound, a faulty turn signal bulb is indicated.
3   If both turn signals fail to blink, the problem may be due to a blown fuse, a faulty flasher unit, a broken switch or a loose or open connection. If a quick check of the fuse box indicates the turn signal fuse has blown, check the wiring for a short before installing a new fuse.
4   To replace the flasher, simply pull it straight out of the fuse block.
5   Make sure the replacement is identical to the original. Compare the old one to the new one before installing it.
6   Installation is the reverse of removal.

Hazard flasher

7   The hazard flasher, a small canister-shaped unit located in the fuse block, flashes all four turn signals simultaneously when activated.
8   The hazard flasher is checked just like the turn signal flasher (see Steps 2 and 3).
9   To replace the hazard flasher, pull it out of the back of fuse block.
10   Make sure the replacement is identical to the original. Compare the old one to the new one before installing it.
11   Installation is the reverse of removal.

8   Steering column switches – removal and installation

Refer to illustrations 8.2, 8.4, 8.5, 8.10 and 8.14
1   Disconnect the negative battery cable.

Headlight dimmer switch

2   The dimmer switch is mounted on the steering column under the dash and is connected to the wiper/washer switch by a pushrod **(see illustration)**.

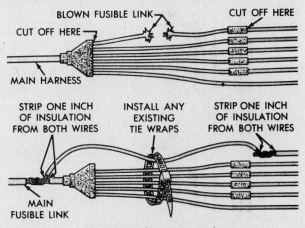

4.3   Fusible link repair details

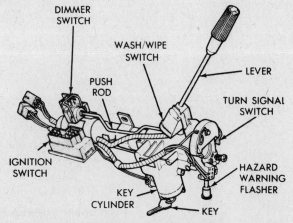

8.2   Steering column switch layout

12

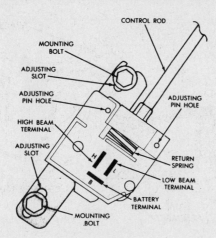

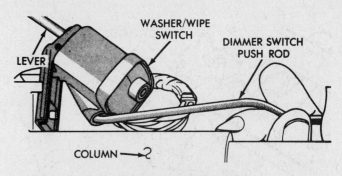

8.5   Engage the pushrod in both the wiper/washer and dimmer switches

8.4   Insert two 3/32-inch drill bits into the dimmer switch adjusting pin holes

3   Unplug the electrical connector, remove the two bolts, disengage the pushrod and lower the switch from the column.
4   To install the switch, seat the pushrod and compress the switch until two 3/32-inch drill bits can be inserted into the adjusting pin holes (**see illustration**).
5   Position the switch, insert the upper end of the pushrod into the wiper/washer switch and install the bolts (**see illustration**). Push the switch back very lightly, tighten the bolts securely, remove the drill bits and plug in the electrical connector.
6   After installation, make sure the switch makes the corresponding clicks when the wiper/washer switch is raised and lowered – adjust it as necessary.

Wiper/washer switch

7   Unplug the electrical connectors from both the wiper/washer and turn signal switches.
8   Remove the four screws and detach the lower column cover.
9   Carefully lift out the horn button and remove the wiper/washer switch hider disc.
10   Turn the ignition switch to the Off position, then turn the steering wheel so the access hole in the steering wheel hub lines up with the turn signal switch screw. Insert a screwdriver through the access hole and loosen the screw (**see illustration**).
11   Detach the pushrod from the switch, unplug the electrical connector and lift the switch off.
12   Installation is the reverse of removal. Be sure to replace the hider disc and engage the pushrod securely.

Turn signal switch

13   Remove the steering wheel (see Chapter 10) and the steering column lower cover.
14   Unplug the electrical connector, remove the screws and lift the switch off (**see illustration**).
15   Installation is the reverse of removal.

---

9   Ignition switch and lock cylinder – removal and installation

Refer to illustrations 9.3 and 9.7
1   Disconnect the negative battery cable from the battery.

Ignition switch

2   Unplug the electrical connector, turn the switch to the Lock position and remove the key.
3   Remove the two mounting screws, lower the switch, then rotate it 90-degrees and detach the pushrod (**see illustration**).

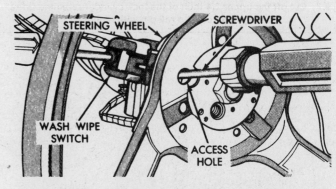

8.10   Insert the screwdriver through the hole in the steering wheel to remove the turn signal/wiper/washer switch screw

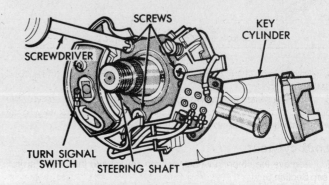

8.14   Use a Phillips screwdriver to remove the turn signal switch screws

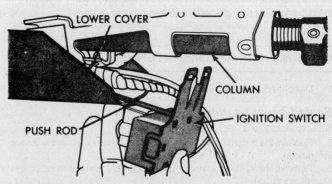

9.3   Lower the switch from the column and turn it 90-degrees so the pushrod can be disconnected

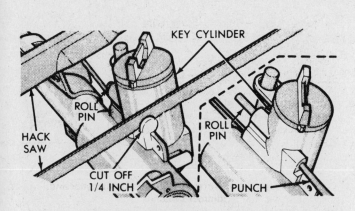

9.7   Cut off the upper 1/4-inch of the lock cylinder retaining boss, then drive out the roll pin with a punch

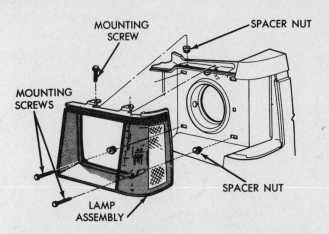

10.2   After removing the screws, the headlight bezel can be lifted off

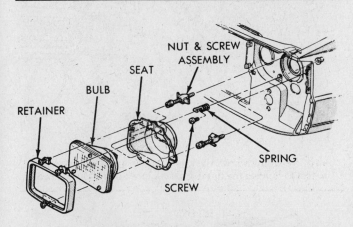

10.3   Headlight components – exploded view

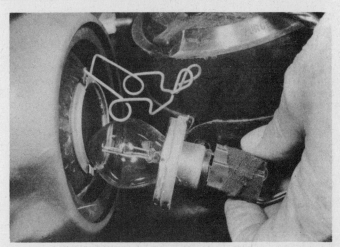

10.9   Release the clip and remove the halogen bulb and holder from the housing

4   Prior to installation, place the switch in the Lock position (the second detent from the top).

5   Hold the switch at a right angle to the steering column, connect the pushrod, then rotate the switch into place and push it back very lightly while installing the screws. Tighten the screws securely.

Lock cylinder

6   Remove the steering wheel, column covers and turn signal switch (see Section 8).

7   Use a hacksaw blade to cut off the upper 1/4-inch of the cylinder retainer boss, then use a hammer and punch to drive out the roll pin **(see illustration)**. Detach the lock cylinder from the steering column.

8   To install the lock cylinder, insert it until it engages the lug, then drive in the roll pin. Insert the key and check for proper operation.

10   Headlights – removal and installation

1   Disconnect the negative cable from the battery.

Sealed-beam headlights

Refer to illustrations 10.2 and 10.3

2   Remove the mounting screws and detach the lamp assembly **(see illustration)**.

3   Remove the retainer screws – don't disturb the adjustment screws **(see illustration)**.

4   Remove the retainer and pull the headlight out enough to allow the connector to be unplugged.

5   Remove the headlight.

6   To install the headlight, plug the connector in, position the headlight and install the retainer and screws. Tighten the screws securely.

7   Place the lamp assembly in position and install the screws.

Halogen headlights

Refer to illustration 10.9

Warning: *Halogen bulbs are gas-filled and under pressure and may shatter if the surface is scratched or the bulb is dropped. Wear eye protection and handle the bulbs carefully, grasping only the base whenever possible. Don't touch the surface of the bulb with your fingers because the oil from your skin could cause it to overheat and fail prematurely. If you do touch the bulb surface, clean it with rubbing alcohol.*

8   Open the hood.

9   Reach behind the headlight assembly, detach the spring clip and pull the holder assembly out for access to the bulb **(see illustration)**.

10   Grasp the bulb base and unplug it from the holder.

11   Insert the new bulb into the holder.

12   Install the bulb holder in the headlight assembly.

11   Headlights – adjustment

Refer to illustration 11.1

Note: *The headlights must be aimed correctly. If adjusted incorrectly, they could blind the driver of an oncoming vehicle and cause an accident or se-*

12

11.1   Headlight adjustment screw locations (arrows)

riously reduce your ability to see the road. The headlights should be checked for proper aim every 12 months and any time a new headlight is installed or front end body work is performed. The following procedure is only an interim step to provide temporary adjustment until the headlights can be adjusted by a properly equipped shop.

1   Headlights have two spring loaded adjusting screws, one on the top controlling up-and-down movement and one on the side controlling left-and-right movement **(see illustration)**.

2   This procedure requires a blank wall 25 feet in front of the vehicle and a level floor.

3   Position masking tape vertically on the wall in reference to the vehicle centerline and the centerlines of both headlights.

4   Position a horizontal tape line in reference to the centerline of all the headlights. **Note:** It may be easier to position the tape on the wall with the vehicle parked only a few inches away.

5   Adjustment should be made with the vehicle sitting level, the gas tank half-full and no unusually heavy load in the vehicle.

6   Starting with the low beam adjustment, position the high intensity zone so it's two inches below the horizontal line and two inches to the right of the headlight vertical line. Adjustment is made by turning the top adjusting screw clockwise to raise the beam and counterclockwise to lower the beam. The adjusting screw on the side should be used in the same manner to move the beam left or right.

7   With the high beams on, the high intensity zone should be vertically centered with the exact center just below the horizontal line. **Note:** It may not be possible to position the headlight aim exactly for both high and low beams. If a compromise must be made, keep in mind that the low beams are the most used and have the greatest effect on driver safety.

8   Have the headlights adjusted by a dealer service department or service station at the earliest opportunity.

12   Bulb replacement

Refer to illustrations 12.3a, 12.3b, 12.3c and 12.4

1   The lenses of many lights are held in place by screws, which makes it a simple procedure to gain access to the bulbs.

2   On some lights the lenses are held in place by clips. The lenses can be removed either by unsnapping them or by using a small screwdriver to pry them off.

3   Several types of bulbs are used. Some are removed by pushing in and turning them counterclockwise **(see illustration)**. Others can simply be unclipped from the terminals or pulled straight out of the socket **(see illustrations)**.

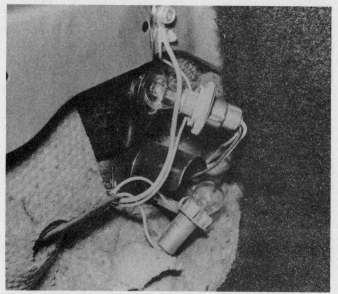

12.3a   After pulling the sockets out of the taillight housing, the bulbs can be removed by pushing in and turning them counterclockwise

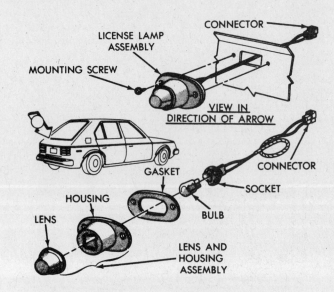

12.3b   License plate light bulb mounting details

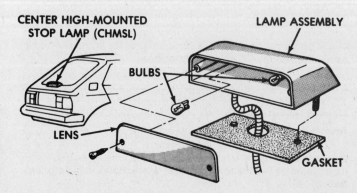

12.3c   High-mounted brake light bulb mounting details

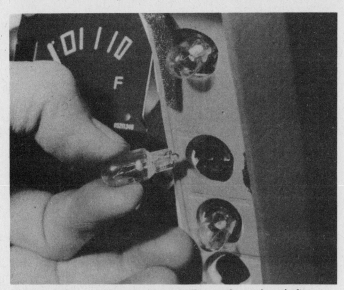

12.4   The instrument cluster bulbs can be replaced after removing the mask lens

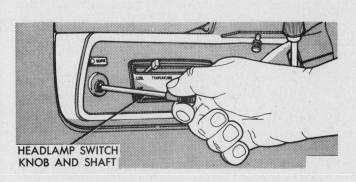

HEADLAMP SWITCH KNOB AND SHAFT

13.2   Depress the release button (not shown) and pull the knob and shaft out of the headlight switch

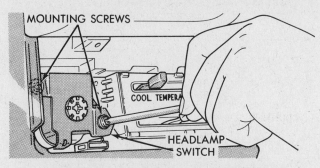

MOUNTING SCREWS

COOL TEMPERA

HEADLAMP SWITCH

13.4a   Remove the screws, detach the switch . . .

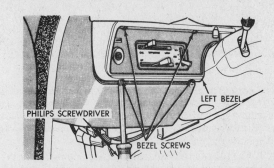

PHILIPS SCREWDRIVER

LEFT BEZEL

BEZEL SCREWS

13.3   Locations of the left side instrument panel bezel screws

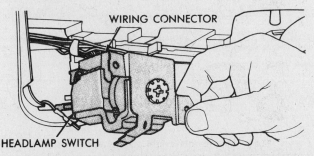

WIRING CONNECTOR

HEADLAMP SWITCH

13.4b   . . . and pull it out for access to the connector

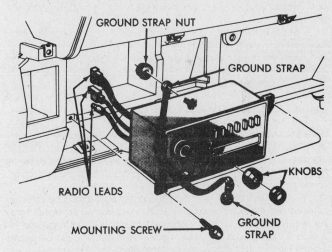

GROUND STRAP NUT

GROUND STRAP

KNOBS

RADIO LEADS

MOUNTING SCREW

GROUND STRAP

14.3   Radio mounting details

---

4   To gain access to the instrument panel lights, the instrument cluster mask must be removed first **(see illustration)**.

13   Headlight switch – removal and installation

Refer to illustrations 13.2, 13.3, 13.4a and 13.4b

1   Disconnect the negative battery cable.
2   Reach up under the instrument panel, depress the release button on the bottom of the switch and withdraw the switch knob and shaft **(see illustration)**.
3   Remove the left bezel **(see illustration)**.
4   Remove the screws, detach the switch from the panel, unplug the

electrical connector and remove the switch **(see illustrations)**.
5   Installation is the reverse of removal.

14   Radio – removal and installation

Refer to illustration 14.3
Caution: *The radio may be damaged if it's operated with the speakers disconnected.*

1   Disconnect the negative battery cable from the battery.
2   Remove the seven screws and detach the center instrument panel bezel.
3   Remove the mounting screws/nuts **(see illustration)**.

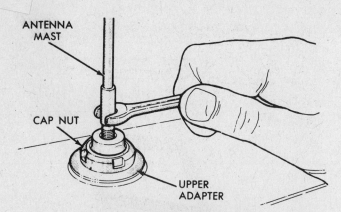

15.3 Unscrew the antenna mast with a small wrench and remove the cap nut and gasket

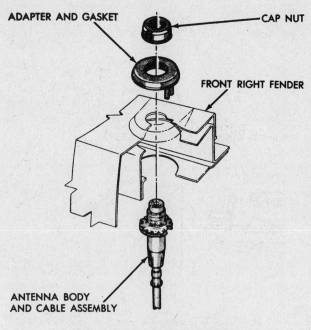

15.5 Antenna mounting details

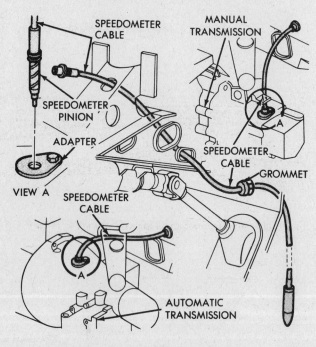

16.2a Speedometer cable routing details

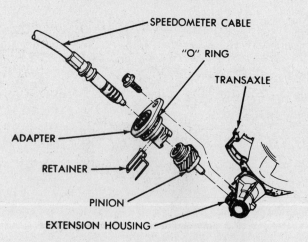

16.2b The speedometer cable can be disconnected from the adapter by removing the retainer

---

4   Pull the radio out of the instrument panel and disconnect the ground lead, electrical connectors and antenna lead.
5   Installation is the reverse of removal.

15   Antenna – removal and installation

Refer to illustrations 15.3 and 15.5
1   Disconnect the negative battery cable.
2   Remove the radio (Section 14).
3   Use a small open-end wrench to unscrew the antenna mast, then remove the cap nut and lift off the upper adapter and gasket **(see illustration)**.
4   Working under the vehicle, remove the three plastic rivets or screws from the rear edge of the inner fender splash shield and pull the shield away for access to the antenna.
5   Detach the antenna from the fender and remove it from the vehicle **(see illustration)**.
6   Installation is the reverse of removal.

16   Speedometer cable – replacement

Refer to illustrations 16.2a and 16.2b
1   Disconnect the negative cable from the battery.
2   Disconnect the speedometer cable from the transaxle **(see illustrations)**. On air conditioned models, remove the left cooler duct.
3   Detach the cable from the routing clips in the engine compartment and pull it up to provide enough slack to allow disconnection from the speedometer.
4   Remove the instrument cluster screws, pull the cluster out and disconnect the speedometer cable from the back of the cluster. On some models, the speedometer connection can be reached after removing the mask lens. Depress the retaining clip on the back of the instrument cluster to detach the cable from the speedometer.
5   Remove the cable from the vehicle.
6   Prior to installation, lubricate the speedometer end of the cable with spray-on speedometer cable lubricant (available at auto parts stores).
7   Installation is the reverse of removal.

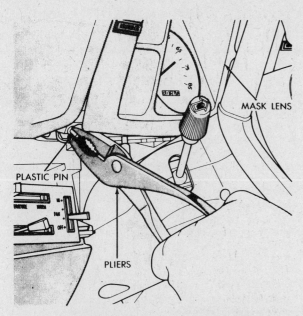

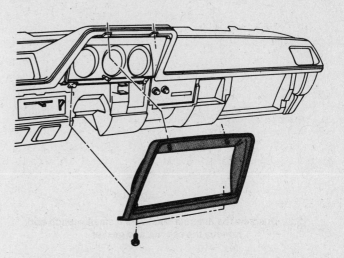

17.2b Instrument cluster bezel mounting details (1983 on)

17.2a On 1978 through 1982 models, use pliers to pull out the two mask lens retaining pins

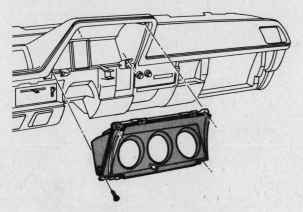

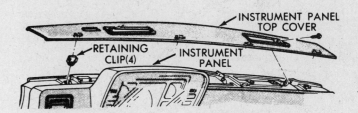

18.2 Instrument panel top cover mounting details

17.3 Instrument cluster mounting details

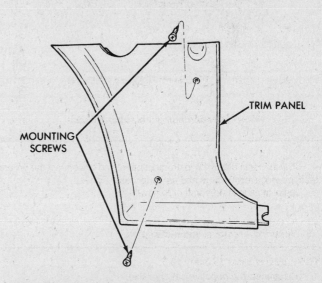

17 Instrument cluster – removal and installation

Refer to illustrations 17.2a, 17.2b and 17.3

1   Disconnect the negative cable from the battery.
2   On 1978 through 1982 models, use pliers to remove the two plastic pins **(see illustration)**, then lower the mask and lens assembly and lift it out of the cluster housing. On 1983 and later models, remove the cluster bezel **(see illustration)**. Remove the screws, lower the mask and lens, then lift it out. **Note:** *The instruments and bulbs can be serviced after mask and lens removal; it isn't necessary to remove the cluster.*
3   On all models, remove the cluster mounting screws, pull the assembly out, disconnect the electrical connectors, depress the clip and detach the cable from the speedometer, then remove the cluster from the vehicle **(see illustration)**.
4   Installation is the reverse of removal.

18 Instrument panel – removal and installation

Refer to illustrations 18.2, 18.4, 18.5, 18.7a, 18.7b, 18.10 and 18.12

1   Disconnect the negative battery cable.

18.4 The side cowl trim panels are secured by two screws

2   Remove the two screws from the outer edge of the defroster openings in the top cover. Pry up the rear edge of the cover and disengage the cover clips. Remove the cover by lifting it up and moving it to the rear **(see illustration)**.
3   Detach the A-pillar trim moldings by removing the two molding screws and the outer screw from the upper windshield garnish molding.
4   Remove the two left side cowl trim panels **(see illustration)**.

12

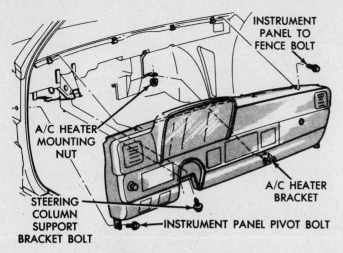

18.5   Instrument panel mounting details

5   Loosen the left and right-hand instrument panel pivot bolts (see illustration).

6   Remove the nut attaching the instrument panel to the air conditioner/heater bracket (see illustration 18.5).

7   On air conditioned vehicles, remove the screws attaching the air conditioner cover to the center distribution duct and slide the cover to the rear (see illustration). Remove the instrument cluster assembly (see illustration). Then, working through the access openings in the cluster area of the instrument panel, depress the speedometer cable retaining clip and disconnect the speedometer cable.

8   On vehicles without air conditioning, reach up behind the instrument panel and disconnect the speedometer cable by depressing the retaining clip.

9   Position the driver's seat all the way to the rear.

10   Remove the fasteners that secure the steering column to the brake pedal support bracket (see illustration) and lower the steering column until the steering wheel rests on the floor.

11   Remove the four screws attaching the instrument panel to the windshield fence (see illustration 18.5).

12   Pull the instrument panel out enough to permit the ground strap to be disconnected, then rotate the panel to the rear and down (see illustration).

13   Disconnect the following components at the wiring connectors:

Headlight dimmer switch
Ignition switch/accessories
Ignition/starter switch
Buzzer switch
Turn signal switch
Windshield wiper switch
Brake light switch

14   Working in the engine compartment, loosen the bolt joining the 40-wire firewall connector.

15   Working under the instrument panel, depress the holding tabs on the firewall connector and pull it out of the plenum.

16   Remove the two nuts and detach the fuse block and relay bank from the left side cowl.

17   Disconnect the side cowl wiring connectors on both sides.

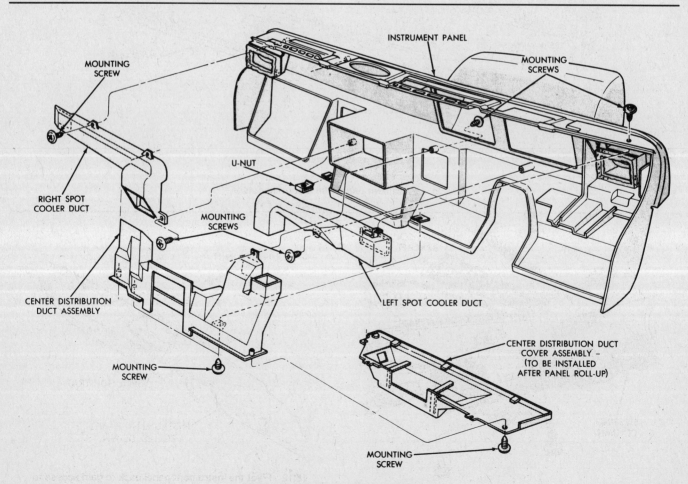

18.7a   Air conditioner/heater duct layout

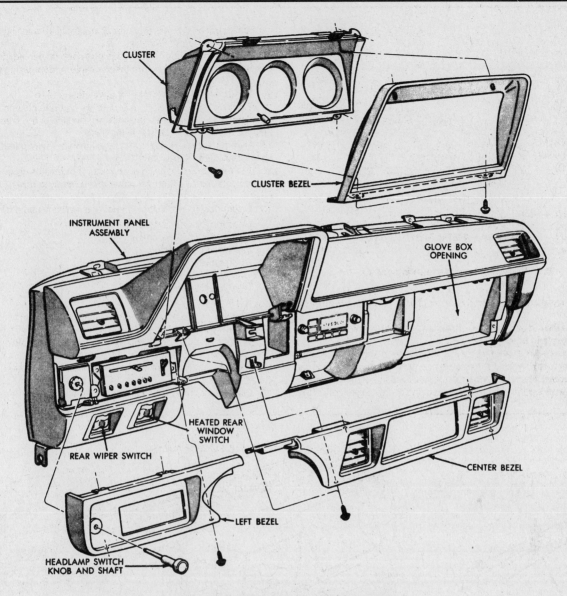

CLUSTER

CLUSTER BEZEL

INSTRUMENT PANEL
ASSEMBLY

GLOVE BOX
OPENING

HEATED REAR
WINDOW
SWITCH

REAR WIPER SWITCH

CENTER BEZEL

LEFT BEZEL

HEADLAMP SWITCH
KNOB AND SHAFT

18.7b   Instrument panel trim mounting details

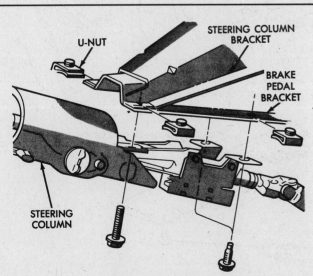

U-NUT

STEERING COLUMN
BRACKET

BRAKE
PEDAL
BRACKET

STEERING
COLUMN

18.10   Steering column mounting details

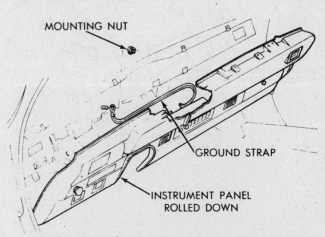

MOUNTING NUT

GROUND STRAP

INSTRUMENT PANEL
ROLLED DOWN

18.12   Pivot the instrument panel back to gain access to
the various electrical connectors

12

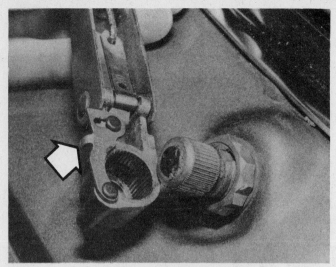

19.2a   Pull up on the lever (arrow) to release the wiper arm from the shaft

19.3   Lift the cover off the windshield wiper motor

18 Disconnect the air conditioner vacuum harness at the quick disconnect fitting.
19 Disconnect the heater or air conditioner control cable.
20 Disconnect the radio antenna and remove the cable from the clips.
21 Remove the nut and disconnect the radio ground strap from the plenum.
22 Disconnect the wiring from the anti-diesel relay (if equipped).
23 Disconnect the blower motor wiring and the resistor block wiring.
24 The instrument panel can now be lifted clear of the side pivot bolts and removed from the vehicle.
25 Installation is the reverse of removal.

---

19   Wiper motor – removal and installation

1   Disconnect the negative cable from the battery.

Windshield wiper motor
Refer to illustrations 19.2a, 19.2b, 19.3 and 19.4

2   Remove the wiper arms, then remove the pivot nuts and washers **(see illustrations)**.
3   Open the hood and lift the plastic cover off the motor **(see illustration)**.

19.4   The wiper motor is fastened to the firewall with three bolts (arrows)

4   Unplug the electrical connector and remove the three wiper motor mounting bolts **(see illustration)**.
5   Detach the wiper pivots and remove the wiper motor and bracket, pivot and link mechanism as an assembly from the vehicle.
6   Installation is the reverse of removal. **Note:** *Make sure the pivot marked L is on the driver's side of the vehicle.*

Rear wiper motor
Refer to illustrations 19.7, 19.8, 19.9 and 19.10

7   Remove the wiper arm, using special tool C-3982 or equivalent **(see illustration)**. Don't try to pry the arm off with a screwdriver or the retaining clip will be damaged.
8   Remove the wiper arm shaft retaining nut, ring and seal from the pivot **(see illustration)**.

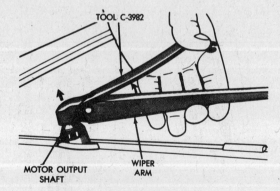

19.7   Use the special tool to remove the liftgate wiper – DO NOT try to pry it off with a screwdriver

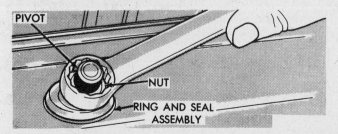

19.8   Use a box-end wrench to remove the pivot nut

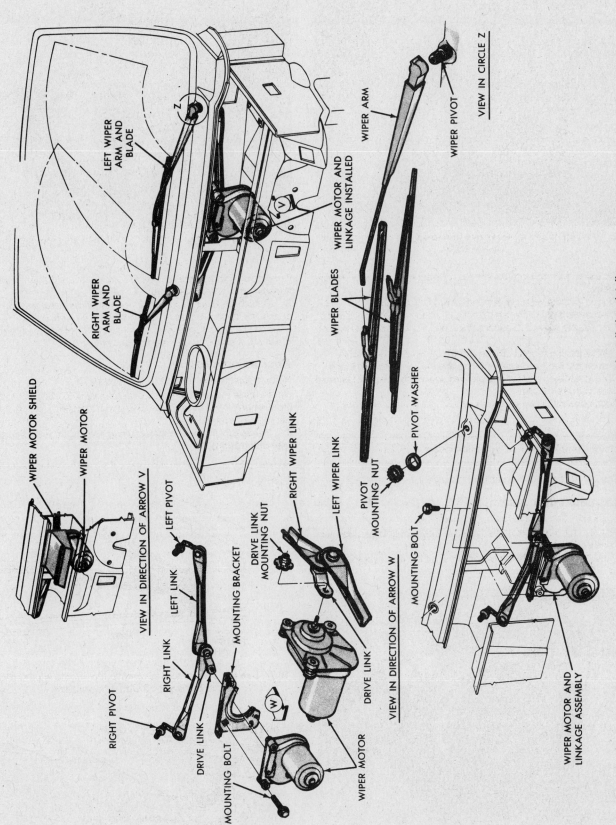

LEFT WIPER ARM AND BLADE

RIGHT WIPER ARM AND BLADE

WIPER MOTOR SHIELD

WIPER MOTOR

RIGHT PIVOT

DRIVE LINK

MOUNTING BOLT

WIPER MOTOR

VIEW IN DIRECTION OF ARROW V

LEFT PIVOT

LEFT LINK

RIGHT LINK

MOUNTING BRACKET

DRIVE LINK MOUNTING NUT

RIGHT WIPER LINK

LEFT WIPER LINK

DRIVE LINK

WIPER MOTOR AND LINKAGE INSTALLED

WIPER ARM

WIPER PIVOT

VIEW IN CIRCLE Z

WIPER BLADES

PIVOT WASHER

PIVOT MOUNTING NUT

MOUNTING BOLT

VIEW IN DIRECTION OF ARROW W

WIPER MOTOR AND LINKAGE ASSEMBLY

19.2b   Windshield wiper and motor installation details

12

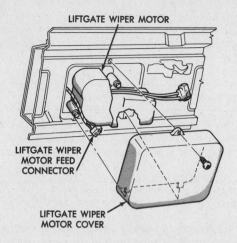

LIFTGATE WIPER MOTOR

LIFTGATE WIPER MOTOR FEED CONNECTOR

LIFTGATE WIPER MOTOR COVER

19.9   Remove the screws and detach the liftgate wiper motor cover

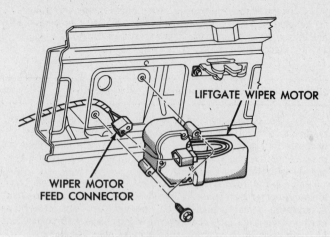

LIFTGATE WIPER MOTOR

WIPER MOTOR FEED CONNECTOR

19.10   Unplug the electrical connector, remove the bolts and detach the motor

COLOR CODE			
BK	BLACK	P	PINK
BR	BROWN	R	RED
DBL	DARK BLUE	T	TAN
DGN	DARK GREEN	V	VIOLET
GY	GRAY	W	WHITE
LBL	LIGHT BLUE	Y	YELLOW
LGN	LIGHT GREEN	*	WITH TRACER
O	ORANGE		

LEGEND			
-⊓⊓-	NORMALLY OPEN CONTACT	-⌁⌁⌁-	RESISTOR
-⊠-	NORMALLY CLOSED CONTACT	-⌁⌁⌁-	VARIABLE RESISTOR
-⊓⊔⊓-	THERMAL ELEMENT (BI-METEL STRIP)	-⊦⊦-	DIODE
-⌒-	CIRCUIT BREAKER	-⊣⊦	GROUND
-⌒⌒⌒-	COIL	o—o—o	SWITCH NORMALLY CLOSED
-⊗-	LAMP	o—⟋—o	SWITCH NORMALLY OPEN
-⌁-	FUSE	o—•—•—o	SWITCH GANGED NORMALLY CLOSED
-⊛-	THERMISTOR	⟶	CONNECTOR
Ω	OHMS	↓↓↓ Y Y Y	MULTIPLE CONNECTOR
-•-	SPLICE	→	MALE CONNECTOR
-⊪-	DENOTES WIRE GOES THROUGH MAIN GROMET TO BODY COMPARTMENT	-<	FEMALE CONNECTOR
		▣	DENOTES WIRE GOES THROUGH 40 WAY DISCONNECT

21.4   Wiring diagram color code and legend

9   Open the liftgate and remove the motor cover **(see illustration)**.
10   Unplug the electrical connector, remove the retaining screws/bolts and detach the motor from the liftgate **(see illustration)**.
11   Installation is the reverse of removal.

20   Cruise control system – description and check

The cruise control system maintains vehicle speed with a vacuum-actuated servo motor located in the engine compartment, which is connected to the throttle linkage by a cable. The system consists of the servo motor, clutch switch, brake switch, control switches, a relay and associated vacuum hoses.

Because of the complexity of the cruise control system and the special tools and techniques required for diagnosis, repair should be left to a dealer service department or a repair shop. However, it's possible for the home mechanic to make simple checks of the wiring and vacuum connections for minor faults which can be easily repaired. These include:

a) Inspect the cruise control actuating switches for broken wires and loose connections.
b) Check the cruise control fuse.

c) The cruise control system is operated by vacuum so it's critical that all vacuum switches, hoses and connections are secure. Check the hoses in the engine compartment for tight connections, cracks and obvious vacuum leaks.

21   Wiring diagrams – general information

Refer to illustration 21.4

Since it isn't possible to include all wiring diagrams for every year covered by this manual, the following diagrams are typical and most commonly needed.

Prior to troubleshooting any circuits, check the fuse and circuit breakers (if equipped) to make sure they're in good condition. Make sure the battery is properly charged and check the cable connections (see Chapter 1).

When checking a circuit, make sure all connectors are clean, with no broken or loose terminals. When unplugging a connector, don't pull on the wires. Pull only on the connector housings.

Refer to the accompanying table for the wire color codes applicable to the diagrams in this manual **(see illustration)**.

12

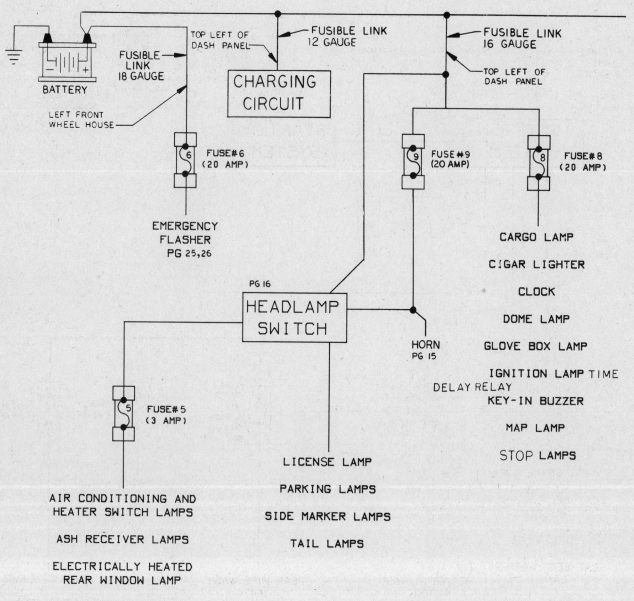

BATTERY

FUSIBLE LINK 18 GAUGE

LEFT FRONT WHEEL HOUSE

TOP LEFT OF DASH PANEL

FUSIBLE LINK 12 GAUGE

CHARGING CIRCUIT

FUSIBLE LINK 16 GAUGE

TOP LEFT OF DASH PANEL

FUSE#6 (20 AMP)

EMERGENCY FLASHER PG 25,26

FUSE#9 (20 AMP)

FUSE#8 (20 AMP)

PG 16

HEADLAMP SWITCH

HORN PG 15

CARGO LAMP

CIGAR LIGHTER

CLOCK

DOME LAMP

GLOVE BOX LAMP

IGNITION LAMP TIME DELAY RELAY

KEY-IN BUZZER

MAP LAMP

STOP LAMPS

FUSE#5 (3 AMP)

LICENSE LAMP

PARKING LAMPS

SIDE MARKER LAMPS

TAIL LAMPS

AIR CONDITIONING AND HEATER SWITCH LAMPS

ASH RECEIVER LAMPS

ELECTRICALLY HEATED REAR WINDOW LAMP

RADIO LAMP

REAR WINDSHIELD WIPER AND WASHER SWITCH LAMP (44)

CLUSTER LAMPS

CONSOLE GEAR SELECTOR LAMP

LIFTGATE RELEASE LAMP (24)

Typical earlier model fuse application chart (1 of 2)

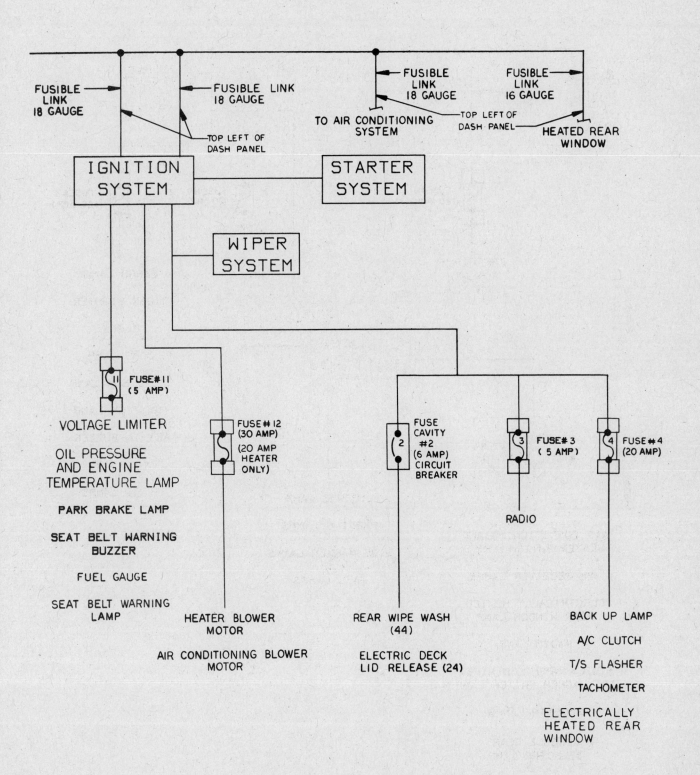

Typical earlier model fuse application chart (2 of 2)

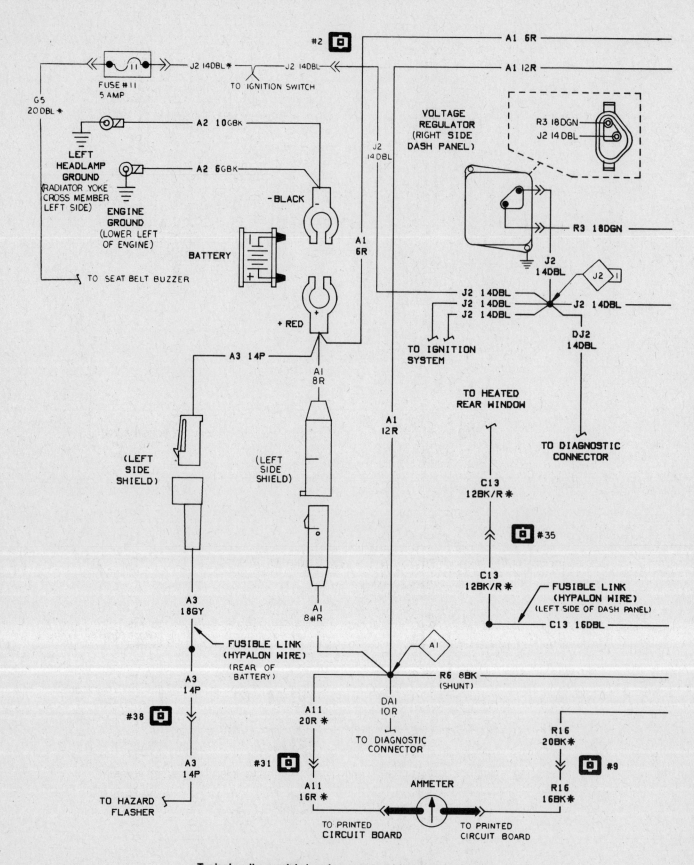

Typical earlier model charging system wiring diagram (1 of 2)

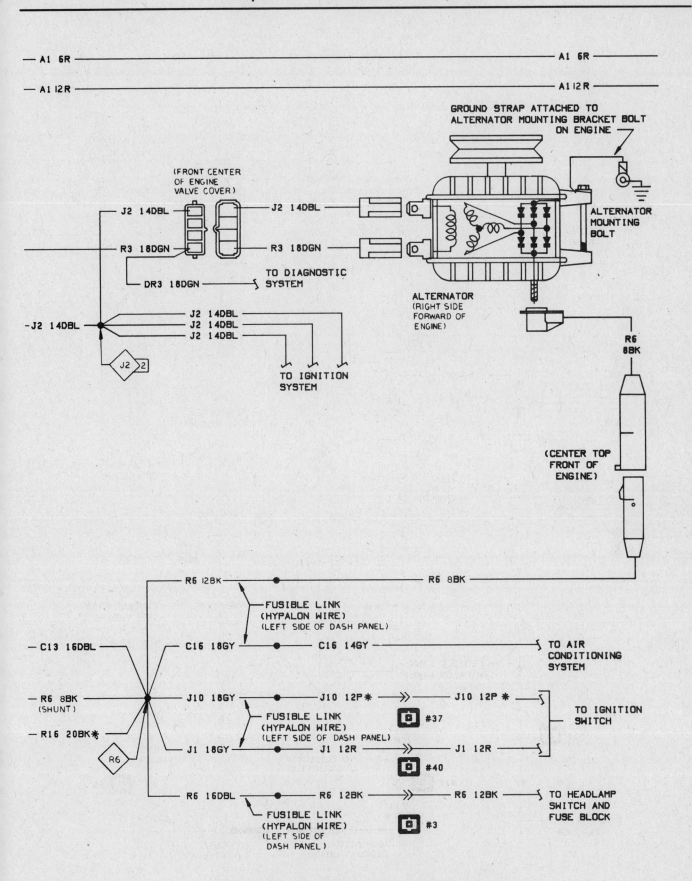

Typical earlier model charging system wiring diagram (2 of 2)

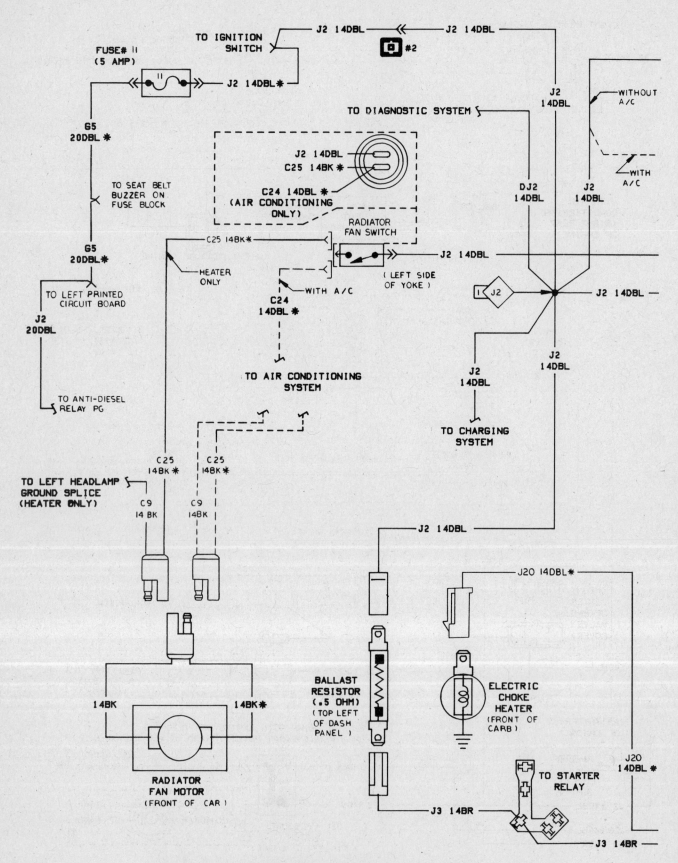

Typical earlier model electronic spark control system wiring diagram (1 of 2)

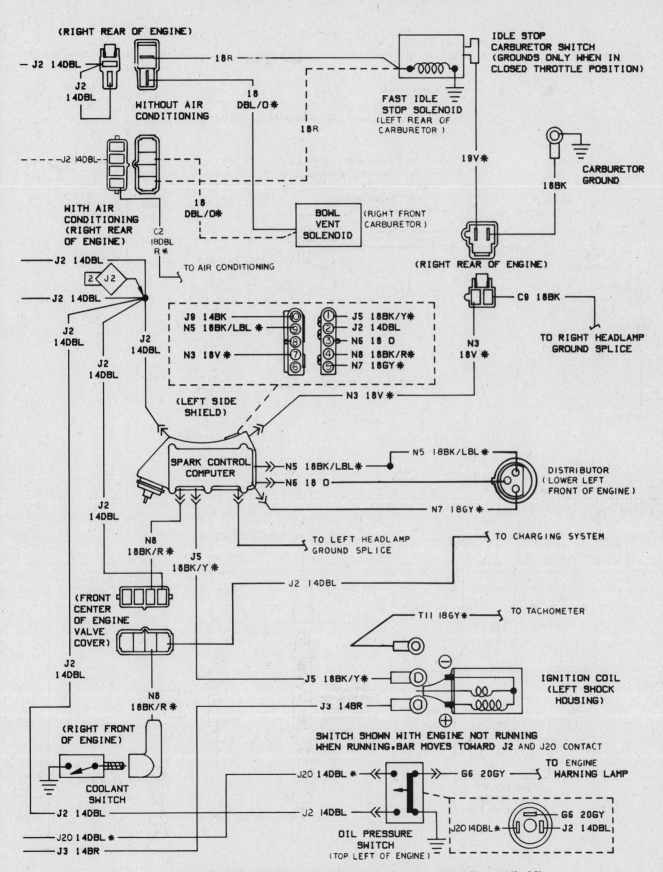

Typical earlier model electronic spark control system wiring diagram (2 of 2)

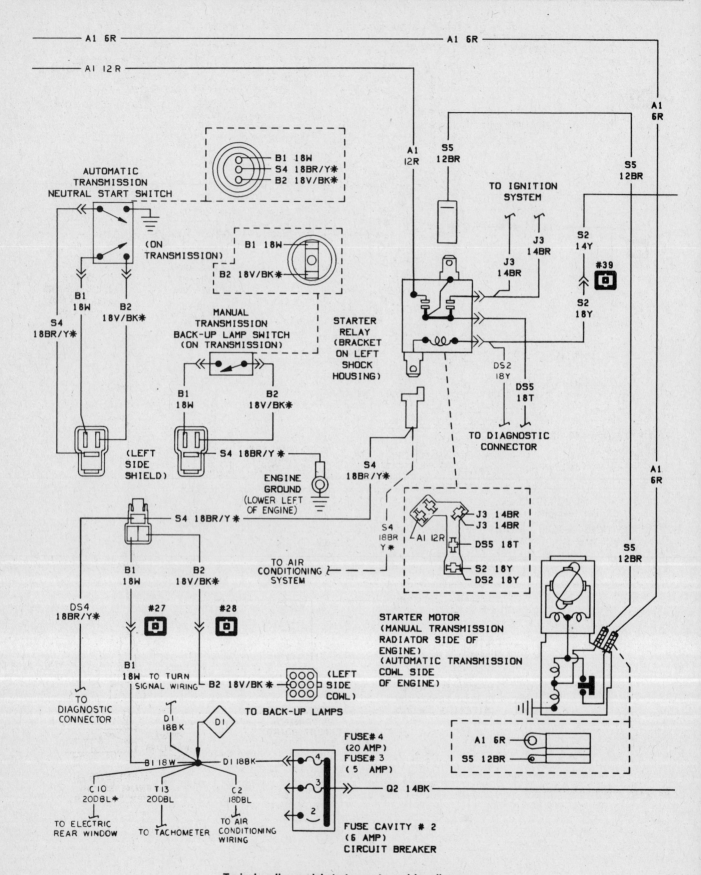

Typical earlier model starter system wiring diagram

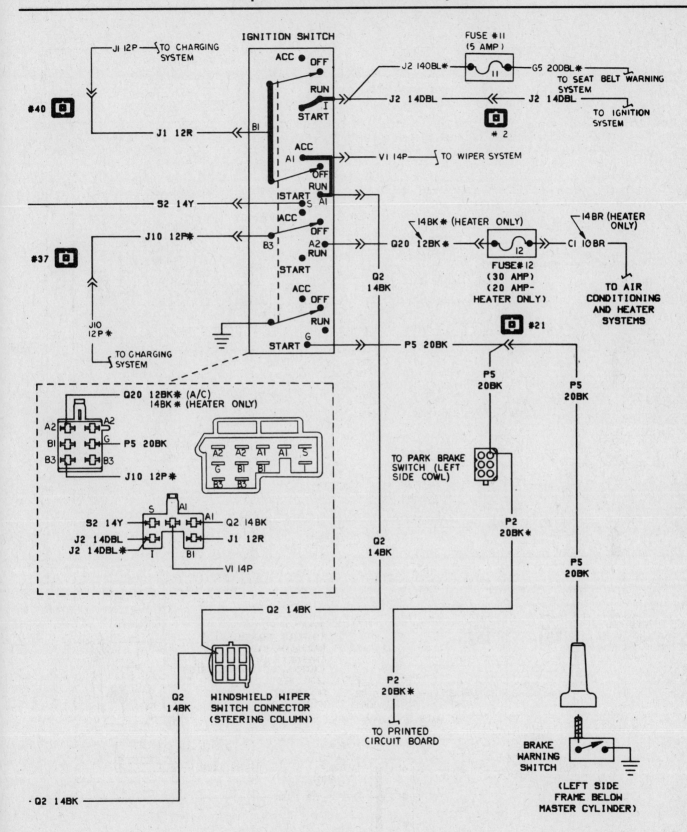

Typical earlier model ignition switch wiring diagram

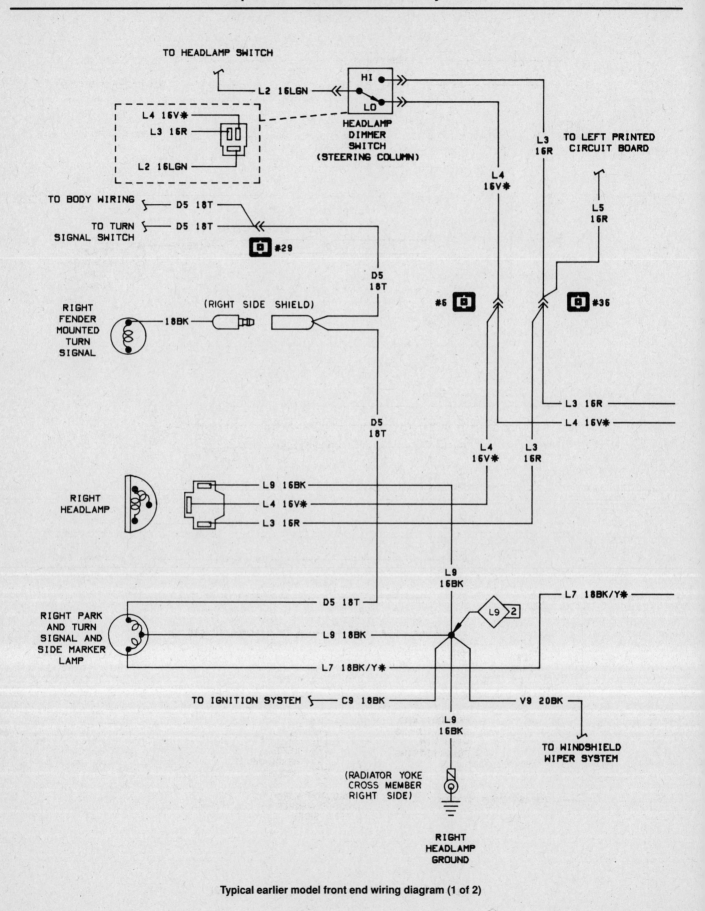

Typical earlier model front end wiring diagram (1 of 2)

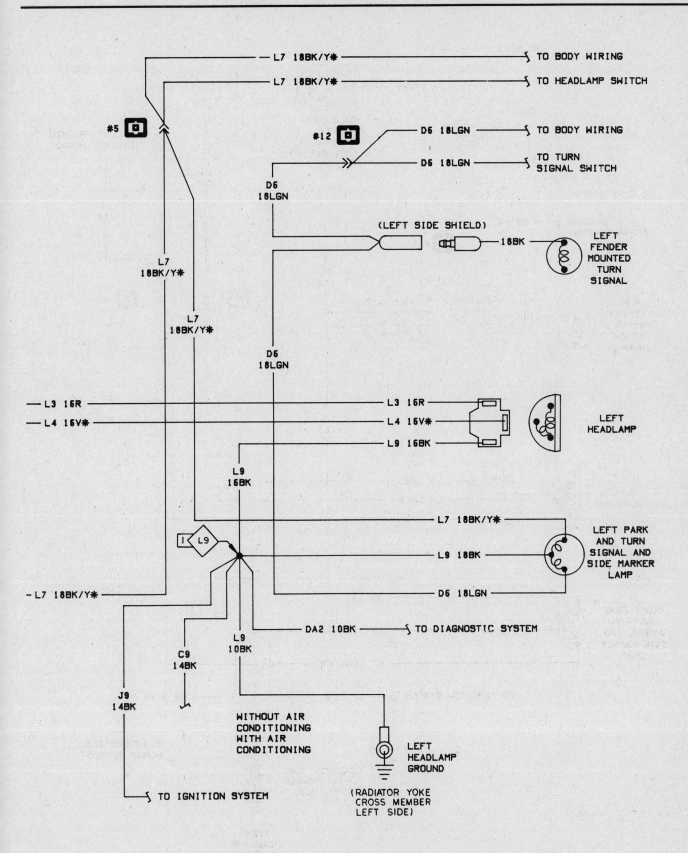

Typical earlier model front end wiring diagram (2 of 2)

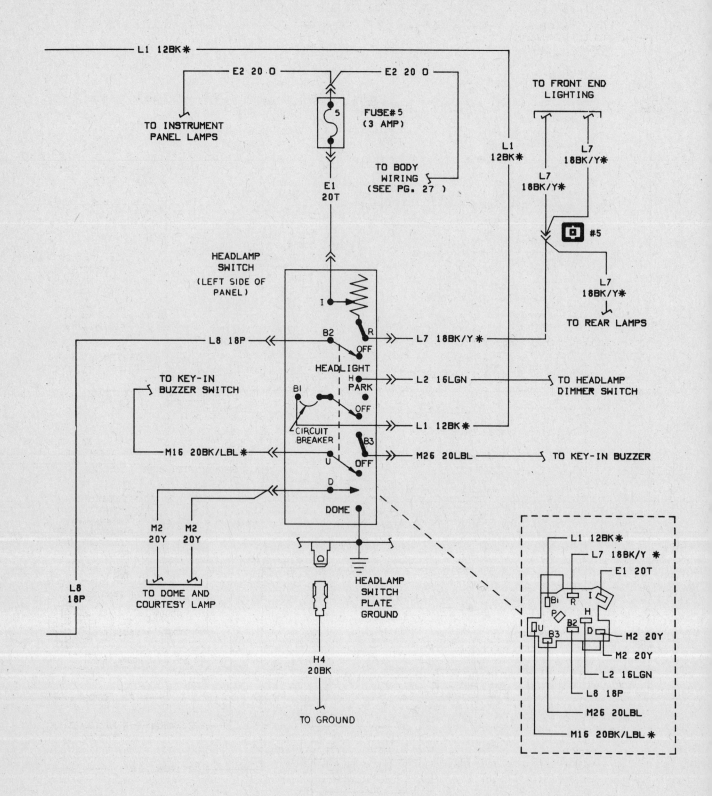

Typical earlier model headlight switch wiring diagram

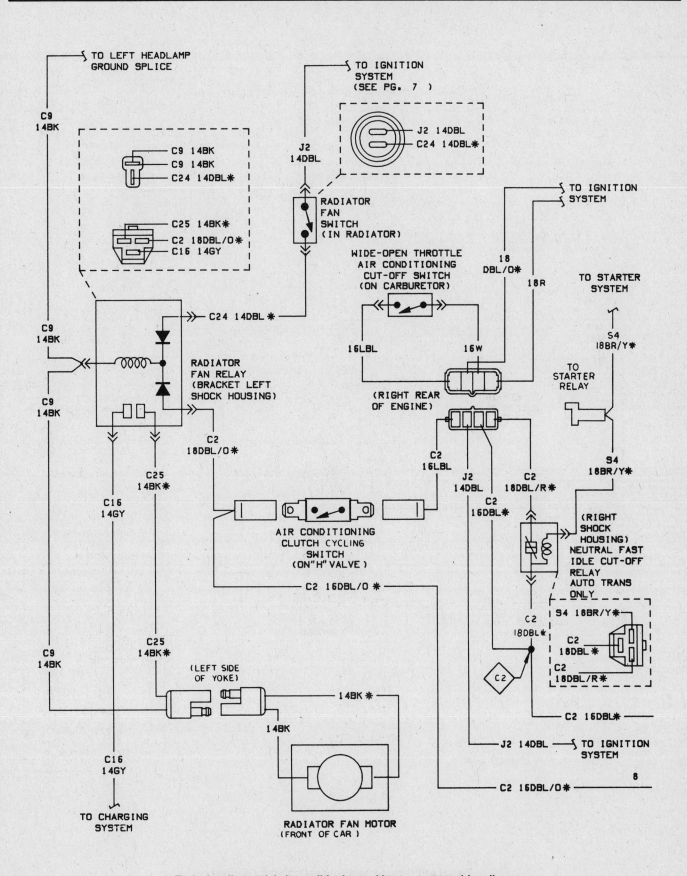

Typical earlier model air conditioning and heater system wiring diagram

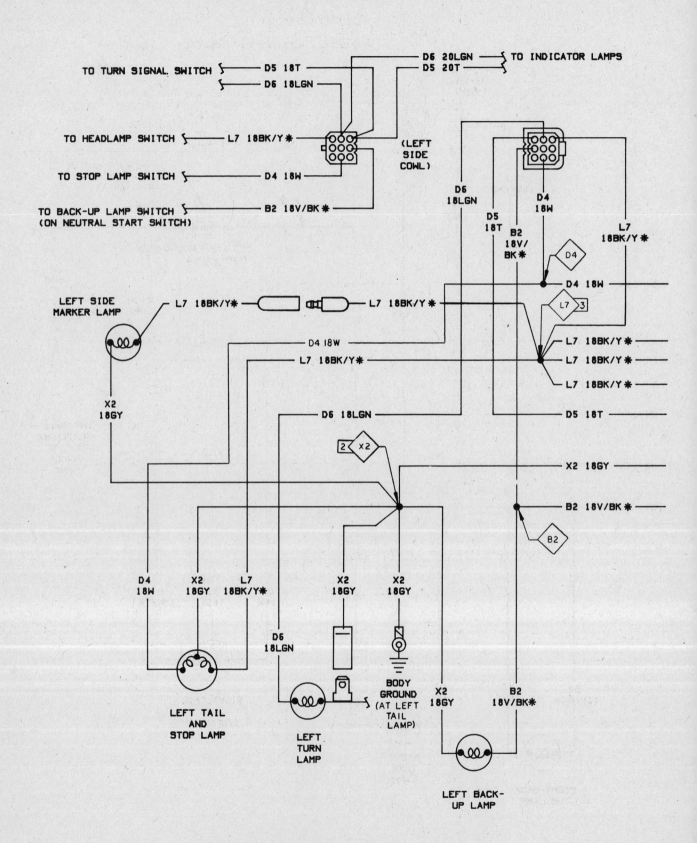

Typical earlier model rear lighting system wiring diagram (1 of 2)

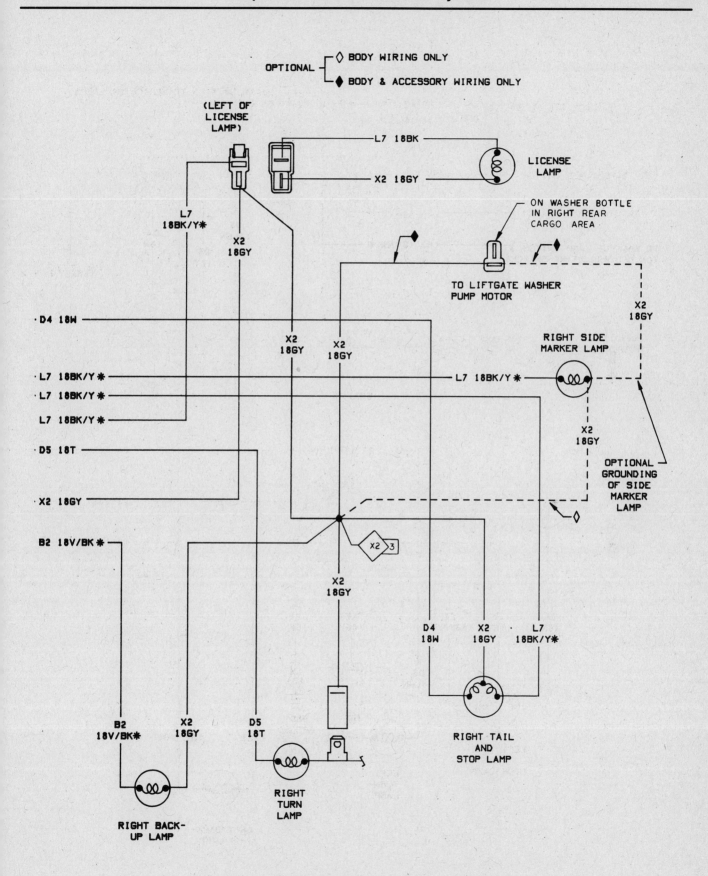

Typical earlier model rear lighting system wiring diagram (2 of 2)

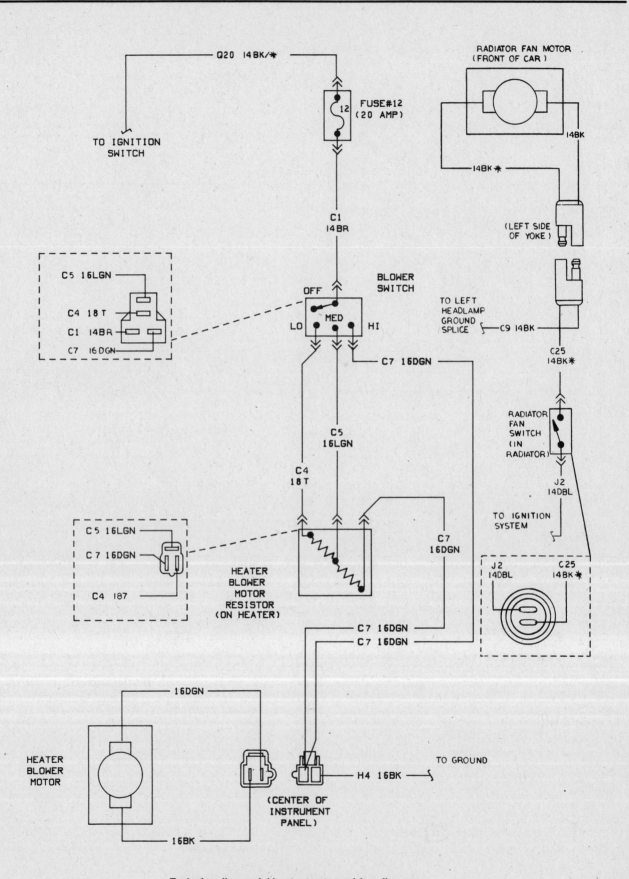

Typical earlier model heater system wiring diagram

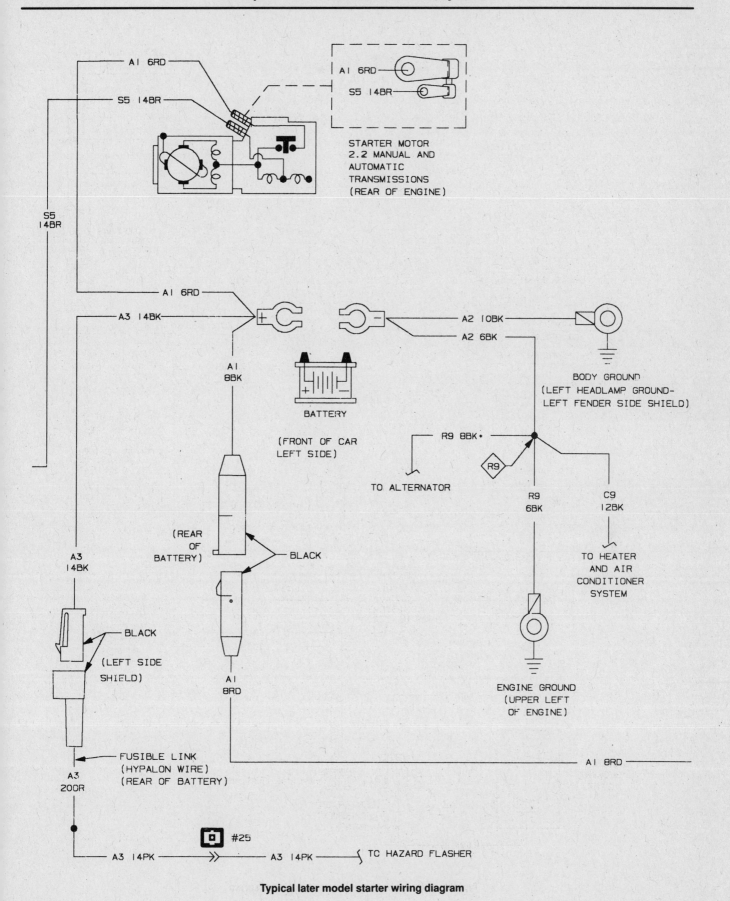

Typical later model starter wiring diagram

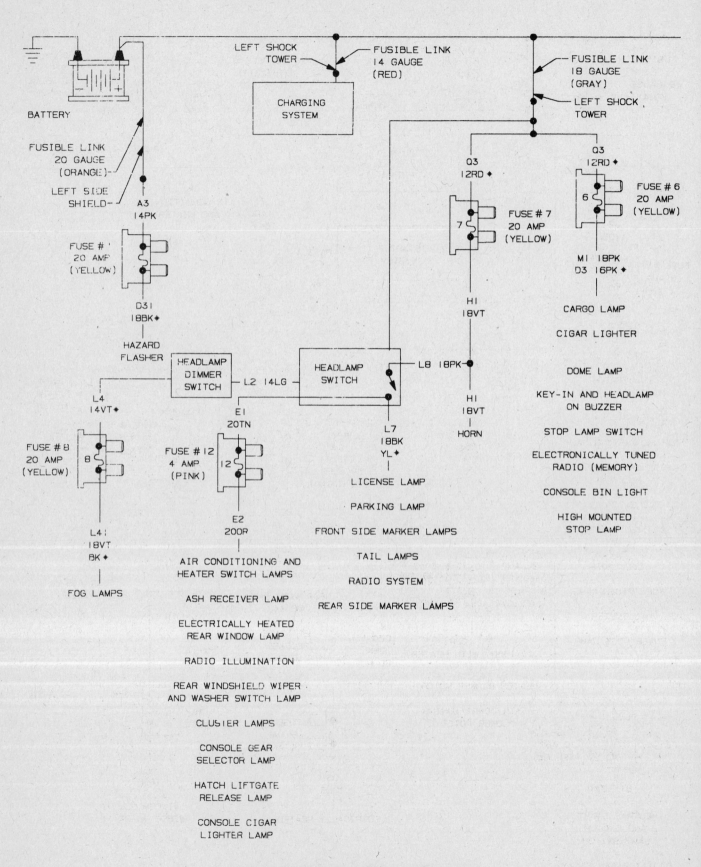

LEFT SHOCK TOWER — FUSIBLE LINK 14 GAUGE (RED)

CHARGING SYSTEM

FUSIBLE LINK 18 GAUGE (GRAY)

LEFT SHOCK TOWER

BATTERY

FUSIBLE LINK 20 GAUGE (ORANGE)

LEFT SIDE SHIELD

A3 14PK

FUSE # 20 AMP (YELLOW)

D31 18BK★

HAZARD FLASHER

HEADLAMP DIMMER SWITCH — L2 14LG — HEADLAMP SWITCH — L8 18PK

Q3 12RD★

7 FUSE # 7 20 AMP (YELLOW)

Q3 12RD★

6 FUSE # 6 20 AMP (YELLOW)

M1 18PK
D3 16PK★

CARGO LAMP

CIGAR LIGHTER

DOME LAMP

KEY-IN AND HEADLAMP ON BUZZER

STOP LAMP SWITCH

ELECTRONICALLY TUNED RADIO (MEMORY)

CONSOLE BIN LIGHT

HIGH MOUNTED STOP LAMP

H1 18VT

H1 18VT

HORN

L4 14VT★

FUSE # 8 20 AMP (YELLOW) 8

E1 20TN

FUSE # 12 4 AMP (PINK) 12

L7 18BK YL★

LICENSE LAMP

PARKING LAMP

FRONT SIDE MARKER LAMPS

TAIL LAMPS

RADIO SYSTEM

REAR SIDE MARKER LAMPS

L4 18VT BK★

FOG LAMPS

E2 20OR

AIR CONDITIONING AND HEATER SWITCH LAMPS

ASH RECEIVER LAMP

ELECTRICALLY HEATED REAR WINDOW LAMP

RADIO ILLUMINATION

REAR WINDSHIELD WIPER AND WASHER SWITCH LAMP

CLUSTER LAMPS

CONSOLE GEAR SELECTOR LAMP

HATCH LIFTGATE RELEASE LAMP

CONSOLE CIGAR LIGHTER LAMP

Typical later model fuse application chart (1 of 2)

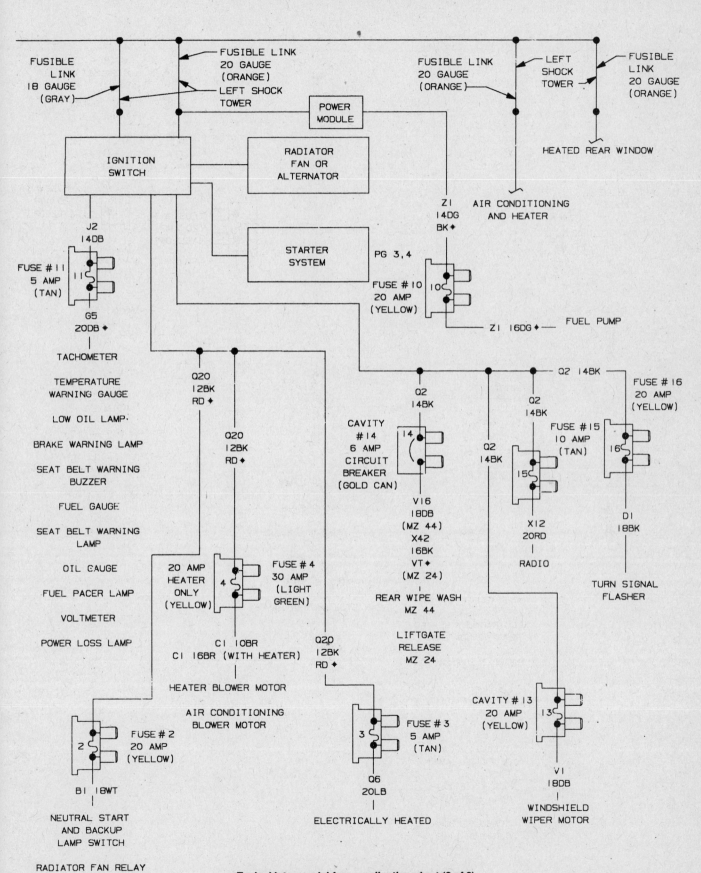

Typical later model fuse application chart (2 of 2)

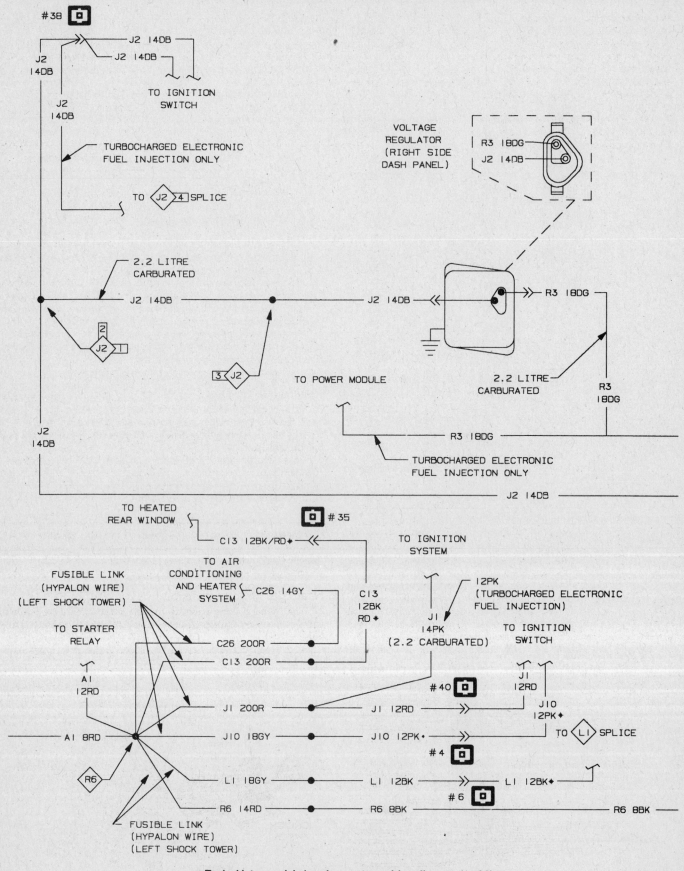

Typical later model charging system wiring diagram (1 of 2)

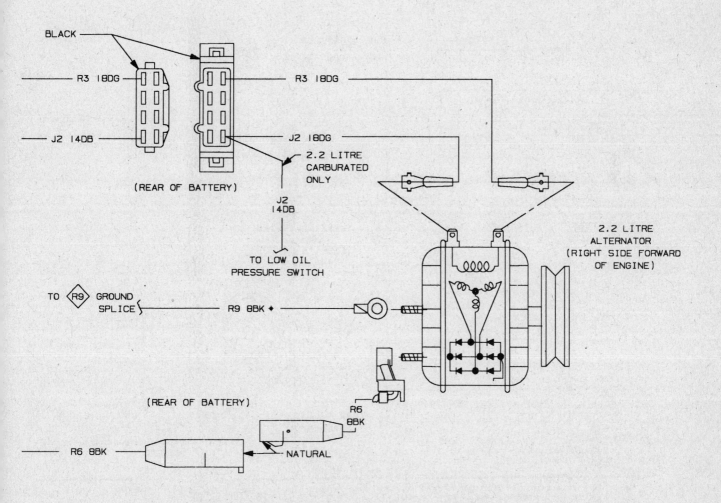

Typical later model charging system wiring diagram (2 of 2)

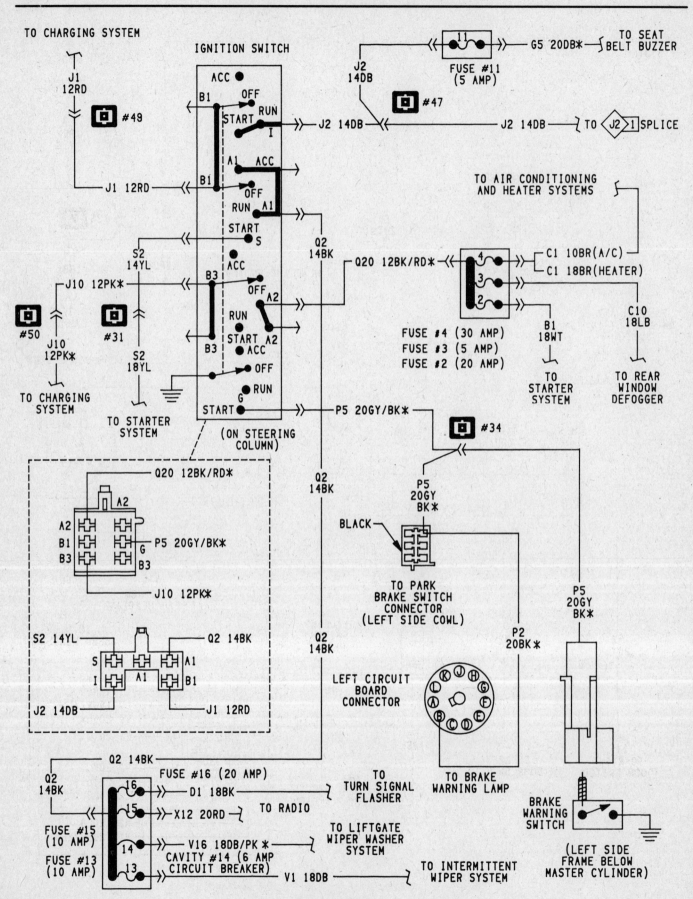

Typical later model ignition switch wiring diagram

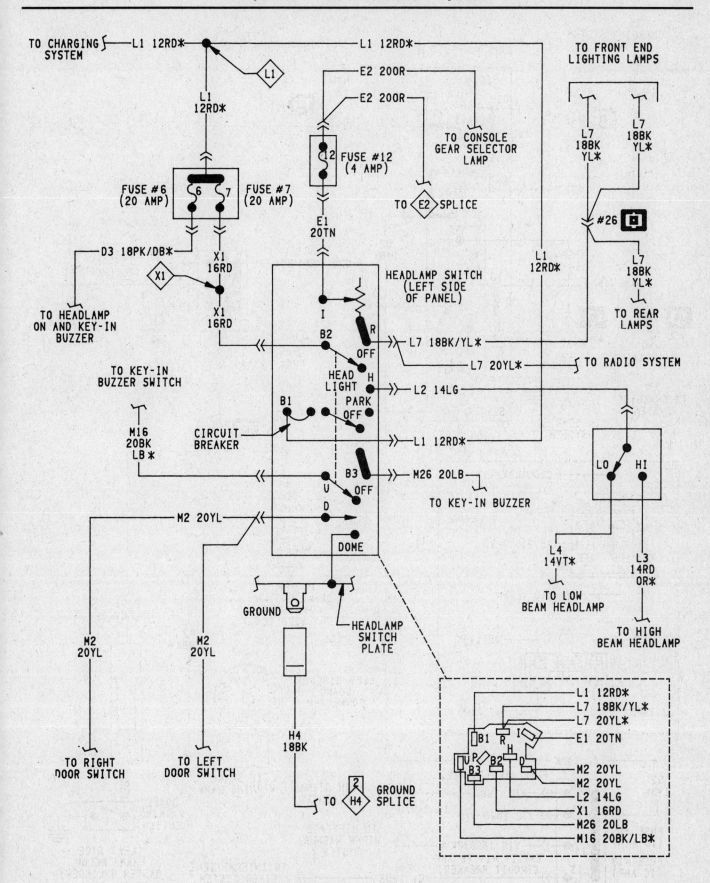

Typical later model headlight switch wiring diagram

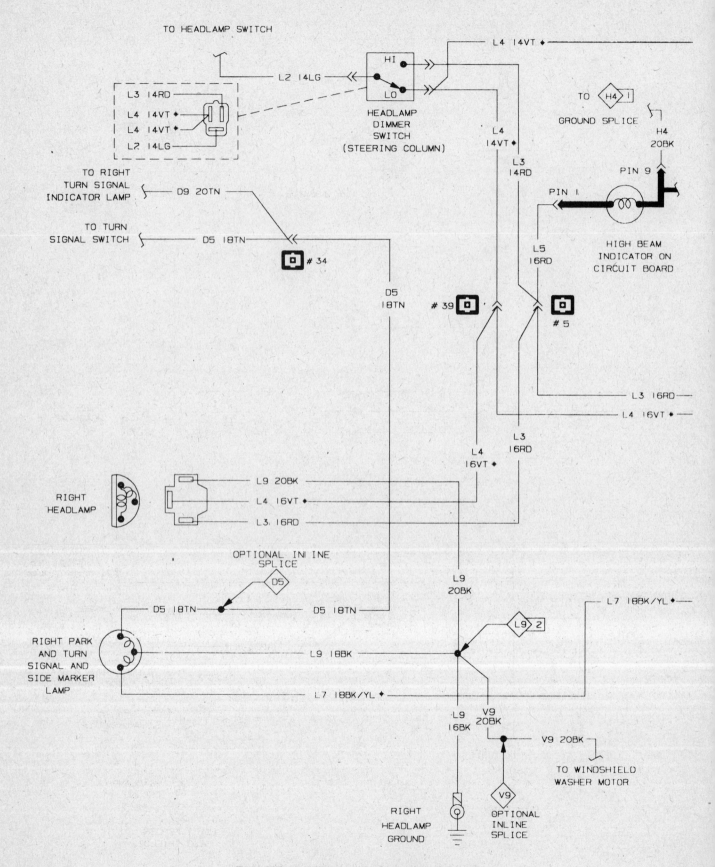

Typical later model front end wiring diagram (1 of 2)

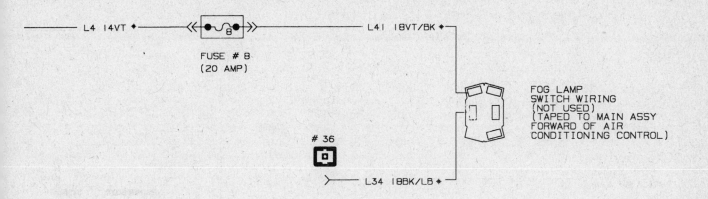

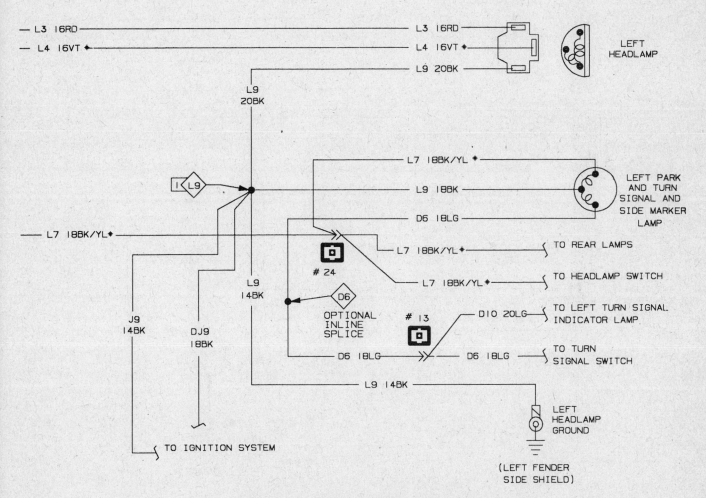

Typical later model front end wiring diagram (2 of 2)

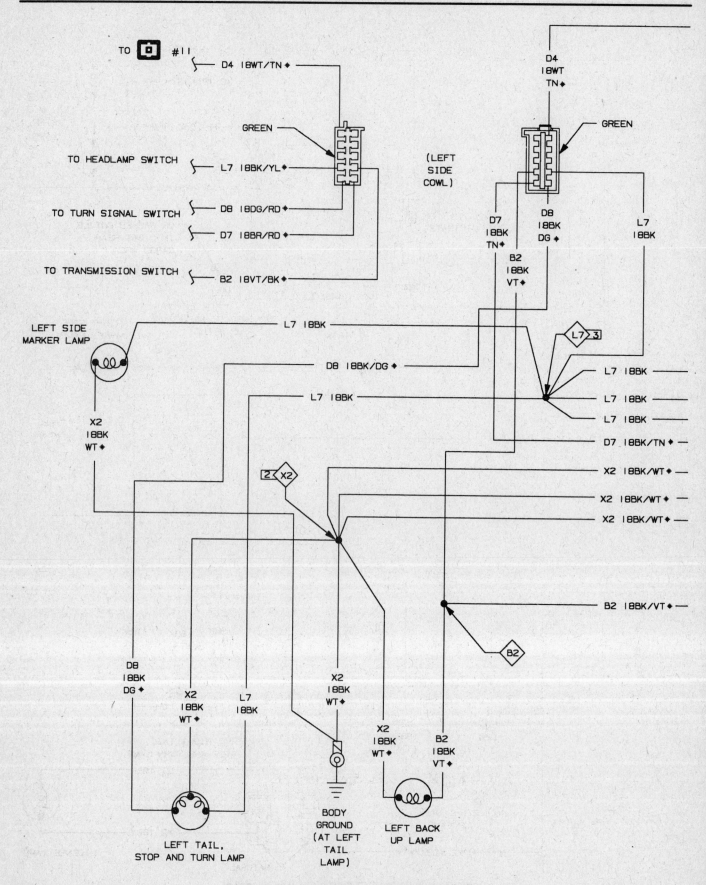

Typical later model rear light wiring diagram (1 of 2)

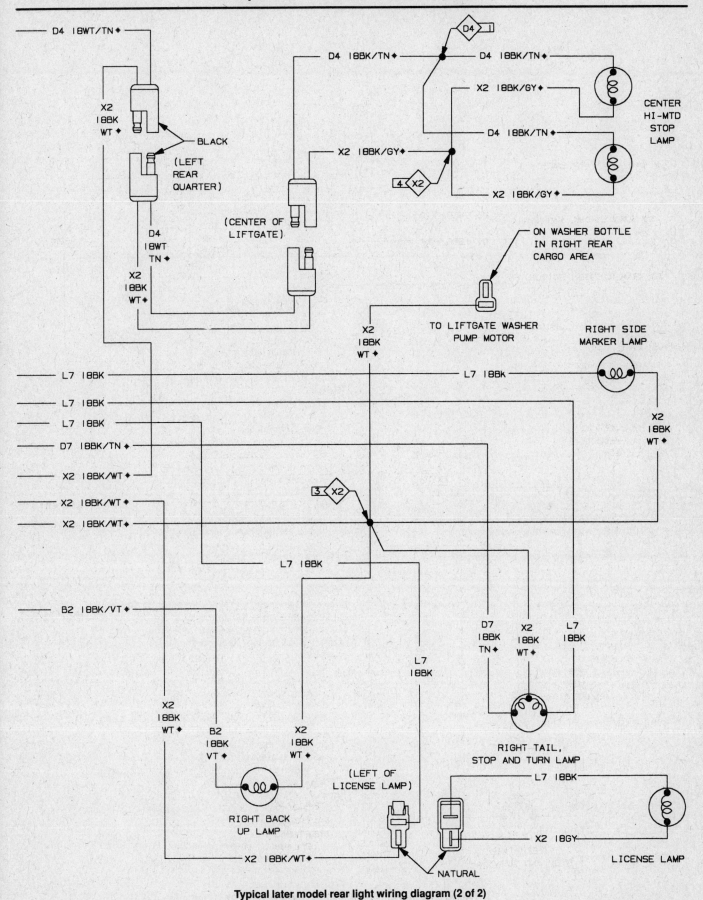

Typical later model rear light wiring diagram (2 of 2)

Index

HAYNES AUTOMOTIVE MANUALS

ACURA
*1776 **Integra & Legend** all models '86 thru '90

AMC
     Jeep CJ - see JEEP (412)
694 **Mid-size models**, Concord, Hornet, Gremlin & Spirit '70 thru '83
934 **(Renault) Alliance & Encore** all models '83 thru '87

AUDI
615 **4000** all models '80 thru '87
428 **5000** all models '77 thru '83
1117 **5000** all models '84 thru '88

AUSTIN
     Healey Sprite - see MG Midget Roadster (265)

BMW
*2020 **3/5 Series** not including diesel or all-wheel drive models '82 thru '92
276 **320i** all 4 cyl models '75 thru '83
632 **528i & 530i** all models '75 thru '80
240 **1500 thru 2002** all models except Turbo '59 thru '77
348 **2500, 2800, 3.0 & Bavaria** all models '69 thru '76

BUICK
     Century (front wheel drive) - see GENERAL MOTORS (829)
*1627 **Buick, Oldsmobile & Pontiac Full-size (Front wheel drive)** all models '85 thru '93
     Buick Electra, LeSabre and Park Avenue; Oldsmobile Delta 88 Royale, Ninety Eight and Regency; Pontiac Bonneville
1551 **Buick Oldsmobile & Pontiac Full-size (Rear wheel drive)**
     Buick Estate '70 thru '90, Electra '70 thru '84, LeSabre '70 thru '85, Limited '74 thru '79
     Oldsmobile Custom Cruiser '70 thru '90, Delta 88 '70 thru '85,Ninety-eight '70 thru '84
     Pontiac Bonneville '70 thru '81, Catalina '70 thru '81, Grandville '70 thru '75, Parisienne '83 thru '86
627 **Mid-size Regal & Century** all rear-drive models with V6, V8 and Turbo '74 thru '87
     Regal - see GENERAL MOTORS (1671)
     Skyhawk - see GENERAL MOTORS (766)
552 **Skylark** all X-car models '80 thru '85
     Skylark '86 on - see GENERAL MOTORS (1420)
     Somerset - see GENERAL MOTORS (1420)

CADILLAC
*751 **Cadillac Rear Wheel Drive** all gasoline models '70 thru '92
     Cimarron - see GENERAL MOTORS (766)

CAPRI
296 **2000 MK I Coupe** all models '71 thru '75
     Mercury Capri - see FORD Mustang (654)

CHEVROLET
*1477 **Astro & GMC Safari Mini-vans** '85 thru '93
554 **Camaro V8** all models '70 thru '81
866 **Camaro** all models '82 thru '92
     Cavalier - see GENERAL MOTORS (766)
     Celebrity - see GENERAL MOTORS (829)
625 **Chevelle, Malibu & El Camino** all V6 & V8 models '69 thru '87
449 **Chevette & Pontiac T1000** '76 thru '87
550 **Citation** all models '80 thru '85

*1628 **Corsica/Beretta** all models '87 thru '92
274 **Corvette** all V8 models '68 thru '82
*1336 **Corvette** all models '84 thru '91
1762 **Chevrolet Engine Overhaul Manual**
704 **Full-size Sedans** Caprice, Impala, Biscayne, Bel Air & Wagons '69 thru '90
     Lumina - see GENERAL MOTORS (1671)
     Lumina APV - see GENERAL MOTORS (2035)
319 **Luv Pick-up** all 2WD & 4WD '72 thru '82
626 **Monte Carlo** all models '70 thru '88
241 **Nova** all V8 models '69 thru '79
*1642 **Nova and Geo Prizm** all front wheel drive models, '85 thru '92
420 **Pick-ups '67 thru '87** - Chevrolet & GMC, all V8 & in-line 6 cyl, 2WD & 4WD '67 thru '87; Suburbans, Blazers & Jimmys '67 thru '91
*1664 **Pick-ups '88 thru '93** - Chevrolet & GMC, all full-size (C and K) models, '88 thru '93
*831 **S-10 & GMC S-15 Pick-ups** all models '82 thru '92
*1727 **Sprint & Geo Metro** '85 thru '91
*345 **Vans - Chevrolet & GMC**, V8 & in-line 6 cylinder models '68 thru '92

CHRYSLER
*2058 **Full-size Front-Wheel Drive** '88 thru '93
     K-Cars - see DODGE Aries (723)
     Laser - see DODGE Daytona (1140)
*1337 **Chrysler & Plymouth Mid-size** front wheel drive '82 thru '93

DATSUN
402 **200SX** all models '77 thru '79
647 **200SX** all models '80 thru '83
228 **B - 210** all models '73 thru '78
525 **210** all models '78 thru '82
206 **240Z, 260Z & 280Z Coupe** '70 thru '78
563 **280ZX Coupe & 2+2** '79 thru '83
     300ZX - see NISSAN (1137)
679 **310** all models '78 thru '82
123 **510 & PL521 Pick-up** '68 thru '73
430 **510** all models '78 thru '81
372 **610** all models '72 thru '76
277 **620 Series Pick-up** all models '73 thru '79
     720 Series Pick-up - see NISSAN (771)
376 **810/Maxima** all gasoline models, '77 thru '84
368 **F10** all models '76 thru '79
     Pulsar - see NISSAN (876)
     Sentra - see NISSAN (982)
     Stanza - see NISSAN (981)

DODGE
     400 & 600 - see CHRYSLER Mid-size (1337)
*723 **Aries & Plymouth Reliant** '81 thru '89
*1231 **Caravan & Plymouth Voyager Mini-Vans** all models '84 thru '93
699 **Challenger & Plymouth Saporro** all models '78 thru '83
     Challenger '67-'76 - see DODGE Dart (234)
236 **Colt** all models '71 thru '77
610 **Colt & Plymouth Champ (front wheel drive)** all models '78 thru '82
*1668 **Dakota Pick-ups** all models '87 thru '93
234 **Dart, Challenger/Plymouth Barracuda & Valiant** 6 cyl models '67 thru '76
*1140 **Daytona & Chrysler Laser** '84 thru '89
*545 **Omni & Plymouth Horizon** '78 thru '90
*912 **Pick-ups** all full-size models '74 thru '91
*556 **Ram 50/D50 Pick-ups & Raider and Plymouth Arrow Pick-ups** '79 thru '82
*1726 **Shadow & Plymouth Sundance** '87 thru '93
*1779 **Spirit & Plymouth Acclaim** '89 thru '92
*349 **Vans - Dodge & Plymouth** V8 & 6 cyl models '71 thru '91

EAGLE
     Talon - see Mitsubishi Eclipse (2097)

FIAT
094 **124 Sport Coupe & Spider** '68 thru '78
273 **X1/9** all models '74 thru '80

FORD
*1476 **Aerostar Mini-vans** all models '86 thru '92
788 **Bronco and Pick-ups** '73 thru '79
*880 **Bronco and Pick-ups** '80 thru '91
268 **Courier Pick-up** all models '72 thru '82
1763 **Ford Engine Overhaul Manual**
789 **Escort/Mercury Lynx** all models '81 thru '90
*2046 **Escort/Mercury Tracer** '91 thru '93
*2021 **Explorer & Mazda Navajo** '91 thru '92
560 **Fairmont & Mercury Zephyr** '78 thru '83
334 **Fiesta** all models '77 thru '80
754 **Ford & Mercury Full-size,** Ford LTD & Mercury Marquis ('75 thru '82); Ford Custom 500,Country Squire, Crown Victoria & Mercury Colony Park ('75 thru '87); Ford LTD Crown Victoria & Mercury Gran Marquis ('83 thru '87)
359 **Granada & Mercury Monarch** all in-line, 6 cyl & V8 models '75 thru '80
773 **Ford & Mercury Mid-size,** Ford Thunderbird & Mercury Cougar ('75 thru '82); Ford LTD & Mercury Marquis ('83 thru '86); Ford Torino,Gran Torino, Elite, Ranchero pick-up, LTD II, Mercury Montego, Comet, XR-7 & Lincoln Versailles ('75 thru '86)
*654 **Mustang & Mercury Capri** all models including Turbo. Mustang, '79 thru '92; Capri, '79 thru '86
357 **Mustang V8** all models '64-1/2 thru '73
231 **Mustang II** 4 cyl, V6 & V8 models '74 thru '78
649 **Pinto & Mercury Bobcat** '75 thru '80
1670 **Probe** all models '89 thru '92
*1026 **Ranger/Bronco II** gasoline models '83 thru '93
*1421 **Taurus & Mercury Sable** '86 thru '92
*1418 **Tempo & Mercury Topaz** all gasoline models '84 thru '93
1338 **Thunderbird/Mercury Cougar** '83 thru '88
*1725 **Thunderbird/Mercury Cougar** '89 and '90
*344 **Vans** all V8 Econoline models '69 thru '91

GENERAL MOTORS
*829 **Buick Century, Chevrolet Celebrity, Oldsmobile Cutlass Ciera & Pontiac 6000** all models '82 thru '93
*766 **Buick Skyhawk, Cadillac Cimarron, Chevrolet Cavalier, Oldsmobile Firenza & Pontiac J-2000 & Sunbird** all models '82 thru '92
1420 **Buick Skylark & Somerset, Oldsmobile Calais & Pontiac Grand Am** all models '85 thru '91
*1671 **Buick Regal, Chevrolet Lumina, Oldsmobile Cutlass Supreme & Pontiac Grand Prix** all front wheel drive models '88 thru '90
*2035 **Chevrolet Lumina APV, Oldsmobile Silhouette & Pontiac Trans Sport** all models '90 thru '92

GEO
     Metro - see CHEVROLET Sprint (1727)
     Prizm - see CHEVROLET Nova (1642)
*2039 **Storm** all models '90 thru '93
     Tracker - see SUZUKI Samurai (1626)

GMC
     Safari - see CHEVROLET ASTRO (1477)
     Vans & Pick-ups - see CHEVROLET (420, 831, 345, 1664)

(Continued on other side)

Haynes North America, Inc., 861 Lawrence Drive, Newbury Park, CA 91320 • (805) 493-6703

HAYNES AUTOMOTIVE MANUALS

NOTE: New manuals are added to this list on a periodic basis. If you do not see a listing for your vehicle, consult your local Haynes dealer for the latest product information.

HONDA
351	**Accord CVCC** all models '76 thru '83
1221	**Accord** all models '84 thru '89
2067	**Accord** all models '90 thru '93
160	**Civic 1200** all models '73 thru '79
633	**Civic 1300 & 1500 CVCC** '80 thru '83
297	**Civic 1500 CVCC** all models '75 thru '79
1227	**Civic** all models '84 thru '91
*601	**Prelude CVCC** all models '79 thru '89

HYUNDAI
*1552	**Excel** all models '86 thru '93

ISUZU
*1641	**Trooper & Pick-up**, all gasoline models Pick-up, '81 thru '93; Trooper, '84 thru '91

JAGUAR
*242	**XJ6** all 6 cyl models '68 thru '86
*478	**XJ12 & XJS** all 12 cyl models '72 thru '85

JEEP
*1553	**Cherokee, Comanche & Wagoneer Limited** all models '84 thru '93
412	**CJ** all models '49 thru '86
*1777	**Wrangler** all models '87 thru '92

LADA
*413	**1200, 1300. 1500 & 1600** all models including Riva '74 thru '91

MAZDA
648	**626** Sedan & Coupe (rear wheel drive) all models '79 thru '82
*1082	**626 & MX-6** (front wheel drive) all models '83 thru '91
267	**B Series Pick-ups** '72 thru '93
370	**GLC Hatchback** (rear wheel drive) all models '77 thru '83
757	**GLC** (front wheel drive) '81 thru '85
*2047	**MPV** all models '89 thru '93
460	**RX-7** all models '79 thru '85
*1419	**RX-7** all models '86 thru '91

MERCEDES-BENZ
*1643	**190 Series** all four-cylinder gasoline models, '84 thru '88
346	**230, 250 & 280** Sedan, Coupe & Roadster all 6 cyl sohc models '68 thru '72
983	**280 123 Series** gasoline models '77 thru '81
698	**350 & 450** Sedan, Coupe & Roadster all models '71 thru '80
697	**Diesel 123 Series** 200D, 220D, 240D, 240TD, 300D, 300CD, 300TD, 4- & 5-cyl incl. Turbo '76 thru '85

MERCURY
See FORD Listing

MG
111	**MGB** Roadster & GT Coupe all models '62 thru '80
265	**MG Midget & Austin Healey Sprite** Roadster '58 thru '80

MITSUBISHI
*1669	**Cordia, Tredia, Galant, Precis & Mirage** '83 thru '93
*2022	**Pick-up & Montero** '83 thru '93
*2097	**Eclipse, Eagle Talon & Plymouth Laser** '90 thru '94

MORRIS
074	**(Austin) Marina 1.8** all models '71 thru '78
024	**Minor 1000** sedan & wagon '56 thru '71

NISSAN
1137	**300ZX** all models including Turbo '84 thru '89
*1341	**Maxima** all models '85 thru '91
*771	**Pick-ups/Pathfinder** gas models '80 thru '93
876	**Pulsar** all models '83 thru '86
*982	**Sentra** all models '82 thru '90
*981	**Stanza** all models '82 thru '90

OLDSMOBILE
	Bravada - see CHEVROLET S-10 (831)
	Calais - see GENERAL MOTORS (1420)
	Custom Cruiser - see BUICK Full-size RWD (1551)
*658	**Cutlass** all standard gasoline V6 & V8 models '74 thru '88
	Cutlass Ciera - see GENERAL MOTORS (829)
	Cutlass Supreme - see GM (1671)
	Delta 88 - see BUICK Full-size RWD (1551)
	Delta 88 Brougham - see BUICK Full-size FWD (1551), RWD (1627)
	Delta 88 Royale - see BUICK Full-size RWD (1551)
	Firenza - see GENERAL MOTORS (766)
	Ninety-eight Regency - see BUICK Full-size RWD (1551), FWD (1627)
	Ninety-eight Regency Brougham - see BUICK Full-size RWD (1551)
	Omega - see PONTIAC Phoenix (551)
	Silhouette - see GENERAL MOTORS (2035)

PEUGEOT
663	**504** all diesel models '74 thru '83

PLYMOUTH
	Laser - see MITSUBISHI Eclipse (2097)
	For other PLYMOUTH titles, see DODGE listing.

PONTIAC
	T1000 - see CHEVROLET Chevette (449)
	J-2000 - see GENERAL MOTORS (766)
	6000 - see GENERAL MOTORS (829)
	Bonneville - see Buick Full-size FWD (1627), RWD (1551)
	Bonneville Brougham - see Buick Full-size (1551)
	Catalina - see Buick Full-size (1551)
1232	**Fiero** all models '84 thru '88
555	**Firebird V8 models** except Turbo '70 thru '81
867	**Firebird** all models '82 thru '92
	Full-size Rear Wheel Drive - see BUICK Oldsmobile, Pontiac Full-size RWD (1551)
	Full-size Front Wheel Drive - see BUICK Oldsmobile, Pontiac Full-size FWD (1627)
	Grand Am - see GENERAL MOTORS (1420)
	Grand Prix - see GENERAL MOTORS (1671)
	Grandville - see BUICK Full-size (1551)
	Parisienne - see BUICK Full-size (1551)
551	**Phoenix & Oldsmobile Omega** all X-car models '80 thru '84
	Sunbird - see GENERAL MOTORS (766)
	Trans Sport - see GENERAL MOTORS (2035)

PORSCHE
*264	**911** all Coupe & Targa models except Turbo & Carrera 4 '65 thru '89
239	**914** all 4 cyl models '69 thru '76
397	**924** all models including Turbo '76 thru '82
*1027	**944** all models including Turbo '83 thru '89

RENAULT
141	**5 Le Car** all models '76 thru '83
079	**8 & 10** 58.4 cu in engines '62 thru '72
097	**12 Saloon & Estate** 1289 cc engine '70 thru '80
768	**15 & 17** all models '73 thru '79
081	**16** 89.7 cu in & 95.5 in engines '65 thru '72
	Alliance & Encore - see AMC (934)

SAAB
247	**99** all models including Turbo '69 thru '80
*980	**900** all models including Turbo '79 thru '88

SUBARU
237	**1100, 1300, 1400 & 1600** '71 thru '79
*681	**1600 & 1800** 2WD & 4WD '80 thru '89

SUZUKI
*1626	**Samurai/Sidekick and Geo Tracker** all models '86 thru '93

TOYOTA
1023	**Camry** all models '83 thru '91
150	**Carina** Sedan all models '71 thru '74
935	**Celica Rear Wheel Drive** '71 thru '85
*2038	**Celica Front Wheel Drive** '86 thru '92
1139	**Celica Supra** all models '79 thru '92
361	**Corolla** all models '75 thru '79
961	**Corolla** all rear wheel drive models '80 thru '87
*1025	**Corolla** all front wheel drive models '84 thru '92
636	**Corolla Tercel** all models '80 thru '82
360	**Corona** all models '74 thru '82
532	**Cressida** all models '78 thru '82
313	**Land Cruiser** all models '68 thru '82
200	**MK II** all 6 cyl models '72 thru '76
*1339	**MR2** all models '85 thru '87
304	**Pick-up** all models '69 thru '78
*656	**Pick-up** all models '79 thru '92
*2048	**Previa** all models '91 thru '93

TRIUMPH
112	**GT6 & Vitesse** all models '62 thru '74
113	**Spitfire** all models '62 thru '81
322	**TR7** all models '75 thru '81

VW
159	**Beetle & Karmann Ghia** all models '54 thru '79
238	**Dasher** all gasoline models '74 thru '81
*884	**Rabbit, Jetta, Scirocco, & Pick-up** gas models '74 thru '91 & Convertible '80 thru '92
451	**Rabbit, Jetta & Pick-up** all diesel models '77 thru '84
082	**Transporter 1600** all models '68 thru '79
226	**Transporter 1700, 1800 & 2000** all models '72 thru '79
084	**Type 3 1500 & 1600** all models '63 thru '73
1029	**Vanagon** all air-cooled models '80 thru '83

VOLVO
203	**120, 130 Series & 1800 Sports** '61 thru '73
129	**140 Series** all models '66 thru '74
*270	**240 Series** all models '74 thru '90
400	**260 Series** all models '75 thru '82
*1550	**740 & 760 Series** all models '82 thru '88

SPECIAL MANUALS
1479	**Automotive Body Repair & Painting Manual**
1654	**Automotive Electrical Manual**
1667	**Automotive Emissions Control Manual**
1480	**Automotive Heating & Air Conditioning Manual**
1762	**Chevrolet Engine Overhaul Manual**
1736	**GM and Ford Diesel Engine Repair Manual**
1763	**Ford Engine Overhaul Manual**
482	**Fuel Injection Manual**
2069	**Holley Carburetor Manual**
1666	**Small Engine Repair Manual**
299	**SU Carburetors** thru '88
393	**Weber Carburetors** thru '79
300	**Zenith/Stromberg CD Carburetors** thru '76

---

* Listings shown with an asterisk (*) indicate model coverage as of this printing. These titles will be periodically updated to include later model years - consult your Haynes dealer for more information.

Over 100 Haynes motorcycle manuals also available

5-94

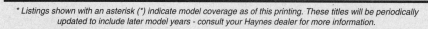

Haynes North America, Inc., 861 Lawrence Drive, Newbury Park, CA 91320 • (805) 498-6703